CASES IN ENTREPRENEURSHIP

THE IVEY CASEBOOK SERIES

A SAGE Publications Series

Series Editor

Paul W. Beamish

Richard Ivey School of Business

The University of Western Ontario

Books in This Series

CASES IN BUSINESS ETHICS

Edited by David J. Sharp

CASES IN ENTREPRENEURSHIP

The Venture Creation Process

Edited by Eric A. Morse and Ronald K. Mitchell

CASES IN OPERATIONS MANAGEMENT

Building Customer Value Through World-Class Operations

Edited by Robert D. Klassen and Larry J. Menor

CASES IN ORGANIZATIONAL BEHAVIOR

Edited by Gerard H. Seijts

CASES IN THE ENVIRONMENT OF BUSINESS

International Perspectives

Edited by David W. Conklin

Forthcoming

CASES IN GENDER AND DIVERSITY IN ORGANIZATIONS

Edited by Alison M. Konrad

ERIC A. MORSE
The University of Western Ontario

RONALD K. MITCHELL
Texas Tech University

CASES IN ENTREPRENEURSHIP

The Venture Creation Process

For information:

Sage Publications, Inc.
2455 Teller Road
Thousand Oaks, California 91320
E-mail: order@sagepub.com

Sage Publications Ltd.
1 Oliver's Yard
55 City Road
London EC1Y 1SP
United Kingdom

Sage Publications India Pvt. Ltd.
B-42, Panchsheel Enclave
Post Box 4109
New Delhi 110 017 India

Printed in the United States of America.

Library of Congress Cataloging-in-Publication Data

Cases in entrepreneurship: The venture creation process / edited by Eric A. Morse, Ronald K. Mitchell.
p. cm.—(The Ivey Casebook Series)
Includes bibliographical references.
ISBN 1-4129-0976-7 (pbk.)
1. New business enterprises—Case studies. 2. Business incubators—Case studies.
3. Venture capital—Case studies. 4. Entrepreneurship—Case studies. I. Morse, Eric A. II. Mitchell, Ronald K. III. Series.
HD62.5.C375 2006
658.1′1—dc22 2005003581

This book is printed on acid-free paper.

05 06 07 08 09 10 9 8 7 6 5 4 3 2 1

Acquisitions Editor: Al Bruckner
Editorial Assistant: MaryAnn Vail
Production Editor: Laureen A. Shea
Copy Editor: Gillian Dickens
Typesetter: C&M Digitals (P) Ltd.
Proofreader: Mary Meagher
Cover Designer: Edgar Abarca

CONTENTS

Introduction to the Ivey Casebook Series **vii**
Paul W. Beamish

Preface **ix**

Introduction: The Venture Creation Process **xiii**

1. Searching for Venture Opportunities **1**
Leveraging Wal-Mart, eBay and USPS 5
Barrie Charity Bingo 8
Takahiko Naraki, the Three Million Yen Entrepreneur 12
Cascadia Water Corporation 20
Russki Adventures 26

2. Screening Venture Opportunities **43**
Kalista's Fine Chocolate 49
Siam Canadian Foods Co., Ltd. 55
Asiasports: Hockey Night in Hong Kong 65
Crystal Corporation of the Philippines 78
Sequel to Success: The Follow-Up to Abatis Systems 86

3. Planning and Financing the Venture **97**
Frontier Adventure Racing: Pack Lightly, Go Like Hell, Never Give Up 116
Borders Hotel Corp. 129
SimEx Inc. 132
Extreme Packet Devices (A) 149
Diabetogen 173
Alpha Personal Dental Care Systems 188

4. Venture Setup **199**
PolicePrep 204
Ben & Jerry's—Japan 213
Textron Ltd. 229
Tapp Technologies Inc. (A) 238
Blinds To Go—Wanted: People to Lead Explosive Growth (A) 240

5. Venture Start-Up **253**
DCF Innovations: Goalie Pad Covers (A) 259
Catfish Creek Canoe Company 271
WaveRider Communications, Inc.: Selling Wireless Internet Access Equipment 275
Omega Paw Inc. 288

6. Ongoing Venture Operations and Growth **295**
Extreme CCTV 298
VanCity Savings Credit Union: Corporate Venturing Into Uncharted Waters 311
Krave's Candy Co.—Clodhoppers (A) 330
Trojan Technologies Inc.: Organizational Structuring for Growth and Customer Service 333
Mainstreet Equity Corp. (A) 338

7. Venture Analytics: Beyond Venture Creation **355**
Creemore Springs Brewery: Branding Without Advertising 371
Fernando Rego and the Fitter 379
Drawn and Quarterly 389
InnoMedia Logic Inc. 399
Quadra Logic Technologies Inc. (A) 412

References **423**

About the Editors **427**

INTRODUCTION TO THE IVEY CASEBOOK SERIES

As the title of this series suggests, these books all draw from the Ivey Business School's case collection. Ivey has long had the world's second largest collection of decision-oriented, field-based business cases. Well more than a million copies of Ivey cases are studied every year. There are more than 2,000 cases in Ivey's current collection, with more than 6,000 in the total collection. Each year approximately 200 new titles are registered at Ivey Publishing (www.ivey.uwo.ca/cases), and a similar number are retired. Nearly all Ivey cases have teaching notes available to qualified instructors. The cases included in this volume are all from the current collection.

The vision for the series was a result of conversations I had with Sage's Senior Editor, Al Bruckner, starting in September 2002. Over the subsequent months, we were able to shape a model for the books in the series that we felt would meet a market need.

Each volume in the series contains text and cases. "Some" text was deemed essential in order to provide a basic overview of the particular field and to place the selected cases in an appropriate context. We made a conscious decision to not include hundreds of pages of text material in each volume in recognition of the fact that many professors prefer to supplement basic text material with readings or lectures customized to their interests and to those of their students.

The editors of the books in this series are all highly qualified experts in their respective fields. I was delighted when each agreed to prepare a volume. We very much welcome your comments on this casebook.

—Paul W. Beamish
Series Editor

PREFACE

We have three objectives in writing this casebook. First, as instructors, we have been successfully using what we call a "process model" of teaching entrepreneurship for more than a decade, and we desire to make it more widely available to colleagues and students. Second, we are convinced of the power of the case-teaching method as an effective means for learners to build the mental bridges needed to transfer theory and concept into practice, and we can see the need for a one-stop volume that links helpful cases to key ideas. Third, in our research, we have identified a clear pattern that links entrepreneurial *thinking* to entrepreneurial *doing,* and we think that it is important for us to share these insights in a usable form for the benefit of both learners and teachers.

The most important idea in this book is that entrepreneurs create new value through the creation of new transactions. There is an old saying in business that nothing happens until somebody sells something—but we think that this is only partially true. Actually, we believe that nothing in business happens until somebody creates some work *and then* sells it to someone else. In essence, when an individual creates a work for others (Mitchell, Morse, & Sharma, 2003), a transaction occurs.

Creating new transactions is the first job of the entrepreneur. Some suggest that the first job is to create or to recognize opportunity. We agree that this is a very important function of the entrepreneur, but there are many who create opportunities, or who recognize them, but who produce less value until this recognition and/or creation is turned into a transaction. Others suggest that the creation of new ventures is the first job of the entrepreneur. Again, we agree that this is an exceedingly important function of entrepreneurs—so much so that this book is focused on this very process. But our admitting this does not change our belief that the creation of new transactions is the first job of entrepreneurs. And then, immediately following the creation of new transactions, comes the creation of a new venture: the combining of new transactions into a continuing stream that—as a new entity—adds new value because it is a new business in our economy. This casebook explains the six steps in the venture creation process: searching, screening, planning/financing, setup, startup, and ongoing operations and growth. 

ORGANIZATION

This book is organized into seven chapters. The first six chapters of the casebook explain the six core elements that are necessary in the process of creating a new venture. These have been previously identified by Karl Vesper (1996) as a part of a larger discussion that goes beyond a specific focus on the explicit six-step sequence of the venture creation process that is the focus of this casebook. The six core elements in the venture creation process are searching, screening, planning/financing, setup, startup, and ongoing operations and growth. Each chapter explains one of these elements by, first, explaining the process; second, by including a student's interpretation of this process; and, third, by providing several cases that can be used to practice the identification of key concepts and the bridging of these concepts into real-world application.

Recent research in developing expert-level performance suggests that there is substantial learning leverage to be gained where deliberate practice is used to enhance a person's thinking system: to improve that person's knowledge base and to expand his or her repertoire of problem-solving processes (Charness, Krampe, & Mayer, 1996). The cases in this text are descriptions of actual situations faced by entrepreneurs. The purpose of using cases is for you to take on the role and responsibility of the entrepreneur in the case and develop your cognitive model of the entrepreneurship process. The process described in the text will give you a head start in what historically has been a trial-and-error learning process. It is our hope that students who make their way through this text and case material will limit the number of mistakes they make in bringing their own ventures to fruition. We see rigorous case analysis as a safe way to take chances and make mistakes—in a sense, on-the-job training with limited downside.

Chapters 1 through 6 are written to provide the opportunity to apply such leverage. Chapter 7 supports another of our main objectives: to share the insights from our research where we have identified a clear pattern that links entrepreneurial thinking to entrepreneurial doing. This chapter explains the three areas of entrepreneurial skill building that are crucial to the creation of new transactions: the development of competition, promise, and planning cognitions. Although most entrepreneurship texts and casebooks emphasize the third necessary element, business planning, we have found that all three are needed for transaction unit-based value creation in entrepreneurship to be effectively accomplished.

You may notice that throughout this casebook we reveal our personal biases about entrepreneurship and entrepreneurship education. Our first bias comes from our training in management strategy, which has created within us an underlying assumption that there is value in top-down information processing. For us, leaders (in this case, entrepreneurs) *can* and do make a difference. Our second bias comes from the circumstances of our own careers. Prior to becoming professors, we each had extensive experience in the world of business operations: Professor Morse has had experience with a variety of businesses through his work for Andersen Consulting (Accenture), as a board member for several startups, and as an entrepreneur, and Professor Mitchell has had experience in public accounting, in corporate entrepreneurship, as a turnaround CEO, as a consultant to high-growth new ventures, and as an entrepreneur. Third, as entrepreneurship scholars and practitioners, we have developed a biased lens regarding people and systems: We tend toward seeing system in service of man versus mankind in service of system, and we see entrepreneurs as the creators, refiners, and employers of a variety of helpful systems. Fourth, we are biased toward cognitive (thinking-based) explanations for learning and teaching entrepreneurship and for the definition of entrepreneurship itself. This means that our focus herein both deliberately and unwittingly centers on enhancing the cognitive (thinking) system of individuals: improving their knowledge base and expanding their repertoire of problem-solving processes (Charness et al., 1996).

It is our hope that you will find this "process" approach to learning and teaching the venture creation process to be elegant: simpler than its alternatives, easily used, efficient (in that it explains a lot with a little), and instinctively satisfying (Michener, 1982, p. 389). We look forward to receiving your comments and suggestions on how future editions can be made even more so.

Acknowledgments

We wish to acknowledge all those who have been formative in our preparation to write this book: our families, especially Charie and Cynthia; supportive colleagues at our respective institutions; those who have been instrumental in our training; and those who have reviewed or contributed cases to this volume. We especially acknowledge the formative influence that Professor Karl Vesper has had on this work. It was Karl who, when the first edition of his textbook, *New Venture Experience,* was published in 1992, clearly identified the process model of venture creation that is the foundation of this work and, since then, has been an exceptionally supportive mentor and colleague. Professor Morse also wishes to acknowledge the support of J. R. Shaw and the Institute for Entrepreneurship Advisory Council for their support. Professor Mitchell also wishes to acknowledge Francis G. Winspear, Jean Austin Bagley, Texas Tech Regents' Endowments, and Dr. Fritz Faulhaber for their financial support.

INTRODUCTION

The Venture Creation Process

Similar to many processes, the venture creation process can be summarized by its underlying attributes: the process sequence, as well as the norms that guide it. The venture creation process has sequence or flow, a set of steps that is ordered by precedence relationships (one thing before another, sometimes with feedback loops). The venture creation process also has norms or standards, the set of criteria by which a person can judge whether a particular step in the sequence has been performed properly. For example, when following a recipe in the cooking process, we must both combine the ingredients in order (the sequence) and not burn the food (a norm) for the meal to be both tasty and what we want to eat.

Venture creation is not so simple that a recipe can adequately describe it, but, in our experience, the venture creation process can effectively be described by a master sequence, which in turn is supported by a set of subsequences that explains the process in more detail. Each step in the sequential process is accompanied by the relevant norms: the standards by which an entrepreneur can assess whether he or she has complied with the normal expectations of those who know the process well and who know what "should" be done.

Interestingly, in our research and experience, we have observed two seemingly contradictory phenomena that bear upon our developing a clear understanding of the venture creation process: (a) that individuals who make the venture creation decision have dramatically different thinking patterns than other businesspeople and, in this sense, may globally be grouped into one similar collection of people with venture creation expertise and (b) that *within* this unique group, there is still much variety, some of which can be described by a person's national culture but other variations that appear to be unique to each single individual (Mitchell et al., 2002). In this sense, entrepreneurship is both universal and unique, and the above-described phenomena are *not* in fact contradictory. The first difference is a *between*-groups difference between entrepreneurs and nonentrepreneur businesspeople, and the second difference is a *within*-group difference among only the entrepreneurs. Why is this distinction important? Because it means that a learner can successfully acquire knowledge of the venture creation process that will make her or him both an entrepreneurial thinker, yet one who is nevertheless distinct from other nonentrepreneur businesspeople.

Generally, in our research and teaching experiences, we have observed that the sequence of the venture creation process is much more likely to be similar among entrepreneurs but that the norms that each entrepreneur uses in the creative processes of entrepreneurship, to effectuate an aspiration or intention, will vary widely depending on the depth of venture creation experience, past life experience, culture, and a whole variety of unique perceptions and perspectives (Sarasvathy, 2001). We explain this at the beginning of this casebook because we think it to be important for both teachers and learners to properly calibrate their expectations as to the likely outcomes of using the process approach to new venture creation. You should therefore expect that the venture creation process, as each learner will understand it, can at the same time become increasingly "like" that of more experienced entrepreneurs while still remaining unique to that individual.

In the following chapters, the master sequence of venture creation will be introduced step by step as follows:

Chapter 1—Searching

Chapter 2—Screening

Chapter 3—Planning/Financing

Chapter 4—Setup

Chapter 5—Start-Up

Chapter 6—Ongoing Operations and Growth

And, as what we hope will be a helpful innovation for the users of this casebook, each of these chapters—after a brief explanation from the authors to set the context—will contain an explanation of the process under discussion from a student's perspective (with only minor edits to enhance clarity). This perspective is not meant to portray an ideal perspective, simply the unique perspective of an individual student. We hope that you will find this a useful jumping-off point for your own reflection and also in discussion with your peers. Cases to practice the concepts and to enable learners to craft their own venture creation process will conclude each chapter.

Consistent with this innovation, we therefore begin with a representation of the "master venturing sequence," as developed by a student who participated in the 2001 Full Immersion Entrepreneurship Program, held at the University of Victoria, and who has authorized its use herein by permission.

As you examine Figure 0.1, you will notice that although there is a step-by-step order to the sequence that follows the one we have suggested, there are also many direct and indirect feedback loops to represent the eventualities that seemed likely to the student-preparer. For example, the bold arrows represent a constant feedback loop, which indicates the instability of the venture creation process: that at any point in the process, one must be prepared to go "back to square 1." Three sets of dotted lines suggest additional possibilities (three feedback Rs) that can be anticipated in special cases as follows:

1. *Repeated* (often called "serial") *entrepreneurship,* as has been represented in Figure 0.1 by the "- – -" designation. This usually occurs once an entrepreneur has created a venture that is now in the ongoing operations/growth stage, and the desire arises to once again create a new venture.

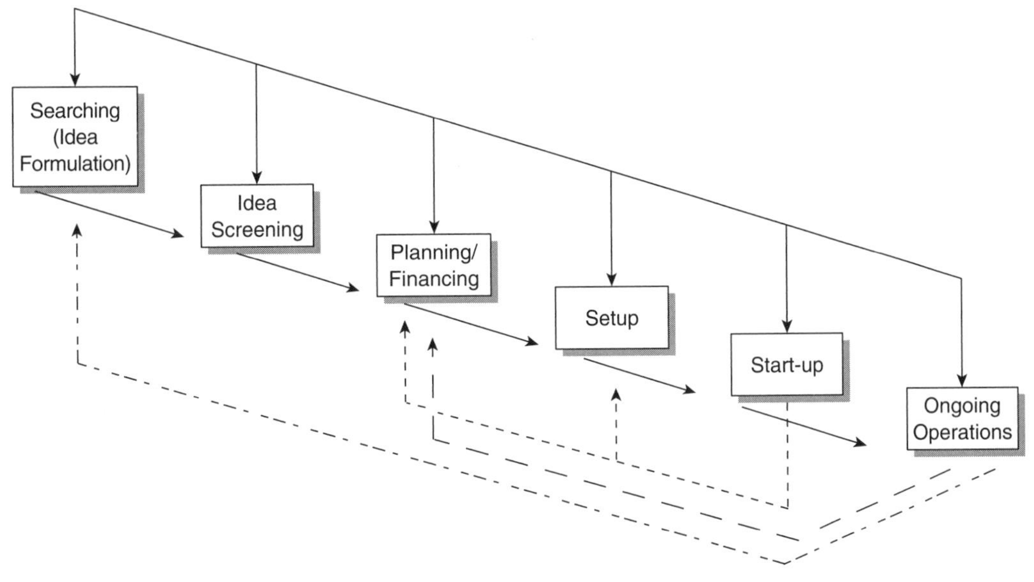

Figure 0.1 Venture Creation Master Sequence

2. *Response to turbulence,* represented by the "– – –" designation. In the life of any business, there can come a time when markets change, disruptive technologies enter the venturing space, or other factors suggest that it is time to make a new plan that is financed accordingly.

3. *Rethinking the venture,* represented by the "- - -" designation. Sometimes, usually during setup or start-up, right after an entrepreneur moves into venture formation mode, certain flaws or surprises come to light that require an immediate response. These are not so serious as to sink the venture, requiring a "return to square 1," but they can and should be anticipated, and preparations should be made to be able to respond effectively should they occur.

A more detailed process, described in the chapters that follow, supports each of the steps in this master sequence. Please remember, however, that the diagrammatic representations and the descriptions of the process that accompany them, although true to the basics of the venture creation process, are nevertheless also truly a representation of the particular individual who prepared them. In our experience over the past dozen or so years, each such representation of the venture creation process is unique—and we have seen hundreds of them. Some script diagrams show a highly constrained process and represent venture creation as a set of cause → effect steps because this is the way a particular individual visualizes the venture creation process. Other script diagrams represent more an effect → cause approach, in which the venture creation process is emergent and depends heavily on the circumstances of that particular individual: "who they are, what they know, and whom they know," for "effectuation" of a new transaction or venture (Sarasvathy, 2001, p. 249). For ease of representation and understanding, the example we include herein is one that is more nearly at a *midpoint* between causal thinking at one extreme and effectuation thinking at the other, including many feedback loops and a recognition that venture creation processes can start or restart at any point. Thus, instead of viewing these process diagrams and descriptions as an ending point for describing, we invite you to please use them as a beginning point for developing an understanding and representation of your own venture creation process.

We begin with searching for new venture opportunities.

To Karl Vesper

1

Searching for Venture Opportunities

The Searching Process

The main purpose of the searching subsequence is to create an idea pool. In our experience, many costly venture creation errors could have been avoided if only the prospective entrepreneur were somehow able to refrain from chasing after the first venture that appeared on the horizon. This error can be described as, "Too little searching leading to inadequate screening."

What this means in real terms is that a great deal of entrepreneurial energy and effort ends up being misapplied on an undeserving venture idea. The way to avoid this error is for the prospective entrepreneur to set, as a minimum goal for the searching phase of the venture creation process, the generation of at least 25 venture ideas—and of sufficiently investigating them so that *at least five potentially viable options* are identified.

We use the words *viable options* deliberately. Recent advances in entrepreneurship scholarship suggest that those more effective entrepreneurs continually manage a portfolio of "real options," which can be thought of as small steps or actions that, when taken, have a maximum upside and a minimum downside (McGrath, 1999). The first step in the venture creation process, then, is to begin by searching for real options. Again, this means generating at least 25 venture ideas and sufficiently investigating them so that *at least* five *real options* are identified.

How can this be accomplished?

As we noted in the Introduction, there is an old saying in business that nothing happens until somebody sells something, but we also noted our opinion that this is only partially true: that nothing in business happens until somebody creates some work *and then* sells it to someone else. In essence: A transaction occurs when an individual creates a work *and* it is purchased by another person (Csikszentmihalyi, 1988; Gardner, 1993), as illustrated in Figure 1.1.

Thus, when in the searching stage of the venture creation process, venture creators are looking for *both* halves of a single real option: (a) a work (a product or a service) that can, in fact, be delivered and (b) a willing second party to purchase it (a market). The elements of the searching subsequence may therefore be divided into these two halves: the activities

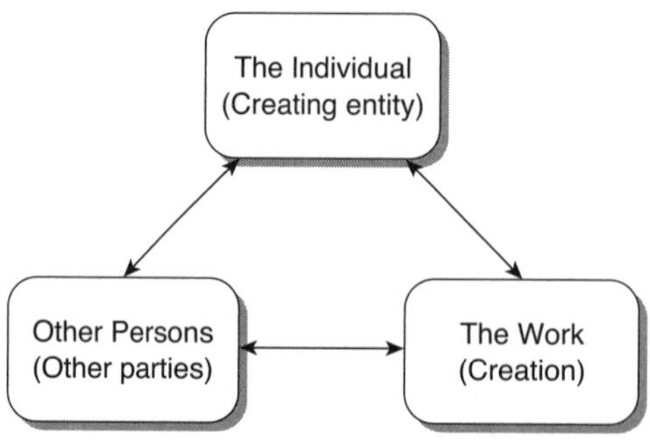

Figure 1.1 The Basic Transaction

Source: Based on Csikszentmihalyi (1988); Gardner (1993).

that lead to the capability to produce a valuable work and the activities that lead to the identification of an unmet need.

Depending on a person's preferences, a variety of methods can be used to generate the information needed in the searching process. Although more and more individuals create their idea pool by using a deliberate searching strategy (e.g., brainstorming, creativity retreats, etc.), most people's venture ideas come from first gaining experience in a particular industry so that they become so well trained in and so attuned to the methods and processes of producing a given product or service that they can recognize a new niche or a better way to do something (Vesper, 1996, pp. 56, 57, 60).

As illustrated in the student representation of the searching process that follows (see Figure 1.2), there comes a point during searching when a person's awareness of his or her productive capabilities combines with awareness of the product or service needs/wants of other persons to produce a new venture idea: a "work" to meet unmet needs/wants in the marketplace (Level 3 in Figure 1.2).

As a stepping-stone toward developing your own searching subsequence, we invite you to more closely examine the searching process as seen through the eyes of one of our former entrepreneurship students.

A Student's View of the Searching Process

The searching process, as viewed through the eyes of an entrepreneurship student, includes the following narrative that accompanies Figure 1.2. This narrative explains the figure and can be used to visualize many of the key elements necessary in the searching process. This student says the following:

My searching process operates in three consecutive levels:

Level 1

In Level 1, the origination level, my ideas stem from three sources:

a. Dissemination of information gathered (ideas collected through research required for scholastic activities, employment, personal interests, etc.)

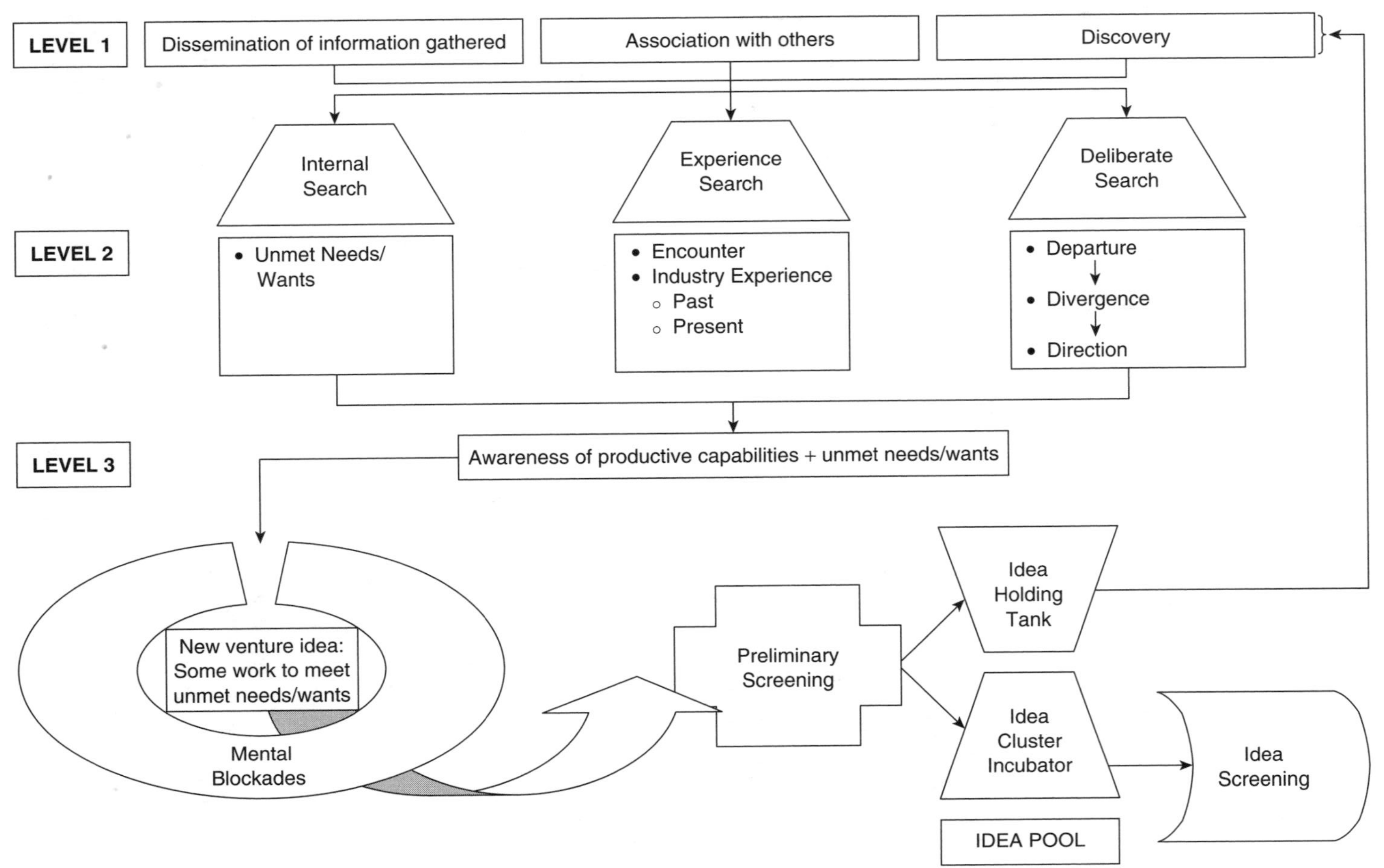

Figure 1.2 Searching (Idea Formulation)

b. Association with others (ideas collected through casual or formal conversation with peers, employers, friends, etc.)

c. Discovery (ideas discovered through cues from the external environment)

Level 2

In Level 2, the ideas that were formulated in Level 1 are now recognized through one of three idea "searches." These searches are as follows:

a. Internal search: a discovery of personal needs/wants that are not being satisfied in the marketplace

b. Experience search: involves uncovering problems and opportunities associated with a familiar domain (i.e., through employment in an industry, involvement in sports or a particular social setting)

c. Deliberate search: involves two stages:

   i. *divergence:* involves abstract, creative thinking designed to mitigate the impact of bounded rationality
   ii. *direction:* involves channeling the creative thoughts into more concrete ideas

The observations from these searches are coupled with unrecognized ideas from Level 1 and together form an awareness of the market's inability to create a successful transaction (with respect to the newly formulated idea).

Level 3

In effect, the searches uncover "cues" or "discoveries" that draw upon awareness of one's productive capability and of unmet needs and wants, to create a recognition of potential opportunities: venture ideas.

After these potential opportunities have been uncovered, however, a critical impasse at this stage is the mental blockade that needs to be overcome if the opportunity is to be uncovered. Such mental blockades are as follows:

i. Difficulty viewing it from different perspectives
ii. Fear of failure/risk
iii. Lack of (correct) information
iv. Discouragement by others
v. Too little time to devote to developing ideas

To overcome such obstacles, positive encouragement from others and from self is needed.

Now that the work needed to satisfy the unmet market needs and wants is uncovered by overcoming mental blockades, focus turns to a preliminary screen or assessment of the work. Questions should be asked, such as the following:

- Do I want to do this (i.e., does it fit my needs, passions, and morals)?
- Will the work satisfy the needs of the market?
- Is it a viable business opportunity (i.e., is it a "buy-a-job," struggling proprietary, etc.)?
- Can I afford to devote my time and effort to developing this idea?

- Why aren't others already capitalizing upon this opportunity?
- Can this venture work?
- Are there other ways to formulate the work?
- Are there other associative unfulfilled market needs/wants?

If the responses to these and other questions are favorable, then the ideas theoretically go to an "incubator" until they are ready to be screened (due to time constraints, other information that is still required, etc.).

If the responses to these questions are not favorable or if complications/problems arise during the preliminary screen, the ideas go to a holding tank for future consideration (until they are "awakened" by some cue). These ideas can be written down and stored in a file or simply left in my mind.

CASES

The following cases have been selected to help learners to develop and become more aware of their own searching processes.

LEVERAGING WAL-MART, EBAY AND USPS

Prepared by Ken Mark under the supervision of Professor Eric Morse

Version: (A) 2004-04-27

INTRODUCTION

David Lewis was mid-way through the second year of his MBA at a prestigious East Coast business school. It was early January 2004, and Lewis had a great idea for a new business, or so he believed:

> With all the perceived time pressures on our busy schedules, I believe that there exists a niche market segment—let's call it the "time-starved" segment—that is willing to pay my future firm to provide product pick-up and delivery services and, in the case of businesses, conserve staff resources. The concept itself is pretty simple: My warehouse is Wal-Mart, my storefront is eBay, my delivery service is the U.S. Postal Service, and customers can contact me directly through my pager, cell phone or by e-mail.

A newspaper clipping from *The Wall Street Journal* had provided the spark for Lewis's new idea. While on a break during a recent shopping trip, Lewis read that:

> . . . many toy retailers say they can't afford to match Wal-Mart prices, particularly those (toys which are priced) below their cost. They note for example that Wal-Mart sells Barbie Swan Lake for $15.84[1]—below the wholesale price of $17 (for smaller retailers), according to a list of manufacturer prices

viewed by *The Wall Street Journal.* Wal-Mart sells Hot Wheels T-Wrecks Play Set for $29.74, below its wholesale price of $42, and Sesame Street Hokey Pokey Elmo at $19.46, below its $24 wholesale price.[2]

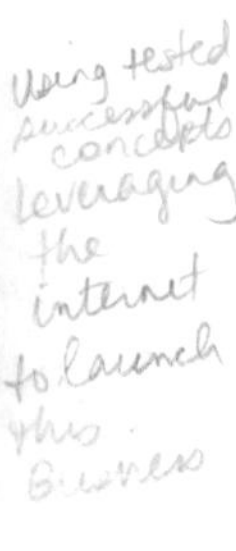

The idea that Wal-Mart sold goods below wholesale prices stuck with Lewis: "If I combined Wal-Mart's low prices with the United States Postal Service's delivery options, I can send an unlimited variety of goods across several time zones on short notice." He did some research on Wal-Mart, eBay and the United States Postal Service:

Wal-Mart as Warehouse

For its fiscal year 2003, Wal-Mart earned $8 billion on revenues of $247 billion. There were 1,568 Wal-Mart Discount Stores in the United States in January 2003, and most of them were open 24 hours a day. With an average store size of 95,000 square feet, Discount Stores carried 80,000 stock-keeping units (SKUs) in 40 departments of merchandise. Table 1 provides a list of the merchandise categories and their contributions to Wal-Mart store sales:

Table 1

Category	*% of WMT Sales*
Grocery, candy and tobacco—Canned goods, snacks, generic chocolates and candy items	24
Hardgoods—Hardware items such as screws, nails, fasteners, lightbulbs, automotive parts, plumbing supplies, utensils, small kitchen appliances	20
Soft goods/domestics—Home and bathroom supplies, towels, clothing, outerwear, underwear	18
Pharmaceutical—Vitamins, over-the-counter medication such as pain relievers and cold/flu syrups, contact lens supplies, footcare products	9
Electronics—Batteries, CDs, DVDs, video games, cameras, film, music supplies	9
Health and beauty aids—Shampoo, soap, dental supplies, mass-market beauty supplies, personal care products	7
Sporting goods and toys—Toys for all ages, footballs, fishing equipment, hockey equipment	6
Stationery—Pens, paper, files, folders, safes, calendars, school bags	3
One-hour photo—Photo-processing on-site	2
Jewelery—Basic jewelery pieces (low-end gold and silver), watches	1
Shoes	1

Source: SEC Filings, accessed 27 January 2004.

eBay as a Storefront

Lewis planned to build his own Web site. He estimated that it would cost him between $200 and $10,000 to outsource Web site construction. To build it himself would cost him two weeks, or 80 hours, of work. Web hosting would cost between $30 and $80 a month depending on the level of service Lewis required.

If Lewis chose to sell packaged combinations of products to online consumers (for example, a "back-to-school stationery set" or an "emergency set of clothing"), Lewis was aware of these fees charged by eBay, shown in Table 2.

U.S. Postal Service as Shipper

Lewis downloaded shipping costs from the U.S. Postal Service's Web site, and he organized the information in the format shown in Table 3.

The rates were for a package sized 30" × 30" × 30" and weighing up to five pounds, shipped from Boston, Massachusetts to San Francisco, California. Lewis believed that the express mail shipping specification represented the heaviest product, in the largest manageable package size, shipped the greatest distance, in the shortest possible period of time. Anything lighter, smaller, shipped closer and delivered later would cost a fraction of $27.30. Lewis had not decided yet if he would offer free shipping.

Other Costs

Lewis knew that he would need, at minimum, a cellular phone ($40 per month) and a pager (same cost). Office expenses, including business stationery, business registration and business cards, would come to approximately $800.

Table 2

Value of Package	*$10.00 to $24.99*	*$25 to $49.99*	*$50 to $199.99*	*$200 and up*
Insertion Fees	$0.55	$1.10	$2.20	$3.30
Picture Services	1st Pic. Free, each additional pic. $0.15	same	same	same
Final Value Fees	5.25% of closing value	5.25% of closing value of initial $25 plus 2.75% of remaining value	same	same

Table 3

Mail Service	*Est. Delivery Time*	*Rate*
Express Mail	Overnight to most areas	$27.30
Priority Mail	2 Days	$27.80
Parcel Post	7 Days	$22.64

Decision Time

Lewis knew there were many different paths he could pursue with this opportunity. Three of his many options were:

- *A concierge service for business service organizations.* Lewis knew many people working at the Big Four accounting firms and the information technology consulting firms. These consultant professionals often spent weeks on the road, visiting a client's many work sites. After a long day, Lewis was certain the last thing the professional wanted to do was to shop for personal or business supplies. So, there existed an opportunity to ship fresh clothing/personal care/stationery sets to consultant professionals staying at hotels nationwide, with the much-needed supplies arriving just in time.
- *An online (basic) gift basket service.* Since almost no organization could match Wal-Mart's buying power (and Wal-Mart itself was not in the gift basket service), Lewis's gift baskets (15 to 30 items, a value of $20 to $50 per gift basket) would not be easily undercut by lower prices elsewhere. Lewis knew there were some online gift basket services already in operation, but he concluded that these gift baskets were targeted at higher-end consumers—the products were often of very high quality and baskets cost upwards of $100.
- *An over-the-counter medication delivery service.* Lewis could pick and ship any combination of over-the-counter medication and other personal supplies to individual vacationers, travel tour groups or business people. Lewis was sure that while visiting local attractions, one of the last things these domestic tourists wanted to do was to seek out the local Wal-Mart and spend time waiting in line. Why not pick up supplies shipped to the hotel?

Lewis remarked:

> I envision my company fulfilling needs of this "last-minute" consumer or business segment in the U.S. market and growing very rapidly. The best part of this idea is that my start-up capital costs are minimal compared to almost any other high-potential businesses.

Lewis believed that he had a high potential business idea and was eager to get going. "After all," he remarked, "Michael Dell did start his now-$40-billion business in his university dorm room. . . ." Eager to jumpstart his company, Lewis wanted to generate as many great opportunities as possible. In addition, he wanted to identify any barriers he might encounter.

Notes

1. All amounts in U.S. dollars.
2. Ann Zimmerman, Joseph Pereira and Queena Sook Kim, "Wal-Mart Fires The First Shot In Holiday-Toy Pricing War," *The Wall Street Journal,* 19 November, 2003.

Barrie Charity Bingo

Prepared by Joe Bubel under the supervision of Professor Eric Morse

 Version: (A) 2004-08-10

It was June 2002, and Kevin Bubel was concerned about the financial drain placed on his company by his latest strategic move. Three months earlier, Bubel had purchased Mayfair Bingo, his only competitor in Barrie, Ontario, due to the threat of an impending smoking bylaw that would have placed both businesses in jeopardy. After purchasing Mayfair, Bubel was left with a 20,000-square-foot building, for which he had little use. Financing the building, utilities and property taxes was now costing him almost $500 a day.

Kevin Bubel and Barrie Charity Bingo

In 1996, at the age of 26, Kevin Bubel assumed managerial control of Barrie Charity Bingo (BCB). The business had been in operation for a total of four years and was making only a small profit. Over the course of the next several years, Bubel bought out all other BCB owners and, by 2001, he held 100 per cent of the business. There were two bingo halls in the Barrie area in 1996: BCB and Mayfair Bingo. Due to its convenient location, high prize giveaways and aggressive marketing, Mayfair Bingo owned 70 per cent of the market, while BCB held the remaining 30 per cent. During Bubel's first year as manager, BCB earned just over $60,000. By 2001, however, BCB was netting over $400,000, and by June 2002, BCB had eaten into Mayfair's market share, with each firm now holding about 50 per cent of the market. With profits increasing each year, Barrie Charity Bingo had become a great investment.

In 1999, BCB moved from its original location to a prime building in downtown Barrie. The building comprised 17,000 square feet, including one restaurant that was integrated into the bingo hall plus a separate restaurant that provided additional rental revenue for BCB. The city of Barrie was experiencing tremendous growth, which had contributed to BCB's success; the population of Barrie was well over 100,000 and the city was forecasted to be one of the fastest growing cities in Canada over the next 10 years.

Under the Ontario Gaming Control Act, charities were responsible for running each program (i.e., bingo session) for which they receive 60 per cent of the gaming revenues. The bingo hall owner (in this case, BCB) received the remaining 40 per cent of the revenue but is responsible for the running of the actual bingo hall, including all related costs such as rent, utilities, labor and debt servicing. Bubel established good relationships with all the charities he worked with, and the charities were especially grateful for the substantially increased revenues during Bubel's years as BCB manager.

The Barrie Smoking Bylaw and Response

In August 2001, Bubel was informed that the City of Barrie was considering the introduction of a bylaw that would prohibit smoking in all public places. As approximately 75 per cent of all bingo players are smokers, Bubel was very concerned that these players would be spending considerably less time and money at BCB if this bylaw were to be implemented. Bubel estimated that the new bylaw would reduce revenues to both of Barrie's bingo halls by 50 per cent.

Bubel concluded that, if this bylaw were to pass, it would be very difficult for both bingo halls to survive. Taking a proactive stance, Bubel immediately called the owner of Mayfair Bingo, and within two days he had signed a purchase agreement for $1.5 million. Bubel believed that the business was worth roughly $400,000, meaning he paid $1.1 million for a 20,000-square-foot building on two acres of prime land in Barrie. One condition of this purchase was that Mayfair would close its doors immediately, leaving BCB a monopoly in the Barrie bingo market.

It seemed very likely that the bylaw would be passed; however, the one remaining requirement was a majority vote from the city's aldermen (area representatives). Taking the argument that this bylaw would result in a $1.5 million loss of revenue for the city's charities, Bubel protested at weekly city council meetings, gave numerous interviews, wrote editorials for the city's newspapers and appeared on the local news. Bubel's argument was well received and, as a result, he was able to convince two aldermen to change their vote, resulting in a final tally of 6–4, giving BCB the only exemption from the bylaw.

BCB would therefore be the only building in the city of Barrie where smoking was not prohibited, and this unique status was guaranteed until at least 2007. Bubel had successfully kept his business alive. Now he had to decide what to do with the empty Mayfair building on Bellfarm Road.

Opportunities

The building on Bellfarm Road was costing Bubel almost $500 a day. He had hoped for a quick sale, but this had not materialized, and approximately $40,000 had already been spent on costs such as debt servicing, property taxes and utilities for the building. Although Bubel was not happy with this financial drain, he felt that the bingo monopoly would net him a further $250,000 per year.

The building itself was in excellent shape and in a good location with ready access to traffic (roughly 6,000 cars passed by daily) and close proximity to Highway 400. Any signage or addition added to the back of the building could be seen from the highway. It was carpeted, heated and fully furnished, with numerous tables and chairs, and it contained an office and a kitchen.

The building sat on two acres of prime land that could be conservatively valued at $400,000 per acre. The building would cost approximately $50 per square foot to build new, and leasehold improvements to fixture the interior in a like manner would cost another $15 per square foot.

Bubel considered his options: the first option would be to sell the building, relieving him of further losses. The second option would be to rent the space, which would cover the cost of holding the building. The third option was to keep it and use it himself. Bubel had done some research on self-storage, and he thought the building might be a good fit for this purpose.

Opportunity No. 1: Sell

When Bubel purchased Mayfair Bingo, his goal was to sell the building and continue running his own bingo hall. A few potential buyers had viewed the building during the past few months, but only one showed even mild interest in its purchase. The asking price was $1.35 million, although Bubel felt that any price over $1.1 million would be acceptable. Clearly the building was not going to be easy to sell. It was difficult to convince retail users that they needed 20,000 square feet, and industrial users were not willing to pay the asking price. Bubel would either have to drop the price or wait for the right buyer.

A slight deviation on the sell option surfaced when the owners of the building next door showed interest in purchasing the back parking lot to expand their own business. They were willing to pay $500,000 for the one-acre lot. This was attractive in that it would relieve some of Bubel's exposure, but it would work only if any new tenant would not need the back parking lot. Another disadvantage of selling the back lot was that the back part of the property could be seen from the highway. Moreover, Bubel was not sure how this deviation would affect the value of the remaining property.

Opportunity No. 2: Rent

Renting the building was another viable option. One possible prospect considered using the building as a large pool hall and bar. This potential tenant was a viable option. However, the tenant was demanding certain provisions, which included leasing only 10,000 square feet at a cost of $14 per square foot, as well as asking for $350,000 in leasehold improvements. Furthermore, they were asking for one year of free rent on a five-year lease.

This option was advantageous, as the rental income would cover the cost of holding the property. It was possible that, with a good tenant, the property value might actually increase in the future, and Bubel could perhaps sell it for a higher figure than the $1.35 million he was currently asking. On the other hand, if the new tenant was unsuccessful, the property may carry the stigma of housing failed businesses, and the building may ultimately be worth less than its current market value. There would certainly be upfront costs incurred in order to transform the building to the desired look required by any new tenant. These costs were estimated to be roughly $25 per square foot in leasehold improvements.

Another potential tenant considered using the building as a banquet hall. Bubel had approached all banquet facilities in the Barrie area and attempted to sell them on the benefits of leasing the building. The fit for a banquet hall was perfect. The building was carpeted and had numerous tables, chairs, a large kitchen and plenty of parking. It could seat approximately 600 people and could be divided into two or even three separate large rooms. Although a few banquet halls had showed serious interest, none had made an offer. Typically, a retailer in the Barrie area would pay around $12 per square foot per year for a large space. However, given the amount of total space involved, Bubel felt that a discount would be necessary, putting the price at around $9 a square foot.

Opportunity No. 3: Self-Storage

A third and totally different alternative involved Bubel opening a self-storage facility in the vacant building. Self-storage is the term used for a facility offering storage units on a month-to-month basis where the tenant can lock up their possessions for a monthly rental fee. A typical storage facility might be on two to five acres of land and would be anywhere in the range of 10,000 to 100,000 square feet. Many facilities offered large roll-up doors and direct drive-up access to conventional (outside) units. Facilities offering climate controlled premises usually offered interior hallways for access to the units.

Barrie had five main storage facilities, ranging in size from 10,000 square feet to 40,000 square feet. Presently, all facilities were at least 85 per cent occupied and were grossing on average $14 per square foot per year. The main niche that Bubel felt he could target would be indoor, heated/cooled mini storage. Only one competitor offered indoor facilities, and they were charging close to $18 per square foot per year in an inferior location. The advantages of an indoor facility included a better atmosphere for an individual's possessions, the ability to target commercial customers due to the sprinkler system and better security.

The building on Bellfarm seemed ideal for self-storage, but there were some reservations. The major concern was that, in order to take advantage of economies of scale, the building should be 40,000 square feet. Of the 40,000 square feet, only about 75 per cent of it would be leaseable due to hallways, an office and other necessary requirements. An expansion to 40,000 square feet would cost $1.1 million for the new construction and another $300,000 for leasehold improvements on the original structure. This financing would be difficult to obtain due to most bank's reluctance to finance self-storage facilities. The other main obstacle was the fact that a new self-storage facility would have difficulty obtaining initial customers. The main advertising source of self-storage was the Yellow Pages, which did not print again until August of 2003.

Now that Bubel had examined these options, he was wondering whether there were other alternatives that he had not yet considered. Would he be able to use the vacant building in another way? Many of his friends and advisors had suggested a banquet hall, while others remained skeptical about retail use for 20,000 square feet. The financial burden continued, and he hoped to come up with something sooner rather than later.

TAKAHIKO NARAKI, THE THREE MILLION YEN ENTREPRENEUR

Prepared by Jason Inch under the supervision of Professor Eric Morse

Version: (A) 2004-09-15

INTRODUCTION

In June 2003, Takahiko Naraki, owner of a Japanese *yuugen-gaisha*[1] called B.I.P. Limited (BIP), sat in his hospital bed in Nagoya after collapsing from an apparent stress-related seizure. He had spent the last two weeks working nonstop and travelling between Nagoya and Tokyo by *Shinkansen*[2] for sales promotion (see Exhibit 1). With his first day off in what seemed like months, Naraki considered the future of his venture. He was so close to success he could almost taste it, but was it worth the toll it was taking on his health and family? Could he find another way to accomplish his entrepreneurial goals without sacrificing so much?

TAKAHIKO NARAKI AND BIP

After graduating from university in 1995, Takahiko "Taka" Naraki joined a small Nagoya-based printing and advertising firm as an account executive. A natural salesman, he epitomized the hectic lifestyle of an on-the-go *salaryman* by having a high customer service ethic and by working around the clock to build relationships. Two years after graduation, he was unsatisfied with the company's expectations that he would stay in his position for the long term with little upside potential, so he left this budding career in advertising and sales to start the first in a series of entrepreneurial ventures.

In Japan at that time, being an entrepreneur was quite rare for somebody in their mid-20s, and it was legally difficult due to government regulations; however, Naraki formed BIP as a *yuugen-gaisha* in July 1997 by raising the legally-required ¥3 million[3] of start-up capital from friends and family. After his first venture in international trade became unprofitable due to the lingering effects of the Asian Economic Crisis that year, Naraki considered switching to Japan-based service businesses that could be positioned as recession-proof investments for BIP's equity.

One such business was education. In Japan, education had always been the path to success, so most parents had high ambitions for their children to attend top schools. Naraki established his own *juku*[4] where he would be both owner and head instructor. The *juku* was modestly successful, but Naraki found that although the revenues were steady, growth was going to be slow. There were two reasons for this: he was using all his free time for teaching, and he had also taken a part-time job working for a catalogue sales company to make some extra money. In 2001, Naraki decided to keep the part-time job but close the *juku*, and then focus on a new technology-based business model he had been considering.

Naraki had wanted to get involved in a high-tech venture since the emergence of the Internet in Japan around 1997. His interest was renewed when NTT DoCoMo introduced mobile phone services that included Web browsing, short message service (SMS) and e-mail. The success of DoCoMo's *i-mode* service for Internet was nothing short of spectacular, with subscriptions growing from four million users in 2000 to more than 30 million just two years later.[5] The keys to DoCoMo's growth were popular functionality, technological advancement and synchronization along the entire value chain. By becoming the

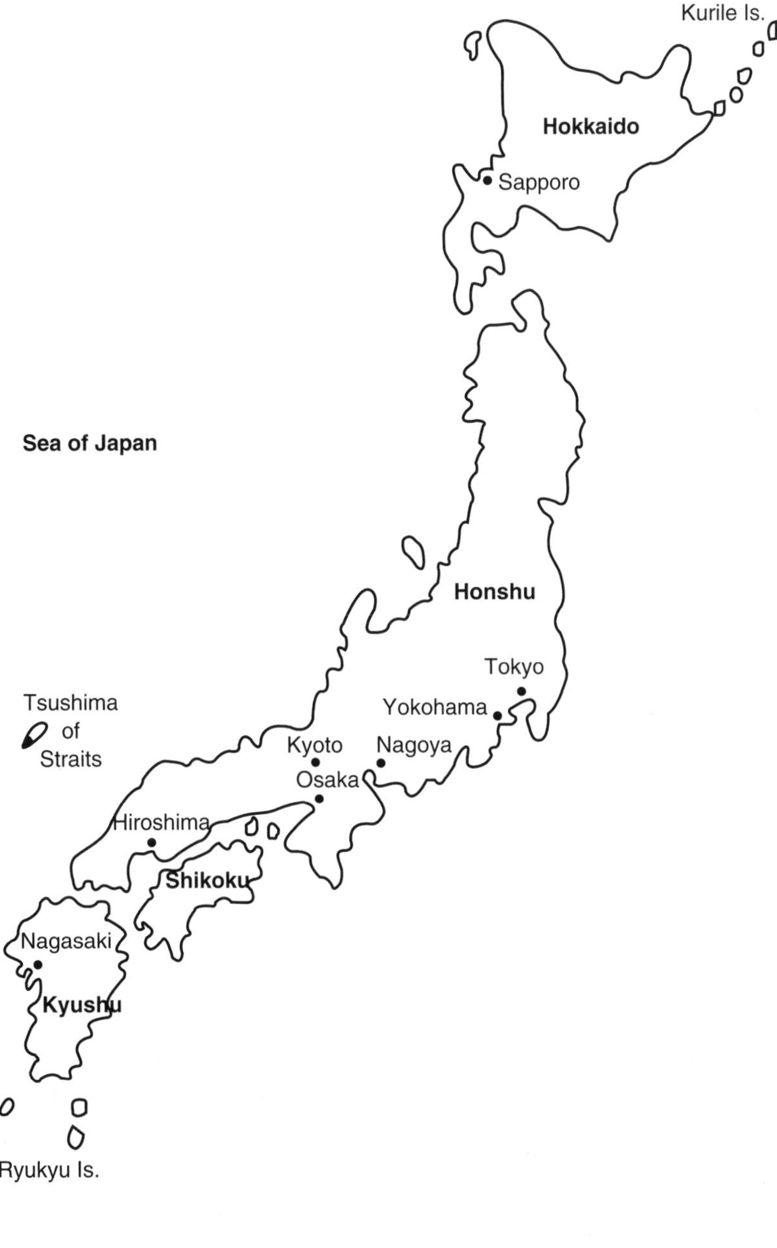

Exhibit 1 Map of Japan

Note: Nagoya is Japan's fourth largest city, located centrally in Japan approximately 366 kilometres from Tokyo, with a population of about 2.17 million (2000 census data, Statistics Bureau, Japanese Ministry of Public Management, Home Affairs, Posts and Telecommunications). By Nozomi train, the fastest type of Shinkansen service, it takes 90 minutes to travel from Tokyo to Nagoya.

nexus of content, service billing and handset hardware, DoCoMo provided a superior user experience.[6] Naraki believed that with the popularity of DoCoMo and increased usage of dial-up and broadband Internet services,[7] he could leverage his experience in sales and advertising to create a product that would deliver personalized content over the Internet to mobile phones in a new way.

The Rebirth of BIP

Naraki began to establish BIP anew in 2001 by attending business mixers and telling associates about his Internet-delivered marketing concept. He worked extensively with a network of mentors and senior businesspeople who helped him in a number of ways, from introducing him to other business people to providing environments for pilot projects. He also continued and expanded his relationship with the president of the catalogue sales company, where Naraki was asked to take charge of the new Internet-based sales activities. Naraki spent a great deal of his time doing personal favors for senior businesspeople—tasks often completely unrelated to BIP—to build relationships for his *jin-myaku.*[8]

At the same time, Naraki started to learn as much as he could about Internet technology itself. He became sufficiently skilled at Web site development to build a prototype of what he called "Next Generation X" (NGX) that was delivered over the Internet by Web browsing software rather than by mobile phones. NGX was designed to deliver messages from a particular company to customers who had requested to be on the company's list. The customers gave their permission for this type of "push" marketing by agreeing to download and install a desktop application from the company's Web site. By building it as a desktop application, Naraki tried to differentiate NGX from similar products such as toolbars in the Web browser or Java applets as part of homepages. Naraki attained early expressions of interest from Dentsu, the world's largest advertising company, and did a pilot project involving World Cup soccer.

This form of so-called permission marketing was based on similar concepts then in use in the U.S. market but differed in the way that Japanese consumers reacted to the company using their personal information. Whereas consumers in the United States were often upset over companies using personal information and violating an implicit or explicit privacy policy, according to Naraki, Japanese consumers often regarded messages from a company they had an interest in to be welcome and an indication of benefit to that consumer not offered to people outside the customer group (i.e., some exclusivity was implied, making the Japanese consumer feel special and unique).

Naraki called this willingness of Japanese consumers to be included on company-sponsored lists the "Natural Permission Method" because it was natural that the consumer would think they were benefiting from, rather than being used by, the transaction. Of course, the company benefited as well, and Naraki ultimately intended to gain revenues from companies that wanted to use NGX as a form of customer relationship management (CRM) to drive promotional campaigns.

Strategic Partnerships

Naraki's investment in networking paid off when he met the president of Affiliate Company (KK) Inc.,[9] Mr. Takayanagi, at a business mixer. The Affiliate Company (Affiliate) specialized in channel marketing to specific consumer groups such as job seekers and students. One of Affiliate's biggest customer segments included companies that wanted to reach, and eventually hire, graduating students during the *shushoku-katsudou* season.[10] Affiliate was interested in developing NGX to support this business model.

NGX needed some technical upgrades and further development since the prototype was originally developed by Naraki and was not ready for usage on a wide scale. Through an introduction by the owner of the office centre where Affiliate's one-person Tokyo satellite branch was located, Naraki met the president of another small company, Mr. Ishikawa of E.X. NetCom (KK) Inc. Ishikawa's company specialized in software development, and Ishikawa himself was of a similar entrepreneurial mindset to Naraki and Takayanagi's, so the three presidents came to a verbal agreement to produce the first true salable implementations of NGX. This software would be marketed to customers of Affiliate under the name Browser SP (see Exhibit 2).

Sales of NGX

The value proposition for the Affiliate version of NGX software worked by connecting job-seeking students to student-seeking companies. Students looking for jobs would be motivated to download one of the NGX installation files from a recruiting Web site or pick up a CD from a company they were interested in. The company could, in fact, compel the job seekers to install the software by offering bulletins and updates only through NGX, and many early customers would elect to do just that, seeing NGX as a clear channel direct to the future employee. Consequently, the main targets for sales of NGX initially would be large Japanese companies with significant hiring programs.

Affiliate, having dealt with this group of corporate customers before by selling Web pages and e-mail programs as the recruitment tools, approached one of its customers, NTT. A few months after the software redevelopment had taken place, a trial was launched with NTT. The trial was successful, and a year and a half later, approximately 50 companies, including NTT, Mitsui & Co., Tokyo Marine and other large corporations, were paying to use one or more versions of the NGX product, generating revenues for Affiliate of ¥480,000 to ¥880,000 per year per customer[11] depending on the features they purchased. Despite the fact that Naraki had come up with the concept and had personally done most of the groundwork, BIP was to receive a share of revenues of only about 25 per cent. The business was expected to grow for the next two years with the current iteration of NGX software.

SuperX

In early 2003, Naraki started to work directly with E.X. NetCom to develop the next generation of NGX, which Ishikawa and Naraki now called SuperX. SuperX was based on the same concept as the earlier NGX, except it now used Macromedia Flash Web publishing technologies that were becoming more popular, and it was designed to be hosted and maintained completely by E.X. NetCom and BIP in an application service provider (ASP) format. SuperX customers would come from segments other than the employee-seeking companies targeted by Affiliate. In fact, Affiliate would not be involved with the development of this next generation product, allowing BIP to retain more of the revenues.

SuperX would include new features that would finally realize Naraki's dream of mobile phone integration of NGX. Taking advantage of the latest mobile and Internet technologies, SuperX could also use video and other multimedia features. The ASP-hosted configuration also included an administrative interface so that customers could better manage their own SuperX applications (a task often provided by Naraki as a free service when selling NGX). SuperX was designed to appeal to a broad range of customers and have many potential applications involving CRM.

Business Operations

During the development and early sales phases of NGX, Naraki continued to support his business through his part-time job—with full-time responsibilities—at the catalogue sales company, which paid him ¥300,000 yen per month

配布方法

User downloads NGX app from webpage, or receives disk or CD.

An NGX or company icon is put on the desktop after installation.

貴社ロゴマークアイコン

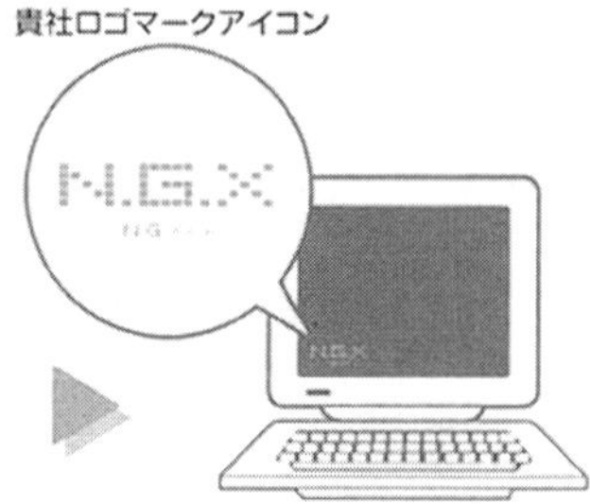

Real-time Message Window, updated as needed.

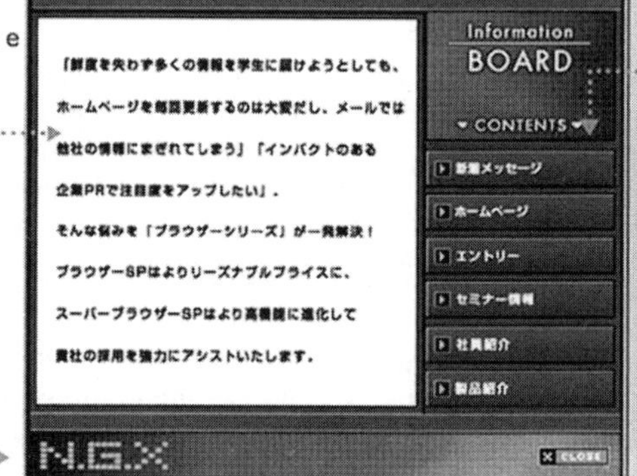

Typical menu items:
Greeting
Homepage link
Applications
Seminars
Meet an Employee
Company Info

Additional customizable branding.

貴社パソコン
Administrator Access

Administrator access site allows:

Real-time updating of content
Ability to send out flash bulletins
Monitor usage of the application

Exhibit 2 Screenshot of NGX, "Browser SP" Version

Source: Company files.

for continuing work on its Internet sales initiative. What Naraki did not spend on supporting his family, he spent on BIP expenses including frequent travel on the *Shinkansen* to Tokyo from Nagoya at ¥21,000 round-trip, capsule hotel stays at ¥9,000 per night, and large mobile phone bills, ¥50,000 per month on average in total from his four separate phones.[12] In a typical month, he might travel to Tokyo seven or eight times, generally staying overnight. Since its establishment, BIP had broken even on the *juku* business, but, from the start of 2002, no significant revenues had come in. The first year's revenues for NGX from Affiliate would be received around September 2003 and were projected to be about ¥7.8 million.

Naraki had no employees helping him in BIP but instead worked with staff from Affiliate or from E.X. NetCom. For example, in the NGX project, Affiliate provided some of the salespeople (Naraki did some sales and promotion management) and E.X. NetCom did some technical development. Naraki saw his role as a facilitator of business between other companies, with BIP acting in the role of intermediary, bringing together companies and relationships from Naraki's personal network.

For financial management, Naraki outsourced his bookkeeping to a Nagoya-based accountant because he was too busy. He had few regular costs and, because of the nature of his business, he used no promotional advertising beyond business cards.

Strategically, although he had a strong vision for the future, Naraki admitted that his day-to-day management of the company was often neglected. He did not yet have a formal business plan. Instead he prepared proposals on a project-by-project basis.

Options

Aside from the most drastic choice of quitting his business and returning to a *salaryman* career, which in itself would be difficult because of age discrimination, Naraki was being forced, by his deteriorating health and financial situation, to at least consider options to manage his time better to reduce stress. *Karoshi*[13] was a risk his family worried about greatly.

Naraki also thought that personal or company bankruptcy was something to be avoided at all costs. While North American entrepreneurs often failed at least once in their business careers and could accept this as a learning or growth opportunity, the same could not be said in Japan, where the statistic for business recovery from bankruptcy is much lower, and failure is not easily tolerated or forgiven. For example, due to the low borrowing rates banks could charge, lenders often pursued friends and family guarantors of company debt. The legal complications and stigma attached to failure are believed to contribute significantly to more than 30,000 annual suicides in Japan each year, 71 per cent by men in 2001,[14] a figure that is proportionately double that of the United States.[15]

Putting these risks aside, Naraki had a drive and energy to keep going, and he refused to think about quitting just when the business seemed to be on the verge of success. To keep going, however, Naraki knew he needed to address the issues of personal time management, business growth and financing.

A key limiting factor for Naraki's business growth was that he was constantly short of time to focus on BIP because of his frequent travel and part-time job at the catalogue-sales company. Additionally, he was in the main sales role, which forced him to go to the customers, who were nearly all in Tokyo. He considered establishing a presence in Tokyo, with either a small office or by moving. Affiliate, a Nagoya-based company, made the decision to open a small office in Tokyo, and it had greatly helped its business to grow, but the cost of establishing an office in Tokyo could also be prohibitive for a business without revenues or capital. A complete move for Naraki and his family would be very difficult and expensive, and he would sever ties with a lot of his Nagoya-based network, while a partial move (such as two weeks in Tokyo, two weeks in Nagoya) might still alienate Tokyo customers, who often demanded near-instant response.

Naraki's agreements with Affiliate and E.X. NetCom were, at this point, quite informal, despite the increasingly large commitment in terms of work and financial support. Naraki, in keeping with his character, thought that contracts and formal agreements were an imposition on his customers and partners, but, even so, he was a little worried. On the one hand, a stronger alliance with Affiliate seemed to promise revenue growth, while a bigger partnership with E.X. NetCom would ensure continued technical development. Both strategic partners were in better financial health than BIP, giving them some leverage in terms of what options they might consider financially. On the other hand, Naraki's marketing expertise and vision of the future of the SuperX project was largely his own, so he could either hire developers and attempt to grow internally or try to build a stronger alliance with E.X. NetCom.

With growth of NGX looking promising, the timing might be right to raise some money, but Naraki felt fiercely independent and didn't want to have additional shareholders in the business. He had already invested ¥3 million of friends and family capital and thought that more than this would shoulder him with too much responsibility for other people's money. Japan's regulated business environment, including rules against preferred shares and employee stock options before 1998, made venture capital or angel investors a rare commodity in the country. While Japan had seen increasing levels of investment in technology companies in the past three years by foreign investors,[16] it still lagged far behind levels of investment in North America, Europe, and other parts of Asia (see Exhibit 3). However, Naraki didn't want his business judgment to be compromised by outside investors who might try to manage him or change his vision. Finally, he could consider bank financing. The perennially low interest rates in Japan, hovering around zero per cent for many years, meant that business loans could be extended at rates as low as two per cent as long as there was a personal guarantor other than Naraki. He had never tried to apply for a bank loan for his business.

The Dilemma

There was extreme pressure on Naraki because of all his conflicting responsibilities in both Nagoya and Tokyo. He was trying to please everybody, partners and customers alike, with extremely good service. In June 2003, after he returned to Nagoya from an especially challenging two weeks, Naraki was driving his car when he suddenly suffered a seizure. It appeared to be some kind of panic attack, which he had never experienced before. Taken to the hospital by ambulance, Naraki soon recovered, but his doctor ordered bed rest. With nothing to do, Naraki's mind wandered to introspection: Should he continue to run BIP when it clearly was having a negative effect on his health? And if he did continue, how should he expand and finance his vision for the company?

Notes

1. Yuugen-gaisha—a Japanese limited liability company. Historically, a barrier to entrepreneurship in Japan has been the legal requirement to have at least ¥3 million of paid-in capital to register as an LLC. In an effort to encourage entrepreneurial activity, the minimum capital requirement law was changed in February 2003 to allow companies to register with as little as ¥1 of capital.

2. Shinkansen—the bullet train.

3. US$1 = approximately ¥120 in 2001.

4. Juku—preparatory school for exams and advanced learning, also known as a cram school.

5. NTT DoCoMo Web site, http://www.nttdocomo.com, accessed February 20, 2004.

6. Vandenbosch, M. and N. Dawar (2002), "Beyond Better Products: Finding, Building and

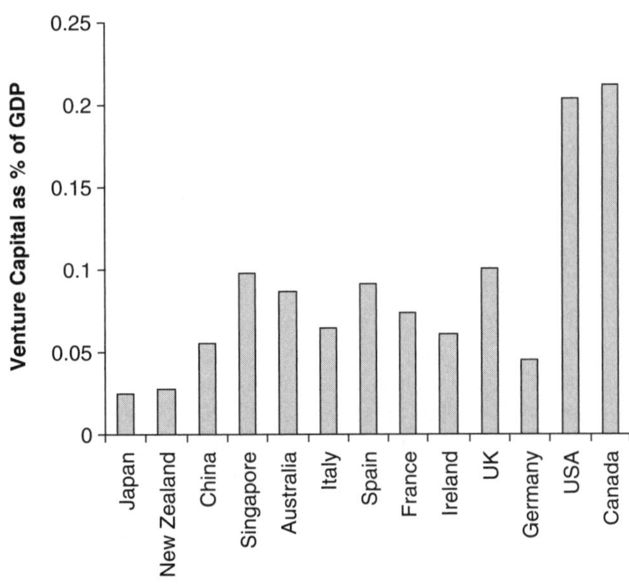

Exhibit 3 Venture Capital Investing in Selected Countries (2002)

Source: Bygrave Reynolds, et al., "Global Entrepreneurship Monitor: 2002 Summary Report," November 30, 2002.

Note: Venture capital comprises investments in seed, early, start-up and expansion stage companies.

Capturing Value in Customer Interactions," Sloan Management Review (Summer).

7. Internet usage had increased to 57.2 million users by December 2002, 5.6 million of them using DSL, for a 44.7 per cent penetration rate. (Sources: ITU Dec 2002 statistic, and Ministry of Home Management, Public Affairs, Posts and Telecommunications DSL adoption historical data: http://www.soumu.go.jp/joho_tsusin/eng/Statistics/number_users031128_1.html accessed February 24, 2004.)

8. Jin-myaku—human network or personal connections.

9. "Inc." is used herein to indicate a Japanese kabushiki-kaisha (KK), an incorporated company with stricter regulatory rules and a larger ¥10 million capital requirement, compared to the smaller yuugen-gaisha designation.

10. Shushoku-katsudou is a Japanese custom of having all new employees apply and later enter as a group at the same time every year to increase cohesiveness and provide an environment for company training.

11. Source: Affiliate promotional specification sheets.

12. Calling people from the same provider network was cheaper or even free, compared with cross-network calls.

13. Karoshi—death by overwork. Most common in the Bubble Economy years of the late '80s, karoshi is still a persistent problem in Japan causing an estimated 317 deaths in 2002 as officially reported by the Japanese Ministry of Health, Labour and Welfare (source: http://www.fpcj.jp/e/shiryo/jb/0334.html accessed February 24, 2004).

14. Japanese National Police Agency statistic for 2001.

15. Based on published World Health Organization statistics, 2001.

16. Yoost, Kerley, Tanaka, "On the Horizon: Private Equity Rising in Japan," *The Asian Wall Street Journal*, August 7, 2001.

CASCADIA WATER CORPORATION

Prepared by Professor Eric Morse

 Version: (A) 2004-10-01

On August 10, 1999, Leo Commandeur founded Cascadia Water Corporation in Victoria, British Columbia, with the intent of owning and operating water reclamation facilities. Commandeur planned to issue a Private Placement Offering Memorandum on September 1, 1999, but first he needed to develop a creative business model that would attract investors.

THE WATER RECLAMATION INDUSTRY

Global population growth, economic expansion, heightened public concern about water quality, growing regulatory and legislative requirements, and an overall decreasing supply of potable (drinkable) water had led to a demand for better methods of wastewater treatment and the necessity to conserve water through water reclamation. Due to the aforementioned factors, but also due to governmental fiscal restraint, much of North America's water and wastewater works needed major upgrading or replacement. Water and wastewater works were deteriorating, maintenance was being deferred, service delivery was less efficient and ecosystems were being stressed in various ways. By doing only critical maintenance in the last 15 to 20 years, many operators of water facilities, primarily municipal governments, had compounded the problem as urban growth had risen exponentially over the same time period. Estimates of the costs to upgrade and regain the existing water and wastewater infrastructure in Canada ranged from $3.8 billion to $4.9 billion.

Public awareness and governmental concern regarding the increasing scarcity of water (see Exhibit 1), the quality of drinking water and the potential health hazards associated with waste products discharged into the environment had resulted in legislation, regulation and enforcement requiring strict standards for potable water and restrictions on the discharge of pollutants in municipal wastewater. Commandeur believed that these measures were likely to result in increased pressure on local governments to upgrade existing water quality.

In many areas of Canada and the United States, aging municipal water and wastewater treatment infrastructure was operating at or near capacity, was in need of substantial capital expenditures and was not well equipped to satisfy increasing regulatory and legislative requirements. As a result, many communities were seeking innovative solutions to their wastewater treatment needs, such as improved technologies and equipment, and various outsourcing and service options, including contract operations and privatization. Outside Canada and the United States, aging infrastructure and, in many cases, underdeveloped infrastructure also required significant capital and advanced technological approaches to address the population's potable water and sewage treatment needs.

Industrial and commercial businesses were mandated to treat their wastewater. Government regulations regarding the disposal of wastewater, combined with public concern regarding industrial pollution, had led to increased awareness on the part of businesses and public utilities as to the benefits of wastewater treatment in waste minimization. In response to increasing water prices and wastewater discharge fees, industrial and commercial businesses had also become aware of the cost effectiveness of recycling their wastewater and often required complex systems

WORLDWIDE FRESH WATER AVAILABILITY TODAY

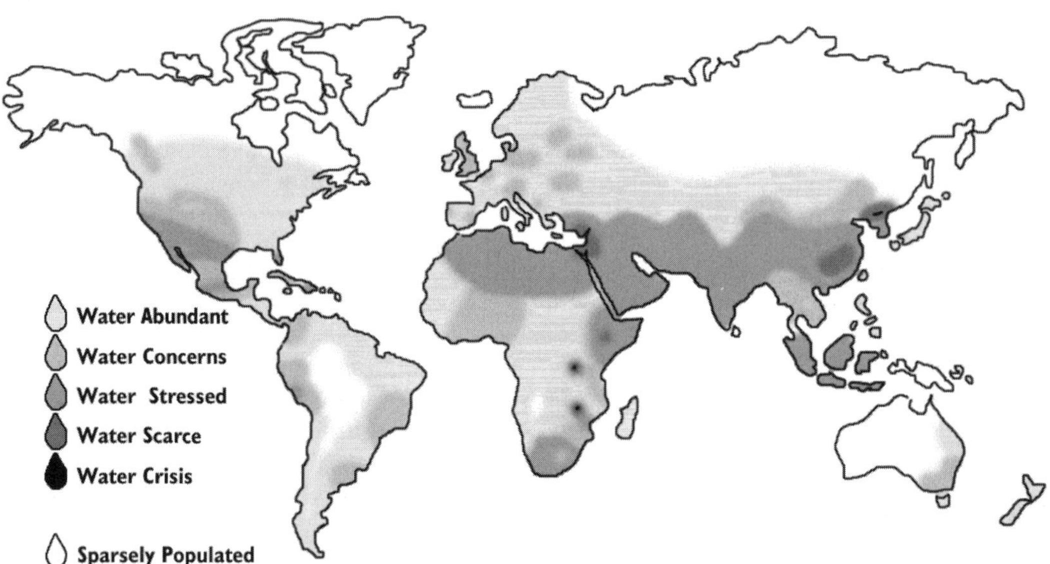

COMPOUNDED BY POPULATION GROWTH AND INFRASTRUCTURE NEEDS (through 2020)

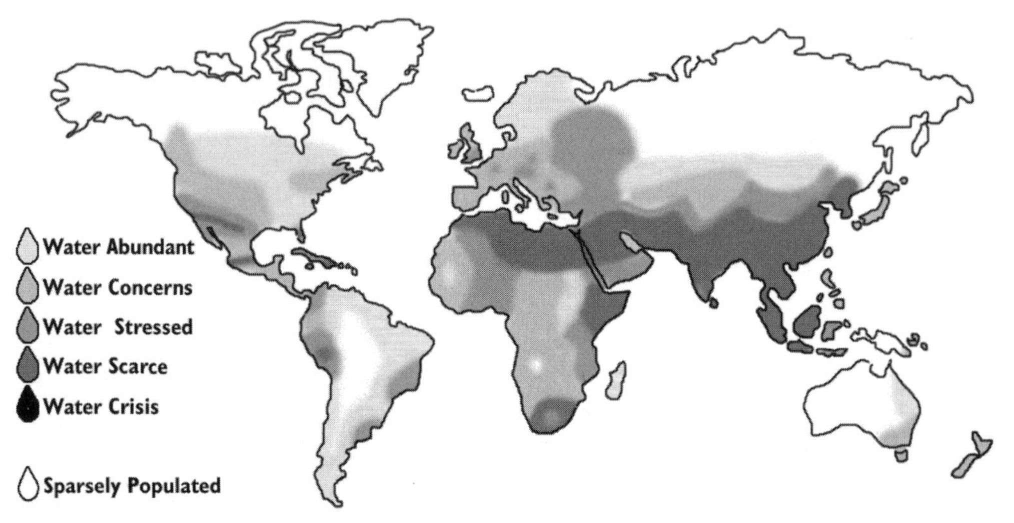

Exhibit 1

Source: United States Filter Corporation, 1998.

and equipment to treat and recycle process water and wastewater.

More and more municipalities were beginning to use Public/Private Partnerships (P3s) to design, build and operate municipal wastewater treatment facilities. The P3 industry was more developed in Western Europe than in North America due to Western European governments' willingness to employ the P3s for their municipal wastewater treatment facilities.

The U.S. and Canadian P3 industry was less developed due to government's historical control of facility operations and maintenance; however, a private industry was beginning to emerge as more and more municipalities realized the benefits of using P3s for water/wastewater facilities. There were an estimated 3,100 private water/wastewater companies based in the United States.

Canadian municipalities had recently begun to investigate P3s for water and wastewater facility operations. The Canadian Council for Public-Private Partnership, located in Toronto, Ontario, had identified 36 such projects under development or under serious consideration in Canada. The opportunity for P3s with local governments in Canada had never been so pronounced. Local governments were seeking greater value for money spent on wastewater space works, reduced risk and more innovation. In order to realize these benefits, local governments were becoming increasingly interested in partnerships with the private sector.

Competition

The wastewater facilities market was extremely fragmented. Wastewater reclamation facilities (WRFs) were sold to institutional, industrial, municipal/government, and military markets worldwide through a direct sales force, original equipment manufacturers and an international network of agents, representatives and distributors. The global market was dominated by a number of very large corporations, including Vivendi from France and its recently acquired subsidiary, U.S. Filter. However, these large international companies tended to focus on larger markets which would allow smaller Canadian or U.S. companies to pursue small municipal works opportunities without significant international competition.

An estimated 40 companies across Canada manufactured water treatment equipment for the domestic market, and more than 100 companies were involved in industrial water treatment systems. In 1999, there were approximately 10 wastewater treatment companies operating in Western Canada. Commandeur felt that as the wastewater treatment industry and P3s became better understood and accepted, the number of wastewater treatment companies in Canada would likely increase dramatically.

Cascadia

Cascadia was founded on the concept that small to mid-sized North American communities had a need for an integrated set of capabilities and technologies to solve wastewater problems. In August of 1999, management of Cascadia was in the planning stage of the business of owning and operating WRFs. These facilities would take wastewater as the raw material and transform it into cleaned water (reclaimed water) that could then be sold to customers who had a demand for non-potable water. Cascadia would own and operate the infrastructure for recycling wastewater into reclaimed water, deriving revenues primarily from ownership and operations contracts. Monthly user fees would provide the Corporation with an ongoing, low-risk annuity.

Only a fraction of the daily residential uses of water was for drinking and bathing. Reclaimed water had many industrial and residential uses, such as irrigation, flushing toilets and urinals, washing cars and other specific industrial purposes.

Although Canadians took clean abundant water for granted, many parts of North America were struggling to meet the current and projected future demand for potable water. Water was already a valuable commodity, and Cascadia believed that it was in a unique position to provide solutions for the demand for potable water by allowing communities and industries to leverage their wastewater into a reusable resource, thus lowering the demand for potable water.

Cascadia intended to develop two WRFs with the proceeds from its upcoming Offering. These facilities would be used to validate and further develop the Corporation's business model and market strategy. Theoretically, Cascadia would be able to generate three streams of revenue from the ownership and operations of the WRFs. Cascadia would first receive a one-time connection fee for every connection to the WRF (this is true only for new construction). Second, Cascadia would receive a monthly processing fee for processing wastewater. Third, a revenue stream would be generated from the resale of the water to customers such as car washes, golf courses, cement plants and other non-potable water users (see Exhibit 2).

Although Cascadia's initial market focus was on providing solutions to small to mid-sized, water-short communities and developments, Cascadia management anticipated growth in the non-potable water industry that would expand the market for WRFs in all water-short communities.

Strategic Alliance With HM&A

Contingent upon the issuance of the Offering Memorandum on September 1, 1999, Cascadia would enter into a strategic alliance agreement with Hill Murray & Associates Inc. (HM&A). HM&A was an engineering, construction, operations and utility management company with expertise in the design and build of wastewater projects and services. A unique advantage of HM&A was that they could design and build facilities that were scalable through the simple addition of incremental processing equipment. This allowed HM&A to build infrastructure in a just-in-time format. This approach was radically different from the existing industry practice that designs and constructs a facility on day one that can meet or exceed the forecasted daily flow rate for the projected ultimate daily wastewater flow of the project.

Trevor Hill, an officer and director of Cascadia, was also an officer, director and controlling shareholder of HM&A. Since its inception in 1993, HM&A had constructed and commissioned 14 WRFs (see Exhibit 3). Under the terms of this alliance, HM&A would design and construct the WRF, and Cascadia would own and operate it. HM&A would be given the opportunity to bid on every WRF design and construction contract that Cascadia was involved with and would have to submit a competitive bid to provide services to Cascadia. Where there was no formal bidding process, the margin that HM&A may make on the project would be as per the amounts outlined in the HM&A Agreement, which were at industry standards. The HM&A Agreement contemplated that Cascadia and HM&A would endeavor to work with each other on every WRF, but both companies agreed that there was no exclusivity in their relationship.

The operations of the WRFs were highly automated, and Cascadia intended to license optimization software created by HM&A, called EnviroSMART. This software would allow Cascadia to maximize operational efficiencies and provide supervisory management of facilities from a central operations theatre. Cascadia also intended to develop an Internet billing system, which would allow easy distribution and payment of invoices for services provided by the Corporation. Cascadia had engaged several consultants to develop an Internet portal. An Internet portal is a central information source on the Web, with links to industry information about water reclamation and reuse. This site would also be used for community education on the uses for reclaimed water and water

Year	*Development Population*[1]	*Total Dwelling Units*		*Total Sewage Flows*	*Current Year*
		Annual[2]	*Accumulated*	*USGPD*[3]	*Capital Requirement*
1999	250	100	100	30,000	$518,515
2000	1,500	500	600	180,000	$1,462,148
2001	2,750	500	1,100	330,000	$1,504,719
2002	4,000	500	1,600	480,000	$
2003	5,250	500	2,100	630,000	$
2004	6,500	500	2,600	780,000	$1,682,186
2005	7,750	500	3,100	930,000	$
2006	8,000	100	3,200	960,000	$
2007	8,000	—	3,200	960,000	$

Year	*Revenue Hook-ups*[4]	*Net Operating Revenue*[5]	*Revenue Sales of Reclaimed Water*[6]	*Total Revenue*
1999	$350,000	$2,611	$1,200	$353,811
2000	$1,750,000	$124,656	$21,600	$1,896,256
2001	$1,750,000	$275,304	$66,000	$2,091,304
2002	$1,750,000	$433,276	$134,400	$2,317,676
2003	$1,750,000	$597,315	$201,600	$2,548,915
2004	$1,750,000	$766,808	$249,600	$2,766,408
2005	$1,750,000	$941,382	$297,600	$2,988,982
2006	$350,000	$946,812	$307,200	$1,604,012
2007	—	$946,812	$307,200	$1,254,012

Exhibit 2 Hypothetical Financial Model—Utilizing Identified Revenue Streams (a particular business model may or may not include any or all revenue streams)

Source: Cascadia Water Corporation, 1999.

1. New development (8,000 people maximum build out).
2. 2.5 people per dwelling unit.
3. Flow is calculated at 100 Imperial Gallons per day per person and converted to USG.
4. $3,500 per Dwelling Unit.
5. $35 per Dwelling Unit per month less operational expenses.
6. $2 per 1,000 USG estimated 200 irrigation days a year. Ten per cent Initial sales increasing 20 per cent per year up to 80 per cent.

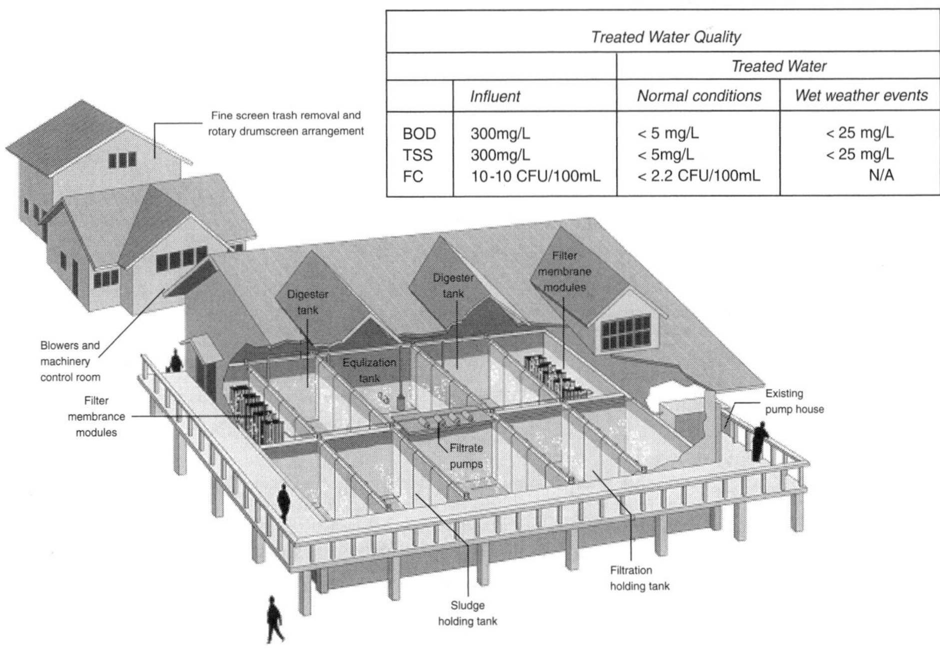

Treated Water Quality			
		Treated Water	
	Influent	*Normal conditions*	*Wet weather events*
BOD	300mg/L	< 5 mg/L	< 25 mg/L
TSS	300mg/L	< 5mg/L	< 25 mg/L
FC	10-10 CFU/100mL	< 2.2 CFU/100mL	N/A

Exhibit 3 Inside and Outside Views of a Large WRF Installation

Source: Cascadia internal documents.

conservation. In concert with the Corporation's Web site, this informational site would evolve over time to allow customers to review their reclaimed water accounts and make payment over the Internet.

Cascadia had acquired a sophisticated tool, called Reuse Investment Opportunity Analyser "RIO," to evaluate potential investment opportunities. RIO was acquired from Trevor Hill, the chairman and director of the Corporation, and Graham Symmonds pursuant to the Software Purchase and Sale Agreement, effective August 10, 1999. Pursuant to the terms of a Software Purchase and Sale Agreement, Cascadia acquired RIO in exchange for common shares in the capital of the Corporation. RIO would eventually be deployed over the Internet so that a sales representative could access it from anywhere in the world. Cascadia would then be able to quickly update RIO to take into account the local rates for power, labor and other consumables as well as capital costs and other relevant parameters of the opportunity. This tool set would enable Cascadia to quickly determine the economies of any opportunity.

Conclusion

Commandeur believed that Cascadia would be able to take a leadership role in the P3 market segment because of its access to the complete spectrum of services provided by HM&A and its clear focus on small to medium-sized municipalities and developments. He was also confident that Cascadia could compete with the existing and new entrants into the wastewater treatment industry. However, Cascadia needed to raise $1 million to acquire its first two WRFs and provide working capital for the continuation of the company.

In order to issue an offering memorandum, Commandeur still needed to figure out a business model that would be financially viable and interesting to potential investors, and he had only until September 1st to get it done.

Russki Adventures

Prepared by Ian Sullivan under the supervision of Professor Paul Beamish

 Version: (A) 2002-12-20

On July 15, 1991, Guy Crevasse and Andrei Kakov, the two major partners in Russki Adventures (Russki), contemplated their next move. They had spent the last year and a half exploring the possibility of starting a helicopter skiing operation in the U.S.S.R. Their plan was to bring clients from Europe, North America, and Japan to a remote location in the U.S.S.R. to ski the vast areas of secluded mountain terrain made accessible by the use of helicopters and the recent business opportunities offered by "glasnost."

During the exploration process, Crevasse and Kakov had visited a number of potential locations in the U.S.S.R., including the Caucasus Mountains near the Black Sea, and the Tien Shen and Pamir ranges north of Pakistan in the republics of Kazakistan and Tadzhikistan, respectively. After close inspection of the three areas, and consideration of many issues, the partners had decided upon the Caucasus region.

After almost two years of planning and research, the thought of making a solid commitment weighed heavily on their minds. Their first option was to accept the partnership offer with Extreme Dreams, a French company that had started a small ski operation in the Caucasus Mountains during the 1991 season. Their second option was to enter a partnership with the U.S.S.R.'s Trade Union DFSO and a Russian mountaineer, and establish their own venture in a Caucasus Mountains area made available to them by a Soviet government agency. Their final option was to wait, save their money and not proceed with the venture at this time.

The Partners

Andrei Kakov, 27, was born in Russia. His family emigrated to Italy, and then to Canada when he was 17 years old. After completing an undergraduate degree in economics at the University of Toronto, he worked with Sebaco for two years before enrolling in 1989 in the Masters of Business Administration (MBA) program at The University of Western Ontario (Western). Sebaco was a Canadian-Soviet joint venture that, since 1980, had been facilitating business ventures in the Soviet Union by acting as a liaison between the foreign firms and the different levels of Soviet government and industry. This job gave Kakov extensive contacts in the Soviet Union and in many of the firms, such as McDonald's and Pepsico, which were doing business in the Soviet Union. Kakov was fluent in Russian, Italian, English, and Japanese.

Guy Crevasse, 28, had an extensive ski racing career which began at a young age and culminated in the World Cup with the Canadian National Ski Team. His skiing career took him to many countries in Europe, North America, and South America. During his travels he learned to speak French, Italian, and some German. After retiring from competitive ski racing in 1984, Crevasse remained active in the ski industry as a member of the Canadian Ski Coaches Federation. He led The University of Western Ontario Varsity Ski Team to four consecutive Can-Am titles as a racer/coach while pursuing an undergraduate degree at Western. Before returning to Western to complete an MBA, Crevasse worked for Motorola Inc. in its sales and marketing departments, where he worked on key accounts, set up product distribution channels, and developed product programs with original equipment manufacturers in the automobile industry. Crevasse had also worked with a ski resort planning and development firm on a number of different projects.

Overview of the Skiing and Helicopter Skiing Industries

Development of the Ski Resort Industry

In 1990, the worldwide ski market was estimated at 40 million skiers. The great boom period was in the 1960s and 1970s when growth ran between 10 to 20 per cent annually. However, the growth stagnation which began during the 1980s was expected to continue during the 1990s. Some of this decline was attributable to increased competition for vacationers' time, the rapidly rising real costs of skiing, and baby boom effects. The only growth segment was female skiers, who represented 65 per cent of all new skiers. The total revenue generated by ski resorts in the United States for 1990 was estimated at $1.5 billion. This figure did not include any hotel or accommodation figures.

Prior to World War II, most skiing took place in Europe. Since there were no ski lifts, most skiing was essentially unmarked wilderness skiing, requiring participants who enjoyed the thrill of a downhill run to spend most of their time climbing. There were no slope-grooming machines and few slopes cut especially for skiing.

The development of ski lifts revolutionized the sport, increased the accessibility to many previously inaccessible areas, and led to the development of ski resorts. After the skiing market matured, competition for skiers intensified and resort operators shifted their efforts away from the risk sport focus towards vacation and entertainment. In order to service this new market and to recover their large capital investments, the large resorts had developed mass market strategies and modified the runs and the facilities to make them safer and easier to ski in order to serve a greater number of customers.

Introduction of Helicopter Skiing

This change in focus left the more adventurous skiing segments unsatisfied. For many, the search for new slopes and virgin snow was always a goal. The rapid rise in the popularity of skiing after World War II increased demand on existing ski facilities and thus competition for the best snow and hills became more intense. Those who wanted to experience the joys of powder skiing in virgin areas were forced to either get up earlier to ski the good snow before the masses got to it, or hike for hours from the top of ski areas to find new areas close to existing cut ski runs. Hiking to unmarked areas was tiring, time consuming, and more dangerous because of the exposure to crevasses and avalanches.

This desire to ski in unlimited powder snow and new terrain away from the crowds eventually led to the development of the helicopter skiing industry. The commonly held conception was that powder skiing was the champagne of all skiing, and helicopter skiing was the Dom Perignon. The first helicopter operations began in Canada. From the beginning of the industry in 1961, Canadian operations have been typically regarded as the premium product in the helicopter skiing industry for many reasons, including the wild, untamed mountains in the western regions. For many skiers worldwide, a trip to a Western Canadian heli-ski operation is their "mecca."

Operators used helicopters as a means of accessing vast tracts of wilderness areas which were used solely by one operator through a lease arrangement with the governments, forest services, or regional authorities. The average area leased for skiing was 2,000 to 3,000 square kilometres in size, with 100 to 150 runs. Due to the high costs in buying, operating, maintaining, and insuring a helicopter, the vast majority of operators leased their machines on an as-needed basis with rates based on hours of flight time.

In the 1970s and early 1980s, the helicopter skiing industry was concentrated among a few players. During 1990 and 1991, the number of adventure/wilderness skiing operators increased from 41 to over 77. The industry could be divided between those operations that provided day trips from existing alpine resorts (day-trippers) and those operations that offered week-long trips (destination-location).

By 1991, the entire global market for both day-trippers and destination-location was estimated to be just over 23,000 skiers per year, with the latter group representing roughly 12,000 to 15,000 skiers. Wilderness skiing represented the largest area of growth within the ski industry in the 1970s and 1980s. Market growth in the 1980s was 15 per cent per year. Only capacity limitations had restrained growth. The addictive nature of helicopter skiing was illustrated by the fact that repeat customers accounted for over 75 per cent of clients annually. The conservative estimate of total margin available to the destination-location skiing industry (before selling and administration costs) was US$12.4 million in 1990. Table 1 gives typical industry margin figures per skier for heli-skiing.

From a cost standpoint, efficient management of the helicopter operations was essential. Table 2 provides a larger list of industry key success factors.

Combination of Resort and Helicopter Skiing

The number of resorts operating day facilities doubled in 1990. Competition in the industry increased for a number of reasons. Many new competitors entered because of the low cost of entry (about $250,000), low exit barriers, the significant market growth, and the rewarding margin in the industry. The major growth worldwide came mainly from the day operations at existing areas, as they attempted to meet the needs for adventure and skiing from

Table 1 Helicopter Skiing Margin per Skier Week (North America)

	$3,500	*100%*
Price Costs:		
Helicopter*	1,260	36%
Food & Lodging	900	26%
Guides	100	3%
Total Operating Costs	**2,260**	**65%**
Total Margin	**1,240**	**35%**

**Note:* Helicopter costs were semi-variable but were based largely on a variable basis (in-flight hours). The fixed nature of helicopter costs arose through minimum flying hours requirements and the rate negotiations (better rates were charged to customers with higher usage). On average, a helicopter skier used seven hours of helicopter time during a one-week trip. A typical all-in rate for a 12-person helicopter was $1,800 per flying hour. Hence the above figure of $1,260 was calculated assuming full capacity of the helicopter using the following: $1,800 per hour for seven hours for 10 skiers + pilot + guide.

Table 2 Helicopter Skiing Industry Key Success Factors

Factors Within Management Control:

- establishing a safe operation and reliable reputation
- developing great skiing operations
- attracting and keeping customers with minimal marketing costs
- obtaining repeat business through operation's excellence
- providing professional and sociable guides
- obtaining operating permits from government
- managing relationships with environmentalists

Location Factors:

- accessible destinations by air travel
- available emergency and medical support
- favourable weather conditions, i.e., annual snowfall, humidity, altitude
- appropriate daily temperature, sunshine, daylight time
- suitable terrain
- quality food and lodging

their clientele. The major concentration of helicopter operators was in Canada; however, competition was increasing internationally. Industry representatives thought that such growth was good because it would help increase the popularity of helicopter skiing and introduce more people to the sport.

In Canada, where helicopter skiing originated, the situation was somewhat different. Out of the 20 wilderness skiing operations in Canada in 1991, only two were tied to resorts. However, for the rest of the world, roughly 80 per cent of all the operations were located and tied closely to existing ski operations. Both Crevasse and Kakov realized that there were opportunities to create partnerships or agreements with existing resorts to serve as an outlet for their helicopter skiing demand.

RUSSKI'S RESEARCH OF THE HELI-SKI INDUSTRY

Profile of the Skier

The research that the Russki group had completed revealed some important facts. Most helicopter skiers were wealthy, independent, professional males of North American or European origin. Increasingly, the Japanese skiers were joining the ranks. The vast majority of the skiers were in their late 30s to mid 60s in age. For them, helicopter skiing provided an escape from the high pace of their professional lives. These people, who were financially secure with lots of disposable income, were well educated and had done a great many things. Helicopter skiing was a good fit with their calculated risk-taker image. Exhibit 1 describes a typical customer. It was not unusual for the skiing "addict" to exceed 100,000 vertical feet of skiing in a week. A premium was then charged to the skier.

Buyers tended to buy in groups rather than as individuals. They typically had some form of close association, such as membership in a common profession or club. In most cases, trips were planned a year in advance.

Geographically, helicopter skiers could be grouped into three segments: Japan, North America (United States and Canada), and Europe. In 1991, they represented 10 per cent, 40 per cent (30 per cent and 10 per cent), and 50 per cent of the market respectively. There were unique features associated with each segment and Crevasse and Kakov knew that all marketing plans would need to be tailored specifically to each segment. In general, they felt that the European and North American customers placed more emphasis on the adventure, were less risk adverse, and had a propensity to try new things.

Analysis of the Competition

Crevasse and Kakov had thought that more detailed information on their competitors would help answer some of their questions. During the winter of 1991, they conducted a complete physical inspection of skiing and business facilities of many helicopter skiing operations. As a result of the research, Russki determined that the following companies were very significant: Rocky Mountain Helisports (RMH), Cariboo Snowtours, and Heliski India. RMH and Cariboo Snowtours were industry leaders and Heliski India was another new entrant trying to establish itself in the market. A close analysis had provided Crevasse and Kakov with some encouraging information.

Rocky Mountain Helisports, the first operation to offer helicopter skiing, was started in 1965 in Canada by Gunther Pistler, a German immigrant and the "inventor" of helicopter skiing. In 1991 his operation, servicing 6,000 skiers, represented roughly 40 to 50 per cent of the worldwide destination-location market. He followed a strategy which cloned small operating units at seven different sites in the interior of British Columbia. RMH's strategy was designed to offer a product that catered to a variety of different skier abilities and skiing experiences. The company serviced all segments that could afford the $4,000 price of admission, including introducing less able skiers to the experience of helicopter skiing. Compared with the revenue of traditional Canadian ski resorts, such as Whistler Resorts in British Columbia, RMH's gross revenue for the 1990 season was larger than any resort in Canada at over $21 million. RMH, which had developed a loyal following of customers in North America and Europe, enjoyed significant competitive advantage because of proprietary client lists, a loyal consumer base, and economies of scale due to its large size.

Cariboo Snowtours, the second largest operation in the world, was established by another German immigrant, Fritz Mogler, at Blue River, British Columbia. In 1991, Cariboo Snowtours served over 2,000 skiers, a number which represented roughly 18 per cent of the market. Mogler developed a strategy of one mega-operation and enjoyed economies of scale in the operations area. Similar to RMH, Cariboo Snowtours had a loyal following from North America and Europe, and catered to a variety of skiing abilities and price levels.

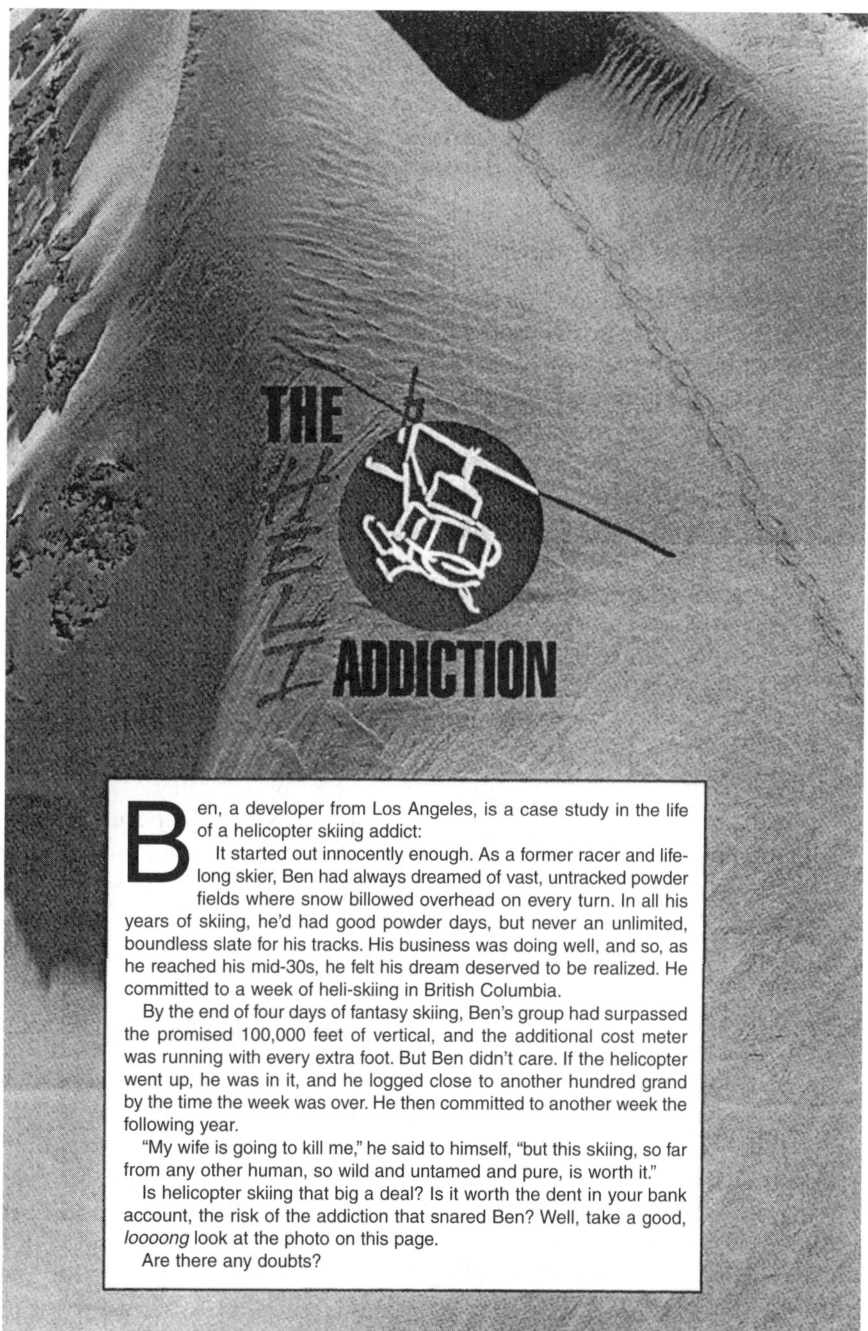

Ben, a developer from Los Angeles, is a case study in the life of a helicopter skiing addict:

It started out innocently enough. As a former racer and life-long skier, Ben had always dreamed of vast, untracked powder fields where snow billowed overhead on every turn. In all his years of skiing, he'd had good powder days, but never an unlimited, boundless slate for his tracks. His business was doing well, and so, as he reached his mid-30s, he felt his dream deserved to be realized. He committed to a week of heli-skiing in British Columbia.

By the end of four days of fantasy skiing, Ben's group had surpassed the promised 100,000 feet of vertical, and the additional cost meter was running with every extra foot. But Ben didn't care. If the helicopter went up, he was in it, and he logged close to another hundred grand by the time the week was over. He then committed to another week the following year.

"My wife is going to kill me," he said to himself, "but this skiing, so far from any other human, so wild and untamed and pure, is worth it."

Is helicopter skiing that big a deal? Is it worth the dent in your bank account, the risk of the addiction that snared Ben? Well, take a good, *loooong* look at the photo on this page.

Are there any doubts?

Exhibit 1 Description of a Typical Helicopter Skiing Addict

Source: Powder, *The Skier's Magazine*, November 1990.

Heliski India was a new entrant to the helicopter skiing business. In 1990, the first year of operation, the company serviced 30 skiers in a three-week period, increasing to 120 skiers during the 1991 season. Heliski India followed a more exclusive and adventurous strategy aimed at the experienced helicopter skiing enthusiast. To cover the high costs and low volume, the operation charged $5,500.

Russki estimated margins and profit dynamics for these three operations. Exhibit 2 contains the projection for RMH. These projected statements were best guess estimates based on discussions with a wide range of industry experts, managers, and investors. Cariboo Snowtours' total profit was estimated as slightly over $2 million, while Heliski India was projected to turn a small profit. Crevasse and Kakov found these figures very encouraging.

Land Usage and Environmental Concerns in the Industry

The helicopter skiing industry was facing some land use issues which were tough on many operators, but which also created new opportunities on which Russki wanted to capitalize. Of particular concern to many helicopter skiing operations, especially European, were pressures from environmentalists who were concerned that noise from helicopters could adversely affect wildlife habitat and start avalanches.

As a result, severe downsizing or complete shutdown of existing European operations had recently occurred, leaving only eight helicopter skiing operations in continental Europe in 1991. The one Swiss and one Austrian operation were under pressure to close, and a 1992 season for the latter was already doubtful. The six small operations in Italy, which worked in conjunction with existing ski areas, were basically the only helicopter skiing available in Western Europe. Flying for skiing in France was illegal due to environmentalists' concerns about a negative impact on the limited areas in the Alps. In Sweden, a few companies operated with a shorter season due to the high latitude, and provided less expensive daily services for visitors who skied within the existing lift systems, but week-long packages were not part of their program.

The North American industry had not been exposed to the same environmental and limited area constraints as the European, mainly because of the vast size of the mountain ranges and good relationships with all interested parties. The American operators, who were associated mostly with the large ski areas, had good working relationships with the forest services, which controlled the areas and issued the working permits.

Canadian operators received their permits from the Ministry of Lands and Forests and the provincial governments. Helicopter skiing had been encouraged because of its ability to bring money into the regions. Due to the vast size of the Canadian mountain ranges and the limited competition for the land use, pressure on the operators in any form had been minimal or nonexistent.

Crevasse and Kakov realized that the environmental and capacity constraints in Europe provided helicopter skiing operators worldwide with significant opportunities. Thus far, it had been mainly the North American operators who had capitalized on this situation, and Russki wanted to find a way to capture unsatisfied demand.

Russian Environment

The Political Environment

Crevasse and Kakov knew that starting a venture in the Soviet Union at this time would be complex. The political situation was very unstable in July 1991, and most expert predictions were not encouraging, including the possibility that the Soviet Union might not exist in the near future. There was a major power struggle going on: the hardliners, most of whom were from the old guard of the Communist Party, were trying to hang on to power; and others, such as Russian President Boris Yeltsin, wanted sweeping democratic changes. The new buzz word on the streets was not "glasnost" or "perestroika" but

Revenues				
Ski Season Duration – peak	20 wks			
– regular	0 wks			
Total Season Duration:	20 wks			
Revenue per Skier – peak		$3,500		
Weekly Group Size: (10 skiers + 1 guide × 4)	44 people			
Total Season Regular Revenue ($3,500 × 40 skiers × 20 wks)			$2,800,000	
Revenue From Skiers Exceeding 100,000 Virtual Feet (10%)				280,000
Total Revenue				**$3,080,000**
Expenses				
Variable: 9 nights lodging/person/night		$80	$720	
9 days meals/person/day		50	450	
Total Variable Cost/Person/Week			$1,170	
Total Annual Variable Costs (20 wks × 44 × $1,170)				$1,029,600
Contribution Margin				$2,050,400
Fixed:				
Helicopter Cost/Weekly Basis (20 week season)			$50,000	$1,000,000
Guides— 1 guide per 10 skiers @				
$50,000 per guide/year	4 guides		$200,000	
Support Staff—5 employees @ $20,000 per employee			$100,000	
Promotional			$250,000	
Total Direct Fixed Costs				**$1,550,000**
Total Margin (Revenue–Dir. Variable Costs–Dir. Fixed Costs)				$500,400
Annual Overhead – communication		$20,000		
– staff travel		50,000		
– office branch		20,000		
– office North America		100,000		
– insurance @ $5/day/person		50,000		
Total Overhead				**$240,000**
Operating Profit				$249,600
Number of Operations: 7				
Total Operating Profit				$1,747,200

Exhibit 2 Russki's1991 Projections: Profit Dynamics of Typical RMH Operation*

*These projected statements were best guess estimates based on discussions with a wide range of industry experts, managers and investors.

"razgosudarstvo," which refers to the breakup of the Soviet state. Secession pressures from many of the republics, such as the Baltics, tested the mettle of the political leaders, perestroika, and the strength of the union itself.

On a regional basis, the future status of some of the regions and republics where the physical conditions met the requirements for helicopter skiing, such as Georgia and Kazakhistan, was unknown. However, Crevasse and Kakov were encouraged by the fact that experts predicted that, no matter what the state of the whole union, Russia would remain intact and continue to function as a unit. This was one of the many reasons why the Russian Republic was selected for the potential initial location.

The Economic Environment

The economy of the Soviet Union was in dire straits. Confusion, lack of focus, and compromise were crippling the process of change from a government controlled economy to a market based one. Real Gross Domestic Product was projected to drop anywhere from three to 11 per cent or more in 1991. Soviet President Mikhail Gorbachev had been given authority to overhaul the economy. However, what changes he would initiate, and whether he still had the support and power to see the process through to completion, were questionable.

Therefore, developing a helicopter skiing operation in the Soviet Union presented Russki with a difficult business environment. Marshall Goldman, Director of Harvard's Russian Research Centre, summed up part of the dilemma facing any new venture in the Soviet Union at this time:

> For those entrepreneurs who think chaos is an ideal environment, this is a perfect time, but for others it is a scary time. The society is collapsing. The economy—both the marketing portion and the planning and administrative sector—is a shambles.

Russki's research indicated that only 20 per cent of the 1,300 joint ventures signed since 1987 were operational because of currency exchange problems, bureaucratic delays, and lack of legal framework to make agreements. Also, it had been very hard for the few operational ventures to realize a return on their investment. In 1991, any business in the Soviet Union had to be viewed with a long-term bias in mind. The big question for many businesses was getting hard currency out of Soviet ventures because there was no international market for the Soviet currency, the ruble. Those who were operating business ventures in the Soviet Union suggested to Russki that it was not an area for the faint hearted to tread. PlanEcon's Keith Crane advised that "even after the agreement has been signed it can be very difficult to get down to specifics and venture into working entities. It took McDonald's 14 years to do it." Due to the political and economic realities of the Soviet environment, firms were making deals with republics, with city agencies, directly with Soviet firms or factories, and sometimes with all of them. More and more frequently, firms had to go to the enterprise level to find the right people and partners. Additionally, foreign firms found the business environment difficult because the concept of business that Westerners had was very different from the one that the Soviets had after 70 years of a controlled Marxist economy. The addition of cultural differences made for a demanding business climate. Russki thought long and hard about the fact that doing business in the Soviet Union had never been easy. In 1991, as the nation wrestled with the gargantuan task of restructuring the country, most firms were finding it more confusing than ever. No road map or blueprint for business development existed.

In addition, without the significant financial resources of a highly capitalized firm that could overlook short-term profits for long-term gains, Crevasse and Kakov realized they would be in a more exposed position if they decided to go ahead with the venture. Political unrest or civil war in the Soviet Union, especially in Russia, could destroy their business and investment. Without a steady supply of repeat and new customers, the venture would be finished as an on-going concern. They knew that credibility from an existing operation or established name would make the task of attracting customers to an uncertain environment easier but, in a time of crisis, would guarantee nothing.

The Opportunities

Despite all the negatives, Crevasse and Kakov thought that helicopter skiing in the Soviet Union would be developed on a large scale in the next few years for a number of reasons. The sport was experiencing tremendous growth, environmental pressures were great in Europe, and capacity at all of the good locations was already stretched.

Therefore, a current opportunity existed in the industry. The partners speculated about how fast they could proceed with their business plan and whether they were exposing themselves to too much risk for the return. Would the opportunity still exist in a couple of years? Could a business of this nature function with the future of the Soviet Union being so unstable? The complete answer to these questions was unknown. Crevasse and Kakov felt as if they were doing a case back at business school where someone had left out half the case facts. Regardless, this was a real-life situation, and a decision had to be made on the knowledge available.

After looking closely at their competition and the general environment, they concluded that, despite the instability in the Soviet environment, there were a number of strong points that suggested that they might be able to make a venture of this nature work. On a positive note, the Canadian Prime Minister, Brian Mulroney, had recently signed the Foreign Investment Protection agreement to ensure stability of Canadian ventures in the U.S.S.R. Also encouraging to entrepreneurs wanting to enter the Soviet Union was the new law that allowed for full ownership of Soviet subsidiaries by foreign firms. Experts suggested that these agreements would be honoured by whatever form of government was in place.

The critical factor in the minds of the Russki partners was the fact that they would be taking in all revenue in hard currency. Thus, the absence of profit repatriation risk decreased this business exposure dramatically. Russki would operate all of the sales and administrative tasks outside of the Soviet Union and, as a result, all of its revenues would be collected in the West in hard currency, thereby eliminating the currency risk completely. This was a position that would be envied by any firm attempting to do business in the Soviet Union. Also, Russki was attractive to all levels of government because the venture would bring desperately needed hard currency into the country.

Mt. Elbrus, the highest peak in Europe and the Caucasus mountain region, was where Russki had options to locate. It was well known throughout Europe and its high altitudes and warm climate offered ideal skiing conditions. Because a strong allegiance already existed between the European customers and the Canadian operators, Russki's Canadian background would sit well with customers. In addition, Russki would deliver comparative cost advantage for the Europeans in a Soviet operation, as shown in Exhibit 3, even if Russki charged similar costs for a week of skiing.

The uniqueness of the region and mystique of Russia offered an interesting alternative for tourism. Russia had a 2,000 year history and a rich culture, which was reflected in the traditions of the local people and the architecture. Furthermore, the Black Sea area which was close to the Caucasus Mountains had been used as a resort area for centuries. The dramatic changes during the early 1990s in the Soviet Union and Eastern Europe had resulted in tremendous interest in these areas.

Since Russki already had the money required for start-up, the company could move quickly without having to take time to raise the capital. The low cost of leasing Soviet helicopters, pilot salaries, service, and fuel as compared with North America was a distinct advantage, and one of the original attractions of Russia. Negotiations with the Russians had shown that this cost advantage was obtainable. The high costs of helicopter operations represented the largest part of the operating costs in helicopter skiing. Lower helicopter costs in Russia would result in cost savings in the range of 50 per cent or more in this expense relative to North American competitors.

The Russki management team was strong. Both men were business-school-trained individuals with international work experience, language skills, and ski industry background. Additional hard-to-copy assets, including access to the "Crazy Canucks" (a World Cup ski team) and European ski stars as Guest Guides, and Soviet knowledge, would be tough for anyone to match in the short term.

Positioning and Marketing of Russki Adventures

Positioning and Pricing

The Russki team had considered two positioning strategies, a high and low pricing strategy. A premium pricing and service strategy like that

North America:

Costs for customer to go Heliskiing in North America from different geographic locations:

Origin of Skier	*Trip*	*Transportation*	*Total*
Japan	$4,000	$2,500	$6,500
Europe	$4,000	$2,000	$6,000
North America	$4,000	$750	$4,750

Russia:

Costs for customer to go Heliskiing in Russia from different geographic locations:

Origin of Skier	*Trip*	*Transportation*	*Total*
Japan	$4,000	$2,000	$6,000
Europe	$4,000	$1,000	$5,000
North America	$4,000	$2,500	$6,500

Conclusion: This comparative analysis of all-in costs to the consumer shows that the Russian operation offers a 20 per cent cost advantage to the European customers.

Exhibit 3 Cost Comparison by Geographic Location

of Heliski India at around US$6,000 would require superior service in every aspect of the operation. The lower priced strategy at $3,500 to $4,000 was $500 below the US$4,000 to US$4,500 pricing of Canadian operators like RMH for the initial season. The second positioning strategy would be designed to target a larger market and concentrate on building market share during the first few years, allowing more time and flexibility to move down the learning curve.

Even with parallel pricing of US$4,000, the "all in" (as shown in Exhibit 3) would give a cost advantage to the European and Japanese customers. Crevasse and Kakov knew that this situation would help challenge customers' traditional allegiance to the Canadian operators.

Based on a "best guess scenario," profit models for the two pricing strategies using conservative sales levels are shown in Exhibits 4 and 5. Though the higher priced strategy was more lucrative, Crevasse and Kakov felt that they had a higher capacity to execute the lower price strategy during the first few years of operations regardless of which partner they chose. They were not sure that they could meet the sales volume for the premium strategy as shown in Exhibit 5, regardless of the realization of savings from use of Russian helicopters. (In the unlikely event that the projected helicopter saving could not be realized, the discounted cash flow in Exhibit 4 dropped from $526,613 to $293,000, and in Exhibit 5 from $597,926 to $194,484.)

These estimates were extremely conservative. One helicopter could service 44 people per week (four groups of 10 skiers and one guide). All projections for the profit dynamics were made with the number of skiers per week below capacity. In addition, the first two years were estimated using 10 and 15 skiers respectively. In subsequent years, the number of skiers was increased, but never to full capacity, in order to keep estimates conservative. Russki realized that operating at or close to capacity on a weekly basis would increase its efficiency and returns dramatically.

Russki also built in an additional $250 in the variable costs per skier per week for contingent expenses such as the cost of importing all food stuffs.

		Year 1	*Year 2*	*Year 3*	*Year 4*	*Year 5*
Revenues						
Total season duration:		10 weeks	15 weeks	15 weeks	20 weeks	20 weeks
Revenue per skier—peak		$4,000	$4,000	$4,000	$4,000	$4,000
Weekly group size:		10	15	20	25	25
Total Season Revenue		$400,000	$900,000	$1,200,000	$2,000,000	$2,000,000
Expenses						
Total Variable Cost:		$100,000	$225,000	$300,000	$500,000	$500,000
(variable cost/skier @ $1,000)						
Contribution margin		$300,000	$675,000	$900,000	$1,500,000	$1,500,000
Fixed						
Helicopter cost: (Assumes Soviet Costs of $10,000/week)		$100,000	$150,000	$150,000	$200,000	$200,000
Guides—1 guide per 10 skiers @ $50,000 per guide/year		$50,000	$75,000	$100,000	$125,000	$125,000
Soviet staff—3 employees @ $5,000 per employee		$15,000	$15,000	$15,000	$15,000	$15,000
Promotional		$100,000	$100,000	$100,000	$100,000	$100,000
Total direct fixed costs		$265,000	$340,000	$365,000	$440,000	$440,000
Total margin						
(Revenues–Direct Variable Costs–Direct Fixed Costs)		$35,000	$335,000	$535,000	$1,060,000	$1,060,000
Total overhead		$35,000	$115,000	$115,000	$115,000	$115,000
Operating profit		0	$220,000	$420,000	$945,000	$945,000
	Year 0	Year 1	Year 2	Year 3	Year 4	Year 5
Investment	$–230,000	0	$220,000	$420,000	$945,000	$945,000
Operating Profit			$220,000	$420,000	$945,000	$945,000
N.A. Partner's Share: 100% Taxes @ 30%		0	$154,000	$294,000	$661,500	$661,500
Profit	$–230,000	0				
DCF Year 1–5 PV @ 20.00%		$526,613				
IRR	71.86%					

Exhibit 4 Profit Dynamics Low Price Strategy With Low Helicopter Costs

	Year 1	Year 2	Year 3	Year 4	Year 5
Revenues					
Total season duration:	5 weeks	10 weeks	15 weeks	20 weeks	20 weeks
Revenue per skier—peak	$6,000	$6,000	$6,000	$6,000	$6,000
Weekly group size:	10	10	15	15	20
Total Season Revenue	$300,000	$600,000	$900,000	$1,800,000	$2,400,000
Expenses					
Total Variable Cost: (variable cost/skier @ $1,000)	$50,000	$100,000	$150,000	$300,000	$400,000
Contribution margin	$250,000	$500,000	$750,000	$1,500,000	$2,000,000
Fixed					
Helicopter cost: (Assumes Soviet Costs of $10,000/week)	$50,000	$100,000	$100,000	$200,000	$200,000
Guides—1 guide per 10 skiers @ $50,000 per guide/year	$50,000	$50,000	$75,000	$75,000	$100,000
Soviet staff—3 employees @ $5,000 per employee	$15,000	$15,000	$15,000	$15,000	$15,000
Promotional	$100,000	$100,000	$100,000	$100,000	$100,000
Total direct fixed costs	$215,000	$265,000	$290,000	$390,000	$415,000
Total margin (Revenues–Direct Variable Costs–Direct Fixed Costs)	$35,000	$235,000	$460,000	$1,110,000	$1,585,000
Total overhead	$35,000	$115,000	$115,000	$115,000	$115,000
Operating profit	0	$120,000	$345,000	$995,000	$1,470,000

	Year 0	Year 1	Year 2	Year 3	Year 4	Year 5
Investment	$–230,000					
Operating Profit		0	$120,000	$345,000	$995,000	$1,470,000
N.A. Partner's Share: 100%		0	$120,000	$345,000	$995,000	$1,470,000
Taxes @ 30%						
Profit	$–230,000	0	$84,000	$241,500	$696,500	$1,029,000
DCF Year 1–5 PV @ 20.00%		$597,926				
IRR	70.78%					

Exhibit 5 Profit Dynamics Premium Price Strategy With Low Helicopter Costs

If Russki proceeded with the lower priced approach, it would position its product just below the industry standard at $4,000 initially. The intent would be to attack the market as the Japanese automobile manufactures had done when entering into the North American luxury car market.

Crevasse and Kakov were encouraged by the numbers because the conservative sales estimates using the low price positioning strategy would allow them to generate a profit in the second year of operations if they could realize the projected savings with Russian helicopters. However, if they didn't, the strategy would still show a profit in the third year. They thought that the return on their investment would be sufficient as far as the internal rate of return was concerned, but they wondered whether the risk of the Soviet environment should increase their demands even more.

Product

Crevasse and Kakov planned to model the Russki product after the RMH operation, which was the best in the industry, by evaluating what RMH had built and improving on its processes. Although Russki wanted very much to differentiate itself from the rest of the industry, the partners were not sure how far they could go within the constraints of the Soviet environment.

Geographical Distribution

Although Russki would focus on the European and North American markets, the former segment was most important. Both Crevasse and Kakov realized that they would need a strong European operation in marketing and sales if they were going to capitalize on the opportunity available. Developing these functions quickly, especially in Europe which was not their home turf, was a major concern. They had to decide on the best sales and marketing channels immediately and set them up as soon as possible if they decided to go ahead with the venture.

Table 3 Marketing Promotion Budget—Year 1

Information Nights With Cocktails @ $1000 /night @ 20 cities	$ 20,000
Travel Expenses	10,000
Trip Discounts (one free trip in 10 to groups)	25,000
Direct Mail	5,000
Brochures	5,000
Commissions	15,000
Celebrity	20,000
	$100,000

Promotion

Due to the small size of the target market and promotion budgets, the new company would have to make sure that the promotional dollars spent were directed effectively. Russki would do this by direct mail, personal selling by the owners, travel agents, and free tour incentives to trip organizers and guides. Long-term word of mouth would be the best promotional tool, but it had to be supplemented especially in the start-up phase of the business.

Additionally, Crevasse and Kakov planned to increase the value to customers by inviting business and political speakers to participate in the skiing activities with the groups in return for their speaking services. Celebrity skiers such as Canadian Olympic bronze medallist and World Cup champion, Steve Podborski, would be used as customer attractions. As outlined in Table 3, they budgeted $100,000 for promotional expenses.

Labour

Where possible, Russki planned to employ Russians and make sure that they received excellent training and compensation, thereby adding authenticity to the customers' experience. Providing local employment would also ensure the

Canadian company's existence and create positive relations with the authorities.

Currency

Through Kakov's contacts, Russki had worked out a deal to purchase excess rubles from a couple of foreign firms which were already operating in the Soviet Union but which were experiencing profit repatriation problems. Russki would pay for as many things as possible with soft currency.

The Partnership Dilemma

During the exploration period, Crevasse and Kakov had well over a dozen offers from groups and individuals to either form partnerships, or provide services and access to facilities and natural resources. They even had offers from people who wanted them to invest millions to build full-scale Alpine Resorts. Many of the offers were easy to dismiss because these groups did not have the ability to deliver what they promised or their skill sets did not meet the needs of Russki. Crevasse and Kakov's inspection and site evaluation helped them to determine further the best opportunities and to evaluate first hand whether the site and potential partner were realistic. This research gave Russki a couple of excellent but very distinct partnership possibilities. They knew that both options had trade-offs.

Extreme Dreams

A partnership with the Extreme Dream group had some definite strengths. This French company, located in Chamonix, an alpine town in the French Alps, had been running the premier guiding service in and around Mont Blanc, the highest peak in the Alps, for 11 years. Chamonix was the "avant garde" for alpinists in Europe and one of the top alpine centres in the world. Extreme Dreams had a 5,000 person client list, mostly European but with some North American names.

What Extreme Dreams had was the operational expertise Russki needed to acquire in order to run the helicopter skiing and guiding side of the business. However, they lacked experience in the key functional areas of business. During the 1991 winter season, it had run a three-week operation servicing 50 skiers in the Elbrus region in the Caucasus Mountains. The Soviet partner facilitated an arrangement with a small resort villa in the area. The facilities, which had just been upgraded during the summer, now met Western standards.

The French company had invested roughly US$100,000, and although it did not have a capital shortage, the partnership agreement that was outlined would require Russki to inject the same amount of capital into the business. The firm would be incorporated in the United States and the share split would be equal amounts of 45 per cent of the stock with 10 per cent left over for future employee purchase. The Soviet partner, a government organization that helped facilitate the land use agreements and permits, would be paid a set fee for yearly exclusive use of the land.

However, Extreme Dreams lacked experience in the key functional areas of business. Possibly, this situation could be rectified by the partnership agreement whereby the management team would consist of three members. Marc Testut, president of Extreme Dreams, would be in charge of all operations. Guy Crevasse would act as president for the first two years and his areas of expertise would be sales and marketing. Andrei Kakov would be Chief Financial Officer and responsible for Soviet relations.

Extreme Dreams had overcome the lack of some food stuffs by importing, on a weekly basis, products not securely attainable in Russia. These additional costs were built into the variable cost in projected financial statements. Russki would do the same if it did not choose Extreme Dreams as a partner.

Trade Union DFSO

The other potential partnership had its strengths as well. The partnership would be with the All-Union Council Of Trade Union DFSO, and with a mountaineer named Yuri Golodov, one of the U.S.S.R.'s best known mountaineers, who had agreed to be part of the management team. Golodov, who had been bringing mountaineers from all over the world to parts of the Soviet Union for many years, possessed valuable expertise and knowledge of the Caucasus area. One of his tasks would be coordination of travel logistics for Soviet clientele. Sergei Oganezovich, chief of the mountaineering department, had made available to Russki the exclusive rights to over 4,000 square kilometres in the Caucasus Mountain Range about 50 kilometres from the area awarded to Extreme Dreams. A small user fee per skier would be paid to the trade organization in return for exclusive helicopter access to the area.

A profit sharing agreement with Golodov, which would allow him to purchase shares in Russki and share in the profits, was agreed to in principle by Russki, the Trade Union DFSO, and Golodov. Under this agreement, Crevasse and Kakov would remain in control of the major portion of the shares. Capital requirements for this option would be in the $230,000 range over the first two years. The two Canadians would perform essentially the same roles as those proposed in the Extreme Dreams agreement. If Crevasse and Kakov selected this option, they would need to bring in a head guide, preferably European, to run the skiing operations. On a positive note, a small resort centre that met the standards required by Western travellers had been selected for accommodations in the area.

As far as medical care in case of accidents, both locations were within an hour of a major city and hospital. Less than an hour was well under the industry norm. In addition, all staff were required to take a comprehensive first aid course.

After discussions with many business ventures in the Soviet Union and with Extreme Dreams, Russki concluded that having the ability to pay for goods and services with hard currency would be a real asset if the situation were critical. Russki would use hard currency, where necessary, to ensure that the level of service was up to the standard required by an operation of this nature.

Crevasse and Kakov knew that selecting a compatible and productive partner would be a great benefit in this tough environment. Yet, they had to remember that a partnership would not guarantee customer support for this venture in the Soviet environment or that the U.S.S.R. would remain stable enough to function as an ongoing concern.

The Decision

Crevasse and Kakov knew that it would take some time for the business to grow to the level of full capacity. They were willing to do whatever it took to make ends meet during the early years of the business. Because helicopter skiing was a seasonal business, they realized that they would need to find a supplementary source of income during the off-season, especially in the start-up phase.

However, they also were confident that, if they could find a way to make their plan work, they could be the ones to capitalize on the growing market. The Soviet Union had the right physical conditions for helicopter skiing, but the business environment would present difficulties. Moreover, the two partners were aware that starting a venture of this nature at any time was not an easy task. Starting it in the present state of the Soviet Union during a recession would only complicate their task further. Yet the timing was right for a new venture in the industry and, in general, they were encouraged by the potential of the business.

Crevasse and Kakov had to let all parties involved know of their decision by the end of the week. If they decided to go ahead with the venture, they had to move quickly if they wanted to be operational in the 1992 season. That night they had to decide if they would proceed, who they would select as partners if they went ahead, and how they would go. It was going to be a late night.

2

SCREENING VENTURE OPPORTUNITIES

THE SCREENING PROCESS

The goal of the screening process is to narrow down the ideas in the idea pool in such a way that the time and effort of the planning and financing process is directed toward the more viable ventures. Some people prefer to narrow the field to just one viable venture, whereas others use the screening process to develop a range of possibilities that can add new value, depending on timing and other practical considerations (e.g., more viable ideas can be "warehoused" for a future venture or sold to more likely venture creators either for cash or for a stake in the new company). In this casebook, we take the approach that the screening process is designed to narrow the field to select *one* more-viable venture idea to pursue further in the planning/financing stage.

Two very broad generalizations supported in the entrepreneurship literature suggest the problems that a better-crafted venture screening process can solve: (a) Entrepreneurs write business plans capriciously, and (b) venture capitalists evaluate entrepreneurial business plans indiscriminately (Mainprize & Hindle, 2003). If the screening process is to be useful in solving these problems, then both entrepreneurs and those who evaluate the venture ideas in business plans need to change somewhat their approach. The change that is needed boils down to properly using the screening process *before* the business plan is produced.

How is this possible? It is the traditional assumption that a business plan must be produced before screening. Interestingly, the Wayne Brown Institute (WBI), a leading sponsor of venture capital conferences throughout the United States and the Pacific Rim, has developed a methodology that removes this constraint. Before a business plan is produced, the venture idea is encapsulated in what is termed an *expanded executive summary,* which then provides the means for an effective review of the essentials.

What are the essentials? Here, some recent additions to venture screening technology, now referred to as the *New Venture Template*™ (NVT) approach to venture screening, come into play. This innovation in the screening process is based on the idea that screening processes should delve more deeply into key underlying attributes of a venture that support the two traditional venture capitalists' questions: (a) Is this a business that can make money, and (b) is the management team sufficiently prepared that the venture has viable long-term prospects—essentially, Is it a business? and Can you keep it? This more topical approach has come to be known as the "espoused criteria" approach—essentially meaning this: Here are the rules of thumb that we venture capitalists use. The deepening of the analysis using actuarial-type methods according to a set of underlying attributes has come to be known as the "known attributes" approach (Mainprize, Hindle, Smith, & Mitchell, 2003).

In a test that compared the accuracy of venture capitalist business plan raters over five years, using the ventures submitted to the WBI as the source of data and following up to ascertain the actual results of these ventures compared to the rating predictions, it was found that although raters using the "espoused criteria" approach achieved a 17% hit rate, raters using the "known attributes" approach more than tripled their accuracy to achieve a hit rate of 52% (Mainprize, Hindle, Smith, & Mitchell, 2002; Mainprize et al., 2003). A simplified paper-based version of the NVT has been included as an appendix at the end of this chapter. The more sophisticated Web-based system is available to individual students and classes for a small annual fee. (The fee includes the Venture Analysis Standards [VAS] workbook, which goes into much more detail of this analysis methodology.) Please contact Ivey Publishing for access.

The NVT venture screening system is presently used by universities and colleges in both Canada and the United States, and, because students and practitioners find it to be so effective, it has become the centerpiece of the screening process that we describe in this chapter, as you will see when you review a student's view of the new venture screening process that follows.

A Student's View of Screening

The screening process, as viewed through the eyes of an entrepreneurship student, is once again presented in the form of a narration that accompanies Figure 2.1. This narrative explains the figure and can be used to visualize many of the key elements necessary in the screening process.

This student says the following:

> The purpose of idea screening is to more thoroughly evaluate the idea before the go-ahead is given to formulate work to satisfy others' needs/wants that are unfulfilled by the market due to transaction costs.

Level 1

There are two parts to Level 1. The first is to conduct a feasibility analysis. This analysis consists of four steps that are as follows:

Step 1: Trend Analysis. This involves examining trends beyond the short-run control of the venture that could significantly alter industry conditions and affect the venture's sustainability. Four major forces are examined:

i. Political/regulatory
ii. Economic
iii. Social
iv. Technological
   - Assess the impact these trends have on the venture.
   - Do they uncover opportunities/problems?
   - Can such opportunities be capitalized?
   - Can such problems be mitigated?
   - Can the venture be sustained?

Step 2: Industry Analysis. This involves assessing whether the industry is attractive to enter. It involves examining five "forces" as follows:

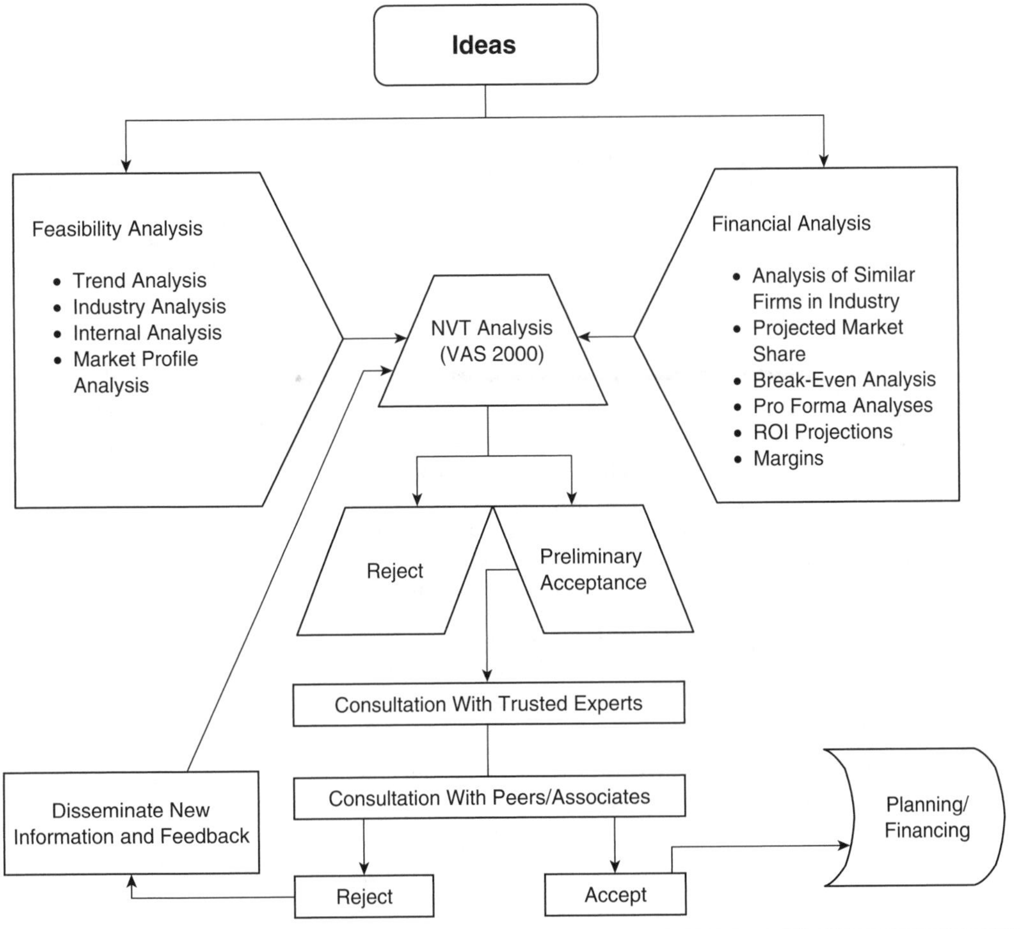

Figure 2.1 Idea Screening

i. Threat of substitutes
ii. Bargaining power of buyers
iii. Bargaining power of suppliers
iv. Rivalry among existing competitors
v. Threat of new entrants
   - Assess the relative importance of each force and gauge the potential impact on the venture.
   - Is this industry attractive to enter?

Step 3: Internal Analysis. Such analyses are usually conducted after the firm has been operating for an extended period of time. It is included here simply as a complement to Porter's (1980) five forces model, as a way to foster thought about the proposed venture's core competencies (that give the firm sustainable competitive advantage). It involves thought about what competencies the venture could have. Four key questions must be answered:

i. Is the competence valuable?
ii. Is the competence rare?
iii. Is the competence inimitable?
iv. Is the competence exploitable?

Step 4: Market Profile Analysis. This involves analyzing the attractiveness of the market. It includes answering four questions:

i. What is the current size of the market, and how large is it expected to be?
ii. What are the current and projected growth rates?
iii. In which stage of the development cycle is the market?
iv. What is the average industry profitability?

The second part to Level 1 is to conduct a financial analysis. This analysis consists of six steps that are as follows:

Step 1: Analysis of Similar Firms in the Industry. This involves looking at financial statements and operations of the key players in the industry.

- What are the returns of these firms?
- What are their turnover ratios, working capital, and so on?
- Could these firms be operating more efficiently?
- What is the level of competence of these firms?

Step 2: Project Market Share. This involves analyzing the relative share of the key industry players and making judgments about how the proposed venture would fare within the industry. This can be done using the information gathered from the market profile analysis and analysis of key industry players.

Step 3: Margin Analysis. This involves projecting the expected margins that can be expected from the venture. Information gathered from the market profile analysis (industry financial ratios) and SIC codes may also be a valuable source of information.

Step 4: Break-Even Analysis. This involves using information gathered from the margin analysis to determine projected break-even volume and break-even sales dollars.

- Is there sufficient volume to sustain the venture?

Step 5: Pro Forma Analyses. This involves forecasting projected income and assets required to generate that income.

Step 6: ROI Projections. This involves projecting the return on investment (ROI) from undertaking the venture.

- What is the opportunity cost of undertaking the venture?

Level 2

Level 2 involves using the information gathered from the feasibility and financial analyses to project the viability of the proposed venture. If the answer to any one of the 15 NVT questions is no, *do not go on.* Go back and review the information collected from the two analyses conducted in Level 1 and redo the NVT analysis. If the answers to all questions are yes, consult with trusted expert and peers/associates.

If, after consulting with these individuals, the idea is still favorable, move onto the planning financing phase. If, after consultation, the idea seems less favorable than anticipated, disseminate this feedback/information and redo the NVT analysis.

Appendix: Simplified Version

Critique Sheet—New Venture Template™

Question:	*Not Known*	*Low*	*Medium*	*High*	*Effort L-M-H*
1. Is it a new combination?	Can't ascertain or get information	① ② ③ The entrepreneurial discovery is not a new technology, product, or service	④ ⑤ ⑥ The discovery is evolutionary—providing a definite improvement over existing competition	⑦ ⑧ ⑨ The discovery is revolutionary—a definite breakthrough	
2. Is there a product market match?	Can't ascertain or get information	① ② ③ I think . . . and that is all.	④ ⑤ ⑥ Strong evidence from sound research (surveys—focus groups) or key partnerships	⑦ ⑧ ⑨ Company has purchase orders or there is a known market for their product	
3. Is there a net-buyer benefit?	Can't ascertain or get information	① ② ③ No clear value to the customer above existing solutions on the market	④ ⑤ ⑥ Clear identifiable value to the customer above existing solutions and switching costs	⑦ ⑧ ⑨ Dramatically improves the customer's life or business	
4. What are the company's margins?	Can't ascertain or get information	① ② ③ Margins below industry standard (rule of thumb—under 15%)	④ ⑤ ⑥ Margins similar to industry standard (rule of thumb—between 16% and 30%)	⑦ ⑧ ⑨ Margins far exceed industry standard (rule of thumb—between 31% and 50% or even greater)	
5. Is sales volume sufficient?	Can't ascertain or get information	① ② ③ Accurate forecast volume is not sufficient to meet business needs given margins	④ ⑤ ⑥ Accurate forecast volume is sufficient to meet business needs given margins	⑦ ⑧ ⑨ Accurate forecast volume exceeds business needs given margins	
6. Does product lend itself to repeat purchases?	Can't ascertain or get information	① ② ③ "Once-only" purchase, or extremely sporadic and unpredictable	④ ⑤ ⑥ Repeat purchases are occasional	⑦ ⑧ ⑨ Purchases are frequent and reasonably predictable	
7. Is there a long-term need?	Can't ascertain or get information	① ② ③ The underlying need served is a fad with limited future need	④ ⑤ ⑥ The underlying need served extends only over the short term	⑦ ⑧ ⑨ There appears to be no foreseeable end to the underlying need served	
8. Are resources sufficient?	Can't ascertain or get information	① ② ③ Resources are effectively nonexistent or limited	④ ⑤ ⑥ Resources are few, or at risk, if growth exceeds plan	⑦ ⑧ ⑨ Resources are plentiful, malleable, and are anticipated to be readily available in the future	
9. Is it inimitable?	Can't ascertain or get information	① ② ③ Easily imitated—no isolating mechanisms (such as patents, copyrights, and other barriers to entry)	④ ⑤ ⑥ Partially protected by isolating mechanisms (this is an evaluation of the strength of those mechanisms)	⑦ ⑧ ⑨ Isolating mechanisms are sufficiently strong so as to permit little or no imitation	

(Continued)

Critique Sheet—New Venture Template™ (Continued)

Question:	*Not Known*	*Low*	*Medium*	*High*	*Effort L-M-H*
10. Is it nonsubstitutable?	Can't ascertain or get information	① ② ③ There are substitutes for the technology, products, or services that directly reduce overall demand	④ ⑤ ⑥ There are substitutes that indirectly reduce the demand for the technology, products, or services	⑦ ⑧ ⑨ There appear to be very few or no substitutes for such technology, products, or services	
11. Is there no slack? (waste)	Can't ascertain or get information	① ② ③ There appears to be a lot of waste and inefficiency in the venture (scrap, rework, low productivity, absenteeism, poor management skill set, low volume production, etc.)	④ ⑤ ⑥ There appears to be some waste and inefficiency in the venture	⑦ ⑧ ⑨ There is little waste and inefficiency in the venture	
12. Is there no hold-up?	Can't ascertain or get information	① ② ③ There are few choices of suppliers or buyers (oligopolistic or monopolistic numbers and attitudes) with little competitive desire to service the venture	④ ⑤ ⑥ There are more choices of suppliers or buyers with some competitive desire to service the venture	⑦ ⑧ ⑨ Suppliers or buyers have little or no economic power over the venture through small-numbers bargaining strength	
13. Is uncertainty minimized?	Can't ascertain or get information	① ② ③ Venture appears to have due diligence concerns—little management control over operational, managerial, or financial risk (lacks insurance, tax planning, employment and intellectual property agreements, etc.)	④ ⑤ ⑥ Venture can pass some key due diligence items	⑦ ⑧ ⑨ Risks are low because venture appears to be well organized and could quickly pass due diligence review	
14. Is ambiguity reduced?	Can't ascertain or get information	① ② ③ Absence of long-term planning with adaptation processes conducted in homogeneous (i.e., key management and board members from the same industry, locality, or family, etc.) rather than a heterogeneous setting	④ ⑤ ⑥ Some planning and a better mix of skills, ideas, and people in the venture	⑦ ⑧ ⑨ Progressive planning and a well-developed and well-rounded skill set among stakeholders of the venture	
15. Management expertise?	Can't ascertain or get information	① ② ③ Venturing team processes little or no experience and specialization in the business	④ ⑤ ⑥ Venturing team has some experience and unique knowledge in the business	⑦ ⑧ ⑨ Venturing team has sufficient industry background and can perform specialized skills critical to the venture's success	
COMMENTS:					**EVALUATOR:**

Source: © Ronald K. Mitchell, 1998, 2000, 2005.

Cases

The following cases have been selected to help learners to develop and become more aware of their own screening processes.

Kalista's Fine Chocolate

Prepared by Paul Artiuch under the supervision of Professor Eric Morse

 Version: (A) 2004-10-01

On August 15, 2003, Graham and Doris Beam sat down at their kitchen table to make a critical decision in the life of their business, Kalista's Fine Chocolate. The couple had just left a meeting with Mr. Smith, the landlord of a pleasing two-story retail and production location, and they now had to decide whether or not to move the business into this new space and out of the basement of their Brantford home. Graham and Doris understood that this decision would be a large step, both for Kalista's Fine Chocolate as a business and for themselves as the owners and operators.

Graham Beam

Graham Beam had always wanted to run his own business. Over the years Graham had explored a number of business opportunities, from a TJ Cinnamons franchise to a kitchenware store, but none of these opportunities had ever progressed beyond the initial research stage.

Eventually, Graham decided to enter the confectionery industry because it allowed him to exercise a high degree of creativity, and, besides, he loved chocolate. The forgiving nature of chocolate, which could be melted and shaped many times, made experimentation with new designs and combinations relatively easy and inexpensive. Graham took pride in his work and the creations that sprang from it.

The choice of the confectionery business was also driven by Graham's 33 years of experience in the food industry. This experience included three years in preparation and decoration of hotel buffets and 30 years in a large kitchen at a Brantford school. Working in a large school kitchen had familiarized Graham with health and safety regulations, food regulations, cleaning and storage procedures and label laws. Graham also learned to manage people, schedule work, create budgets and institute quality control processes. To supplement the skills acquired throughout his career, Graham enrolled in business and management development courses, focusing on labor laws and people management.

Doris Beam

Doris Beam shared her husband's desire to own a business. Doris's ideas and skills were complementary to Graham's and therefore eased the decision to enter the confectionery business.

Doris's work experience was more administrative in nature. Following high school, she had worked at a bank as a teller for a few years. She spent the next 27 years working in an administrative position at a Brantford law firm. Her responsibilities included reception, ordering supplies, banking and bookkeeping. This work allowed Doris to meet many influential people in the Brantford community.

Doris's role at Kalista's Fine Chocolate was administrative by necessity, although she also enjoyed the artistic part of the business. Courses in painting and flower arranging, as well as a genuine interest in the creative side of the business, cultivated her ability to innovate and design new products. Doris's goal in the short term was to leave her job at the law firm and concentrate on marketing and product design at Kalista's Fine Chocolate.

Kalista's Fine Chocolate

The idea for Kalista's Fine Chocolate originated in 1998. The Beams took a trip following Graham's recovery from cancer, and they began to talk seriously about pursuing their own business. Initially, they decided to look into repackaging high-quality candy for resale in Canada. Some months later, they spoke to a relative in Cambridge who was also interested in pursuing a similar type of venture. On the drive home, they discussed various business ideas and focused on the possibility of working with chocolate.

As a first step, Graham decided to learn more about the industry by inquiring at an Ancaster chocolate manufacturer. This company informed him of an upcoming chocolate-making course that could answer his questions. Graham took the course in January 1999 and decided that this was the business he wanted to be in. In May 1999, the couple took out a business licence for Kalista's Fine Chocolate.

The location for production and retail was the basement of the Beams' home, which was finished and equipped in the middle of 1999. The couple began to experiment with chocolate recipes and designs, and the first sale was made in October of 1999.

In February 2000, the Brantford Mall offered Kalista's Fine Chocolate an attractive deal on a kiosk for the Valentine's Day season. The Beams agreed and set up a small kiosk to sell their product line. The kiosk proved to be a success, and the business expanded from its home base to include the new location during Christmas, Easter and Valentine's Day. The respective annual year-end sales for 1999 to 2002 were $1,700, $14,700, $25,300 and $25,200. Half the sales each year were made over the Christmas season. The percentage of sales generated by the mall kiosk grew from about 28 per cent in 2000 to 42 per cent in 2002.

Throughout the operation of the business, the Beams learned a great deal about the confectionery industry and about the chocolate business in particular. They experimented with their product line to the point where, in August 2003, it included 12 different varieties of truffles, various seasonal chocolates and custom products such as boxes and roses. Research was also done by sampling and analysing competitors' products from local chocolate stores.

The truffle became the signature item for the business. Each type of truffle had a different filling, which had a distinct taste. The filling was hand-rolled and dipped in high-quality, Swiss-made Lindt chocolate. White, dark and milk chocolates provided the outside coating on the truffles. The final step was the decoration, which was done using colored chocolate (see Exhibit 1). The high-quality ingredients and Graham's expertise in creating outstanding truffle recipes quickly became the strengths of the business.

Kalista's Fine Chocolate was advertised both in the Yellow Pages and through limited postings in the local paper. This was supplemented by promotions during a number of bridal shows and local charity events. Kalista's Fine Chocolate attracted a small but loyal clientele of mostly upper-income Brantford citizens as well as family and friends.

Considerations

In the summer of 2003, Graham became eligible for retirement from his job at the school. Taking early retirement would allow him to work full time on opening and running the new Kalista's Fine Chocolate location. Graham's pension

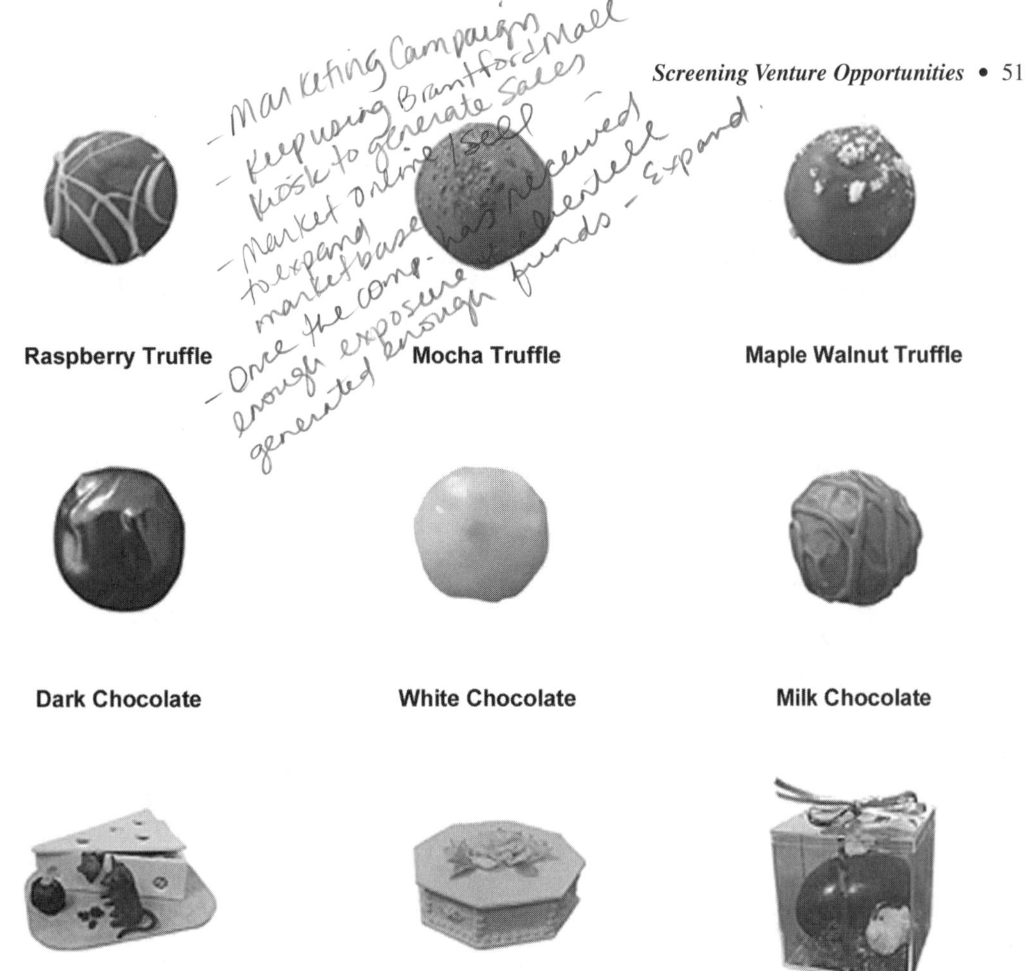

Exhibit 1 Kalista's Fine Chocolates

income would be $7,200 less than his working salary and this difference would need to be made up by the business. Doris would retain her job at the law firm until the business could sustain two full-time employees.

After three years of mainly home-based operations and occasional mall retail sales, the demand for Kalista's Fine Chocolate products began to outstrip the supply. The biggest issue was the time pressure that the Beams faced while working their full-time jobs and operating the business at the same time. During the 2002 Christmas season, they both worked three hours a day during the week and all weekend just to keep up with the demand. The couple knew this could not be sustained for another season.

Customer acquisition occurred through word of mouth, as the Beams did not have much marketing experience. For this reason, most of their loyal clientele, who purchased chocolate at the kiosk and from the Beams' home, were well known by the couple. However, the Beams began to recognize the downside of this situation, as potential customers who were unfamiliar with the business may be hesitant to purchase chocolate from a home-based operation. This was viewed as a major obstacle in the further growth of the business.

The financial goal of Kalista's Fine Chocolate was to supplement Graham's pension income and to allow Doris to leave her job at the law firm. Although a large financial return was not a priority, the couple could not afford to lose money on the business. As of August 2003, the Beams had approximately $180,000 in home equity, bank accounts and RRSPs worth $5,000 and $65,000 respectively, and cars worth $10,000. Kalista's Fine Chocolate has assets worth $18,900 and liabilities of $5,500 (see Exhibit 2). Doris secured a $25,000 personal line of credit and was confident

Income	
Retail Sales	$25,231.05
Cost of Goods Sold (COGS)	12,129.72
Gross Profit	13,101.33
Expenses	
Advertising	701.80
Bank Charges	208.85
MC/Visa Charges	35.00
Donations	297.50
Freight and Delivery	68.40
Interest Expense	102.50
Laundry	13.98
Licences and Permits	436.90
Mileage	193.19
Miscellaneous	220.17
Office Supplies	398.18
Postage and Delivery	125.15
Printing and Reproduction	591.64
Professional Development	472.08
Professional Fees	650.00
Reference Materials	63.85
Rent	325.00
Supplies—Marketing	323.57
Supplies—Kitchen	329.96
Telephone	2,070.93
Travel and Entertainment	337.57
Meals	703.06
Uniforms	229.68
Total Expenses	8,898.96
Other Income	60.00
Net Income/Loss	$4,262.37
Assets	
Current Assets	
Bank Account	$733.36
Accounts Receivable	32.60
Inventory	2,461.42

Exhibit 2 Income Statement (for the year ending December 2002) *(Continued)*

Total Current	**3,227.38**
Fixed Assets	
Computer Equipment	13,657.58
Accumulated Amortization	(4,717.04)
Production Equipment	9,963.29
Accumulated Amortization	(3,256.39)
Total Fixed	**15,647.44**
Total Assets	**18,874.82**
Liabilities and Equity	
Current Liabilities	
Mastercard	4,183.70
GST Payable	(382.60)
PST Payable	1,647.10
Total Liabilities	**5,448.20**
Equity	
Capital Contributed	36,051.83
Retained Earnings	(26,887.58)
Net Income	4,262.37
Total Equity	**13,426.62**
Total Liabilities and Equity	**$18,874.82**

Exhibit 2 Income Statement (for the year ending December 2002)

that she could get another $50,000 if she used the house as collateral.

In August of 2003, the business had sustainable relationships with suppliers of all the materials needed to support the product line. The new retail location would require a larger product line, and therefore the Beams would have to acquire and manage more suppliers. In the past, some problems with suppliers had arisen due to the small order quantities of the materials required by Kalista's Fine Chocolate. Although the Beams had many ideas for their own products and for some outside merchandise that they could carry, they were having trouble finding the time for experimentation and development.

The city of Brantford had a predominantly blue-collar population of 86,000 people. The growth rate in the population was about two per cent (six per cent for Ontario), and the average income was $40,000 ($47,000 for Ontario). Brantford had a relatively wealthy upper class; however, the Beams were not sure if it was large enough to sustain Kalista's Fine Chocolate. Although Brantford was not a major tourist destination, a new downtown casino drew traffic from the surrounding areas. Other nearby cities included Ancaster and Paris. Ancaster, a 20-minute drive away, had a population of about 28,000 people with an average income of $61,000. The relative wealth of the town made it attractive as another possible location for the business. Paris, a town of about 10,000 people, was located about 20 minutes away. Paris was not as wealthy as Ancaster, with an average income of just over $42,000; however, it was a popular tourist location. The three cities made up the bulk of the potential market, with other larger cities such as Cambridge and Hamilton further away but still within a reasonable driving distance.

Research into the competitive situation in the area indicated that Kalista's Fine Chocolate had two potential rivals in Brantford. The first, a Laura Secord at the local mall, sold lower quality moulded chocolate in a variety of sizes. The second was a home-based business that specialized in custom orders for moulded chocolates. Other businesses within driving distance included the Nut Bean (Paris), Adrian's Candy & Nut Shop (Cambridge) and Choclotastic (St. Jacobs). All three specialized in confectionery items such as nuts, candy and lower quality chocolate. Graham felt that his closest competition in terms of product line and quality came from a store in Oakville named Ultimate Chocolate and another in Burlington called Rockers Chocolates. Both competitors specialized in quality chocolate truffles and other chocolate products including slab-work and custom artistic designs; however, they were located a greater distance from Brantford.

The Beams considered selling their product wholesale to other retailers but decided against it for quality control reasons. Their concern was that losing control over how the product was transported, stored and displayed could adversely affect the perceived quality and reputation of the business.

The Location and Lease

The proposed location for the new retail and production space was in a two-story house on a busy road in the centre of Brantford. The proximity to Brantford General Hospital and to a retirement home was also viewed as beneficial. The space included 1,000 square feet on the main floor, a bathroom, office and a spare room upstairs, as well as an unfinished basement. The landlord had a small office in the back of the building with a separate entrance. There were several parking spots available for customers at the side of the building.

The rough terms of the lease agreed on during the first meeting included rent payments of $1,000 per month for a 24-month term with the option to renegotiate after the expiration of the lease. The utilities for the whole building and upkeep of the outside would be the responsibility of Kalista's Fine Chocolate. Property taxes would be split between the landlord and the tenant. An understanding was reached that Kalista's Fine Chocolate would take care of any minor repairs while the major items would be handled by the landlord. Finally, Kalista's Fine Chocolate would receive first right to buy the property in the event that it should be put up for sale.

Following the first meeting, the Beams were very impressed with the landlord, who seemed very helpful and interested in their idea. He also offered to enter into a partnership with Kalista's Fine Chocolate, an offer the couple respectfully declined. Overall, it seemed that the landlord was a sincere and trustworthy individual and a good person with whom to establish a business relationship.

The Decision

As the Beams considered their options before the second meeting with the landlord of the new property, they realized that many issues were still unresolved. The physical layout of the retail and productions space would have to be designed. A new fridge, cupboards, shelves, production equipment, display cabinets and retail counter would also be required. Graham's estimate for renovating the location and preparing it for production and retail would be about $40,000. The Beams were also unsure of the labor requirements to staff the store or even whether they could afford them. Lastly, the working capital needs were uncertain, as was the demand for Kalista's Fine Chocolate products. As the couple looked back at their goals and vision of the business, they realized the magnitude of the decision. With the meeting coming up in two short days, they had to decide on the next step for Kalista's Fine Chocolate.

Siam Canadian Foods Co., Ltd.

Prepared by Tom Gleave under the supervision of Professors John Kennedy and Tony Frost

 Version: (A) 2002-10-17

In July 1996, Jim Gulkin, Managing Director and founder of Bangkok-based Siam Canadian Foods Co., Ltd., was considering the emerging business opportunities in neighbouring Burma (also known as Myanmar). Although relatively undeveloped compared to the rest of Southeast Asia, Burma had been experiencing increasing levels of foreign investment activity in recent years. Gulkin, who had considered entering Burma in the past but declined, needed to determine if the time was now appropriate for him to enter the market.

Company Profile

Siam Canadian Foods Co., Ltd. (SC) was a brokerage business based in Bangkok, Thailand. It was started in April 1987 after Canadian Jim Gulkin quit his job in the oil industry and invested his life savings of Cdn$130,000 in the business. Gulkin was raised in Montreal where he remained until he graduated from grade 11 "with a stratospheric 51 per cent average." With school out of the way, he began travelling and working in various parts of the world and became enamoured with Thailand after holidaying there in 1979. SC's role as a food broker was to identify overseas customers, usually food importers, and negotiate sales with them on behalf of food processors in Thailand. SC's initial activity was limited to brokering canned pineapple and tuna; however, it gradually expanded its offerings to include a wide range of products such as frozen seafood, frozen poultry, canned and frozen fruit and vegetables as well as dehydrated fruit and juice concentrates. Over time, SC also began to source various products from both Burma and India on an ad hoc basis.

When first starting out, Gulkin was admittedly very inexperienced in the food brokering business. He commented:

> I didn't have a clue what I was doing . . . I didn't know what a letter of credit, invoice or cross-check was. I didn't even have a business plan or a marketing plan.

Adding to this inexperience, Gulkin found that local processors were reluctant to deal with him, despite the fact that he spoke fluent Thai. As a newcomer to an industry tightly controlled by Thailand's highly assimilated Overseas Chinese community, Gulkin struggled to develop comfortable levels of trust and confidence with the processors.

The food brokerage business generally operated on low margins, thus necessitating movements of large volumes of goods in order to achieve profitability. As the business evolved, SC began to focus mainly on brokering frozen seafood because the commissions were the most attractive. The company earned an average commission revenue of 1.25 per cent on sales contracts, usually denominated in U.S. dollars, that it negotiated on behalf of the food processors. During the late 1980s and early 1990s, the frozen seafood business was in a state of expansion in North America and Europe. At the same time, Thailand was quickly becoming a globally recognized source of frozen seafood, largely on the strength of overseas market acceptance of Black Tiger Shrimp. Gulkin estimated that Thailand harvested about 200,000 tons of Black Tiger shrimp in 1995, 90 per cent of which came from aquaculture facilities.

The following is an estimate of Thailand's recent fresh and frozen shrimp exports:

Year	**1990**	**1992**	**1994**
Baht (Billions)	20.5	31.7	49.2

25 Baht = US$1.00

In 1991, Gulkin opened up a representative office in Vietnam with the help of Philippe Vo. Vo was born in France to a French mother and Vietnamese father and, prior to moving to Vietnam, managed a seafood exporting business in California. The purpose of the representative office was to procure frozen seafood products for sale to overseas importers. Several months later, Gulkin, Vo and another local partner started a separate importing and distribution business, SC Food Services, in Ho Chi Minh City.

In 1992, Gulkin began to investigate the possibility of setting up a representative office in Burma but decided against it because he felt "very uncomfortable" with the local players in the seafood industry. This investigation made him realize that, apart from the necessary start-up capital which would be required, he also needed "connections" to people favoured by the ruling military junta, SLORC. He returned to Burma in 1994 when he discovered that new activity in the seafood industry was being generated by independent, non-politically connected businesspeople. Discussions with the new players gave him a much higher level of comfort that business could be done in Burma without the need for buying favours. However, Gulkin also found that these new players were "sincere but incompetent" given that his attempt to export US$100,000 of frozen seafood collapsed due to insufficient raw material supplies of acceptable quality, resulting in a net loss to SC of about US$30,000. He later recalled that "it was a cheap lesson for the market knowledge we gained."

In 1994, SC secured one of the most significant contracts in the company's history on the strength of the relationship it had established with one of its key German importers. The contract called for SC to procure 600 tons of breaded shrimp to be shipped for ultimate sale to McDonald's Restaurants in Germany. A second contract for 450 tons was awarded to SC in 1995, with shipments this time going to McDonald's in Germany and Austria. The trading value of the 1995 shipment was US$7 million to US$8 million. Under the terms of the contracts, SC received a commission from the processor as well as a supervision fee paid by the importer. The latter was paid because SC dispatched quality control personnel to the processor's site to oversee the production and packaging of the breaded shrimp.

SC first achieved profitability in 1991 and had remained in the black ever since. In 1995, SC's trading volume was valued at about US$85 million, 90 per cent of which was attributable to frozen seafood. By 1996, SC employed 15 staff who were involved in sales, quality control and administration. The main destinations for the company's shipments were importers from the following countries, in descending order of sales value: United States, France, Germany and Canada.

The combination of increasing success in the food brokering business and the growing affluence in Bangkok in recent years led Gulkin to form a separate sister company, Siam Canadian Gourmet Ltd., in early 1996. This importing and distribution business was initially focused on importing wines and coffees for sale to hotels, restaurants and specialty food retailers. It was later expected to expand its product range to include imported cheeses, sauces and other gourmet cuisine items. Initial results were considered "very promising."

SC's Vietnamese Experience

Gulkin's motivation for entering Vietnam in 1991 was largely based upon his assessment that, as an undeveloped country with a large, intelligent and hard-working population, many opportunities were becoming available to small firms with limited resources such as SC. As well, entering Vietnam was also consistent with Gulkin's view that, in order to succeed in the food brokering business, firms had to adopt a diversification strategy in terms of both supply sources and product line offerings. Furthermore, the amount of foreign investment in Vietnam had been escalating, due largely to the implementation of the Vietnamese government's so-called "doi moi" or "renewal" policy, which was designed to attract foreign investment. This meant that there would be a limited window of opportunity for SC to enter the market before being shut out permanently by bigger players. Therefore, with the help of Vo, Gulkin opened up Siam Canadian Foods (Vietnam) in order to gain access to frozen seafood for shipment overseas. Apart from Vo, SC (Vietnam) employed four quality control staff and an administrative assistant. Gulkin held 100 per cent ownership of SC (Vietnam) while maintaining a 50 per cent profit-sharing arrangement with Vo. Later, Gulkin, Vo and a local Vietnamese partner opened up SC Food Services, a separate distributorship that imported meats and dairy products, and sourced local fruits and vegetables, for sale to hotels and restaurants in the Ho Chi Minh City area.

Gulkin's view on the performance of SC Foods (Vietnam) was mixed. The business had experienced modest profitability since its inception, something that he felt was "very good, all things considered." On the other hand, daily operations were frustrating, particularly with respect to the honoring of contracts by food processors. Gulkin offered the following as a simple, typical example of a Vietnamese contract gone bad:

> We enter into a contract with a Vietnamese processor to supply us with 30 metric tonnes (mt) of frozen cuttlefish tentacles per month for 12 months. We, in turn, contract to sell this quantity of product to a European buyer. One month into the contract the Japanese, all of a sudden, become interested in this particular commodity. The raw material price, therefore, goes up and out of 360 mt contracted, we might get to ship 15 or 30 mt. The Vietnamese processor has absolutely no intention of honouring our contract if it means that he loses money or even makes less than he originally hoped. The contract is meaningless to him. It is nothing more than a piece of paper. His word or his reputation are not tangible concepts to him. My company, however, has to find a way to pacify our buyers who are none too happy. Sometimes it costs some money but fortunately our relationships with our buyers are strong. We do tend to make it very clear to our buyers beforehand that a contract in Vietnam is basically worthless and we, therefore, give ourselves a very wide notwithstanding clause in any contract we involve ourselves in.

These frequent experiences left Gulkin with the impression that local processors only considered the short-term implications of their business, often leading him to ponder the question "why bother?"

Burma

Burma, also known as The Union of Myanmar, was the largest mainland country in Southeast Asia and had a population of about 47 million. The country bordered on Bangladesh and India in the northwest, China in the northeast, Laos in the east and Thailand in the southeast. It was a diverse nation with over 135 distinct cultural groups, the predominant one being the Bamars, representing about 69 per cent of the population. The country was considered by the World Bank to be among the poorest in the world, with a per capita income of US$676, based on purchasing-power parity. The capital city of Rangoon (also known as Yangon) had a population of approximately six million and was the nation's main port through which over 90 per cent of all ocean-going trade passed. The physical geography of the country was a mixture of tropical mountains, plains and delta lowlands. Burma had a coastline that totalled over 2,830 kilometres bordering along the Andaman Sea and the Bay of Bengal. The country was thought to have abundant natural resources, particularly in teak wood, oil and seafood. (See Exhibit 1 for a Regional Map of Southeast Asia and Exhibit 2 for Recent Economic Indicators on Burma.)

Exhibit 1 Map of Southeast Asia

Source: E-I-U Country Report, First Quarter 1995.

	1991/1992	*1992/1993*	*1993/1994*
Nominal GDP (kyat—billions)	187	248	339
Real GDP* (kyat—billions)	50	55	58
Real Per Capita GDP (kyat—millions)	1,202	1,289	1,341
Real GDP Growth Rate (%)	–0.6	+9.3	+6.0
Consumer Price Index (1986 = 100)	349.30	460.49	541.51
Total Exports (kyat—millions)	2,932	3,655	4,071
Total Imports (kyat—millions)	5,337	5,365	7,218
GDP Area of Economic Activity (%)			
Agriculture	37.5	38.5	38.3
Trade	22.1	22.1	22.1
Processing/Manufacturing	8.9	8.8	9.2
Livestock/Fishing	7.6	7.3	7.2
Social Administration	7.2	6.7	6.7
Rental and Other Services	4.8	4.5	4.4
Transportation	4.0	4.0	3.9
Construction	2.9	3.0	3.0
Other	5.0	5.1	4.2

Exhibit 2 Recent Economic Indicators—Burma

Source: Investing in Myanmar, Union of Myanmar Investment Commission, 1995.

*Real GDP figures given use 1985/1986 fiscal year as benchmark.

1994 exchange rates: US$1.00 = 5.08 kyat; Cdn$1.00 = 3.78 kyat

Burma's seafood resources were plentiful given its exclusive economic fishing zone of 486,000 square kilometres along its coastline. Prior to 1994, the Myanmar Fisheries Enterprise, a state-run company controlling the nation's seafood harvesting and processing, was the dominant player in the Burmese fishing industry. This company was dissolved in 1994 in an effort to improve the industry through attracting private investment. The total marine harvest for Burma was estimated to be as follows:

Year	**1990**	**1992**	**1994**
Tonnes (Thousands)	645.7	650.7	689.0

Gulkin estimated that the total current annual harvest of all shrimp species in Burmese waters was about 20,000 tons. Given that the state of development within the seafood industry was relatively low, he felt that the placement of modern fishing fleets and aquaculture facilities, spurred on by recent measures to liberalize the industry, would increase Burma's seafood output considerably over the next several years, but not to the extent that it would match Thailand's output.

In 1988, Burma passed the Foreign Investment Law which, much like Vietnam's "doi moi" policy, was designed to attract foreign capital to industries which would promote exports and provide for the acquisition of new technologies. This Law was seen by the Burmese government as a market oriented measure because it allowed 100 per cent foreign ownership of firms, repatriation of capital and an "unequivocal guarantee" against the nationalization or expropriation of businesses. Firms operating under the guidelines of the Law paid a flat tax of 30 per cent; however, there existed numerous provisions which could be used to lessen a firm's tax burden, including the following:

- a tax holiday period of three consecutive years inclusive of the year of start-up with a possible extension if the Myanmar Investment Commission deemed it appropriate
- exemption or relief of tax paid on profits which were held in reserve and re-invested into the firm within one year
- accelerated depreciation of capital assets
- exemption or relief from customs duties paid on various equipment and instruments imported during the start-up phase of the firm

By 1994, 113 enterprises involving foreign ownership were engaged in a variety of agricultural, seafood processing, manufacturing, mining, energy and transportation activities in accordance with the provisions of the Law, eight of which were directly related to the seafood industry. (See Exhibit 3.)

Firm	*Activity*	*Origin of Foreign Investor*
1. Myanmar Bangladesh Fisheries Ltd.	Shrimp farm management	Bangladesh
2. Myanmar American Fisheries Co., Ltd.	Fish and marine products	United States
3. General Fisheries Co., Ltd.	Fishing, breeding, processing of fresh and saltwater products	Thailand
4. Myanmar Niino Joint Venture Co., Ltd.	Culturing and marketing of high quality pearls	Japan
5. Hanswaddy Fisheries Co., Ltd.	Fishing, prawn farming, processing and marketing of fresh and saltwater products	Thailand
6. Myanmar P.L. International Ltd.	Prawn farming, processing and marketing	Singapore
7. Myanmar Garming Fisheries Ltd.	Shrimp cultivation, fish processing and marketing	Hong Kong
8. Myanmar Seafoods Ltd.	Procurement, processing, handling and marketing of fresh and saltwater products	Singapore

Exhibit 3 Recent Joint Venture Investments in the Burmese Fisheries Sector

Recent Political History

In April 1947, Burma took a significant step towards gaining independence from British colonization by having its first free elections after WWII. The winner of the election was Aung San, the leader of the Anti-Fascist People's Freedom League (AFPFL). On July 19, 1947, Aung San, along with six of his senior cabinet colleagues, was assassinated. This became known as Martyr's Day. U Nu, the ranking AFPFL politician remaining, took over the leadership of the country and gained Burma's independence from Britain in early 1948. During these early years, U Nu attempted to establish his party's concept of Buddhist-based socialism. However, in March 1962, General Ne Win led a left-wing military takeover of Burma in support of the Burmese Socialist Programme Party (BSPP) and subsequently imprisoned U Nu and his supporters. In July 1962, several students who protested this takeover were shot to death at Rangoon University. These killings were followed by the complete destruction of the student union building on the campus. In the ensuing years, Ne Win began to direct the country towards the "Burmese way to socialism" in accordance with the doctrine of the BSPP. As a consequence, virtually all businesses were nationalized and there was a gradual closure of trade with most of the outside world. This eventually led to the collapse of the Burmese economy.

In 1987 and 1988, many Burmese organized mass demonstrations protesting the legacy of incompetence of the Government and calling for the removal of Ne Win. In July 1988, Ne Win stepped down following six weeks of bloody confrontations between pro-democracy demonstrators and the military, in which an estimated 3,000 people were killed. The BSPP did not relinquish power, however. In September 1988, a BSPP backed military coup was staged resulting in the establishment of the new State Law and Order Restoration Council (SLORC), under the leadership of General Saw Maung, Commander-in-Chief of the armed forces. Saw Maung immediately imposed a state of martial law while promising to hold a democratic election in the near future. This quickly led to the forming of the National League for Democracy (NLD), a coalition of parties opposed to the BSPP, under the leadership of Aung San's daughter, Aung San Suu Kyi. The NLD went on to win the election which was held in May 1989, despite allegations that SLORC had attempted to manipulate the outcome. After the election, SLORC refused to allow the NLD to assume the role of government and arrested the party's leadership and soon after placed Suu Kyi under house arrest.

On July 10, 1995, Suu Kyi was released from house arrest after six years of detainment, and four years after she had won the Nobel Peace Prize, in absentia, for her dedication to democratic reform in Burma. Despite SLORC's warning that Suu Kyi should abstain from political activism, she continued to hold press conferences and political rallies outside of her housing compound on University Avenue in Rangoon. Furthermore, she repeatedly called upon the United States and the European Community to impose economic sanctions against Burma as a means to force democratic reform in the country and was successful to some degree. During 1995, the four U.S. cities of Santa Monica and Berkeley, California, Ann Arbor, Michigan and Madison, Wisconsin passed "selective purchasing" legislation which barred these cities from buying goods and services from companies doing business in Burma. Similar legislation had also been tabled and was awaiting ratification by the cities of Oakland, San Francisco, New York and Colorado Springs.

By July 1996, several recent events had caused the issue of human and democratic rights in Burma to gain political attention and press coverage worldwide. Two months previously, in May, the Burmese government arrested 262 NLD members, thus preventing them from holding their first national congress since the 1990 election. This incident was followed by the mysterious death of James Nichols, a Burmese resident and former honorary consul in Burma for Denmark, Finland, Norway and Switzerland, who died in jail under vague circumstances. The 69-year-old Nichols, a close friend of Suu Kyi, had served two months of a three-year prison sentence for possessing an unlicensed fax machine.

These events led Suu Kyi to escalate her call to the Western powers for sanctions against Burma. At one point, she was able to have a video-taped speech smuggled out of the country. The message, which was played to members of the European Parliament, prompted the European Union to support Suu Kyi's position that economic sanctions were needed in Burma in order to move the democratic reform process forward. The culmination of these events led Heineken to announce on July 1 that it would divest itself of its interest in its Burmese joint venture. Soon after, Carlsberg announced that it had cancelled its plans to develop a brewery in the country. These announcements occurred about four months after Pepsi sold off its 40 per cent stake in a Burmese joint venture.

That same July (1996), leaders from the Association of Southeast Asian Nations (ASEAN), whose members included Thailand, Vietnam, Malaysia, the Philippines, Brunei, Singapore and Indonesia, met in Jakarta for their annual conference. ASEAN was a forum used to discuss issues that were of mutual interest to its members, including political, economic, security and environmental concerns. Burma had been invited to the conference as an observer for the first time, a move that was seen by many as the first step towards eventually granting it full membership status. Interestingly, by the time the conference concluded in late July, the United States Senate had passed a bill approving the use of sanctions against Burma if SLORC engaged in any acts which suppressed the pro-democracy movement of the NLD. The only hurdle which remained for full passage of the bill was the signature of President Clinton who, only several months previously, approved the Helms-Burton Bill, a measure designed to penalize firms and firm managers who continued to conduct business with Cuba.

The issue of democratic and human rights abuses in Burma was very prominent at the conference. However, while the United States and the European Union considered applying economic sanctions on Burma, ASEAN's policy position called for "constructive engagement" with SLORC. ASEAN's view was that the region's economic and security interests would be better served if Burma was not isolated. To this end, many ASEAN firms were encouraged by their governments to invest in Burma. In fact, Singapore-based Fraser and Neave immediately offered to take over Heineken's ownership stake in its Burmese joint venture. Similarly, discussions about building a new brewery between the Golden Star Group, Carlsberg's former Burmese partner, and Malaysia's Asia-Euro Brewery were already underway, less than three weeks after Carlsberg announced its pull-out.

Gulkin's Perspective on Burma's Politics

In considering his position on the question of democratic and human rights in Burma, Gulkin offered the following:

> Aung San Suu Kyi is a decent, intelligent, well-intended, brave and selfless person. I realize that the politically correct trend is to call for sanctions against Burma, but economic isolation simply does not work. Take a look a Cuba, Chile, North Korea and Iraq. All of those countries have experienced economic sanctions of varying degrees, but their leaders still remained. People will often use South Africa as an example that sanctions work, but their case was unusual. The new South Africans were an island of Europeans isolated both within their own country and from the rest of the world.
>
> Economic empowerment raises hope for democracy. Just take a look at Taiwan, South Korea and even here in Thailand. All of these countries went from dictatorships to democracies as their level of wealth increased. In 1992, when the Thai military tried to take over the government, the people said "No!" and what happened? Democracy prevailed. Many Thais had started to enjoy the benefits of increased economic power and were not going to give them up. It is the economically deprived that

lack money and education. These people are easy to keep in place.

On the question of human rights, Burma is no worse than Indonesia or China. The Indonesian government has brutally occupied East Timor for over 20 years. As for China, there are tens of thousands of executions happening there each year, some even for economic crimes. Amnesty International is constantly citing China as a major human rights offender but I don't see Pepsi or Carlsberg pulling out of there.

Reconsidering Burma in 1996

Gulkin recognized that time was of the essence if he was going to finally commit to Burma. On the positive side, Rangoon had seen the development of at least five new seafood processing plants in past two years financed by independent firms. Having had preliminary discussions with some of the independents, Gulkin's instincts led him to believe that corruption would not be a problem and that he would be able to quickly develop relationships of trust and confidence with them. As well, the lack of economic development within the country meant that smaller firms such as his own might be able to gain a sustainable foothold before many larger, well-financed firms entered the market. It was Gulkin's view that bigger multinational corporations could afford to be "politically correct," while smaller firms needed to take advantage of the windows of opportunity while they existed. A further incentive for establishing operations in Burma was his belief that, given the underdeveloped state of the Burmese seafood industry, he would be able to realize significantly larger commission margins than he was currently receiving in Thailand or Vietnam.

Investment in Burma was also consistent with Gulkin's business philosophy of developing and managing diverse supply sources and product ranges. This was particularly important when he considered that the Thai seafood market was simultaneously experiencing increased levels of competition as well as dwindling supplies of raw materials. He estimated that the seafood industry in Thailand had reached the saturation point in terms of the number of processors operating and that raw material supply levels would gradually deplete to the point where the industry would be in definite decline within ten years. At the same time, relations between Thailand and Burma had moved in a decidedly favourable direction in recent months. In March 1996, Banharn Silpa-archa became the first Thai Prime Minister in 16 years to visit Burma. The primary objectives of the trip were twofold: first, to re-establish border trade between the two countries, given that cease-fires between insurgent ethnic groups along the border had been sustained, and second, to give Thai business interests a chance at gaining a stronger foothold in the country given the recognition of increased interest that other nations in the region were showing in Burma.

Gulkin's view was that most of the other nations in the region did not offer the same potential for developing his seafood exporting business further. For instance, although neighbouring Cambodia had a sizeable coastline along the Gulf of Siam and thus strong potential as a seafood exporter, the country was still experiencing the devastating effects that years of brutal war and governance under the Khmer Rouge had brought to the country. A strong consensus among many business people living in Thailand was that Cambodia was not a secure place to travel, let alone conduct business. Evidence of this insecurity was shown by the recent kidnapping of a British landmine disposal expert, along with 20 Cambodian colleagues who were working on behalf of the Mines Advisory Group. Additionally, in a highly publicized incident in 1994, three foreign backpackers were kidnapped and subsequently murdered by the Khmer Rouge.

Gulkin had also dismissed the possibility of entering Malaysia because it had experienced very strong economic growth in recent years which, in turn, allowed the seafood exporting industry to become well developed. Gulkin viewed Indonesia as having potential, given that it was a large, resource-rich archipelago; however, he dismissed this option because of its considerable distance from Thailand. Furthermore, Indonesia was currently experiencing political turmoil of its own, brought on by the arrest of Megawati Sukarno, daughter of Indonesia's founding President Sukarno and the principal political foe of the current President, General Suharto.

Several factors existed which were working to dissuade Gulkin from making the leap to Burma, however. First, Gulkin was concerned about competing against PL Corporation, a local seafood exporting company controlled by General Ne Win's son-in-law, particularly since local companies were often shown preferential treatment by local suppliers and producers. Additionally, there was increased interest in the region from two of SC's key competitors, the Hong Kong-based Sun Wah Trading Company and a sourcing division for the Japanese trading giant, Mitsui. Sun Wah was a well-financed firm which maintained its own fleet of transport ships and had a well-established reputation in the seafood trading business. Its solid financial position allowed the firm to extend million dollar financing arrangements to processors, thus enabling them to remain open in times when cash flow was squeezed, something SC was not able to do for its customers. Mitsui's sourcing division was interested in Burma's raw material supply so that other members of the Mitsui keiretsu would be assured of having inputs for their value-added food processing operations. Gulkin viewed Mitsui, as well as the increasing interest of Japan's other big trading companies, as his largest threat in Burma. This was because the Japanese giants would be able to outbid many of the smaller players, and in turn, limit their ability to secure reliable supply sources. Additionally, the recent trend of the Japanese Yen was also cause for some concern because its rising value gave the Japanese greater purchasing power throughout the world.

The recent political attention given to Burma also worried Gulkin. While Gulkin viewed economic isolation as harmful, he also needed to consider the view of his overseas customers. He remained cautiously optimistic that his customers would not view his possible foray into Burma as unduly harmful. At the same time, however, he realized that if the economic sanctions movement gained momentum, some of SC's customers might "black list" Burma. Adding further confusion to this situation was the recognition that an increasing number of Asian firms were making inroads into Burma, despite the calls for sanctions elsewhere in the world. It was quite clear that Asia's view of Burma was considerably different from that of the Western powers.

The level of development of Burma's infrastructure was also cause for some concern. It would clearly be difficult to conduct business in a country which lacked an adequate system of roads or communication linkages. The port facility in Rangoon was especially problematic and was considered to be the biggest bottleneck in the country. It was not uncommon for vessels to wait for several days or even weeks before they could be loaded or unloaded. The matter was so grave that it prompted several foreign investors from Singapore and Hong Kong to begin the development of a new port across the river from Rangoon; however, it was expected to be about a year before the port became operational.

Decision

In considering his Burmese investment decision, Gulkin had to consider several trade-offs. Could he afford to take a "wait and see" approach to Burma while other Asian firms started to tap into the market? Similarly, could he afford to allow this opportunity to pass him by given that other seafood exporting opportunities in the region were quite limited? Alternatively, if Gulkin entered Burma, could he be assured that his investment was secure given the state of political governance in the country? At the same time, would he run the risk of losing some key clients who would discontinue doing business with him because of his involvement in Burma?

Asiasports: Hockey Night in Hong Kong

Prepared by Andrew Delios

Version: (A) 2000-02-03

On March 5, 1999, Tom Barnes, executive director of Asiasports Limited (Asiasports), spent several hours in a meeting with the two main shareholders of the private company, Shane Weir and Bill Gribble. In the meeting, the trio discussed the business strategy for Asiasports for the next five years. Asiasports, a sports management company, was involved in the development of ice hockey in Hong Kong. Barnes, Weir and Gribble had to make decisions about whether the company should promote hockey outside of Hong Kong and its choice of sports properties. An implementation plan also had to be developed for the chosen strategy.

Tom Barnes

Tom Barnes, 32, was born in St. Louis, Missouri, in the United States. He had been active in hockey since his high school days, where he served as captain of his high school team. After completing an undergraduate degree in organizational behavior at the University of Miami at Ohio, Barnes worked for Enterprise Leasing in St. Louis and Seattle, Washington. In February 1993, following the suggestions of relatives who were living in Hong Kong, Barnes moved there. Once he arrived in Hong Kong, Barnes began to work for the large cable programmer, Star TV. This job gave Barnes an entry back into the sports world as he worked as a program researcher for the prime sports channel of Star TV. Six months into his term at Star TV, Barnes discovered the existence of a hockey league in Hong Kong while on a hiking trip in rural Lantau Island. In the fall of 1993, he joined the fledgling ice hockey league, which was the predecessor of one of Asiasports' main properties.

History of Hockey

Ice hockey had been played for several hundred years. Forerunners to the present version of the game were played on frozen lakes and ponds in Great Britain, France and Holland in the 18th century. From these beginnings, hockey began to take more shape in the 19th century in Canada. A primitive variant of today's game emerged near Halifax, Nova Scotia, Canada in the early 1800s. Local schoolboys adopted hurley, a form of field hockey played with a stick and ball, to winter conditions. In the 1870s, students at McGill University in Montreal, Quebec, Canada assigned a set of rules to hockey and played the first exhibition game. The first formal ice hockey league was launched in Kingston, Ontario, Canada in 1885.

Ice hockey was originally played with seven players on the ice. In 1911 the seventh position, the 'rover,' was dropped. Later amendments to the rules permitted player substitutions, and the number of players on a team began to exceed ten. Various other initiatives and rule changes shaped the game into its 1990s version. These rule changes facilitated the opening-up of the game, and made hockey into a faster sport.

In the 1990s, hockey was a sport of power, speed, agility and knowledge. Players had to master the ability to skate; they had to learn to control the puck (the sport's ball) with a stick while maneuvering at high speeds; they had to interact well with team-mates; and they had to have endurance and strength. Speed was one of the compelling aspects of the game. The fastest players skated at speeds of 50 kilometres per hour, and the hardest shooters propelled the puck at nearly 200 kilometres per hour. Hockey also had an aggressive aspect. Body contact between players was allowed, but not to the extent seen in rugby or American football.

International Spread of Hockey

From its beginnings in Eastern Canada, hockey gradually spread to Western Canada and the northern states of the U.S. Hockey also spread east across the Atlantic to Scandinavian countries like Sweden, Finland, Norway, and other northern European countries like Russia, Belarus, Lithuania, Latvia and the Czech and Slovak Republics. Later, regions in Europe with warmer climates, Great Britain, Switzerland, Germany and Italy, embraced the sport.

This spread led to hockey's inclusion in the inaugural Olympic Winter Games, held in 1924 in Chamonix, France. Participating countries were drawn from Western European and North American countries. In the 1950s, Eastern Europe countries began to participate in Olympic and World Championship events. This growth continued, and in 1998, Japan and China also competed in Olympic hockey.

Women's hockey made its debut in the 1998 Winter Olympics. Prior to that, women's hockey had been recognized internationally, through sanctioned World Championships. At a national level, women's hockey leagues were prominent in the U.S., where several college leagues had operated since the mid-1970s. In the 1990s, women's hockey was played in North America, Europe and Asia. China, Japan and South Korea were the principal countries in Asia in which women's hockey was played. In Canada, close to 20,000 women were enrolled in hockey leagues in 1997. In the U.S. this number was greater as participation had grown four-fold since 1990.

When hockey spread internationally, its growth in new countries was supported by two factors. The first factor was that hockey had to be seen as an exciting and attractive sport for both viewing and participation. Hockey faced competition for the participant and viewer from a variety of other sports. In the United States, for example, hockey had to compete with team sports such as baseball, American football, basketball and soccer, as well as individual sports like tennis and golf. The second factor was that hockey had to develop at a grassroots level. Children had to have the opportunity to play hockey when young, to help develop an interest that would carry over into participation as a player, viewer, and volunteer in hockey associations when an adult.

Hockey Associations

International Ice Hockey Federation[1]

Representatives of Bohemia, Switzerland, France, Belgium and Great Britain founded the International Ice Hockey Federation (IIHF, or Ligue Internationale de Hockey sur Glace) in 1908. The aim of the IIHF was to control the sports of ice hockey and in-line hockey and to organize international competitions.

In its first ten years, the IIHF was purely a European institution. However, in the last two decades of the 20th century, and with the growth of in-line hockey, the sport of hockey became increasingly global. The IIHF grew along with hockey. In 1999, it consisted of 55 member federations.

The IIHF was involved directly with a number of tournaments and leagues, such as the European Senior Championships, the World Senior and Junior Tournaments, the Asia/Oceania Junior Championships and the European and World Women Championships. The IIHF had indirect, but substantive, involvement in other tournaments. These tournaments included the well-known Olympic Games, as well as lesser-known ones like the Continental Cup and the Super Cup. Aside from ice hockey tournaments, the IIHF helped to organize several in-line competitions and tournaments. These were organized at the grassroots level, for generating new interest in specific cities and countries, and at a national competitive level. Finally, the IIHF ran a development program for hockey. This program focused on development in four areas: coaching, officiating, playing and administration.

National Hockey Associations

A number of European, North American and Asian countries had national-level ice hockey associations. These bodies oversaw the development and promotion of the sport within the national domain, as well as in national competitions. National associations, such as the Canadian Hockey Association or USA Hockey, ran development programs for coaches, players and officials. The associations organized national championships and put together the junior and senior teams that competed in international championships.

As an example, the Canadian Hockey Association (CHA) was the sole governing body of amateur hockey in Canada. It worked in conjunction with 13 branch associations, the Canadian Hockey League, and the Canadian Inter-University Athletic Union. The CHA maintained offices in several major cities in Canada and operated on an annual budget of Cdn$15.1 million (US$9 million, see Exhibit 1). With a relatively small budget, it relied on the co-operation of volunteers to fulfil its mandate to the approximately 500,000 registered hockey players in Canada.

Source	*Funding (Canadian dollars)*
Sponsors	4,055,000
Program/Event Revenue	4,690,000
Membership/Service Fees	1,809,000
Merchandise	1,743,000
Sport Funding Agencies	1,465,000
Government	1,110,000
Other	268,000
Total	**$ 15,140,000**

Exhibit 1 Sources of Funding for Canadian Hockey Association (1997 to 1998)

Source: Canadian Hockey Association Web page: http://www.canadianhockey.ca/e/index.html, April 1999.

Note: Major sponsors included Nike Inc., Royal Bank of Canada, Esso (Imperial Oil) and Air Canada.

National Hockey League[2]

The National Hockey League (NHL) was the premier hockey league in 1999. The league had teams based in Canada and the U.S. The players in the NHL had a variety of nationalities: American, British, Canadian, Czech, Finnish, German, Russian, Slovak and Swedish, to name a few. The largest group of players was Canadian, but in the 1990s the percentage of players from the U.S. and Europe had been increasing.

The NHL, which was not the first professional league formed in North America, commenced operations in 1917. Initially, it had four Canadian teams: the Montreal Canadiens, the Montreal Wanderers, the Ottawa Senators and the Toronto Arenas. After several decades of sporadic growth and a bout of competition from a since-disbanded rival league, the World Hockey Association, in 1999 the NHL had expanded to 27 teams.

In the 1990s, the NHL adopted an aggressive marketing stance in which promotional activities in the U.S. and elsewhere in the world were an important component. The NHL ran several programs designed to grow the game of hockey. NHL Skate was one of these. NHL Skate aided the creation of multi-purpose ice skating facilities. A related program was NHL Hockey Playground. This program had the goal of creating off-ice hockey rinks in urban environments. A third program, NHL A.S.S.I.S.T., helped youth organizations defray costs associated with playing the sport: equipment costs, costs of travel and the cost of renting an ice rink. NHL A.S.S.I.S.T. had a worldwide mandate and had financed teams in Canada, China, Hungary, Ireland, Romania and the United States.

As a further aid to the promotion of the sport, the NHL actively sought greater penetration of U.S. television markets. Despite success as a television product in Canada and several European countries, the popularity of professional hockey on U.S. television had waned in the late 1990s. To increase television viewership, the NHL had continued to increase the number of U.S.-based franchises through the 1990s. In the late 1990s, the NHL planned to add new teams in such places as Atlanta, Georgia in the U.S. The 30-team league would have teams placed throughout North America, including cities in the south and southwest portions of the U.S.

It was in these cities, in which snow and ice were a rarity, that the NHL had faced its greatest growing pains in the 1970s and 1980s. However, in the 1990s, expansion had been successful because the game's premier player was a member of a Los Angeles-based team for the first half of the 1990s. The adoption of hockey in the south was also aided by an innovation: the creation of the in-line skate.

In-Line Hockey

In the mid-1980s, two brothers in Minnesota developed an in-line skate that could be used to play hockey. Their efforts led to the incorporation of the Rollerblade company. Subsequently, the popularity of in-line skating as a form of recreation and exercise exploded in the U.S. and elsewhere in the world. In the late 1980s and early 1990s, in-line hockey leagues began to mushroom in the U.S. In-line hockey was particularly well liked in the southern states of the U.S., in places where ice hockey had traditionally had difficulty gaining acceptance as a legitimate sport. California, where in-line skating had been adopted enthusiastically, saw the growth of several professional, semi-professional, amateur and development in-line hockey leagues. Children's participation in in-line hockey was also widespread and growing.

To deal with the rapid growth of in-line hockey, national hockey associations worked to organise the sport on a national and sub-national basis. For instance, in December 1994, USA Hockey created USA Hockey InLine to address the growth in demand for playing, coaching and officiating programs within in-line hockey in the U.S. Accordingly, the mission of USA Hockey was "to promote and facilitate the growth of in-line hockey in America and to provide the best possible experience for all participants by encouraging, advancing and administering the sport."[3]

USA Hockey InLine provided many services to its members. It offered resources and educational programs to coaches, referees and league administrators. It organised and sanctioned tournaments for players of all ages and skill levels. It co-ordinated national teams that competed in IIHF-sanctioned tournaments.

National associations were not the only ones to adopt and help in-line hockey. As part of its efforts to expand the sports fan base, the NHL created the NHL Breakout program. This program sponsored street and in-line hockey in 22 NHL North American cities in 1999. The tournaments concluded with a National Championship, which was held in January 2000. The NHL Breakout tournament was open to players of all ages and skill levels. Games were played on portable, inflatable in-line hockey rinks, which were also developed by the NHL.

Private companies also became involved in the promotion and organisation of in-line hockey. TOHRS was one such company. TOHRS was an in-line hockey tournament organisation that was sanctioned by USA Hockey. It provided 50 tournaments in the U.S. each year, drawing a total of more than 100,000 participants. Players from all ages and all levels competed in these tournaments. The majority of these tournaments were held in southern U.S. states such as Florida, California, Texas and Georgia, places where ice hockey was played infrequently at a grassroots level.

One reason for the popularity of in-line hockey in southern locations was its suitability to warm weather conditions. Unlike ice hockey, which required an outdoor ice surface (and a cold climate) or an indoor ice arena, in-line hockey could be played anywhere there was a hard, paved surface. Parking lots were a popular location for in-line hockey games as were indoor roller skating rinks. In-line hockey was also played on portable rinks. The NHL Breakout tournament was played on this type of rink. Other tournaments and leagues also used these rinks. California's Pro Beach Hockey Series, which was broadcast on ESPN and ESPN2, was played on a portable Pro Beach Hockey rink. This rink (50 metres by 23 metres) was three-quarters the size of an ice hockey rink. It had 1,200 seats for spectators.

ASIASPORTS

Sports Management

Asiasports was a sports management company (sometimes called a sports marketing company). Sports marketing companies generally carried out a variety of activities. Among these were the organization of fund raisers and sport event design and development, event production and consulting, sponsorship sales and management, media advertising, direct marketing, sales promotion and public relations.

Sports marketing companies often became synonymous with a particular form of sport. For example, Ryno Sports, which was based in California, principally promoted beach volleyball and beach softball. It sold sports that typified the California lifestyle. In connection with these sports, Ryno Sports provided a variety of services ranging from complete event management to professional athletic exhibitions, instructional clinics, turnkey events, consulting and the merchandising of gifts and merchandise.

Some sports marketing companies held a variety of sports properties. Lanier Sports Marketing, which operated out of Cary, North Carolina in the U.S., created, marketed and produced several types of sports in North Carolina. The company helped to create a boxing event called "King of the Ring," and it broadcast boxing. The company's other projects included sponsoring of golf tournaments and distributing and selling tickets for the local university basketball team. Finally, aside from these promotional activities, the company had an advertising arm that created and produced commercials and provided media planning and placement services.

Structure of Asiasports

Asiasports was formally incorporated on July 1, 1996. It was a widely held private company. The main shareholders were Shane Weir and Bill Gribble, each with a 30 per cent share. Barnes possessed 10 per cent, a Hong Kong venture capital company owned 10 per cent, and the remaining 20 per cent was held by thirty other people. The company had a board of directors. Seven to eight shareholders sat on the board; however, Weir and Gribble held most of the decision-making power. While it was a widely held company, its financial resources were limited to the pockets of Weir, Gribble and Barnes, which were not exceptionally deep.

Barnes made quarterly reports to the board, and the company had an annual general meeting. The board helped to set the strategic direction of the company, while Barnes had the autonomy to make day-to-day operating decisions. To aid his tasks, Barnes had one assistant, Keith Fong, and he contracted out secretarial support. When needed, Asiasports made use of volunteers comprising hockey league members and their families. However, all of the hands-on work for the company was done by Barnes and his assistant.

Growth of Asiasports

Weir, Gribble and Barnes founded Asiasports in response to opportunities for the promotion of hockey in Hong Kong. Prior to the founding of Asiasports, hockey in Hong Kong had been played on an informal basis for many years. Following the conclusion of a hockey tournament in March 1995, Barnes spoke with Weir and Gribble about their idea to create a sports marketing company for the promotion of hockey in Hong Kong. Barnes, who was looking for a new position at that time, began working for Asiasports on a full-time basis in July 1996.

Asiasports was founded with the mandate to manage hockey and other activities. In 1999, Asiasports was still in the entrepreneurial stage and Barnes was considering adding a variety of new hockey and non-hockey-related sports properties. It was by the addition of new properties and the expansion of existing ones that sponsorship income had increased by 50 per cent from 1996 to 1999. During the same period, player fees had grown by 20 to 25 per cent on an annual basis. With the exception of the World Ice Hockey 5's event, all sports properties were individually profitable. Even so, the company had experienced a loss on its 1998 operations.

In its first three years of operations, Asiasports had organised and managed several leagues and events. Some of these were hockey-related, while others involved other sports such as slo-pitch softball and golf. Hockey itself did not have as high a profile in Hong Kong as other sports such as horse racing, soccer and tennis. Horse racing was a popular spectator event, with nightly broadcasts of race results on Hong Kong's main TV channels. Soccer and tennis were the main participant sports. A multitude of tennis courts and soccer fields were squeezed into the tight land space in Hong Kong.

Sources of Revenues

As a sports management company, Asiasports derived its revenues from a variety of sources. Its two primary sources of revenues were player fees and sponsorship income. Player fees represented money collected from participants in the leagues and tournaments organised by Asiasports. As an example, for a player in the South China Ice Hockey League (SCIHL), the fee for the 1998–99 season was HK$1,800 (US$230) (also see Exhibit 2).

For most of Asiasports' activities conducted in Hong Kong, player fees represented 50 per cent of its income. The other 50 per cent came from sponsorship income. Asiasports had engaged a number of sponsors for the SCIHL, and for its annual ice hockey tournament, the World Ice Hockey 5's. The main sponsors for the SCIHL were Budweiser, the SUNDAY network, Nortel networks, the Hong Kong Yellow Pages, Caltex and Jack-in-the-Box. The number of sponsors for the World Ice Hockey 5's was the greatest, as shown in Exhibit 3.

In return for sponsorship, Asiasports gave sponsoring companies exposure. The principal sponsor for the ice hockey tournament was identified in the tournament's title—SUNDAY World Ice Hockey 5's. Tournament and league sponsors also had their names placed on the sweaters of competing teams, a practice similar to European hockey and football leagues, and auto-racing circuits in the U.S. and Europe. Sponsors were likewise identified in programs developed for tournaments. Sponsors also received name exposure through print and electronic media coverage of Asiasports-sponsored events. The two primary events, or sports properties, were the South China Ice Hockey League and the World Ice Hockey 5's.

Asiasports Properties

South China Ice Hockey League

The South China Ice Hockey League (SCIHL) stimulated much interest in hockey in Hong Kong. The league began in the fall of 1995 with four teams and about 60 players. In the 1996–97 season, six teams competed in the league which involved about 100 players. In the fourth and most recent season (1998–99), six teams and more than 100 players competed in the first division, and another six teams competed in the second division. The first division was the competitive league. The second division was a developmental league. Both men and women who were new to hockey, and children, were members of second division teams.

The SCIHL was originally founded in response to Hong Kong expatriates' desire to play hockey while living in Hong Kong. However, the current coverage of SCIHL extended beyond that original objective. The players came from many of the expatriates that lived in Hong Kong: Canada, China, Finland, France, Japan, Sweden,

CONSOLIDATED FINANCIAL STATUS		
Revenue (all sources)	Gordie Howe Event	235,520
	Sponsorship	542,000
	Players' Fees	148,759
	Merchandise	40,110
	Total Revenue	**966,389**
Expenses (all sources)	Gordie Howe Event	389,826
	Tournament Costs	843,970
	Total Expenses	**1,233,796**
Net Profit		**(267,407)**
TOURNAMENT COSTS		
Expenses	Asia Sports Management Fees	85,000
	Video Production	30,000
	Working Staff	70,000
	Ice Rental	450,000
	Program Production	43,000
	Merchandise	88,750
	Other Expenses	77,220
	Total Expenses	**843,970**
GORDIE HOWE EVENT		
Revenue	Friday Dinner and Gala	65,000
	Gala Dinner	170,520
	Total revenue	**235,520**
Expenses	Appearance Fee	78,000
	Friday Dinner	11,626
	Books	68,000
	Personnel Costs	30,000
	Hotel Costs	194,000
	Miscellaneous Costs	8,200
	Total Expenses	**389,826**
Net Income—Gordie Howe Event		**(154,306)**
SPONSORSHIP		
Revenue	Title Sponsor Sunday	—
	Co-Title Sponsor Nortel	250,000
	Associate Sponsor (Yellow Pages)	80,000
	Associate Sponsor (Budweiser)	80,000
	Dragon Centre/Sky Rink Team Sponsorship	30,000

Exhibit 2 Revenues and Expenses for World Ice Hockey 5's Tournament (1999) (HK$) *(Continued)*

	Distacom—Team Sponsorship	30,000
	French Restaurant—Team Sponsorship	15,000
	Cap. Z—Team Sponsorship	15,000
	Ski at Whistler—Team Sponsorship	15,000
	Lan Kwai Fong Holdings	10,000
	Drink Sponsors	—
	HK Land	7,000
	Dresdner Bank	5,000
	Kan and Co.	5,000
	Total Sponsorship Revenue	**542,000**
PLAYER FEES AND MERCHANDISE SALES		
Player Entrance Fees	Foreign	83,359
	Local	65,400
	Total Player Fees	**148,759**
Merchandise Sales	**Total**	**40,110**
Total Player Fees and Merchandise Revenues		**730,869**

Exhibit 2 Revenues and Expenses for World Ice Hockey 5's Tournament (1999) (HK$)

Source: Company documents.

Main Sponsors	*Other Sponsors*
SUNDAY	Hong Kong Land
Nortel Networks	Distacom
Budweiser	Ski AT Whistler
Yellow Pages	Fred Kan & Co.
Swire Coca Cola	The Hong Kong Tourist Association
Air Canada	Hong Kong St. John's Ambulance
The Festival Walk	Texon Media
The Empire Hotel	Empire Brew
	Hong Kong Club
	Conrad International Hotel
	Dresdner RCM Global Investors
	API Prism
	Comforce Advertising and Promotion
	Asia Business Group
	Can-Am Ice Hockey Association

Exhibit 3 Sponsors for World Ice Hockey 5's (1999)

Source: Company documents.

Place of Birth/Nationality	*Number of People*	*Per Cent of Population*
Place of Birth		
Hong Kong	3,749,332	60.30
China and Macau	2,096,511	33.72
Elsewhere	371,713	5.98
Nationality for Elsewhere Category		
Filipino	118,449	1.91
Chinese	57,393	0.92
British	44,703	0.72
United States American	18,502	0.30
Japanese	17,999	0.29
Indian, Pakistani, Bangladeshi	17,379	0.28
Thai	15,494	0.25
Canadian	10,816	0.17
Australian	7,777	0.13
Portuguese	323	0.01
Others	62,878	1.01
Total	**6,217,556**	**100.00**

Exhibit 4 Population and Nationality of Hong Kong Residents (1996)

Source: 1996 Population By-census. Census and Statistics Department, Hong Kong.

Note: People born in Hong Kong, China and Macau held a variety of nationalities.

Switzerland and the United States, among other countries (see Exhibit 4). The majority of the players in the second division were from Hong Kong.

The growth of participation of players from Hong Kong echoed the mushrooming popularity of hockey throughout Asia. Barnes believed Asia's fascination with ice skating owed much to the exposure to figure skating in the Winter Olympics and the success of Asian figure skating champions, like Michelle Kwan, Chen Lu and Kristi Yamaguchi. This interest, he said, often leads skaters to turn to ice hockey. Barnes noted, "Once you master skating around in circles, you'll eventually get bored and want to try something else like ice hockey."

In the SCIHL, as in other areas of Southeast Asia, games were played in ice rinks located in shopping malls. There were five ice rinks in Hong Kong in 1999, with the most recent built in 1998. The venue for the SCIHL was the Skyrink, which was located in the Dragon Centre Shopping Mall, Kowloon. The size of a shopping mall rink was two-thirds that of a standard rink. Consequently, five players—two forwards, two defence and one goaltender—played on a team, rather than the six used in a standard ice hockey game (see Appendix). Fewer players meant that the game was faster and higher scoring than the six-player version. It was more entertaining for the casual spectators that watched the game while shopping in the mall.

World Ice Hockey 5's

The World Ice Hockey 5's was an annual event that had been held since the early 1990s. The idea for the tournament had sprung from a group of American and Canadian hockey players who played hockey at the City Plaza Rink, in Tai Koo Shing, Hong Kong. Four teams competed in this tournament, in which five games were played over a weekend. It was named Hockey 5's because five, rather than six players, played for each team (see the Appendix for a summary of rules for this game).

The first World Ice Hockey 5's tournament was held in 1994. The Swedish company Ericsson sponsored this tournament which saw three local teams and three overseas teams (Beijing, Bangkok and Bahrain) compete for the title. The number of teams grew to nine in 1995, with Moosehead as the lead sponsor.

The event continued to grow through the next three years. In 1996, ten teams competed, with overseas teams from Tokyo, South Korea, Dubai, Bangkok, Singapore and Beijing. In 1997, the number of teams grew by 50 per cent and the name, World Ice Hockey 5's—Hong Kong, was coined. This tournament also marked the introduction of women's teams, from Hong Kong, Japan and Harbin, China, to the tournament. With the continued expansion of the tournament, two venues were used to stage the tournament.

The 1998 tournament saw the introduction of a Kids' Division and an All-Asia Men's Division. The number of teams in this tournament more than doubled to 34. Sixty-four games were played over four days at the Skyrink and the City Plaza rink. The 1999 tournament was billed as Asia's largest ice hockey tournament and the world's largest ice hockey 5's tournament. It had more than 40 teams competing in four divisions: Kid's Division, Women's Division, Men's Division 1 and Men's Division 2 (see Exhibit 5). Because of the growth in the tournament, it was held over a period of 10 to 11 days, rather than one weekend.

The growth in the number of teams in the tournament sparked wider media coverage of the event. The tournament had 49 clippings and stories written about it in Chinese and English language print media in Hong Kong, and in

Kids' Division	*Women's Division*	*Men's Division 1*	*Men's Division 2*
Number of Teams:			
11 Teams	6 Teams	15 Teams	10 Teams
Sources of Teams:			
Hong Kong	Canada	Canada	Hong Kong
Philippines	Hong Kong	Bangkok	Macao
Singapore	Japan	Hong Kong	Philippines
Taiwan	Philippines	Japan	Singapore
	Singapore	Singapore	United Arab Emirates
		Taiwan	
		United States	
		United Arab Emirates	

Exhibit 5 Participation in World Ice Hockey 5's Tournament (1999)

Source: Company documents.

print media in Japan and Canada. In the electronic media, ATV, a Hong Kong broadcaster, covered the tournament's final two days. A special five-minute feature was also carried on TVB Pearl. Other coverage was received from CNN and the Asia Sports show.

Asiasports' special guest for the 1999 tournament, Gordie Howe, enhanced media coverage because Howe was widely regarded as one of the greatest players in the sport of hockey. Both local and international media mentioned Howe's attendance at the tournament in their coverage of the 7th annual World Ice Hockey 5's.

In observing the tournament, Howe noticed parallels between the present situation for hockey in Hong Kong, and that in the southern United States in the 1970s. Howe said, "When I heard they played hockey in Hong Kong, I had the same reaction as when they started playing hockey in Florida" (reported in Hong Kong Standard, 12/03/1999). In 1999, Florida had two professional teams competing in the NHL.

Other Properties/Events

Asiasports organised a number of other hockey tournaments in different parts of Asia and Southeast Asia. In 1997, Asiasports ran tournaments in Macao, Bangkok, Thailand and Jakarta, Indonesia. In 1998 and 1999, the company continued to be active in Asian tournament hockey. Manila in the Philippines, Dubai, and Bangkok were each the site of an Asiasports hockey tournament. Asiasports also assisted with signing up teams for a tournament in 1998 in Ulaan Baatar, Mongolia.

Aside from running hockey tournaments, Asiasports supported the development of hockey. It ran programs for coaches and training programs for children who wanted to play ice hockey or in-line hockey. Occasionally, Asiasports promoted non-hockey sporting events, such as softball or golf, but when it did this, it competed directly with other sports management companies in Hong Kong. When Asiasports concentrated on hockey, it had no direct competition in Hong Kong and little across the rest of Southeast Asia. Even rink operators were not competitors because ice skating rinks were concerned with attracting a figure skating audience.

Future Growth

Setting for Expansion

By the spring of 1999, Asiasports had been successful in developing the SCIHL and the World Ice Hockey 5's tournament. However, these properties alone were not enough to meet the company's mandate and Barnes' goal of bringing hockey to prominence in Southeast Asia. In 1999, hockey still existed as a fringe sport in Hong Kong and other Southeast Asian countries like the Philippines, Taiwan, Thailand, Malaysia and Singapore. No national bodies organised the sport in these countries.

The growth of hockey in these countries had been sporadic and slow, especially compared to the more northerly Asian countries, China, Japan and South Korea. In Japan, for example, hockey was played at many levels. Developmental leagues existed for children, many universities had their own teams, a variety of people played in informal leagues, and a semi-professional (semi-pro) league, similar to what could be seen in Europe, China and South Korea, also existed. Women's hockey in all three countries was strong. China's women's national team was the third best in the world in the latter half of the 1990s.

The growth in the popularity of hockey in China, Japan and South Korea had attracted the attention of the IIHF. It was involved in linking ice hockey in these countries to the hockey world at large. However, ice hockey in Hong Kong and other Southeast Asian countries had yet to draw any serious attention from the IIHF. Even so, the IIHF was aware of Asiasport's activities in Hong Kong. Unlike the IIHF, the NHL had expressed some interest in hockey in Southeast Asia. It had offices in Japan and Australia. It played two league games in Japan each year. Further, the NHL had provided Asiasports with merchandise and logos for Asiasports' events.

Options

Several options existed for Asiasports. These options included both geographic and product diversification, as well as an increased focus on existing products. Barnes wanted to bring hockey to Asia, but in considering these options, he thought "he would take Asiasports where the money was, to keep the company alive."

1. **Set up hockey leagues in Southeast Asia.** In 1999, the only established hockey league in Southeast Asia was SCIHL in Hong Kong. The opportunity existed to set up similar leagues in Bangkok, Manila, Taipei, Singapore and Ho Chi Minh City. The state of hockey in these cities was similar to that in Hong Kong in the early 1990s, and each city possessed a viable rink on which hockey could be played. Further, Bill Gribble was located in Taiwan, and he had done some groundwork on establishing hockey in Taipei.

2. **Develop and expand existing tournaments.** Asiasports organized four to five tournaments each year across several cities in Southeast Asia. One option was to deepen its involvement in these tournaments. It could do this by committing more time to developing sponsors for the various events, by seeking a wider coverage of cities for the tournaments, and by giving tournament partners in various cities access to players that competed in the SCIHL.

3. **Develop in-line hockey.** In 1999, in-line hockey did not enjoy as good a penetration in Hong Kong as ice hockey because it was still new. Furthermore, in-line skating was difficult to do as a recreation in Hong Kong because of the danger caused by the crowded roads and steep inclines found on many roads. Even so, in-line hockey had begun to sprout in Hong Kong and was played at two locations: Discovery Bay on Hong Kong Island, and Diamond Hill in Kowloon. An advantage to developing in-line hockey was that the NHL had expressed an interest in promoting in-line hockey in Hong Kong. If this option was pursued, there was the chance for Asiasports to develop a tie-in with the NHL for the promotion of the sport and the sale of NHL-branded merchandise.

4. **Develop other properties.** This option included the development of a series of golf and softball tournaments. While this activity would bring Asiasports into more direct competition with other sports management companies in Hong Kong, it would broaden the base of Asiasports' properties and increase the number of potential participants and sponsors.

5. **Develop a semi-pro league in Hong Kong.** This option represented a shift in the way Asiasports did business. Developing a semi-pro league meant that players would receive a salary for playing, rather than paying a fee. The loss of user revenues and the higher cost structure would have to be offset by increases in sponsorship revenues. A semi-pro league would have a higher profile, as did the World Hockey 5's tournament, than the SCIHL. As well, the league could be an avenue by which hockey in Hong Kong could be linked to that in China, Japan, South Korea and perhaps elsewhere in the world.

As Barnes considered these options, he could not divorce himself from the context of Asiasports. It was a young, entrepreneurial company that had the financial and human resource constraints typically faced by such companies. It could not pursue all options, and its biggest challenge might be to solidify its current activities in Hong Kong before expanding. Even so, whichever option was selected, it had to be selected soon because the 1999–2000 season was approaching rapidly.

Notes

1. Information in this section was derived in part from the International Ice Hockey Federation's homepage: http://www.iihf.com., April 1999.
2. Material in this section was drawn from material available on the National Hockey League's official Web site: www.nhl.com., April 1999.
3. The mission statement and other material on USA Hockey were sourced from USA Hockey's Web site: http://www.usahockey.com., April 1999.

Understanding the game of ICE HOCKEY 5's

The rink

Basically, a hockey rink is a large rectangle with rounded corners. The ice surface of a standard NHL rink is 200 feel by 85 feet, but dimensions can vary. The surface at Skyrink and City Plaza is 120 feet by 60 feet, ideal for a smaller five-a-side team format.

The markings

The rink is marked with two blue lines which designate offensive and defensive zones and used in determining offside violations. The goal line is the red line at each end of the rink that is used in determining whether a goal has been scored. The rink also has two faceoff circles at each end and another at center ice. The dots located just outside the blue lines at each end of the rink also are used as faceoff locations.

The nets

The goal nets have openings that are four feet high and six feet wide. The nets are anchored to the ice by pins that give way when players crash into the goals.

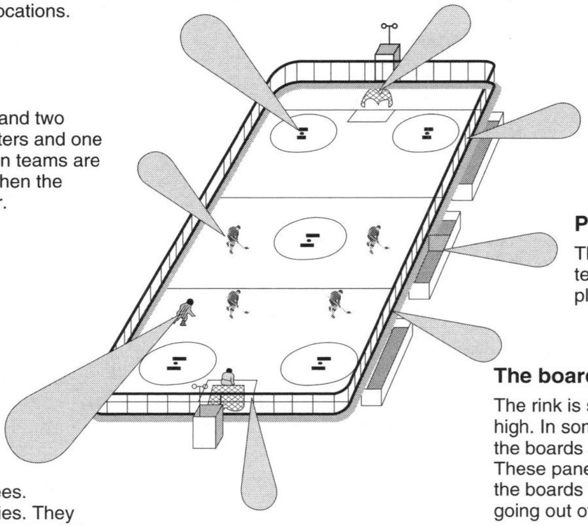

Players

Teams are allowed to dress 12 skaters and two goalies. Teams generally have four skaters and one goalie on the ice. Exceptions occur when teams are short-handed because of penalties or when the goalies pulled in favor of an extra skater.

Team benches

The team benches are on the same side of the rink but at opposite ends to each other.

Penalty box

The penalty box is located between the two team benches at center ice. This is where players go to serve penalties.

The boards

The rink is surrounded by boards that are four feet high. In some portions of the rink, extending from the boards are plexiglass panes, or ìthe glass.î These panes generally extend several feet above the boards which often prevents the puck from going out of play.

Officials (Referees)

The game is officiated by two referees. They call offside passes and penalties. They have also been known to break up confrontations and, on occassion, fights.

The crease

The red square area marked in front of each goal is the crease. No player from the attacking team is allowed inside the crease unless the puck is there.

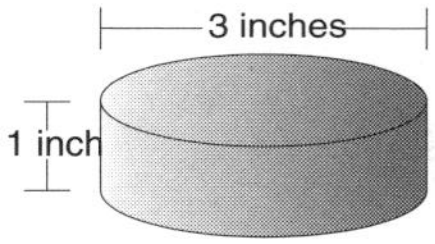

3 inches

1 inch

The puck

A four-ounce vulcanized rubber disc that is one inch thick and three inches in diameter. Pucks generally are frozen for a few hours before a game to make them less flexible and more likely to slide instead of bounce.

Source: Company documents.

CRYSTAL CORPORATION OF THE PHILIPPINES

Prepared by Professor Don Lecraw

 Version: (A) 1997-07-15

Mr. Jose de Valencia, Speaker of the House of Representatives of the Philippines, sat in his office one day in early 1994. But instead of thinking about laws and regulations and Philippines politics, he was thinking about crystal: blown, hand-cut, 32 per cent leaded crystal glasses, vases, bowls and chandeliers. "Should my group and I invest in a plant to make blown, hand-cut, leaded crystal here in the Philippines? Yes or no?" thought Mr. de Valencia.[1]

HISTORY OF AN IDEA

In 1987, while on a trip to Ireland, Mr. de Valencia had had the idea of producing blown, hand-cut crystal in the Philippines. On a tour of the Waterford crystal factory, Mr. de Valencia had learned that the production of hand-cut crystal was a dying industry. Labor costs in Ireland, France, and Czechoslovakia had risen over the past decades—and labor costs represented about 70 per cent of the direct costs of manufacturing blown, hand-cut, leaded crystal. Consequently, crystal prices had risen dramatically relative to other glassware. In response, some producers had reduced quality by reducing lead content from 32 per cent to 24 per cent and gone from hand-cutting the crystal to machine-pressed crystal. As well, modern lifestyles had moved away from formal, sit-down dinners in stately mansions. Now, most people owned, at most, an ornamental vase or bowl.

At the time, however, Mr. de Valencia had thought that this might be an opportunity for the Philippines. The Philippines had a plentiful supply of highly educated, easily trainable workers. Labor costs were relatively low, although not as low as in China, Indonesia or Vietnam. The phrase Mr. de Valencia liked was "cost effective" labor. The Philippines also had a tradition of craftsmanship. For example, it produced some of the finest ladies sleepwear in the world, sold in top stores in the U.S. and Europe. On the other hand, the Philippines had no tradition or expertise in producing crystal or other ornamental glass. Even regular glass manufactured in the Philippines were priced significantly below imports from Hong Kong, Korea and China, to say nothing of imports from Europe, the U.S., or Japan.

When Mr. de Valencia returned to the Philippines, the idea of producing cut crystal in the Philippines was placed in the back of his mind, as he turned his energies to rebuilding the industry and political system of the Philippines in the years after the downfall of President Marcos in 1986. Mr. de Valencia and his family were heavily involved in the industrial and political fabric of the Philippines. His brother Oscar was president and chairman of Basic Petroleum, an oil exploration and drilling company. Besides oil, Basic Diversified had operations in construction and real estate. Mr. de Valencia has been elected to the House of Representatives. He was an early backer of General Fidel V. Ramos for the presidency of the Philippines. In 1992, General Ramos was elected president of the Philippines and Mr. de Valencia became Speaker of the House of Representatives.

About this time, the idea of producing crystal in the Philippines received another push. Starting in the late 1980s and into 1990, the U.S. had been in protracted negotiations with the Philippine government, under President Aquino, over the extension of the U.S. lease on military facilities in the Philippines, most notably the huge navy base at Subic Bay and the airbase at Clark Field, about 100 kilometers north of

Manila. In 1990, a base agreement was reached; but the agreement was rejected by the Philippine Senate. Subsequent negotiations between the U.S. and Philippine governments failed to reach a mutually acceptable arrangement, and the U.S. undertook to withdraw its personnel from the Philippines and turn over the bases "as is" to the Philippine government within three years.

In June 1991, however, Mt. Pinatubo, 30 kilometers from Subic Bay and 20 kilometers from Clark, blew up in the largest volcanic explosion the world had seen in more than a century. Subic was buried under 12 inches of "ash fall" (much like wet sand), and Clark received six inches of ash fall. Just prior to the main explosion, the U.S. had withdrawn most of its personnel from Clark to Subic when daily minor explosions had shown that the mountain was about to erupt. The eruption devastated both bases as buildings collapsed under the weight of the ash fall and over one hundred major earthquakes. The U.S. military never returned to Clark. Instead, on schedule, they turned the ruined base "as is" (covered with ash fall) to the Philippine military. Within days the base was stripped of everything that could be carried or trucked, right down to door hinges (and the doors) and light sockets. The U.S. military remained in Subic and partially restored the base. As well, Richard Gordon, the mayor of Olongapo, the city outside the base, forewarned by the looting of Clark, mobilized the people of Olongapo to guard the base as the Americans withdrew over time.

Faced with this situation, the Philippine Congress, under the leadership of Mr. de Valencia and President Ramos, set up a Bases Conversion Development Authority with a mandate to turn the former bases into world-class source of production and employment. To spur investment in the bases, they were granted duty free status as export processing zones and offered a number of investment incentives, such as tax holidays, low-cost leases on facilities, and improved infrastructure.

Mr. de Valencia had also talked extensively with other like-minded Filipino businesspersons about investing in a company to manufacture crystal. These investors had expressed a strong interest in being part of the venture—if it proved to be feasible. The groups of investors had even decided on a name for the proposed company: Crystal Corporation of the Philippines (CCP). The group has also decided that the venture should be 100 per cent Filipino owned. They envisioned CCP as a Standard bearer to show the world that the Philippines and Filipinos were capable of producing export products of the highest quality.

Mr. de Valencia had also brought in Mr. William Mullins, an Irishman with extensive experience in the business, as an adviser. Through Mr. Mullins, the group had identified Mr. Joseph Foley, of Tipperary Crystal, a crystal in Ireland, who had agreed to act as chief technical consultant to CCP. Mr. Foley had told Mr. de Valencia that there would be no problem hiring skilled Irish crystal blowers and cutters to train CCP's workers due to the massive restructuring of the Irish crystal industry. Through Mr. Foley, Mr. de Valencia had also contacted Mr. Smythe, one of five partners in Irish Crystal, an importing and distributing company in the U.S. Mr. Smythe had expressed interest in helping with CCP's export marketing efforts in the U.S. Mr. Smythe had said that it would be possible for him to market all CCP's exports to the U.S.—provided they met or exceeded the basic quality standards for the industry, and the price was right. Mr. Smythe had suggested that he would set up a separate sales/distribution company, to be wholly owned by him, to market all CCP's exports to the U.S. The reason for setting up a separate company was that Irish Crystal already handled accounts from Irish companies that would be in direct competition with CCP's products.

The U.S. Crystal Market

The U.S. market for crystal can be divided into three segments based on quality and price: high end, medium, and low end. The price structure for the major producers is in Table 1. Waterford, with sales in the $100 million range, dominated

Table 1 Major Manufacturers of Crystal Products for Market Segments in the United States

	Average U.S. Retail Price (per piece) Manufacturer of Better-Selling Stemware Line
High End:	
Lalique (France)	$70–80
St. Louis (France)	70–80
Baccaral (France)	60–70
Waterford/Wedgewood (Ireland)	45–60
Orrefors (Sweden)	45–55
Middle:	
Tarquia (Portugal)	$30–40
Galway Crystal (Ireland)	30–40
Lenox (United States)	25–35
Gorham (Germany)	35–45
Noritake (Germany)	35–45
Saski	25–35
Miller Rogaska (Yugoslavia)	20–30
Mikasa (Germany)	15–25
Low End:	
Colony	$10–20
Durand (France)	5–15
Bormiolo (Italian)	5–10
Toscany	5–10

the high end of the market with an estimated 70 per cent of the market.[2] It was followed by Orrefors (10 per cent) and Baccarat (eight per cent). No other manufacturer had over five per cent of the high end of the market.

In the late 1980s through the early 1990s, however, Waterford had been battered by events in the U.S. economy: The fall of the U.S. dollar against major currencies (including the Irish punt) by over 30 per cent had forced it to raise prices dramatically in the U.S. The U.S. recession in the early 1990s had reduced overall demand for crystal. In 1991, Waterford/Wedgewood had introduced a separate line of medium-priced crystal produced in factories in Germany, Yugoslavia and Portugal under the name Marquis by Waterford Crystal. The Marquis line had its own branding and packaging; sold for $30 to $40 per piece compared to $45 to $50 for Waterford Crystal; was lighter and more modern and less ornate in design. Waterford management hoped that the Marquis line would both expand Waterford's target market and serve as a stepping-stone for new purchasers who would eventually upgrade into the higher-priced Waterford Crystal lines. Waterford management had termed sales of the Marquis line as "encouraging" but did not release separate sales figures. All told, by the mid-1990s, employment at Waterford was less than half that of a decade earlier.

In the lower segments of the market, the amount of hand work in forming and cutting the crystal was reduced and the lead content was reduced as well. This not only reduced labor costs as a percentage of total costs, but also decreased the costs of the raw material in the crystal. At the bottom end of the market, the crystal was moulded, not hand blown, and the designs were pressed by machines, not hand cut.

Each of the three market segments could be further divided into three subsegments: stemware and giftware, premium and incentive, and catalogue mail order. The stemware and giftware subsegment included the bridal market, which accounted for 40 per cent of the U.S. market and two-thirds of the high-end market. Through the early 1990s, this had been the fastest-growing subsegment of the market. By the mid-1990s, this subsegment had sales of about $120 million.

The premium and incentive segment was composed of trade sales (dealer and sales incentives), consumer premiums, and business gifts. The business gift market was seen as having the greatest potential for sales growth. Catalogue sales in the U.S. were projected to grow at eight or nine per cent per year, with catalogue sales of medium and high-priced gifts, such as crystal, projected to grow at about this rate.

As of the mid-1990s, department stores still represented the major distribution channel for crystal, accounting for about 38 per cent of sales. The share of sales through department stores had declined, however, along with the market share of department stores in total retail sales. Crystal sales through manufacturer-owned stores and catalogues had increased their shares (see Table 2).

The Philippine Economy

Since most of the output from the proposed investment would be exported, the major factor in the Philippine economy that would affect on the feasibility of the investment was the labor supply. Over the past 20 years, the Philippine economy had not performed well. The tenure of President Marcos had witnessed an era of "crony capitalism," during which large fortunes were made by those with close connections to the government. During this period, the economy had stagnated, and the external debt of the Philippines had risen to almost $30 billion. When Mrs. Aquino became president in 1986, economic growth spurted briefly. Under the weight of natural disasters (flooding, earthquakes and the Mt. Pinatubo explosion) and repeated coup attempts, economic growth stagnated again. With the orderly transition of power from President Aquino to President Ramos in 1992, there was some optimism that economic growth would take off, but by mid-1994, economic growth rates had not as yet begun to increase significantly.

Taken together, these factors had led to a poor performance for the Philippine economy: the real GNP per capita in the early 1990s was below its level in the late 1970s, real wages were below their level in the late 1960s, there were high levels of unemployment and underemployment, and there was a mass exodus of millions of skilled,

Table 2 Major Distribution Channels of Crystal Products

Category	*Per Cent of Retail Sales*
Department stores	38
Jewelry stores	19
Manufacturer-owned retail stores	11
Specialty stores	12
Mail order	9
Door to door	6
Craft stores	3
Others	2
	100

educated Filipinos to work abroad in jobs ranging from domestic helpers and seamen to bank managers and computer systems analysts. Remittances from these four million workers were estimated at $4 to $6 billion per year. These remittances, together with increased capital inflows, had led to the improvement of the exchange rate from 30 in 1986 to 25 pesos per U.S. dollar in 1994, even though the accumulated inflation rate over the 1986–1994 period had been 30 per cent higher in the Philippines than in the U.S.

There were two other important features of the Philippine labor market that affected Crystal. First, although most of the labor force was not unionized, unions in the Philippines were relatively strong and politically active. Although only a small percentage of the non-government labor force was unionized, through periodic mass demonstrations and political action, unions had managed to steadily raise the minimum wage and achieve strong benefits packages and work rules. By 1994, the minimum wage was about 125 pesos per day (about $5), with benefits about 30 per cent of wages. Probationary and short-term (six month) contract workers did not receive benefits. Although wages of $5 per day were far below those in high income countries, they were three to four times higher than the wages in neighboring Indonesia (a country with comparable GNP per capita), Vietnam and China and about the same as wages in Thailand, a country with twice the level of GNP per capita.

Most workers, however, did not receive anywhere near the minimum wage, either because their industry was excluded from the legislation or the companies for which they worked skirted or violated the law.[3] Many companies employed a high percentage of short-term workers for whom they did not have to pay benefits and who could be terminated without compensation. Many other companies used "contract labor" for whom the company contracted with a labor contractor for a lump sum. The workers were paid by the contractor—often at wages significantly below the minimum wage.

Second, the Filipino people had a strong drive for education. Based on its colonial heritage, English was both taught as a subject in the schools and used as a medium of instruction in many classes and textbooks. Most of the colleges, universities and technical schools were privately owned with relatively low tuition, about $150 per semester. This education system had two results: the percentage of the relevant age group enrolled in school (high school and college) was dramatically higher in the Philippines than in countries of similar income levels, but technical graduates tended to have little hands-on training due to the cost of equipment relative to tuition costs.

Stagnant GNP per capita, a dual wage system, and the rapid labor force entry of well-educated graduates had led to high unemployment and underemployment, long waiting lists of well-qualified workers for minimum wage jobs, many well-educated workers taking jobs below their skill and educational levels, and substantial overseas contract employment.[4]

Clark Air Field and Subic Bay

Clark Field had had a checkered history as an airbase. Near the beginning of the Japanese entry into World War II, Japanese planes had caught the U.S. air force planes based at Clark by surprise and destroyed most of the planes on the ground. During the Vietnam War, B52 bombers stationed at Clark had played a major role in the high level bombing in Vietnam. Subic had been the largest U.S. military base outside the continental U.S. The construction of the runway at Subic had been the largest earth moving project in the history of the U.S. Navy Seabees. After the Vietnam war, there was a dramatic decrease in activity at Clark, and to a lesser extent at Subic. Nevertheless, by the time of the termination of the bases' agreement, their combined employment of Filipinos made them the largest employer in the Philippines outside the government. Beyond direct employment, there were extensive spillover effects into the adjacent cities due to the spending of U.S. military and civilian personnel and their dependents. As well, despite extensive fencing, there was substantial smuggling and pilferage from the bases, especially from Clark with the goods sold in Dau (near Clark) and Olongapo.[5] The U.S. government estimated that together, Clark and Subic, comprised about four per cent of the Philippine economy.

Although Clark Field had been less affected by the Mt. Pinatubo explosion than had Subic, redevelopment at Clark had lagged behind that of Subic for several reasons: the U.S. military had not attempted to clean up Clark after the explosion; there had been extensive looting; Subic's port made it ideal for export-oriented manufacturers; and Subic's Richard Gordon had aggressively promoted Subic as an investment site. In addition, Clark was much closer to Mt. Pinatubo than Subic.[6] By 1994, both Subic and Clark had attracted investment in huge duty-free stores, hotels and other service facilities, but Clark had not been nearly as successful as Subic in attracting manufacturing investment.[7]

Crystal Production

The production of leaded, hand-blown, hand-cut crystal is both skilled labor and capital intensive. The ingredients—silica, lead and additives—are placed in a large pot. The pot is placed in a furnace and heated for eight to ten hours until it is molten. The blower then puts the end of a six-foot hollow rod into the molten crystal, removes it with a glob of crystal at the end, and blows through the other end of the rod making a bubble of crystal. The bubble is reheated and blown further as the rod is turned to make the bubble symmetric. As part of this process, as the crystal bubble is being blown, it is placed and turned in metal moulds held by other members of the blowing team. This process is continued until the crystal bubble is the correct size and shape. The bubble is then cut off the pipe and placed inside an annealing oven at temperatures of 400 to 450°C. After several hours, the annealing oven is turned off and the crystal wares are left to cool off until the next day. The cooled bubble is then cut so that it is open on one end and closed on the other. At the end of this process, the crystal looks like an uncut object in the desired shape: drinking glass, vase, dish, and so on.

Next, the crystal is inspected for flaws in size and shape. The design to be cut is then drawn onto the crystal. Cutters, using wet grind stones, cut the design into the crystal. After the cutting, the crystal is polished and finished. Finally, it is again inspected for flaws. No two pieces of crystal are exactly the same. There are always minute air bubbles in the crystal and small deviations from design. These small "imperfections" are one of the distinguishing characteristics of handmade, blown, cut crystal.

The quality of the crystal depends on the percentage of lead it contains (ranging from 24 per cent to 32 per cent), its symmetry and shape and the fineness of the cutting. In Ireland, training a cutter takes almost one year; training a blower takes almost two years.

The Investment

In early 1994, Mr. de Valencia had identified two former warehouses on the Clark base that could be converted to be suitable for manufacturing crystal. These warehouses were available at very attractive lease terms. But they would have to have extensive renovations, repair, remodelling and cleanup. In addition to the attractive lease terms, Mr. de Valencia and the other investors preferred to invest at Clark in order to assist the redevelopment of the base and to create jobs in the surrounding area, which had not recovered well from the effects of the eruption, the base closing, and continued flows of lahar over nearby river systems and rice lands.[8]

Mr. de Valencia had commissioned feasibility studies of the investment projecting investment amount required, sales, costs, profits and the internal rate of return (IRR) of the project under different scenarios. The biggest "investment" would be in training the cutters and blowers. A team of six skilled crafts persons—two blowers, two cutters, one finisher, and one production supervisor—would have to be hired by Mr. Foley in Ireland. This team would have a total cost of about $50,000 per month. Mr. Foley had estimated that it would take 24 person months of the six-person team to train Crystal's workers to the point at which they would no longer need training and supervision and they could in-train other new workers as the need arose.

All the cutting machines and pots would be imported from Ireland. The pots had a usable life of about four to six weeks. Since Crystal was planned to be located at Clark and it would be exported oriented, all machinery (and raw materials used for export products) could be imported duty free. The two furnaces would be made in Crystal's plant, with the assistance of Irish technicians to train the cutters and blowers. Initially, uncut crystal glasses, vases and so on would be imported from Ireland until Crystal's blowers developed the expertise to produce crystal wares of acceptable quality, size and shape. Initially, the productivity of both the blowers and the cutters would be low; but over time, it was hoped to rise to the levels that existed in Ireland. As well, initially breakage and wastage would be high. This did not mean lost materials, however, since the shattered crystal could be reheated and reused.

For Waterford in Ireland, for a vase with cost of goods sold (direct costs) of $100, $70 was labor and 30 per cent was materials and power to run the furnace and cutting machines. Irish workers earned about $10 per hour. For production in the Philippines, shipping costs would add 15 per cent to raw material costs. (Shipping costs for finished goods to the U.S. were about the same from the Philippines as they were from Ireland.) For crystal sold in the Philippines, Crystal would have to pay 40 per cent duty and taxes on locally produced crystal wares that were sold on the domestic market. Crystal planned to sell its output at 100 per cent over its cost of goods sold. The agent/distributor would receive a 10 per cent commission. This pricing structure would allow Crystal's wholesale price to be about 10 per cent below prices demanded for crystal produced in Europe.

The initial projections for an investment in two furnaces had not been encouraging. The up-front training costs (including the costs of the trainers) were too high to be offset by projected profits starting in year three when full production was reached and the Irish technicians would no longer be needed. If, however, at the end of the second year, Crystal were to invest in two more furnaces (which could be located in the second warehouse), it could double output without appreciably increasing administrative overhead. This projection assumed that Crystal's blowers, after two years training, could in turn train the new blowers. Since blowers worked in teams of four to six, new blowers could be placed in the teams with experienced blowers and gradually be trained by them, without a substantial loss of productivity or increase in wastage. Cutters, however, worked individually at single machines. Hence, training had to be one on one. If Crystal planned to double production at the end of year two, at the outset, it would have to invest in enough cutting machines and hire enough cutters to increase shifts to have the cutting and finishing capacity for full production with four furnaces, i.e., all its cutters would have to be trained in the first two years by the Irish.

If Crystal were to produce 32 per cent leaded crystal and were able to sell at the high end of the market, at full capacity, sales would be in the $6 to $7 million dollar range, with two furnaces and double that for four furnaces. Under this scenario, investment plus accumulated losses would be in the $4 to $5 million dollar range by the end of the second year. With the departure of the Irish and going to full, four-furnace capacity, Crystal was projected to be highly profitable with a substantial positive cash flow: if the assumptions underlying the projections were correct.

With the cooperation of Mr. Foley and Mr. Smythe, projections of the internal rate of return of CCP had been made under different scenarios. The implications for IRR for producing at two different quality (and hence price) points—high end and medium—had been calculated as well as the implications of two different wage and labor force structures (see Table 3). Mr. de Valencia had rejected the alternative of producing for the low end of the market, since the potential advantage of the Philippines was in its labor force.

Table 3 IRR by Quality and Labor Cost

Quality/Labor	*Contract*	*Minimum Wage*	*Premium Wage*
High	36%	34%	31%
Medium	32%	30%	27%

Note:
1. Long-term borrowing rate was 14% in 1994.
2. Figures have been disguised, but essential relationships have been maintained.

As Mr. de Valencia stared at these projections, he remained uncertain about the quality level at which CCP should produce and its target market segment. All else equal, he and the other investors would prefer to have CCP compete at the high end of the market. But was this the wisest choice? After all, at the end of the day, the investors would expect a good return on their investment relative to the risks they were taking.

Mr. de Valencia's uncertainty over CCP's targeted quality and market segment were intertwined with his uncertainty over the best labor policy for CCP to follow. After all, CCP's prime competitive advantage was in its access to low-cost labor. So it seemed prudent to reduce labor costs as far as possible. Moreover, if CCP paid the minimum wage and used short-term, contract workers, Mr. de Valencia had no concerns about CCP's ability to hire highly educated and qualified production workers. Once trained, there was no danger of these workers being hired by competitors, since there were none, or to go abroad to work in the crystal industry, since foreign labor laws would not allow hiring in industries in which there already was substantial unemployment.

Finally, whatever product and labor strategy he chose, Mr. de Valencia's ultimate concern was over the viability and profitability of the project itself. Was this the right investment for the Philippines at this time? Or had he and the other potential investors been carried away with the vision of "Made in the Philippines" adorning crystal wares on tables around the world?

Notes

1. The financial and operating data have been disguised to protect confidential information.
2. Waterford had purchased Wedgewood, a producer of fine china, in 1986.
3. For example, salespersons received between 30 and 50 pesos per day (outside Manila and Cebu), agricultural workders received 40 to 60 pesos per day, and workers in many small and medium-sized enterprises received 50 to 60 pesos per day.
4. In 1994, over four million Filipinos were working abroad as contract workers, out of a population of 68 million.
5. The smugglers' market in Dau occupied an area of about one hectare (2.4 acres) comprised of hundreds of shops selling everything from Hershey's chocolate bars to winches.
6. Subic had received more ash fall during the explosion due to a tropical depression in the South China Sea which had reversed the usual wind pattern to be toward Subic and away from Clark.
7. As part of the investment incentives, the government allowed each Filipino $200 per year (later reduced to $100) in duty-free purchases; residents of the areas surrounding Clark and Subic were allowed $200 per month; and all visitors and returning Filipinos were allowed $2,000 duty-free shopping at the two bases within 48 hours of arrival in the Phillipines.
8. Lahar flows occurred when heavy rains combined with the ash covering the ground and flowed down the mountain slopes into the rivers, creating moving walls of liquid sand up to 15 feet high. Lahar flows had inundated neighboring towns so that only rooftops protruded above the lahar and covered agricultural lands with sand up to 50 feet thick.

SEQUEL TO SUCCESS: THE FOLLOW-UP TO ABATIS SYSTEMS

Prepared by Michael Crump under the supervision of Professor Eric Morse

 Version: (A) 2004-10-13

Paul Terry slammed his fist down forcefully on his coffee table. "There comes a time," Terry said to the entrepreneurs gathered in his living room, "when you have to stop pontificating and just jump out of the airplane."

In the room were several former employees of Abatis Systems, including Adam Lorant, the co-founder, and John Seminerio, the chief executive officer (CEO). Since September 2001, the group had been meeting to develop ideas for a new high-tech business venture. It was now March 2002, however, and people were getting frustrated and impatient.

They had narrowed the choice down to two different business concepts. Lorant knew it was time to decide whether to make the leap.

BACKGROUND

In late 1997, Lorant and Terry had both been product managers at Newbridge Networks, an Ottawa-based company founded by the charismatic technology entrepreneur, Terry Matthews. For the past year, the pair had been working in Vancouver at the request of Matthews, who had asked them to establish a new west coast "centre of excellence" for Newbridge.

With that project complete, Lorant and Terry were free to return to Ottawa. However, they had their eyes on an even bigger challenge: starting a company of their own. With Matthews's mentorship and assistance, they left Newbridge, and in February 1998 they founded Abatis Systems in Vancouver.

Abatis focused on developing technology that could inspect packets of data traveling over an Internet Protocol (IP) network, then prioritize and route the packets according to their function.[1] For example, voice and video packets could be given higher priority than e-mail packets. Abatis's technology allowed Internet service providers to offer additional services, such as videoconferencing, with guaranteed levels of service.

Within a year, Lorant and Terry began looking for a seasoned CEO to help refine their market strategy and attract funding. They recruited John Seminerio, an experienced data communications executive, in March 1999. By the end of the year, the company was conducting field trials of its first product and was growing rapidly, eventually employing 150 people.

In early 2000, Abatis began looking for strategic investors to finance its product launch. Within a few months, however, the company made an announcement that stunned the local business community. Redback Networks, a U.S. company based in Silicon Valley, was acquiring Abatis for Cdn$1.2 billion—the largest valuation ever paid for a private high-tech company in Canada. As Lorant noted, "We delivered a return to our investors of over $2 million for each day of Abatis's life."

Following the acquisition, Lorant, Terry and Seminerio all stayed on with the company to assist with the transition and integration. The three executives subsequently left Redback in the spring of 2001.

MAGELLAN ANGEL PARTNERS

After leaving Redback, Lorant, Terry and Seminerio were forced to ask themselves an important question: What do we want to do with our lives? Lorant recalled:

> We all decided we were too young to retire. Abatis had been way too much fun. Coming to work every day had been such a rush. It filled us with pride to know that this great company was here because we had a dream and took the leap.

Furthermore, the three men had become good friends and enjoyed working together as a team. They believed that their individual backgrounds, expertise and personalities created a highly complementary skill set (see Exhibit 1).

They decided to form an angel investors group, backed by their personal assets. As angel investors, the group hoped to do for Vancouver what Terry Matthews had done for the Ottawa region—build a local cluster of technology companies by providing mentorship and seed capital. In the summer of 2001, they formed Magellan Angel Partners and began looking around Vancouver for new seed-stage investment opportunities.

At the same time, they decided to gather together a group of five to six former Abatis employees with entrepreneurial ambitions and assist them in launching their own start-up. Their idea was for Magellan Angel Partners to act as mentors to the group and then eventually separate themselves from the day-to-day management of the company. The three partners had great confidence in the team of Abatis alumni they had assembled. What they needed now was a great business plan.

John Seminerio	*Adam Lorant*	*Paul Terry*
Financing Sales Negotiations	Marketing Product Management Distribution	Strategy R&D Product Management

Adam Lorant

Lorant was a co-founder of Abatis Systems and its vice-president of product management and marketing. Before Abatis, Lorant worked with Newbridge Networks and Northern Telecom Canada in senior product development and marketing roles. Lorant received his MBA from the Richard Ivey School of Business in 1992 and a bachelor's degree in electrical engineering from the University of Toronto.

Paul Terry

Terry was a co-founder and chief technology officer of Abatis Systems. Before Abatis, Terry worked at Newbridge Networks in technical, marketing, product management and strategic roles. He was one of the youngest lecturers at the University of Liverpool, specializing in advanced computer systems. He holds a PhD in Electronics, honors degrees in physics and electronics, and received his MBA from the Cranfield Business School in England.

John Seminerio

Prior to serving as CEO of Abatis, Seminerio was employed for more than 17 years in the networking and telecommunications industries. Seminerio played a senior role in sales, marketing and business development aspects of several companies, including MPR Teltech, DSC Communications and Nortel Networks. Seminerio received an MBA from the University of Southern Mississippi and a bachelor's degree in systems design engineering from the University of Waterloo.

Exhibit 1 Magellan Angel Partners' Backgrounds

Note: Although each have their primary competencies, there is an overlap of skills between the partners.

The Brainstorming Process

In September 2001, Lorant, Terry and Seminerio first met with the Abatis alumni to brainstorm ideas for the new company.

"Starting with a blank sheet of paper is scary," Lorant noted. To get the ball rolling, he and Terry threw out a few quick concepts they had conceived over beers at the University of British Columbia golf club. Soon, other people in the group were proposing ideas of their own.

The group believed that significant innovations occur when expertise from one field is transferred to an entirely different area. Thus, they looked for opportunities to apply their telecom skills—designing reliable, scalable, manageable networks—to another high-tech industry.

They also looked for inspiration in magazines and journals and tried to forecast what kinds of problems different high-tech sectors might confront in the near future. As Lorant observed, there was no shortage of ideas:

> The great thing about high-tech is that there are an infinite number of business opportunities. You are limited only by your imagination and people's willingness to buy. Technology itself is never a limitation. If you can think of a need, you can always find someone to build the technology to meet it.

Over the next four months, the group held weekly meetings in Terry's home to brainstorm new concepts and critique previous ideas. At the start of each meeting, they appointed one person to capture all new ideas on a portable whiteboard. At the end of the meeting, the new ideas were divided up among group members for further research and evaluation. Each new idea needed to be assessed against the group's basic screening criteria. When the group reconvened, each person reported the results of the analysis. Lorant remarked:

> It's a very fluid, iterative process. Often, we find that several concepts don't work on their own, but elements from each can be combined to make something exciting and viable. We're constantly going back and tweaking old ideas to make them better.

Ideas Considered

In all, the group evaluated more than 40 different business concepts. These ideas spanned a wide range of high-tech products and services, as illustrated by the following examples:

Personal Intelligent Agents

Intelligent agents are software programs that autonomously carry out tasks on behalf of users. The group proposed to develop and commercialize a Personal Intelligent Agent software product that would act as a virtual personal assistant. For example, a user might tell the software, "I need to book a trip to Montreal next week." The agent, using artificial intelligence and linguistic tools, would go online to find airline, hotel and rental car reservations, and seven-day weather forecasts for Montreal—just as a personal assistant would.

Database Accelerators

The group proposed to design specialized hardware for handling large database applications. Existing database applications ran on general-purpose servers that handled many different kinds of software. A custom-designed system would improve the price-performance of these applications.

Solid-State Disk Drives

The group proposed to design a solid-state disk drive.[2] Existing disk drive technology used magnetic disks, spun at high speed under a moving device that would read and write data. The group believed that solid-state technology could be used to make disk drives that were 100 times faster at accessing data than existing products.

Consumer Internet Appliances

The group proposed to design an inexpensive, user-friendly Internet device with only limited functionality (such as e-mail and web browsing). Unlike personal computer systems, the device would require no technical skill to use. Customers could simply take the device out of its box and plug it in, much like a toaster or a television. The devices would be marketed to the "techno-phobic" segment of the population and would lower the barrier for this group to access the Internet.

Web Content Management

The group proposed to develop software that would greatly simplify the process of publishing content to Internet or intranet websites. They proposed to market the product to medium-size companies with corporate intranets that need frequent updating of content. The software would enable people at all levels throughout the organization to publish new content to the intranet, thereby lowering the cost and complexity of maintaining these systems.

Screening Criteria

Each new idea was evaluated against six basic business criteria that Magellan Angel Partners had provided:

1. Simple to understand and sell.
2. Big market (more than $500 million; no one with more than 20 per cent market share).
3. Compelling value proposition solving a pressing need (e.g., 10 times the performance of existing products).
4. Innovative technology that can be protected from imitation.
5. Quantifiable return on investment (payback within 12 months).
6. Ability to design and build.

According to Lorant, the process of screening new ideas for real business potential was "like watching baby turtles scampering to the ocean. Most don't make it."

By January 2002, the group had narrowed the ideas down to two concepts. They began meeting daily to draft a full business plan around each concept.

Concept 1: Data Center Equipment

Internet data centres (also known as "hosting centres") are facilities that physically house web servers, database servers, application servers, storage devices and networking equipment in a central, controlled environment. Data centres provide companies the option of moving their in-house IT systems into specialized offsite facilities—effectively outsourcing many of their IT needs to third-party specialists.

The group proposed to design, build and sell specialized computer equipment for use in Internet data centres (IDCs). They believed existing suppliers were not meeting the business needs of IDCs and that future trends would exacerbate this problem. They envisioned new technology that would allow data centres to achieve the same service quality and cost-efficiency as telecommunications companies.

Product and Technology

In 2002, data centres used high-end, general-purpose computers (servers) connected together with general-purpose networking equipment.

The group recognized several problems associated with using general-purpose computers as the underlying infrastructure for IDCs. Firstly, it meant the IDC needed to store and manage too many "boxes and cables." This resulted in increased power and space requirements for the facility and made management of the equipment an extremely complex job. Secondly, general-purpose hardware and software (such as the Windows or Linux operating systems) were not designed for the extremely high reliability and availability requirements that customers demanded. As a result, data centres were often forced to provide redundant hardware to prevent downtime. Finally, the existing equipment did not allow unused computing power on a server to be reallocated elsewhere, resulting in chronic underutilization of computing capacity.

The group believed that it could solve all these problems by replacing general-purpose computers with specialized equipment that would be purpose-built to meet the equipment needs of IDCs. They proposed to redesign data centre technology from the ground up, with reliability and manageability as core principles.

Market and Competition

It was widely recognized that the data centre industry was poised for rapid growth, fueled by the phenomenal growth of the Internet. However, the group found several differing estimates on growth rates and market size. Various market research firms estimated that capital equipment expenditures by data centres would reach between $4.2 billion and $27 billion by 2005.[3] The group believed the actual market size would be at the lower end of this range.

In 2002, most IDCs had not achieved profitability, and many were in poor financial health. A sharp downturn in the technology sector had resulted in excess capacity and eroding margins among both data centres and their equipment suppliers. Consolidation was occurring throughout the market, as bigger data centres tried to find profitability in economies of scale.

One of the lessons learned by early IDC companies was that revenue efficiency, or revenue per square foot of data centre space, was a critical metric to be managed. Data centres were attempting to increase their revenue efficiencies in several ways. One way was to sharply control their operating and capital costs. Another way was to move into higher-value services. In 2001, the bulk of industry revenue came from simple Web site hosting services. In the future, however, revenues were expected to diversify and margins were expected to improve as customers outsourced more and more of their mission-critical IT applications, such as data backup, security, corporate e-mail, sales force automation and CRM.[4]

Data centre companies could effectively be split into several tiers, segmented by size and customer base (see Exhibit 2). Tier 1 data centres tended to make bulk purchases and signed long-term supply contracts with brand-name suppliers. Tier 2 and 3 customers made their equipment purchasing decisions almost entirely on the basis of price.

	Tier 1	*Tier 2*	*Tier 3*
Annual Revenues	> $100 million	$10 million–$100 million	< $10 million
Market Share by Revenue	25%	75%	25%
Customer Base	Large “Fortune 1000” companies	Small- and medium-sized firms	Very small, local firms
Servers Under Management	> 3,000	500–3,000	10–500
Profitability	None are profitable, due to large capital investments. Restructuring to deal with excessive debt.	Some are close to being profitable. Biggest position and burn rate.	Some are already profitable, but barely. Concerns are cash.

Exhibit 2 Data Centre Market Segmentation

Competition among major equipment suppliers to IDCs was fierce. Competitors included some of the biggest players in the computer industry: Sun Microsystems, IBM, Hewlett-Packard and Dell. In early 2002, Sun launched its N1 architecture, a new equipment solution targeted specifically at data centres. N1 would make Sun a direct competitor.

Strategy and Business Model

Under the group's proposed business model, their company would design, manufacture and sell highly specialized computer equipment to Internet data centres.

The group proposed to enter the North American market with a direct sales and distribution model. Their early strategy would be to build relationships with a few initial reference customers. These early adopting customers would help to "harden" the product by testing it for functionality and reliability, providing valuable feedback, and collaborating with product engineers to improve it. Reference customers would also provide the company with credibility when approaching future customers.

After establishing a foothold in North America, the company would expand to international markets and begin leveraging third-party distribution channels to lower sales and support costs.

The group planned to target the medium-sized, tier 2 companies. To gain traction with this segment, they needed to change the customers' purchasing decision criteria away from initial capital cost and toward total cost of ownership. They intended to do this with a very tight, compelling message. By designing new equipment specifically to meet the special needs of IDCs, they could enable these companies to both control operating costs and move into higher-margin services (see Exhibit 3).

The group had met with a few potential IDC customers to research the market and get feedback on their concept. The feedback was very positive. Potential customers were very excited at the prospect of better utilization rates for their capital investments. They were also quite interested in the prospect of lower operating costs.

It was expected that the hardware technology would be composed of commercially available components connected together with a proprietary architecture. The company would build and maintain an extensive patent portfolio to protect its architecture from imitation. In addition, the company would develop value-added software and firmware that would complement its hardware.[5]

The group felt confident that their product would be so radically different from existing solutions that they would have no trouble differentiating themselves from any larger competitors—even

	Existing "General-Purpose" Equipment	*Proposed "Purpose-Built" Equipment*
Number of Computer Units ("Boxes")	1,000	8
Number of Switches	12	2
Number of Routers	2	2
Number of Racks	26	1
Number of Cables	5,044	32
Power Consumption	320 kW	20 kW
Total Cost of Ownership Over Two Years	$4.5 million	$3 million

Exhibit 3 Data Centre Infrastructure Comparison

Sun's N1 products. They perceived these companies as slow and not very innovative. Lorant commented on the competitors:

> With an entirely new class of product like this, it takes more than a year for a new entrant to really hit the big players' radar screen, and another year or two for us to really start to cause them the pain that would force them to react. So we've got one to three years head start on the big guys. That's enough time for us to build technology, reference customers, revenue and a brand.

The group's exit strategy for investors was to take the company through an initial public offering (IPO).

Concept 2: High-Performance Computing

High-performance computers, or "supercomputers," are used by industry and academic centres for large-scale simulation, modeling, data mining and other computationally intensive applications. A climatologist may be modeling weather patterns, a biologist sequencing the human genome or a product engineer simulating car crashes—many real-world problems require massive computing resources. In 2002, a typical supercomputer was 500 to 1,000 times more powerful than a typical desktop computer.

The group proposed to apply their telecommunications engineering skills to the field of high-performance computing (HPC). The team believed there was an opportunity to design a new supercomputer architecture that would offer tremendous advantages over existing solutions in terms of price-performance, scalability, reliability and manageability.

Product and Technology

As the scale and scope of problems being solved through computational analysis had increased in recent years, so had the strain these applications placed on their computing systems. All supercomputers were designed to use many microprocessors connected together and working in parallel. The bottleneck in scaling the performance of these systems (i.e., adding more processors) was the ability to efficiently move data between processors.

In 2002, two different supercomputer architectures dominated the industry, and each used a different means of connecting processors. The first architecture, known as SMP, or "symmetric multiprocessing," consisted of multiple processors sharing the same memory. These were extremely powerful, but expensive, custom-built supercomputer systems. With the second architecture, known as the "cluster" design, supercomputers were built using a patchwork approach. Large numbers of general-purpose computers were linked together with off-the-shelf networking equipment. Cluster systems, while dramatically less expensive than SMP systems, became extremely complex to use and manage as they got bigger and more powerful.

The group recognized the underlying problem of communicating data between processors as essentially a *networking* problem, and believed their telecom expertise could find a better solution. They aimed to design a new type of supercomputer that would combine the best attributes of both existing segments.

Market and Competition

The North American market for high-performance computing systems was estimated to be approximately $4.7 billion in 2002. The demand for computational power was expected to continue growing. Market research firms estimated that supercomputer sales revenues would expand at a 6.1 per cent compound annual growth rate between 2002 and 2007.

In the past, many new companies had tried and failed to enter the HPC market. Most had attempted to develop their own proprietary microprocessor—a very expensive, resource-intensive process. As Lorant observed, "the industry is littered with the carcasses of failed supercomputer startups."

The past several years had seen the emergence of industry standards in HPC technology. In microprocessors, the industry was converging on the popular x86 architecture.[6] Likewise, Linux had rapidly emerged as the standard operating system, replacing a wide assortment of custom-written, proprietary software.

In 2002, approximately 80 per cent of revenues came from sales of SMP systems, with the remaining 20 per cent from cluster systems. However, cluster systems were quickly gaining market share, due to their very compelling price-performance.

The group aimed to provide a solution that would combine the best attributes of both SMP and cluster systems. With a huge price-performance improvement, they felt they could significantly expand the role of high-performance computing in many segments, and thereby grow the entire market for HPC systems. They expected to attract new customers who were unable to afford the capital investment or operational costs of existing supercomputer systems.

The market for supercomputers was extremely fragmented. Customers were commonly segmented based on the dollar size of their equipment (see Exhibit 4). Customers could also be segmented into vertical markets. In 2001, the largest of these vertical markets were biosciences (22 per cent), scientific R&D (21 per cent) and mechanical design (12 per cent).

The purchase process for large supercomputer systems (priced at more than $1 million) tended to be very long and formal, including requests for information (RFI), requests for proposal (RFP) and joint funding agreements. Purchasers, who bought computer systems for specific applications, usually had fixed equipment budgets. For smaller systems, the process was typically much more streamlined, and these systems were often used for a variety of applications. In either case, the buying decision was largely driven by the price-to-performance metrics of competing products. In larger enterprise businesses, the stability and maturity of their equipment supplier was also a strong consideration.

The supercomputer market was dominated by technology industry behemoths, such as IBM, Hewlett-Packard, Compaq, Sun Microsystems and Silicon Graphics, each with roughly equal market share. Cray, a specialized manufacturer of high-performance computers, was also a significant competitor.

Strategy and Business Model

The group's proposed business model was straightforward: they would design, build and sell high-performance computers to a variety of market segments.

In many ways, the group's strategy for market penetration and growth was similar to that of the Data Center concept. The first two years would be spent building an engineering team, designing the product and developing the necessary technology. Following the product launch, they would initially rely on direct sales and distribution of departmental and divisional scale systems. They would target universities, national research laboratories and government agencies in North America. The group believed that these vertical markets were the "early adopters," willing to experiment with new technologies and work closely with new suppliers. Once again, they intended to use these early adopters as reference customers who would help them refine their product and provide them with credibility in other vertical markets.

The group planned to expand quickly into a wide variety of vertical market segments. They would use indirect sales channels to reach overseas markets and other vertical markets. Eventually, they also planned to move upmarket into the enterprise and technical capability market segments.

To demonstrate the value of their product, they planned to exploit industry benchmarks for price-to-performance. They felt confident that they could gain a lot of attention and publicity within the industry by smashing some existing performance records. The group hoped to achieve a price-performance metric that was 10 times greater than existing products (see Exhibit 5).

The group had met with several potential reference customers in the supercomputer market. Overall, customers' reactions to the concept were positive, but highly skeptical. Quite simply,

	Technical Capability Segment	*Enterprise Segment*	*Divisional Segment*	*Departmental Segment*
HPC Equipment Cost	Very, very expensive	> $1 million	$250k–$1 million	< $250k
Type of Application	Dedicated to one extremely large, demanding problem	Used for multiple different problems	Used for multiple different problems	Used for multiple different problems

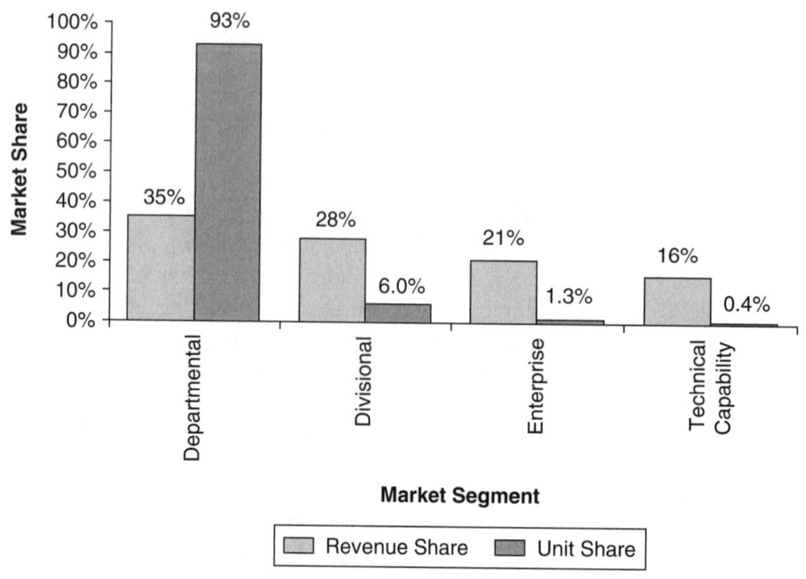

Exhibit 4 High-Performance Computer Market Segmentation

customers were unconvinced that the group could achieve the kind of performance improvements they claimed. Lorant noted:

> Basically, their feedback is: "Wow, if you can really do that, we'd definitely be interested." But they're skeptical.

The group foresaw three major proprietary technology innovations that would need to be patent-protected. The first would be a unique hardware architecture that would *directly* connect x86 processors together, bypassing both the shared memory of symmetric multiprocessing (SMP) and standard networking equipment (the cluster). The second technology would be a management system that would simplify the user interface with the computer, while also providing self-diagnostic and self-repair capabilities to improve reliability. The final innovation would be a subsystem that acted as a "co-processor" to the supercomputer's main processors.[7] This subsystem would handle highly repetitive algorithms (such as those found in data mining or encryption) to significantly accelerate the performance these applications.

	SMP System	*Cluster System*	*Direct-Connect System*
Price-Performance: ($/gigaflop)[1]	$15,000	$1,000	$1,500
Reliability—Minutes of Service Outage per Month	10	100	1
Total Cost of Ownership per Year	Medium	High	Low
Scalability—Increase in Computing Power With Double the Processors[2]	Fair	Poor	Good
Scalability—Maximum Number of Processors	64	Thousands	Thousands

Exhibit 5 High-Performance Computer Architecture Comparison

1. As a measure of computer speed, a "gigaflop" is a billion floating-point operations per second (FLOPS).
2. As measured from 10 processors to 20 processors. In an ideal world, doubling the number of processors would yield a 100 per cent increase in computing power. However, inefficiencies in moving data between processors limit the practical scalability of HPC systems.

The group also recognized the need to carefully navigate around competitors' patents to ensure they did not infringe, as the HPC space changed constantly due to the extensive R&D performed in this industry segment. Nonetheless, the group believed they could compete against larger competitors on the basis of superior technology.

The group's exit strategy for investors was to take the company through an IPO.

Decision Time

By March 2002, the group had informally discussed both concepts with venture capitalists who were intrigued but stated that they would not fund either concept unless the three Magellan partners stayed actively involved as the company's full-time management.

Adam Lorant studied the faces of the people gathered in Paul Terry's home. After months of research and debate, he could see the group was impatient to make a decision and get going. He thought about his own future as well. Did he really want to leave angel investing to manage the launch of another start-up? And if so, which business concept should they select?

Notes

1. IP = Internet protocol, the industry standard for transmitting data over computer networks.
2. "Solid-state" is a term referring to an electronic device that consists of only solid components (no moving parts).
3. All monies are in US$ unless otherwise specified.
4. CRM = Customer Relationship Management software.
5. Firmware is a read-only software routine that is embedded directly in a hardware device. Firmware is effectively a combination of software and hardware.
6. "x86" is the generic name of a microprocessor architecture first developed by Intel, but later manufactured by a number of competing semiconductor companies.
7. A "co-processor" is any computer chip that acts as an "assistant" to the main processor by handling very specialized chores. A co-processor is faster at its specialized function than the main processor, and it relieves the processor of some work.

3

Planning and Financing the Venture

The Planning/Financing Process

There is perhaps more written in entrepreneurship textbooks about the venture planning process—the business plan—than about all the other venture creation processes combined. In this casebook, we have combined the venture planning and financing processes because they are so closely tied together in the practitioner community, and discussing them together seems both more effective and efficient. The goal in this chapter is therefore to provide sufficient detail that instructors and students will find a ready context within which the venture planning cases that follow can be analyzed and discussed, and actual venture planning and financing skills can be gained.

In our minds, the planning and financing processes are connected within what we call the "harvest system" of financing. The harvest system is based on the fundamental elements of any system: Input → Process → Output, as suggested in Figure 3.1. As we have worked with a variety of systems in our careers, it has become clear to us that an effective way to build a system is to start first with the outputs to answer the question, "What do you want to get done?" What "output" is expected? Following this, it is next helpful to look at inputs to ascertain just exactly what is available or can be made available to enter the system and be subject to the processes that transform inputs to outputs. Finally, the focus turns to the process itself: the means whereby the transformation sought is brought about. We discuss these in this order: outputs, inputs, and process.

Editors' Note: It is far beyond the scope of this casebook, and therefore is not our intention, to comprehensively address the many highly specific and technical processes that occur in connection with financing a venture. Many excellent works treat these topics comprehensively, using an entire textbook to but scratch the surface. Our intention here is to sufficiently describe "what needs to get done" so that students can, from the entrepreneur's perspective of venture leader, envision many of the necessary elements for the management of an effective financing program.

Inputs	*Process*	*Output*
Level 1: Product/Service Level • Effective Product Concept	 • Position	Harvest: • Target Market Value
Level 2: Venture Level • Well-Built Venture: e.g., NVT, debt vs. equity • Prepared Venturer • Stakeholder Relationships	 • Prepare • Practice • Present • Persist	Harvest: • Sell: o Public o Private • Hold

Figure 3.1 Financing: The Harvest System Model

Outputs: The Harvest

In business venturing, the main output has been called the venture harvest (Stevenson, Roberts, & Grousbeck, 1994), where value is distributed, generally, to those who helped to create it. The purpose for creating the venture under these assumptions is therefore the generation and distribution of value for and to the stakeholders: all those who can affect or are affected by the venture (Freeman, 1984). Value comes in many forms and can be computed using many "bottom-line" conceptions of value. One idea that is gaining currency in a multifaceted global business world is the notion of creating value that is sustainable, using the measure of a "triple bottom line," which suggests a multiple focus: on economic, social, and environmental performance. This idea of broader value creation was first introduced in the Brundtland Report, produced by the United Nations World Commission on Environment and Development (WCED, 1987). Of course, value creation can also be cultural, spiritual, artistic, quality of life, or more and hence is not limited only

to a specified set of outputs. Within this casebook, we use economic value as a representative output to retain consistency with other contributing business disciplines, but we encourage those whose ideas of value creation are more comprehensive to see that sustainable entrepreneurial value creation is possible across a much wider spectrum of outcomes (Cohen, Smith, & Mitchell, 2004; Cohen & Winn, 2003; Dean & McMullen, 2002).

As shown in Figure 3.1, there are at least two levels at which a value harvest can be expected. Product/service-level value (Level 1) consists of the value created when the venture produces and delivers a product or service to customers in some target market. The planning and financing process that occurs at the product/service level has as its objective the enabling of value creation and retention and relies on such techniques as market research to ascertain consumer needs and wants, market segmentation analysis, demographic analysis, and so on. Based on this information, the plan can be adjusted to ensure that the market is attractive, that the venture can attain sufficient market share, and that the product or services planned for the venture can meet user needs and wants.

In our estimation, there are three general harvest system outcomes at Level 2, the venture level, where the venture itself is a financing product: sell public (which to us means taking a company public), sell privately (which can mean either its acquisition by another entity or its liquidation), or hold (usually to continue to receive the value stream, such as cash flows, created by the venture). Of interest to prospective venturers is the implication of the harvest existing *within* a system: The type of harvest you desire will be closely tied to the types of inputs you choose. This idea will become more evident as we now turn to a discussion of harvest system inputs and address both the product/service-level (Level 1) and venture-level (Level 2) inputs.

Inputs: A Well-Built Venture

The inputs at the product/service level (Level 1) of the venture lead to an effective product concept. Inputs are linked to outputs in this part of the harvest system because it is crucial to determine the extent to which the products/services intended for the venture meet the needs and wants of the target market. Some of the activities that are undertaken at this point in the venture creation process include the determination of a value creation strategy, which includes the generation of a value statement, a technical assessment, design, and product positioning. The key idea here is for potential entrepreneurs to ensure that the product envisioned comports well with the value intended for the target market.

Depending on circumstances, the inputs necessary for achieving an effective harvest at Level 2 may go beyond the scope of a casebook that focuses specifically on the venture creation process and, in addition to creating a well-built venture as illustrated in Figure 3.1, can require having both a prepared venturer and the necessary stakeholder relationships (how can your venture fail if all the stakeholders are willing to make it succeed? [Lenn, 1993]). In the specific case of planning and financing the venture, however, the key input elements concern the capital structure: Should the venture be financed using debt, equity, or some combination of both?

Answering this question is crucial to the Level 2 harvest because a mismatch between inputs and outputs can easily compromise the planning/financing process. For example, if the harvest objective is to take the venture public, having a large debt load can be viewed much more negatively than having an extensive and broadly based set of equity investors. Conversely, if the harvest objective is to hold the business for a steady cash flow stream, it would be unwise to have taken investments from equity investors who have as their goal a profitable exit in three to five years.

Compromise of the planning and financing process occurs when inputs and outputs are improperly matched due to the underlying social assumptions that accompany debt versus equity financing. These social assumptions consist of a balanced agreement between the provider of capital and the entrepreneur as its user. In the case of debt financing, the expectation of lenders is "money back plus interest," and this is secured by collateral: assets of value in excess of the amounts borrowed that can be seized and sold to ensure that the "social deal" of money back plus interest is honored. In the case of equity financing, the expectation of investors is "many times my money" and is secured by some type of voting power—often control—that these investors can exercise if things go wrong. The debt deal contains the expectation of an additive return. The equity deal contains the expectation of a multiplicative return. For a failure to meet the terms of debt, you lose your "stuff." For a failure to meet the terms of equity, you may lose your venture—or at least control of it.

In the case of the debt/equity decision, a well-built venture is therefore one wherein the inputs are tailored such that a venture plan can be implemented to match the expectations for a financial harvest. Thus, attention now turns to the planning/financing process itself.

Process: Planning and Financing

The planning/financing process also occurs at two levels: the product/service level and the venture level. We begin by discussing the product/service level.

The Product/Service Level

The planning process at the product/service level turns an effective product concept into target market value. In Figure 3.1, we refer to this as *positioning,* which is a more expanded use of that term than is used in the marketing texts. Still, the idea that there is a process that can be planned and enacted to make a product concept valuable in a specific market is a powerful one, and we cannot think of a better word to describe it than to *position* the product/service.

What makes something valuable in a target market? In the section that follows, the student example (see Figure 3.2) suggests that value in a target market can be assessed by such questions as the following: Are consumers willing to pay the price needed? Will consumers be able to differentiate this offering? Can the venture compete as the low-cost provider?

Answers to these questions come more easily with a plan that leads to effective positioning. As suggested in the New Venture Template™ approach to venture screening, product/service value results from having (a) a new combination and (b) a product-market match that (c) can deliver net buyer benefit.

New Combination. Drucker (1985) defines entrepreneurship as an act of innovation that involves endowing existing resources with new wealth-producing capacity. Noted Austrian economist Joseph Schumpeter (1934) labels the innovative acts that endow old resources with new value "new combinations." Finding new combinations involves a process of entrepreneurial discovery that, once understood, will become an engine that can drive your entrepreneurial career for as long as you desire. In the free enterprise system, two major categories of entrepreneurial discovery exist. They are

1. scientific discovery and
2. circumstantial discovery.

Scientific discovery occurs when a physical/technological insight is obtained. Scientific discovery occurs when something is invented and when that something invented is applied in a new and valuable way.

Circumstantial discovery refers to insight that is obtained though specific knowledge of time, place, or circumstance. Circumstantial discovery yields an opportunity simply because of what (whom) and when you know something of economic value.

Scientific or circumstantial discovery can occur within five different domains of new combination (Schumpeter, 1934):

1. the introduction of a new good or an improved good,
2. the introduction of a new method of production,
3. the opening of a new market,
4. the conquest of a new source of supply of raw materials or components, or
5. the reorganization of any industry.

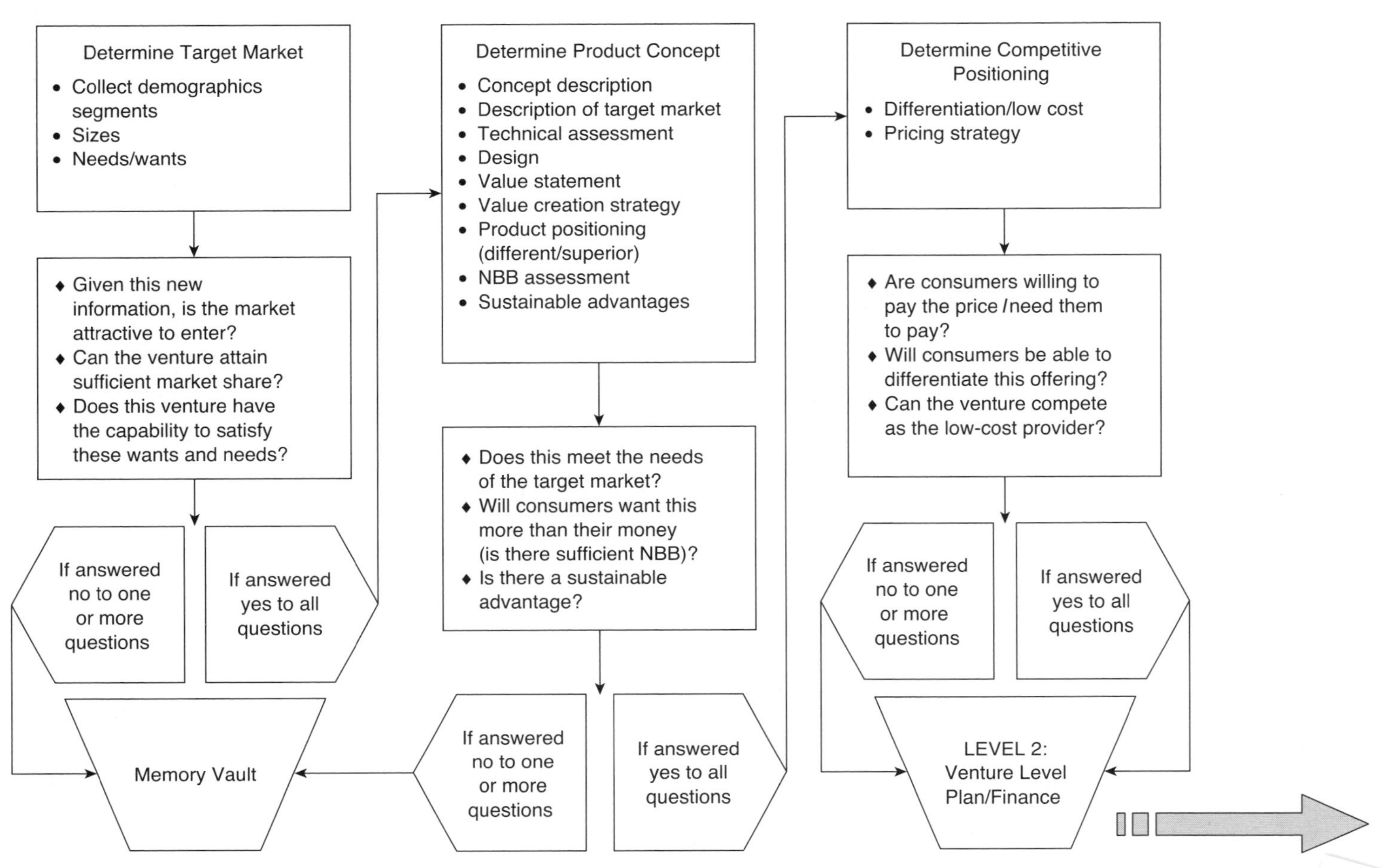

Figure 3.2 Planning/Financing—Product/Service Level

Each of the above types of new combination may vary in the level of innovation present. This, to some extent, is a judgment call, which should be made by comparing your idea to products/services in the same category. So if you have an idea for a new computer game, you could judge its new combination level by examining how closely it imitates existing products/services of the same type. If the "true" (not imagined) differences are great, then the new combination level is high. If your computer game idea is very similar to games that are presently in existence, then its new combination level is low.

Product-Market Match. Without a product-market match, an idea or product/service is *not* the basis for a business at the product/service level. The critical test of a product-market match (PMM) is often quite simple. It begins with the question, "Where is the purchase order?"

A purchase order shows something important. It shows that someone in the "real" marketplace values your product/service more than he or she values money (more on this in the next topic review note: net buyer benefit). If you cannot show a purchase order, you do not have a business.

Now the number of reasons, justifications, and excuses that novice venturers can concoct to avoid answering this question is arguably almost infinite. But the point remains—that unless someone is willing to place an order for a product/service at an asking price, the product or service is not the basis for a business.

Therefore, at this point in the planning process, it is essential to be honest with yourself. A highly realistic assessment of the product-market match at this point in the venture minimizes most of the cost of unproductive new venture failure. If you answer this subquestion wisely and objectively, then you can save yourself most of the emotional and financial anguish that surrounds a new venture that fails. Resources can be conserved. Money and enthusiasm can be saved for the day when they can create wealth instead of waste. And if an entrepreneurial discovery is still in the research project stage, then it can be funded as such, without the broken promises and disappointments that come from prematurely treating a research project a business.

How does one go about determining whether there is a product-market match? The means to accomplish this are as varied as the number of product and service ideas that are generated. There are, however, two or three standards to use to conduct a "smell test." They are as follows:

1. If you would not buy it yourself, there probably is not a product-market match.
2. If a focus group of potential customers from the target market would not buy it, there probably is not a product-market match.
3. If customers in a test market will not buy it or if the purchasing agent of a distributor will not issue a purchase order, there probably is not a product-market match.

This is not to say that counterexamples (times when the above three tests were proven wrong) do not exist. They do. But are you willing to bet at 100:1 odds (or worse) that you will get lucky despite the evidence—or do you want to have your efforts and capital count for something?

If the answer to the product-market match subquestion is not yes, then do not go on. Stop. Fix the problem. And if the problem can't be fixed, then walk away (because you don't have a business anyway), or operate the effort as the research project or charity that it truly is. If you want a business, then find a product or service where there is a match with the market.

Yes, it is possible that someone else will take "your idea" and strike it rich. But the reality, if this happens, is that their situation and yours were not the same. Ventures work because opportunities and entrepreneurs somehow fit each other. Realistically, in a lifetime, each of us has several such "opportunity fits" presented to us.

So our job is not to pry ourselves into a deal in a "forced-fit" mode. The force-fit approach is a lot like trying to force the "ugly sister's foot" into Cinderella's glass slipper. It still does not fit despite all the effort and embarrassment. Instead, our job as venturers is to prepare for the time when the fit is right . . . and the key leading indicator that this is right is that the answer to the product-market match question is yes! At this point, you can then go on and assess the other elements of the venture in logical order, confident that your further efforts will not be wasted.

But also remember the risks. Lack of purchase orders (lack of PMM) means that the business idea/product concept is in trouble. There are too many stories of venturers who "augured in" (had to quit) because they spent too much time and energy on a no-win PMM problem. So if in doubt, cut your losses now, and build a better venture on a sound PMM foundation.

Net Buyer Benefit (NBB). In 1991, an author named Ghemawat coined a term that is very useful. It is not one that was used often in the business literature prior to that time. It is the concept of net buyer benefit.

The concept of something that is "net" presumes that there is something minus something to compute a result: a "net." So we will have to define exactly what a net buyer benefit is to be able to ask that of a product/service, with the idea being that there must be a net buyer benefit, meaning that somehow there must be value to the consumer, the person who is actually getting the product.

First of all a definition: Because net buyer benefit is a *net,* it involves a subtraction. So to get net buyer benefit, what we are doing is subtracting the price we are charging for the product/service from what we will call "gross buyer benefit": *overall satisfaction with what a customer is getting, what she or he is buying.* Gross buyer benefit is what makes a customer want whatever that product is, more than money. The difference between how much a customer wants it—how satisfied he or she is—and the price that the venture is going to charge for that product/service; that difference is the net buyer benefit. In summary, then, the definition of net buyer benefit is gross buyer benefit minus the price you charge.

Net buyer benefit (Ghemawat, 1991) is the first of two types of value within a target market: value to the customer, with the second being margins—value to the venture, as illustrated in Figure 3.3.

The third positioning step in the planning process is the creation of NBB. Ultimately, your customers must want your product or service more than they want the portion of their money that your product/service will cost.

When the net buyer benefit for your product/service is large, you have room to raise the price if you need to. Here high demand prevents raised prices from materially decreasing the quantity sold. Economists refer to this situation as inelastic demand. Alternatively, when the net buyer benefit is small, you will feel "price pressure" (i.e., you will either not be selling, or your customers will be demanding a discount). Here price is "elastic" because any increase in the price dramatically reduces demand.

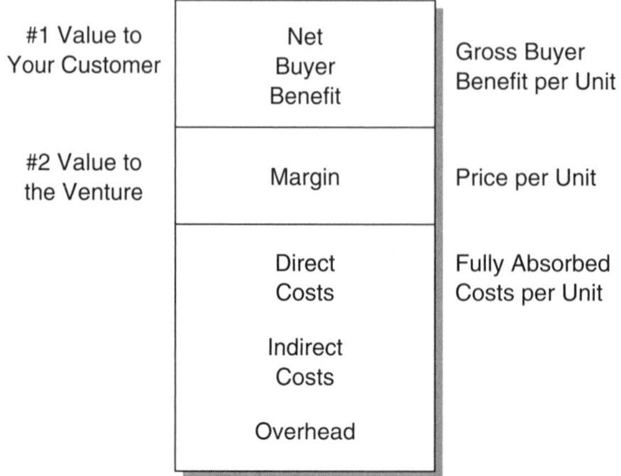

Figure 3.3 Two Types of Value

Source: Ghemawat (1991).

Customer value in a target market (net buyer benefit) is created when you persuasively position your product/service to communicate to your customers the differences your product/service possesses when compared to others on the market. As customers clearly perceive these differences, gross buyer benefit goes up. As gross buyer benefit goes up, the amount of customer value (net buyer benefit) increases accordingly. When viewed this way, net buyer benefit can be seen in its most simple form. Net buyer benefit exists only because of customer perception—hence, "positioning" is the key planning process.

One key task of an entrepreneur, then, is to create and manage the way that customers "see" or "perceive" a product/service. This job done well is the key to customer value. This job done poorly leaves an *inadequate* foundation for a venture. The two key elements in value creation are effective pricing and effective product differentiation (Porter, 1980). The job function that normally handles the creation and the management of customer perception is the marketing functional specialty, and we encourage you to go to your marketing text for a detailed look at creating value within this function.

At the product/service level, several key ideas should be the focus of the business planning/financing process, and these ideas can be well described by the term *positioning* of the product/service. Next we examine the venture creation planning/financing process at the venture level.

The Venture Level

In recent years, much more has become known about essentials in the process of business planning and financing at the venture level. In fact, one recent analysis also used a systems approach to ascertain the essentials of this planning/financing process (Mainprize & Hindle, 2003). Interestingly, the process identified by these authors comports well with the four Ps shown in Figure 3.1: prepare, practice, present, and persist—two explicitly and two implicitly.

Explicitly, recent research suggests key guidelines for the "preparation" and "presentation" of entrepreneurial business plans and implicitly suggests attention to "practice" and "persistence." In this chapter, we focus on the two explicit processes: preparation and presentation.

Preparation. Two possible approaches to business plan preparation present themselves at this point in the chapter: (a) describe what should go into a business plan and (b) describe what a well-prepared business plan should get done. Because the approach that we have taken in this casebook is to look to a "harvest" as the key output, and because the descriptions about "how to" put together a business plan are readily available on the Internet, in a wide variety of text and popular press books, or even in our reference section (e.g., Sahlman, 1997), it seems logical to us to take the second approach and to try and provide to you, as student or instructor, information that is not so easily obtained.

Mainprize and Hindle (2003) make the case that two key dimensions guide the preparation of entrepreneurial business plans (EBPs) that are intended to effect a harvest: (a) ability to communicate the nature of the uncertain future and (b) credibility, as indicated by the mechanisms available to encourage and enable a living business plan, providing for revision and iteration.

Mainprize and Hindle (2003) assert that uncertainty in an entrepreneurial business plan is markedly greater than in a plan for an existing business and that this difference stems from the "liabilities of newness" (Stinchcombe, 1965, p. 148). They argue that liabilities of newness are the greatest challenge for a new venture and that clear communication of the future and its uncertainty in the EBP is one of two main roles of the planning process in new ventures creation.

These authors further assert that because all organizations must deal with uncertainty, it is therefore dangerous for them to articulate and adhere inflexibly to one rigid strategy. According to Mintzberg (1987), whom they cite, setting oneself on a predetermined course in unknown waters is the perfect way to sail straight into an iceberg. Steadfast planning in business may inhibit changes in two ways. First, it discourages the organization from considering disruptive alternatives (Mintzberg, 1994, p. 178). Second, it might inhibit creativity. A conflict lies with a desire to "retain the stability that planning brings to an organization . . . while enabling it to respond quickly to external changes in the environment" (Mintzberg, 1994, p. 184).

Somewhat in response, Hindle (1997) coined the term "provision of flexible credibility" (p. 111) to describe the dynamic nature of entrepreneurial business planning. Credibility of an EBP is achieved if the document effectively matches the entrepreneurial team's (resource seekers') resource needs with the investors' (resource providers') expectations and criteria. The credibility quotient is necessary but not sufficient. The EBP must also be flexible and able to adopt and adapt the reader's criteria. An EBP "which presents a 'take it or leave it' set of propositions or has its financial forecasts 'set in cement' has a high likelihood of failure" (Hindle, 1997, p. 111).

When these two dimensions are juxtaposed in graphical form, we get an idea of the type of business that is portrayed when communication and credibility are both taken into account (see Figure 3.4).

According to Mainprize and Hindle (2003), the effective preparation of an EBP requires that five principles should be considered for each dimension, as suggested in Table 3.1. A brief explanation of each principle follows.

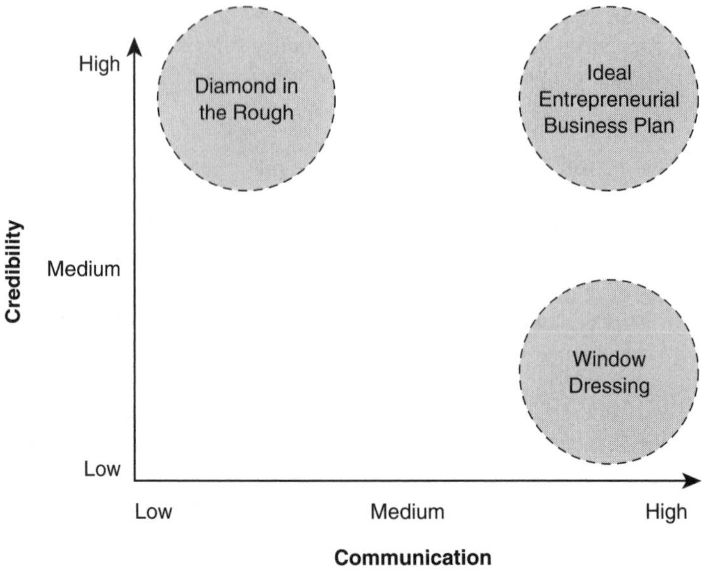

Figure 3.4 Credibility and Communication of Entrepreneurial Business Plans
Source: Mainprize and Hindle (2003).

Principle 1: Expectations. Preparation of an EBP requires translation of the vision of the venture and how it will perform into a format compatible with the expectations of its readers. Readers of EBPs seem to have this in common: They use the plan to aid in decision making about "provision of resources to the venture" (Hindle, 1997, p. 11).

In the deal screening stage, an EBP is expected to communicate that (a) key success factors and risks can be clearly identified and are understood; (b) the venture has a large projected market with good potential market penetration; (c) a strategy for commercialization, profitability, and market dominance is present; and (d) a strong proprietary and competitive position can be established and protected (Mainprize & Hindle, 2003).

Principle 2: Milestones. Hindle (1997) suggests that the writer of an EBP must "identify all major plan objectives, primarily as financial targets" (p. 123). This process of identification is often referred to as setting milestones in the venture planning process, which consists of anchoring key events in the plan with specific financial and quantitative values. The milestone approach satisfies the dual need for planning and flexibility and makes obvious the hazards of neglecting linkages between certain events. "Milestone planning takes entrepreneurs to the next important stage at the lowest possible cost, where they can make informed decisions, rather than blunder along adhering to a fixed plan that out of ignorance they have based on faulty projections" (Block & MacMillian, 1985, p. 196). Quantitative values rather than chronological dates must anchor milestones (Mainprize & Hindle, 2003).

Principle 3: Opportunity. Because no opportunity lasts forever and because consumer trends and tastes, the competitive landscape, and technological innovation all evolve over

(Text continues on page 110)

Table 3.1 Checklist for Preparing Entrepreneurial Business Plans (EBPs)

Dependent Variables	*Independent Variables (Principle)*	*Assessment Questions*	*Rating*	*Criteria*
Communication	Expectations	Does this EBP meet my expectations for efficient provision of sufficient information upon which to make the screening decision? As a venture capitalist, I am expecting the following: ❐ key success factors and risks can be clearly identified and are understood; ❐ the venture has a large projected market with good potential market penetration; ❐ a strategy for commercialization, profitability, and market dominance is present; ❐ a strong proprietary and competitive position can be established and protected.	Low	Only one or two of the expectation items are present in the EBP.
			Med.	Three of the expectation items are present in the EBP.
			High	All four of the expectation items are present in the EBP.
	Milestones	Milestones in the EBP are clearly communicated primarily as ❐ quantitative values, ❐ financial targets.	Low	Either there are no milestones or they are without any quantitative values or financial targets.
			Med.	Some of the milestones use quantitative values or financial targets.
			High	All milestones use quantitative values or financial targets.
	Opportunity	Does this EBP fully describe the venture opportunity by describing the following: ❐ the new combination of the venture, ❐ the magnitude of the opportunity (market size), ❐ market growth trends, ❐ venture's value from the market (percentage of market share proposed or market share value in dollars)?	Low	Only one or two of the opportunity items are described in the EBP.
			Med.	Three of the expectation items are described in the EBP.
			High	All four of the opportunity items are described in the EBP.

(Continued)

Table 3.1 (Continued)

Dependent Variables	*Independent Variables (Principle)*	*Assessment Questions*	*Rating*	*Criteria*
	Context	Does this EBP demonstrate awareness of the context by describing the following: ❒ industry structure, ❒ competition, ❒ the predicted changes to the industry over time, ❒ factors that will inevitably change but cannot be controlled by the team?	Low	Only one or two of the content items are described in the EBP.
			Med.	Three of the context items are described in the EBP.
			High	All four of the context items are described in the EBP.
	Business Model	Does this EBP outline the business model by explaining the following: ❒ who pays (paying customer), ❒ how much (average transaction value), ❒ how often (repetition)?	Low	Only one of the business model items is explained in the EBP.
			Med.	Two of the business model items are explained in the EBP.
			High	All three of the business model items are explained in the EBP.
Credibility	Team	Does this EBP describe the entrepreneurial team by addressing the following: ❒ what they know, ❒ whom they know, ❒ how well they are known?	Low	Only one aspect of the entrepreneurial team is addressed in the EBP.
			Med.	Two aspects of the entrepreneurial team are addressed in the EBP.
			High	All three aspects of the entrepreneurial team are addressed in the EBP.
	Elaboration	Does this EBP elaborate the overall strategy into subplans by ❒ linking the milestones to subplans, ❒ using a timeline to show how tasks, milestones, and subplans interconnect?	Low	Either there are no subplans or they are without any linkage to milestones.
			Med.	Some of the milestones are linked to subplans.
			High	All milestones are linked to subplans, and a timeline shows their interconnectedness.

Dependent Variables	*Independent Variables (Principle)*	*Assessment Questions*	*Rating*	*Criteria*
	Scenario Integration	Does this EBP employ simulation techniques to obtain a variety of plausible future scenarios by establishing a ❐ most likely case, ❐ best case, ❐ worst case?	Low	Only one scenario is presented.
			Med.	Two scenarios are presented.
			High	Three scenarios are presented.
	Financial Link	Does this EBP link the selected strategy discussed in the body of the plan to the financials by addressing the following: ❐ how much money the company needs over what period, ❐ the level of sales to break even, ❐ when established, how much profit the company is likely to make, ❐ when cash flow turns positive, ❐ what the main assumptions are that the forecasts are based on?	Low	One or two aspects of the financial link are addressed in the EBP.
			Med.	Three aspects of the financial link are addressed in the EBP.
			High	Four or five aspects of the financial link are addressed in the EBP.
	The Deal	Does this EBP articulate a value-added deal structure by describing ❐ funds required—the amount of cash investment required for growth and the use of the proceeds; ❐ the offer—for equity financing, the offer is almost always stated as a percentage of the equity in the venture; ❐ the return—commonly stated as an annual return on investment; ❐ exit strategy—the most likely mechanism in which the investor can expect to receive the initial investment back plus the return; ❐ exit horizon—the approximate length of time the investment will be illiquid?	Low	One or two aspects of the deal are addressed in the EBP.
			Med.	Three aspects of the deal are addressed in the EBP.
			High	Four or five aspects of the deal are addressed in the EBP.

Source: Mainprize and Hindle (2003).

time, an initial opportunity inevitably changes. Four aspects must be described in an EBP to fully articulate the opportunity principle: (a) the new combination of the venture, (b) the magnitude of the opportunity or market size, (c) market growth trends, and (d) venture's value from the market (percentage of market share proposed or market share value in dollars) (Mainprize & Hindle, 2003). Here the EBP should "distinguish the venture's business concept, distinctive competencies and sustainable competitive advantages" (Hindle, 1997, p. 122).

Principle 4: Context. Four key aspects should be covered by an EBP to adequately describe the context within which the new venture is intended to function (Sahlman, 1997). First, entrepreneurs should demonstrate how the new venture's context helps or hinders their specific proposal. Second, EBP writers should demonstrate how the venture's context will change, describe how those changes might affect the business, and discuss the range of flexibility of response that is built into the venture. Third, the EBP should spell out what management can (and will) do in the event the context grows unfavorable. Fourth, the EBP should explain the ways (if any) in which the entrepreneurial team can affect context in a positive way.

Principle 5: The business model. In an EBP, the business model should be described with simplicity. The business model is a brief statement of how an idea actually becomes a business that creates value. It tells who pays, how much, and how often. The same product or service may be brought to market with several business models. Any entrepreneurial task is made up of a combination of individual activities. When they are represented systematically in relation to one another, the result is a business model. The business model describes the activities a company needs to perform to produce its product, deliver it to its customers, and earn revenue. Essentially, the EBP must describe an attractive, sustainable business model—one that is possible to create a competitive edge and defend it (Mainprize & Hindle, 2003; Sahlman, 1997).

Mainprize and Hindle (2003) suggest that a clear description of a business model shows potential investors that the entrepreneurial team has thought through the key drivers of the venture. Three Cs—business *concept,* distinctive *competency,* and sustainable *competitive* advantage—form a trinity of message content that describes the business model that empowers the EBP reader (Hindle, 1997, p. 265). Empowerment through the description of a business model "involves employing information that makes the potential investor to feel competent to make a decision" (Hindle, 1997, p. 123).

Principle 6: Team. At this point in the preparation of an EBP, the credibility of the venture comes into play, and the first principle of credibility relates to the decision makers—not necessarily because the people part of the new venture is the most important but because without the right team, none of the other parts really matters (Sahlman, 1997). Sahlman (1997) further suggests that investors require an EBP to answer three questions about an entrepreneurial team: (a) What do they know? (b) Whom do they know? (c) How well are they known? Interestingly, this list of queries (if one were to add, Who are you?) quite closely parallels the requirements for the "effectuation-type" thinking that forms the foundation for a flexible response to opportunity (Sarasvathy, 2001).

Principle 7: Elaboration. The capability to elaborate, to break down individual tasks into their subparts (Block & MacMillian, 1985), is also critical to new venture credibility. Elaboration of strategy is the "decomposition of the codified strategy into a three-part hierarchy: sub strategies; ad hoc programs and specific action plans" (Hindle, 1997, p. 25). When elaboration is used effectively, the step-by-step approach to risk taking, known as real options reasoning (McGrath, 1999), in which each step maximizes the upside while minimizing the downside, becomes possible (Hindle, 1997; Mainprize & Hindle, 2003).

Principle 8: Scenario integration. Sahlman (1997) suggests that claiming an insuperable lead or a proprietary market position is naive. Mainprize and Hindle (2003) suggest that building a new venture is like chess: To be successful, the entrepreneur must anticipate several moves in advance, to view the future as a movie versus a snapshot.

Principle 9: Financial link. In the presentation of financials in an EBP, the key assumptions related to market size, penetration rates, and timing issues of market context substantiated in the text of the EBP should be linked directly to the financial statements (Hindle, 1997). This means that the income and cash flow statements must be preceded by operational statements setting forth the primary planning assumptions about market size, sales, productivity, and basis for the revenue estimate (Mainprize & Hindle, 2003).

Principle 10: The deal. If the main idea behind the planning process is to enact a harvest, then one of the primary purposes of an EBP is naturally to attract an investor, thereby linking input and output through the planning/financing process. To this end, Hindle (1997) suggests that the EBP must "create a value-adding deal structure" (p. 124).

With the foregoing principles in mind, an entrepreneurial business plan (EBP) can be prepared at the venture level, which will substantially support the output specification of the planning/financing process: a valuable harvest. The second explicit process that links inputs to outputs in the harvest system model is "presentation." Some ideas for effective presentation as a part of the planning/financing process follow.

Presentation. Making an effective presentation is a critical process that entrepreneurs use to fuse available inputs to desired outputs. Although many popular press books exist on how to make effective presentations, our belief is that the real key to presenting business plans effectively is focused practice. We encourage students to go to and participate in venture capital conferences, as well as to present their own business plans in as many different forums as possible (e.g., student-targeted business plan competitions).

In this chapter, we have attempted to provide sufficient detail in the planning/financing process that instructors and students can find a ready context within which the venture planning cases that follow can be analyzed and discussed, and actual venture planning and financing skills can be gained. Before the cases, however, we next present how one student sees the planning/financing process.

A Student's View of the Planning/Financing Process

This entrepreneurship student's perspective on the planning/financing process is, as in prior chapters, presented in the form of a narration that accompanies Figures 3.1 and 3.2. This narrative explains the figure and can be used to visualize many of the key elements necessary in the searching process.

This student says the following:

Level 1

Level 1 of my planning/financing process deals with planning the product or service. It consists of three essential steps.

Step 1: Determine Target Market. This involves four key elements that must be undertaken in sequential order. The purpose of this step is to collect information that can be used to develop the product concept.

Stage 1: Collect demographic information. This involved collecting information about the characteristics of individuals that comprise the market population.

Stage 2: Determine segment sizes. This involves using the information gathered from the segmentation analysis to assess the attractiveness of serving one or more of the segments. This may involve taking a larger sample of the population to ensure a more representative sample (upon which size projections can be made).

Stage 3: Determine segment needs/wants. This involves identifying what differentiates the segments in terms of individuals' needs and wants.

After assessing the proposed target market, the three questions listed in the script sequence diagram must be answered. If the answer to any one question is no, the opportunity is sent to the "memory vault." This memory vault is similar to the idea holding tank (of the idea formulation subscript), where the potential opportunities are sent until a cue from the environment signals more thought about how the opportunity could "work." If the answers to all questions are yes, then Step 2 is conducted.

Step 2: Determine Product Concept. The purpose of this step is to develop a framework for the product/service that meets the needs/wants of the market. This step consists of two stages.

Stage 1: Develop concept description. This stage consists of three parts:

i. Description of target market (for whom is the product/service designed?)
ii. Technical assessment (how will the product/service provide what it does for the target market?)
iii. Design (what is the product/service and what does it do?)

The purpose of establishing a concept description is to turn the idea into a concrete conception of what the venture will offer.

Stage 2: Develop value statement. This stage consists of four parts:

i. Value creation strategy (how can we create value for the customer—from a customer's perspective, how valuable will she or he perceive these strategies?)
ii. Product positioning (given the target market's attributes and concept description, how will consumers perceive the offering to be superior or different?)
iii. NBB assessment (given the value creation strategy, why would consumers care about our offering? How much would they care?)
iv. Sustainable advantages (what are the sources of sustainable competitive/comparative advantage?)

The purpose of formulating a value statement is to take a consumer's perspective and determine if the offering is desired more than money (that there is significant NBB). The answers to the three questions listed in the script sequence diagram will determine whether the idea transfers to the memory vault or to Step 3.

Step 3: Determine Competitive Positioning. The purpose of this step is to determine how the product/service will compete in the marketplace. It consists of two stages.

Stage 1: Differentiation/low cost. This stage involves choosing a competitive strategy upon which the product/service will compete in the marketplace. As opposed to the product positioning assessment that was conducted for the value statement, this stage conceptualizes how the product/service will be positioned against competitive offerings in the marketplace. Specifically, should a low-cost or differentiation strategy be emphasized?

- How can this offering be differentiated from others?
- How can this venture compete on the basis of low cost?

Stage 2: Pricing strategy. Developing such a strategy involves thought about the characteristics of the target market, the attributes and repetitiveness of the product/service, and the value that the customer can be expected to derive. Attention must also be given to the margins and financial analyses derived/conducted in the screening phase.

- If prices are low, will consumers view the offering positively/negatively (i.e., as poor quality)?
- If prices are high, how will sales be affected (price elasticity)?
- What price would generate a positive reputation for the offering while maximizing revenues?

The answers to the three questions in the script sequence diagram will determine whether the idea transfers to the memory vault or to Level 2 of the planning/financing subscript.

Then, Level 2 is discussed (see Figure 3.5).
For Level 2, the student further says the following:

Level 2 deals with planning the venture and attaining financing. This level involves three steps.

Step 1: Determining Requirements of the Venture. This step involves three stages. Its purpose is to promote thought about the venture requirements that will have to be used in the business model to attract financing.

Stage 1: Determine venture output requirements. This involves all the things needed to ensure a harvest. Basic requirements are as follows:

i. Evaluation of the harvest system
ii. Evaluation of the expectations of the stakeholders

Stage 2: Determine venture input requirements. This involves all of the things needed to bring into the venture to produce the Level 2 work for others: the venture as a financing product. Basic requirements are as follows:

i. Debt versus equity analysis
ii. Proper management team
iii. Supplier and other key stakeholder ID

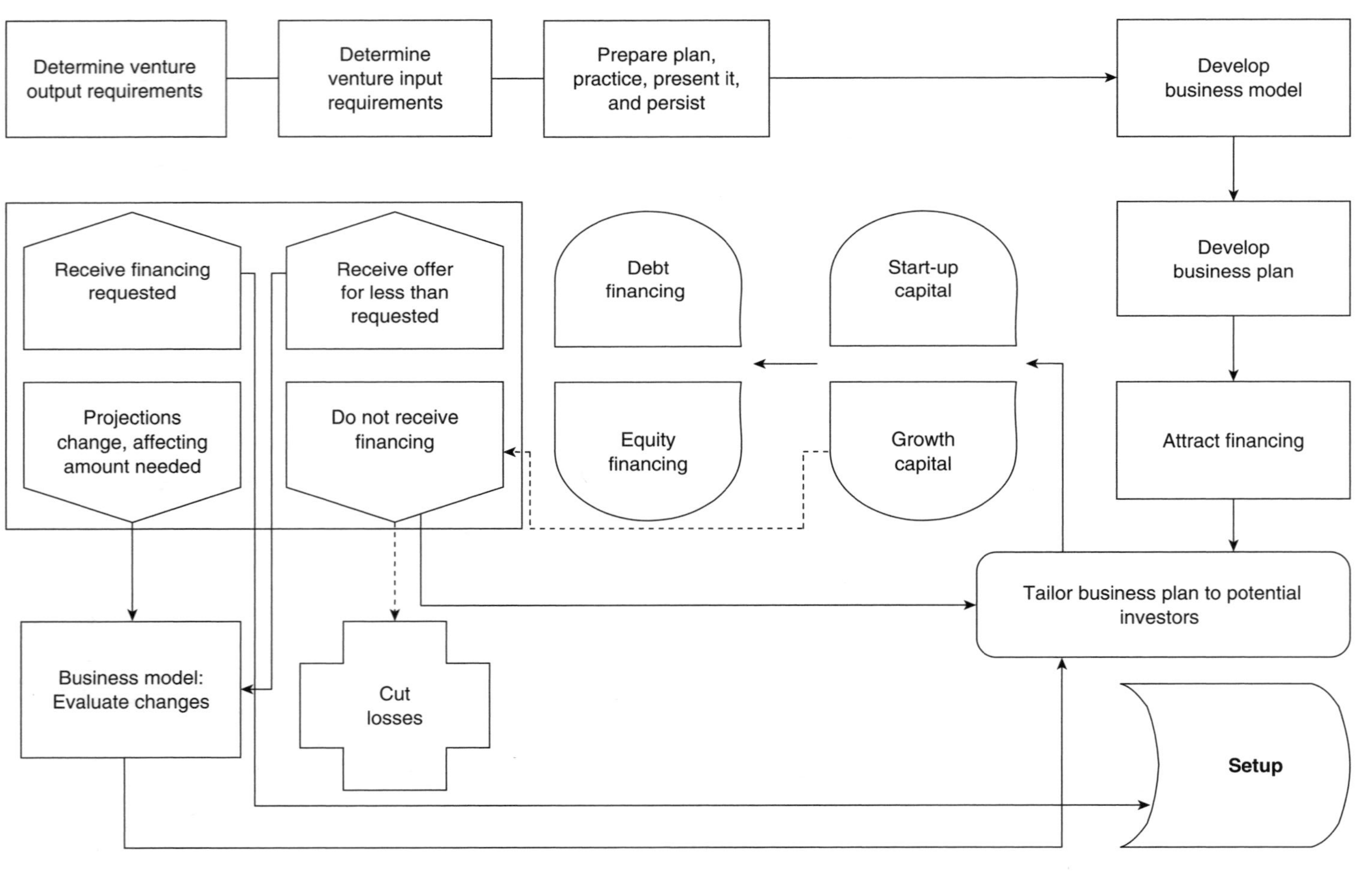

Figure 3.5 Planning/Financing—Venture Level 2

iv. Working capital arrangements
v. Key information resources

Stage 3: Venture planning and financing processes. This involves all of the things needed to transform the inputs into outputs. Basic requirements are as follows:

i. Prepare plan ideas to match inputs with outputs
ii. Practice the presentation with key advisers
iii. Present it to key stakeholders for input and to obtain "buy-in"
iv. Persist until the plan is sufficiently refined

After all possible requirements have been exhausted and associated costs have been projected, the development of a business model and business plan comprises the last step before financing.

Step 2: Develop the Business Plan. This step involves three stages. Its purpose is to develop a business plan to present to investors.

Stage 1: Develop business model. The purpose of this stage is to articulate an excellent understanding of the business logic of the proposed venture that comes from the prior planning/ financing process. The business model measurements include the following:

i. Summation of sources and uses of funds
ii. Opening balance sheet
iii. Pro forma income statement
iv. Cash flow projection
v. Year-end balance sheet

Stage 2: Develop business plan. The last stage before financing is sought is the development of a business plan that will be presented to investors. It involves amalgamating the work done in Level 1 and Level 2. Specifically, the business plan should include the following elements:

i. Opening
ii. Description of product/service
iii. Market analysis
iv. Pricing considerations
v. Operations
vi. Spending plans
vii. Financial analysis
viii. Appendices

Stage 3: Attract financing. This stage involves nothing more than thinking about what the potential investor will be interested in knowing about the venture (i.e., a venture capital firm may want to know if it can receive many times its money, whereas a financial institution may be interested in knowing if there is sufficient cash flow to meet debt obligations). The next stage would be to tailor the business plan to the needs of the investor sought.

Step 3: Attaining Financing. This step involves the assessment of whether the capital desired is for a new venture or for growth. If capital is needed for growth (or to stay competitive) and if financing is not attained, it may be time to cut losses and dismantle the business (represented by the dashed line on Level 2 of the planning/financing subscript).

In any event, the pros and cons of attaining debt or equity financing were weighed when the business plan was tailored to the investor(s) being sought. The business plan is now presented to the debt or equity financier, who then offers the financing required or offers less than the requested amounts.

If the financing sought is attained, then setup of the venture can be conducted. If projections about the amount of financing needed change or if any offer for less than what was requested is received, then these changes must be included in the business model, and the business plan must again be presented to potential investors if warranted. If it is deemed that the offer that was made (for less than the requested amount) could sustain the venture, then setup of the venture could be conducted. If this is not the case (or if no financing was received), then more investors must be pursued.

It must be emphasized that only in the case of growth capital when no financing can be attained should losses be cut. In the case of a new start-up, all possible options should be exercised before such a notion should even be considered.

Cases

The following cases have been selected to help learners to develop and become more aware of their own thoughts on the planning and financing processes.

Frontier Adventure Racing: Pack Lightly, Go Like Hell, Never Give Up

Prepared by Professors Charlene Zietsma and Stewart Thornhill

 Version: (A) 2002-01-30

Dave Zietsma, president of Frontier Adventure Racing (FAR), went over the numbers again in dismay. It was February 2001. Despite the amazing popularity of FAR's Raid the North Adventure Racing Series (FAR's most popular races sold out in less than a minute from the opening of Web site registration), Zietsma already knew that the season would end in September with the company making little or no profit for the fourth year in a row.

The competition was beginning to move into FAR's niche space, and they were hurting FAR's image with potential corporate sponsors. So far, they posed no threat with adventure racing competitors however, as FAR's races were recognized as "the most important race series in Canada."[1] FAR had great products, a solid international reputation for putting together excellent races and good name recognition among adventure racers. Zietsma himself was the captain of Canada's top adventure racing team (Team Subaru Outback), and his passion for the sport had led to significant media coverage, with Zietsma being named as one of McLean's top

100 Canadians under the age of 30 in 1999. Team Outback regularly competed in international adventure racing events, lending credibility and respect to FAR by association. Yet with all these assets, FAR was still not making a reasonable return on investment.

While passion had carried Zietsma this far, some hard decisions would have to be made if some way weren't found to generate profits. And they had to be made now: TSN and OLN (the Sports Network and the Outdoor Life Network) had offered Zietsma two hours of television coverage (one hour in prime time) and half of the ad spots during the show if FAR could pay the production costs of $75,000. FAR's share of the ad spots, at TSN's current rates, was worth only $15,000, but the show would boost the visibility of the sport and FAR, and might be later sold to other networks outside of Canada. The visibility gained might go a long way in encouraging corporate sponsorship of FAR's race program. If this opportunity slid by, Zietsma felt that he would have much more trouble in 2002 gaining the TV coverage and sponsor support he needed to make the business profitable.

History of Adventure Racing[2]

Adventure racing can be defined as a non-stop, multi-day, multi-sport, mixed team event. In many ways it can be likened to an expedition with a stopwatch. The goal of the competition is to be the first team to get all members across the finish line together. The course should take competitors through remote wilderness where they must travel without outside assistance. Each team must use strategy to determine the best route, equipment, food and pace to win. Teams must pass through various checkpoints en route, and each team carries an emergency radio in case they become lost or hurt. Since a significant part of the challenge is in the planning and problem-solving, race information is given on a "need to know" basis only (often you won't even know where the start line is until the day before the race). By doing so, the actual problem-solving and planning must be done quickly and efficiently during the competition.

There are many different reasons why people compete in adventure races, but most of them will relate back to the idea of taking on a larger-than-life challenge and beating it. The sense of reward that comes with it is overwhelming and the bigger the challenge, the bigger the reward.

The origins of adventure racing lie in a multi-sport race (mountain running, kayaking and mountain biking) that takes place in New Zealand called the Coast to Coast. Started in 1980, this was the first multi-sport, wilderness endurance race. It was actually created when someone misunderstood a conversation they overheard suggesting some Americans were looking to create a wilderness challenge, the next step in our endless pursuit of the ultimate challenge. In an attempt to beat the Americans to the punch, Coast to Coast and another race known as the Alpine Ironman were created. Not long after and completely unrelated, the Americans actually did dabble in the extreme with a race called the Alaska Mountain Wilderness Classic, which was started in 1983. While Coast to Coast has grown into one of the most heralded multi-sport races, the Alaska Mountain Wilderness Classic has stayed very grassroots, advertising by word of mouth only, and all profits from the race being given back to the competitors. It is still very much as it was in 1983.

The next big step was the Raid Gauloises (commonly known as the Raid), first held in New Zealand in 1989, the first mixed team multi-sport, multi-day wilderness endurance race. Created by Gerard Fusil, the Raid quickly popularized the sport of adventure racing in Europe (particularly France, Fusil's home turf), Australia and New Zealand through Fusil's superb marketing. To many, this was seen as the ultimate test of human endurance. The Raid travelled to a different exotic location around the world every year, leaving room for a new race in the homeland of the sport, The Southern Traverse. Started in 1991, The Southern Traverse maintained the true spirit of adventure racing established by the Raid but over a shorter, three-to-five-day period (although the winning team has traditionally done it in less than three days).

Although the popularity of the sport grew rapidly in Europe, Australia and New Zealand, it was still relatively unheard of in North America. It wasn't until a two time Raid competitor and talented entrepreneur, Mark Burnett,[3] created the Eco-Challenge that the sport caught on in North America. The first race took place in Utah in 1995 and grew to a status equalled only by the Raid. Other race locations have included Canada, Australia, Morocco, Argentina, Borneo and New Zealand. Since 1995, many new races have begun to pop up all around the world, although not all of them have established themselves as legitimate and viable.

In the wake of the heavy media attention around events like the Eco-Challenge, a new, more accessible style of adventure race has emerged: the weekend race. The 5+ day races around the world require not just a huge time commitment for preparation and competing but also a substantial financial investment. The weekend race (typically 36 hours in length) offers a more realistic starting point for those looking to test themselves in the adventure racing arena. Weekend races require substantially less time preparation and training, technical skill requirements are minimal and the cost is much lower, yet they are still long enough and challenging enough to test the limits of most weekend warriors. They also provide an ideal training ground for those looking to compete in longer races. The result of this new trend: participation in adventure racing is exploding, bringing it perilously close to mainstream! Participation in the sport has grown by 275 per cent in Canada since 1998, while the number of races has grown by 312 per cent (see Exhibit 1).

FAR Company History

FAR was founded in 1998 by Dave Zietsma, a former management consultant. His experience as an international adventure racing competitor gave him enough insight into the sport to be able to introduce it to Canada. In just three years, FAR's Raid the North series has introduced adventure racing to many Canadians and has become one of the top race series in North America. According to the FAR Web site (www.far.on.ca):

> Frontier Adventure Racing is about offering people the opportunity to test their limits. Whether through our 36 hour race series, our five day Extreme race, an adventure racing training program or one of our new Adventure Weekends, participants can expect to face unpredictable challenges in a wilderness setting.

Zietsma himself is a purist: while other companies have diluted the adventure racing experience to ensure that most competitors succeed in completing the race, FAR's races are hard. On average, only 25 per cent of the teams finish each race intact within the allotted time limits. Teams are disqualified if they use their radio to contact FAR headquarters for medical or navigational assistance, or if one member withdraws, though the other team members are often allowed to continue the race unranked. Zietsma's involvement in adventure racing as a leading competitor is what keeps FAR Inc. at the forefront of the sport. All Raid the North race courses are designed and tested by Zietsma so participants are assured an authentic adventure racing experience and a world-class challenge. While Zietsma stresses that his 36-hour races are targeted at, and meant to be doable by, the weekend warrior and newcomer to adventure racing, there is no doubt that they are meant to be challenging. FAR races are well known for their impeccable logistics, in a sport where disorganization can have dire consequences for competitors.

Paquette and Zaglia, authors of *Extreme Adventure,* a recent book on Adventure Racing, said the following about FAR:

> The courses are well designed and extremely demanding—challenging mixed teams of four, racing with or without a support crew, to kayak, canoe, mountain bike and mountaineer through the rugged mountains, icy rivers and dense forests of Quebec, Ontario and British Columbia.[4]

Products

FAR's product line is summarized in Exhibit 2.

FAR began with one 36-hour race in Ontario in 1998. The following year saw the expansion of

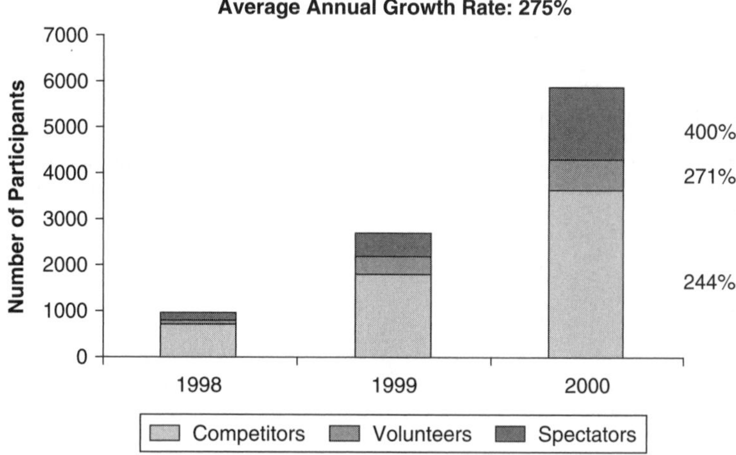

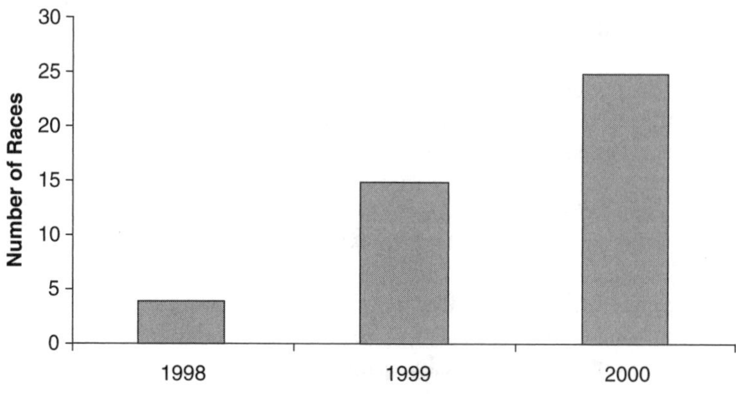

Exhibit 1

the Raid the North series from one race to three races (in Ontario, Quebec and British Columbia) and the introduction of Raid the North Extreme, designed to be the pinnacle of adventure racing in Canada. All four races were featured on the Outdoor Life Network in Canada as well as in numerous magazines.

In 2000, adventure race training courses were introduced to help new people enter the sport by learning the tricks of the trade from some of Canada's top racers. Adventure Weekends were also added:

> Targeted at those who are captivated by the thrill of adventure racing but not necessarily interested in competing, these 3 day programs take participants on an educational and inspirational guided tour of an adventure race.[5]

In 2001, five 36 hour races are offered (two in Ontario, one in Nova Scotia, one in British Columbia and one in Quebec). A two-and-a-half day series championship in Ontario has also been added, and the Raid the North Extreme race is scheduled for Newfoundland. The fastest team in

Raid the North Races	*Adventure Race Training*	*Adventure Travel*
Sprint: 7 Adventure Challenge Races (3- to 6-hour races plus 1-hour format for Kids' Raid the North)	Adventure Race Training: 18-week seminar and 11-week intensive	1 Adventure Weekend
Mid-Length: 5 Raid the North Races (36 hours) 1 Raid the North Championship race (2½ days)		Corporate Training (under development)
Expedition: 1 Raid the North Extreme Race (5 days)		

Exhibit 2 FAR's Product Line

the 36-hour races usually completes the race in about 24 hours, while as many as half the teams do not complete the race within the 36 hours. In 2001, FAR added an 'advance loop' for race leaders so that the best teams could challenge themselves with an additional race leg, but the finish line would remain accessible for most teams.

Adventure Challenge races—three-to-six hour, 40-kilometre races held in conjunction with Raid the North races—have also been added in 2001, enabling FAR to capture more revenues to defray fixed expenses of co-ordinating the races. Details have not been fully worked out yet, however. In Elliott Lake, a Northern Ontario town that has been an enthusiastic and supportive host for FAR races for three years now, FAR will be offering a Kids' Raid the North in conjunction with a 36-hour race in 2001. Both the Adventure Challenge races and the Kids' Raid the North race will bring more people out to the finish line, increasing visibility for sponsors, and providing competitors of the 36 hour races with much-needed applause from a sizable crowd as they finish the race. The Adventure Challenge races were requested by Salomon, one of FAR's sponsors, as a way to increase their visibility.

As a sideline to the business activities of FAR Inc., the staff was very active in the not-for-profit Frontier Adventure Racing Club. With regular training and informational activities in the Toronto area and a strong Internet presence, the club has become a meeting place for competitors and a valuable information tool to adventure racing hopefuls across Canada. Many competitors have used the club as their first step into learning about the sport and finding training partners and teammates.

Revenues

FAR's income statement is shown in Exhibit 3. Because of his commitment to keeping adventure racing accessible to the average person, Zietsma has fought to maintain relatively low entry fees for his races. Thirty-six hour races are priced at $1,400 per team, while the Extreme race is priced at $4,200 per team. Comparable races in other locations are typically priced at about $2,000 for the 36-hour races and between $5,000 and $9,000 for longer races. While the Ontario races made money because the company was based in Ontario, races in British Columbia traditionally lost money because of the increased travel expenses for race staff, the cost of renting vehicles, and the higher cost charged in British Columbia for equipment rentals (e.g., canoes or kayaks). British Columbia races were also difficult to design and manage because variable weather in the mountains increased the risk and the time required to design the course.

	RtN			Adv. Product			
	RtN Series	*Extreme*	*Adv. Chall.*	*ART*	*Wkds*	*Sales#*	*Total*
Revenue							
Total Entry Revenue	512,900	214,600	16,500	39,600	14,400	3,000	801,000
Other Operating Revenue	15,000	2,520					17,520
Less: GST (7%)	–36,953	–15,198	–1,155	–2,772	–1,008	–210	–57,296
Net Operating Revenue	490,947	201,922	15,345	36,828	13,392	2,790	761,224
Operating Expenses:							
Watercraft Rentals	35,294	1,133		800	800		38,027
Communications System	21,830	590		540	540		23,500
Jerseys/Banners/ Bike Plates	22,538	3,792	1,210				27,540
T-Shirts/Giveaways	20,189	4,253	1,000	400	240		26,082
Competitor Materials	20,189	3,384	3,435				27,008
Base Camp/Banquet	29,146	5,730		1,200	1,200		37,276
Course Safety/Staff	50,032	12,390					62,422
Other Course Expenses	33,512	8,850		2,000			44,362
Course Setup/Travel	13,393	6,195		1,000	800		21,388
Accommodations	7,080	3,540		8,000	640		19,260
Prizes	58,115	30,090	1,800				90,005
Photographer	11,210	2,950					14,160
Additional Service Expenses	9,160	2,201	7,445	1,200			20,006
Product Costs						2,100	2,100
Total Operating Expenses	331,688	85,098	14,890	15,140	4,220	2,100	453,136
Net Operating Profit/Loss	159,259	116,824	455	21,688	9,172	690	308,088
Overhead Allocation							
Promotional*	30,267	18,585	531	1,593	1,593	531	53,100
Salaries/Wages	183,049	36,434	6,170	12,190	2,434	737	234,433
General & Admin.	60,296	8,956	1,267	1,055	510	345	71,862
Total	273,612	63,975	7,968	14,838	4,537	1,613	359,395
Net Income/Loss Before Sponsorship	–114,353	52,849	–7,513	6,850	4,635	–923	–51,307
Sponsorship Revenue							
Title Sponsor	?						
Presenting Sponsor	?						
Official Category Sponsor	?						
Miscellaneous Sponsorship Revenue	5,000						
Less Sponsor Agent Fees	–35,000						
Net Sponsorship Revenue	–30,000						

Exhibit 3 Raid the North Income Statement *(Continued)*

	RtN			Adv. Product			
	RtN Series	Extreme	Adv. Chall.	ART	Wkds	Sales#	Total
***Promotional Budget (excludes OLN TV production)**							
Website/Internet	12,000						
Print Material	16,000						
Tradeshows	13,000						
Advertising	3,600						
Other (stickers, CD videos, . . .)	8,500						
Total Promotional	53,100						
# **Product Sales** are T-shirts, hats and videos.							

Exhibit 3 Raid the North Income Statement

The Quebec races have also been net money losers. The costs of translating and printing all promotional material into French, as well as the cost of hiring a French-speaking local representative to negotiate site arrangements, pulled these races into the red. The Extreme race, on the other hand, was more profitable: the entry fee was three times as much, but the costs were less than twice as much, leaving more profit margin.

Zietsma didn't track expenses separately among the 36-hour races because he felt it was necessary to have races in each of the locations in order to be recognized as a Canadawide adventure racing company. "To look at them individually and drop unprofitable races would be changing our positioning as a national series," Zietsma commented. On the other hand, he was a newlywed, and he was getting tired of all the travelling.

Adventure Race Training Seminars were designed to enhance image and defray overhead during non-race times. Adventure Weekends were designed to open a door for FAR into the corporate market. Neither the training seminars nor the adventure weekends made money, partly by design, and partly because start-up and promotional costs and low demand due to the newness of the programs have limited their contributions to fixed costs. The three-to-six-hour Adventure Challenge races were run on a cost-recovery basis: designed to increase visibility and bring a crowd, entry fees were very low. The Challenge races also benefited from being able to use the same canoes and crews as the 36-hour races.

Staff

As with many small businesses, FAR had trouble attracting and retaining good staff members. Zietsma commented:

> We get some pretty good applications because of the sex appeal of adventure racing but we can't pay enough for very qualified people to take it seriously. With new staff, it takes two to three months for them to be useful enough that I don't want to fire them anymore. I completely recognize that I have no time to train them properly. It is extremely difficult for people to conceptualize an adventure race until they have been to one, and they are quite different than typical sporting events. This makes it difficult to get new staff focused on the right elements.

Staff turnover was high, and FAR frequently started with a whole new staff each race season. Zietsma and three others (a logistics manager, a course designer and a public relations person) worked year round. An intern was brought on board during the busy summer season for race co-ordination. Web site updates were outsourced. Much of the work during the races was done by volunteers, who arrived for training the day before the race began.

While the PR role was expected to also include marketing responsibilities, to date, no staff person has had the experience or initiative to do both. Zietsma has thus absorbed most of the marketing function himself. Zietsma may consider outsourcing the PR function in the future—a contractor could cost slightly more, but would require less supervision.

Sponsorship

To make up the shortfall in race revenues and provide a pool of prize money for the winners, FAR depended heavily on sponsorship money. Sponsors invested in sports sponsorship to gain visibility with particular demographic segments that participate in or follow a sport. While interest in adventure racing was growing, it was still a very young sport. It left much to be desired as a spectator sport, since the races were held in wilderness locations, and the competitors covered vast distances, often invisible in dense bush. Television coverage has been more successful as a way to show adventure races, as camera crews who specialize in getting to remote locations captured the intensity of the challenge. Coverage of the Patagonia Eco-Challenge was shown during primetime in April 2000 on Discovery Channel. The Sunday evening telecast ranked 14th overall in prime time and was the number one sporting event on cable in prime time for the night, beating Major League Baseball on ESPN and Davis Cup Quarterfinals on ESPN2. The Monday evening coverage ranked number eight overall among basic ad-supported cable shows, and was the number one sports program in prime time on cable (excluding wrestling).

TV audiences in Canada remained relatively low; however, the Outdoor Life Network generally commanded an audience of 20,000 to 30,000 during adventure racing programming, while TSN (The Sports Network) captured 60,000 to 80,000 viewers. Viewership information for Discovery Channel Canada was unavailable, but their demographics are as follows: 54 per cent male, 59 per cent between the ages of 25 and 54 years old, and 38 per cent business owners, managers or professionals.

Sierra Designs has been the title sponsor for Raid the North races for three years, and other sponsors such as Salomon have provided significant revenues. In the three years that Sierra Designs has sponsored the race, however, there have been three different individuals managing the relationship. Mistakes were made. In 2000, no one from Sierra showed up at the races, and competitor gifts were skimpy and there were no gifts for volunteers. Sierra did not promote their sponsorship of the race. "They didn't get what they needed out of the sponsorship, and we didn't make them get what they needed," says Zietsma. "We don't have a full-time sponsor co-ordinator to follow up with them to ensure they get value out of the deal." Sierra did not renew their sponsorship in 2001.

Because of this experience, Zietsma decided to outsource the sponsorship function. He contacted a company in the summer of 2000 to ask them to take on the project. After two months of waffling, that company not to take on the project. Zietsma hired PSG group in November 2000 for $20,000 of upfront development costs, and $15,000 per month commencing in January 2001.

PSG group was able to get a number of interviews with companies who were interested in looking at FAR as a sponsorship option. Unfortunately, most had fully allocated their money for 2001 by the time PSG contacted them. In addition, Zietsma felt they needed passion to make the sale, and PSG representatives didn't have the passion that Zietsma himself had. By mid-February, PSG had been able to raise only $5,000, versus the $120,000 that Zietsma had raised himself the previous year. Facing the prospect of having almost no money from sponsors, a $35,000 bill for sponsorship, and a need for $75,000 for TV production over and above FAR's normal cash requirements, the situation looked difficult at best.

"There are some opportunities out there," Zietsma claimed. Subaru was a sponsor of Zietsma's Canadian competitor, Adventure Racing Canada. Adventure racing was a good fit for SUV manufacturers because it appealed to the right demographic: the average age of FAR competitors was 31, and over 60 per cent of them were professionals. These were the people who had the wherewithal to purchase SUVs. The demographics of FAR's competitors were shown in Exhibit 4.

Subaru was also the sponsor of Zietsma's competitive team. Subaru had so far refused to sponsor FAR because they sponsored Team Subaru Outback—they got the promotional value out of Dave Zietsma through his team, not his company. Other SUV manufacturers were reticent to sponsor FAR because of Zietsma's relationship with Subaru, though one of them indicated significant interest this year. Zietsma thought that another good possibility would be a wealth management company: he argued that he could draw quite a parallel between managing the risks in adventure racing with managing investment risks. Another option might be a Global positioning system manufacturer, though a company that had expressed interest said it must wait until next year. Salomon would return as a significant sponsor, probably covering the cost of PSG group for 2001.

Zietsma suggested there were two other possible sources of revenue to explore: the government and the military. Last year, Quebec Tourism sponsored a race in Charlevois, Quebec called "Raid Ukatak." Only seven teams competed in the race, some of which probably had their entry fee paid by the government. The government also paid journalists to cover this event, hoping for worldwide exposure of Quebec as an adventure tourism destination. Zietsma felt his company could do a much better job managing this kind of race for the government because of his experience and contacts. However, even identifying the right person to contact in the government is a tricky task, and time and staff constraints have limited his ability to follow up.

The 2001 Raid the North Extreme race will be held in Newfoundland, a remote and wildly beautiful place with chronic economic problems. The Newfoundland government has been quite supportive of Raid the North's foray into its province, and the location appeal has also attracted journalists and competitive teams from around the world. "Picture kayaking next to massive icebergs," Zietsma said. "The footage will be terrific." Other provinces have regional economic development bodies that might be interested in providing assistance and financial support for bringing races and TV coverage to their areas, but it has been difficult to spend the time to identify who needs to be contacted in each area.

The Canadian military is another option. Enrollment has been so low recently that Canada is in danger of losing NATO status. The military recently allocated additional money to public relations to try increase enrollment. The military has a problem with image. Adventure racing doesn't have an image problem: it is hip and trendy, and very appealing to high school students and others. Yet the parallels between adventure racing and the military are striking: in adventure racing, civilians are sent out to remote locations where their progress is monitored by radio communications, an infrastructure is developed quickly and efficiently to manage the flow of people through remote locations, and search and rescue operations are performed if something goes wrong. The military could send infantry members as teams, could use its resources to assist in co-ordinating adventure races, use adventure racing as training exercises, or perhaps run a separate race just for military, like Eco-Challenge does with the U.S. Armed Forces. Zietsma feels he could create a strong presentation tying in adventure racing and the military which he could take to high schools to increase enrollment in the military.

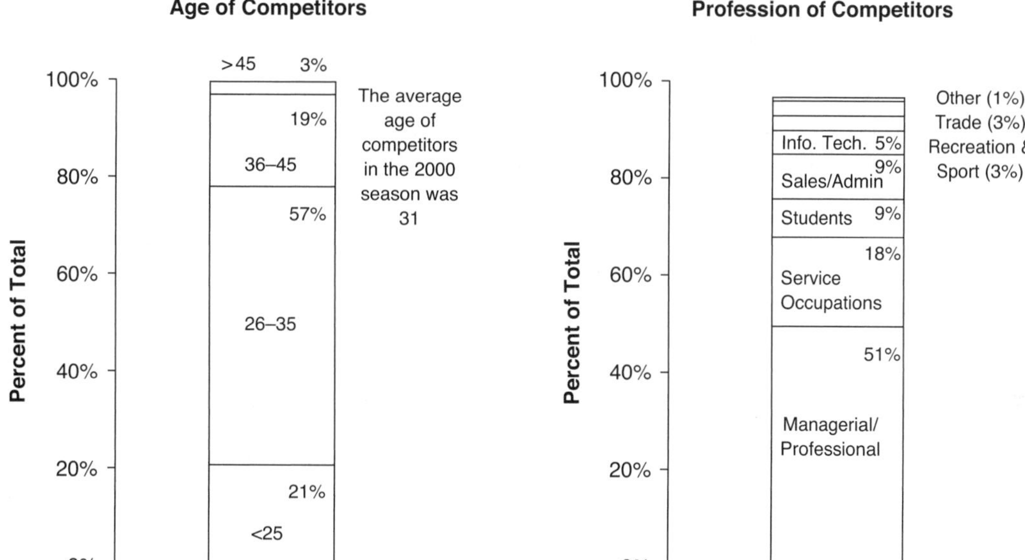

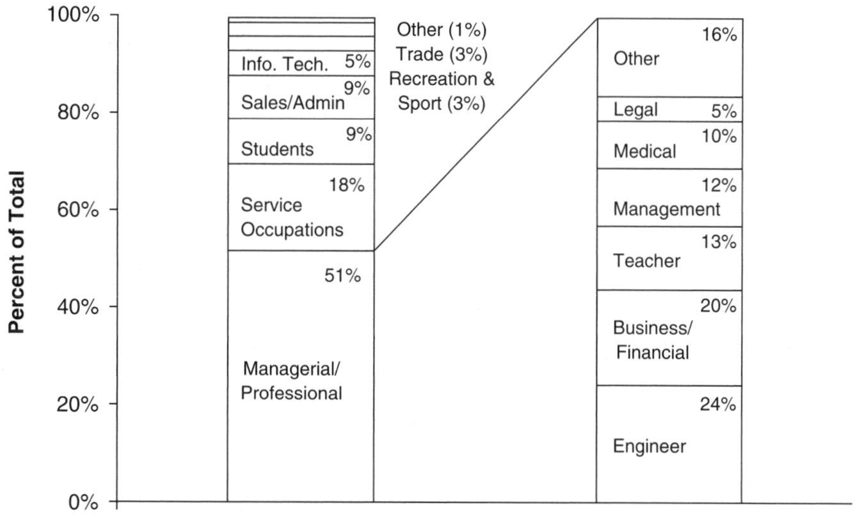

Exhibit 4 Demographics of Raid the North Competitors (2000)

Source: 2000 Raid the North competitor database. $n = 572$.

While another source of revenue might seem to be adventure travel, Zietsma claimed this was also a passion-driven business without a significant amount of money. While Burnett and Eco-Challenge developed an adventure travel program, it was probably not all that successful.

Competition

FAR was competing with other adventure racing companies in four ways: for participants, resources (e.g., equipment rentals), sponsors and media coverage. In 2000, FAR had a 38-per-cent share of total Canadian participation in adventure racing, up from 26 per cent in 1998 and 34 per cent in 1999.

The company was also competing in the three major segments of adventure racing: the sprints (usually several hours), the mid-length races (24 to 48 hours), and the expedition races (four-to-five-day races). Each segment had different competitive characteristics and key success factors (see Exhibit 5). A further Elite category, featuring seven to 10 day races, was dominated by Eco-Challenge and Raid Galoises.

For the sprint races, there were few barriers to entry, and organizers didn't need to know much about adventure racing. In fact, most FAR competitors wouldn't consider the Sprint races to be adventure racing at all. Successful sprint race organizers were good marketers: they could sell the race not only to competitors, but also to sponsors. Because of the low barriers to entry and the

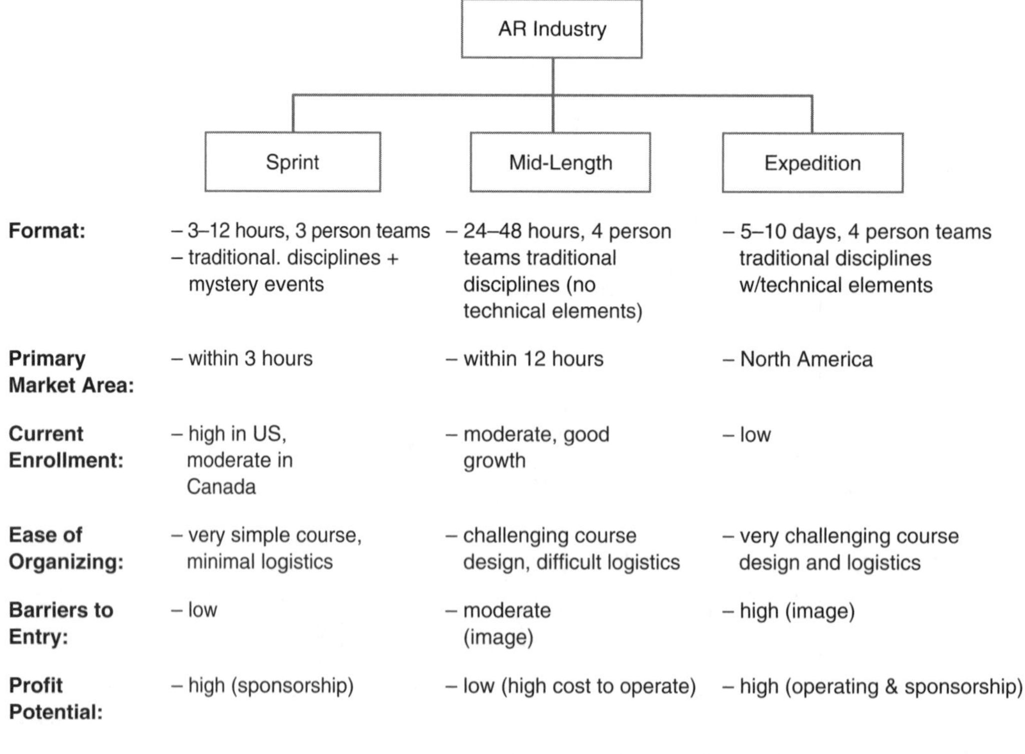

Exhibit 5 Overview of the Adventure Racing Industry

rising popularity of adventure racing, there have been hundreds of these short races popping up every year.

For the mid-length races, course design and logistics were very important, and thus at a minimum, knowledgeable staff in these areas had to be available. However, these races also required sponsorship, considerable equipment and good marketing to competitors. Image and reputation were more important, as competitors were putting their personal safety in the hands of race organizers.[6]

For expedition races, course designers needed an intimate knowledge of adventure racing that was acquired only from doing it themselves. Image and reputation were big barriers to entry, and logistics and course design were critical. Expedition races attempted to attract the best competitors from around the world.

In Canada, FAR owned the expedition segment. The 2001 race in Newfoundland sold out with 10 teams on the waiting list and competitors from eight countries represented. FAR's mid-level races have also been highly successful and very well thought of because of their consistently good course design and logistics. FAR has not seriously entered the sprint race category until this year (the Adventure Challenge races), and then only at the behest of sponsors and only in conjunction with a mid-level or expedition race.

Adventure Racing Canada (ARC), sponsored by Subaru, has been leading provider in the sprint race category. This company has done an excellent job at marketing, particularly to sponsors. ARC has been actively seeking sponsorship from the same companies as has FAR, and more successfully. PSG reported that potential sponsors have been told by ARC that FAR is for elite athletes only, not weekend warrior types, and that FAR races are held in remote areas, reducing the likelihood that they will bring visibility to sponsors. Zietsma countered by suggesting that ARC held its races in similar locations to FAR, and that the FAR demographic (30-something professionals) was a much better target market for high priced SUVs and other consumer goods than the young, edgy crowd that ARC appealed to. Recently, ARC began to offer 30-hour races, which competed more directly with FAR's Raid the North races.

Internationally, races in the mid-level and sprint categories typically drew their participants from local competitors. Expedition races drew from the international pool of adventure racers. These races were often considered informally as qualifying races for the elite Eco-Challenge and Raid Galoises races. While the expedition category organizers do compete with each other to some extent, they also all collaborate in raising the visibility of adventure racing as a sport. These races drew new participants from their local markets (where travel costs for participants were low), while regular adventure racers often participated in several races internationally. Direct competitors were the Southern Traverse in New Zealand, the Mild Seven Outdoor Quest in China, and the Beast of the East in the United States.

A Change in the International Adventure Racing Scene

A new international adventure racing association, under the umbrella of Discovery Channel, was formed in 2001. Discovery Channel was instrumental in creating media profile for Eco-Challenge, but withdrew its sponsorship of the event in 2000. Discovery Channel is now mounting its own elite race as a competitor to Eco-Challenge. Seven of the top expedition category adventure racing companies around the world (including FAR) have agreed to cross-promote each others' races, and act as qualifying races for Discovery Channel's new race in 2002. The media visibility that should result can provide a big boost to the sport as a whole. The Discovery Channel race is likely to be well received by regular Eco-Challenge competitors who have begun to express some dissatisfaction with Eco-Challenge since Burnett has been distracted with the Survivor series.

The Adventure Racing World Series includes: *Adrenalin Rush* (United Kingdom/Ireland); *The Beast of the East* (USA); *Expedicao Mata*

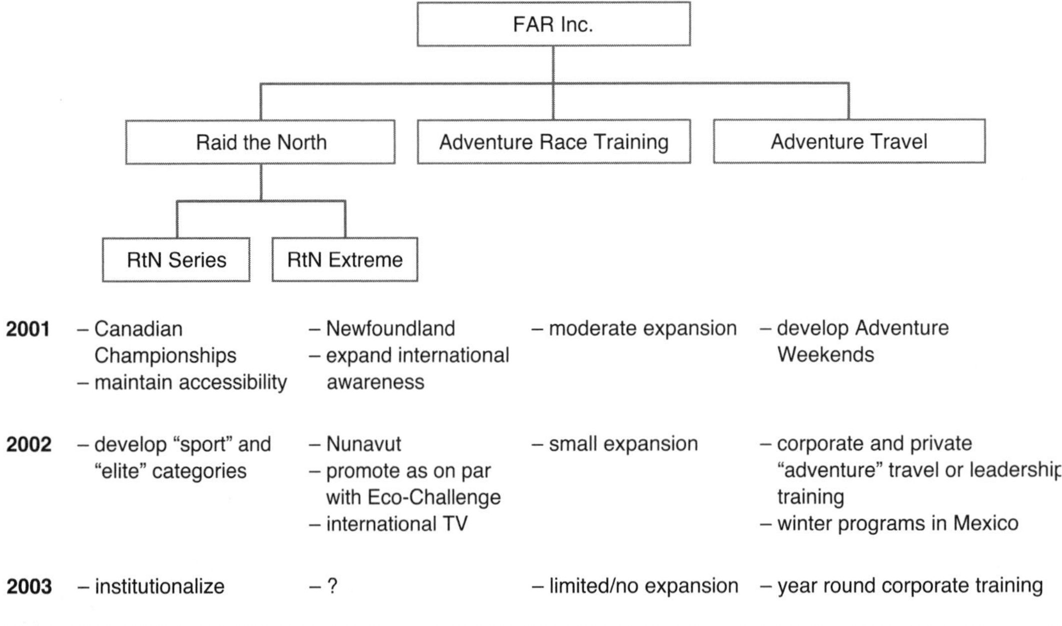

Exhibit 6 Frontier Adventure Racing Inc. Three-Year Plan

Atlantica (EMA) (Brazil); *Hi-Tec Adventure Quest* (Africa); *NOC Merciless Mountain Melee* (USA); *Raid The North Extreme* (Canada); and the *Southern Traverse* (New Zealand). Discovery Channel will be the exclusive media sponsor of the series. Discovery Channel is one of the world's largest cable television networks, serving more than 185 million subscribers in 152 countries across the globe. Discovery Channel presents high quality programming spanning science and technology, nature, history, human adventure and world culture genres.

Zietsma expressed high hopes for the Adventure Racing World Series and FAR's future. His three-year plan (shown in Exhibit 6) looks very promising. The Nunavut race planned for 2002 is expected to attract government support (because of the race's ability to impact the local economy), international media (because the remote location is considered "sexy"), and international competitors. Zietsma expects this race to compete in the elite category with Eco-Challenge. But making it through 2001 will be a very difficult for FAR without some additional sponsorship or financing. FAR has a highly respected product that sells well, but profitability now and in the future seems elusive. For the past four years, FAR has been following its own motto: Pack lightly, go like hell and never give up. But resources are now too light, and the company may have reached the limit of how far it can go. Zietsma wondered if he should give up.

Notes

1. Paquette, Martin & Zaglia, Carlo (2000: 50). *Extreme Adventure.* Quebec: Martin Paquette Photo Enr.
2. Quoted from www.far.on.ca.
3. Burnett is also the founder of the Survivor television series.
4. Paquette, Martin & Zaglia, Carlo (2000: 50). *Extreme Adventure.* Quebec: Martin Paquette Photo Enr.
5. www.far.on.ca.

6. Wilderness rescues and first aid treatment are a part of every race. Competitors also rely on the proper functioning of emergency radios, rock-climbing equipment, and canoes or kayaks. Maps must also be carefully developed so that competitors can navigate their way to various checkpoints. Checkpoint staff must be there to greet all competitors. Missing or poorly located checkpoint staff can leave competitors searching for frustrating hours through the wilderness.

Borders Hotel Corp.

Revised by Professor David Shaw
(originally prepared by Richard Nason under the supervision of Professor John Humphrey)

Version: (A) 2002-08-14

The Problem

On November 13, 2001, Karen Daniels, president of Borders Hotel Corp (BHC), had just returned from a meeting with the directors of BHC. The meeting had discussed three financing proposals to raise $2,275,000 for BHC. Daniels was uncertain of the impact of the three proposals on the financial viability of BHC and on the returns to herself and other investors. The meeting ended with the directors asking her for a recommendation on the preferred financing for a teleconference in two weeks.

History

After several years as a hotel manager for a national chain, Daniels had established herself in the tourist accommodation business close to the Canada-U.S. border near the Sarnia, Ontario, Canada and Port Huron, Michigan, U.S.A. border crossing. Daniels chose this location because the route was heavily traveled by tourists during the spring and summer months. In 1988, she formed a company known as Huron Motor Courts, Inc., acquired an attractive lot of land and erected an elaborate, modern motel on this site. The buildings provided complete tourist accommodation, shelter for automobiles and spacious dining facilities with entertainment for guests. Daniels considered Huron Motor Courts, Inc. a very successful venture.

With the introduction of the North American Free Trade Agreement (NAFTA), existing and new businesses in the area grew significantly. These businesses were not along the main tourist route on which Huron Motor Courts was situated; consequently, they did not in any way adversely affect the attractiveness of the site as a potential tourist stopover. However, the general expansion in the area attracted many business people who, not infrequently, found it necessary to remain in the area overnight.

The BHC Project

With these developments in mind, Daniels approached a number of industries in the vicinity in the summer of 2001, with a proposal regarding accommodation for visiting businesspeople. Her suggestion was well received, and several manufacturing concerns expressed an interest in maintaining permanent accommodation for visitors on business. With this encouragement, and in view of the overflow of visitors experienced to date from the tourist business, Daniels conceived the idea of constructing a modern hotel that would attract year-round business by arrangement with the local industries, and could be used to catch the overflow from the Huron Motor Courts during the tourist season.

Daniels then considered the type and size of hotel that would be desirable, and tried to estimate the costs of such a project. A property close to the Huron Motor Courts, which Daniels owned, was 200 feet wide and 350 feet deep, and was appraised at $975,000. After consultation with a local architect, Daniels developed a plan for a hotel building on this site that fulfilled the apparent prerequisites. The plan called for a three-storey structure, containing four suites of two rooms each, 31 twin bedrooms, 30 double bedrooms, a large front store, seven smaller stores and other facilities, which Daniels felt might eventually accommodate a travel agent, hair salon, business center and fitness room.

Daniels then attempted to estimate the profitability of such an establishment. Based on her experience with the motor court business, the income from the four suites and the bedrooms would be $8,100 per day, presuming that all accommodation was occupied. The income from leases of other parts of the building she estimated at $15,000 per month, again with 100 per cent occupancy. Rent would be charged as a per cent of sales and was expected to vary with occupancy. Other income eventually would be derived from gift counters, newspapers, display space and from a large central area, 100 feet by 20 feet in the lower level, for which a purpose had not yet been planned.

Apart from the incorporation expenses, which were expected to be about $50,000, Daniels estimated her yearly operating expenses, again based on 100 per cent occupancy (see Exhibit 1).

Daniels felt that in forecasting the profitability of the hotel, an estimate of 75 per cent average occupancy over a year was realistic, and 50 per cent occupancy the lowest possibility. All store and office spaces were to be leased on a yearly basis. Income taxes were estimated at 40 per cent.

	Total Variable Cost	*Fixed Costs*
Advertising		$120,000
Heat, light, water	$51,000	54,000
House supplies	52,000	
House wages	227,000	
Repairs and maintenance	41,000	98,000
Insurance		45,000
Salaries		350,000
Laundry	62,000	
Office expenses		51,000
Miscellaneous		12,000
Linen	11,000	
Telephone, fax, etc.		59,000
Automobile and travel	10,000	10,000
Municipal taxes		60,000
Computer systems		224,000
Depreciation		320,000
	$454,000	$1,403,000

Exhibit 1 Annual Operating Expenses at 100% Occupancy

The estimated cost of erecting a brick, concrete and steel hotel, such as the one proposed, was set at $2,300,000. After considerable investigation, Daniels set the estimated cost of furnishing the hotel at $1,100,000. She judged that working capital of $75,000 would be required in order to operate the business. Further, since her estimate of the profitability of the new hotel seemed to warrant a venture into this expanded field of business activity, she was certain that the required capital could be raised.

Accordingly, Daniels met with her associates in the Huron Motor Courts venture, to discuss the establishment of the new business. It was decided, in view of the degree of speculation involved in a new venture of this kind, and also because of the possibility of future expansion in the hotel business, that the business should be established as an independent corporate body with no financial connection whatsoever to Huron Motor Courts, Inc.

Thus, the new company, to be known as the Borders Hotel Corp., was to be incorporated as a company to operate hotels. The head office would be established on the property of Huron Motor Courts, Inc. Daniels would become the president and chairman of the board of directors. The new company would have an authorized share capital as follows:

8% Cumulative preferred shares par value $25	500,000 shares
Common shares without par value	1,000,000 shares

BHC Financing Proposals

Considerable progress had been made in planning operations. Daniels felt that attention must be turned now to the matter of providing the permanent capital, which had been previously estimated at $4.5 million: working capital, $75,000; land, $975,000; building, $2,300,000; furnishings, $1,100,000 and organization costs, $50,000.

Daniels foresaw the desirability of beginning construction as quickly as possible, so that the interior work could be completed in the winter. It was anticipated that the new structure would be completed in time for the 2002 peak season. Since considerable time would be required to raise the necessary capital, the five outside members of the board and Daniels each invested $25,000 and received 2,500 common shares. This provided the funds to begin construction immediately. The necessary arrangements were completed and construction of the new hotel commenced in September 2001.

As the next step in the financing, BHC would enter into an agreement with Daniels to purchase the land on which the hotel was to be built for $975,000. Under the purchase agreement, BHC contracted to give Daniels 97,500 shares of common stock in consideration for this land.

To finance the furnishings, BHC would negotiate a 10 per cent, five-year term loan of $1,100,000 with the furnishings suppliers. Blended annual payments of $290,160 were due starting at the end of the first fiscal year.

After these three financing arrangements, BHC had raised $2,225,000 with $2,275,000 still required. Daniels arranged preliminary discussions with her associates to decide the most feasible method of raising the capital. She had entertained the thought of a first mortgage on the company's real estate. The mortgage would be for $2,275,000, 20-year term, at eight per cent.[1] The annual principal and interest blended payments would be $231,000, with payments due at the end of BHC's fiscal year. However, Daniels was concerned that the fixed payments might prove too great a risk, with future earnings prospects uncertain.

Daniels' associates made a second proposal: the sale of 24 units at $100,000 per unit with each unit consisting of 10,000 common shares. Legal and other expenses for the issue were expected to be $125,000. Daniels was not enthusiastic about the common stock proposal, as her proportion of the profits would be substantially reduced.

A third proposal, which also involved units, was presented. This time each unit consisted of 3,000 preferred shares and 2,500 common shares. The units would sell for $100,000 with legal and other costs of $125,000. There would

4 units sold. The preferred shares would have a par value of $25, a preferred dividend rate of eight per cent and dividends would be cumulative. These preferred shares would be redeemable within the first five years of issue at $26 per share. If dividends were passed for two consecutive years, the preferred shares could elect a majority of the board of directors.

After the development of the three proposals, the meeting adjourned. The directors asked Daniels to investigate the three options and report to the board with a recommendation at a meeting scheduled via teleconference on November 27.

Note

1. At this time, long treasury bonds were yielding 5.75 per cent.

SimEx Inc.

Prepared by Nancy Roberts under the supervision of Professor David C. Shaw

Version: (A) 2002-12-02

Note: We relied heavily on an article published in the *Business Quarterly Magazine,* Summer 1995 Issue, for some historical information contained within this case. The article entitled "From Venture Capitalist to Entrepreneur" was written by Michael Needham.

Introduction

Michael Needham, president and CEO of SimEx Inc., Geoff Cannon, director of sales and marketing, and Gerry Townsend, vice-president finance & contracts, struggled with the concept of the Mars Odyssey simulation and the various options it presented as they prepared their proposal to the Texas Development Corp (TDC). They had to develop the specifics of the various options in terms of required equipment, time to view, amount of investment, aesthetics, etc. The resources required to undertake the project, the price to charge the public for the attraction, the operating costs for the various options, and the financial terms of the contract, all must be included in the proposal presented to the TDC for the "Astronaut Space Camp" centre, which was scheduled to undergo renovations in the fall of 1996.

The "Mars Odyssey" simulation was the most ambitious project yet undertaken by SimEx, but Michael, Geoff and Gerry were confident that they could put together an attraction that would generate an enthusiastic response from the public, be a major drawing card for the theme park, and provide an attractive return to the investors. Now the task was to get their ideas focussed and their presentation organized. Other competitors for the "Astronaut Space Camp" would mount effective proposals and spectacular presentations; but SimEx had the digital film of Mars developed from the NASA Pathfinder Initiative's film of the planet ready to go, and the experience of other simulated adventures to build their case. Michael, Geoff and Gerry knew the "Mars Odyssey" simulation was a compelling winner. Now they had to convince the TDC. This project was central to SimEx's success and warranted close attention. Michael, Geoff and Gerry decided to put together a special team of people from all areas of the company to analyze the options available to SimEx. This team was led by Allen Yamashita, Creative Director of SimEx Digital Studios.

Michael Needham

Background

After graduating from the MBA Program at the Western Business School in the late 1960s, Michael Needham and an acquaintance formed a venture capital firm called Helix Investments. Together, they raised $10 million, which they invested in a number of start-up companies in return for minority equity positions. To quote Michael, "The people and enterprises we supported eventually built Mitel, Newbridge, Corel Systems, Cast Containers, Hummingbird Communications and GEAC Computers."[1]

In 1982, Moses Znaimer, a former employee of Helix, who was subsequently funded by Helix to form CITY-TV, and his accountant Gerry Townsend, a partner in a large public accounting firm, approached Helix with an idea. They wanted to start a company that would build attractions for the public that were similar to the simulation training Znaimer received while obtaining his pilot's licence. Although the building of simulation attractions had been attempted by others with little success, Helix was impressed by Znaimer's enthusiasm and creativity, not to mention his success with CITY-TV. Thus, in 1983, Helix formed a company called Interactive Entertainment Inc. (IEI). Michael retained his position as president of Helix and also became vice-chairman of IEI. Moses became chairman of IEI on a part-time basis and Gerry joined IEI on a full-time basis as chief operating officer. Their first installation was called "Tour of the Universe®," located in the CN Tower in Toronto. This attraction opened in 1986 at a total cost of $15 million, $7 million over budget. Although the attraction was successful and profitable, its inherent operating weaknesses proved to be too great and after six years, it was sold to CN by Helix.

Rapid Growth

The period from 1983 to 1990 was one of rapid growth for IEI, particularly in Japan. The first Japanese attraction opened in 1988 at the Shikoku EXPO and was successful. Thereafter, attractions in Japan were constructed on a joint-venture basis with a company called "Saison Group." A member of an influential Japanese family, known to IEI through Helix, owned Saison Group. Saison Group helped IEI establish credibility in the Japanese market. IEI also diversified into live theatre and video productions in North America.

The rapid growth and diversification caused an ongoing cash shortage, and forced Helix to take a closer look at the management of the company. Clearly, a full-time CEO was warranted. As Michael explained,

> In 1989, I was given the task of finding a CEO. I could not find anyone in Canada who had the kind of experience we needed in film and simulation attractions, and people in the United States were too expensive. I ended up managing the company myself while still serving as president of Helix. After a year, I offered to buy the simulated attraction assets of IEI from Helix. I thought if I had the film library and the ongoing attractions and if I focused the business on providing simulated experiences, I could make a go of it. Helix agreed.[2]

In 1991, Michael formed SimEx Inc. to buy the assets of IEI. Gerry Townsend, one of several management shareholders in the new company, stayed on with Michael as vice-president responsible for administration, contracts and project management.

Geoff Cannon

As part of the transition, Michael convinced a good friend, Geoff Cannon, to join SimEx as the director of marketing. Geoff had operated his own marketing, publishing and advertising company. He was aware of the financial difficulties IEI had encountered and was reluctant at first to join. He agreed to work as a consultant on a part-time basis. After one year with this part-time arrangement, Geoff sold his company and joined SimEx full-time as the Director of Sales and Marketing, working out of the Toronto Head Office. According to Geoff,

> I scouted opportunities. Who did we want to go after, what types of things did we want to do, and what did we need in terms of materials to make that happen? How could we get the message across and how could we position ourselves so that we ultimately provided the client with the solutions they were looking for?
>
> We discovered that the battles were won or lost with software. That's what it was all about, not so much the hardware. What mattered was what you put on the screen, being able to create enough of it, and having enough places where you could actually show it to get a return on your investment.

By shifting the focus of the company from one that was always geared around the simulator hardware to one that concentrated on a much more macro scale of delivering attractions, SimEx became a technology leader in the industry and improved its financial stability. However, major capital expenditures were still made cautiously as a several million dollar loss could be calamitous.

The Attractions

Each SimEx film was an entertaining adventure anchored to a science event or phenomenon. Each adventure had a quest. SimEx strove to design an environment that stimulated learning and set the conditions for critical thinking and insight, always working for a skillful balance between information and entertainment. Ideas were researched with science advisors and authorities in the field, and were co-written with educators using traditional story structure—Prologue, Act 1, Act 2 and Epilogue. Refer to Exhibit 1.

SimEx built many simulator attractions for educational facilities. SimEx also built simulator attractions for amusement parks and EXPOs. The attractions integrated the simulators with show sets and video and audio programs. The motion systems were synchronized with special format simulator films by motion programming systems. These electrically powered motion systems (based on aircraft simulator technology) were available in sizes from four seats to 50 seats.

Simulators

SimEx offered two types of simulators: a closed cabin simulator and an open platform simulator.

In the open platform simulator design, visitors were seated on a platform that was installed in front of the screen. In this scenario, only the platform moved. Screen sizes varied to fit the limitations of each theatre. They could be either flat or curved and as large as 25 feet by 50 feet. If the theatre was dome-shaped, the screen could be larger still and actually extend over the viewers' head. Refer to Exhibit 2.

In the closed cabin simulator design, the screen comprised the cabin interior and so it moved with the simulator. The screen was curved, 15 feet by seven feet in size, and completely filled the viewers' vision. A digital laser-based sound system with 11 speakers encompassed the entire theatre, adding to the sense of realism and completing the package. Refer to Exhibit 3.

Similar attractions familiar to most people were rides like "Body Wars" and "Star Tours" or the "Back to the Future" ride at Universal Studios.

Actuators

An actuator was the machinery below the platform or cabin floor that enabled the cabin flight simulators to move in all directions. IEI had used hydraulic actuators because they were the best then available. But, Michael had changed motion system suppliers when he formed SimEx. The new actuators were purchased from a company called MOOG. MOOG supplied the TVC (thrust vector control) hydraulic actuators for NASA's space shuttle and brake actuators for the Shuttle Orbiter. In the early 1980s, MOOG initiated development of an electric replacement for the Shuttle main engine TVC actuator. The new thrusts were more than four times that of the best hydraulic actuators on the market. A great deal of engineering development was required to enable MOOG electric actuators to meet NASA's requirements. Marshall Space Flight Centre worked with MOOG to develop the necessary

(Text continues on page 138)

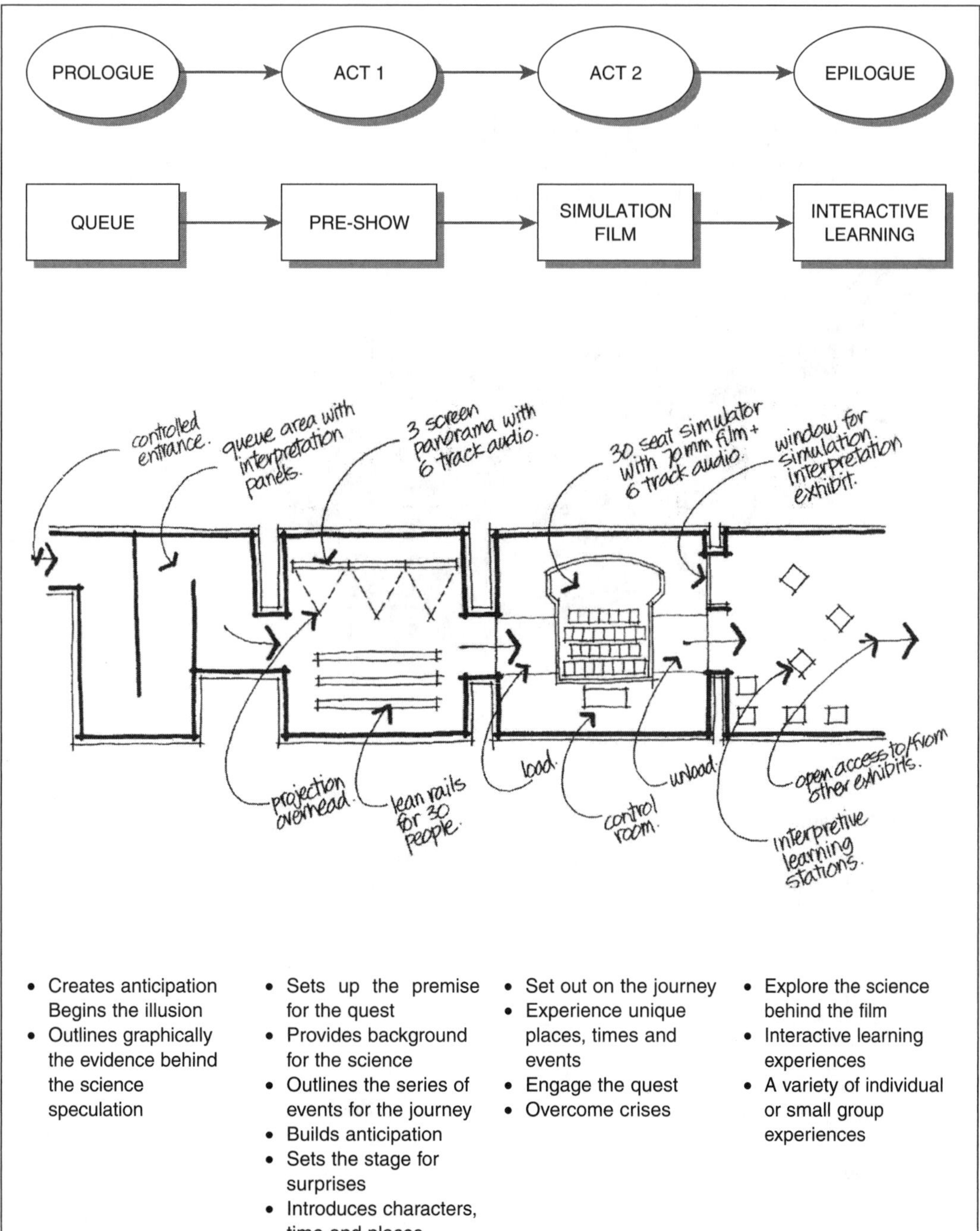

Exhibit 1 Story Outline

Source: Company files.

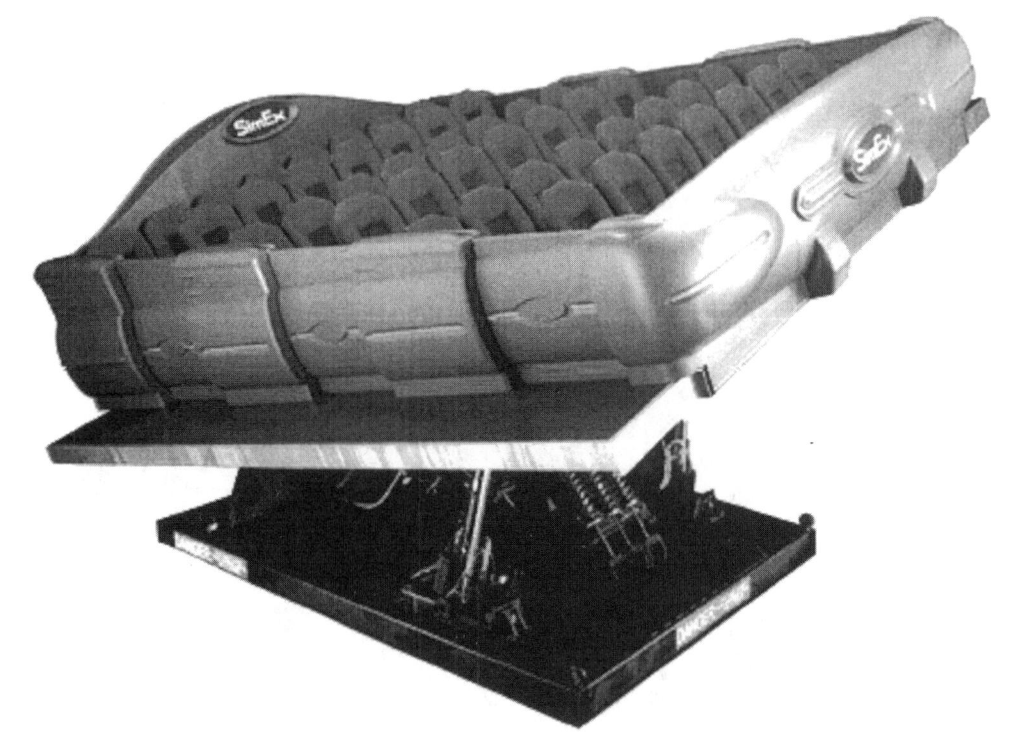

Product Description

Four degrees of freedom, electric motion simulator in an open configuration with off board projection system and screen. Ideal for large format or dome film projection.

Features

- Average up-time 99.4 per cent
- Flight quality motion system
- Transportable
- Space efficient
- Multiple films/reprogrammable in 30 seconds
- Multiple platforms can be configured around single theatre screen

Seating Capacity	**Cost ($US)**
• 42 seats providing up to 504 people/hour capacity	$1,000,000

Exhibit 2 SimEx Open Platform Electric Simulators

Source: Company files.

Product Description

Four degrees of freedom, electric motion simulator with enclosed cabin theatre and built-in screen for a thoroughly immersive experience.

Cabin

A fireproof, lightweight, vibration free structure constructed of rigid honeycomb laminate.

Standard themed cabin interior.

Features

- Average up-time 99.6 per cent
- Flight quality motion system
- Transportable
- Space efficient
- Multiple films/reprogrammable in 30 seconds

Seating Capacity	**Cost ($US)**
• 36 seats providing up to 432 people/hour capacity	$1,100,000

Exhibit 3 SimEx Closed Cabin Electric Simlulators

Source: Company files.

technology. In 1990, when the electric unit was complete, MOOG partnered with SimEx as a means to obtain commercial applications for this product, and now SimEx offered only MOOG electric simulators.

SimEx had exclusive rights to MOOG's electric motion systems for the attractions industry and was the only company offering an electric simulator. The electrically actuated motion system was capable of manipulating a load of up to 15,000 pounds in four degrees of freedom: roll, pitch, vertical heave and longitudinal surge; or six degrees of freedom: roll, pitch, vertical heave, longitudinal surge, yaw and sway. SimEx believed its large capacity four degrees of freedom model was its best product. Refer to Exhibit 4 for a comparison of hydraulic and electric simulators.

SimEx Digital Studios

SimEx Digital Studios was a fully equipped, state-of-the-art computer graphics facility which employed 18 people. The centre was led by Allen Yamashita, Creative Director, who had 17 years of experience in film making and was considered to be an expert in the production of special format simulation films. In fact, Allen had been recognized by American Cinematographer as one of the most innovative film makers in the industry. He had produced several large format films including two for World EXPOs. Allen supervised a team of world class animators and film makers, among them, Richard Yuricich, a three-time Academy Award nominee for "Star Trek," "Close Encounters of the Third Kind" and "Blade Runner." The studio had the capability of producing two five-minute simulator films per year.

Digital Filming

Most SimEx films, up to this point, had not been digital. "Mars Odyssey" was the first one. Digital filming meant that everything was done on the computer instead of having a camera and shooting a model or shooting a live action. Images were created in digital format and then transferred into film format. There were no cameras.

Not every film had to be done digitally. Sometimes it didn't make sense. If the adventure involved live action, like taking a trip down the Amazon River, it was more cost effective to do that with real film. However, if the adventure involved space travel or elements that were extinct or futuristic, digital filming offered many advantages. Once the image was stored in a data base, it could be manipulated to complete different moves very easily and stored for use in future adaptations to achieve economies of scale.

High quality digital filming was very time-consuming. If you amortized the total length of production with the finished film length, it amounted to one to two seconds per day of final material. Frequently the two formats were mixed, as with the production of "Who Framed Roger Rabbit" or "Jurassic Park." A typical SimEx film would be between four-and-one-half minutes and five minutes in length when completed.

The Consumer

As a science interpretation medium, simulation appealed to a youthful audience who quickly adapted to a high tech entertaining experience. They were computer literate and preferred fast-paced stimulating encounters. SimEx met these needs by creating a science-grounded simulation experience. It used large format images to create places and times that were impossible, yet believable.

The Market

The interactive media market was estimated at $10 billion. Traditionally, this business developed around destination attractions, educational facilities and theme parks, places like Science Centres, EXPOs, Disneyland and Universal or MGM Studios. Now there was a huge move toward "family entertainment centres" (FECs) and "location-based entertainment" (LBEs). Geoff explained,

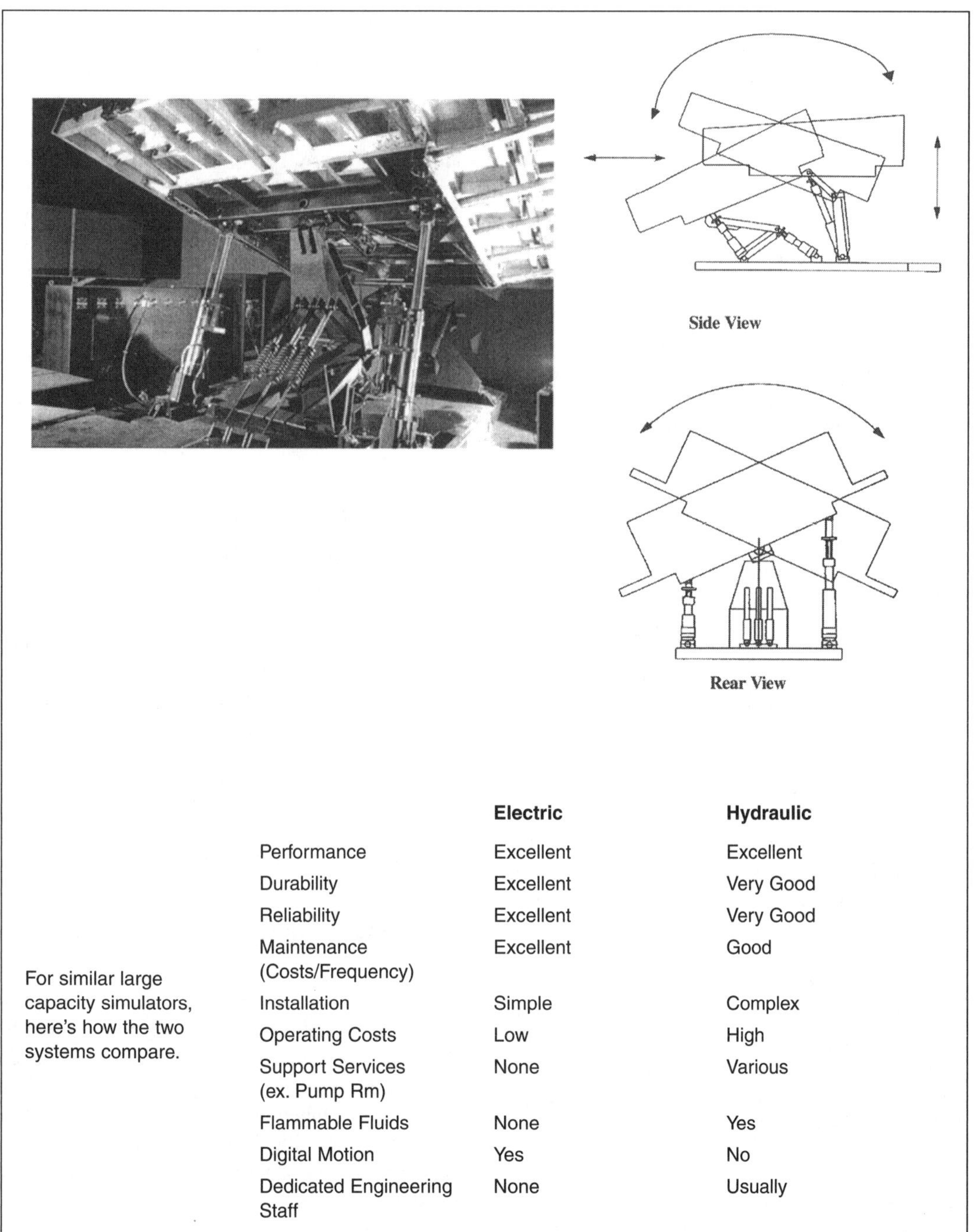

	Electric	Hydraulic
Performance	Excellent	Excellent
Durability	Excellent	Very Good
Reliability	Excellent	Very Good
Maintenance (Costs/Frequency)	Excellent	Good
Installation	Simple	Complex
Operating Costs	Low	High
Support Services (ex. Pump Rm)	None	Various
Flammable Fluids	None	Yes
Digital Motion	Yes	No
Dedicated Engineering Staff	None	Usually

Exhibit 4 Comparison of Hydraulic and Electric Actuators

Source: Company files.

> Large screen theatres and multiplex cinemas are being located where local crowds or tourists gather. The landlords are searching for other forms of entertainment to add to that mix. Simulation and virtual reality are components that have an application in these areas.

Recently SimEx had introduced a new attraction concept it called "Virtual Voyages" (VV). By offering its VV packages, SimEx could change each experience with minimal effort. Unlike attractions that simply changed the film, like IMAX theatres, VV packages included the software to change the movie, the pre-show, and the motion movements with the touch of a button. Each SimEx simulator theatre could hold up to three software programs at any one time. This flexibility was of key importance for any place that was concerned with repeat visitors. Previously, simulator attractions were single-themed attractions often located in major theme parks, e.g., "Back to the Future." At these major theme parks, visitors returned every three to four years on average, and did not object to the attraction being unchanged. Theme parks were not a large market for SimEx.

The Attractions

Generally, SimEx did not become involved in the construction of premises to house its attractions. Usually SimEx asked for attraction-ready space and installed a turn-key attraction into it. For example, at Ontario Place, SimEx utilized two existing silos located at the west end of the park, that formerly housed the Northern Ontario Exhibit. On a joint venture basis, SimEx installed a futuristic attraction called "Sea Trek®." Refer to Exhibit 5 for a schematic sketch of the Sea Trek® layout at Ontario Place.

Sea Trek

At Ontario Place, the silos were painted and themed to look like a deep sea submarine base. After purchasing their tickets, the customers entered "the suiting bay." Although themed consistently with the prologue in a story, its real function was to operate as a queue line. People saw diving suits and tanks and lockers; water bubbling through pipes and other show sets that indicated they were in a deep sea submarine base and under water. The queue area could hold up to three audience groups. Since Sea Trek® was a 30 seat simulator, this meant roughly 90 people.

In the Sea Trek® adventure, customers met the "Ocean Rangers" by video monitor. The Ocean Rangers had a mandate to protect the oceans against pirates and polluters. There was Keith, an Australian deep sea diver; Mike, the Canadian technical specialist in his hockey sweater; and Sarah, an American scientist, who liked practicing her trombone too much.

The Pre-Show

Every seven minutes or so, 30 customers moved from the queue line to the Pre-show (Act 1). They were met by a small robot named Sonar, the maintenance boss of the base, who served as the host of the pre-show, which was about five minutes in length. During Sonar's briefing an emergency arises. Geoff explained,

> Lisa, one of the Ocean Rangers, is out looking for treasure and has found a sunken galleon. But uh-oh! A pirate had arrived on the scene and captured her. We now have to go and save her.

The Submarine Ride

At this point, visitors entered the simulator. The simulation experience was five minutes in length and equated to Act 2 in the process. When loading and unloading time was taken into account, approximately seven-and-one-half minutes were taken up in the submarine trip. The numbers were critical to designing an attraction, because this business was capacity limited. There were finite levels.

The Epilogue (Post-Show)

As visitors exited the simulation ride they passed through interactive exhibits that used

Sea Trek is a thrilling underwater adventure that combines multi-media technology, animatronics, video programs and a large format special effects film with an electric motion simulator

1. Sea Trek Exterior
2. Suiting Bay
3. Transition Corridor
4. Sonar Pre-Show
5. Submarine Ride

Exhibit 5 Attraction Layout Sea Trek
Source: Company files.

material presented in Acts 1 and 2. If souvenirs and printed materials were available, they were placed in this area. In the case of "Sea Trek®," the existing structure at Ontario Place did not permit such an area; thus, a free standing structure called the "Sea Trek® Boutique" was built beside the exit doors.

At Ontario Place, SimEx was provided with the shell, the heating, ventilation and air conditioning (H-Vac) and the power requirements based on the specs given by SimEx. Everything else—the interior theming, the monitors, the simulator, the pre-show and the animatron—was designed and installed by SimEx which essentially made "Sea Trek®" a turn-key attraction.

Revenue Negotiations

No two deals were the same. Sometimes SimEx just sold or leased the simulator hardware for an attraction. Sometimes, SimEx simply provided the film and accepted a rental payment. Sometimes another group made the film and provided the theming and SimEx simply provided the motion platforms and projectors.

Sometimes SimEx acted as a supplier and sometimes as a joint-venture partner. As a typical example of a joint venture, SimEx had just completed negotiations to install a Sea Trek® attraction in Lisbon. The park managers in Lisbon were providing the land and the building. SimEx had to make the space attraction-ready and install the Sea Trek® attraction, an investment of about US$2 million. A joint-venture company was formed to operate the attraction. All proceeds after operating expenses of about $300,000 per year were to be split on a 70/30 basis with the larger share going to SimEx. The only cost included in the operating expenses that was allocated to one of the partners was a $150,000 fee per year, to SimEx, for the software rental. About 300,000 visitors were expected to pay an average of $4.00 (U.S. equivalent) at the Lisbon attraction. This type of arrangement was fairly typical.

The Competition

When SimEx first started under the name of "Interactive Entertainment," there were no competitors. SimEx pioneered this industry. Now three firms—Iwerks, Showscan and Bigscreen—shared the field with SimEx. For the most part, when people thought of the simulation attraction business, these three names, not SimEx, came to mind. As Michael commented,

> We started the simulation attraction industry and we should own it. But we do not. We share it with three U.S. companies, all of whom got their start from a connection with us and now all are larger than SimEx. When we started in 1983, we had all the money we needed, a considerable amount of expertise and excellent connections. That is not usual for most start-ups. Nevertheless, despite the rich-kid advantages we had, the company is not anywhere near where it should be. We lost six years of management energy and a substantial amount of money on a diversification strategy that diluted our efforts and which eventually went sour. We should have changed strategies much earlier than we did.[3]

What SimEx needed was a blockbuster attraction in a really good location. Given that Bigscreen already had a large screen theatre located in the "Astronaut Space Camp," Michael felt certain that Bigscreen would be presenting a proposal to the TDC. Although Bigscreen had the financial capabilities to build a simulated attraction, Bigscreen did not have "Mars Odyssey." "Mars Odyssey" was an exceptional production. No other competitor in the market today had a film that could compete with this one. This was the chance to truly cement SimEx as a formidable competitor, and the renovation of the "Astronaut Space Camp" centre was ideal.

The New Attraction

"Mars Odyssey"

"Mars Odyssey" was originally designed for the World City Exposition scheduled to open in Tokyo in 1996. The budget for the film had been $4 million. SimEx hoped to place "Mars Odyssey" at eight other locations over the next five years and in each case secure a three-year film rental agreement.

"Mars Odyssey" was a high quality, computer graphics, digital effects film. The story was about Man pushing space exploration to Mars and completing NASA's Pathfinder Initiative in 2100 A.D. The space colony on Mars had depleted its energy resources and was facing a life threatening "energy down" situation. An energy transporter rescue mission, manned by Wattohm, a robotic space pilot, had been organized to try to save the colony. Refer to Exhibit 6. Wattohm was given the dangerous mission of transporting the "new energy source" to Mars. We, the visitors, were allowed to accompany the rescuers. The visitors left for their mission from a space station on earth. Refer to Exhibit 7. The buildings in the

Exhibit 6 Wattohm

Source: Company files.

Exhibit 7 Layout of the Space Station on Earth

Source: Company files.

background behind the space station on earth were Neo Tokyo.

The "Mars Odyssey" script was written by SimEx in conjunction with NASA and Jet Propulsion Laboratories (JPL) scientists. For the surface of Mars, SimEx took JPL photos from NASA's Space Probe and copied these onto a computer. They removed the distortion, mapped these photos into the system, and added texture and colour to create the surface of Mars. SimEx had mapped from latitude 40 North to latitude 40 South, all the way around Mars using exact JPL photos.

The Astronaut Space Camp Centre

The "Astronaut Space Camp" centre was located within close proximity to the Houston Air Force Base and was affiliated with NASA. The TDC and NASA collaborated on the attractions and centre design, with final approval resting with NASA; however, the TDC alone managed the centre. Management of the centre came open for tenders every 10 years. The TDC had just recently won the bid and would be in charge of the centre for the next 10 years.

The TDC was a very large profitable company that managed food and beverage concessions at international airports and stadiums. The TDC was expanding and had just closed a deal to manage a famous national park in the United States and now, the "Astronaut Space Camp." The TDC was an expert in the management of food and beverage concessions but knew very little at this stage about the management of attractions.

Within the centre there was a large display of rockets and exhibits of space gear, a gift shop, a Bigscreen theatre, an art gallery and several eating establishments. Patrons could either walk through the exhibits or could take bus tours of the various NASA facilities. There were few other attractions at the centre and no major attractions within close proximity to draw tourists. Over the past few years, attendance at the park had been dropping. Current park attendance was approximately 1.8 million, down from 2.8 million in 1990.

Roughly 80 per cent of all visitors to the park took the bus tour. Thus, the TDC and NASA hired an economic research group to survey individuals on the bus as a means to identify the park's market. The surveys were conducted at four different times throughout the year. Combining the results revealed the following:

- Roughly 50 per cent of all visitors were families.
- 75 per cent were first-time visitors.
- 85 to 95 per cent of all visitors were tourists, a high proportion of which had visited major theme parks and popular tourists attractions, and had a sophisticated basis of comparison.
- The average visit ranged between three to six hours.

NASA wanted to put excitement back into space travel, to recapture the feeling the public had when man first walked on the moon. To this end, the survey asked respondents to identify their favourite subject for future exhibits and shows. Forty-six per cent were interested in future exploration, 43 per cent in the space shuttle and 36 per cent in life as an astronaut. Clearly, the public's interest deviated from the park's existing theme, which focussed on what NASA had accomplished in the past. Therefore, the TDC and NASA decided the park needed to be renovated.

The objective was to create a first-class tourist attraction, one that would be suitable for Heads of State and other dignitaries to visit. That meant that any new attractions must be spectacular enough to actually draw visitors to the centre, and priced accordingly so that visitors would pay to view the attraction and the investors would receive a reasonable return. There also had to be a sufficient range of activities for each age group. The TDC hoped the renovations would increase existing attendance by one-third.

The Attraction

Michael, Geoff and Gerry were aware that they would have to convince the TDC to consider a simulated attraction. Unlike the people at NASA, the TDC did not understand what simulation was all about: how it worked, how it fit in, and how it benefitted them. There was an education process involved. The TDC would be concerned with lengthening the time visitors remained at the park. The longer the visitors stayed, the more they would spend on food, beverages and souvenirs.

Michael intended to present the TDC with some recent studies. These studies indicated that the way to increase park attendance, ticket prices and per capita spending was to periodically add a blockbuster attraction that acted as a "showcase" for the centre. Today's most popular "showcases" at many theme parks were simulated attractions. Given that any new attraction for the centre would have to be endorsed by NASA, SimEx intended to stress that simulation and flight simulators were fundamental to the training of a NASA astronaut, and that SimEx had worked with NASA in the past.

In his attraction, Michael wanted to include the following:*

- Present a vision of future Earth, Mars and space exploration that was exciting, uplifting and tangible, and to accomplish this in a dynamic manner.
- Present a vision about how the current NASA space exploration initiative called Pathfinder was important and what it could result in 100 years in the future.
- Present a vision of how the current and near future endeavours of the Space Station, Earth to Orbit Transportation, Life Sciences Research, and Robotic Precursor Missions would enable Man to eventually colonize Mars.

SimEx Options

SimEx management envisioned two possible attractions. The first "Blockbuster" option would require the construction of a large dome-shaped building. Michael envisioned an 8,000 to 10,000 square foot, four-story facility which could hold three 42-seat open platform units plus 24 non-motion seats. Given the importance of this project, SimEx was prepared to design, finance and build the facilities to house the attraction, as well as to install and operate it. SimEx would expect the TDC to provide the building and basic facilities. SimEx would collaborate with the TDC on marketing, ticketing and attraction programming. As compensation, SimEx would offer the TDC a percentage of revenues.

Michael expected at least 50 per cent of the visitors to the "Astronaut Space Camp" centre to visit SimEx's attraction. The story line or possible dialogue for each segment of the "Blockbuster" attraction was outlined as follows:*

- Prologue/Queuing Area

Mars, long an object of fascination in both science and science fiction. With humour and insight, the prologue examines popular entertainment media from the writing of Jules Verne and H. G. Wells to films of the last 50 years. Russian and American scientific exploration of the planet decades ago and the current NASA Pathfinder series of satellites, probes and rovers are highlighted.

- Act 1/Pre-Show

The year is 2100. One hundred years ago, America set the goal for all of humanity with the Pathfinder Initiative, a program to identify and develop the necessary technologies to live and work in space and on other worlds. We are members of a delegation from Earth to the Mars colony to celebrate the end of that bold era of human advancement and enter a new one.

Our companion craft will be delivering the trigger device for a new energy source for the colony. We will witness that event and participate in the conference on exploration of the stars.

A report of a meteor shower that will hit the planet in the next 24 hours underlines the risk of space travel. We are cautioned that while travel to Mars has become routine, it is still a dangerous journey.

---

*Source: Company files.

- Act 2/Ride Film

Visitors would view the "Mars Odyssey" film. The beginning and the ending of the "Mars Odyssey" film would be amended so that space station earth would be located in the same city as the space ride attraction. In this case, space station earth would be located in Houston.

- Epilogue/Interactive Learning

A possible post-show could include interactive monitors where the visitors could dial up information that was interesting in relation to the film they had just viewed; or how simulation worked; or how the special effects were produced. Another option would be to highlight information about NASA and space projects.

Michael felt that a "Blockbuster" dome SimEx theatre would be best for the centre. There was no doubt that such a "Blockbuster" attraction would help keep people at the "Astronaut Space Camp" centre longer and justify a higher general admission price. However, questions remained: would it attract new visitors to the centre, and was it too similar to the space film experience at the centre's Bigscreen theatre to attract enough visitors? The anticipated cost for the SimEx "Blockbuster" attraction, not including the cost of the "Mars Odyssey" film, was approximately US$12 million. This figure included an additional $500,000 in software development to adapt the "Mars Odyssey" film to a dome theatre.

SimEx considered another option. A somewhat less expensive means of utilizing "Mars Odyssey" was to avoid the construction of a large, custom-made dome structure and make use of an existing 5,000 square foot building on the TDC site. Not big enough for a domed theatre, it did have a 20 foot ceiling height which would allow SimEx to install separate 36-seat, closed cabin simulators. Based on current attendance, SimEx envisioned using three closed cabin simulators to demonstrate astronaut training and the experience of future space travel.

There would be an area that provided a "walking on Mars" experience; a pre-show that used interactive techniques to demonstrate the development of space travel; and a post-show that explored interactively the reason why people found space and space fiction fascinating and why far-fetched theories had a habit of becoming reality. Although SimEx planned to initially use the film "Mars Odyssey," it had two other high quality space simulation films—"Jove's Hammer" and "Destination Jupiter"—that would also work well under this scenario. "Jove's Hammer" was produced in 1996 at a cost of $1 million and "Destination Jupiter" was produced in 1984 at a cost of $2 million.

Making use of the closed cabin simulators certainly offered an entirely different experience to the Bigscreen theatre, however, the three closed cabins provided less capacity than the dome theatre. SimEx felt that this attraction would have to be priced lower than the "Blockbuster" attraction. SimEx's cost for supplying this option was approximately US$8 million.

Refer to Exhibits 8 and 9 for an estimation of expenses for both options.

Bigscreen Options

Given there was already a traditional Bigscreen theatre in the "Astronaut Space Camp" centre, Bigscreen had a vested interest in the changes that were taking place. It seemed only logical that Bigscreen would resist SimEx's proposal and/or make a counter proposal. As Geoff remarked,

> The existing Bigscreen theatre is a typical large format theatre. It's not a ride or an experience, just a movie. Mind you it's a spectacular image, and the space/astronaut story is emotive, but it's still just a movie.

It was possible that Bigscreen would propose to build a three dimensional (3-D) large format theatre. A 3-D theatre could have a large flat screen that would cost approximately US$15 million to construct, or a dome screen that would cost US$20 million. Although Bigscreen had a number of 3-D films in its library, only one had a space theme and it was not really suitable to show at the "Astronaut Space Camp" centre. Therefore, Bigscreen would have to create one or more films at the cost of $6 million each for a flat screen and $10 million each for a dome

Simulators:	*Dome Building*	*Existing Structure*
*Cost of Three 42 Seat Open Platform Simulators and 24 Non-Motion Seats:	$3,000,000	
*Cost of Three 36 Seat Closed Platform Simulators:		$3,300,000
*(Includes: Motion system and related motion equipment, seats, deck, platform walls & gates, theming, projection system, lens design and production, theatre lighting, audio system, show control, assembly and testing in Toronto, freight insurance and packing, local services and installation.)		
Facility Related Cost: (sub contracted)		
Building/Dome incl. Screen	$3,834,000	Supplied by TDC
Internal Partition Construction/Acoustics	$777,000	$850,000
HVAC Distribution/Electric etc.	$389,000	$350,000
Total Facility/Dome Related Costs	**$5,000,000**	**$1,200,000**
Theming Cost of Pre-show; Film Adaptation, Post-Show and Facade:		
Hardware Systems, Sets, Queue Theming and Facade Fully Installed:		
Pre-Show	$708,000	$708,000
Post-Show	$708,000	$708,000
Construction	$472,000	$472,000
Lighting/Audio	$118,000	$118,000
Engineering Drawings, Documents and Approval Support	$36,000	$36,000
Spare Parts	$88,000	$88,000
Software Development	$1,870,000	$1,370,000
Total Pre-Show and Facade Costs	**$ 4,000,000**	**$ 3,500,000**
Grand Totals:		
Motion Platforms	$3,000,000	$3,300,000
Facility Related Costs	$5,000,000	$1,200,000
Theming Cost of Pre-Show, Post-Show and Facade	$4,000,000	$3,500,000
Grand Totals	**$12,000,000**	**$ 8,000,000**

Exhibit 8 Estimated Costs for SimEx Options (in U.S. dollars)

Source: Company files.

screen. The average ticket price for a traditional Bigscreen film was US$7 per person. For a 3-D film the cost rose to US$10 per person.

The second option for Bigscreen was to construct a simulation experience. Bigscreen had just entered the simulation attraction business. The type of simulators Bigscreen used in their attractions only seated 18 people and each cost the same as one of SimEx's 36 seat cabins or one of SimEx's 42 seat open simulators. Michael felt Bigscreen would propose this option but it would be an expensive option given the number of Bigscreen simulators required to handle the expected attendance.

All Bigscreen films were filmed with a 70 mm film with 15 perforations per inch, versus

Average Operating Hours:		
Number of Operating Hours per Day (10:00 a.m. to 8:00 p.m.)	10	
Number of Operating Days per Year	360	
Current Park Attendance:	*# Days*	*# Visitors*
Poor Attendance	129	2,500
Average Attendance	173	5,000
Good Attendance	34	8,750
Very Good Attendance	24	12,500
Dome Option:		
Proposed Average Net Ticket Price (not incl. sales tax):	*Price*	*Attendance Ratio*
Adults (13 years and older)	$6.00	56%
Children (3 to 12 years old)	$4.00	14%
Groups	$4.00	30%
Hourly Capacity:	8 shows per hour	
Operating Expenses:	$500,000	
Closed Cabin Option:		
Proposed Average Net Ticket Price (not incl. sales tax):	*Price*	*Attendance Ratio*
Adults (13 years and older)	$5.00	56%
Children (3 to 12 years old)	$3.50	14%
Groups	$3.50	30%
Hourly Capacity:	7 Shows per Hour	
Operating Expenses:	$400,000	

Exhibit 9 Revenue Assumptions for SimEx Options (US$)

Source: Company files.

SimEx's 70 mm film with five perforations per inch, which was less costly and a more suitable format for simulator attractions. Michael knew that Bigscreen did not have any films in the 15 mm format that were suitable for showing at the "Astronaut Space Camp" centre but that they could propose to make one.

The Proposal

There was a large difference in cost in the various options open to the TDC and each represented a totally different experience. SimEx believed it would have to make astronaut training by simulator a big part of the presentation. The TDC would be looking at the capital cost to them of each attraction, the revenue split and how long it would take to realize payback and profits. Generally, a larger share of revenues went to the party that financed the capital expenditures. When the capital expenditures were recovered, the revenue split was often renegotiated.

Audience cannibalization was also important. What was the expenditure threshold of the average visitor? How many attractions could each visitor afford without compromising the amount spent on other park items more profitable to the

TDC? How long was the average visitor willing to stay at the centre? Could they fit in all the attractions? These were the types of issues Michael anticipated having to deal with.

The proposal to the TDC was scheduled for two months from today. That meant Allen and his team had six weeks to prepare their presentation to Michael, Geoff and Gerry. The presentation needed to include the following:

- a recommendation as to which option to choose, if any, and why
- a detailed explanation of the attraction chosen including concepts and theming for each segment: Prologue, Act 1, Act 2, Epilogue
- the resources required to undertake the suggested project
- an estimate of associated costs for equipment requirements and operating expenses
- the price to charge the public and capacity limitations
- a revenue-sharing agreement between SimEx and the TDC
- a determination of the cash flows in time and the value of the project
- a payback component for SimEx investors
- an exploration of the risks, financial and otherwise, to SimEx
- an examination of Bigscreen's likely response and SimEx's counter moves

As the parts of the presentation started to come together and everyone in the company had an opportunity to see the film and experience the thrill of space, the tensions grew and the excitement level increased dramatically. Everyone remembered Michael's vision:

> I want each element of the attraction to knit together to provide an unforgettable experience. That means richly themed queue lines; interactive pre-shows that allow visitors to actively participate in learning about space; a climactic simulated space adventure and interactive post-show learning activities.

The date when Allen and his team presented their ideas to Michael, Geoff and Gerry, June 10, 1996, loomed large in everyone's minds. On Friday June 21, Michael, Geoff and Gerry would make the pitch to the TDC. While negotiations would continue beyond that date if the reception was positive, a negative reaction would kill the project and destroy a lot of high hopes. The proposal to the TDC was a key success factor for SimEx. Not only did management have to decide which option to present; they had to decide the financial and operational details of the proposal.

Notes

1. Michael Needham, "From Venture Capitalist to Entrepreneur," *Business Quarterly Magazine,* Summer 1995, p. 77.
2. Michael Needham, "From Venture Capitalist to Entrepreneur," *Business Quarterly Magazine,* Summer 1995, p. 79.
3. Michael Needham, "From Venture Capitalist to Entrepreneur," *Business Quarterly Magazine,* Summer 1995, p. 81.

Extreme Packet Devices (A)

Prepared by Adrian Ryans

 Version: (A) 2001-07-12

Introduction

In October 1999, Bruce Gregory, the recently appointed president and chief executive officer (CEO) of Extreme Packet Devices (Extreme), was reviewing the business plan the company had just completed. Gregory viewed this plan as a critical document, since it would guide the company's actions over the coming months and would be the key document as Extreme raised additional funds. Gregory wanted the plan to be ambitious and have a clear vision so that it would capture the imagination of employees, customers and financial supporters, while at the same time providing a disciplined road map for the organization and benchmarks for the venture capitalists funding the company.

The Founding of Extreme Packet Devices

Mark Janoska, Albert Heller and Henry Chow, three engineers from Newbridge Networks, and Mark Waite, from Toshiba America Electronic Components, had founded Extreme in late March 1999. Janoska, Heller and Chow had worked in the next-generation switch group at Newbridge, a large Canadian supplier of telecommunications equipment. All three men had resigned from Newbridge in February 1999. The founders recognized that many large technology-based companies were increasingly acquiring technology from external suppliers, rather that relying on internal research and development groups. This helped the large companies respond to increasing time-to-market pressures. The group thought that the technology area they were working in at Newbridge might represent an area where some companies would be willing to buy solutions from an external supplier. At the time that they resigned from Newbridge, they had not selected the specific opportunity they would pursue.

Once the trio's departure from Newbridge had been confirmed, Terry Matthews, the founder and chairman of Newbridge Networks, decided to back them. He put the founders in touch with Tom Valis, a partner at Celtic House International, Matthews' personal venture capital firm. Debbie Weinstein, an Ottawa lawyer, introduced them to Dave Furneaux, a partner in Furneaux & Company, a Massachusetts-based venture capital firm.

By May 1999, the founders had been successful in raising Cdn$3 million[1] of seed funding from the two venture capital firms and from some individual investors. With Matthews' connections, the fledgling company was able to lease space in Kanata Research Park in the Ottawa, Canada, area (there was a severe shortage of high-quality office space in the area in 1999), and Extreme moved from Albert Heller's basement to the new space in June 1999.

The Opportunity

In the late 1990s, the global telecommunications industry was experiencing tremendous growth as a result of the bandwidth explosion (about 200 per cent per year) that had been created by the growth of e-commerce, Internet services, entertainment and the deregulation of the industry. This growth had brought many new communications carriers into the industry. Almost all the growth in demand was the result of growth in data traffic, rather than in voice traffic. This growth, plus the future anticipated growth, had led to the development of high-capacity, long-haul optical networks for carrying data traffic across continents and oceans. In 1999, the highest capacity "pipes" were OC-192 systems, which were able to carry 10 billion bits (or gigabits) of information per second. The capacity of these pipes could be increased by an approach called Dense Wavelength Division Multiplexing (DWDM), which enabled several virtual channels to be created in one optical fibre by using slightly different colors (or wavelengths of light). Thus, a forty-channel OC-192 had the capacity to carry 400 gigabits of information per second. One forty-channel OC-192 system had sufficient capacity to allow about 10 million people to make simultaneous telephone calls; all the signals were carried over a single strand of optical fibre. Nortel Networks, a telecommunication equipment manufacturer based in Canada, was the global leader in the OC-192 market.

As more and more traffic was being sent over the telecommunications infrastructure, massive traffic management problems were created for the switches that managed the data in the network. Often, thousands of lower speed links were aggregated onto one high-speed link, such as an OC-192. Next generation switches, which would be in the terabit per second class,[2] were close to being deployed, and would have 10 gigabit per second ports. Different data streams had different priorities called Quality of Service. The ports to the high-speed link had to do a number of things, including making sure that the highest priority traffic got fast access to the link, while lower-priority traffic was held for fractions of a second in a buffer before being sent onto the high-speed link. As the amount of traffic coming into these ports increased, the design of the traffic management system became extremely complex and required very complex, application-specific, integrated circuits (ASICs) that typically took a team of 10 to 15 engineers 18 to 24 months to develop. By March 1999, the founders had decided that this was the initial market opportunity that Extreme Packet Devices would pursue.

The Recruiting of the CEO

In their early discussions, the venture capitalists encouraged the founders to think about hiring an executive with complementary skills, who could become Extreme's CEO. While the founders were not totally convinced that they needed to hire a CEO, a search did begin for potential candidates after Extreme received its seed funding. Valis and Furneaux played a lead role in identifying potential candidates. In mid-May, Furneaux approached Bruce Gregory, the vice-president, of technology of Cadabra Design Automation, an electronic design automation software company that had been founded in Ottawa. Gregory was responsible for Cadabra's research and development, technology definition, customer support and design services. Prior to that, Gregory had worked as an engineer in hardware design.

Gregory met with both Valis and Furneaux and with the founders. He believed that he could work very effectively with all of them, but he recognized that the founders were not really convinced that they needed an external CEO. Gregory also knew that in a sense, he would be "taking the company away from the founders." In order to demonstrate that he could add real value, Gregory proposed that he lead a strategy session for the founders, and Valis and Furneaux. During the June strategy session, they identified seven critical activities that they had to complete in 1999, if Extreme were to be successful. These activities were:

- Raise $10 million;
- Generate "buzz" about Extreme;
- Secure two early access partners (EAPs), who could work with Extreme to help it refine its product;
- Secure a manufacturing agreement. Since Extreme Packet Devices was going to be a "fabless" semiconductor company, it would have to find a partner who could make these very complex devices;
- Hire at least 20 people. This was not a trivial task in an environment where highly skilled engineering talent was in extremely short supply;
- Secure five design wins with customers. This would be a challenging sales and marketing task. Extreme would have to identify potential customers and identify the decision-maker(s) in a large company who would be in a position to decide to outsource the development of these chips to a third party. In a large, complex company such as Nortel Networks it would be difficult to identify the key decision-makers, sell them on outsourcing and sell them on Extreme, a start-up, as the company to develop the chips;
- Complete four one-million gate, application-specific, integrated circuits (ASICs). This was an extremely challenging engineering task with a minimum design cycle of 14 to 18 months.

Gregory then asked each of the founders to check off which tasks they were working on, or planning to work on over the next six months. At the end of the exercise, it became clear to everyone at the meeting that all of the founders were planning to be involved in most of the activities, but the task that was least likely to get the necessary attention was the development of the four ASICs. Clearly, if this did not get the focused attention of the founders, Extreme would fail.

After this exercise, the founders realized that Gregory could play the key leadership role and take primary responsibility for several of the activities, freeing up the founders to focus much of their attention on building the engineering team and designing the ASICs. Gregory officially joined the company as Employee Number 11 on July 5, 1999.

Early Moves

Development of the Business Plan

Prior to Gregory's arrival at Extreme, there had been a significant amount of customer contact. Much of this contact had been of a promotional nature and there had been little progress in terms of identifying and closing an early access partnership. The management at Extreme felt that an ideal time to engage these critical customers was when about 80 per cent of the ASIC architecture was in place. The final 20 per cent of the design could be responsive to the issues and design needs of the customer.

Extreme had initially decided to target established Tier 1 suppliers,[3] even though this meant dealing with large, complex organizations, where a substantial amount of time could be spent just understanding the decision-making structure and its key players. Shortly after joining Extreme, Gregory began visiting potential customers, often accompanied by Janoska, Extreme's chief technology officer. On these early calls it became clear to Gregory that, while many of the key elements of Extreme's business strategy were in place, all the elements of the plan did not hang together as well as he would like. This made it difficult for him to articulate a clear vision of where Extreme was heading. Therefore, in August, he decided to give high priority to developing a formal business plan that could be used both internally and externally as he tried to attract EAPs and customers, and as he prepared to seek additional funding from the venture capital community in the late fall.

Gregory, Heller, Janoska, and Shail Paliwal, the new director of finance, were all involved in the development of the plan. Gregory took prime responsibility for developing the plan, but the other three provided critical input to its development. The market data used in the plan was developed from a variety of often-conflicting information sources, but it also reflected the judgment of the Extreme management team. The plan went through several drafts, and was essentially complete in October 1999. The October version of the business plan is included in Exhibit 1. Gregory planned to update the plan periodically to reflect new developments and iterations in the Extreme strategy.

"Framer" Opportunity

On June 29, 1999, Cisco Systems, one of the largest telecommunications equipment manufacturers, announced that it was acquiring StratumOne Communications Inc. in a deal valued at US$435 million. StratumOne was developing chips for the framer layer in line cards in 10 gigabit per second ports. This was an opportunity very close to the traffic management one that Extreme was pursuing. Cisco announced that it planned to use StratumOne's technology exclusively in-house and would not sell it to other telecommunications equipment manufacturers. This meant that other manufacturers that had planned to use the StratumOne solution were now scrambling for a new source for these semiconductors.

One of the early decisions that faced Gregory was whether Extreme should pursue this second opportunity. Superficially, it looked quite attractive: there was a clear opportunity in the market since a number of companies had been counting on the StratumOne solution, and it would be easier and faster for the Extreme engineering team to develop these ASICs than the traffic management ones. Extreme management felt that they could bring a product to market in less than one year.

(Text continues on page 171)

Business Plan

Extreme Packet Devices Inc.
309 Legget Drive, Suite 204
Kanata, Ontario
K2K 3A3
Canada
Tel: 613.599.6088
Fax: 613.599.6081
www.extremepacket.com

NOTE: This business plan contains disguised data and parts of the plan have been omitted from this case exhibit.

Business Plan

Table of Contents

1 **EXECUTIVE SUMMARY** **3**

2 **THE OPPORTUNITY** **5**

3 **EXTREME PACKET DEVICES PRODUCT PORTFOLIO** **7**

3.1 OVERVIEW OF PRODUCT SPACE 7
3.2 TRAFFIC MANAGEMENT DEVICES 9
3.2.1 OC-192c Traffic Management Data Path Element .... Not included
3.2.2 OC-192c Traffic Management Buffer Manager Element .... Not included
3.2.3 OC-192c Traffic Management Scheduler Element .... Not included

4 **MARKETING PLAN** **10**

4.1 POTENTIAL CUSTOMERS 10
4.2 ESTIMATED MARKET FOR TRAFFIC MANAGEMENT DEVICES 11
4.3 MARKETING STRATEGY 11
4.4 MARKETING MILESTONES 12
4.5 PRODUCT PRICING 12
4.6 SALES FORECAST 13

5 **COMPETITIVE ANALYSIS** **14**

5.1 OEM VS. MERCHANT SILICON 14

6 **THE EXTREME TEAM** **15**

6.1 MANAGEMENT
15
6.2 ORGANIZATION CHART 18

7 **FINANCIAL DATA** .... **NOT INCLUDED**

7.1 FINANCIAL HISTORY .... NOT INCLUDED
7.2 EXPANSION REQUIREMENTS AND BUDGETS .... NOT INCLUDED
7.3 FINANCIAL PROJECTIONS .... NOT INCLUDED
7.4 REVENUE AND GROSS MARGINS .... NOT INCLUDED
7.5 CORPORATE CAPITALIZATION .... NOT INCLUDED
7.6 STAFFING PROFILE .... NOT INCLUDED

8 **APPENDICES** .... **NOT INCLUDED**

8.1 INCOME STATEMENT AS AT SEPTEMBER 30, 1999 .... NOT INCLUDED
8.2 PRO FORMA CASH FLOW STATEMENTS .... NOT INCLUDED
8.3 PRO FORMA INCOME STATEMENTS .... NOT INCLUDED
8.4 PRO FORMA BALANCE SHEETS .... NOT INCLUDED
8.5 PRO FORMA REVENUE & GROSS MARGIN PROJECTIONS .... NOT INCLUDED
8.6 CORPORATE CAPITALIZATION .... NOT INCLUDED
8.7 STAFFING PROFILE .... NOT INCLUDED

Exhibit 1 Business Plan *(Continued)*

1 Executive Summary

Extreme Packet Devices Inc. (Extreme) is a fabless semiconductor company focused on delivering high speed communications devices.

Extreme operates as a system-on-a-chip supplier to the OC-48/OC-192 Multi-protocol switch/router equipment market. Extreme's products will perform IP and ATM traffic management and packet processing functions in Carrier-Class, Edge, and Access Routers and Switches ("switches"). Extreme's devices will enable the next generation line cards for terabit switches to meet speed, capacity and price targets at the leading edge of the market window.

The initial product is focused on Traffic Management and Extreme is delivering a chipset that provides Quality of Service for IP and ATM networks based on the next generation of switch fabrics with 10 Gb/s ports from companies such as IBM, Abrizio (PMC-Sierra), Growth Networks and Power-X. The need for Traffic Management is driven by the need to create multi-service switches that can transport integrated delay sensitive and demand traffic. The need for a 10Gbps traffic management solution is driven by both the immediate desire to create large switches, and the future desire to be able to support OC-192c transmission links.

Extreme will follow the initial offering with a solution to address the Packet Processing and Classification functions that combine with Traffic Management to form the heart of the line card. The market for Extreme's devices is projected to grow from $1.5M in 2000 to over $35M in 2002 as the number of 10Gb/s switch ports deployed ramps from field trials in 2000 to widespread deployment in 2002.

Extreme was formed out of the core System Architecture group at Newbridge Networks that was responsible for architecting Newbridge's next generation of high speed switches. This core group has been augmented with highly skilled design, verification and management talent from companies such as Newbridge, Nortel, Toshiba, Mitel and LSI Logic.

Extreme is addressing a specific customer group that is facing enormous time to market pressures on the next generation of switches and routers. The trend to outsourcing in this market is clear, over the last five years the communications IC market has grown from about US$100M to over US$8B in annual revenue. Extreme is focused on the next logical step for outsourcing by leading communications OEMs as they get ready for wide spread deployment of OC-192C capable equipment.

Extreme Packet Devices Inc. is the only independent semiconductor company with announced plans to deliver a solution in this space in the next year. Extreme is a company driven by partnerships, at both the OEM level, partnering on their next generation products, and at the supplier level forming strategic alliances with other vendors to ensure interoperability between devices on the line card.

Extreme's product development is well in hand, with 35 employees, 30 of which are directly developing the chips. Extreme is backed by a stable and committed investor

Exhibit 1 Business Plan *(Continued)*

Business Plan

group that has experience in growing early stage companies such as Intel, Compaq, Newbridge, Cambrian and Skystone. With plans to grow the company to 52 people by year end, and startup funding of CDN$3M fuelling the early growth of the company, Extreme is in the process of securing a second round financing of CDN$12M to complete product development and take the company to early revenue generation.

Exhibit 1 Business Plan *(Continued)*

2 The Opportunity

Rapid expansion of the Internet, primarily driven by e-commerce applications, has placed enormous strain on existing infrastructure. As more and more traffic is forced onto the Internet, the raw bandwidth of the underlying switches is being forced to expand in order of magnitude increments. The next generation of switches will be in the terabit/second class and the distinguishing feature will be the port speed of the switch fabric - capable of handling OC-192C, and commonly referred to as 10Gb/s ports. As this bandwidth is deployed, and thousands of lower speed links are aggregated onto one high speed link, Quality of Service (QoS) is critical to the successful deployment of the network.

The Carrier-class SONET/SDH-based IP Router/Switch Equipment market is dominated by less than ten major Global companies, as is the SONET/SDH-based ATM Switching market.

Carrier-class SONET/SDH-based IP Router/Switch Market US$5B 1999

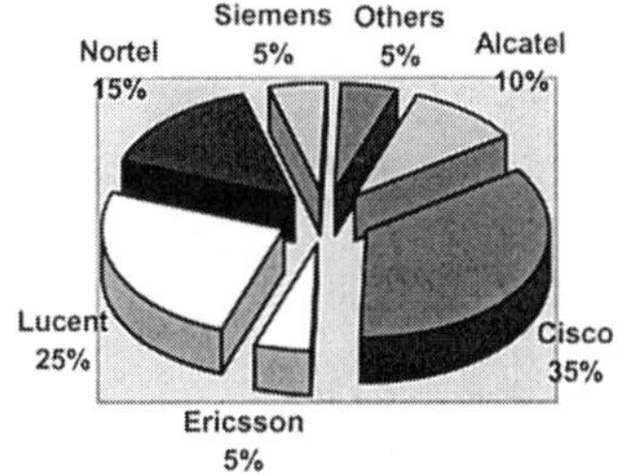

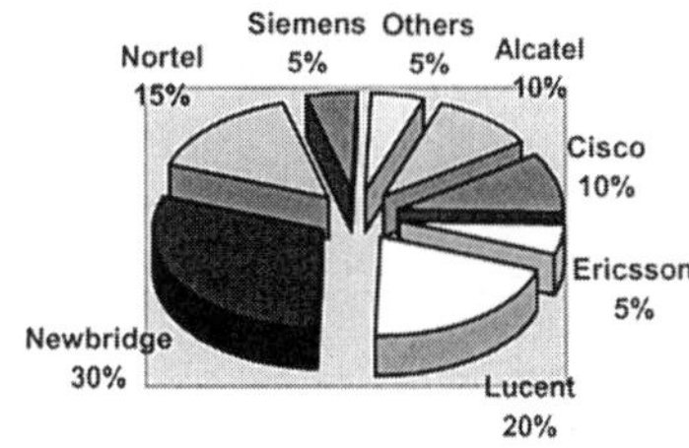

The list of companies racing to deploy these 10Gb/s ports is of very high quality, led by names such as Cisco, Lucent, Nortel, Ericsson, Newbridge, Siemens and Alcatel. The Carrier Class IP switch/router and ATM switch market was $9B in 1998, with a third of that being OC-48/OC-192. The market for terabit switches alone is expected to grow to $11B in 2002, representing a silicon market opportunity for Extreme of over US$35M in 2002.

At the same time, OEMs are faced with a monumental task in bringing these switches to market. Complexity of design, scarce design resources, high internal cost of development and tight deadlines are driving the OEMs to look for merchant silicon solutions wherever possible. A typical System Level ASIC takes 18-24 months to develop, with a team of 10-15 engineers, so it is critical that OEMs deploy their valuable engineering talent in the right areas.

Exhibit 1 Business Plan *(Continued)*

Extreme Packet Devices has identified the Traffic Management function as being well positioned for outsourcing, as the required functionality is well understood, but the device complexity and core algorithms require a large investment in order to bring the chips to completion. By focusing initially on the TM functionality, Extreme enables OEMs to focus on areas such as Packet Processing and Classification that are not clearly defined. As these areas become standardized, Extreme will become active in designing Packet Processing and Classification devices, but the initial focus is squarely on Traffic Management.

The initial deployment of Extreme's TM chipset is being timed to coincide with the early field trials of terabit switches from the Tier 1 OEMs. By locking up the early sockets, Extreme will be ensuring a stable customer base that will drive future growth.

Exhibit 1 Business Plan *(Continued)*

3 Extreme Packet Devices Product Portfolio

3.1 Overview of Product space

The primary focus of Extreme lies within the line cards used in the creation of telecommunication switches. This section will familiarize the reader with the domain that Extreme intends to target with its product roadmap. The overview begins with the description of a generic switch as illustrated by Figure 3-1.

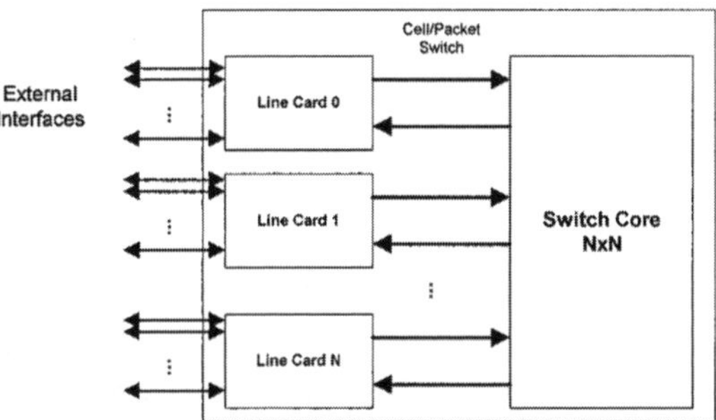

Figure 3-1: Generic Switch Model

In general, this consists of line cards and a switch core (the control plane of the switch is ignored for this discussion). The function of the line card is to terminate external line interfaces, such as ATM/SONET, Packet/SONET or Packet/Gigabit Ethernet; perform cell/packet level processing, such as congestion management and scheduling; and to transmit the cells/packets to the switch core. The function of the switch core is to route the cells or packets to one or more of the output ports. This is achieved via a routing tag within the cell/packet header, or via a request/grant mechanism between the line cards and an arbiter on the switch core.

Exhibit 1 Business Plan *(Continued)*

The generic structure of the line card is illustrated by Figure 3-2.

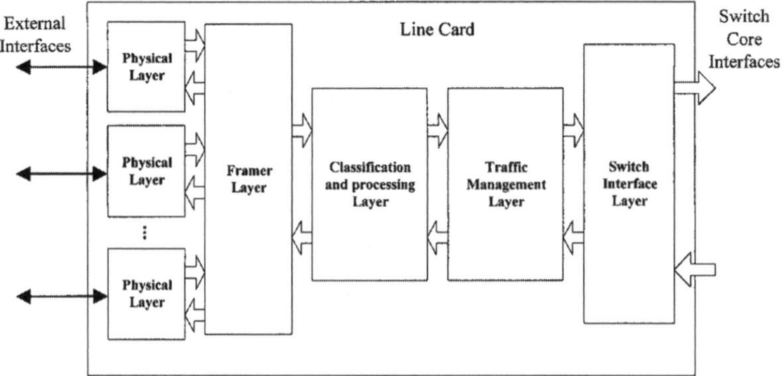

Figure 3-2: Line Card Model

This consists of a physical layer, a framer layer, a cell/packet classification and processing layer, a traffic management layer and a switch interface layer.

The physical layer terminates the external optical or electrical signals, performs clock recovery/generation and serial-parallel conversion functions. Examples are long reach optical fiber or twisted pair electrical transmission media.

The framer layer receives/transmits parallel information from/to the physical layer. Its primary function is to process overhead channels and delineate frames of information. Examples are SONET carrying either ATM cells or Packets, and Gigabit Ethernet carrying Packets.

The classification layer receives/transmits cells or packets from/to the framer. Its primary function is to determine how cells or packets should be handled within the switch. Typically this involves association of the cell or packet with a connection or flow and the addition of a connection/flow identifier to the cell or packet. Examples are ATM, where the classification is based on the VCI/VPI of the cell header, and IP, where the classification is based on the source/destination address. In addition to classification, this layer is also used to perform encapsulation manipulations on packet flows. In general, this involves increasing or decreasing the size of the packet.

The Traffic Management layer receives/transmits cells or packets from the classification layer. This layer determines how cells or packets should be buffered, how to perform intelligent discard during times of congestion, and how to schedule the cells or packets for transmission to the switch core and the external lines. Examples of buffer management and scheduling models are the ATM Forum service classes (CBR, VBR, ABR and UBR), and the differentiated services model being proposed by the IETF.

Exhibit 1 Business Plan *(Continued)*

The switch interface layer is used to interconnect the traffic management device with the switch core. This provides functions such as termination of backpressure information from the switch core, and the addition of switch routing tags.

3.2 Traffic Management Devices

Figure 3-3 illustrates the first chipset being offered by Extreme, which provides a traffic management solution for the development of 10Gbps line cards for high capacity switches.

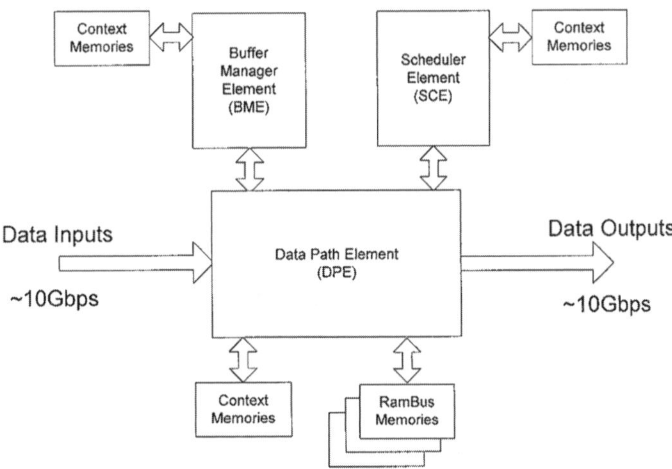

Figure 3-3: 10Gbps Traffic Management Chipset

This consists of three chips, the Data Path Element (DPE), the Buffer Manager Element (BME) and the Scheduler Element (SCE). These chips, along with their external memory sub-systems provide a unidirectional 10Gbps traffic management solution that can be used by a switch manufacturer to create high capacity switches with 10Gbps line cards having external interfaces ranging from OC-12 to OC-192.

The need for traffic management is driven by the need to create multi-service switches that can transport integrated delay sensitive and demand traffic. The need for a 10Gbps traffic management solution is driven by both the immediate desire to create large switches, and the future desire to be able to support OC-192c transmission links.

[Several pages, which described in detail Extreme's proposed technical solution, have been omitted from this exhibit]

Exhibit 1 Business Plan *(Continued)*

4 Marketing Plan

4.1 Potential Customers

The customer base for Extreme's products is comprised of systems manufacturers engaged in supplying equipment for the switching or routing of high speed data networks. The distinction between telecom and datacom is blurring as network reliability issues that are driven by telecom applications are being solved in datacom equipment. For the purposes of this plan, the customers can be segmented into Tier 1 and Tier 2 customers, where Tier 1 customers have a significant revenue stream and Tier 2 is largely comprised of startup companies.

Extreme will focus primarily on the mature vendors in order to maximize the potential return on any design win. A partial list of vendors is included below.

Customer Company	Product In Development with 10G ports
TIER 1	
Alcatel	High Speed Switch Router
Cisco Systems EWAN – San Jose	Multiple High Speed Switch Router Products
Ericsson – Silver Springs, MD	High Speed Switch Router
GEC/Fore Systems – Warrendale, PA	High Speed Switch Router
Juniper Networks – Mountain View, CA	High Speed Switch Router
Lucent Technologies	Multiple High Speed Switch Router Products
Newbridge Networks – Kanata, ON	Terabit Switch
Nortel Networks	Multiple High Speed Switch Router Products
Siemens Unisphere – Burlington, MA	Multiple High Speed Switch Router Products
Tellabs – Chicago, IL	Multiple High Speed Switch Router Products
TIER 2	
Avici	Terabit Switch Router
Crescent Networks	High Speed Switch Router
Charlotte's Web	Terabit Router
Equipe Communications Inc.	Multiple High Speed Switch Router
Foundry Networks	High Speed Switch Router
Ironbridge Networks	High Speed Switch Router
Pluris	Terabit Network Router
Tenor Networks	High Speed Switch Router

Exhibit 1 Business Plan *(Continued)*

4.2 Estimated Market for Traffic Management Devices

The market size estimate for Extreme's TM chipset is based on an estimate of the number of 10Gb/s switch ports that will be deployed over the next three years. Data was collected from Dataquest, IDC, RHK and industry sources in order to build up a profile from 2000 through 2002. The data shows the number of 10Gb/s ports growing from 200 in 2000 to almost 7,000 in 2002. The revenue generated by the equipment vendors is estimated to be US$11B in 2002 and the revenue for TM silicon is estimated at US$35M in 2002.

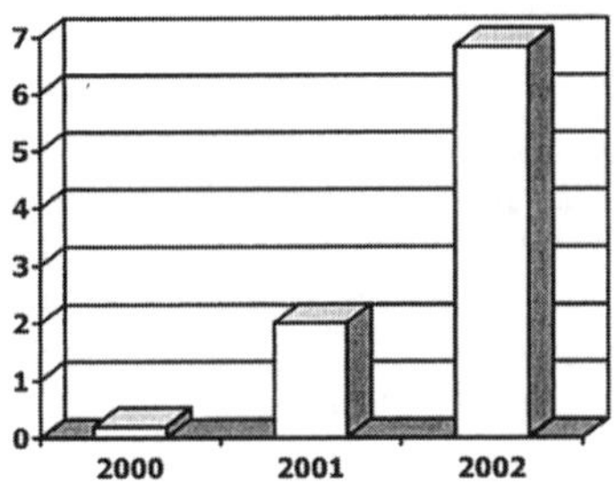

□10Gb/s Ports - Units Shipped (000s)

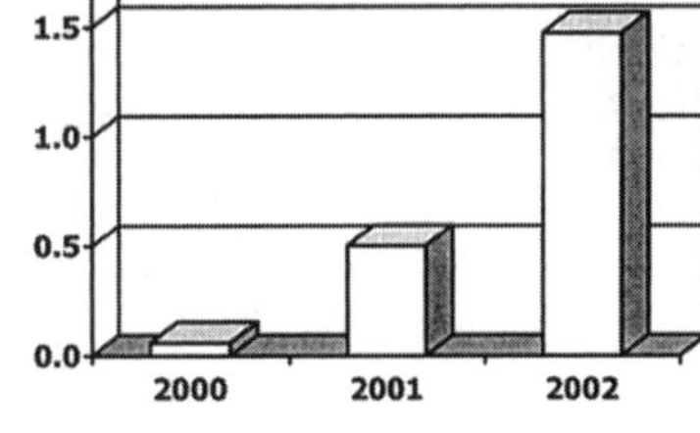

□10Gb/s Ports - Revenue $B

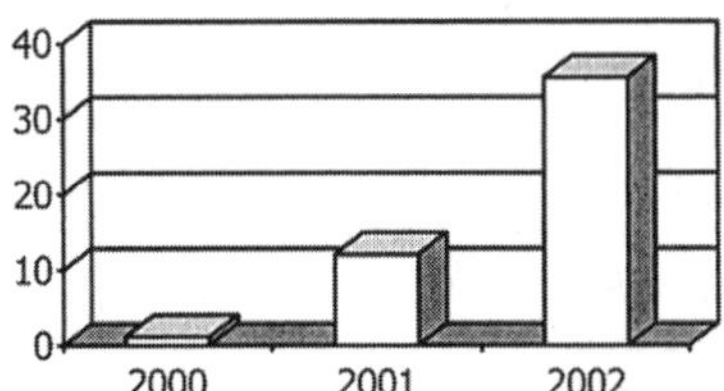

□TM Silicon Market for 10Gb/s Ports $M

4.3 Marketing Strategy

The Traffic Management solution being delivered by Extreme is a complex, high end solution and sales will be accomplished through direct contact with our target customers. Our marketing strategy will emphasize the marriage of system and silicon expertise that has been brought to bear on a difficult problem. The focus will be on time to market and how the Extreme solution will enable an OEM to bring a fully featured product to market faster and with less risk than with an internally developed solution. To this end, Extreme

Exhibit 1 Business Plan *(Continued)*

will invest the time necessary for customers to convince themselves of the technical merits and feasibility of the Extreme solution. This is accomplished through a combination of offsite reviews at customer offices and onsite technical due diligence where customers are allowed to review Extreme's design documentation and have discussions with the development team.

Extreme is in the process of forming strategic alliances with other silicon vendors that supply critical components on the line card or in the switch core, companies such as Intel, PMC-Sierra and AMCC. As these joint development and joint marketing agreements are signed, we will leverage the combined solution as a system level sale with the partners providing all the major silicon blocks required, freeing up the OEM to concentrate on product differentiation through software and firmware.

Finally, Extreme will engage in Early Access Partnerships (EAP) with key customers in order to provide access to the early design specifications and to keep the EAP customers focused on the Extreme solution. Executing on the EAP strategy is key to locking up the early design wins that will provide a strong base for future revenue growth.

For all customers our approach will be based on the fact that we are the only merchant silicon vendor providing a solution for Traffic Management at 10Gb/s.

4.4 Marketing Milestones

We have held discussions under non-disclosure with all the major OEMs in North America. The basic technology has been validated, and we are now focused on securing the first two Early Access Partners. It is expected that Extreme will secure two design wins before the end of the calendar year.

We have also held detailed discussions with two complimentary silicon vendors, one operating in the switching fabric space, the other providing framers and network processors, and have reached agreement in principle to proceed with joint development of the interfaces. The two companies in question were recently merged into one enterprise (through an acquistion) and we expect to be able to announce the agreements in the near future.

4.5 Product Pricing

Product pricing is based on a value model of an OC-192 line card. It is the intention of Extreme to maintain a 60% gross margin. The only manufacturer that has announced an OC-192 line card is Nexabit (now part of Lucent) at US$225K per port. Table 4-1 ***[not included in this case exhibit]*** shows the average price of a 10Gb/s port based on product available today. It is key to note that we have decoupled the line rate from the port speed. As the high speed switch fabrics are deployed, the need to terminate OC-12 and OC-48 will not diminish for a number of years, but rather it will be necessary to aggregate multiple lines onto a single line card feeding a 10Gb/s switch port. Hence our definition of a 10Gb/s port is 16 X OC-12, 4 X OC-48 or 1 X OC-192. This places one 10 Gb/s port at an average sales value of $375,000 today. The anticipation is that the price per 10G port will decline over time to an average of $150,000 to $170,000 in 2002.

Exhibit 1 Business Plan *(Continued)*

Using industry standard components for all functions except Traffic Management, the total cost for a line card including Extreme silicon is estimated at US$70,000 today. As can be seen from Table 4-2 ***[not included in this case exhibit]***, the target price for the three-chip Extreme TM solution is US$3000 in the year 2000. This is in line with the percentage of cost allocated to TM for a typical line card in the OC-12 or OC-48 market place.

4.6 Sales Forecast

Forecast sales figures are summarized in Figure 4-1. A volume ramp that follows the market model used to determine the total available market was used, with the following assumptions: of the total market available, it is assumed that 50% will go with OEM internally developed solutions. Of the remaining market, we are assuming that our leadership position will allow us to capture a minimum 40% market share. This leads to revenues in 2002 of US$7.4M.

Figure 4.1 Three Year Sales Forecast (US$M) by Quarter

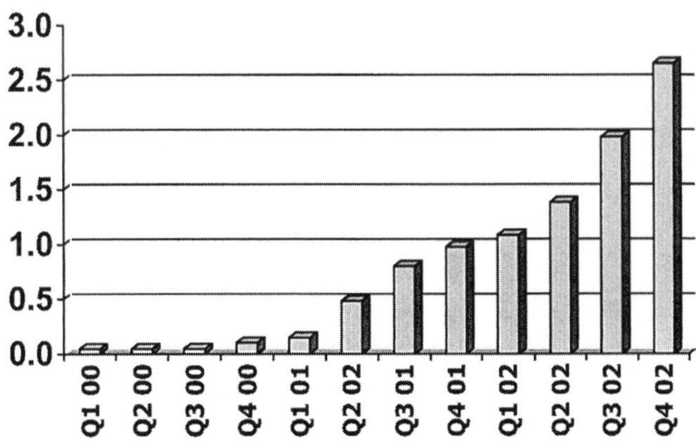

Revenue Profile Calendar 2000-2002

Q1/00	Q2/00	Q3/00	Q4/00	Q1/01	Q2/01	Q3/01	Q4/01	Q1/02	Q2/02	Q3/02	Q4/02
$46K	$46K	$46K	$102K	$147K	$482K	$804K	$978K	$1.1M	$1.4M	$2.0M	$2.7M

All Figures US$

Exhibit 1 Business Plan *(Continued)*

5 Competitive Analysis

5.1 OEM vs. Merchant Silicon

To the best of Extreme's knowledge, there are no other companies currently offering a merchant silicon solution for 10Gb/s Traffic Management. While competition is expected, it is our feeling that the system expertise at Extreme, combined with the early start in developing the technology will make it very difficult for a late starter to make serious inroads in the market. Of the potential competitors, we believe that companies active in the network processor market will emerge as competitors in the traffic management space. However, all of the known network processor companies, including Intel and IBM, have announced plans for OC-48 wire speed devices and are currently occupied by ongoing development. It has been made clear to us by the customer base that there is an architectural schism between OC-48 and OC-192, and a clean sheet design is required. Products based on multiple RISC processors will not be able to scale in performance to 10Gb/s, again providing Extreme with a lead in the market.

The true competition will come from the ASIC design groups within the OEMs. Traditionally system companies have considered complex functions such as TM to be proprietary value added functions. As such, they were wary of outsourcing the development of such a key component. However, over the last three to five years, the trend to outsourcing has been driven by the need to get ever more complex systems to market under continuously shrinking design cycles. The battle within the OEM is no longer one of convincing them to outsource, but rather one of establishing credibility and offering concrete plans to mitigate the risk introduced by using an outside source.

Exhibit 1 Business Plan *(Continued)*

6 The Extreme Team

Extreme has brought together a talented team of individuals with complimentary business and technical skills, and proven track records in developing early stage companies and delivering complex System Level Integrated Circuits

6.1 Management

Bruce Gregory, President and CEO

Bruce Gregory is President and CEO of Extreme Packet Devices Inc. In this capacity, he is responsible for leading the senior management team in the development and execution of the company's strategic plan.

Mr. Gregory joins Extreme Packet Devices from Cadabra Design Automation, a successful electronic design automation software company founded in Ottawa and currently headquartered in Santa Clara, California. During his three years at Cadabra, Gregory held the position of Vice President, Technology and helped grow the company from 8 employees to 70 as it expanded to service a global customer base. Gregory was responsible for Cadabra's research and development, technology definition, customer support and design services.

Prior to Cadabra, Gregory held positions at LSI Logic Corporation as Director of ASIC Engineering and at Newbridge Microsystems as a hardware design engineer. Gregory holds a Bachelor of Engineering degree from Carleton University.

John Langevin, Vice President, Marketing

John Langevin has more than 16 years of experience in sales, marketing and business development with high technology companies. He joins Extreme Packet Devices from Cimaron Communications Corp., a successful startup company that was engaged in the design and development of SONET/SDH framing integrated circuits. As Director of Business Development, he was responsible for developing new business, marketing, establishing and maintaining strategic relationships, and strategic planning. Cimaron was acquired by Applied Micro Circuits Corporation in March 1999.

Prior to Cimaron, Mr. Langevin was at Aware, Inc. Aware is a developer of digital subscriber line (xDSL) technology. During his four years at Aware, Mr. Langevin was Director of OEM Business and Marketing Manager for Telecommunications. Aware had a successful IPO in August 1996.

Mr. Langevin worked at M/A-COM from 1983 to 1994, where he had positions of Program Manager, Director of Marketing, Area Sales Manager, and Sales Engineer.

Mr. Langevin has a Masters degree in Business Administration from Boston University, and a Bachelor of Science degree in Computer Engineering from Lehigh University.

Exhibit 1 Business Plan *(Continued)*

Dr. Mark Janoska, P. Eng., Chief Technology Officer

Mark Janoska is co-founder and Chief Technology Officer for Extreme Packet Devices Inc. In this role he is responsible for guiding the company's technology innovation.

Dr. Janoska joins Extreme Packet from Newbridge Networks, where he was responsible for device and full switch architecture design of next generation high capacity switches, ATM and IP traffic management and packet processing ASICs. Prior to that, he was with Westinghouse where he worked on the software development of X.25 packet switches and digital signal processing for sonar systems in submarine applications.

Dr. Janoska holds a Bachelor of Engineering and a Ph.D. in Electrical Engineering from McMaster University and is a licensed Professional Engineer.

Albert Heller, Vice President, Research and Development

Albert Heller is co-founder and Vice President of Research and Development for Extreme Packet Devices Inc. In this capacity, he is responsible for overseeing the company's product development and technical direction.

Mr. Heller is an electrical engineer who brings over eight years of design and project management experience to Extreme Packet. Most recently he held leadership engineering positions with Newbridge Networks where he was responsible for designing and developing device-level and system-level next generation network switches. He is credited with architecting and developing one of the first high complexity, high density embedded DRAM ASIC devices for high capacity ATM switch fabrics.

Prior to joining Newbridge, Mr. Heller was a design engineer with Unisys Canada. He holds a Bachelor of Science in Electrical Engineering from the University of Manitoba.

Henry Chow, Chief Architect

Henry Chow is a founding member of Extreme Packet Devices Inc. and is Chief Architect for the company. He is responsible for overseeing the design of the company's core traffic management devices.

Mr. Chow has over 17 years of design and management-level experience developing TDM and ATM switching systems and high complexity ASICs. Most recently, he was with Newbridge Networks, where he held Senior Design, Engineering Management and Technical Planning positions. In these roles, he was responsible for architecting and developing high capacity ATM and IP switching systems.

Prior to joining Newbridge, Mr. Chow was a designer with Mobile Data International (MDI) and Mitel. He holds a Bachelor of Science in Electrical Engineering from the University of Saskatchewan, Saskatoon.

Exhibit 1 Business Plan *(Continued)*

Shail Paliwal CA, Director of Finance

Shail Paliwal is the Director of Finance for Extreme Packet Devices Inc. In this role he is responsible for managing the company's financial systems.

Mr. Paliwal is a Chartered Accountant with ten years experience working primarily in the technology sector. Prior to joining Extreme Packet, Mr. Paliwal was the Vice President, Operations and Chief Financial Officer at the Ottawa Centre for Research & Innovation (OCRI). While at OCRI, Mr. Paliwal was an integral part of the executive management team, providing significant input into the development of both long-term strategic plans and the formulation of corporate objectives. At an operational level, Mr. Paliwal formulated organization wide internal operating policies and assumed control of a significant part of the day-to-day operations, including human resource issues.

Prior to his position at OCRI, Mr. Paliwal was Vice President, Finance & Administration with a small group of private entrepreneurs.

Exhibit 1 Business Plan *(Continued)*

Business Plan

6.2 Organization Chart

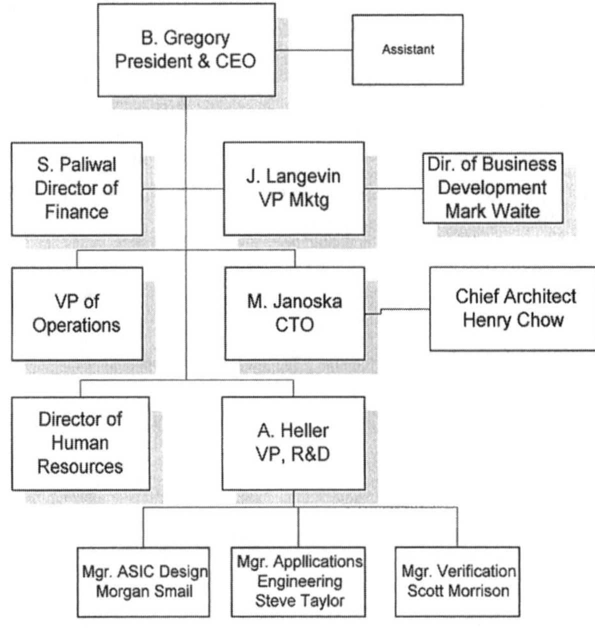

CONFIDENTIAL NDA #_____ Page 18 24/01/01

Exhibit 1 Business Plan

Gregory ended up strongly recommending against pursuing the new opportunity. He argued that they had a strategy and that they should not deviate from it. Extreme didn't know the framer opportunity in enough depth, and it could cause them to lose focus. Since the technology was less complex, Gregory also felt that competition would develop quickly. At a board meeting in August, he recommended that Extreme should stay focused on the traffic management opportunity and that it should not pursue the framer opportunity. Subsequently, it became clear that other companies were actively pursuing the framer opportunity. It would have been a very competitive market.

Building the Infrastructure and Hiring Staff

When Extreme moved into Kanata Research Park, it initially leased 6,000 square feet. While it was still using only a fraction of this space, the company had an opportunity to acquire the rights to lease an additional 6,000 to 7,000 square feet. Knowing how difficult it was to get prime space in the Kanata area, Extreme decided to acquire the extra space for its anticipated growth.

Initially, Extreme had trouble attracting high-quality engineering talent. In August 1999, the company made about 20 offers of employment, but only two of these offers were accepted. The recruiting and selection process was consuming a lot of engineering and management time that could have been better employed elsewhere. Therefore, Janoska and Gregory decided that they would do the final "sales interview" with each of the candidates they wished to hire. Janoska's role was to sell the prospective employee on Extreme's technology and its potential, and Gregory's role was to sell the candidate on the company. When they adopted this approach, the success rate rose dramatically, and by October, the company had 35 employees, 30 of whom were involved in chip development.

A major investment area for companies designing ASICs was electronic design automation tooling for the engineers. One of the major problems in many start-ups was that the engineers often sat around waiting for tools to be available so that they could move ahead with their part of a project. Gregory decided that Extreme would invest heavily to provide Extreme's engineering staff with enough of the best tools available so that tools would not be a constraint on time-to-market. Extreme decided to work closely with Synopsys, a leading California-based designer of high-end electronic design automation tooling. Initially, Extreme spent $1.5 million on licenses, but in October, Gregory went to Extreme's board with a proposal to sign a $4-million agreement over three years with Synopsys. Under this agreement, Synopsys would provide whatever design automation tools Extreme needed at a particular time for 90 engineers. This gave Extreme great flexibility since the types of tools it would require would depend on the stage of the ASIC development process. The Extreme board approved the agreement at an October meeting.

Customer Acquisition

Extreme's initial strategy had been to target on Tier 1 telecommunications equipment manufacturers, such as Lucent, Nortel, Newbridge and Tellabs. However, these companies were proving difficult to sell. It was hard to penetrate the organizations to reach the right people, and even when Extreme did find the right people, they were difficult to convince. These organizations had the engineering capability to do the traffic management ASICs themselves, even though Extreme felt it could develop better ASICs in less time. Furthermore, based on events such as Cisco's acquisition of StratumOne, some potential customers were concerned about going with an outside supplier, since this supplier might be acquired by one of their competitors.

As a result of this, Gregory decided to focus more of Extreme's attention on high-potential startups (Tier 2 companies in the Extreme business plan). In August, they were approached by PMC-Sierra, a Vancouver-based company that was a leading manufacturer of high-speed, high-density broadband communications semiconductor architectural solutions. PMC-Sierra was working with a Tier 2 company and needed a traffic management system so that its customer would have a complete solution. It had proposed to this customer that it should consider the Extreme Packet Devices product.

The challenge for Extreme, one that it faced with all potential customers, was to demonstrate that it could develop a real leading edge product that would be available in the promised time frame. In essence, Extreme had to convince potential customers that it was selling more than "foil ware." The approach that Gregory used to deal with this issue was to ask the customer: "What do we have to do to prove it to you?" In the case of PMC-Sierra's customer, the customer decided to send an engineering team to Ottawa for a week to meet Extreme's engineering and management team and to take an in-depth look at its architecture. The team was impressed with what they saw and it began to look like Extreme might have found its first EAP, although no formal agreement had been reached by early October.

On October 4, 1999, John Langevin joined Extreme as vice-president of marketing. Gregory viewed Langevin as a key hire. Prior to joining Extreme, Langevin had been the director of business development at Cimaron Communications Corp., a successful start-up that had developed specialized semiconductors for telecommunications equipment manufacturers. Cimaron had been acquired by another company in March 1999. In his role at Cimaron, Langevin was responsible for developing new business, marketing, establishing and maintaining strategic relationships, and strategic planning. His skill set complemented those of Gregory and the other members of the management team at Extreme. Langevin was based in Boston.

Preparing to Raise $12 Million

When Gregory joined Extreme, the venture capital firm partners had told him that he would not need to spend a lot of time on the securing of finances. The venture capitalists felt that they could look after the financing if Gregory made sure that the other key activities were well under control. However, it soon became clear that while the venture capital partners could get introductions and raise investor interest in Extreme, the CEO had to build the relationship and make the pitch for the funds. As the summer wore on, and the time approached for securing a second round financing of Canadian $12 million, Gregory found that this was taking more and more of his time.

It was clear to Gregory that although progress was being made on many of the critical activities identified in June's planning meeting, the business plan was going to play a big role in securing the next round of financing. As he reviewed the latest draft of the plan in mid-October, Gregory wondered if it successfully addressed the three big questions that venture capital firms and institutional investors would be asking:

- Is there a market?
- Does Extreme have a product to address this market?
- Is Extreme going to win in the market?

Notes

1. The average exchange rate in 1999 was Cdn$1.00 = US$0.67.
2. A terabit is 1,000 gigabits.
3. A list of the Tier 1 companies is included in the Extreme Packet Devices business plan in Exhibit 1.

DIABETOGEN

Prepared by Dave Martin under the supervision of Professor James E. Hatch

Version: (A) 2002-09-23

In early January 2000 Michael Crowley, vice president of Business Development at Robarts Research Institute in London, Ontario, was contemplating the steps he should take in order to raise financing for Diabetogen, a biotech company spun out of Robarts. Commercialization of biotech drugs was a lengthy process in which development costs escalated dramatically as a drug moved closer to market. Moreover, there was a high level of uncertainty surrounding the success of a drug as it passed from testing in animals to the various phases of clinical testing in humans. As a result, the risk, especially for early stage investors, was enormous. Michael was wondering how much Diabetogen was worth, and how ownership should be distributed among the many stakeholders. Finally, with the risk so high, what proportion of the company would have to be given up to the first round investors?

THE BIOPHARMACEUTICAL INDUSTRY

Biotechnology

Because DNA is our genetic "blueprint," it plays a major role in determining who we are. DNA produces an intermediate "message molecule," RNA, which, in turn, produces protein molecules. Proteins perform many of the critical functions in the body: they provide the construction materials for cells, and they also activate the functions of cells. Diseases are often the result of inherited or mutated DNA, a situation that leads to an inability to create essential proteins, or the production of inappropriate proteins that have destructive behavior. Biotechnology researchers focus their efforts on the discovery of DNA, RNA and proteins, looking for those that are associated with disease in the hope that the missing molecules can be replaced or the effects of damaging molecules minimized. Drugs developed from DNA, RNA and proteins are called biopharmaceuticals.

For many inherited diseases, scientists were confident that cures would be developed following completion of the Human Genome Project, a multi-billion dollar global effort to determine the entire sequence of human DNA. By January 2000, only a fraction of the genes responsible for the 4,000 human genetic diseases had been identified, but already biopharmaceuticals had been developed as a result of some of these discoveries. Some of the successful first generation biopharmaceuticals included human insulin, produced by bio-engineered bacteria and sold by Eli Lilly; Activase, produced by Genentech for stroke and heart attack; and Epo, produced by Amgen for treatment of anemia. Biotech innovations that were expected to revolutionize medicine in the near future included vaccines for AIDS, viruses that target and kill only cancer cells leaving normal cells unaffected, and biotechnologies for nerve, organ and tissue regeneration.

Overview of the Industry

The development of biopharmaceuticals held great promise because, while conventional drug treatments often only alleviated symptoms, biopharmaceuticals would act to cure disease. Moreover, because biopharmaceuticals were natural molecules, many of the toxic side effects associated with conventional treatments could be avoided.

The industry was attractive for various business reasons. Patent protection extended to 20 years or longer in most countries, and the complex nature of biopharmaceutical research meant that even when a drug came off patent, it would be extremely difficult to copy. Barriers against entry were high due to the capital and knowledge needed to identify, purify and develop a process to produce commercial quantities of a therapeutic DNA, RNA or protein molecule. Once production was scaled-up, however, it cost relatively little to produce these molecules in high volumes. Gross margins in the industry were, therefore, very high. Furthermore, demographics indicated that as baby-boomers aged, there would be a very high demand for new pharmaceuticals.

Together, these forces had combined to make the biotech sector "very hot." Over the last five months, both Canadian and American biotech stock indices had doubled, and many investors who had ridden the dot.com wave over the last two years were now pouring money into biotechs. Biopharmaceutical companies were also attractive acquisition targets for the conventional pharmaceutical companies who had their origins rooted in the nineteenth century, since many of these firms had major drugs soon coming off patent with nothing in the development pipeline to replace the revenues that would be lost. Only three months earlier, Warner-Lambert had acquired a California-based biotech company called Agouron Pharmaceuticals for US$2.1 billion. Agouron had developed protease inhibitors that were standard components of the AIDS drug cocktail that had extended the lives of AIDS patients significantly.

In early 2000, over 1,300 biopharmaceutical companies already existed in the U.S., and while the technology was lagging in Canada, several major biotech companies had been established in this country. For example, Montreal-based Biochem Pharma discovered and developed the world's leading AIDS and hepatitis drugs based on modification of a DNA component molecule. In December 1998, Biochem Pharma had recorded annual revenues of Cdn$225 million, with a net income of Cdn$114.8 million and the company had a market capitalization of Cdn$4.8 billion (see Exhibit 1 for market information on other biopharmaceutical companies).

Michael knew that in the biotech industry, even before testing in humans, many years and

Company/ Country	*Product(s) Stage*	*Development Share*	*'98 EPS*	*Current Price*	*Market Cap*
Amgen, US	Biopharmaceuticals for cancer, anemia.	FDA approved	$1.02	$66 5/16	$67.74 billion
Biogen, US	Biopharmaceuticals for MS, Lupus.	FDA approved	$1.40	$117 7/8	$17.71 billion
Onyx, US	Viruses to treat cancer.	Phase III	($1.29)	$28 1/16	$324 million
Entremed, US	Biopharmaceuticals for cancer.	Phase I	($1.99)	$62 5/8	$921 million
QLT, Can	Biopharmaceuticals for cancer and blindness.	FDA approved	($0.55)	$94.00	$2.57 billion
Biomira, Can	Vaccines for cancer.	Phase III	($0.65)	$25.00	$1.11 billion
Bioniche, Can	Biopharmaceuticals for vet and human cancer.	Human—Phase III Vet—on the market	($0.01)	$4.00	$99 million

Exhibit 1 Comparative Company Information

possibly millions of dollars would be spent identifying and purifying molecules, testing their activity in the test-tube, then testing toxicity and pharmacological effects in various animal species. Luckily for scientists, this early stage research was often funded by government grants, and took place in university laboratories or hospital-affiliated institutes where fundamental research was funded with the intention of building knowledge, not profit. Michael estimated that approximately $7 million had been spent already bringing Diabetogen's drugs to their current stage of development.

As he sat contemplating the issues surrounding Diabetogen, Michael was aware that since 1988 over 100 biopharmaceuticals had been approved for human use in North America. Furthermore, 350 of the drugs currently under evaluation by the U.S. Food and Drug Administration (FDA) were biopharmaceuticals, and global sales of biopharmaceuticals in 1998 totalled more than US$13 billion—this was expected to reach $24 billion by 2006. While these facts bode well for the biopharmaceutical industry, Michael also knew that only a fraction of the 1,300 biopharmaceutical companies in North America would make it to market with a successful drug. The low probability of success in the development of drugs was largely due to failures during the rigorous clinical trial process, a process in which drugs were tested for safety and their ability to fight disease (efficacy).

The Clinical Trial Process

Before newly discovered drugs could be marketed to humans they had to enter a rigorous testing and approval process that was instituted in countries around the world. In the U.S., clinical testing and approval of drugs for human use were administered by the FDA, whereas in Canada, the Health Protection Branch (HPB) handled this responsibility (Exhibit 2 describes the phases of human clinical testing that drugs must pass through prior to receiving approval). As mentioned earlier, many drugs failed at various times during the testing and approval process, as most drugs that showed promising results in the laboratory setting eventually proved to be unsafe or not effective in humans.

Human clinical trials could take 10 years and required many millions of dollars since it could take hundreds or even thousands of patient tests to generate statistically significant results. Usually, money at the earlier stages of human testing would come from venture capital firms and, for these early-stage investors, the rigorous clinical trial process meant that there were extremely steep odds against a drug making it to market. Michael had access to statistics from the U.S. FDA and the Canadian Health Protection Branch indicating the average success rate of drugs at each stage of testing. These rates are indicated in Table 1.

Michael drew a diagram that included these probabilities and he included risks that were associated with each stage (Exhibit 3). He felt that his diagram would help in his valuation of Diabetogen. Further, he believed that, if he could show first-round investors that many of the risks traditionally associated with early-stage biotech companies had been reduced or mitigated in Diabetogen, the company would warrant a higher-than-normal valuation.

Despite the low odds of success, drugs that eventually gained approval and were used in the treatment of major illnesses yielded multi-billion dollar businesses: the market capitalizations of Amgen and Genentech, two U.S. biotech pioneers, exceeded US$40 billion each. In recent years, early-stage biotech venture capitalists had become more sophisticated and often employed or contracted the services of biotech experts to assess the fundamental value of a company's science.

DIABETOGEN'S SITUATION

Diabetogen was incorporated in December 1997 to commercialize the work of three world-renowned scientists in the field of diabetes who, among them, had published over 200 articles on the disease. The scientific founders of Diabetogen included Dr. Terry Delovitch and Dr. Bhagi Singh, both of whom had joint appointments with Robarts and The University of Western Ontario, and Dr. Jean-Francois Bach who was

Pre-Clinical Development: Pharmaceutical and biotechnology companies spend many years screening compounds for activity against certain disease models. Once a compound that carries promise for disease treatment has been identified, pre-clinical or animal studies are carried out to determine the safety and biological effect of the compound. Pre-Clinical Trials typically require two to three years to complete, and on average, 12 per cent of compounds in the pre-clinical, animal-testing stage will proceed to the next step.

Investigational New Drug Application (IND): The filing of an IND with the U.S. FDA or the Canadian Health Protection Branch is the first step in entering human clinical trials. The IND contains all data generated in the pre-clinical trials. The package also specifically outlines protocols to be utilized in the Phase I round of human testing. The filing and approval process takes approximately one year, and on average, 90 per cent of compounds will gain approval to enter human clinical testing.

Phase I: The first time a human patient population is exposed to the drug in question is during Phase I clinical trials. Usually, the patient population is composed of between 20 and 100 healthy volunteers. The trials are conducted to provide initial data about safety of the drug in humans. Phase I testing takes approximately one year, and on average, 20 per cent of drugs yield results that indicate the drug is free of intolerable side effects and can pass into Phase II trials.

Phase II: Phase II clinical trial data are collected on a patient population afflicted with the disease being studied. The trial is designed to provide initial data on the therapeutic benefit of the drug. Dose response relationships are studied and additional toxicity data are gathered. These trials take approximately two years to complete and include 50 to 300 patients. On average, 29 per cent of drugs show a therapeutic benefit sufficient to warrant entrance into Phase III clinical trials.

Phase III: Phase III clinical trials involve testing an expanded patient population at geographically dispersed centres to establish safety and efficacy. Patient populations range from 250 to thousands depending on statistical significance. Phase III trials take approximately three years, and on average, 61 per cent of drugs are successful at this stage.

Approval: Once the risk/benefit relationship for a drug is determined, a submission to receive marketing approval is made to the FDA or HPB. Submissions include the drug's chemical name, proper name, and the product's biological, pharmacological, and toxicological properties. In addition, an establishment license application must be filed for the production of a product, and test sites must be approved for drug manufacturing. The review of the submission usually takes one year, with an average success rate of 74 per cent, but the company can commence selling the drug through an Emergency Drug Release provision during this time period.

Phase IV: Phase IV trials are designed to monitor the long-term benefits and risks of a drug after it has received marketing approval. The number of patients involved can range from 1,000 to 10,000.

Exhibit 2 The Clinical Trial Process

Source: "Biotech/Pharmaceutical Focus on Near-Term Milestones," Douglas Miehm, RBC Dominion Securities.

a director of several clinical research units at Hôpital Necker in France. Previously funded by government grants, the scientists of Diabetogen had reached a point where continued research and development of Diabetogen's five drug candidates would require substantial private investment, and this capital would be needed within four months if the program was to continue.

One of the five drugs, called anti-CD3 (described later), had shown positive results in pre-clinical animal testing and Diabetogen was ready to file an IND application to begin human trials with the drug. Anti-CD3 was further along in development than Diabetogen's other molecules, and was considered the company's "lead drug." At the same time that Michael was preparing to file the IND, he was also working to finalize the licensing rights that would allow Diabetogen to develop and commercialize anti-CD3 for the treatment of diabetes. This licensing process had

Table 1

Stage of Development	*Ave. Probability of Success of Proceeding to the Next Stage*
Pre-Clinical	12%
IND Application	90%
Phase I	20%
Phase II	29%
Phase III	61%
Drug Submission	74%

to take place because, although Dr. Bach was a founder of Diabetogen and it was he who discovered that the molecule could cure diabetes in mice, the rights controlling development and commercialization of the drug were held by his employer, Hôpital Necker.

The anti-CD3 molecule itself had been discovered 10 years earlier at Oxford University by an immunologist named Dr. Hermann Waldmann. Oxford and Dr. Waldmann sold the rights to the molecule to a biotechnology company called Leukosite. Leukosite was subsequently purchased in 1999 by Millennium Pharmaceuticals, a Boston-based biotech company, who initiated a research program to develop anti-CD3 as a drug to reduce immune rejection of transplanted organs. At the same time that Millennium was focusing on transplantation, Dr. Bach was investigating the potential of anti-CD3 in the treatment of Type I diabetes. In his lab at Hôpital Necker in Paris, Dr. Bach showed that anti-CD3 could cure diabetes in mice with a 70 per cent success rate, and now the molecule had reached the point where it could be tested in humans. Michael had already secured a licence for the diabetes application from Hôpital Necker. The agreement stipulated that the hospital would receive royalties of two per cent of gross revenues once anti-CD3 reached the market for use in the treatment of diabetes. Now he had to finalize a licensing agreement with Millennium for composition (use) of the molecule.

The nature of the Millennium licence would have a major impact on the strategic focus and valuation of Diabetogen going forward since the roles that Diabetogen and Millennium would play, and the cash flows to Diabetogen depended greatly on the specifics of the agreement. Michael believed that for a biopharmaceutical company to become an ongoing entity, it must eventually develop its own sales and marketing infrastructure, but he also knew that in the early stages of building a biotech firm, the market penetration of a company's first drug could be increased substantially with a strong strategic partner who had an established sales force and regulatory, manufacturing and distribution infrastructure. Balancing these two objectives, Michael planned to negotiate with Millennium (a fully integrated biopharmaceutical company) a deal that would allow Diabetogen to commercialize anti-CD3 for diabetes, and to leverage the sales force and manufacturing capabilities of Millennium in some markets, while marketing and selling the drug itself in others.

Based on previous discussions with Millennium, Michael had prepared what he believed would be an acceptable licensing proposal. In it, Millennium would license anti-CD3 to Diabetogen for use in diabetes and finance the Phase III clinical trials. In return, Millennium would gain rights to manufacture, market and sell anti-CD3 in North America, paying Diabetogen a royalty of 15 per cent of the gross revenues, and also paying Hôpital Necker its two per cent royalty fee. In other markets such as Europe, Michael planned to retain sales and marketing rights as part of his plan to build internal competencies and an infrastructure in these areas. For these markets, Michael planned to outsource the manufacturing of anti-CD3 to Millennium, paying Millennium 20 per cent of revenues for this service.

As well as financing the IND application for anti-CD3 and Diabetogen's portion of the

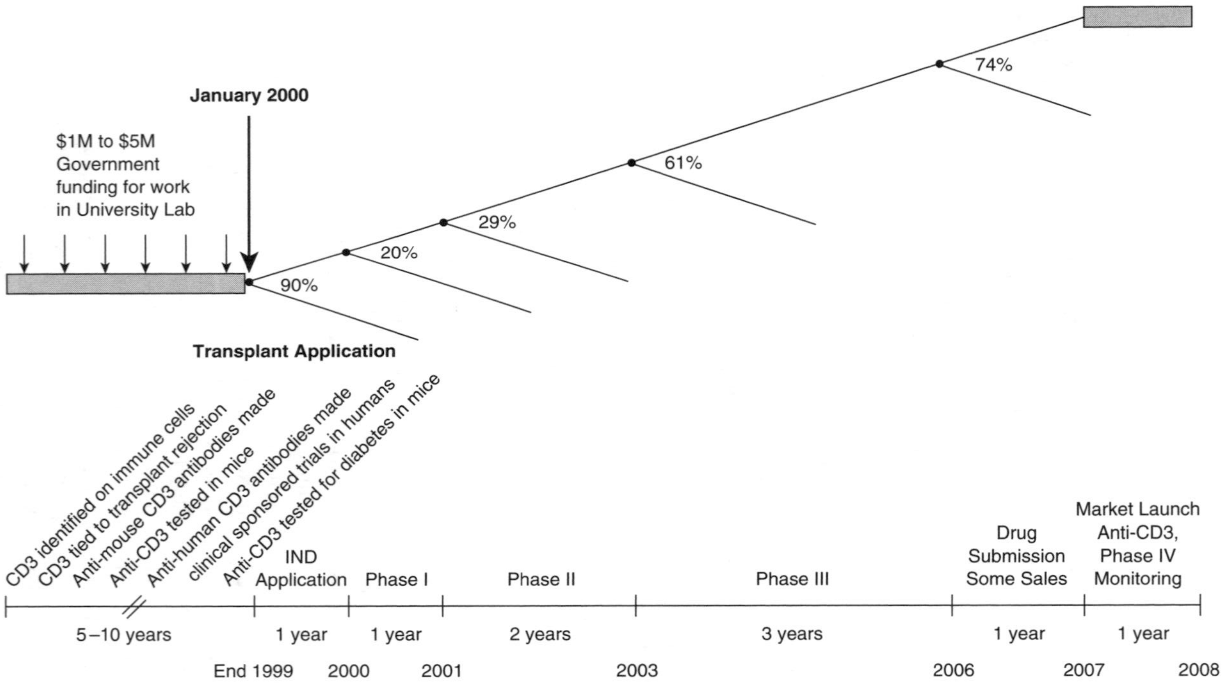

January 2000

$1M to $5M Government funding for work in University Lab

90%

20%

29%

61%

74%

Transplant Application

CD3 identified on immune cells
CD3 tied to transplant rejection
Anti-mouse CD3 antibodies made
Anti-CD3 tested in mice
Anti-human CD3 antibodies made
clinical sponsored trials in humans
Anti-CD3 tested for diabetes in mice

		IND Application	Phase I	Phase II	Phase III	Drug Submission Some Sales	Market Launch Anti-CD3, Phase IV Monitoring
	5–10 years	1 year	1 year	2 years	3 years	1 year	1 year
		End 1999 – 2000	2000 – 2001	2001 – 2003	2003 – 2006	2006 – 2007	2007 – 2008
Risks		Incomplete or poor application.	Anaphylactic reaction. Wrong dosage. Immune suppression.	No significant effect. Wrong dosage. Wrong endpoint sought.	No significant effect.		Poor product launch. Delays in bringing manufacturing facility on-line.
Risk Mitigation		Competency in filing INDs with FDA and HPB. Strong pre-clinical documentation.	Strong clinical trials group. Good pre-clinical testing. Already tested in humans by Millennium.	Strong clinical trials group. Good pre-clinical Testing.	Strong clinical trials group.		Strategic partners for manufacturing, marketing and sales.

Exhibit 3 Drug Development Probability and Risk Diagram

clinical trial expenses, Michael also needed to raise capital to build corporate and R&D infrastructure, fund working capital, and support ongoing work on the company's four other drug candidates.

Management and Governance

Michael had already started work assembling a management team, a board of directors and scientific and medical advisory boards. He had extended a conditional offer to Mr. William McGinnis for the position of president and CEO, and Mr. McGinnis had agreed to retire from his current post as director of Institutional Accounts and vice president of the Endocrine Unit at Eli Lilly United States to take the position at Diabetogen. Eli Lilly, interestingly, was the world's leading provider of insulin, and the recruitment of Mr. McGinnis was a major success for Diabetogen. Michael felt that Mr. McGinnis excelled in all of the skills that would be required to advance Diabetogen in the development and commercialization of its drugs. He had extensive knowledge of the entire diabetes field, hands-on experience with business development in the pharmaceutical industry, and a strong network to build a corporate team. Furthermore, with 27 years at Lilly, Mr. McGinnis had a great deal of experience in managing scientists and business personnel during his various executive appointments. The offer was, as mentioned, conditional on securing first-round financing. Since the plan was to bring Mr. McGinnis on board by May 1, 2000, both the anti-CD3 licensing and the first round of financing had to be in place before this date.

The position of chief scientific officer was held by Terry Delovitch and, at present, Michael was acting as chief operating officer and chief financial officer although he realized that he would soon have to recruit for these positions since his primary appointment was with Robarts. Robarts was also providing, at the moment, the services of an Intellectual Property Manager, Hamza Suria, and administrative support.

Michael had partially assembled the board of directors. So far the appointments included two seasoned executives with a strong interest in finding a cure for Type I diabetes. One of the two had agreed to serve as chairman. Mark Poznansky, president of Robarts, and William McGinnis would also sit on the board. Interestingly, all of the board members had children who suffered from Type I diabetes. Michael envisioned that the board would be filled out with at least one more scientific delegate and several venture capital representatives or their designates.

As a biopharmaceutical company, Diabetogen would also have a Scientific Advisory Board. The scientists from Diabetogen would serve on this board along with other scientists who were leaders in the fields of Type I diabetes, immunology and cancer research. The board would also include four medical doctors from Canada, the U.S. and Europe. One of the medical advisors, Dr. Jeffery Mahon, was an associate professor of Medicine and clinical trials, and Michael believed that Dr. Mahon's expertise in clinical trials would be invaluable for the company.

Diabetogen's Products

Type I diabetes is an autoimmune disease, meaning that the immune system wrongly destroys cells that should normally survive in the human body. In the case of diabetes, it is cells in the pancreas called beta cells that are destroyed. Since beta cells are responsible for producing insulin, and insulin controls the amount of sugar being delivered by the blood to the body's cells, the destruction of beta cells by the immune system results in a condition in which body sugar levels fluctuate dangerously. Without insulin to control blood sugar levels, cells in the human body can be exposed to excessively high levels of sugar at certain times, and dangerously low levels at other times. These fluctuations can lead to comas, blindness and many other medical problems. While monitoring of blood sugar levels combined with dietary control and injection of insulin can reduce the medical risks, even when properly managed, diabetics often develop heart problems, kidney failure, blindness and limb circulation problems over time. Diabetes is the fourth leading cause of death in North America and direct medical expenses attributed to the disease total $38 billion annually. It costs approximately US$10,000 per year to maintain a diabetic individual on insulin.

The disease progression of diabetes could be split into three stages: early, intermediate and late, corresponding to the average age of individuals in each stage (3–10 years, 10–20 years, and 20+, respectively) and the extent of destruction of the beta cells. The scientists involved in Diabetogen had discovered five bio-molecules, each with the potential to permanently block the progression of the disease in early stage individuals, or cure the disease in intermediate and late stage diabetics (see table below).

The drugs worked by blocking the destructive activities of the immune system. Involved in diabetes were three types of immune cells: T killer cells which normally attack diseased cells, T regulatory cells which suppress the activity of T killer cells, and APCs which break down and present components of target cells to the T killer cells, stimulating an attack by the T killers. Diabetes develops, as with other autoimmune diseases, when T killer cells are over-activated, T regulatory cells are under-activated, or APCs present components of normal cells to the T killers as candidates for destruction.

Anti-CD3: CD3 was a protein that was embedded in the surface of all T regulatory cells. It acted as a "stimulating receptor" which meant that when it was activated, it sent signals into the T regulatory cells causing the cells to proliferate (produce more of themselves) and activate (produce and release biochemical signals). It was these biochemical signals, released by T regulatory cells in response to CD3 activation, that dampened the activity of T killer cells, blocking their destruction of pancreatic beta cells. Ten years earlier at Oxford, Dr. Waldmann had utilized standard biotech techniques to produce an antibody that could bind specifically to the CD3 protein receptors, and through this interaction, stimulate the T regulatory cells.

This antibody was called anti-CD3. Antibodies were normally produced in the body to aid in fighting infections, but over the last decade, scientists had been developing antibodies in the laboratory to act as biopharmaceuticals. The antibody developed by Dr. Waldmann, anti-CD3, bound specifically to CD3 and it had the ability to activate CD3 when this happened.

While Millennium was investigating the ability of anti-CD3 to reduce organ rejection following transplant surgery, Dr. Bach investigated its use in diabetes. What Dr. Bach found was that treatment with anti-CD3 could reverse late stage disease in diabetic mice with complete remission in 60 to 80 per cent of mice. It was believed that even in late stage diabetics, some pancreatic beta cells remained, and that when the mice were treated with anti-CD3, beta cells re-established themselves to near normal levels by a process called proliferation. Millennium had already developed a human version of the anti-CD3 antibody (Waldmann's antibody only bound to mouse CD3), had received IND approval, and had initiated Phase I clinical trials for anti-CD3 in humans undergoing transplant surgery. Now the time had come for Diabetogen to test the molecule in humans for its diabetes potential. Securing a supply of human anti-CD3 from Millennium was part of the licensing agreement that Michael would negotiate with Millennium. In fact, it was in Millennium's best interest to allow Diabetogen to develop the drug for diabetes as Millennium had no interest or expertise in the disease. For Millennium, out-licensing anti-CD3 for diabetes would be a relatively inexpensive

	Early Stage	*Intermediate Stage*	*Late Stage*
Drugs in Development	ApoE Anti-CD28	APL-GAD Zeta-Zap	Anti-CD3

way of generating additional revenues from the anti-CD3 platform.

Anti-CD28: One of the scientific founders of Diabetogen had, himself, produced antibodies that reacted with another T cell receptor protein, CD28. In mice that normally develop diabetes, the anti-CD28 antibodies blocked early-stage disease progression with 100 per cent success if administered to mice at ages that correspond to one to five years of age in humans. The next steps in the development of anti-CD28 would be the generation of antibodies against the human version of CD28 (since only antibodies against the mouse CD28 protein existed); the testing of these antibodies in vitro (in test tubes), then on cells, then finally, in humans. Antibody synthesis work could be contracted out to labs that specialized in this technique, but the testing would be conducted in Diabetogen's laboratories. Anti-CD28 was discovered by Dr. Delovitch at Robarts, and although Diabetogen had not yet signed a licence for the molecule, Michael knew that this would be only a formality. The molecule had the potential for Diabetogen, like anti-CD3 for Millennium, of becoming a broad platform molecule for which other medical applications could be investigated either internally or through sublicensing to other biopharmaceutical companies.

ApoE: ApoE blocked diabetes by impairing the ability of APCs to present beta cell components to T killer cells. This drug was most effective if administered at ages corresponding to one to five years in humans. ApoE would not have to be humanized like anti-CD28; however, the mechanism of its action still had to be determined. ApoE was discovered by Dr. Singh at The University of Western Ontario and would be licensed to Diabetogen. Like anti-CD28, ApoE had the potential to become a broad platform molecule for treatment of immunological conditions.

Zeta-Zap and APL-GAD reversed intermediate stage diabetes in laboratory mice by dampening the activation of T killer cells. These drugs were most effective if administered to mice at ages corresponding to 15 to 20 years in humans, and more work would have to be done in mice before the molecules could be brought to the human testing stage. Both were discovered by scientists at Neurocrine BioSciences Inc. (a San Diego-based biotech company), and negotiations were underway to license development and commercialization rights for the molecules to Diabetogen.

There were currently no cures for diabetes. There were, however, several established pharmaceutical companies also seeking cures or better treatments for the disease (Exhibit 4). Some of the companies were taking the same approach as Diabetogen (i.e., developing molecules that would suppress the immune system allowing maintenance or restoration of the pancreatic beta cells). Others were trying to produce modified insulin molecules with better therapeutic properties. Other approaches included gene therapy and beta cell transplantation. While the competitors were at various stages of development, and any one might have a breakthrough, Michael was confident that Diabetogen had been founded by the top diabetes researchers in the world, and that the company's partnership with Millennium would facilitate the most efficient development of a superior drug.

Revenue and Profit Forecasts

Because work on anti-CD28, ApoE, APL-GAD and Zeta-Zap was so early-stage, Michael could only project development costs for these drugs. Anti-CD3, on the other hand, was closer to commercialization and Michael was able to generate forward-looking profit/loss statements based on projected sales of the drug. Exhibit 5 shows these projections.

He knew that sales of anti-CD3 were not anticipated until 2007 but, based on the most recent version of the Millennium licence, Diabetogen should begin to receive funding for Phase III clinical trials, in the form of milestone payments, beginning in 2004. Furthermore, as early as 2001, Michael anticipated that the company would

A review of agents currently in clinical trials for the treatment of Type I diabetes is shown below:				
Drug	*Company*	*Mechanism of Action*	*Cure/ Treatment?*	*Clinical Trial Phase*
Pramlintide	Amylin	Insulin Substitute	Treatment	Phase III (USA)
Native Insulin	National Institutes of Health	Preventative Insulin Supplementation	Cure	Phase II (USA)
Modified Insulin	Pfizer/Inhale, Novo Nordisk/Eli Lilly	Insulin Replacement	Treatment	Phase II (USA)
AI 401	Eli Lilly/Autoimmune	Immunosuppressant	Cure	Phase II (USA)
Phosphatase Inhibitors	Sugen	Improve sugar	Treatment uptake	Pre-Clinical (USA)
	VivoRx, Sertoli, CytoTherapeutics, Neocrin	Beta cell transplantation	Cure	Pre-Clinical (USA)
Anergix	Anergen	Immunosuppressant	Cure	Pre-Clinical (USA)
	Transkaryotic, Eli Lilly	Gene Therapy	Cure	Pre-Clinical (USA)
Interleukin	Hoffman LaRoche, Immunex	Immunosuppressant	Cure	Pre-Clinical (USA, Europe)
Antibodies	Becton Dickinson, Boehringer Ingelheim	Immunosuppressant	Cure	Pre-Clinical (USA, Europe)
Rapamycin	Wyeth-Ayerst	Immunosuppressant	Cure	Pre-Clinical (USA)

Exhibit 4 Competitors

receive sponsored research payments from Millennium and other partner companies. At the expected market launch of anti-CD3 in 2007, Michael projected the number of potential patients who would likely be treated in the first two years of sales. There were currently about two million Type I diabetics in North America and Europe, and each year up to 60,000 new patients were diagnosed. The number of newly diagnosed diabetics was expected to increase by 0.5 per cent per year. Approximately 10 per cent were late-stage disease sufferers, and using the epidemiological statistics, Michael projected that by 2007, there would be approximately 110,000 late-stage diabetics in North America and 150,000 in Europe. From this information, Michael projected the North American and European sales revenues that could be expected for anti-CD3. In his base-case projections, he assumed that Diabetogen's drug would be used by 15 per cent of the late-stage diabetics in the North American and European markets in the first year (increasing to 19 per cent in the second year). Although the price to the end-user was not

anti-CD3		*1999*	*2000*	*2001*	*2002*	*2003*	*2004*	*2005*	*2006*	*2007*	*2008*
North American	Patients									113,306	113,873
Sales by Millennium	Penetration	0%	0%	0%	0%	0%	0%	0%	0%	15%	19%
	Revenue/Patient	$0	$0	$0	$0	$0	$0	$0	$0	$5,000	$5,000
	Gross Revenue	$0	$0	$0	$0	$0	$0	$0	$0	$84,979,500	$108,178,904
	Royalties to Diabetogen	$0	$0	$0	$0	$0	$0	$0	$0	$12,746,925	$16,226,836
European Sales	Patients									147,298	148,034
Sales by Diabetogen	Penetration	0%	0%	0%	0%	0%	0%	0%	0%	15%	19%
	Revenue/Patient	$0	$0	$0	$0	$0	$0	$0	$0	$5,000	$5,000
	Gross Revenue	$0	$0	$0	$0	$0	$0	$0	$0	$110,473,500	$140,632,766
	Cost of Goods Sold	$0	$0	$0	$0	$0	$0	$0	$0	$13,256,820	$16,875,932
	Selling, General & Admin.	$0	$0	$0	$0	$0	$0	$0	$0	$22,094,700	$28,126,553
	Royalties to Hôpital Necker	$0	$0	$0	$0	$0	$0	$0	$0	$2,209,470	$2,812,655
	Pre-Tax Cash Flow	$0	$0	$0	$0	$0	$0	$0	$0	$72,912,510	$92,817,625
Other Revenues		$0	$0	$650,000	$1,000,000	$1,000,000	$19,400,000	$11,300,000	$10,800,000	$12,866,554	$7,104,782
Milestone and Sponsored Research Payments											
Expenses (allocated to anti-CD3)		$140,886	$290,289	$1,500,000	$2,700,000	$2,700,000	$11,210,763	$11,311,398	$10,872,073	$1,851,701	$1,727,909
Pre-Tax (Loss)/Profit		–$140,886	–$290,289	–$850,000	–$1,700,000	–$1,700,000	$8,189,237	–$11,398	–$72,073	$96,674,288	$114,421,334
Other Drugs Expenses		$0	$750,000	$1,000,000	$1,500,000	$2,000,000	$2,500,000	$3,500,000	$4,500,000	$5,500,000	$6,500,000
Total Net Burn		($140,886)	($1,040,289)	($1,850,000)	($3,200,000)	($3,700,000)	$5,689,237	($3,511,398)	($4,572,073)	$91,174,288	$107,921,334

Exhibit 5 Profit/Loss Statements as at December 31

worked out, Michael conservatively projected that Diabetogen (in Europe) and Millennium (in North America) would receive $5,000 for each patient treated.

For earnings from North American sales, Diabetogen would receive royalties of 15 per cent of gross revenues from Millennium. Royalties to Hôpital Necker would be paid directly by Millennium.

For earnings from European sales which would be handled by Diabetogen, Michael subtracted manufacturing costs that would be paid to Millennium ($600 per patient treatment), selling, general and administrative expenses which were each projected to be 20 per cent of revenues, and Hôpital Necker royalties which would be two per cent of revenues.

The projected milestone and sponsored research payments from Millennium were added to the positive cash flows at scheduled points on the development timeline, then general expenses that Michael allocated to the anti-CD3 program were subtracted to generate a projected pre-tax profit/loss.

Financing Needs

Michael had determined that to build a corporate R&D infrastructure, fund further development of anti-CD3, and continue research on Diabetogen's four other drugs, he would need to raise roughly $12.5 million. For the anti-CD3 program, this money would allow Diabetogen to finance the IND application and Phase I and II clinical trials. With Millennium funding the Phase III trials, it appeared that anti-CD3 would be completely developed for diabetes with no further equity capital. Despite this, Michael anticipated that Diabetogen would be well positioned to go public with a high valuation by the end of 2003. This date corresponded to the projected completion of anti-CD3 Phase II clinical trials, a milestone that sent many biotech companies to the public markets. Since Michael projected that the company would need minimal, if any, money at this stage for anti-CD3 development, the initial public offering (IPO) might just be a secondary offering in which early-stage investors could sell their shares to public investors. On the other hand, if Diabetogen's other drugs continued to show promise in 2003, the company would likely require an infusion of capital at the IPO date.

For the $12.5 million currently needed, Michael had already secured $5 million through a government grant called the Challenge Fund. This money was truly a grant as it was provided to finance pre-clinical research programs, and would not have to be paid back. Therefore, Michael calculated his net cash needs to be $7.5 million.

He was aware of several venture capital firms (VCs) in Canada and the U.S. that specialized in biotech investments (see Exhibit 6), and he wondered which of the firms might be most interested in funding Diabetogen.

Before he approached the VCs, however, he knew that he had to determine a value for Diabetogen. How much of the company would first-round investors expect for their $7.5 million investment?

Valuation

Valuing Diabetogen would be difficult because positive cash flows from operations would not occur for several years, and these cash flows were highly speculative, depending on development successes at many stages. Furthermore, although Diabetogen was developing five drugs, only anti-CD3 had progressed to the stage where Michael felt investors would recognize value based on projections of cash flows from future sales. In other words, having the four other drugs made Diabetogen attractive because it reduced risk that the company would be worth nothing if anti-CD3 was not successful in clinical trials, but only cash flows from anti-CD3 would be considered in a valuation of the company. Under these constraints, Michael considered several options to value Diabetogen.

Firm	*Location*	*Investment Range*	*Biotech Expertise*	*Other*
KPCB	San Francisco	up to $200 million	Yes	Pioneers in biotech venture capital.
Advent International	Boston	up to $200 million	Yes	World's largest private equity firm.
BB Bioventures	Boston	$5–$50 million	Yes	Some investments in Canada.
Sofinov	Montreal	open	Yes	Prefer Quebec investments.
Ventures West	Vancouver/Toronto	$0.5–$5 million	Yes	
MDS	Toronto	$0.25–$10 million	Yes	Largest Canadian Biotech Investor.
CMDF	London, Ontario	up to $10 million	Yes	Fund administered by MDS.

Exhibit 6 Venture Capital Firms

Multiples: For the first valuation, Michael returned to his revenue and earnings projections (Exhibit 5). He knew that with tax-loss carry-forwards and cash-refund research tax credits called SREDS, Diabetogen would not be required to pay taxes for several years and, therefore, the pre-tax profit could be considered net earnings. He also knew that in the biotech industry, companies traded with forward price/earnings multiples ranging from 20x to 80x. He felt that because Diabetogen would be a multi-platform company, it conservatively deserved a 40x forward multiple. Therefore, for year-end 2007, he projected that the company would be worth approximately $4.58 billion (40x$114.4 million) based on 2008 earnings from anti-CD3. Next, Michael knew that he would have to discount this value back to the present. He returned to his Drug Development Probability Diagram (Exhibit 3) to verify the standard lengths of each stage of drug development, then using industry-standard IRRs (internal rates of return) that had been provided by a VC who worked for a firm well-known in the Canadian biotech industry, he determined a present value (PV) for Diabetogen. The IRRs that were blended to account for changes in risk as a drug got closer to market are shown in Table 2.

Table 2

Stage of Development	*Required IRR*
Pre-clinical	200%
IND application	75%
Phase I	60%
Phase II	50%
Phase III	40%
Drug submission	25%
Market	20%

Since Diabetogen was currently applying for the IND for anti-CD3, Michael discounted the $4.58 billion at a rate of 75 per cent over eight years, inferring a present value of $52 million. Michael was interested to see what the company would be worth as anti-CD3 passed through the clinical trial process. Using the IRR specific for each stage, and the projected drug development timeline, Michael generated projected values for each year prior to the commercialization of anti-CD3.

This work is presented in Table 3.

Table 3

Year End	*Entering (or in) Stage*	*Discount Rate*	*Value*
2007	Market Launch	20%	$4,576,853,350
2006	Drug Submission	25%	$3,661,482,680
2005	PIII	40%	$2,335,129,260
2004	PIII	40%	$1,667,949,472
2003	PIII	40%	$1,191,392,480
2002	PII	50%	$602,713,198
2001	PII	50%	$401,808,799
2000	PI	60%	$170,501,074
1999	IND Approval	75%	$52,031,052

Michael then used a probability valuation method in which the projected value was multiplied by the probabilities of success at each stage between the present time and the IPO date (i.e., $4.58 billion × 90% × 20% × 29% × 61% × 74%). This generated a value of $107.8 million which he discounted back over the entire eight years at 30 per cent, a rate that reflected the portfolio rate of return that would be demanded by venture capitalists. This generated a present value of $13.2 million, which was substantially lower than the financial value calculated above.

While the two methods generated drastically different results, Michael averaged the two results and came up with $47.8 million.

Michael felt there were several strong reasons why Diabetogen warranted a valuation higher than $13.2 million. First, industry-standard probabilities had been used in the calculation, and Diabetogen was better positioned than most pre-clinical biotech companies. The company had very strong management and unusually enthusiastic support in the global scientific community. Many key players shared Michael's opinion that Diabetogen's scientists were at the top of the global diabetes research field. Furthermore, anti-CD3 had already been tested in humans in Phase I trials by Millennium (for transplant rejection), and in human clinical sponsored trials in Europe for the diabetes indication. Clearly, with the drug already in humans and showing no adverse effects, Diabetogen's probability of success was increased, and the probabilities, especially at the early stages of the clinical trials program should reflect this. Michael believed that, in fact, the IND application was certain (i.e., 100 per cent), and that the probability of successfully completing Phase I trials was also close to certainty (i.e., 90 per cent). Returning to his model, Michael plugged these probabilities into his valuation, and generated a PV of $66.1 million.

Before he moved on to his next valuation, Michael tested a key sensitivity, revenue per patient. He was aware that a recently approved biopharmaceutical for arthritis was on the market at $17,000 per patient. With this in mind, Michael tested various pricing points. He found, for instance, that if Diabetogen or its partners received $9,000 instead of $5,000 per patient, the present value of Diabetogen jumped to $119 million.

Concept of Value: Next, Michael determined the costs that had already been incurred to bring anti-CD3 and the other drugs to their current state. These costs he estimated to be about $7 million. Then he added the $5 million granted by the Challenge Fund to arrive at a pre-money valuation of $12 million. Adding the $7.5 million that would be raised with the first-round financing, the company should have a post-money value of $19.5 million.

"Rule-of-Thumb" Valuation: Michael was also aware that Canadian venture capitalists often applied a blanket valuation to startup Canadian biotech companies. This valuation ranged between $1 million and $3.5 million, post-cash, meaning, for example, that if a VC invested $500,000, the VC would require 14 per cent to 50 per cent of the company. Obviously, the fact that Michael was seeking $7.5 million complicated the use of this method.

Finally, he considered another option: raise the $7.5 million as a convertible debenture, at a conversion rate to be determined at a later date and based on an independent valuation of the firm at that date.

What was the value of Diabetogen? What ownership percentage would have to be offered to the first-round investors for their $7.5 million. Michael knew that shares and options would be issued to other stakeholders including the founding scientists, Dr. Waldmann, management, directors, the planned ESOP program, Robarts, and strategic partners. It was especially important for the founding scientists to have a meaningful stake at this stage of financing since it was their reputation, knowledge and skills that had created value in the company, and future drug discovery and development required their participation. In addition to shares, some stakeholders would receive royalty payments directly or indirectly. For instance, Hôpital Necker, Robarts and The University of Western Ontario (UWO) would receive direct royalties on the drugs that were developed in their laboratories. Specifics of the royalty payments would be laid out in licensing agreements reached with the institutes. Michael knew that indirectly, founding scientists also received royalties, usually about half of the payments made to their respective institutions. For instance, Dr. Bach would receive a portion of Hôpital Necker's anti-CD3 royalties.

In addition to the institutes and the scientists, Michael knew it was standard in the biotech industry to reserve a certain number of shares for employee and management stock options, and he wondered how these options and the remainder of the equity of Diabetogen should be distributed. Table 4 lists all of the stakeholders in the company.

Table 4

Stakeholder	*Shares*	*Royalties*	*Marketing Rights*	*Salary*
Dr. Waldmann	yes			
Millennium	to be negotiated		yes	
Hôpital Necker	yes	yes—2% of anti-CD3 revenues		
Robarts	yes	yes—for anti-CD28		
UWO	yes	yes—for Apo E		
Scientists	yes—options	yes—indirectly		yes
Management	yes—options			yes
Board Members	yes—options			fees for service
Michael Crowley	yes—options			yes
First-Round Investors	yes			

To divide the pre-money equity, Michael considered that the $5 million raised through the Challenge Fund had been secured through the efforts of three London-based organizations: Robarts (80 per cent allocation), UWO (10 per cent allocation) and University Hospital (10 per cent allocation). Next, Michael valued the science of the company at $6 million with 50 per cent attributed to Hôpital Necker, 25 per cent to Robarts, and 25 per cent to UWO. Similar to royalties, founding scientists would receive their equity from their associated institute. Finally, $1 million was reserved for the value that current and future management would bring to the table. This would take the form of options, half being zero cost options to be vested over a three to four year period, with the remainder being at- or above-money options. Ninety per cent of both classes would go to the managers already committed to the company, with the remaining 10 per cent reserved for future managers and employees.

With all of these issues on his mind, Michael set to work preparing the investment memorandum that would be presented to the potential first-round investors.

Alpha Personal Dental Care Systems

Prepared by Barbara Czyzowski under the supervision of Professor James E. Hatch

 Version: (A) 2003-02-10

Peter Butler and Julie McBride hurried to the car through the snow-covered parking lot. It was late December 1988 and they were on their way to a meeting with Peter's attorney to discuss the contents of the offering memorandum the attorney was preparing. Their firm, Alpha Personal Dental Care Systems (Alpha), required risk capital to further develop their new invention: a toothbrush with a unique double-locking connector mechanism which permitted the head to be easily and safely replaced. As they drove away, Peter and Julie started to discuss just what elements would be included in the offering memorandum, and began thinking about the potential investors they would approach for funds.

Peter Butler arrived in Canada from England in 1961, and brought with him nine years of training and experience in the graphical skills associated with packaging design. After engaging in several business ventures, Peter joined three partners to create Design Associates, a London, Ontario-based graphic arts firm. The company continued in business for over 20 years designing both the artwork and the packaging for manufacturing-based businesses. Julie McBride joined the firm as an account manager in 1985 and, as time passed, found herself working more closely with Peter. During this time, Peter and Julie acquired extensive experience in the packaging, advertising and marketing activities related to retail and industrial products.

Following a failed merger with another firm Peter and one of his original partners, Brian Williams, launched their own venture, Butler, Williams and Friends. The plan was to share key resources and overheads, but each was expected to develop and manage his or her own client base. Julie became an employee of this firm, handling all aspects of office management as well as engaging in client-related work.

In addition to their joint business venture, Peter and Brian, through separately incorporated companies, each owned 50 per cent of two properties in the London area. The first company owned the building in which the two partners operated and one acre of land on which the building was situated. The remainder of the building was rented to other commercial tenants. They owned a second building on four acres of land. Butler and Williams together shared the costs and the lease revenues associated with these buildings. The two also shared ownership in another company that held eight acres of vacant land adjacent to their business premises as well as 290 acres of vacant land near Woodstock, Ontario.

Due to its proximity to two major highways between London and Toronto, the Woodstock property had sparked the interest of many prospective developers over the years. Although Peter was not aware of the current value of either of the pieces of land or the building, the Woodstock property had been acquired in 1980 for approximately $500,000.

The Evolution of the Idea

Peter had a former neighbour and friend of 20 years who was a dentist named Don Thomas. Thomas maintained a practice in London, Ontario, and was part-owner of a dental clinic. He lived near Bayfield, Ontario, and taught part-time at the dental school at The University of Western Ontario. In January 1986, the two friends were discussing Thomas's business when the dentist mentioned some concerns he was having. He felt that his patients were not replacing their toothbrushes regularly, and he believed that this neglect could trigger the onset of periodontal disease or systemic health problems. He also feared that this issue had led many patients to experience accelerated tooth decay which, in turn, increased the probability that patients would require dentures. He was aware that the Canadian Dental Association recommended replacing toothbrushes every two months and that studies had shown that the duration of the common cold could be reduced if toothbrushes were changed at the time when the patient first noticed signs of the cold.

Thomas also felt patients should use dry (not wet) toothbrushes to brush their teeth to obtain the maximum benefits intended from the brushing process. Since toothbrushes currently used were comprised of nylon bristles which required 24 hours to properly dry out, this would mean that a patient who brushed twice per day would require two toothbrushes. Thomas believed that if dentists could find a way for patients to change their toothbrushes more regularly and to always use dry brushes, the patients could save considerable money in dental work and would increase their chances to keep their teeth. He had statistics which indicated that having dentures shortened life expectancy by four years, and he felt this risk could be avoided with improved oral hygiene. Peter and Don, feeling that a market existed for a toothbrush that could address these issues, decided to pursue the idea further.

The Product Concept

The original concept was to develop a product which resembled a safety razor which was in wide use. The toothbrush would have two distinct sections: a retainable handle and a disposable head. The disposable heads would be marketed in convenient multi-unit packages to encourage more frequent toothbrush replacement. Buying a quantity of heads would have the additional advantage of lowering the costs of packaging, which they found were about 50 per cent of the cost of the toothbrushes currently being sold. The handle and heads would be standardized and made available in a single colour, likely white, to keep costs of production low.

They also envisioned that the retainable handle would help change the consumer's concept of the toothbrush from a disposable entity to an item of higher personal value which could open up a number of niche markets. This could be achieved by having the handles personalized, or developed from various attractive materials, such as plastic, brass, or stainless steel. Other additions to the line might include floss holders, mirrors, interproximal brushes, gum massagers, and related items. Another enhancement they considered included providing a hygienic bathroom holder or travel case for consumers to store their toothbrushes.

Technological Development

Early in their investigation, Peter and Don learned that there were already a number of toothbrush products in the market that purported to meet the need they wanted to address. However, they found that the products all suffered from an inadequacy in the device which locked the handle to the head. Consequently, they began to devote their efforts to developing a better locking device that would eliminate the potential hazard to users caused by the head separating from the handle. At the same time, they were mindful that production costs would have to be low enough to keep the price of the final product competitive.

Peter tried dozens of approaches to secure the two parts, but all possessed weaknesses—some were too difficult to secure, others were too costly. One day in May 1987, while travelling with Julie, Peter suddenly got the idea for a new type of double-locking connector. The connector literally had two locking mechanisms which ensured that the head would safely stay on the handle. Moreover, the design made it apparent to the user if the lock was not in place. He sketched a rough version of his idea on paper and over the next several weeks, Peter refined his concept into a series of diagrams. Peter then took these sketches to an engineering firm in London that developed a preliminary mechanical drawing and, subsequently, a plastic prototype that utilized his design concept. This process was completed in the same summer.

Peter was very excited about his invention but he knew that many steps were still required before the invention could be commercially viable. The first was to take the mechanical drawings to a top patent attorney in Toronto who was also an engineer and ask him to conduct a preliminary patent search. Peter knew that the idea of a detachable toothbrush head could not be patented since he had seen products of this type in the market. However, he had hopes that the double-locking connector was unique. The lawyer initially expressed his doubt that the connector would be patentable because there were literally thousands of patented connectors in the market. Despite his skepticism, the lawyer agreed to conduct a patent search and to advise Peter of his findings. Peter hoped that his idea would be the first of its kind and decided that, if it was not patentable, he would have to return to the drawing board.

Later in the summer, Peter was delighted to hear from the lawyer that there was some possibility that the connector could be patented. This was already a major achievement but Peter had no time to rest on his laurels. Through the patent attorney, the services of an industrial designer were obtained in order to specify the exact product characteristics and designs. Patent applications required very detailed drawings depicting precisely how the product was constructed and utilized. The drawings were challenging to create since they were required to visually explain the product characteristics in the absence of any supporting text.

At the same time, Peter had to begin addressing a number of issues surrounding the ability to manufacture the product. Issues such as product style, the types of molds required, the engineering specifications, collapsibility, the tolerances involved and the tooling requirements, in addition to the fine tuning needed to make the product attractive to the consumer, had yet to be determined. In order to obtain the necessary expertise, a friend recommended that Peter secure the input of a well-known industrial designer who was located in Montreal.

Don and Peter flew to Montreal to meet with the designer, but the meeting did not go well due to differences between the designer's goals and those of Peter and Don. However, Peter still needed the expertise of an experienced industrial designer, and he subsequently located a highly qualified professional in Toronto who also taught industrial design part-time. This designer made considerable changes to the product's connection process, and ultimately designed a new product prototype which could be provided to the patent attorney and others so that they could visually see how the product would function.

In the autumn of 1987, Peter's lawyer had advised that his concept could possibly be patented, and the application process was initiated. By July 1988, a patent application was filed in the United States. The U.S. patent was sought first because of the lawyer's belief that if a duplicate process did not already exist in the United States, there would be a high probability that a similar process also did not exist in another country. Peter expected that corresponding applications would be filed in Canada and other foreign countries by July 1989.

A patent application usually has three essential components: the *patent drawings* that are completed by a registered patent artist, the *patent claims* which provide a description of the invention (i.e., what the product or process actually claims to do) in simple yet broad terms, and finally, the actual *patent* itself which sets out in detail the words that will constitute the document that the applicant company will ultimately use as protection against imitation by another firm. Peter's lawyer was employed by a firm that specialized in patents and he was, therefore, able to provide all of these patent elements in-house. All were contained in the July submission to the patent office.

The patent process involves the investigation of all claims of the concept seeking protection, and normally takes from three to five years from the date of application before a patent is awarded. The process is typically an iterative one, wherein the patent office reviews the claims and requests changes to narrow the scope of the patent. This is because companies seeking patents usually keep their descriptions broad to provide them as much latitude as possible for defending their claims. The patent office, on the contrary, is concerned with maintaining very specific descriptions in order to avoid confusion or disputes that might arise due to overlaps among several patents.

Incorporation and Licensing

Peter's patent attorney referred him to a corporate lawyer and on his advice two new companies, Click Connections Corporation (Click) and Alpha Personal Dental Care Systems Inc. (Alpha) were incorporated in June 1988. Peter owned 90 per cent of Click and Julie owned the remainder. The corporate lawyer had suggested the patent to the double locking connecting device be owned by Click, to minimize disputes concerning patent uses and applications. Alpha was created to cover all dental applications only, while non-dental applications would be pursued through other companies.

Click and Alpha entered into an agreement whereby Click licensed to Alpha the exclusive worldwide rights to use and commercialize Click's invention for any dental or dental hygiene application. The license was effective for the life of the patent and also covered any improvement or enhancement subsequently made to the invention by either Click or Alpha. Alpha was not required to pay any royalties to Click for the license agreement, as the license was granted in consideration of monies spent and efforts put forth to date by Alpha's shareholders. Under the terms of the agreement, Alpha was entitled to sublicense to third parties, including manufacturers, the rights to use the invention, but only within the specific field of dental care. Alpha also filed Canadian and U.S. applications for registration of the trademark "Click" for use in association with its dental applications.

Advisory Team

Concurrent with the patent application, Woods Gordon was also developing a Business Plan for the idea. In the meantime, Peter and Julie started bringing others together who could contribute their expertise. The two partners believed that the input from the team was critical to the product's successful development and these individuals joined Peter and Julie as an advisory council. The council was formally comprised of four dentists (including Dr. Don Thomas), although several other acquaintances also offered informal assistance from time to time. For example, one of the acquaintances was an experienced manager in a manufacturing corporation that had extensive contacts with industrial designers, and raw material suppliers. Another held a senior financial management position in a medium-sized corporation. To compensate them for their contributions in what Alpha called "sweat equity," individuals who functioned in an advisory capacity were provided with common shares in Alpha. A number of people (including Peter) contributed funds amounting to $47,000 in return for additional shares. In addition to his financial contributions, for the past two years Peter had also devoted a significant part of every day to the Alpha project. In recognition of this commitment, he was provided with a number of shares. All shareholders of Alpha were parties to a shareholders' agreement dated April 1988. Exhibit 1 provides a summary of the holders of common shares and Exhibit 2 contains a copy of the Shareholders' Agreement. This agreement would require modification if any additional shareholders invested in the company. Finally, in recognition of their contribution, Peter agreed to allocate one per cent of the profits of Click to be divided among the original investors in Alpha.

Business Strategy

Although there was little formal market research, Peter and Julie conducted a survey at three dental clinics to determine the buying behaviour of individuals and to assess whether or not they would be receptive to the new product idea. The 400 responses to the survey were very favourable.

Name	*Number of Common Shares Held*
P. R. Butler	424,000
J. E. McBride	195,000
D. R. Thomas	111,000
J. M. Black	107,000
J. B. Morgan	73,000
W. G. Taylor	57,000
C. J. Carter	11,000
J. F. Masse	11,000
T. L. DeVriese	11,000
I. S. Sherban	315
Total Common Shares	**1,000,315**

Exhibit 1 Holders of Common Shares

From the Woods Gordon study they learned that Nielsen had conducted studies which concluded that total over-the-counter retail sales of oral hygiene products through drug, food and chain merchandisers in the United States were approximately US$3 billion in 1987, and total sales of toothbrushes in the United States during the same period were about US$245 million. They anticipated the Canadian market would represent approximately 10 per cent of that in the United States. They also realized that dentists themselves represented a large market, with many providing a new toothbrush to patients during their periodic examinations. Other opportunities existed in the institutional (hospitals, health clinics, schools), and corporate (hotel chains, airlines, dental insurance companies) sectors, among others.

From the beginning Peter had no interest in manufacturing the product himself. The team was cognizant of the many competitors currently operating in the dental hygiene market in both Canada and the United States. They were primarily large multinational corporations, including the Gillette Company (which produced the Oral B toothbrush), Johnson & Johnson, and the John O. Butler Company, among others. All of these companies were aggressively involved in marketing and promoting their dental care products, most of which competed directly with Alpha's proposed concept. Consequently, the group felt that their best strategy would be to license Alpha's technology to one or more of the existing manufacturers. The group believed that the manufacturers or their distributors would have the resources necessary to effectively market Alpha's concept to a broad range of consumers, resources which Alpha currently lacked. Peter believed that the rights to sell the toothbrush could be licensed for four to seven per cent of revenues.

The Funds Required

Peter knew that he needed additional funds to develop and exploit the concept. He had already spent a considerable amount of money to reach this stage (see Exhibit 3). Although Peter was

(Text continues on page 198)

THIS AGREEMENT made as of the day of April 1988

AMONG: ALPHA PERSONAL DENTAL CARE SYSTEMS INCORPORATED (Hereinafter called the "Company")

AND: EACH AND ALL OF THOSE HOLDERS OF COMMON SHARES in the capital of ALPHA PERSONAL DENTAL CARE SYSTEMS INCORPORATED who may from time to time, either before or after their acquisition of any of such shares, become party to this Agreement

(Hereinafter collectively referred to as "Shareholders" and individually referred to as "Shareholder").

WHEREAS the authorized capital of the Company consists of an unlimited number of common shares (the "Common Shares");

AND WHEREAS, of the authorized capital of the Company, Common Shares have been issued and are held by the Shareholders in the numbers set forth in Schedule "A" hereto;

AND WHEREAS the parties hereto have agreed to enter into this Agreement to establish a continuing basis of relationship among themselves and amongst any other persons who from time to time become shareholders of the Company;

NOW, THEREFORE, IN CONSIDERATION of the mutual covenants and agreements herein contained and the sum of $1.00 paid by each of the parties to each of the other parties (receipt and sufficiency of which is hereby acknowledged), the parties agree as follows:

1. *Warranties*

Each Shareholder warrants that he is the beneficial owner of the Common Shares registered in his name and that he has full entitlement and capacity to enter into and give effect to this Agreement. Each Shareholder who shall hereafter acquire Common Shares or additional Common Shares, as the case may be, warrants that such Common Shares shall be issued and registered in his name and that at that time (and assuming all such Common Shares have been validly allotted and issued as fully paid and non-assessable) he shall have full entitlement and capacity to give effect to this Agreement.

2. *Management*

(a) The Shareholders shall cause such meetings of the Company to be held, shall vote at all such meetings and shall generally take all steps necessary to cause such resolutions to be passed, by-laws to be enacted, documents to be executed and all things and acts to be done by the Company to ensure the following continuing arrangements with respect to the management, operation and control of the Company as hereinafter set forth in this Section 2.

(b) The board of directors of the Company shall consist of nine directors.

(c) The officers of the company shall be elected or appointed by the board from time to time and shall, as of the date hereof, be as follows:

Chairman of the Board and Chief Executive Officer and President	P. R. Butler
Vice-President	D. R. Thomas
Secretary-Treasurer	J. E. McBride

(d) By notice given to every director at least 10 days before the date of the meeting, the Shareholders shall cause meetings of the board of directors to be held at least once in every three month period and at each such meeting the parties hereto shall cause the Chairman or the President to report fully to the board with respect to the current status of operations of the Company and any major developments or planned action involving the Company. In addition, the parties hereto shall cause full current financial information concerning the business and affairs of the Company to be presented at each such meeting of the board. The Shareholders shall cause the by-laws of the Company to provide that meetings of the board may be called

Exhibit 2 Shareholders' Agreement *(Continued)*

by the Chairman or the President or any two directors, that a quorum for meetings of the board shall consist of * directors, that at any meeting of the board of directors the Chairman shall not be entitled to a second or casting vote, and that all matters submitted to the board must be approved by at least * directors.

(e) The Shareholders agree that it shall be a condition of the employment by the Company of any new employee that such employee enter into an employment agreement with the Company, effective at the commencement of the employee's employment, providing in terms satisfactory to the Company's counsel that the employee, inter alia, (i) will not compete with the Company, (ii) will not divulge any confidential information relating to the Company or its customers, and (iii) will disclose and assign over to the Company all ideas, suggestions, improvements, patent rights, etc., which the employee makes during the term of his employment and which relate to the Company's business.

3. *Dealing with Common Shares*

(a) Except as hereinafter set forth, no Common Shares shall be transferred, assigned, pledged or in any way encumbered by any Shareholder. No purported dealing with any Common Shares in violation of this Agreement shall be valid and the Company shall not transfer any of the Common Shares dealt with in violation of this Agreement in the records of the Company nor shall any voting rights attaching to such Common Shares be exercised, nor shall any dividends be paid on such Common Shares during the period of such violation. Such disqualification shall be in addition to and not in lieu of any other remedies to enforce the provisions of this Agreement.

(b) Each of the Shareholders agrees that he will not, without the consent required by the Company's charter documents, sell or offer to sell any of the Common Shares owned by him.

(c) If at any time the Company shall complete a public offering, then all the Shareholders shall be entitled to sell Common Shares owned by them as part of the public offering, provided that the ability of the Shareholders to sell any Common Shares owned by them as part of the Public Offering will be subject to the discretion of the Company's underwriter. If the Company's underwriter imposes a limit on the total number of Common Shares which may be disposed of in a public offering will be subject to the discretion of the Company's underwriter. If the Company's underwriter imposes a limit on the total number of Common Shares which may be disposed of in a public offering (the "Available Common Shares"), Shareholders wishing to sell Common Shares shall be entitled to sell that percentage of the Available Common Shares that the number of Common Shares owned by such Shareholder is of the total number of Common Shares held by Shareholders wishing to sell Common Shares under the provisions of this paragraph.

(d) In the event that any Shareholder (hereinafter called the "Seller"):

(i) dies; or
(ii) becomes bankrupt or insolvent; or
(iii) does, permits to be done or omits to do any act in breach of this Agreement and such breach or default has continued for 30 days following written notice thereof to the Seller by any other Shareholder;

then the Seller or his legal representatives shall offer to sell and the remaining Shareholders shall each have the right, but not the obligation, to purchase all of the Common Shares owned by the Seller immediately prior to the event referred to in clause (i), (ii) or (iii) hereof, as the case may be. Any shareholder exercising a right to purchase hereunder is hereinafter referred to as the "Purchaser" and all such Purchasers are hereinafter collectively referred to as "Purchasers."

(e) The purchase price for the Common Shares to be sold pursuant to Section 3(d) shall be the [book value per share], as determined by the Company's Auditor.

(f) The Purchasers shall purchase the Common Shares to be sold by the Seller pursuant to Section 3(d) on a pro rata basis, being the proportion that the number of Common Shares held by each of the Purchasers respectively as at the date of the event requiring such offer to sell under Section 3(d) is to the number of Common Shares held by all Purchasers as at that date.

Exhibit 2 Shareholders' Agreement *(Continued)*

(g) Within 30 days following a determination by the Company's auditor of the book value per share the Seller or his legal representatives shall sell and the Purchasers shall purchase the Common Shares of the Seller and each Purchaser shall make payment in full therefor in cash or by certified cheque on closing or, at the option of the Purchaser, in equal periodic instalments over a period not exceeding two years. In the event that an election is made by a Purchaser for payment in instalments, the outstanding portion of the purchase price shall bear interest at a per annum rate equal to the Bank prime rate of * plus * per cent and such Purchaser shall, unless other security arrangements are made which are satisfactory to the Seller or his legal representatives, pledge to the Seller his portion of the Common hares purchased as security for the due payment of the outstanding portion of his purchase price; provided that, until a default in payment has occurred and remains unremedied after 10 days' notice thereof, the Seller or his personal representatives shall not be entitled to exercise any voting privileges or other rights of ownership in respect of the Common Shares so pledged.

(h) Notwithstanding paragraphs (b) and (c), a Shareholder wishing to sell or assign some or all of his Common Shares (the "Initiating Shareholder"), other than as part of a Public Offering, may do so by first obtaining a bona fide offer to purchase such Common Shares (the "Offer") which, to be effective, shall be in writing and shall include a covenant that the Purchaser will become bound by the terms and conditions of this Agreement. Such Offer may not be accepted without first communicating it and the terms therein contained to the other Shareholders shall be open for a period of 31 days. If any of the other Shareholders accepts the offer of the Initiating Shareholder within the said period of 31 days, the Initiating Shareholder shall sell his Common Shares to the Shareholder or Shareholders so accepting his offer on a pro rata basis, being the proportion that the number of Common Shares held by each accepting Shareholder is to all the Common Shares held by all accepting Shareholders. If none of the other Shareholders accepts the offer of the Initiating Shareholder within the said period of 31 days, the Initiating Shareholder shall be entitled to sell all, but not less than all, of the Common Shares which are the subject of the Offer, in accordance with the terms of the Offer, provided such sale is completed within 30 days following the expiration of the above-mentioned period of 31 days.

(i) In addition to the foregoing, subject to applicable law, any Shareholder shall be entitled at any time to sell or transfer any or all his common Shares (i) to a corporation wholly-owned by such Shareholder or by such Shareholder and one or more members of his immediate family, or (ii) directly to one or more members of such Shareholders' immediate family provided in either case that no such sale or transfer shall be effective until such corporation or such family members, as the case may be, has entered into an agreement with the other parties hereto whereby such corporation or such family members, as the case may be, agrees to assume and be bound by all the terms and conditions of this Agreement and, in particular, the obligations and restrictions to which the selling Shareholder is subject hereunder. No such sale or transfer shall relieve the selling Shareholder of his obligations hereunder.

(j) Any of the Shareholders may mortgage, pledge, charge or otherwise encumber or grant security interests in some or all of its Common Shares as security for a bona fide loan made to such Shareholder by a single lender acting at arm's length with such Shareholder, provided always that the secured party first specifically agrees as follows:

(i) in the event it exercises any power of foreclosure, the secured party shall execute and be bound by the terms of this Agreement;

(ii) prior to exercising any power of foreclosure or sale or any other remedy which it may have, the secured party shall give to the other Shareholders 60 days' prior written notice of its intention to do so and shall given such other Shareholders the opportunity, during such 60-day period, to pay to the secured party all amounts owing to it by the Shareholder in default and obtaining a valid transfer and assignment of the secured Common Shares, on a pro rata basis, being the proportion that the number of Common Shares held by each Shareholder wishing to exercise such right is to the Common Shares then held by all Shareholders wishing to exercise such right, free and clear of any mortgage, pledge, charge, encumbrance or security interest; and

Exhibit 2 Shareholders' Agreement *(Continued)*

(iii) prior to the expiration of the 60-day period referred to in clause (ii) hereof, the secured party shall make no demand requiring that the Common Shares held by it as security be transferred into the name of the secured party or its nominee.

(k) If on the closing of any disposition under Section 3(d) or Section 3(h), the selling party shall neglect or refuse to complete the transaction, the purchasers or transferees shall have the right upon such default, without prejudice to any other rights which they may have, to pay such defaulting party's share of the purchase price to the Company's bankers in trust and to the credit of such defaulting party and each of the Shareholders hereby irrevocably constitutes the Company and the other Shareholders its true and lawful attorneys to complete the said transaction and to execute any and every document necessary in that behalf.

(l) Any vendor of Common Shares pursuant to Section 3(d) or Section 3(h) hereby warrants that it has, and will at the closing of any sale have, good and marketable title to the Common Shares free from all encumbrances. Should any person hold an encumbrance on the Common Shares contrary to the provisions hereof, then the encumbrance shall be of no force and effect and the Common Shares when sold pursuant hereto shall be free or any encumbrance. Where there is an encumbrance on the Common Shares and it is permitted pursuant to Section 3(j) and a permitted sale is made to one or more of the other Shareholders, then the purchasing Shareholders shall take free and clear of the permitted encumbrance and any purchase price, notwithstanding anything herein contained to the contrary, shall be paid to the permitted encumbrancer and to the selling Shareholder jointly, as their interests shall appear.

4. *Party to Agreement*

The Company shall not issue any of its Shares or approve any transfer of its Shares to any person who is not a party to this Agreement.

5. *General Provisions*

(a) Any costs in determining the book value per share shall be borne by the Company.

(b) All certificates for Shares in the capital of the Company issued from time to time shall have endorsed thereon a memorandum substantially as follows:

"This Certificate is issued to and held by the party to whom it is issued subject to the terms of a Shareholders' Agreement entered into among the Shareholders of the Company and the Company."

(c) Any notice, direction or instrument required or permitted to be given hereunder shall be given in writing and be mailed, postage prepaid, or delivered by one party to another as follows:

if to a Shareholder, at his address as set out in the records of the Company;
if to the Company,

Alpha Dental Care Systems Incorporated
R.R. 1
Hyde Park, Ontario
N0M 1Z0

Any notice, direction or other instrument aforesaid, if delivered, shall be deemed to be given or made on the day on which it was delivered or, if mailed, shall be deemed to have been given or made on the third business day following the day on which it was mailed, provided that no mailing shall be deemed to have been given or made if mailed during a time or actual or threatened postal disruption or dispute in Canada. Any party hereto may, from time to time, give notice of any change in its address and, in such event, the address of such party shall be deemed to be changed accordingly.

Exhibit 2 Shareholders' Agreement *(Continued)*

(d) Except as expressly contemplated herein, this Agreement or any benefits or liabilities hereunder shall not be assigned by any of the parties without the prior written consent, executed under seal, of the others.

(e) This Agreement embodies the entire agreement and understanding between the parties hereto and supersedes all prior agreements and undertakings, whether oral or written, relative to the subject matter hereof.

(f) This Agreement may be amended only as follows:

(i) by resolution of the Shareholders passed by the favourable votes of the holders of not less than $66\,^{2}/_{3}$ per cent of the number of Common Shares represented at a meeting of Shareholders duly convened for the purpose and held in accordance with the provisions of the Company's by-laws at which the holders of more than 50 per cent in number of the Common Shares then outstanding are present in person or by proxy; or

(ii) by instrument in writing signed in one or more counterparts by the holders of not less than 75 per cent in number of all the then outstanding Common Shares.

(g) The parties hereto agree from time to time after the execution of this Agreement, to make, do, execute or cause or permit to be made, done or executed all such further and other lawful acts, deeds, things, devices, conveyances and assurances in law whatsoever as may be required to carry out the true intention and to give full force and effect to this Agreement.

(h) Unless otherwise specified, all statements of or references to dollar amounts in this Agreement shall mean Canadian dollars.

(i) Time is expressly declared and stipulated to be of the essence of this Agreement in respect of all payments to be made hereunder and all covenants and agreements to be performed and fulfilled. Any extension of time hereunder shall not be deemed to be or to operate in law as a waiver of this provision.

(j) If any provision of this Agreement shall fail to be strictly enforced or any party shall consent to any action by any other party or shall waive any provision as set out herein, such action by such party shall not be construed as a waiver thereof other than at the specific time that such waiver or failure to enforce takes place and shall at no time be construed as a consent, waiver or excuse for the failure to perform and act in accordance with this Agreement at any past or future occasion.

(k) This Agreement may be executed in several counterparts each of which when executed by any person shall be deemed to be an original and such counterparts shall together constitute but one and the same instrument.

(l) Words used herein importing the singular number only shall include the plural, and vice versa, and words importing the masculine gender shall include the feminine and neuter genders, and vice versa, and words importing persons shall include firms and corporations.

(m) The division of this Agreement into sections and the insertion of headings are for convenience of reference only and shall not affect the construction or interpretation of this Agreement.

(n) This Agreement shall be governed by and construed in accordance with the laws of the Province of Ontario.

IN WITNESS WHEREOF the parties hereto have caused this Agreement to be executed under seal as of the date first above written.

Exhibit 2 Shareholders' Agreement

Nature of Expense	*Amount*
Initial Patent Searches	$3,562
Corporate Legal Services	3,055
Legal Services Relating to Patent	6,497
Legal Services—Shareholders' Agreement	1,200
Business Plan	10,756
Industrial Designer	14,121
Prototypes—Initial Version	1,029
Prototypes—Subsequent (five times actual size)	6,110
Prototypes—Most Recent Versions	3,159
Administration & Miscellaneous	568
Market Research	34
Total Expenses Incurred	**$50,091**

Exhibit 3 Summary of Expenses Incurred to Date

able to contribute more of his personal assets to the business, he thought it advisable to secure investors from outside the company.

In order to proceed further with the toothbrush design, the manufacturability of the product would have to be tested. The test involved ensuring that the toothbrush could be produced using a collapsible core moulding technique that had been recommended. It also allowed the manufacturer to gauge the cycle time for production. Other testing was required on aspects such as stress and structural analysis of the parts, of the integrity of materials and of the mould opening and closing process. These tests would be performed by a firm in Toronto that was experienced in prototype design using a computer-assisted design process. The result would be a "testing brief" that Alpha would use as part of its future solicitations to potential investors, manufacturers, or multinationals. Peter felt that the costs of testing further product design, styling, and professional services would total at least $50,000.

The Challenge

Peter's lawyer had been confident that the required funds could be raised from individual investors and suggested a private placement. Peter knew little about the equity market or the methods employed in selling shares in a firm. Although he was a strong believer in the merits of his invention, he had doubts that it would be possible to sell shares in a concept that was at such an early stage of development. However, the attorney had been associated with a number of very successful offerings in the 1980s and he persuaded Peter that such an offering would have a high probability of success.

Before approaching investors, a number of decisions had to be made including: who should be approached, the type of instrument to be offered, the price of the instrument and the contents of the offering memorandum which would be provided. Peter and Julie felt a rising sense of excitement as they drove to the lawyer's office to hear his recommended strategy.

4

VENTURE SETUP

THE SETUP PROCESS

The venture setup process consists of the set of activities required to create an organization that is able to produce some work that is competitive in the marketplace. Setup requires an entrepreneur to identify and then create appropriate structures, systems, and even cultures, which enable a competitive product or service to come into existence. Thus, setup is primarily organizational, where the key resources (e.g., material, human, technical, etc.) are assembled and combined in such a way that product/service positioning, differentiation, competitive advantage, comparative advantage, and, in sum, value creation, result.

In the market system, success in the process of competitively assembling resources (Hunt & Morgan, 1995) ultimately shapes the fate of a new venture. This is why, before initiating the start-up process, it is critical to ascertain—even test—the extent to which a product or service can be fashioned effectively. For products, building, costing, and testing a prototype do this job. For services, developing clear service specifications, and then also testing them for cost and "doability" within a target market, does the job. Concurrent with these processes, entrepreneurs should become aware of and consider protecting, through appropriate copyright, patent, trademark, and so forth, the unique and competitive features of products/services—your intellectual property.

The result of the setup process is organization, and organization is enacted through structure. In this sense, *setup* and *structuring* are synonyms. In the setup process, structuring is *inwardly focused,* by which we mean that the focus of an entrepreneur's attention during the setup process is on the venture itself rather than on its customers. (The *outward focus* on customers is the main objective of the start-up process.)

What must be organized/structured during setup?

The list of possibilities for what must be structured varies somewhat depending on the nature of the venture, but, in our experience, structuring includes at least the following:

- Forming an advisory board
- Forming relationships with new venture employees
- Establishing internal reporting relationships, policies, and procedures
- Identifying and engaging legal and accounting services
- Forming the venture entity/legal structuring
- Making make-or-buy decisions

- Establishing relationships with suppliers
- Establishing production or service delivery systems and/or facilities
- Establishing banking relationships
- Establishing an accounting and financial reporting system
- Obtaining needed licenses and insurance
- Deciding location issues
- Arranging helpful alliances (e.g., industry or buying groups)
- Updating the business plan (to reflect the reality of new relationships)

You may notice that each of the above structuring processes involves your entering into some type of relationship. In this respect, structuring can be thought of as a kind of relationship building. This concept is important because it is the solution to one of the most frustrating aspects of learning the venture setup process.

In our experience, many learners who encounter the setup process for the first time expect there to be an extensive list of "how-to" checklists that, if followed, will result in proper venture setup. However, effective setup (which we have previously defined to be competitively assembling resources) is a judgment-based process that is unique to each venture. The reason for this is that resources are heterogeneous (Hunt & Morgan, 1995), meaning that each resource comes in an indivisible bundle that is to some degree unique (Penrose, 1959). Furthermore, the way in which you, the entrepreneur, intend to apply these resources is also heterogeneous, meaning that the product or service that you plan to offer is intended to be unique and special enough that it is competitive in the marketplace. Thus, we have concluded that our suggesting or providing a checklist approach to venture setup would be misleading and possibly destructive to your venturing aspirations.

Instead, we suggest that you consider the resource assembly process that is at the core of the setup process to be your opportunity to use the setup process to enact your competitive advantage in the marketplace. Since 1995, this has been referred to as the resource advantage approach to competing (Hunt & Morgan, 1995). The insight that we hope that you will take from this chapter is that gaining resource-based competitive advantage occurs during the setup process and that the way for you to effectively enact the setup process is through the relationship-building process. And we believe that your success in building relationships with your stakeholders will be through your capability to reliably identify definitive stakeholder relationships (Mitchell, Agle, & Wood, 1997).

Accordingly, it is very helpful during the setup process for first-time venturers to form an advisory board—even if it is done informally—because in our observation, there is no substitute for experience in the formation of all the new relationships that are essential to an effective start-up. An advisory board can assist first-time venturers by contributing some of the judgment necessary for relationship-building-based resource assembly to result in resource-based competitive advantage.

In the end, however, it will be through your own experience that you will gain the skills necessary to build the relationships necessary to set up a competitive new venture. In the next section of this chapter, we look at a student's view of the setup process.

A Student's View of the Setup Process

The setup process, as viewed through the eyes of an entrepreneurship student, includes the following narrative that accompanies Figure 4.1. This narrative explains the figure and can

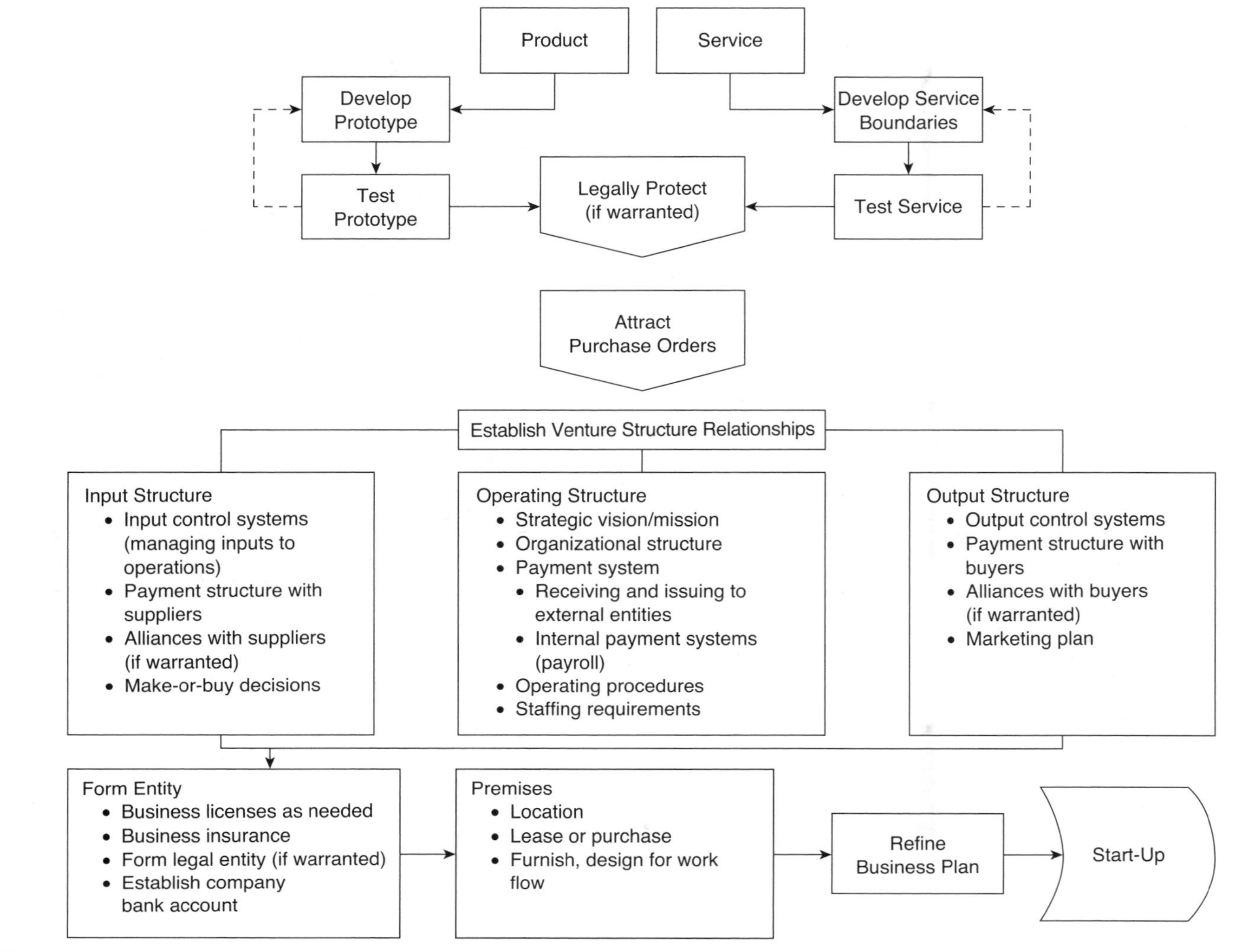

Figure 4.1 Setup

be used to visualize many of the key elements we have just described to be essential to the setup process.

This student says the following:

After the financing is secured, the setup process begins with the development of the product or service prototype. The product/service offering is then tested until the optimal product/service is developed. Legal protection for the product/process can then be sought (if it is warranted). The final step in testing would be to try and attract purchase orders, to ensure that all competitive assumptions are valid. After this step, the venture's structure must then be developed.

Step 1: Establishing Venture Structure. This step involves three critical stages: establishing the input structure, establishing the operating structure, and establishing the output structure.

Stage 1: Establishing the input structure. This stage first involves putting a system in place to track and manage inputs to operations. A payment structure with suppliers also needs to be established, outlining volume/time discounts and credit terms. If possible, alliances with suppliers should be established. Such alliances could include exclusivity agreements or the joint establishment of systems required to develop a just-in-time (JIT) inventory system. Finally, make-or-buy decisions will also have to be made on the basis of, "Is it most efficient to make this in-house or to buy?"

Stage 2: Establishing the operating structure. This stage first involves developing a strategic vision as to where the venture should be in *x* number of years down the road. Its purpose is to strive to attain goals, giving the venture meaning. An organizational structure is also needed. Rather than create a functional structure with the total autonomy for decision making held by the "top personnel," a structure should be created that fosters and promotes creativity and induces employee involvement in the venture. A payment system also needs to be established to perform two functions: first, to receive and issue payments to external entities (suppliers, professional entities) and, second, to issue payments to staff. How much these individuals will receive in compensation must also be defined (the planning phase has already incorporated a general dollar outflow estimate for staffing and professional services). Operating procedures must then be defined, outlining job descriptions, workflow, and how tasks are to be performed and in what time they are to be performed. Last, staff must also be pursued. This involves seeking likely candidates for employment and screening applicants until the positions are filled.

- The structure should cultivate a culture of creativity and continuous learning.

Stage 3: Determining output structure. This stage first involves implementing output control systems. Such systems include using software to keep track of inventory turnover, receivables turnover, gross margins, and so on. The purpose of an output control system is to periodically measure the venture's performance and to then measure the variance in expected results and actual results. The questions to be asked are as follows:

- Are the actual results superior or inferior to those projected?
- Why are the actual results superior/inferior?

- Were the causes for the variance beyond the control of management? If so, is this trend likely to continue? If it is likely to continue, how can it be mitigated/capitalized upon?

A payment structure with buyers also needs to be established. It must be determined if the offering will be offered on credit terms and what payment terms the venture should accept. Alliances with buyers should be made (if warranted), again locking in exclusivity agreements where possible and packaging the product with other complementary products.

- When formulating alliances with buyers, beware of opportunism of other parties. Think about why the other party would enter into an agreement with you.
- When formulating alliances with buyers, always keep in mind how such an agreement could affect the reputation of the firm.

Last, a marketing plan needs to be established that outlines how the value of the offering will be communicated to potential consumers.

- What is the best means to reach the targeted demographic given the constraints of the budget imposed?
- What will be emphasized in the message?
- How many consumers is this plan likely to attract to the venture?

Once the venture's structure has been established, Step 2 can be conducted.

Step 2: Entity and Premises. This step involves two principal stages.

Stage 1: Form entity. This stage first involves determining whether the venture should be a legally incorporated entity. It involves an assessment of the risks of liability associated with proprietorships, but, generally speaking, it is probably most attractive to incorporate. Thus, one part of this stage is to form a legal entity (registering the company name, etc.). Business licenses and insurance must also be purchased and a company bank account established.

Stage 2: Premises. This stage involves choosing the location for the venture given all of the product/service requirements as well as the operating requirements. Thus, the first part of this stage is to choose a location. It must then be determined if a lease or purchase agreement is most attractive. Finally, given a limited budget, the premises must be furnished and designed for the workflow requirements that were developed when operating procedures were formulated.

After the entity has been established, licenses and insurance have been purchased, and the premises determined, the business plan must be refined to account for any changes that have been made during the setup phase. After the changes have been made, the start-up phase can be conducted.

Cases

The following cases have been selected to help learners to develop and become more aware of their own thoughts on the venture setup process.

PolicePrep

Prepared by Deland Jessop under the supervision of Professor Stewart Thornhill

 Version: (A) 2004-12-15

Introduction

Deland Jessop was driving back from Conestoga College after another meeting with the dean of social science, Bill Jeffrey. It had been almost one year since he completed his MBA from the Richard Ivey School of Business, and he had experienced both triumphs and failures over the last year. With his two partners, Jessop had successfully launched PolicePrep, an e-learning company dedicated to preparing potential police applicants for their entrance exams. The three partners had just completed some major development work and had to talk about future options. Jessop's two partners both had full-time jobs, and Jessop had to consider seeking employment while treating PolicePrep as a part-time job, or investing time and effort in further developing the business. On top of that, if Jessop were going to go forward developing PolicePrep, the entire business relationship and ownership structure would probably have to change.

Hiring Process

In order to be hired as a police officer in jurisdictions across North America, individuals had to complete a lengthy and challenging application process. Many services charged up to \$300[1] to simply apply and partake in Stage 1 of the application process (see below). The minimum requirements were quite basic: a high school diploma, a clean criminal record, a valid driver's licence and 18 years of age. The majority of applicants, who otherwise met the basic requirements, failed to advance beyond the initial round of screening tests.

Although each service had its own unique hiring process, most followed a standard format. Generally, anyone was entitled to partake in Stage 1, but could advance through the stages only after successfully completing the stage prior.

The written exams usually incorporated multiple choice questions (anywhere from 72 to 150 questions), which covered areas such as basic math, pattern solving, identification, mapping, judgment and other police-related topics. In addition to the multiple choice exam, most police services had a written exam and/or essay component. Interviews generally consisted of both behavioral style questions and questions about a particular community service or police service. Behavioral tests often required applicants to respond to video images of actual police experiences, such as a neighbor dispute. The applicant would then be judged on their ability to communicate a solution to the problem. Psychological tests were performed using standard formats, such as the Minnesota Multiphasic Personality Inventory-2, and a thorough background investigation was performed by police officers of that service.

Potential Customers

Every year in Canada police services received approximately 40,000 applications for positions as police officers, while in the United States, this number was closer to 700,000. In Ontario, nearly 70 per cent of applicants were between the ages of 18 and 29. Eighty per cent were male and one-third had completed programs in law and security or police foundations training (see Exhibits 1 to 3).

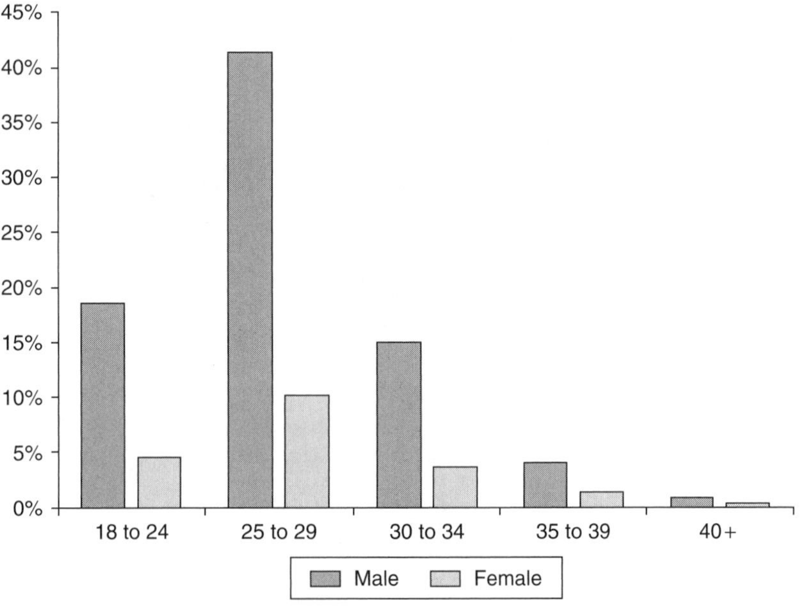

Exhibit 1 Statistics on Ontario Police Applicants by Age

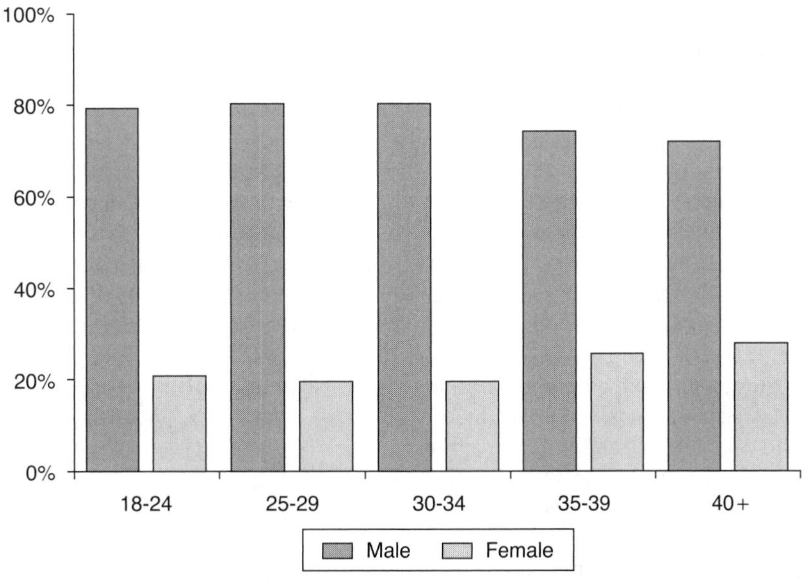

Exhibit 2 Statistics on Ontario Police Applicants by Age and Sex

Source: Company files.

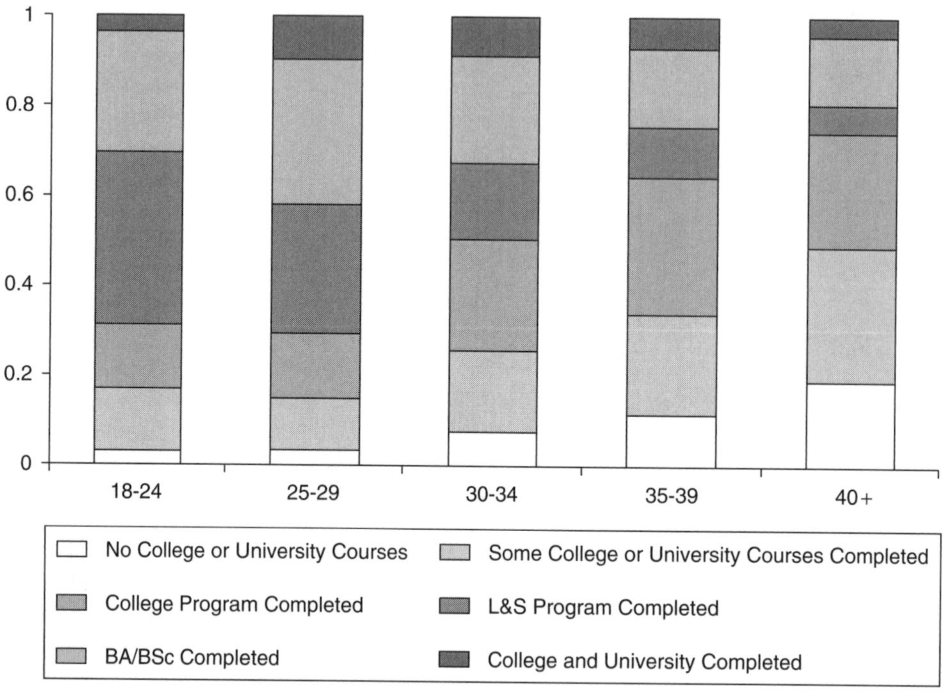

Exhibit 3 Statistics on Ontario Police Applicants Application Education

A focus group conducted at Fanshawe College revealed that many students in police foundation programs had often dreamed of becoming a police officer from a very young age and worked for years to achieve this dream. Although in Ontario the requirements called for high school education only, applicants often spent thousands of dollars and several years attending community colleges to receive diplomas in police foundations and law and security programs or completing relevant university degrees. Some police recruiters considered the college courses redundant training, as new recruits had to complete an intensive three-month training program at the Ontario Police College in Aylmer, Ontario. This training program covered almost all of the material that was taught in the colleges. Students took the college courses to give themselves any possible advantage over fellow applicants.

In addition to educational expenses, applicants were also required to pay a non-refundable fee ($300) when they applied to the majority of Ontario Police Services. As well, applicants who were unsuccessful with a particular stage of the testing were required to wait a minimum period of time before they could reapply. These periods could be up to one year, depending on the particular police service. This wait could be very discouraging to potential applicants and caused many of them to give up on the process or take a job they were less interested in. After the year had expired, they had to perform the tests again and pay another fee.

Industry

The test preparation industry was very large across North America and was dominated by two large firms: Kaplan and Princeton Review. These firms focused mainly on standard test formats that catered to very large markets (GMAT, LSAT, MCAT, etc). Traditional delivery methods in the standardized testing industry included small classroom sessions occurring on weekends and preparation books that could be purchased through major book retailers. Sales and marketing efforts were generally focused on institutes of higher learning such as colleges and universities across North America.

Standardized tests had been evolving to take advantage of technology and were often administered using computers. The preparation industry responded by upgrading its delivery methods to include CD-ROM products as well as Internet learning courses where students received practice tests and teaching material directly online. Universities and colleges around the world also moved into this area, offering curriculum through the Internet in courses ranging from MBA programs to sociology degrees.

One factor that prevented the larger firms from entering the police preparation market was the non-standardized nature of tests that existed among different police services.

The police preparation industry could be classified as very young with a great deal of fragmented local providers in regions across North America. There were very few barriers to entry as no strong brand name had established itself as an expert in the field. Also, the costs associated with starting up a firm were very low, and there were several different delivery formats that could exist for the material.

Competition

The competitors supplying police preparation packages could be broken down into four major groups:

Standardized Books

There were several books on the market across North America that aimed to prepare applicants for the testing process. The books included material on the interview process, qualities that police services were looking for in candidates, practice exams and teaching material on the subjects covered in the exams.

Strengths

- Practice exams designed for specific police services (New York, Chicago, etc.).
- Distribution covering North America through major bookstores.
- Relative inexpensive product (approx. $50).

Weaknesses

- No products designed for Canadian market.
- Not interactive.

Online Sites (Marketing)

There were several American Web sites offering material on police exams and interviews. Their primary goal seemed to be marketing-oriented as their sites attempted to solicit the purchase of a book.

Strengths

- Same benefits as the books.
- Minimal information free over the Internet.

Weaknesses

- No products designed for Canadian market.
- Not interactive.

Online Sites (Products)

There was one Web site that offered online practice exams. The product included a single exam and didn't provide any teaching material or preparation material for interviews, résumés or psychological tests.

Strengths

- Practice exams designed for specific police services (New York, Florida, etc.).
- Cost efficiency on delivery of material.
- Relative inexpensive product (US$50 for one online practice test).

Weaknesses

- Start-up site poorly put together. The site that had the online exam didn't offer any preparation material.
- No products designed for Canadian market.

Classroom Instruction

There were several small firms (often run by an individual police officer) that offered one-day instructional courses to help prepare potential applicants for the entrance exam.

Strengths

- Products designed for the specific tests that applicants are interested in.
- Classroom instruction far more effective teaching process.
- Expert advice from qualified personnel.

Weaknesses

- Higher cost to the program—$180.
- One day of assistance only.
- Limited times and regions available.

COLLEGES

In 2002, there were 19 community colleges across Ontario that had either a police foundations program or law and security program. There were a total of 2,388 students in the first year of these programs (see Exhibit 4). Several of the colleges had plans to double the number of students entering a first-year program over the next four years. The primary goal of these students was to gain an education that would give them an advantage in the hiring process of police services.

The colleges taught a curriculum that focused on the skills required to be a police officer and included courses such as introduction to law, sociology, police procedures, fitness, community policing and more. Several of the colleges were attempting to change their designation by partnering with recognized universities to offer a bachelor's degree in justice studies. The college programs were professionally run with qualified and skilled instructors who often came from a policing career. Their mandate did not include a focus on the application process and, while one or two of the schools offered a one-day course to go over the testing requirements (Stage 3), most did not offer any preparation in this matter.

During the focus group at Fanshawe College, concerns were raised about the lack of preparation offered by colleges. Police foundation program co-ordinators were considering a means of preparing their students for the application process in a cost-effective manner.

OTHER OPPORTUNITIES

Other than policing, there were many other opportunities to provide standardized test preparation. Fire departments across North America used multiple choice exams but were even more fragmented than police departments in terms of testing and application procedures. Fire department training in Ontario was followed a pattern similar to that taken by police training several years ago. There are two or three colleges that offered fire training diplomas in Ontario, but demand from applicants far exceeded the supply of available positions. Other areas for possible expansion included ambulance, nursing, pilot tests, etc., other countries around the world (Australia, Britain, France), other language offerings and even new delivery formats (classroom sessions, books, etc.).

POLICEPREP IS BORN

In his second year of the MBA program, Jessop saw a major downturn in the economy, which was intensified by the events of September 11 and several high-profile corporate scandals. Consulting firms were no longer actively recruiting and were, in fact, laying off some of their own staff. Jessop decided to start exploring different entrepreneurial ideas with fellow classmates.

		Police Foundation		
College	*City*	*Year 1*	*Year 2*	*Law & Security*
Algonquin	Nepean	315	200	126
Fanshawe	London	300	215	0
Conestoga	Kitchener	210	175	84
Niagara	Welland	200	180	85
Seneca	North York	200	175	0
Durham	Oshawa	150	125	60
Loyalist	Belleville	150	100	55
Georgian	Barrie	144	120	58
Canadore	North Bay	100	80	40
Sheridan	Oakville	74	55	111
Cambrian	Sudbury	50	35	20
Confederation	Thunder Bay	150	110	60
Humber	Toronto	50	40	20
Lambton	Sarnia	50	44	20
Mohawk	Hamilton	50	25	20
St. Clair	Windsor	50	37	20
St. Lawrence	Brockville	50	38	20
Sir Sandford	Peterborough	50	40	20
Northern	Timmins	45	32	0
	Totals	**2,388**	**1,826**	**819**

Exhibit 4 College Enrollment 2002
Source: Company files.

One night while at a local bar, Jessop was describing the application-and-testing process that he had gone through to become a police officer. Adam Cooper, a classmate of Jessop's, mentioned that he used to work as an instructor for Kaplan, a company that taught people how to prepare for the GMAT. The two men began exploring the idea of offering an online preparation course for the application process in Canada. Kalpesh Rathod, another classmate, was brought on board due to his expertise with Internet development.

The three partners worked throughout second year developing the material, performing focus groups at community colleges, meeting with Ivey staff about marketing and development issues and contracting an Internet developer to build the site. As the site was nearing completion at the end of the MBA program, Cooper and Rathod both pursued employment opportunities. Since the company would not be able to generate enough revenue to support three full-time employees at the offset, Jessop agreed to focus a greater deal of time further developing the site and initiating sales and marketing activities. The original site included tests designed for the Royal Canadian Mounted Police (RCMP) exam and the GATB (General Aptitude and Test Battery) exam, which qualified applicants for most police services across Ontario.

Marketing

PolicePrep was marketed as s a complete online solution, customized for specific police services. It took a premium pricing strategy, offering full access to five RCMP and five GATB tests, plus all teaching and preparation material (math, grammar, interview, résumés, fitness, etc.) for $197 per year. The three partners did not have a great deal of money as they were just graduating from business school, so the promotion efforts consisted of contacting the colleges about the product and giving presentations at schools to professors and groups of students. Fliers were posted around Ontario, and postcards were produced to hand out at recruiting drives held by police services in Toronto.

Development

Further tests were developed for different jurisdictions including Alberta, Saskatchewan, New York, California and Florida. Some experimentation occurred with the product mix, including offering single-test options for a cheaper price ($50) and developing books based on the Web content for Canadian exams. Video images were added to the site to cover behavioral tests that were used in both Canada and the United States.

Partnership

When the partnership was formed, a very loose agreement was put in place whereby each partner would have signing authority and an equal share of the profits. One concern that Jessop had was the extra hours that he put into the development after the launch. While the other two partners were working full time, Jessop had performed the vast majority of site and sales development. There had been no formal agreement on how Jessop would be compensated for his extra work, but both Rathod and Cooper had acknowledged that Jessop had performed a great deal more work and that compensation would be made. This put a strain on the relationship between the partners and made Jessop reluctant to pursue the company as a sole source of personal income.

Victories

All three partners shared many victories due to their efforts on PolicePrep. Both Rathod and Cooper leveraged the experience they gained from launching the site to successfully land full-time jobs. PolicePrep reached the break-even mark in December 2002, just six months after the site went live (see Exhibit 5 for financials). Several colleges opened their doors to PolicePrep to pitch the product to their students, and one school contracted PolicePrep to design a course for its students as part of the fall 2003 curriculum. Sales were consistent from January 2003 to June 2003, with word of the product spreading. The standard Ontario test changed on July 1, 2003, but because of PolicePrep's flexible platform, the site was upgraded within two weeks to offer the new exam. Customer feedback was outstanding (see Exhibit 6).

FINANCIALS—POLICEPREP BALANCE SHEET			
	31-Dec-02	*31-Mar-03*	*30-Jun-03*
Assets			
Current Assets			
Cash	$10,721	$19,051	$15,256
Accounts Receivable	—	2,312	1,520
Prepaid Hosting	85	—	—
Total	10,806	21,363	16,776
Fixed Assets			
Web Site	16,942	18,018	18,018
Less: Accumulated Depreciation	(6,257)	(10,620)	(14,856)
Total	10,685	7,398	3,162
Total Assets	21,491	28,761	19,938
Liabilities and Shareholders' Equity			
Current			
Accounts Payable	541	1,026	2,447
Long-term Debt	—	—	—
Owners' Equity			
Invested Capital	16,500	16,500	16,500
Retained Earnings	4,450	11,235	991
Total	20,950	27,735	17,491
Total Liabilities and Shareholders' Equity	$21,491	$28,761	$19,938

FINANCIALS—POLICEPREP INCOME STATEMENT A1			
	31-Dec-02	*31-Mar-03*	*30-Jun-03*
Revenue	**(6 months)**		
Sales	$22,086	$15,867	$17,515
Expenses			
Credit Card	753	589	632
Development*	2,666	485	4,908
Payment Processing	378	306	333
GST Tax**	1,450	1,123	—
Administrative	344	556	418
Refund Expense	—	—	660
Hosting	510	1,234	267
	6,101	4,293	7,218

Exhibit 5 Financials—PolicePrep Balance Sheet *(Continued)*

	31-Dec-02	31-Mar-03	30-Jun-03
Operating Profit	15,985	11,574	10,297
Marketing Expense	4,432	—	13,329
Internet Marketing	797	423	2,977
Banking Fees	50	2	—
	5,279	425	16,306
EBITDA	**10,706**	**11,149**	**(6,009)**
Net Income	**$4,450**	**$6,785**	**$(10,244)**
Retained Earnings Beginning		4,450	11,235
Dividends			
Net Income	$4,450	$6,785	$(10,244)
Retained Earnings Ending	**$4,450**	**$11,235**	**$991**

Exhibit 5 Financials—PolicePrep Balance Sheet

Notes: *One-time development fee of $3,000 to paid to partner for development in third period. **GST incorrectly recorded as an expense in first two periods. No salaries paid to any parties.

Source: Company files.

Use		*Overall Satisfaction*		*Recommend*		*Value for Money*		*Exam Success*	
Daily	18	Satisfied	45	Absolutely	46	Satisfied	45	Pass	12
Weekly	16	Neutral	1	Don't Know	1	Neutral	1	Not Written	34
2 to 3 Times a Month	14	Unsatisfied	2	Unlikely	1	Unsatisfied	2	Failed	2

Exhibit 6 Survey Statistics From Users

Source: Company files.

SETBACKS

Although sales had grown steadily, PolicePrep still wasn't at a stage to justify a full-time salary for day-to-day operations. Tests could be added, but partners were reluctant to create exams for jurisdictions outside of Canada due to very slow sales in the United States. PolicePrep attempted a marketing campaign during April 2003 that involved bathroom media advertising, which proved costly and ineffective. Despite the fact that customers were extremely satisfied with the product, PolicePrep was a one-off sale, without any further products to offer these satisfied customers. The deal with the college hit several snags, which reduced the potential income during the first year.

LOOKING FORWARD

When PolicePrep was initially developed, the partners agreed to set it up in a manner such that very little work would be required to maintain the system. This was done in case all three partners landed full-time jobs and wanted to keep the site running as a passive income generator. If he were going to focus exclusively on PolicePrep, Jessop would need to structure a deal with his partners wherein his time was directly compensated, or he would have to agree to buyout the other partners. But how much would the company be worth at this stage? If Jessop were going to focus all his time on the company, what other opportunities should he explore? Or would it be best to leverage the experience of developing and launching a moderately successful company to land a career with a firm and treat PolicePrep as a part-time hobby?

Note

1. All amounts in Canadian dollars unless otherwise indicated.

Ben & Jerry's—Japan

Prepared by James M. Hagen

Version: (A) 2001-10-31

On an autumn evening in Tokyo in 1997, Perry Odak, Angelo Pezzani, Bruce Bowman and Riv Hight gratefully accepted the hot steaming oshibori towels that their kimono-bedecked waitress quietly offered. After a full day of meetings with Masahiko Iida and his lieutenants at the Seven-Eleven Japan headquarters, the men from Ben & Jerry's welcomed the chance to refresh their hands and faces before turning to the business at hand. It had been just over nine months since Odak had committed to resolving the conundrum of whether to introduce Ben & Jerry's ice cream to the Japan market and, if so, how. The next morning would be their last chance to hammer out the details for a market entry through Seven-Eleven's 7,000 stores in Japan or to give the go-ahead to Ken Yamada, a prospective licensee who would manage the Japan market for Ben & Jerry's. Any delay in reaching a decision would mean missing the summer 1998 ice cream season, but with Japan's economy continuing to contract, perhaps passing on the Japan market would not be a bad idea.

Perry Odak was just entering his eleventh month as CEO of the famous ice cream company named for its offbeat founders. He knew that the Seven-Eleven deal could represent a sudden boost in the company's flagging sales of the past several years. He also knew that a company with the tremendous brand recognition Ben & Jerry's enjoyed needed to approach new market opportunities from a strategic, not an opportunistic, perspective. Since meeting Masahiko Iida, the president of Seven-Eleven Japan just 10 months earlier, Odak was anxious to resolve the question of whether entering the huge Japan market via Seven-Eleven was the right move or not.

Ben & Jerry's Background: 1978 to 1997

1978 to 1994: Growth From Renovated Gas Station to $160 Million in Sales[1]

Brooklyn school mates Ben Cohen and Jerry Greenfield started their ice cream company in a defunct gas station in Burlington, Vermont in 1978, when both were in their mid 20s. The combination of their anti-corporate style, the high fat content of their ice cream, the addition of chunky ingredients and catchy flavor names like "Cherry Garcia" found a following. In addition to selling by the scoop, they began selling pints over the counter and the business grew. With the help of less visible team members, Jeff Furman and Fred (Chico) Lager, the founders took the company public to Vermont stockholders in 1984, later registering with the Securities and Exchange Commission (SEC) for nationwide sale of stock. The company name was Ben & Jerry's Homemade, Inc. and it began trading over the counter with the symbol, BJICA.

Stockholder meetings were outdoor festivals where standard attire included cut-offs and tie dyed T-shirts and where Cohen was liable to call the meeting to order in song. In addition to being a fun company, Cohen and Greenfield determined that it would be a socially responsible company, known for its caring capitalism. Highlighting its community roots, Ben & Jerry's would only buy its cream from Vermont dairies. In the case of one of its early nut flavors, "Rain Forest Crunch," the nuts would be sourced from tribal co-operatives in South American rain forests where nut harvesting would offer a renewable alternative to strip cutting the land for wood products, and where the co-op members would hopefully get an uncommonly large share of the proceeds. As another part of its objective of "caring capitalism," Ben & Jerry's gave 7.5 per cent of pretax profits to social causes like Healing Our Mother Earth, which protected community members from local health risks, and Center for Better Living, which assisted the homeless.

The product Cohen and Greenfield were selling was exceptionally rich (at least 12 per cent butterfat, compared with about six to 10 per cent for most ice creams). It was also very dense, which was achieved by a low overrun (low ratio of air to ice cream in the finished product). This richness and density qualified it as a superpremium ice cream. Haagen-Dazs (founded in New Jersey in 1961) was the only major competitor in the superpremium market. While Haagen-Dazs promoted a sophisticated image, Ben & Jerry's promoted a funky, caring image.

As Ben & Jerry's began to expand distribution throughout the Northeast, it found increasing difficulty obtaining shelf space in supermarkets. Charging Haagen-Dazs with unfairly pressuring distributors to keep Ben & Jerry's off their trucks, Greenfield drove to Minneapolis and gained national press coverage by picketing in front of the headquarters building of food giant Pillsbury which had earlier acquired Haagen-Dazs. His homemade sign read "What is the Doughboy afraid of?," a reference to Pillsbury's mascot and to the company's apparent efforts against the underdog ice cream makers from Vermont. This David versus Goliath campaign earned Ben & Jerry's national publicity and, when combined with some high powered legal action, it gave them freer access to grocery store freezer compartments.

A policy was in place that the highest paid employee would not be paid more than seven times what the lowest paid worker earned. Part of the anti-corporate culture of the company was a policy which allowed each employee to make up his or her own title. The person who might otherwise have been called the public relations manager took the title "the Info Queen." Cohen and Greenfield took turns running the company. Whether despite, or because of, these and other unusual policies, the company continued to grow (see Exhibit 1). In 1985 the company bought a second production plant, this one in nearby Springfield, Vermont. A third plant was later built in St. Albans, Vermont. By the late 1980s, Ben & Jerry's ice cream had become available in every state of the union.

1994 to 1997: Responding to Fallen Profits

By 1994, sales exceeded $150 million, distribution had extended beyond the U.S. borders and the company had over 600 employees. The future was not encouraging, though, with 1994 actually bringing in a loss. While Ben & Jerry's unquestionably held the second largest market share (at 34 per cent compared to Haagen-Dazs' 44 per cent) of the American superpremium market, the company had started to lose market share. Net income had also suffered badly since reaching a high in of $7.2 million in 1993 (Exhibit 2). While Cohen was most often the company's CEO,

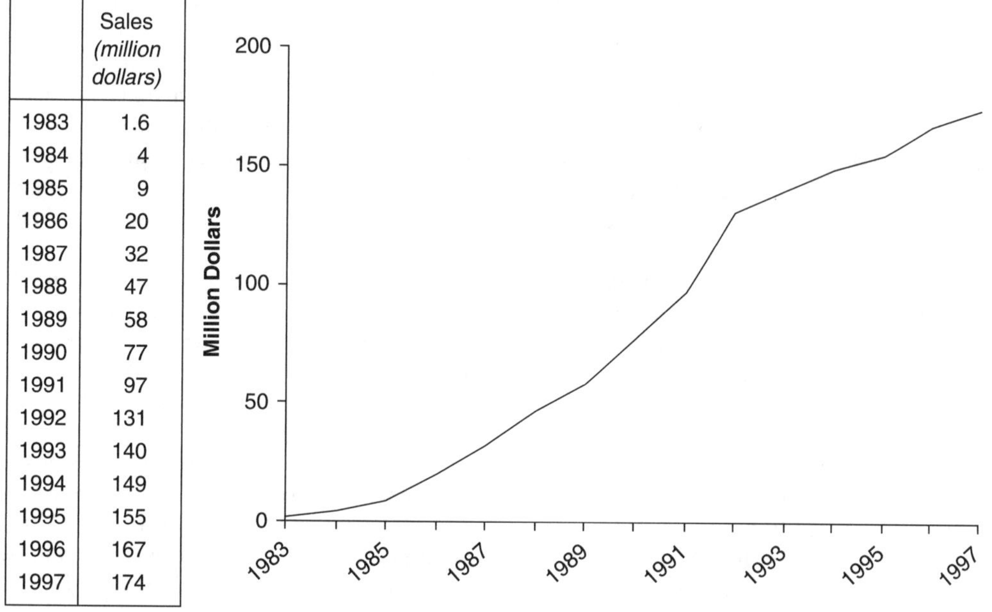

	Sales *(million dollars)*
1983	1.6
1984	4
1985	9
1986	20
1987	32
1988	47
1989	58
1990	77
1991	97
1992	131
1993	140
1994	149
1995	155
1996	167
1997	174

Exhibit 1 Ben & Jerry's Annual Sales

Source: Ben & Jerry's annual reports.

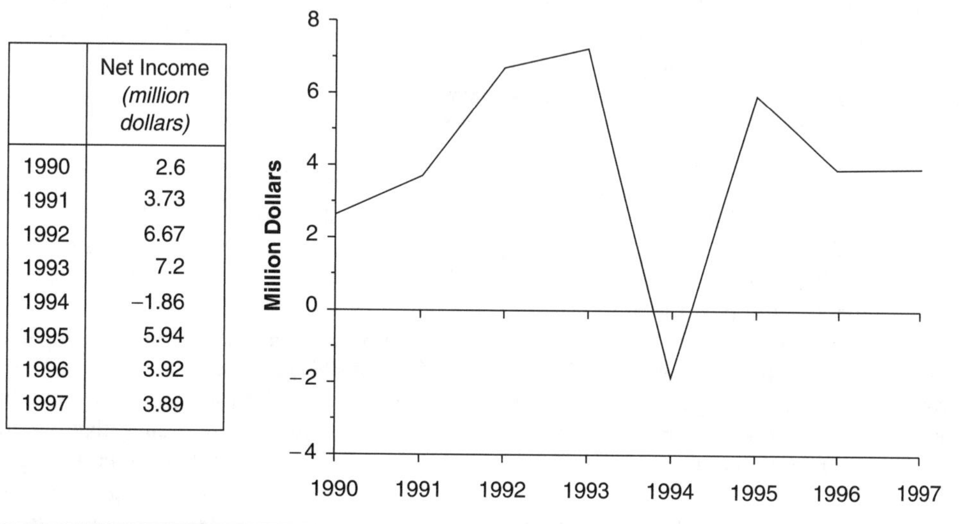

	Net Income *(million dollars)*
1990	2.6
1991	3.73
1992	6.67
1993	7.2
1994	−1.86
1995	5.94
1996	3.92
1997	3.89

Exhibit 2 Ben & Jerry's Net Income

Source: Ben & Jerry's annual reports.

much of the company's growth occurred while Chico Lager was either general manager or CEO between 1982 and 1990. Ben was particularly engaged in efforts to further the cause of social justice by such activities as attending meetings of similarly-minded CEOs from around the world. Board member Chuck Lacy had taken a turn at the helm, but he lacked aspirations for a career as a CEO, just as the company's namesakes did. The slowdown in growth and retreat in market share comprised a threat to the company's survival and to the continuation of its actions and contributions for social responsibility.

The company had never had a professional CEO and it had avoided commercial advertising, relying for publicity on press coverage of its founders' antics and social interest causes. This approach was apparently losing its effectiveness and the company could no longer feature an underdog image in its appeals for customer support. Relaxing the rule on executive compensation, the company launched a highly publicized search for a CEO, inviting would-be CEOs to submit a 100-word essay explaining why they would like the job. In 1996, Bob Holland, a former consultant with McKinsey & Co., took the presidency, bringing a small cadre of fellow consultants with him. All of Holland's highly schooled management sensibilities were put to the test as he took over a company that had lacked effective management in recent years, commencing employment for a board of directors that was suspicious of traditional corporate culture. By this time, Cohen, Greenfield and Furman still had considerable influence over the company, controlling about 45 per cent of the shares. This permitted them, as a practical matter, to elect all members of the board of directors and thereby effectively control the policies and management of the firm. Holland's relationship with the board didn't work and eighteen months later he was out, the company's decline had not been reversed and morale among the employees was at a low.

While the board was willing to pay a corporate scale salary to its CEO, it was unwilling to let go of the company's tradition of donating 7.5 per cent of before tax profits to not-for-profit social causes. A spirit of socially responsible business management would need to continue, as that was still the company's stock in trade as much as the ice cream was. With this, as well as the need to survive, in mind, the board hired Perry Odak at the recommendation of one of its members at a base salary of $300,000, with a start date in January 1997.

While Odak had grown up on a dairy farm in upstate New York, it was not this dairy background that landed him the job as CEO of Ben & Jerry's. His experience at turning around troubled companies was far more important. Odak was recruited away from a consultancy assignment at U.S. Repeating Arms Company, which he had been instrumental in turning around from its decline into red ink. This followed diverse experiences ranging from senior vice president of worldwide operations of Armour-Dial, Inc. to president of Atari Consumer Products, along with numerous consultancies and entrepreneurial activities that included the start-up team and management of Jovan, a fragrance and cosmetic company. A professional manager who thrived on challenges and abhorred mere maintenance of a company, Odak had entered the business world with a degree in agricultural economics from Cornell University topped with graduate coursework in business.

The Market for Superpremium Ice Cream

Ice cream is noted as far back as the days of Alexander the Great, though it was first commercially manufactured in the United States in 1851. By 1997, almost 10 per cent of U.S. milk production went into ice cream, a $3.34 billion market. The ice cream brands that dominated American supermarket freezer cases are given in Exhibit 3 and Exhibit 4. National (as opposed to regional) branding of dairy products, including ice cream, was a recent phenomenon. Dreyer's (owned in part by the Swiss food giant, Nestle,

	Sales *(million dollars)*
ALL BRANDS	3.34
Store Brands	1.00
Dreyer's/Edy's Premium	0.46
Breyer's Premium	0.40
BlueBell Premium	0.17
Haagen-Dazs	0.15
Ben & Jerry's	**0.12**
Healthy Choice Premium	0.10
Starbucks Premium	0.03
Homemade Premium	0.02
Breyer's Free Premium	0.02

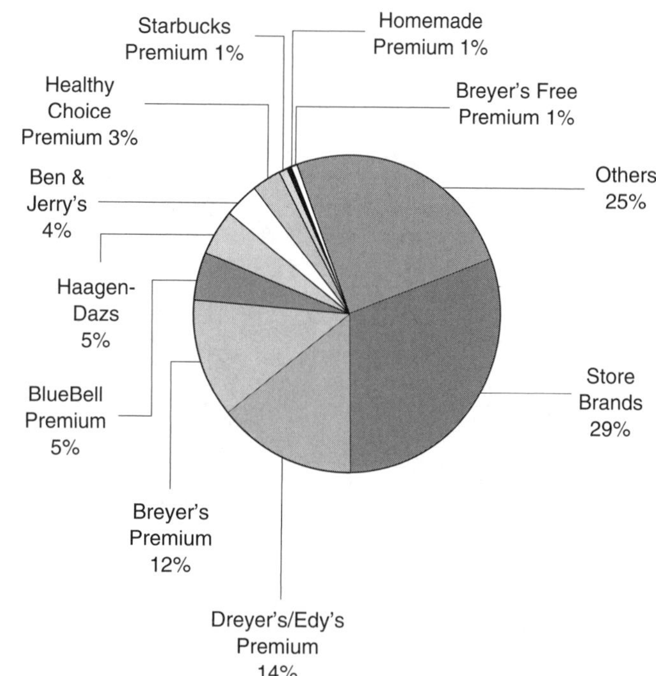

Exhibit 3 Top U.S. Ice Cream Brands, 1996 to 1997
Source: Ben & Jerry's.

and branded Edy's on the East Coast) was the biggest brand at 13.9 per cent of the U.S. market, in terms of value. The next biggest was Breyer's, a unit of the Dutch-English firm, Unilever, at 12 per cent. Blue Bell (from Texas) was fourth biggest at 5.2 per cent, and Haagen-Dazs (owned by the U.K. beverage and food company then known as Grand Metropolitan) was at 4.6 per cent. Ben & Jerry's came in at about 3.6 per cent of the market. Healthy Choice Premium ice cream (owned by the agribusiness and consumer food firm ConAgra) was close behind with 3.2 per cent. Starbucks (one of Dreyer's brands) had 1.0 per cent. The biggest share of the market (some 30.2 per cent) came from the retailers' private label products and a number of economy brands (with which Ben & Jerry's did not regard itself to be competing) made up the balance.

There are considerable economies of scale in ice cream production, so despite the advantages of having dispersed production in order to reduce costs of transporting the frozen finished product or the highly perishable cream, milk and egg yolks that are principle raw ingredients, each major manufacturer generally had only a few plants to serve vast markets. Market leader, Haagen-Dazs, had just two plants in the United States, while Ben & Jerry's had three. Even with relatively few plants, Ben & Jerry's was operating at only about half of plant capacity in 1997.

While the Ben & Jerry's brand had the country's fifth highest share of the ice cream market (in terms of value), it still accounted for only a small 3.6 per cent of the market. Ben & Jerry's, though, measured its competitive strength not in general ice cream sales (including many store

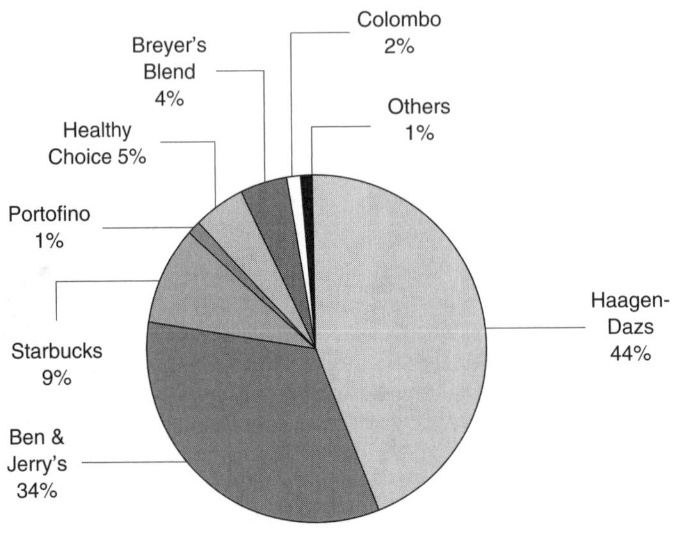

Exhibit 4 Share of Superpremium Ice Cream Brands, U.S. Market

Source: Ben & Jerry's.

brands and economy ice creams), but rather in sales of superpremium (high fat content) ice cream. The market for this product was much less fragmented, with Haagen-Dazs getting 44 per cent and Ben & Jerry's getting 34 per cent of the $361 million of supermarket (excluding convenience store and food service) sales measured and monitored by scanner data. If the two companies' frozen yogurts and sorbets were included, their market shares would be 36 per cent for Ben & Jerry's and 42 per cent for Haagen-Dazs. Both companies specialized in superpremium products, with additional sales being derived from sorbets, frozen yogurts and novelties. Haagen-Dazs had really pioneered the category back in 1961 when Reuben Mattus in New Jersey founded the company. The company was later acquired by the giant food company, Pillsbury, which in turn was bought in 1989 by the U.K. liquor and food giant, Grand Metropolitan.

Both Ben & Jerry's and Haagen-Dazs had achieved national distribution, primarily selling their product in supermarkets and convenience stores. Ben & Jerry's had 163 scoop shops, compared to 230 Haagen-Dazs shops. Dairy Queen (with 5,790 shops worldwide) and Baskin Robbins dominated the scoop shop business, though their products were not superpremium. Prices for Ben & Jerry's and Haagen-Dazs would range from $2.89 to $3.15 per pint, often more than twice as expensive as conventional (high overrun/lower butterfat) ice cream and premium brands. Starbucks and Portofino ice creams were other much smaller contenders in the United States with their "premium plus" products, characterized by a butterfat content slightly under that of the superpremium category.

Statistical evidence indicated that ice cream consumption increased with income and education. Starting in the mid 1990s, though, sales growth started to fall off and Ben & Jerry's experienced a decline in profits, even suffering a loss in 1994. Haagen-Dazs and Ben & Jerry's product sales were very widely available across the entire U.S. market and it was clear that future growth would have to come from new products or from new (non-U.S.) markets. More troubling was that Ben & Jerry's was beginning to lose market share in both the total ice cream market and, more importantly, the superpremium market.

Ben & Jerry's International Sales

Ben & Jerry's was intentionally slow to embrace foreign markets. Cohen was opposed to growth for growth's sake, so the company's few adventures overseas were limited to opportunistic arrangements that came along, primarily with friends of the founders. Meanwhile Haagen-Dazs had no such hesitation. By 1997, it was in 28 countries with 850 dipping shops around the world. Its non-U.S. sales were about $700 million, compared to about $400 million of domestic sales. Ben & Jerry's, on the other hand, had foreign sales of just $6 million, with total sales of $174 million. In terms of non-U.S. superpremium ice cream sales, Haagen-Dazs and Ben & Jerry's were still the leading brands, but Haagen-Dazs was trouncing Ben & Jerry's.

Canada

Ben & Jerry's first foreign entry was in Canada in 1986, when the company gave a Canadian firm all Canadian rights for the manufacture and sale of ice cream through a licensing agreement. While about one-third of the product was exported from the United States, high Canadian tariffs (15.5 per cent) and particularly quotas (only 347 tons annually) made export impractical. In 1992 Ben & Jerry's repurchased the Canadian license and as of 1997 there were just four scoop shops in Quebec. The Canadian dairy industry remained highly protective even after enactment of the North American Free Trade Agreement.

Israel

Avi Zinger, a friend of Cohen's, was given a license, including manufacturing rights, for the Israel market in 1988. His 1997 sales totalled about $5 million, but the only revenue accruing to Ben & Jerry's Homemade, Inc. would be licensing income and this amount was negligible. To assure quality coming from the plant in Yavne, Israel, Zinger and his staff received training at the Waterbury factory. As of fall 1997, there were 14 Ben & Jerry's scoop shops in Israel, with the shops selling such items as gifts, baked goods and beverages, in addition to the ice cream. Zinger also sold Ben & Jerry's products through supermarkets, hotels, delis and restaurants.

Russia

The company entered into its first foreign joint venture in 1990 by establishing the firm Iceverk in the Russian republic of Karelia, which is Vermont's sister state. This grew out of Cohen's travel to Karelia as part of a sister state delegation in 1988. A goal of the joint venture effort was to promote understanding and communication between the peoples of these two countries. The joint venture agreement specified the following division of ownership shares: Ben & Jerry's—50 per cent; the Intercentre cooperative—27 per cent; Petro Bank—20 per cent; and Pioneer Palace (a facility similar to a YMCA, that provided the location)—three per cent. Half of any profits would stay with the Iceverk and the balance would be divided among the partners. Ben & Jerry's contributed equipment and know-how to the venture, while the local partners provided the facilities for the factory and for two scoop shops. After considerable, mostly bureaucratic, delays, the shops opened in July 1992. By 1993, there were three scoop shops and about 100 employees. Iceverk opened several more scoop shops and the venture began to sell pints in supermarkets locally, as well as in Moscow. Ben & Jerry's hired James Flynn to put his University of New Hampshire marketing degree to good use by serving as marketing rep in Moscow. Sales improved as food service customers increasingly bought the product. In 1996, Ben & Jerry's terminated the joint venture, giving its equity and equipment at no cost to its joint venture partners. A retrospective view of that decision is that the company felt that the management time needed to keep the partnership going was too demanding, given the perceived potential. Iceverk no longer uses the Ben & Jerry's name, though it does continue to make ice cream in Petrozavodsk, Karelia's capital.

United Kingdom

In 1994 there was much discussion at Ben & Jerry's headquarters in Burlington about whether the company was ready to strategically (rather than just opportunistically) move into international markets. Susan Renaud recalled the consensus being that no, they were not, but just three months later the company shipped a container of product to Sainsbury, an upscale supermarket chain in the United Kingdom. Cohen had met a Sainsbury executive at a meeting of the Social Venture Network and the executive had encouraged him to ship over some product. This launch was made with no idea of what the pricing would be, nor any knowledge of what kind of packaging and ingredients were acceptable in that market. The company was shipping a 473 ml package, while the standard was 500 ml. With its foot in the door, the company thought it best to try other outlets in England, as well. It tried out one distributor, which had agreed to donate one per cent of its Ben & Jerry's turnover to charity. Sales did not materialize and another distributor was tried, this time without the charity constraint. The product had a distinctive market position, with one radio commentator alleged to have said, "If Haagen-Dazs is the ice cream you have after sex, Ben & Jerry's is the ice cream you have instead of sex." By 1997, U.K. sales totalled $4 million.

France

In 1995, the company entered France with great ambivalence. CEO Holland was all for entering the French market and the company sent off a container of product to Auchan, a major retailer Cohen was introduced to through Social Venture Network ties. As global protests grew over French nuclear testing, though, there were discussions in the company about withdrawing from the French market or vocally protesting against the French government. With this internal disagreement concerning the French market, there was no marketing plan, no promotional support and no attempt to address French labelling laws. The company hired a French public relations firm, noted for its alternative media and social mission work, and separately contracted with a sales and distribution company. But there was no plan and nobody from Ben & Jerry's to coordinate the French effort. In 1997, sales in France were just over $1 million.

Benelux

Ben & Jerry's entry into the Benelux market was also without strategic planning. In this case, a wealthy individual who had admired the company's social mission asked to open scoop shops, with partial ownership by the Human Rights Watch. By 1997, there were three scoop shops in Holland. Sales totalled a mere $287,000, but there was the prospect of using the product reputation from the scoop shops to launch supermarket and convenience store sales.

In short, Ben & Jerry's fell into several foreign markets opportunistically, but without the consensus of the board and without the necessary headquarters staff to put together any kind of comprehensive plan. As the company had never developed a conventional marketing plan in the United States, it lacked the managerial skill to put together a marketing campaign for entering the foreign markets.

As a result, by 1997, Ben & Jerry's international sales totalled just three per cent of total sales. While the company had nearly caught up with Haagen-Dazs in U.S. market share, Haagen-Dazs was light years ahead in the non-U.S. markets. With declining profits and domestic market share at Ben & Jerry's, it was beginning to seem time to give serious attention to international market opportunities.

Focus on Market Opportunities in Japan

Background on the Market for Superpremium Ice Cream in Japan

In the 1994 to 1996 period when Ben & Jerry's was having its first taste of a hired professional CEO (Bob Holland), it struggled with the prospects of strategically targeting a foreign market and developing a marketing plan for its fledgling overseas operations. In particular, the company made inquiries about opportunities in Japan, the second largest ice cream market in the world, with annual sales of approximately $4.5 billion (Exhibit 5). While the market was big, it was also daunting. Japan was known to have a highly complex distribution system driven by manufacturers, its barriers to foreign products were high and the distance for shipping a frozen product was immense. Ben & Jerry's would be a late entrant, more than 10 years behind Haagen-Dazs in gaining a foothold in the market. In addition, there were at least six Japanese ice cream manufacturers selling a superpremium product. A major Japanese frozen desserts company, Morinaga Seika, had made proposals to Ben & Jerry's on two different occasions in 1995. In both cases the proposals were rejected. In January 1996, Morinaga actually conducted focus groups to evaluate Ben & Jerry's products. It was beginning to seem appropriate to taking a closer look at the Morinaga proposals and other options.

Despite the challenges of entering Japan, that market had several compelling features. It was arguably the most affluent country in the world, Japanese consumers were known for demanding high quality products with great varieties of styles and flavors (which practically defined Ben & Jerry's) and it seemed that the dietary shift toward more animal products was still underway. By 1994, Japan's 42 kilogram annual per capita consumption of milk was less than half

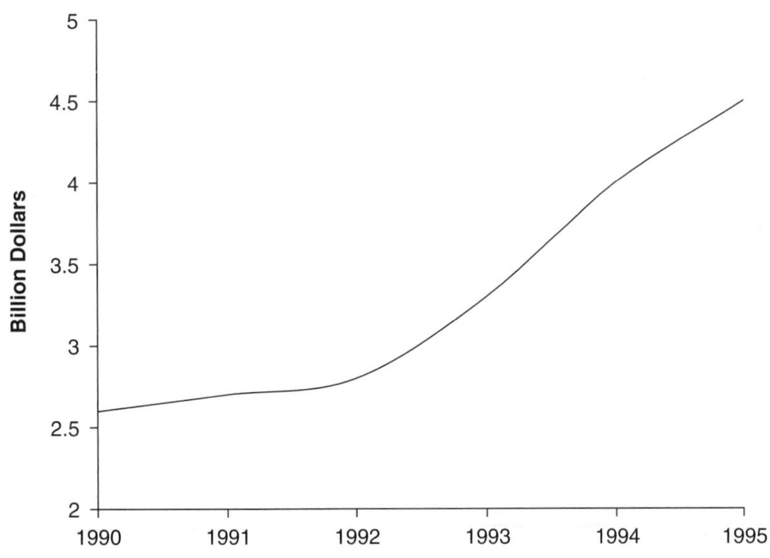

Exhibit 5 Japan Ice Cream Market Size

Source: Ben & Jerry's.

that (103 kg) of the United States, and cheese consumption was about one-tenth that of the United States. Commercial dairy sales had really only taken off after World War II, when school lunch programs were initiated with milk as a regular component. Incomes in Japan increased dramatically from the 1950s to the 1980s so that animal-based food products and home refrigerators were affordable to a large number of people.

Though Haagen-Dazs' financial figures were not published by its parent, Grand Metropolitan, market intelligence suggested that the ice cream maker had Japanese sales of about $300 million, with Japan providing the highest margins of any of its markets. Haagen-Dazs had managed to capture nearly half the superpremium market in Japan. It entered the market as an imported product and later began production in Japan at a plant owned jointly by Haagen-Dazs, Sentry and Takanashi Milk Products. About 25 per cent of Haagen-Dazs' sales there appeared to be from scoop shops. In addition to gaining visibility through scoop shops, Haagen-Dazs operated a fleet of ice cream parlor buses, with upper deck cafe tables, at exhibitions and other public gatherings. On the one hand, Haagen-Dazs would be a formidable competitor that would likely guard its market share. On the other hand, there would be no apparent need for Ben & Jerry's to teach the local market about superpremium ice cream. The market seemed to welcome imported ice cream and expectations of falling tariffs on dairy products suggested new opportunities for ice cream imports from abroad. Haagen-Dazs' flavors were generally the same as U.S. flavors, with some modifications, such as reduced sweetness. While prices were attractive in Japan, about $6 per pint, it was unclear how much of that would go into the pockets of the manufacturer versus various distributors.

In contemplating an entry in the Japan market, it was hard to avoid thinking about the case of Borden Japan. Borden introduced a premium ice cream to the market in 1971 through a joint venture with Meiji Milk. The product was highly successful and Borden was leader of the category. In 1991, the Borden-Meiji alliance came to an end and Borden had extreme difficulty gaining effective distribution. Borden did not follow industry trends toward single serving cups of ice cream and it suffered greatly when distributors started lowering the price of the product, sending the signal to consumers that Borden was an inferior product. After sales had fallen by more than two-thirds in just two years, Borden withdrew from the Japan market. Desserts were uncommon in Japan, leaving ice cream primarily for the snack market. Thus, single serving (about 120 ml) cups became popular, accounting for about 45 per cent of sales (Exhibit 6) and ice cream came to be sold increasingly in convenience stores. By 1993, about a quarter of all ice cream sales were in convenience stores, compared to 29 per cent in supermarkets (Exhibit 7).

One concern at Ben & Jerry's was its size. With total worldwide sales of just over $150 million, it was very small in comparison to Haagen-Dazs, which had estimated sales of $300 million in Japan alone. At least five Japanese companies already in the superpremium market were larger than Ben & Jerry's, with leaders Glico, Morinaga, Meiji and Snow Brand all having total ice cream sales three to four times that of Ben & Jerry's and, in each case, ice cream was just part of their product line.

Cohen was not very enthusiastic about the sort of financial or managerial commitment that was apparently required to enter the Japan market and he couldn't see how entering that market fit in with the company's social mission. Others on the board shared his attitude. Two immediate problems were that entering Japan would not be the result of any social mission (the concepts of social mission and corporate charity being very foreign in Japan) and the company's lack of international success suggested that it may already have been spread too thin in too many countries. Jerry Greenfield, however, was interested enough to visit Japan on a market research tour in early 1996. The purpose was to see just how Ben & Jerry's might gain distribution if the company were to enter the Japanese market. Valerie Brown of Ben & Jerry's fledgling marketing department accompanied Greenfield.

	Brand	*Size (ml)*	*Price (Yen)*
Home Cup	Bleuge	950	950
Pint	H. Dazs	474	850
	Lotte	470	850
	Meiji	470	950
Personal Cup	H. Dazs	120	250
	Meiji	145	250

Others 22%
Home Cup 9%
Pint Cup 24%
Personal Cup 45%

Exhibit 6 Japan Superpremium and Premium Sales by Package
Source: Fuji Keizai Co.

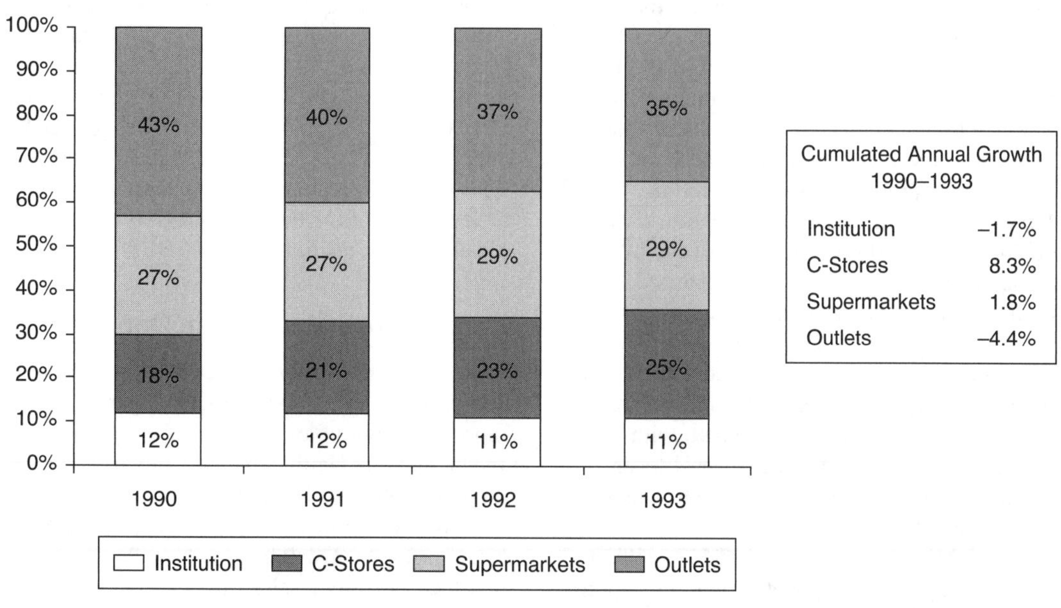

Exhibit 7 Japan Ice Cream Market by Channel
Source: Ice Cream Data Book (Morinaga)

Contacts for the visit came primarily from Valerie's classmates at Harvard Business School, from a consulting company and from the Japan External Trade Organization.

Alternative Strategies for a Ben & Jerry's Entry Into Japan

In his visit to Japan, Greenfield was willing to consider entry into Japan through such diverse distribution channels as Amway Japan, Domino's Pizza and department stores. One of his meetings was with the Japanese distributor of Dreyer's, the American company with partial ownership by the Swiss food giant Nestle. Dreyer's, not being perceived as a direct competitor, was Ben & Jerry's largest distributor in the United States. Dreyer's had licensed its trademark with a joint venture operation in Japan in 1990. Sales had since fallen and the joint venture seemed to have had difficulty with its biggest customer, Seven-Eleven Japan. The retailer's demands for just-in-time delivery required Dreyer's to maintain large inventories and the retailer demanded the right to rapidly drop flavors which did not meet sales expectations.

Another meeting was with a high level team of Seven-Eleven executives, including Masahiko Iida, the senior managing director, and Yasayuki Nakanishi, the merchandiser of the Foods Division. Iida expressed interest in selling Ben & Jerry's ice cream, suggesting that Ben & Jerry's could sell directly to Seven-Eleven, avoiding some of the distribution costs that are typical of the usual multi-layer distribution system in Japan. On the other hand, a major American beverage distributor in Japan warned that it would be the kiss of death to enter the market through some kind of exclusive arrangement with a huge convenience store chain like Seven-Eleven. The balance of power would be overwhelmingly in the retailer's favor.

Meiji Milk Products (with $447 million of ice cream sales), in combination with its importer, the giant Mitsubishi Trading Company, expressed interest in distributing Ben & Jerry's products. This team clearly had very strong distribution resources, including an exclusive supply contract for Tokyo Disneyland. One concern was that Meiji already had a superpremium brand called Aya. Despite Meiji's strong interest, though, this option had probably become a long shot on account of earlier protests by Ben & Jerry's leadership of deforestation practices by another division of Mitsubishi.

Other marketing possibilities that had surfaced in 1996 included an arrangement with the advertising agency that had charge of Japan Airlines' in-flight entertainment, as well as a chance to open a scoop shop at a highly visible new retail development about to be built at Tokyo Disneyland. If anything, the many options, focus groups and proposals made the decision about what to do with Japan even more difficult. The fact that the Ben & Jerry's board was divided on whether the company even had any business in a Japan launch discouraged further action.

By late 1996, Holland was following up discussions with a well-recommended Japanese-American who was available to oversee marketing and distribution of Ben & Jerry's products in Japan. Ken Yamada, a third generation Japanese American from Hawaii, had obtained the Domino's Pizza franchise for Japan. His compensation would be a margin on all sales in Japan. When Bob Holland's employment with Ben & Jerry's ended later in the year, he was still in discussion with Yamada, but he was still lacking the enthusiastic support of the board of directors for a possible entry into Japan.

A Fresh Look at the Japan Options

Perry Odak assumed leadership of Ben & Jerry's in January 1997, inheriting the file of reports on possible strategies for entering the Japan market. Neither the file nor institutional memory indicated much momentum leading toward any one of the Japan strategies. In being hired, however, Odak had the board's agreement that the company's sales (and especially profits) must grow and that non-U.S. markets were the most likely key to that growth.

In February 1997, Odak added a business-related detour to a scheduled trip to Thailand with his wife. He stopped by Tokyo for a courtesy call to Mr. Iida, the President of Seven-Eleven Japan, a controlling parent company of 7-Eleven U.S.[2] This was to more or less make up for Ben & Jerry's inability to send a CEO to a January "summit" meeting in Dallas at which Mr. Iida and the head of the U.S. 7-Eleven operations had wished to meet face to face with the leaders of its major suppliers. 7-Eleven U.S. was, in fact, Ben & Jerry's biggest retail outlet and Ben & Jerry's was a major supplier to Seven-Eleven.

After about 10 minutes of pleasantries at this introductory meeting at the Seven-Eleven headquarters in Tokyo, Iida asked Odak point blank: "Is there anyone at Ben & Jerry's who can make a marketing decision? We'd like to sell your product, but don't know how to proceed or with whom." Rather taken aback at this surprisingly direct inquiry, Odak replied that he could indeed make a decision and he resolved to sort through the Japan options and get back to Iida in short order.

Back in Burlington, Odak installed Angelo Pezzani as the new international director for Ben & Jerry's Homemade. Odak had known Pezzani since 1982 when they both started work at Atari on the same day. Pezzani's position was then general consul of Atari Consumer Products Worldwide. Going over the options with Pezzani, it appeared that partnering with Yamada was still the strongest option for entering Japan, but the Seven-Eleven option had not yet been well developed for consideration. Yamada represented considerable strength with his Domino's success and with the fact that Domino's already offered ice cream cups as part of its delivery service in Japan. Possible drawbacks were his insistence on having exclusive rights to the entire Japan market, with full control of all branding and marketing efforts there.

Pezzani and Odak decided to continue negotiations with Yamada, keeping that option alive, and to simultaneously let Iida know that they wanted to explore options with Seven-Eleven. They requested an April meeting with Iida in Japan to move things along. The April meeting would include Mr. Nakanishi, the head of frozen ice desserts for Seven-Eleven Japan, and Bruce Bowman, Ben & Jerry's head of operations. To work out ground arrangements for the meeting, Odak and Pezzani needed someone on the ground in Japan and they called on Rivington Hight, an American who had learned Japanese in the U.S. intelligence service, married a Japanese woman and had been living in Japan for much of the past 30 years. No stranger to Odak or Pezzani, Hight had also worked for Atari in 1982 as president of Atari Japan. Like Odak and Pezzani, he had held a variety of management positions and consultancies in the years since.

The April meeting in Japan was basically intended to lay the framework to begin hashing out the many details that would be involved if Ben & Jerry's were to enter the Japan market through Seven-Eleven. It was a chance for the critical players in each company to get together. Perry brought Pezzani, Bowman and Hight. Arriving at the Ito-Yokado/Seven-Eleven headquarters building at the foot of Tokyo Tower, the Ben & Jerry's team walked into a lobby full of sample-laden salespeople and manufacturers nervously awaiting their chance to put their products on the shelves of some 7,000 stores. The receptionist quickly identified Odak and company and immediately put VIP pins on their dark lapels, directing them to the VIP elevator that went straight to the executive suite on the 12th floor. A hostess there immediately guided the group across the plush white carpeting to a spacious meeting room, where they were served tea while awaiting Iida and Nakanishi. Odak arrived with more questions than answers, but he was determined that any product Ben & Jerry's might sell in Japan would be manufactured in Vermont, where the company had considerable excess capacity. Also, the costs of labor and raw dairy products were higher in Japan than the United States, so the 23.3 per cent tariff and cost of shipping seemed not to be prohibitive. As a result of the Uruguay Round of GATT, the tariff would be reduced to 21 per cent in the year 2000. The introductory meeting went well, but they had not yet addressed any of the difficult issues except to establish that it would be possible to export the product from Vermont to Japan.

Wrestling With the Details of the Seven-Eleven Option

Odak, Pezzani and Bowman had a full plate of issues to resolve. The first question was market. Iida had said he was interested in Ben & Jerry's product because it was something new to Japan and particularly unique with its chunks. Seven-Eleven had even tried to get a Japanese company to co-pack a chunky superpremium ice cream, but the Japanese packer was unsuccessful with its production processes. Research supporting a clear market for this novel product in Japan was scant, though it seemed unlikely that Seven-Eleven would commit shelf space to a product it had any doubt about and both Iida and Nakanishi certainly knew their market. A skeptical view of Seven-Eleven's interest in bringing Ben & Jerry's to Japan was that Seven-Eleven's combined U.S. and Japan operations would become so important to Ben & Jerry's (potentially accounting for a substantial portion of its sales) that Seven-Eleven could, in some fashion, control the ice cream maker. Even if that were not part of Seven-Eleven's motivation, it could be a concern.

While Ben & Jerry's management was leaning toward an entry into Japan, it was not a foregone conclusion. The entry would require a commitment of capital and managerial attention. As the product would be exported from the United States, there would be the risk of negative exchange rate movements that could make exports to Japan no longer feasible, thus making Ben & Jerry's financial picture less predictable. Commodity risk was also a serious concern in that the price of milk could rise in the United States, hurting Ben & Jerry's relative to competitors producing ice cream in Japan.

Assuming that an entry into the Japanese market was desirable, there were a number of apparent options for gaining distribution there, making it necessary to seriously consider the pros and cons of entering by way of Seven-Eleven. The most obvious pro was immediate placement in the freezer compartments of over 7,000 convenience stores in that country. In the early 1990s, the convenience store share of the ice cream market had increased and it appeared that these stores were now accounting for at least 40 per cent of superpremium ice cream sales in Japan. Equally positive was the fact that Seven-Eleven had taken advantage of its size and its state-of-the art logistics systems by buying product directly from suppliers, avoiding the several layers of middlemen that stood between most suppliers and Japanese retailers. These cost savings could make the product more affordable and/or allow a wider margin to protect against such risks as currency fluctuation.

On the negative side, if the product was introduced to the market through a convenience store and it was just one of many brands there, would it be able to build its own brand capital in Japan like Haagen-Dazs had? Would the product essentially become a store brand? Without brand capital it could be difficult to distribute the product beyond the Seven-Eleven chain. An alternative approach of setting up well located scoop shops, along with an effective marketing or publicity campaign, could give the product cache, resulting in consumer pull that could give Ben & Jerry's a price premium, as well as a range of marketing channels. Would committing to one huge retail chain be a case of putting too many eggs in one basket? A falling out between Ben & Jerry's and Seven-Eleven Japan could leave the ice cream maker with nothing in Japan. Even during discussions with Ben & Jerry's, the retailer was known to be terminating its supply agreement with the French ice cream manufacturer Rolland due to allegedly inadequate sales. Presumably Seven-Eleven could similarly cut off Ben & Jerry's at some future date.

While weighing the pros and cons of the business arrangement, there were also production issues which Ben & Jerry's had to consider. Nakanishi insisted the ice cream be packaged only in personal cups (120 ml) and not the 473 ml (one pint) size that Ben & Jerry's currently packed. The main argument for the small cups was that ice cream is seldom consumed as a family dessert in Japan, but rather is consumed as a snack item. A secondary argument was that, for sanitation purposes, customers liked their own individual servings. Cake, for example, was generally served in restaurants with each slice individually wrapped. Nakanishi's insistence was despite the fact that Seven-Eleven stocked Haagen-Dazs and some of its local competitors in both sizes.

Bruce Bowman embraced the challenge of designing a production system that would accommodate small cups that the company had never packed before. It seemed that about $2 million of new equipment would be needed, though it could be installed in the existing buildings. The sizes of some of the chunks would have to be reduced in order for them to not overwhelm the small cups. Besides requiring these known adjustments to production operations, Seven-Eleven might be expected to request other product changes. Japanese buyers were known for being particularly demanding in their specifications.

Ben & Jerry's had long been shipping ice cream to the West Coast and to Europe in freezer containers. Shipments to Japan were feasible, though the Seven-Eleven approach to just-in-time inventory procedures would make delivery reliability especially key and, of course, costs would have to be minimized. Logistics research indicated it would likely take at least three weeks shipping time from the plant in Vermont (the St. Albans plant would be used if the Japan plan were implemented) to the warehouse in Japan. Because of the Japanese label needed in Japan, production would have to carefully meet the orders from Seven-Eleven. The product could not be shifted to another customer, nor could another customer's product be shifted to Japan.

A number of sticky points needed to be resolved. In addition to changing the package size, Seven-Eleven wanted to provide its own design for the package art and the design would definitely not include a photo of Ben and Jerry. Packaging had always been an important part of the Ben & Jerry's product. Funky lettering and the images of Ben and Jerry are part of what made the product unique. If Seven-Eleven were given control over the package art, what would that do to the benefits of developing a global branded product? Would consumers be confused about the placement of the product as they travelled? On the other hand, the carton designs had already been evolving somewhat and maybe a bit more evolution would satisfy Seven-Eleven. In fact, the earlier focus groups by Morinaga brought out the concern that it was too bad the "strange Ben & Jerry's packaging" had to detract from the good ice cream.

Ben & Jerry's sent a number of samples to consider and Nakanishi developed a short list that would be tested (if the deal went forward) in a couple dozen Seven-Eleven stores so that the top five flavors could be identified for the market entry. "Chunky Monkey" was near the top of Nakanishi's list, though the name absolutely had to change, he said. It turned out that only minor ingredient modifications would be needed to reduce the sweetness and to replace "vegetable gum" with "protein solids."

Through numerous communications and several meetings during the summer of 1997, a number of issues were discussed and resolved. For example, Seven-Eleven would acquire only a six-month exclusive right to Ben & Jerry's and even that would be only for the specific flavors being sold to Seven-Eleven. Because of its relatively small size and inability to cover a loss, Ben & Jerry's was asking for sale terms that would transfer title (and all risk) for the product at the plant gate. It also was asking for 12 weeks lead-time on any order to allow for sourcing of ingredients, as well as efficient production scheduling. It appeared that these requests would not be too burdensome for Seven-Eleven. The sensitive issue of price was intentionally left until late in the discussions. Haagen-Dazs was being sold for 250 yen per 120 ml cup and Seven-Eleven wanted to position Ben & Jerry's at a slightly lower price point. This would be problematic for Odak, who had recently increased the domestic price for Ben & Jerry's ice cream in part to support the product's position as equal or superior in quality to Haagen-Dazs.

A concern yet lurking in the boardroom in Burlington, Vermont was what would be the company's social mission in Japan. Since the early 1990s, the company had moved beyond using its profit to fund philanthropy. The new imperative was to make the workplace, community and world a better place through regular day-to-day operations. On the other hand, profits were still needed in order to even have day-to-day operations and a new market (such as Japan) could be the ticket to those profits. In the meantime, no particular social mission had emerged from the summer discussions of entering the Japan market.

The Approaching Deadline for a Summer 1998 Japan Launch

Odak and his staff had made steady progress narrowing and developing their Japan options during the summer of 1997. If they were to enter the Japan market for the summer 1998 season, though, they would have to commit to one plan or another no later than autumn 1997. Two distinct entry options had emerged.

The Yamada option was largely the same as it had been at the beginning of the year. His proposal was to have full control of marketing and sales for Ben & Jerry's in Japan. He would position the brand, devise and orchestrate the initial launch and take care of marketing and distribution well into the future. He would earn a royalty on all sales in the market. By giving Yamada full control of the Japan market, Ben & Jerry's would have instant expertise in an otherwise unfamiliar market, as well as relief from having to address the many issues involved in putting together an entry strategy and in ongoing market management. Yamada knew frozen foods and he had an entrepreneurial spirit and marketing savvy, evidenced by his success in launching and building up the Domino's pizza chain in Japan. Giving up control of a potentially major market, though, could not be taken lightly. Because Yamada would invest his time in fleshing out and executing a marketing plan only after reaching agreement with Ben & Jerry's, there was no specific plan available for consideration. Even if there were, Yamada would retain the rights to change it. For the near term, however, Yamada would expect to add selected flavors of Ben & Jerry's ice cream cups to the Domino's delivery menu, providing an opportunity to collect market data based on customer response.

The Seven-Eleven option would leave Ben & Jerry's in control of whatever market development it might want to pursue beyond supplying Seven-Eleven in Japan. While Seven-Eleven would provide an instant entry to the market, the company would not be in a position to help Ben & Jerry's develop other distribution channels in Japan. The retailer thought it could sell at least six cups per day at each store, which would be the minimum to justify continuing to stock Ben & Jerry's. Looking at the size of Seven-Eleven's ice cream freezer cases suggested that this would require approximately 10 per cent of Seven-Eleven's cup ice cream sales to be Ben & Jerry's products. Ben & Jerry's was as yet unknown in Japan and it did not have the budget for a marketing campaign there. Sales would have to rely primarily on promotional efforts by Seven-Eleven, but the company was making no specific commitment for such efforts.

Another option was increasingly compelling—that of holding off on any Japan entry. Japan's economy was continuing to languish, with increasing talk that it could be years before recovery. A financial crisis that had commenced with a devaluation of Thailand's currency in July 1997 seemed to be spreading across Asia. If the pending Asia crisis hit an already weakened Japanese economy, the economics of exporting ice cream from Vermont to Japan could become infeasible. Though the value of the yen had recently fallen to 125 yen to the dollar, Ben & Jerry's could still sell the product at the plant gate at an acceptable profit with room for both shipping expense and satisfactory margins for Seven-Eleven and its franchisees. If the rate went as high as 160 yen to the dollar, then the price in Japan would have to be raised to a level that might seriously cut into demand, especially relative to Haagen-Dazs, which had manufacturing facilities in Japan.

It would be a long evening meal as Odak, Pezzani, Bowman and Hight gave their final thoughts to the decision before them. Not only had Odak promised Iida that he could make a decision, but Yamada needed an answer to his proposal as well. In any event, Ben & Jerry's had to proceed with one plan or another if it was going to have any Japanese sales in its 1998 income statement.

NOTES

1. Monetary values are in U.S. dollars unless otherwise noted.

2. A brief explanation of the relationship between the Japan Seven-Eleven organization and the U.S. 7-Eleven organization is in order. 7-Eleven convenience stores originated in Texas in 1927 as a retail concept of Southland Corporation, which had been in the ice business. Southland began using the 7-Eleven banner in the 1950s because the stores would be open from 7 a.m. to 11 p.m. The business grew through company-owned and franchised stores. Southland gave a master franchise for Japan to the Ito Yokado Company, a large supermarket operator there, which in turn established Seven-Eleven Japan to conduct the 7-Eleven business in Japan through company-owned and franchised stores. In the 1980s, Southland was in financial distress and Ito Yokado, along with its subsidiary, Seven-Eleven Japan, bailed out Southland, acquiring a controlling interest in the company. In this light, Odak's dinner with Iida in Japan constituted a sort of executive summit between Ben & Jerry's and its largest customer.

TEXTRON LTD.

Prepared by Lawrence A. Beer

 Version: (A) 2002-01-24

INTRODUCTION

Gary Case, executive vice-president of Textron Ltd., sat at his desk and slowly drew a circle around the words *ethics* and *social responsibility*. Above the circle he wrote in bold letters the phrase "public opinion," and sat back to ponder his symbolic illustration of a potential problem that only he seemed to envision.

Case was thinking ahead and letting his mind focus on an issue that seemed out of the realm of the tenets of basic managerial principles that his undergraduate and MBA studies had prepared him for during his scholastic years. While he well appreciated the strategic decision-making concepts of running a transnational business, he felt himself personally wondering how to approach the complex subject of applying global ethics and social responsibility to an international venture that was being pushed on his company.

BACKGROUND

Textron Ltd. was a 65-year-old, family-held business based in Youngstown, Ohio. As a producer of cotton and sponge fabricated items for the beauty trade, selling to intermediate users as components in their make-up compact cases as well as direct to the retail trade for onward sale to consumers, the company was under constant attack from Far Eastern manufacturers. The need to enter into some type of offshore manufacturing enterprise was now evident in order to maintain a cost competitive position for the firm to continue to prosper and grow.

As a maker of cotton puffs for the application of make-up cosmetics, the company had grown from a loft in Brooklyn, New York, back in the mid-1930s to a medium-sized enterprise with sales of $25 million and pre-tax earnings of $1 million plus. In the category of cosmetic applicators, Textron's fine reputation had been built on years of excellent service to the trade with attention to detail. Using, at first, the hand sewing abilities of seamstresses from the garment centres of lower Manhattan, the company had been a pioneer in developing customized machinery to produce quality cotton puffs to the precise custom requirements of modern cosmetic manufacturers. Today, 100 per cent virgin cotton rolls would enter Textron's factory at one end and exit as soft velour pads in numerous shapes, contoured sizes and colors at the other end of the process.

These puffs would be either sewn or glued with ribbon bands and satin coverings bearing the well-known brand names of the major franchised cosmetics companies of the world from Revlon, Estee Lauder, Maybelline and Max Factor as well as numerous others. They might also contain the names of retail store house brands or the internationally recognized trademarks of their own company. Currently, a new collection had been created through a licensing arrangement bearing the name of a highly respected fashion beauty magazine, whose instant recognition with the teenage trade was propelling the company to new sales levels. While historically Textron Ltd. primarily had produced components, supplying cosmetic companies with custom applicators tailored to their cosmetic ingredient requirements, the growth of its retail business in this subcategory was developing at a rapid pace. Major drug store chains, supermarkets and specialty shops featured Textron brands and their lines were becoming synonymous with the best in cosmetic applicators and assorted beauty accessories. With the launch of an additional range under the guise of a high fashion authority, featuring highly stylized "cool shapes" and "hot colors" designed to entice younger adolescent buyers, their reputation was achieving enhanced public notice. Such products using uniquely descriptive trendy phrases evoked an image of "hip to use applicators" and a whole new generation of teenage users was being developed.

The firm also was a key purveyor to the entertainment industry directly servicing the Hollywood movie and TV production companies, Broadway and the theatrical community, along with indirect sales to professional make-up artists and modeling studios thanks to the quickly developing beauty store trade. All in all, the future for Textron Ltd. was most promising.

Gary Case, a college friend of the company's president and principal owner, was brought into the business because of his experience at the retail sales and marketing level. The chief executive officer, who possessed an engineering background, was more than capable of overseeing the manufacturing side of the business; however, the strong movement of the organization into direct consumer goods, coupled with the overall expansion of the company, necessitated Case's hiring.

As the company began to prosper in the early 1970s, other stateside competitors emerged, but none could match the quality and inherent reputation of Textron Ltd. Their attention to detail and expertise of their original equipment manufacturer (OEM) sales staff servicing the franchise cosmetic companies gave Textron a competitive edge. They were called upon to work closely with their industrial customers to develop cotton puffs that matched the trends in new cosmetic ingredients and application methods at the research and development (R&D) stage of such developments. Such progressive fashion-oriented but facially skin-sensitive cosmetic formulas required applicators that matched the demanding specifications of these new advances in the cosmetic field. Cotton materials were needed to sustain the look on the skin and provide the user with the same result that the cosmetic cream, lotion or powder promised. While women, the prime purchasers of such products, wanted to obtain the dramatic results the franchise cosmetic companies advertised, professional make-up artists had long known that the choice of applicators to transfer the pressed powder in the compact, the lotion in the bottle or the cream in the jar, was the key to the process. The right puff was therefore needed to complement the make-up process.

In the late 1980s, Far Eastern manufactures of cosmetic applicators began to emerge, offering cheaper versions of such items. While the detailed processing of the raw cotton material used in such production was inferior to the quality and exacting details of those manufactured by Textron Ltd., the cost considerations necessitated a strong consideration of their offerings by the company's clients. As textile manufacturing began to develop in the Indochina region and more and more American firms brought their expertise to the area, the overall quality of goods as well as the base materials used began to improve. As an outgrowth of improvements in the generic textile business emerged, better methods of production, selection of raw materials and attention to quality filtered down into the cosmetic cotton applicator category.

Case, along with the president of the company, David Grange, and the head of product development group, Nancy Adams, had made periodic trips to the Hong Kong Beauty Exhibition to constantly gauge Far Eastern competitors. For many years, they observed a display of poor offerings and found themselves returning from such visits confident that the threat of offshore competition was not yet emerging as a viable alternative for their clients. Their regular customers, both beauty companies and retailing organizations, were rarely evident at such conventions and hence their positive feelings were continuously strengthened.

Current Issues

Over the last few years, however, it became evident that startup companies, beginning as derivative plants of the large textile manufacturers throughout China, Taiwan, Korea and Thailand, could become a real danger to their ever-growing global business. While many of these enterprises still produced inferior merchandise, Textron noticed that a number of their American competitors were now forming alliances with such organizations. These associations brought with them the knowledge of how to deal with the beauty industry both in America and Europe, instilling in them a deep appreciation for quality and endurance of raw materials to work with the new cosmetic preparations. Once such considerations took a foothold and a reputation for delivering such competitively detailed quality merchandise with vastly lower costs was discovered by Textron's clients, the company could be in for some rough times ahead. During the last visit to the Hong Kong show, Grange had bumped into a number of his key franchise cosmetic component buyers as well as a few of his retail chain merchandise managers. They had all acknowledged the quality advances made by these emerging new players. It was felt however that the distance of such suppliers from their own factories and key decision-making staffs and the fact that the shapes and designs were still not up to the innovative expertise of the Textron company created a hesitation among clients wanting to deal with them. Grange knew full well however that with advanced global communication technology and the alliances with American-based representative organizations, the gap would be closed shortly. If such alterations were made and a fully competitive quality product could be offered with the inherent deep labor and overhead cost advantages that Far Eastern firms possessed, Textron was due for some major sales competition in the future.

After their last trip to the Asian convention in September of 1999, Grange and Case spent the hours on the return trip discussing strategic alternatives for the company in the years ahead. This wasn't the first time such matters were approached and, in fact, two years earlier, the company entered into an alliance with a United Kingdom manufacturer for the production on a joint basis of cosmetic sponges. Grange had always been reluctant to place his production facilities out of his geographical everyday domain. He was a "hands on" entrepreneur who felt strongly that all facets of one's business should be at arm's reach. Grange was deeply committed to his people and his door was always open to everyone in his organization. He was involved in every area of the business and it was not until Case joined Textron that Grange began to relinquish control over selective daily operations.

This desire to closely preside over and monitor his people was born out of a heritage of family involvement as exemplified by his father. His dad had instilled in Grange a great empathy for workers and staff, and even today the company's culture still carried such roots of benevolent carrying.

When the firm had moved from the greater New York area to Youngstown, key personnel were given liberal incentives to move to the new location, and great care was given to those who could not make the journey. Still today, the company showed great pride in its relationship with employees. Textron's human resources department was not merely a conduit for processing applications for employment and overseeing payroll but a large fully functional multitalented group that ran off-site improvement seminars and cross training exercises. Besides offering a full array of benefit packages, the company had a well-supervised child-care facility on the premises at no charge to employees. The human resources director attended all managerial meetings, thereby maintaining a strong presence in all company decision-making and the position was considered on par with senior management executives. The commitment to maintaining hands-on control of his organization and the strong, caring relationship with his people made for a close-knit family and a kind of patriarchal role for Grange. He prided himself on the fact that union attempts to organize his factory labor force never got off the ground, as his employees felt that they were best represented by Grange himself.

Years ago, a satellite retail packaging assembly plant and distribution facility in San Antonio, Texas, which had been part of the purchase of a small professional beauty applicator business, was dissolved in favor of consolidating all operations in Youngstown. All personnel at this redundant factory were given an opportunity to relocate in Youngstown or they received good termination benefits.

The United Kingdom alliance was finalized due to Grange's long and valued friendship with the principal of that company. The two also shared similar feelings about managing people and a common cultural background. Both parties had spent many years working together and enjoyed a special relationship, which had been fostered by the fact that the U.K. managing director's family resided in Ohio, thereby bringing the two executives together on a monthly basis as the Englishman came home often. Grange also visited the British facility every two months and the two executives spoke weekly on the phone. Both men viewed the alliance as more of a partnership than an arm's length sourcing arrangement.

Grange always felt that one of his prime differentiated product marketing characteristics was that up until the U.K. association for sponge material applicators, all his products were made in the United States. He believed that such designation symbolized quality of material and manufacturing excellence as well as innovative styling and technologically advanced, state-of-the-art compliance. Even with the English sponge production unit, all the cotton puff applicators were still made in the States. To drive home this important selling issue, all packages of retail cotton finished goods bore the American flag proudly stamped on them next to the words "Made in the U.S.A." Grange had recently seen consumer products bearing the slogan "Designed in America" as well as "Product Imported From China and Packaged in the U.S.A." but felt that the global customer still valued the U.S.A. slogan indicating the country of origin on his retail line. But in Grange's recent discussions with component buyers in the cosmetic and fragrance industry, such designation did not seem so important, given the fact that both the sponges and cotton puffs were slightly undistinguishable or hidden parts in the total presentation of the makeup compact, the accent being on the brand name, ingredients and plastic case; imported items could be utilized if quality was maintained. The recent acceptance of the sponges made in England by Textron's clients gave credence to the fact that quality, price and service were the prime criteria for the industry, rather than the country of origin.

Decision-Making Time

Following the conference on the plane ride home from the Orient, Grange and Case had assembled their managerial staff and charged them with putting together a preliminary plan to form an association with a Far Eastern manufacturer of cotton puffs. At the initial briefing meeting, samples of cotton puff merchandise collected from a variety of Far Eastern producers were evaluated by the manufacturing quality control people as well as by representatives of the marketing and sales groups from the retail and OEM divisions. The immediate consensus was that with a little direction in fashion styling composition and adjustment in fixative dyes to sustain color in the cotton velour, a quality comparative range to supplement their domestic manufacturing output could be produced abroad. When Case presented the factory cost quotations for the samples being reviewed, the vice-president of finance exclaimed, "Such values were way below our own manufacturing standard costs before administrative overhead." He further added that "even with anticipated duty and freight via containerized shipments, the projected landed price at our door would eclipse our costs by a good 20 per cent or more reduction." When Case noted that "these foreign price quotations were based on minimum quantities and could be subject to economies of scale discounting," all participants quickly realized that their projected stock keeping unit (SKU) sales for 2000 would easily allow for even greater margins.

When the meeting broke up, Chris Jenkins, the vice-president of finance, cornered Grange and Case in the hallway.

> Guys, if these numbers can be confirmed, and if future production of these Chinese puffs can be modified to accommodate our quality stability color standards and slightly altered for design modification, we need to jump on this as soon as possible. Better still, if we can manufacture over there ourselves via our own factory or through a joint venture, our profit potential would be magnified at least three times.

Alternative Proposals

It was now six months since that initial meeting. In the interim, Case had been back and forth a number of times, holding substantial discussions with what was now a short list of two potential alliance candidates, both of which were co-operative ventures, with local Chinese governmental bodies holding a share in them. While these companies' abilities to alter their production to accommodate changes in the color additive process and make design modifications were verified, and the exchange of cost quotations were proceeding well, Case had not yet proposed the final type of alliance he wanted.

In the back of his mind, Case wanted to form his own subsidiary but felt that such initial market entry strategy was both costly and risky, given the large investment required. Besides Case and Grange, the company did not have any other executives familiar with managing abroad. Given such considerations, Case's discussions to date with his Chinese associates had produced only two feasible alternatives to begin the relationship:

1. An initial three-year guaranteed outsourcing purchase agreement wherein, following the detailed specifications of Textron Ltd., supplies of cotton powder puffs would be produced at base prices. Such quotations would be subject to preset quantity discounting but offset slightly by an inflationary yearly adjustment. The right to pre-approve the samples of each and every shipment before departure would also be included in the arrangement. In essence a simplistic arm's-length purchasing association was contemplated.
2. The creation of a joint venture wherein Textron Ltd. would own 48 per cent of the company and the alliance partner would own the rest. Textron would be primarily responsible for sales and marketing worldwide along with periodic on-site technical assistance as to product design, quality assurances and engineering considerations by their technical staff. The plant facility, the manufacturing process itself and everyday operations would be under the direct control of the Chinese partner. Textron Ltd.

> would contribute a yet-to-be-finalized small dollar investment to help upgrade machinery and in general modernize the physical facilities. The partners would share the revenue generated by the sales efforts of Textron for the items produced in the plant.

Although exacting details of either proposed strategy needed to be worked out, with the former option requiring more legal and regulatory considerations, Case was confident that both situations could be accomplished. With the additional help of some local Chinese alliance specialists whom Case had utilized during the days when he had actually lived and worked in Hong Kong for a former employer, all seemed to be progressing nicely. Case knew he had to give additional thought to many other operational and administrative issues, and he wanted to obtain some sound advice from his internal teams before deciding which alternative to pursue. Questions as to the capital investment and how such funds would be utilized would require more discussions with the potential partners if the joint-venture route was chosen, but such issues would be addressed during Case's next trip to the Far East.

China as the Prime Choice of Supply

The focus on China was due mainly to Case's familiarity with the people and business environment. He felt very comfortable, given his prior experiences in the region and his knowledgeable appreciation of the culture and the way relationships were constructed. Beyond Case's personal considerations, the Chinese manufacturers he had encountered already had the necessary machinery and were well versed in the production of cotton puffs. Many already supplied the worldwide beauty trade but did not possess the sophisticated marketing and sales competencies practised by Textron, nor had they gained the reputation Textron historically enjoyed with the franchise cosmetic industry. An alliance with Textron would enhance the Chinese manufacturers' technical abilities and provide them with a wider entrée to the trade. The annual beauty show in Hong Kong attracted a global following, which would allow Textron to even create an offshore sales office and showroom close to the prime production facility to entertain prospective clients. Besides the Chinese connection, Case had opened initial discussion with makers of sponge applicators and other beauty accessories in Japan and Korea so that his trips to the China could be combined with other business opportunities he wanted to pursue in the Far East.

Case had entertained pursuing a Mexican manufacturer, as he had had prior dealings with companies producing a variety of cotton products in Mexico. Given the background of many of them in the cotton and aligned textile trade, this seemed a natural consideration, especially given the NAFTA accords and geographical proximity to Textron's major market, the United States. All potential companies Case visited, however, were located in the central part of the country, none near the border where the *Maquiladoras* were available. Case's Mexican contacts were not familiar with the specific production of cotton puff applicators as their cotton experience was in the manufacturing of surgical dressings, bandages, feminine hygiene pads and simple cotton balls. They would need to buy machinery and train a staff in such manufacturing operations. If Textron would fund such investment and provide technical assistance, a number of them agreed to manage such a facility on the U.S.-Mexican border through a joint venture. Case was hesitant to provide the funding, and he was worried that starting up a new plant would not let Textron achieve the inherent historical benefits that the more mature existing production in China would instantly allow.

Besides the economic considerations, Case found the Mexican manager's attitude a bit troublesome. Textron had once used a Mexican plant to supply, in final packaged form, cotton pads for the removal of facial cosmetic make-up. While his dealings with the principles of this family owned and operated business were most cordial and personally gratifying, Case had found that their attention to manufacturing details left much to be desired. The quality inspection of the raw cotton coming into their plants had given Case cause for concern. Many openly told him they mixed first quality fibres with "seconds" and remnants from the textile manufacturers in their local areas to achieve cost efficient production. As Textron always claimed its materials for cotton puff applicators were of "100 per cent virgin cotton," such an assertion might be difficult to enforce and supervise, given the pronouncements by his prior supplier. When discussions as to the importance of schedules to insure timely supply arose, the Mexican sources seemed to give the impression that they would do their best to comply. This slight hesitation bothered Case, as his component buyers demanded on-time delivery and were always changing specifications at the last minute.

Case had deep reservations on the business competencies exhibited by such Mexican firms, as his communications with them in the past, wherein days would go by before he heard from them, had left a poor impression on him. Many times, when he had repetitively inquired by e-mail, fax and telephone as to shipping dates for packaged finished products, he was eventually told that third-party suppliers of the packaging materials for the cotton pads caused the assembly delay. Inquiring further, during a visit with his Mexican supplier, Case learned that when local Mexican firms contract with each other, time promises are flexible and it seemed that an attitude of "when they are available, we get them" took precedence over definite schedules. During the year the company utilized the Mexican supplier, not one shipment was dispatched within the required period, and Case had given up contacting them, even paraphrasing the Mexican explanation when queried by his own inventory/warehouse manager.

The decision to go with a Chinese partner in some format seemed to be the best solution.

Case's Personal Reflections

As Case pondered what other matters needed to be resolved, his mind began to focus on his three-year posting, back in the early 1990s in Hong Kong, with an electronics manufacturer to oversee their Chinese network of suppliers. When Case and his family had first arrived in the then-British colony, the excitement of this new foreign land and it's unique culture had made a lasting impression on him. He had marveled at the sights, sounds, smells and overall ambience of the city state that mixed East and West. Coming from a middle class American lifestyle, the treatment the family received was like being transformed into a rich conclave of the elite. His children went to a specialized English-type boarding school and rarely mixed with local natives of their own age. In fact, such young Chinese children were lucky to get a basic elementary school education before being forced out into the real world and into the working community. The outskirts of the city, and even sections within, contained deep pockets that were below some extreme poverty levels Case had seen in other depressed regions of the world. Within a severely overpopulated area that was strained every day with new immigrants from the mainland, the concept of work, any job, took on a new meaning. People would work for what seemed like slave wages to Case, and he wondered how they survived, just attaining a mere sustenance level. His wife could afford household maids and cooks that were more like indentured servants than domestic employees. They worked long hours at meagre wages and never complained.

During Case's visits to plants in mainland China, both during his expatriate posting years and subsequent trips back in the mid-1990s, the conditions at such facilities had initially deeply disturbed him. The environments he witnessed were nothing like he had ever seen in the United States. Factories were like prison compounds. The laborers seemed to toil at their job stations never looking up, never smiling and always looked like they were staring out with blank facial expressions. Rarely had Case seen them take a break, with many workers eating lunch at their desks and at their worktables or machinery. He seldom witnessed the laborers even taking bathroom breaks. The air in the facilities was always stale with no ventilation except for a few fans, and it was always very hot or very cold, depending on the outside temperature. He witnessed children, younger it seemed that his two adolescent kids, toiling in the plants alongside the elderly. He watched infants placed alongside their mothers on the floor of the factories being rocked by feet as the mothers' hands moved on the table above them. As these visits became more frequent, Case's disdain for such initially horrific working conditions began to lessen and he began to accept what he saw.

Many times, in social conversations with other executives and managers, Case had voiced his concerns about the treatment of the workers. He listened as they tried to get him to understand and appreciate that while the conditions were terrible, the alternative might be even worse. With the expanded population, growing at a massive rate, the supply of people outstripped employment opportunities. In order to survive, people would take any job and children as well as the elderly all had to work. Public governmental assistance was not only inadequate but almost impossible to administer, even if the resources could be found. The old communist philosophy of all society working for the good of the common proletariat, and hence the state, had been indoctrinated with the birth of the Mao regime; people saw it as their duty and obligation to endure hard times.

Case's Chinese friends had often remarked that if China were to catch up to the Western capitalistic nations and be a participant in the world's expanded trading economies, its people were its greatest competitive asset. In order to be a member in the world community and to provide enrichment for future generations, sacrifices had to be made. Capital for the improvement of factory environmental conditions was secondary to the need to update basic machinery and gain technology. The government had to build a sound internal infrastructure of roadways, rail and port facilities to ship its goods before the physical welfare of its people could be considered. With power still a scarce commodity, any electricity flowing into a factory needed to be first used to run the machinery and not for hot or cool air to be produced. The only way to achieve the goal of making mainland China competitive with the rest of the world was through the exportation route which was founded in the country's ability to produce cheaper goods than the rest of the globe. This simple fact necessitated low labor and overhead operating costs that contributed to poor working conditions in the factories.

Obviously, Case understood this economic argument was the main reason his company—and therefore he himself—had come to the region. In order for his own organization to remain competitive in the cotton puff business both at home and abroad, it would have no choice but to locate a portion of its operations in China or some other emerging nation.

Case had seen the TV footage of the protesters at the 2000 WTO conference in Seattle who had destroyed that meeting and in later months had done the same in Washington, D.C., and Ottawa, Canada. He heard them voicing and physically demonstrating their deep concerns against governments and transnational companies as to worker rights and environmental conditions in emerging and developing nations. Case was well aware of the attention the press gave to large multinational companies like Levi Strauss, Reebok and others over their treatment of employees, accusing them of almost slavelike practices in their foreign factories. Even personalities who lent their names to the labels of garments, like Kathy Lee Gifford, had come under strong pressure for allowing their third party licensees in the United States to operate sweat shops and mistreat workers. Companies that did not even have a direct relationship wherein they exercised straight control over employee conditions were still questioned about the suppliers they used abroad as the social conscience of the world seem to be focused on these issues.

Although Case himself deplored the hiring of adolescent children, he understood the economic and social context that existed in China for their use. China wasn't America. Young kids grew up much faster and much more was expected of them as contributors to the family unit. Even the government mandate, made within the framework of the message of a collective good of the nation for families to have only one child, did not alleviate the problem. In fact, in many families it just made the burden deeper. Most Chinese families were made up of extended relatives who grouped together to pool their resources for their common survival. In these family units, all members had to work. The simple luxury of going to a public school, playing games and watching TV, as American children enjoyed, was not part of their world. In numerous families, children, mostly young girls, were sent away from their rural villages to emerging urban industrial centres to look for work. After paying large portions of their meagre weekly salaries back to their employers for dormitory housing and food within the confines of the factory compound, any amount left over was sent to the family.

Even the elderly felt such pressure to work, as retirement after years of service and a reasonable pension was almost a non-existent consideration. No true governmental program like social security existed, and the family had to care for the elderly in their homes, putting a great burden on the whole extended unit. Political dissidents and even criminals were conscripted into the labor force to help offset the cost of the State having to provide for them. Plant conditions, treatment of workers and even caring about the environment were not primary issues for an emerging country trying to first find work for its population during the transformation process into a competitive world economic nation.

Case pondered if it was time for the company to prepare a written corporate moral compass. Should it publish a code of ethics, as many transnational firms had been doing? What should it consist of, what specific criteria defining norms of behavior should be stated? and should it be incorporated as an obligation in the arm's length purchasing agreement being considered with the Chinese supplier? If the announced provisions were violated, should this be viewed as an automatic right for Textron to terminate the agreement, or should there be a time frame in which to cure such conditions? Case also wondered how his firm could monitor such matters to ensure compliance. If the alternative joint venture were chosen, how should such values be incorporated into the partnership agreement and how should Case process such matters during the negotiation?

Case was comfortable with discussions on costs, quality and delivery specifications as they had a finite measurable logic to them. Social responsibility and ethics touched upon many emotional areas that were harder to define. He had seen firsthand how different cultures approached them from divergent viewpoints, and he had gained a respect for the saying "when in Rome do as the Romans do." He also, however, maintained the feeling that there were core human values that at times transcended such local traditions and social context.

Moral Dilemmas—Unanswered Questions

What worried Case was even if the business decision was the right one, could the company be entering a relationship that might some day backfire? If a factory that Textron bought merchandise from or, because of the joint venture, was more deeply involved in was alleged to be mistreating employees, would public opinion injure the company's reputation? Was the focus of the world now on China and its historic practices of human rights abuse? Would someone be watching companies more closely that associated themselves with Chinese partners in any form?

What if Textron's buyers of components, the franchised cosmetic houses, were themselves chastised for using slave-type labor in the supplies used in their own manufacturing of their brand named products? Would they in turn cease to buy from Textron Ltd.? What if consumers of the retail packaged lines decided to boycott the products for similar reasons? What if the licensor of the new collection felt that such foreign sourcing of items bearing their trademark was injurious to their image and reputation, and they objected?

Given his company's strong traditional organizational culture of placing employees first, Case also wondered what effect any such ethical and social responsibility issues stemming from a Chinese association could have on his own domestic operational employees.

He wondered about such matters again as he thought to himself that going global was more than just an exercise in financial, legal and operational logistical decision making; it involved taking a moral position in Textron's commercial relationships with overseas entities.

TAPP TECHNOLOGIES INC. (A)

Prepared by Lesley Menzies under the supervision of Professor David Shaw

Version: (A) 2002-10-17

Jay Tapp, president and CEO of Tapp Technologies Inc. (Tapp Tech) contemplated expanding the size and role of his board of directors. Tapp Tech was a total packaging systems company serving the wine industry through the production and sale of pressure sensitive wine labels and the distribution of label application equipment. The company was experiencing rapid growth, every phase of the business was straining with the workload. Jay's own time was fully committed. He knew that the continued growth of the company required different skills that neither the present board nor his management team had. Jay was worried that outside directors on the board would slow down his decision making, interfere with his vision for the company and increase costs during a period when cash was in short supply.

COMPANY HISTORY

The wine industry in North America traditionally used a particular type of label for its bottled wines called a glue label or a sheet cut label. The wine label industry demanded extremely high quality and detail-oriented labelling. The sheet cut label fulfilled the high level of print quality that the wine label industry demanded.

An alternative labelling method was called "pressure sensitive" labels. Most other industries around the world had converted to a pressure sensitive label over the last 15 years. The wine industry, notably in North America, was resisting the conversion for two specific reasons: (1) the level of graphic reproduction demanded by the North American wine label market was not available in pressure sensitive labels; (2) new equipment was required to affix the pressure sensitive labels.

The total wine label market was approximately a $200 million business, with the pressure sensitive label component at 15 per cent of that market. Tapp Technologies had a 40 per cent share of that 15 per cent segment. Jay expected that 50 to 60 per cent of the wine industry would convert to pressure sensitive labels over the next three to five years.

Gallo, a large winery, was responsible for 50 per cent of the wine gallonage within North America. Gallo had just decided to convert to pressure sensitive labels. The conversion of Gallo to pressure sensitive labels injected $25 million worth of pressure sensitive label volume into the market.

Jay Tapp wanted to continue to operate the business as a total packaging system, relying upon the unique characteristic of having the ability to service both the label and equipment side of the market. Tapp Tech had about 35 applicators out in the field, and out of the 35 companies with the application equipment, 30 were wine label customers. The same sales force was responsible both for the sale of labels and of the equipment, and experience had shown that the company was most successful when it is able to sell the whole system.

While Jay was employed in London, England, he became aware of the technology that allowed a high level of print quality to be used on pressure sensitive labels. He returned to Canada and formed a company to sell both the labels and the equipment components, the total packaging system.

Jay formed Tapp Technologies in October 1992 to introduce the new technology to the North American wine industry. The incorporation of the company under the Canadian Business Corporation Act required that a board of directors be established. Jay chose a board consisting of the four investors in the company; Jay Tapp, Larry Tapp, Maureen Tapp and Bob Kite. Jay did not believe that the board would interfere with his vision for the company nor question his decision-making in the start-up phase of the company. Each board member offered a particular skill or attribute. Larry Tapp, (Jay's father) former CEO of Lawson Mardon Inc., a global printing and packaging company, and a member of several boards, offered experience in the printing and packaging business, along with broad corporate experience; Maureen Tapp (Jay's wife) worked for Tapp Tech in marketing planning, and Bob Kite, vice president of operations, managed a large facility that supplied the wine industry with glue labels prior to his agreeing to come to work for Tapp Tech.

Jay appointed his father, Larry Tapp, as chairman of the board; Jay knew that Larry's priorities would focus on the best interests of the company, and his business experience would contribute to the efficient handling of the board's agenda. Jay was confident that he would be able to maintain a healthy working relationship with his father as chairman.

In January 1993, Jay attended the major wine industry trade show in California which was the largest in North America. At this time, Tapp Tech was a fledgling company without manufacturing capabilities. Jay decided to test the level of interest in the new technology by displaying sample orders from a company in France and showing the required equipment to attach the labels. The wine industry responded with a keen interest, and Tapp Tech achieved quick penetration into the market.

There were about seven companies worldwide with the capability of Tapp's printing technology, four in France, one in Italy and one in England. The wine industry within North America was growing at a double digit rate. Because there was not enough wine being produced in North America to fill the demand, wine was imported from other countries and bottled by the wineries here.

Pressure sensitive labels addressed two separate dimensions within the wine label market: the time savings in set-up and change-over production and the marketability of wine through innovative label design possibilities. Production-driven wineries focus on reducing costs per litre of wine produced, while other wineries rely heavily upon packaging as a method of selling. In the wine industry, packaging comprises 80 per cent of the customer decision to purchase. Tapp Tech was servicing both dimensions of the wine label market.

In April 1993, Tapp started manufacturing labels with one press. There were many challenges in getting the technology up to a commercial level. The manufacturer of the equipment lacked the expertise to run the equipment; and, there were no raw materials available in the formats desired by Tapp Tech. Tapp Tech had to develop its own expertise in running the equipment and create its own raw materials for the formats required. The demand for Tapp Tech's product was higher than its ability to supply, forcing management to become preoccupied with the issues of capacity, efficiency, quality control and waste control. The company adopted a manufacturing focus. The problems and opportunities associated with growth demanded more of Jay's time and resources, which meant that management capabilities were being spread thin.

Working capital requirements were increasing as well. The company was dealing with the Bank of British Columbia for its funding needs. This relationship worked well while Tapp Tech was a start-up company; however, once rapid growth occurred, the Bank became uncomfortable with the increased need for funds.

Tapp Tech's revenue base was split between selling the machinery and the labels. Sales revenues were $5.6 million, $2.3 million for equipment sales and $3.3 million for the wine label graphics side of the business. Both areas were growing rapidly.

The Board of Directors Situation

Jay realized that he must deal with issues arising from the fast growth of his company. Decisions were becoming more complex and more difficult to change once made due to the number of interrelated factors. He needed to establish further credibility with financial institutions and corporate suppliers. Jay also wanted to gain access to capabilities and contacts within his industry. When he had specific problems, he wanted to draw on the experience of others. Consultants were an option, but they were expensive and too focused.

Jay learned from other entrepreneurs that boards can focus on operating issues and slow the process to a crawl with demands for information; legal and tax issues; costs, liability, customer concerns and sole supplier issues. While he wanted advice on specific operating issues, mostly he wanted to look to the board for strategic matters such as entering new markets, exporting his product, or increasing capacity. He wondered how to keep the board "on topic."

Jay thought that expansion of the board to include two to four additional members could give him both general experience and specific expertise to draw on, along with objectivity and credibility. But, an outside board of directors meant that Jay would have to teach the new directors the inner workings of the industry and the strategy and operations of the company, so the benefits could not be expected quickly, and came at a high time investment cost. A board would require more of his time, and he would have to commit to produce reports and organize and attend all meetings. He would have to compensate directors and pay for their travel and accommodations when they attended meetings, which was an issue for a company caught in a cash crunch. Jay believed that a director should have a financial stake in the company, so he would have to convince a potential director to buy shares, which raised a whole new set of problems regarding credibility, valuation and control of the company.

Jay thought he had covered the pros and cons of the decision. At first, he had listed the names of potential directors as part of the decision; but, then he concluded that he should make the decision of whether to expand the board independent of the potential candidates.

Blinds To Go—Wanted: People to Lead Explosive Growth (A)

Prepared by Ken Mark under the supervision of Professors Fernando Olivera and Lyn Purdy

Version: (A) 2002-11-19

Introduction

Pointing at a large map of North America, Stephen Shiller, president of Blinds To Go (BTG), declared his plans to "blanket the continent with our stores and factories, one region at a time." Red-colored pins, all 120 of them, dotted the eastern region of the map, which had been the target of Blinds To Go's first expansion phase. Backed by Harvard Private Capital (HPC), the investment arm of Harvard University, this Canadian window dressing retail fabricator had more than quintupled its revenues to US$100 million in the 20 months prior to June 2000. Pacing around the "War Room" in his Montreal headquarters, Stephen Shiller announced,

> First, we'll complete our expansion into Florida; then we'll decide either to tackle the West Coast or proceed to march our stores across the United States in a westernly direction. By the end of next year, we plan to have 200 stores. We can envision sustained revenue growth of 50 per cent per year. Some estimates indicate that our revenues could top half a billion dollars in three years—selling blinds! But one thing that concerns me is. . . .

Stephen Shiller stopped in mid-sentence, swiveled around slowly and intoned,

> . . . four vice-presidents have left the company in the last two years and we've had a mixed record hiring senior managers. This is our core team and we really need senior talent to help guide our growth.

Blinds To Go—A Retail Fabricator of Window Dressings

In 1954, David Shiller, the patriarch of the Shiller family, started his own company in Montreal, Canada by selling bedding products from the trunk of his family's station wagon. Opening a retail location one year later, David Shiller started to sell carpets, floor coverings, draperies, and fabrics. When his son, Stephen, joined the business in the mid-1970s, he convinced his father to focus his efforts on selling blinds. Their retail operation was called "Au Bon Marche" and the Shillers began to create the production system that allowed them to cut the normal six- to eight-week delivery time frame for custom-made blinds to 48 hours. In fact, in that original store, they were eventually able to deliver custom-made blinds to customers in one hour or less. "The factory was literally next to the store and we offered our one-hour delivery guarantee, which kept our customers happy," Stephen Shiller explained.

The Shillers were, in their own words, aggressive salespeople. They loved crafting deals to satisfy their retail customers and remarked that it was better to sell eight products to eight different customers and make a dollar profit from each one than to make an eight dollar profit from one customer. For two decades, "Au Bon Marche" was known for its aggressive merchandising efforts and energetic television commercials in the Quebec region.

When the Shillers started to open more stores in 1994, they were taken aback by the tremendous sales growth at each one. At that point, they realized that they had a great concept on their hands.

Stephen Shiller exclaimed,

> Our sales were higher for each consecutive store opened, and none of our competitors could replicate our model. They were either manufacturers or retailers: none were both. None could hope to deliver the 48-hour turnaround we promised, had our unique sales model, which was 100 per cent commission-based, or had our attention to customer needs. We knew we had to do something fast before someone else beat us to the punch.

The All Window Coverings (AWC) market itself was stagnant, realizing only one to two per cent growth per year in this US$2 billion market. A sub-segment of this market, however, the retail fabricator market (vertically integrated manufacturer/merchandisers of blinds), of which BTG was a part, was growing at least nine per cent per year. A report by the Sullivan Marketing Group forecast that retail fabricators, constituting 12 per cent of the market and growing, would play an increasingly visible role in the AWC market.

Preparing BTG for Rapid Expansion

Their appetites whetted by sales growth in each successive store, the Shillers decided to plan their expansion. Studying the North American market in 1995, they asked themselves if they should expand west to Ontario or south to the

United States. They knew that if they failed south, they could focus on Ontario and Western Canada. "We wanted to try something difficult—we knew that, to repeat a cliché, if we could make it there, we could make it anywhere," explained Stephen. An introduction to Harvard Private Capital led them to discussions with this investment arm of Harvard University. Harvard was a careful strategic investor, reviewing a portfolio of 600 companies a year but investing in only about a dozen. Stephen continued,

> I recommended to my father that we take a leap of faith—we were a private company, making more money than we could intelligently spend. If we went with Harvard, we would not take money out—we would reinvest it so that eventually we could take the company public and reward our employees who had been with us for years. Harvard never put pressure on us to grow. It was more important for them to see my vision to build a great company.

Realizing that outside management had to be brought in to lead this growth, the Shillers knew that their first hire would be the most important. While working with HPC, they were impressed by the work performed by Nkere Udofia. Stephen remarked,

> Udofia was working at that time as the managing director of Harvard Private Capital and I knew that we needed him at BTG for our expansion. But I had to be sensitive about my approach. As their representative, he would come in once a month and I would invite him to go jogging, and have dinner with me and my family. We became good friends and I liked his long-term vision. Having spent eight years backing retail companies at Harvard, it was clear Udofia was bored and thinking about options outside of Harvard.
>
> When Udofia announced that he was leaving HPC on his own accord, I jumped at the chance to invite him aboard. South Africa was in the midst of taking down apartheid, and Udofia, wanting to help out, was spending time down there, seeing what he could do. Udofia wanted to see if he could help build a private investment infrastructure in South Africa. This meant he spent considerable time out of country. I re-invited him to help out with BTG one to two days a week when he was in the country to which Udofia agreed.
>
> Udofia eventually grew tired of the Boston-Johannesburg-Montreal commute. One to two days became two to three, and before long, Udofia was with BTG full-time. At BTG, Udofia worked with me and my father, helping build the senior management team and guiding the company in its rapid growth stage.

BTG "Owner-Manager"

Collaborating with the Shillers, Udofia identified what he believed would be a key driver of success—a consistent corporate culture that meshed with BTG's retail culture. They discussed the need to strengthen and "professionalize" the management team, while retaining the entrepreneurial, hands-on culture that had made the company successful. They outlined a number of important aspects of this environment. They believed that the ideal senior manager would need to compliment the Shillers and be an "owner-manager." At BTG, an "owner-manager" was someone who was hands-on and strategic, highly committed, possessing a grasp of the entire business, able to develop people, and focused on long-term value creation (see Exhibit 1).

Along with the need to be both detail-oriented and strategic, the Shillers and Udofia (Executive Team) expected senior managers to operate within tight quality standards. Additionally, in order to execute the overall strategy, they expected senior managers to discuss their work plans with them. At the same time, they wanted senior managers to be visionary, to share and believe in BTG's ultimate goal of being a multi-billion dollar North American retailer. Lastly, they expected their team to be aggressive, entrepreneurial, possess high personal and work standards, and be highly accountable for their actions. Individual members would need to be open to feedback—able to learn from their mistakes and adapt.

One of the changes that Udofia made when he joined the organization was the practice of

BTG Management Bars

Manager

- Responsible for identifiable functional/project area
- Good perspective and experience in at least one function
- Strong supervisory skills and on-the-ground leadership
- Able to develop project workplans with guidance
- Able to drive straightforward initiatives to resultsñproven track record as a doer

Director

- Able to run major day-to-day operations role
- Able to focus and prioritize with minimal guidance
- Thinks strategically and tactically about the business
- Able to take general direction and structure an approach to resolve issues
- Able to drive complex initiatives to significant results
- Able to influence others outside of immediate areas of responsibility
- Able to build and leverage cross-functional ties
- Can handle multiple major initiatives simultaneously

Vice President

- Broad view of the company and its objectives across multiple functions
- Able to help set strategic direction
- Well established credibility across the company
- Able to bring thought leadership at senior management level and in multiple functions
- Clear value-added contribution at the company-wide level
- Proven ability to train and develop people
- Team-builder, has a following (disciples)
- Owner-Manager; Personal ownership for overall business; Able to think, and make decision as an owner

CORE BTG VALUES

Exhibit 1 Blinds To Go Management Bars

openly discussing problems as soon as they appeared. Stephen explained,

> We surface problems rather than sweep them under the rug. It's very hard to hide problems anyway in a small organization like ours. We have a healthy respect for lessons and mistakes—better surface and learn from mistakes. We ask people to be direct and honest with their people. We will go out of our way to let you know how you're doing. This comes from Udofia's philosophy—it wasn't always this way at BTG.

Building the BTG Senior Management Team

In building the senior management team, the Executive Team (David & Stephen Shiller and Udofia) began by creating a master list of duties to be handled by the team (see Exhibit 2). The list was then divided into these three functions:

Retail Operations

Responsible for all the retail operations consisting of store operations, store merchandising, people development and marketing. Store operation, retail planning, and human resources teams worked together to find, attract, develop, and retain the talent needed to support the field operations. Marketing and merchandizing focused on getting the right product into the stores and promoting the BTG brand to consumers.

Manufacturing Operations

Responsible for sourcing, developing, and manufacturing custom BTG products and delivering to stores. BTG sourcing and product development team worked with suppliers to produce unique products for BTG and with the BTG plants to manage raw material inventories. The core manufacturing team worked with human resources to attract, train, and develop the plant workforce necessary to product BTG products. The manufacturing process was very labor-intensive.

Administrative/Support Operations

Outside of the two major business units, BTG needed various corporate support functions. Real estate development was responsible for finding and building new stores to support the rollout. Finance/control team was responsible for providing accurate, timely financial information to and with operating managers to enhance profitability. The IS team worked closely with all senior managers to ensure that information systems were reliable, secure and that the infrastructure expanded to support the growth.

Udofia felt that with senior managers covering these positions, BTG would be ready to tackle its expansion plan.

In recruiting senior management personnel, BTG was able to offer industry-competitive salaries to its senior management team because of its highly profitable, cash-rich position. Furthermore, the package of stock options that would be granted to each member of the senior management team, along with a schedule of performance targets for additional stock, was very enticing. Lastly, BTG believed that the fast-paced environment of a rapidly growing company would attract qualified talent.

Udofia and Stephen described the BTG culture as fundamentally non-hierarchial. Both Udofia and Stephen felt as comfortable dealing directly with an entry-level analyst or coordinator as with a director or vice-president (VP). BTG was careful about conferring titles, believing that the individual had to have at least an equal amount of experience and success as his or her future peer group before being promoted. It was BTG's philosophy that titles needed to represent demonstrated value-added contribution at BTG—thus it was common to have a director performing the same duties as would a VP as they worked towards demonstrating their value. Udofia's view on promotion was as follows: To be promoted into a VP position from the director level was like being voted into a partnership where one went from being a department or functional manager to being a general manager or partner with a very broad view of the company and its objectives.

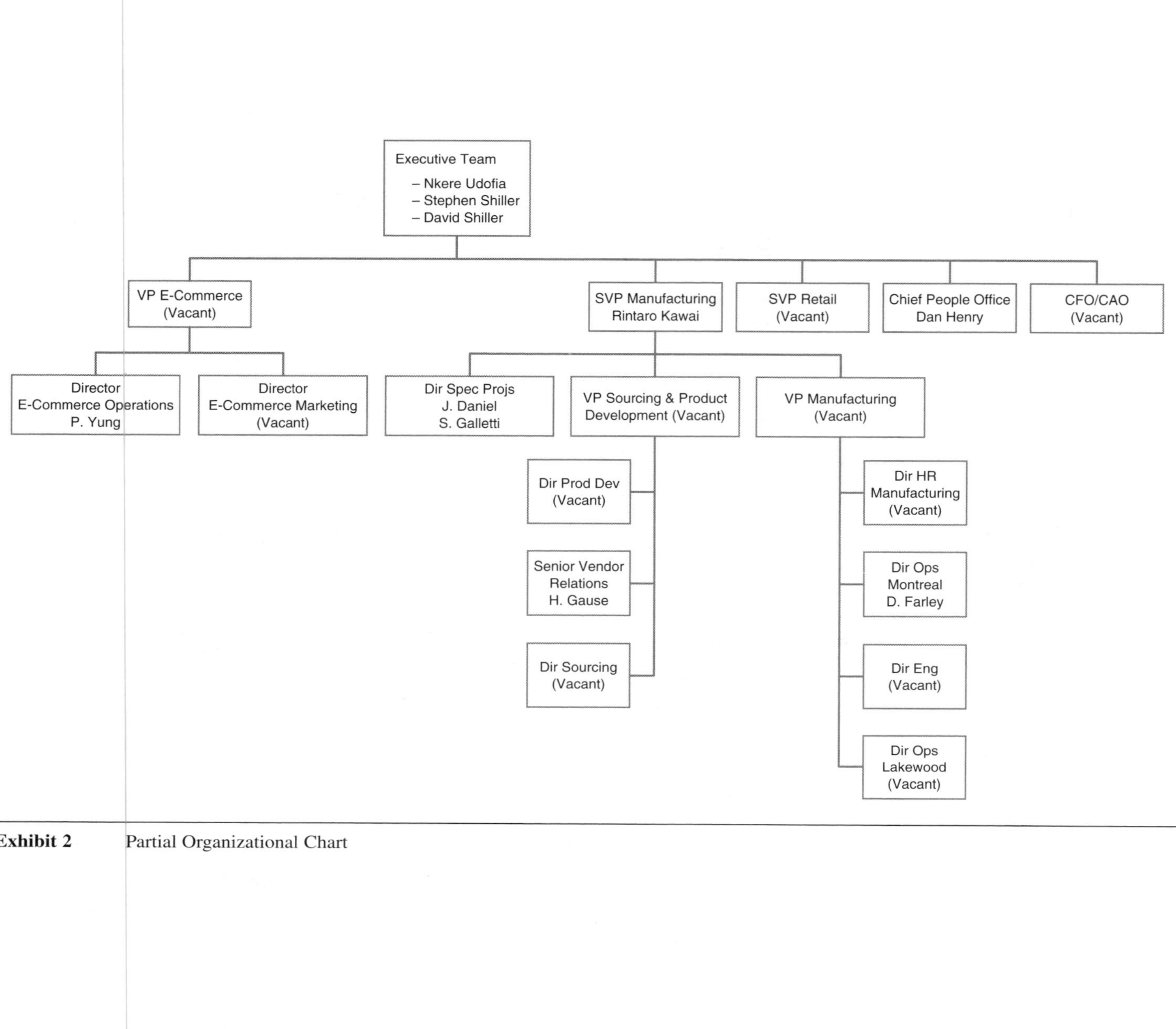

Exhibit 2 Partial Organizational Chart

Hiring Process

The hiring process for senior managers at BTG was as follows—each potential hire was interviewed first by Udofia or Stephen, then on an individual basis by four or five existing senior managers. The senior management team decided as a group if they were ready to extend an offer, with Udofia and Stephen being the ultimate decision makers. Udofia commented,

> We wouldn't bring VPs or directors aboard without buy-in from the rest of the management group—all our VPs, even the ones who have left, were screened by our management team—they have to fit. When we hire a VP, we're basically hiring for experience and what we are trying to determine is the relevancy of their experience to what we're trying to do. We have an owner/manager culture which is very hands-on—you own part of the business through stock-options. This, however, puts a huge demand on the company when you bring on senior management.
>
> We have had a mixed history of hiring VPs. There are lots of people out there who are strategic, but most likely not detailed-oriented or hands-on enough to operate in this environment. As for culture and fit, we do not want people to do something because they feel they have to do it, we want everyone to do it because they believe it is right. We do it to add value. That's the difference. We want people thinking about this business as if it's their own. Long-term thinkers.
>
> At BTG, we've not had a hard time attracting applicants, but we have had a hard time finding people who fit. To grow at a slow rate would be easy (slow to us means 20 to 30 per cent), but we're growing at 50 to 60 per cent per year! That is why I still spend 75 per cent or more of my time recruiting, and Stephen spends up to 50 per cent of his time in the same capacity.

Once hired, getting a new VP started meant that he or she learned about how blinds were sold at the retail level, and then actually worked for a period of two to four weeks in the capacity of a sales associate. After this hands-on training, the VPs would be given increasingly difficult projects in their department to start learning the business, finally working up to managing their department after a few months.

Udofia and the Shillers had been disappointed in the past two years that four of their seven VPs departed BTG due to issues of underperformance. All four VPs who left had come to BTG with a history of success at other companies. They were attracted to BTG for the same reasons—fast-growth, entrepreneurial environment, attractive compensation. Udofia believed that this mixed record had to do with several issues: there was a steep learning curve for new VP hires at BTG and the four that left might have been unwilling to make the effort to indoctrinate themselves in the BTG corporate culture and value system. Udofia explained,

> This business is different. It's not a typical retailer. It's integrated, not a pure retailer. It's sales, not merchandising-driven. It's extremely people-dependent and not process-dependent. And it's owner-managed and operated and hands-on. All this requires the typical exec to learn—a lot of their former experience is not relevant. If you are not willing to learn this business, if your ego or experience gets in the way, you will fail.

Another issue that surfaced was the VPs' lack of ownership and short-term focus.

Stephen continued,

> We have focused on building something great and long-lasting—long-term value creation. Fundamentally, we want our people to help solve the problems and help build a great company. If your focus is on using band-aids to get to an IPO and then cash out, we don't want you here. It is really hard to get this level of motivation without working with someone.

Udofia also observed that the VPs who left after only a relatively short period of employment were the ones who were defensive and unable to learn when given constructive feedback about their mistakes. Understanding the steep learning curve, Stephen and Udofia worked closely with each department VP in an attempt to coach and develop them, but with limited success. In coaching them, they tried to be as direct and straightforward as possible because that was how they expected the VPs to deal with their employees. In addition, the coaching sessions were never personal attacks—according to Udofia, everyone at BTG should be working towards the same goal and should be able to take feedback constructively. Udofia added,

> I've never met a perfect candidate. We can only assess the likelihood of success—if you have identified the risk areas, then you try to manage the risks. When we hire someone and they leave, nine out of ten times we have identified the risks but were ultimately unable to manage them to success. This is a dynamic environment. You have to be willing to learn and grow.

Jeff Rayner, VP marketing, offered,

> Why have people left? Incompetency, personality clashes. Others were competent, but their egos did not allow them to be part of our team. That said, we need to parachute in fast-growth managers, people who are doers. I had a recent hire, with whom I spent significant time trying to train but she would not roll up her sleeves to do what she perceived as the grunt work—she thought selling blinds in-store was beneath her.
>
> Frankly, if you're not turned on by the culture of the people working here, it's "strike one." If you can't see the concept, "strike two." This is not the safe zone, we're in a challenging arena. Not to worry because Udofia and Stephen have developed an environment that functions best if you check your ego at the door. Don't let your ego get in the way.

The Ex-VP Store Operations

The former VP of store operation had been brought in from a major U.S. clothing retailer. BTG was impressed by the fact that she was in charge of opening the retailer's Canadian stores and had been through the whole store and staff set-up process. She brought 15 years of experience in retail, including regional management duties.

One of her major changes was a move away from commission-based compensation at retail to a straight per hour wage. Udofia commented,

> The move away from commission, in retrospect, goes counter to our culture. She never got it. She sent out 500 memos in 16 months, trying to enforce standards one way or another. We would walk into the store and realize that people had never read the memos. Actually, half of them didn't read the memos, and the other half that did, didn't care. She tried to impose a structure of uniformity. "Dress alike, act alike." When we hired her, we were trying to bring in professional experience.

She lasted only 16 months at BTG and was terminated in July 1998.

> Udofia's overall impression was that she was too administrative, not hands-on enough, not willing to work hard. Her ego, Udofia explained, never allowed her to learn the business. He recounted that her experience in merchandising-driven, operations-intensive retail businesses led her to come to the wrong conclusions about how to run BTG's store operations. The store operation at BTG is largely people or sales-driven. To the day she left, she never appreciated this distinction. In addition, she disliked travel and was unwilling to make the necessary time and effort commitments to BTG.

The Ex-VP Operations

Having 10 years of manufacturing experience, the first VP of operations had been a senior VP at a competing blinds manufacturer and a VP at a painting company.

His employment at BTG lasted from January 1998 to October 1, 1999. Udofia saw that this VP was short-term focused, not hands-on, and believed that he had nothing new to learn from BTG. In addition, he did not take feedback well.

Udofia outlined,

> He was too short-term focused and not a team player. Every decision he made was done to manipulate the books, or sweep problems under the rug—he got up everyday trying to appear to move the ball forward instead of really moving the ball forward. We had to intervene because we believe that people tend to emulate their leaders—we did not want him to instill his behavior in our manufacturing organization. We spent the first six to eight months trying to teach him the business. We

> worked hard with him, bent over backwards to help him. Tried to coach him to be more hands-on, accept feedback, but he kept humoring us, trying to hide problems. The next six months, we tried to change him, get him to be more long-term focused and we hoped that he would work out. In the end, HOPE IS NOT A STRATEGY—we failed with this guy. In hindsight, his short-term focus and selfish nature made him a bad fit from Day One. We wasted lots of time and energy with him.

The Ex-VP Finance

Udofia indicated that the former VP finance had 20 years of finance experience in the retail industry and had been the CFO of a large U.S. regional retailer.

> He had come from a large corporation where two to three per cent operating profit was normal and thinking that five per cent was a great number, he could not understand why BTG was dissatisfied with 15 to 20 per cent operating profit. His subsequent reluctance to seek ways to improve what he thought was already a stellar number led to his dismissal in January 1999, less than six months after he had been hired. We have learned, if you get it wrong, cut it short. Failure at this level is too tough on the organization.

Current Staffing of Top Management Roles

In contrast, there were other hires at the VP and director levels at BTG that had turned out to be successful (see Exhibit 3).

The current director of finance, Sonia Girolamo, was originally thought to be very high risk when she was hired. Udofia stated that although she had ten years of retail auditing experience, she came in lacking operational experience and people management skills. After only two years, she had developed into one of the most highly regarded managers at BTG. Taking over duties from the previously mentioned ex-VP Finance, Girolamo initially had to be persuaded that she was not yet ready for the title of vice-president. Udofia continued,

> Sonia's paid off tremendously for us. After an initial tough transition, she has been a great student and has really grown into a good general manager. We identified her development needs and were able to work through them primarily because she bought into our vision.

Roberto Delgadillo, director of management information systems, added,

> Sonia's doing well because she understood what the rules were, and can live with them, and she does have enough leverage so she does not feel frustrated. She earned their respect. Other people were frustrated by decision making here—Udofia and Stephen still get involved in any important decision. You've got to accept that decisions are made by one of those two offices. If you don't accept that, you get frustrated. Because of the pace imposed, they seem to become bottlenecks at times—sometimes the decision making slows down so much that it seems ineffective. But you've got to understand that this is a relatively new company and if you decide these guys know where they are going, you've got to place your trust in them and leave your egos at the door . . . it's difficult at times.

Sonia Girolamo commented,

> Last year, I was pushing for the VP position, but this year, titles have been recalibrated, and with the new VPs in after the shakeout, we saw that the skill sets changed as the company evolved. People who would have been fine two years ago wouldn't cut it as VP today. On the street, it could be perceived as BTG can't retain managers, but insiders know that it benefits the corporation. We're hiring people to help build a great organization as opposed to working for an average company.
>
> The BTG culture is so special that even with my staff, there is a lot of turnover. There are tons of work to do, so you can imagine that some VPs have difficulty accepting the hands-on approach. You've got to realize that we've got limits in our power of decision. A lot of VPs were used to running units by themselves. Here, if you gain their confidence, you'll be ok. But first you have to gain their confidence.
>
> The exposure one gets here can contribute to increased turnover. Tons of people can identify the problem, but not many can implement the

SENIOR MANAGEMENT PROFILE

DAVID J. SHILLER
Chairman and Founder

Founder of Blinds To Go™ Inc. and Au Bon Marché™, Inc., the predecessor company, David has been in the blinds and shades business for over thirty years. Prior to Au Bon Marché™, David founded and developed several other successful retail businesses. David has been in the home fashion business since 1954 when he left a family business and ventured out on his own. David is one of Montreal's best known entrepreneurs and a leader in the business community. David is the key visionary behind the Blinds To Go™ expansion. David, together with his son Stephen, is the General Partner of The Shiller Group, a private investment partnership that owns the controlling interest in Blinds To Go™, Inc. The Shiller Group also owns a portfolio of real estate investments in Canada and the United States.

STEPHEN J. SHILLER
President and CEO

Stephen is co-founder and the key operating executive behind the development of Blinds To Go™, Inc. Stephen is responsible for moving the company into manufacturing and for expanding the company outside of the Montreal area. Stephen has over twenty one years of general management experience in the blinds and shades industry. Stephen, together with his father David, is the General Partner of The Shiller Group, a private investment partnership that owns the controlling interest in Blinds To Go™, Inc. The Shiller Group also owns a portfolio of real estate investments in Canada and the United States.

NKERE UDOFIA
Vice Chairman

A private investor and advisor, Nkere has been working with the company since July 1996, helping to develop the strategic, financial and management resource plans to support the company's expansion. Nkere has more than ten years of experience in private investments, consulting and product management, including eight years managing private investments of retail and consumer companies. From 1989 to 1996, Nkere was a private investment professional at Harvard Private Capital Group, Inc., and was elected Managing Director in 1993. While at Harvard, Nkere served on the board of directors of over a dozen portfolio companies. From 1987 to 1989, Nkere was employed by the Procter and Gamble Company. Nkere is a graduate of Massachusetts Institute of Technology with Bachelor of Science and Master of Science degrees, and holds a Master of Business Administration degree from Harvard Business School.

Exhibit 3 VP Profiles *(Continued)*

SENIOR MANAGEMENT PROFILE

RINTARO KAWAI
Senior Vice President, Manufacturing Operations

Rintaro joined the company in September 1999 as the senior manufacturing executive. Most recently Rintaro was a Principal in the Operations Practice at Booz-Allen & Hamilton, Inc., a leading management consulting firm, where he helped companies achieve significant improvements in operational performance. Previously, he spent over ten years in the automotive industry in various product development and manufacturing positions at General Motors and at Chrysler. Rintaro holds a Masters of Science in Management from MIT Sloan School of Management and a Bachelor of Science in Mechanical Engineering from GMI Engineering and Management Institute.

BRANSON EDWARDS
Vice President, Real Estate Development

Branson joined the company in December, 1999 as the senior real-estate development executive. Branson has over 10 years of retail, real estate and general management experience. Most recently, Branson was a Regional Vice President for Hollywood Entertainment, Inc. where he created the company's first regional real estate team and opened over 100 new locations. Branson holds an AB degree in English from Duke University and an MBA in Real Estate Finance from the University of North Carolina.

HERSCHEL GAVSIE
Vice President, Purchasing and Product Development

Herschel joined the company in April 1996 as the senior merchandising and product development executive. He has over ten years of senior management experience in the window covering industry. His experience includes extensive international sales and marketing activities in addition to merchandising and product development background. From 1985 to 1996, Herschel was President of Vertico Industries, a manufacturer and wholesaler of window shades and blinds. His experience in the industry includes significant product innovation, having developed new concepts in both the horizontal and vertical blind categories. Herschel holds a Bachelor of Civil Law degree from McGill University and a Juris Doctor from Nova South Eastern University.

DAN HENRY
Vice President, Chief People Officer

Dan joined the company in November, 1999 as the senior human resources and people development executive. Dan has over 12 years experience building strategic approaches to leveraging human capital. He has extensive experience in acquisition integration, labor relations and organizational development. Dan has held a number of human resource and general management positions with Staples, Inc., Pepsi-Cola and Reebok International. Dan holds a degree from Cornel University.

Exhibit 3 VP Profiles *(Continued)*

SENIOR MANAGEMENT PROFILE

JEFFREY RAYNER
Vice President, Marketing

Jeff joined the company in January 1997 as the senior marketing executive. Jeff has over ten years of marketing and general management experience in both manufacturing and retail businesses. Most recently, Jeff was Vice President and General Manager of Credit Card Enhancement Services for Citibank. Previously, Jeff was the Director of Marketing of the Waldenbooks division of Borders Group Inc. Jeff began his career in brand management with General Mills Inc. in 1984 and has also worked at Kraft General Foods. Jeff holds a Masters of Business Administration from New York University and a Bachelor of Science in Management, from the State University of New York.

DEBORAH SHANLEY
Vice President, Store Operations

Debbie joined the company in May 1997 as Director of Stores and was promoted to Vice President in July 1998. Debbie manages the field organization and has over fifteen years experience managing store organizations with several specialty retailers. Prior to Blinds To Go, Debbie spent five years as Regional Director of Stores with Gymboree and held district and regional management positions with Pottery Barn and Sesame Street. Debbie began her retailing career in 1982 with Filene's Basement as an assistant manager and subsequently spent five years with August Max and several other divisions of US Shoes. Debbie attended Suffolk University.

Exhibit 3 VP Profiles

Source: Company files.

solution—and that is the difference. We all will be limited in some capacity, but some people don't have enough spine to take the blame. One of my previous directors said to me, "Sonia, sign this check because I'm not sure it's right and I don't want my signature on it." Nobody's going to make a huge mistake that will kill the company because for most important decisions, you're going to go through Udofia and Stephen first.

Step back and you'll see that we're growing 50 per cent, and we will all make mistakes. As Udofia says, "Don't manage my expectations—I would rather you spend your time increasing the odds for success."

Conclusion

Rintaro Kawai, senior VP of operations, concluded,

> What are the toolkits you need to work with our dynamic growth, unique model? Do you get the people or do you grow them? How would you help outsiders understand the situation and use what they had experienced in the past and fit it in here? We had VPs who shouldn't have been VPs—but how would you have handled the recalibration? Udofia is spending more than 50 per cent of his time hiring; what else could he be doing?

5

Venture Start-Up

The Start-Up Process

Venture start-up has two parts: (a) the process of actually engaging in sales of the work (product/services) of a venture to specific customers in the marketplace and (b) the process of actually turning out the products/services that are sold. In these respects, start-up enables and facilitates an effective and efficient exchange of value in a market transaction by developing or increasing trust and decreasing potential transaction-destroying frictions that are associated with the wariness and overprotectiveness that occur in new relationships (in the case of marketing and sales) and by developing or increasing reliability/quality in production and service processes. Frictions related to low trust, among other things, have aptly been named "liabilities of newness" (Stinchcombe, 1965, p. 148) or transaction costs (Arrow, 1969, p. 48).

In a typical business school curriculum, concepts for increasing trust and overcoming liabilities of newness/transaction costs in exchange processes come from disciplines such as law, organization behavior (OB), and human resource management (HRM), with the key discipline in this part of the start-up process being marketing. In our observation, law, OB, and HRM provide key ideas in support of the marketing concepts and practices, upon which successful start-up depends, and include primarily marketing strategy and tactics implementation, sales force management (deployment), customer relationship management (initiation and trust development), marketing communications (including product launch tactics), market research (test marketing, confirmation of buyer behavior, and decision analysis), services marketing, and inventory management, among the several marketing topic areas.

In a typical business school curriculum, concepts for increasing trust and overcoming liabilities of newness/transaction costs in production/service processes come from disciplines such as production/operations management (POM), organization design (OD), and managerial accounting (MA). Each of the foregoing disciplines supports the idea of total quality management (TQM) with its fundamental axiom of minimal variation (Deming, 1986), which is at the core of an effective production start-up process.

Interestingly, then, start-up involves increasing trust in *both* marketing/sales and production processes. Because no other work in entrepreneurship presently addresses start-up in these terms, we focus the remainder of our discussion of the start-up process on this key element: increasing trust through the sales process and increasing trust through TQM in production/service processes.

The Marketing/Sales Process, Increased Trust, and Effective Start-Up

Fundamentally, marketing/sales processes solve information problems that threaten trust: Venturers who do not know their customers, as well as customers who are unaware of the features and benefits of products or services, are unlikely to enter into exchange relationships of value to both parties due to liabilities caused by the newness of the relationship. Marketing processes—strategy, tactics, customer relationship management, communications, research, and so on—focus extensively on the identification and solution of these problems.

Sales processes focus on direct contact with a customer that leads to reductions of transaction frictions, thereby yielding sales. According to world-renowned sales expert Zig Ziglar (1982, p. 79), six critical factors create conditions of trust in a transaction setting:

1. the transfer of human feeling;
2. the use of empathy (thinking as a seller *and* as a buyer) as the source of feeling cues;
3. sufficient preparation for customer interaction that creates genuine feeling;
4. the possession of the physical, mental, and spiritual reserves that support optimal transfer of the most positive levels of human feeling;
5. a realization that, in fact, love is the dominant factor in sale; and
6. a commitment to honesty, conviction, and integrity in selling relationships.

When selling is viewed as an essentially human process that is based in an optimal transference of feeling, it is our observation that transaction-preventing frictions in relationships are dramatically reduced and, accordingly, that start-up of the new venture—effectively establishing its connection to the key stakeholders, the people and entities that "really count to the venture" (Mitchell et al., 1997, p. 853)—is much more effective.

TQM in the Production Process, Increased Trust, and Effective Start-Up

It is not widely expressed that at the core of TQM is the idea of increased trust. Indeed, the idea of quality is now closely linked to the idea of trustworthy or reliable production systems (see Table 5.1), an idea conceived by W. Edwards Deming and popularized by Genchi Taguchi, Joseph M. Juran, Phillip Crosby, and others (Magnier, 1999; Tortorella, 1995). A simple characterization of TQM is as a management system that aims at continuous increases in customer value: better quality at continuously lower real costs. For our purposes, TQM is about continuously improving a customer's net buyer benefit and increasing trust in our customer relationships.

Table 5.1 Deming's 14 Points for Management

Point #	*Principle*
1.	Create and publish to all employees a statement of the aims and purposes of the company or other organization. The management must demonstrate constantly their commitment to this statement.
2.	Learn the new philosophy, top management and everybody.
3.	Understand the purpose of inspection, for improvement of processes and reduction of cost.
4.	End the practice of awarding business on the basis of price tag alone.
5.	Improve constantly and forever the system of production and service.
6.	Institute training.
7.	Teach and institute leadership.
8.	Drive out fear. Create trust. Create a climate for innovation.
9.	Optimize toward the aims and purposes of the company the efforts of teams, groups, and staff areas.
10.	Eliminate exhortations for the workforce.
11a.	Eliminate numerical quotas for production. Instead, learn and institute methods for improvement.
11b.	Eliminate MBO (management by objectives). Instead, learn the capabilities of processes and how to improve them.
12.	Remove barriers that rob people of pride of workmanship.
13.	Encourage education and self-improvement.
14.	Take action to accomplish the transformation.

Most important, it can be observed how trustworthy production processes, which are essential to an effective start-up, can be achieved in the venture creation process.

Summary

The result of the start-up process is exchange, and exchange is enacted through a conception of marketing—the marketing mix—that includes both sales and production: product, price, promotion, and place. In this sense, *start-up* and *marketing* are very closely related. In the start-up process, exchange-based activity (both of sales and of production) should be *outwardly focused,* by which we mean that the focus of an entrepreneur's attention during the start-up process is on the market environment surrounding the venture rather than on internal processes. (The *inward focus* on venture attributes is the main objective of the preceding chapter, which addresses the setup process.)

Thus, in the case of marketing and sales, by developing or increasing trust and decreasing potential transaction-destroying frictions that are associated with the wariness and overprotectiveness that occur in new relationships and, in the case of production, by developing or increasing reliability/quality in production and service processes through TQM,

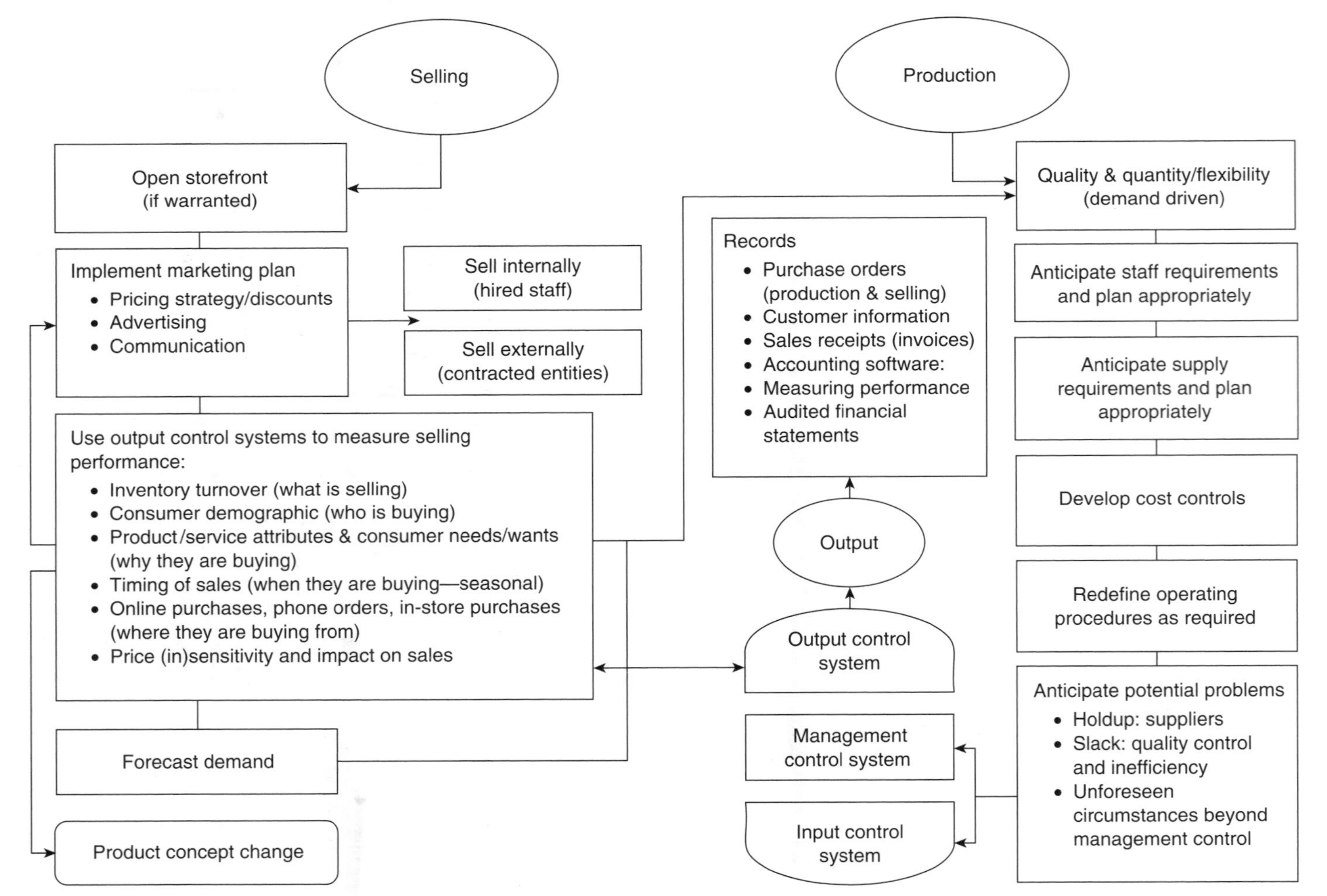

Figure 5.1 Start-Up

the effectual linking of the venture to its external environment—the crucial objective of the start-up process—can be accomplished.

A Student's View of the Start-Up Process

The start-up process, as viewed through the eyes of an entrepreneurship student, includes the following narrative that accompanies Figure 5.1. This narrative explains the figure and can be used to visualize many of the key elements we have just described to be essential to the start-up process.

This student says the following:

This phase involves three primary functions: selling, production, and output.

Step 1: Selling. After opening a storefront (if warranted) and a location where operations are conducted, two stages are conducted.

Stage 1: Implement marketing plan. This involves implementing the marketing plan that was formulated during the setup phase. It involves implementing the pricing strategy that was formulated in Level 1 of the planning/financing phase, choosing communications mediums, and communicating the value of the offering to the consumer and developing name recognition for the offering. After the marketing plan has been implemented, and assuming it is generating purchase orders, the offering is then sold to interested parties. It is also assumed that the marketing plan will not be able to generate significant interest from all members of the target population. Keeping this in mind, it may be worthwhile to contract with external entities that have established contacts and know the distribution network and how the "distribution channel" works. It is necessary to have sales staff in-house to generate purchase orders and to perform boundary-spanning roles.

Stage 2: Use output control systems to measure selling performance. This involves using the data collected and maintained in the output control system, as well as the intuition and knowledge of sales staff (internal and external), to determine what consumers want and how price sensitive they are (or are likely to be if the novelty of the offering wears off). It involves answering five key questions.

- What is selling?
- Who is buying?
- Why are they buying?
- When are they buying?
- Where are they buying from?

Once these questions are answered and a price sensitivity analysis has been conducted, the conclusions drawn are used for three sources. First, the marketing plan is revisited, and the conclusions are used to more effectively target the consumers. Second, if it is found that few purchase orders are made or if the consumer is using the product for something other than what was planned, the product concept may need to be altered or changed altogether. Third, the conclusions drawn can also be used to forecast demand. These forecasts are then used as inputs to the second step—production.

Step 2: Production. This step consists of one step that comprises a number of elements. The fundamental element that must be understood is that production must be flexible and demand driven. Quality and quantity must be based on the boundary-spanning inputs from the selling step, and communication between the two groups is essential to the success of the firm.

Stage 1: Production planning. This stage first involves anticipating the staff and supply requirements. As production is demand driven, it is very important that the production process be as dynamic as possible to avoid slack time and ensure the efficient production of the offering (no bottlenecks). After the staff and supply requirements have been determined, it is important to develop cost controls, such that variance between actual and expected performance can be determined.

It is assumed that after the determination of staff/supply requirements and cost controls, the physical production of the offering is commenced. Once commenced, operating procedures are refined as required to ensure that operations are conducted as efficiently as possible. Employees should actively participate in this process, as they are the individuals that are conducting the procedures, and it can be assumed that they have immense knowledge as to how production may work better (this is also consistent with fostering a culture of creativity and innovation).

Finally, the last element of this stage listed in the start-up subscript is "anticipate potential problems." This element is not the last part of this stage but is something that should be considered at all stages of production. Planning must be done in the event that holdup by suppliers occurs or if there are quality control problems (as a result of employees or equipment). Solutions to these potential problems must be formulated to avoid excessive cost increases and damaging the firm's reputation from being unable to "deliver" a quality product on time.

Step 3: Output. After the product has been produced, records must be kept, which are kept in the respective control system (input, management, or output). Purchase orders are kept to determine how much was paid for certain services or supplies/materials. If profitability suffers or is enhanced, the variance between recent and past purchase orders can be investigated. Customer information is also kept. When possible, demographic information should be attained. This, however, is not the principal reason for keeping such records. Coupled with the records of sales receipts, customer information should be deemed as providing service to the customer. If the consumer has problems with the good/service that was purchased, his or her information can be found and the problem resolved much easier than if no record was kept at all. Such records would also reduce fraud on behalf of the customer, and mail-outs of information to the customer can be conducted (or thank you notes, etc.).

As part of the control system, accounting software must also be used to measure financial performance (margins, turnover, etc.) and to produce the legally required financial statements.

Now that the business is up and running, focus turns to the next phase: continuing operations and growth.

Cases

The following cases have been selected to help learners to develop and become more aware of their own thoughts on the venture start-up process.

DCF Innovations: Goalie Pad Covers (A)

Prepared by T. J. Flood under the supervision of Professor Mark Vandenbosch

Version: (A) 1998-10-23

In March 1995, T. J. Flood, a graduate from the Ivey School of Business and the Marketing Director of DCF Innovations (DCF), set out to develop a strategy to bring to market DCF's patented goalie pad cover concept. As he sat in his basement office, he reviewed his market research and began to develop a complete marketing plan to present to his partners, Grant Conrad and Vince DiCesare.

DCF Innovations

DCF was formed by three high school friends, in order to pursue the goalie pad cover concept. Equipped with approximately $40,000 in financing from bank loans and venture capital, DCF was successful in receiving patent protection on its product concepts. At a cost of $10,000 for the patent rights, DCF was left with approximately $30,000 to market its products.

The Sport of Hockey and Goaltenders

The sport of hockey was played in various forms. The traditional style, ice hockey, was played on ice surfaces. Players used skates to transport themselves around the ice. The object of the game was to score more goals than the opposing team. Players used hockey sticks to maneuver a hockey puck into the opposing team's hockey net to count goals. It was the role of the goaltender to protect the net and prevent the players of the opposing team from scoring. Players continually shot the puck with their sticks towards the net in an attempt to score. Goaltenders attempted to block or deflect the puck away from the net with their bodies or sticks in order to prevent goals from being scored.

Ice hockey pucks were constructed from an extremely hard and durable rubber. As a result, goaltenders wore a vast amount of protective equipment to protect themselves (Exhibit 1). Goalie pads were used to protect the legs of goaltenders from contact with the puck as well as from abrasion from contact with the ice surface when they were forced to the ice in attempts to block or deflect the puck. Goalie pads were constructed with leather or a synthetic leather outer layer encasing a protective inner layer made from foam or various shock-absorbing materials. The goalie pads protected the goaltender's legs from above the foot to the middle of the thigh. The goalie pads were affixed to a goaltender's legs with a series of straps.

During the early 1990s, a new form of hockey began to develop in North America. With the development of in-line skates, which replaced skate blades with wheels that allowed the same manoeuverability as ice skates on non-ice surfaces such as concrete or asphalt, came the evolution of in-line hockey. The game was virtually identical to ice hockey with the exception that it was played not on ice but on surfaces such as concrete or asphalt. This game was heavily adopted in the United States because the climate of many regions was not conducive to maintaining ice surfaces. The role of the goaltender was identical in in-line hockey as it was in ice hockey. In-line hockey goaltenders had the same protective gear as did their ice hockey counterparts.

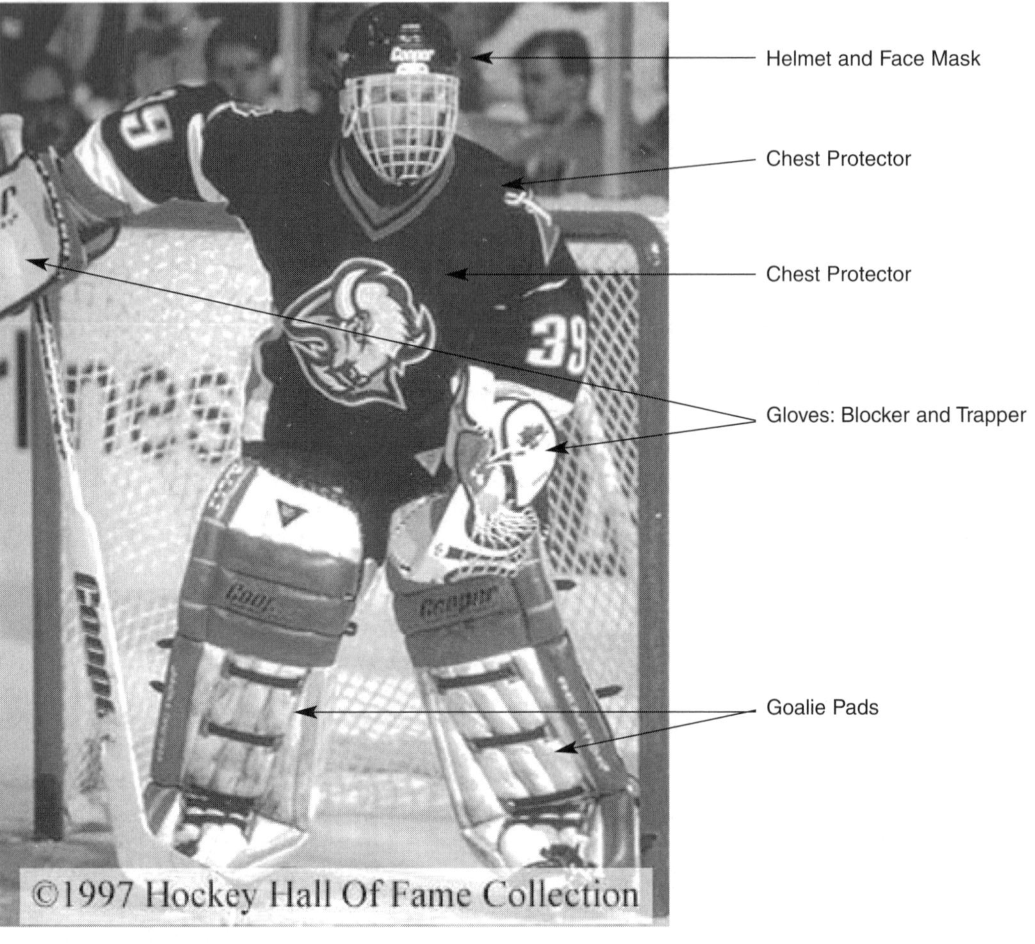

Exhibit 1

Goalie Pad Covers

DCF had fully developed the goalie pad cover concept. Goalie pad covers were lightweight, removable covers that conformed to goalie pads like a second skin. From an aesthetic point of view, the goalie pad covers allowed goaltenders to match their pads with current team colors and/or customize the look of their pads in order to complete their uniform (Exhibit 2a and 2b). The idea was derived by Conrad during the 1994 Winter Olympics. The goaltender for Team Canada, Corey Hirsh, was outfitted with goalie pads colorfully adorned with red maple leaves. A goaltender himself, Conrad realized that this type of customized pad design would cost well over $1,000. He then thought it would be a great idea to develop a product that would allow goaltenders to adapt the look of their goalie pads at an affordable price. Consequently, the concept of goalie pad covers was born.

The features and benefits to goaltenders of this product were many. Along with customizing the look of goalie pads, the covers protected the goalie pads against the wear and tear of continued use. Further, if covers were used on currently

Exhibit 2a Customized Ice Hockey Goalie Pad Cover With Matching Hockey Jersey

Exhibit 2b Customized Ice Hockey Goalie Pad Cover

Exhibit 2c In-Line Hockey Goalie Pad Cover

owned or used goalie pads, the goaltender could avoid the arduous process of breaking in new pads.[1] The covers did not alter the existing goalie pad in any way and included a patented Gill System of Universal Fit to ensure that the covers would fit any design or size of goalie pad and could be easily attached. Essentially, the product would provide the goaltender with the look of brand new, high quality pads for less than a third of the price of new goalie pads.

In-Line Hockey Opportunity

During the summer of 1994, all three partners played in an organized in-line hockey league. It was through this experience that the concept for a second product was developed.

In-line hockey was extremely popular but was in its infancy in terms of becoming an organized sport. The partners of DCF came to understand that a major problem existed in the recruitment of goaltenders for this new sport. This situation was an obstacle that had to be overcome for in-line hockey to continue its progress towards establishment as a competitive mainstream sport in North America and abroad. It was felt that the lack of interest in this key position could be directly attributed to the inherent awkwardness and excessive costs currently involved with playing goal in in-line hockey.

The awkwardness of in-line goaltending could be attributed to the goaltender's lack of lateral mobility while on in-line skates and the limited sliding capabilities of goalies in the down position. While in-line skates were effective in allowing goaltenders forward and backward diagonal movement, quick lateral movements (proven in ice hockey as a great asset to goaltenders) were virtually impossible due to friction between blades, pads and the in-line playing surfaces. This awkwardness resulted in a major competitive disadvantage for in-line goaltenders compared to those playing the similar ice hockey position.

The greater costs associated with goaltending versus other positions were twofold. First, a goaltender had to be completely outfitted with expensive goalie equipment for which the cost was at least three times that of being outfitted for other positions. Secondly, due to the nature of the position, this equipment experienced wear to a much greater degree than that of other players, especially on the high friction in-line playing surfaces.

In response to these two major problems, DCF developed its second model of goalie pad cover specifically designed for in-line hockey (Exhibit 2c). The product was similar to the ice-hockey version in that it was a removable, lightweight goalie pad cover that form-fitted to any goal pad like a second skin. However, its surface was fitted with strategically placed "Duraflex" plastic in the knee area as well as on its sides. This provided goaltenders ice-like sliding ability and lateral movement on the various in-line playing surfaces while protecting existing goal pads from the inevitable wear and tear associated with the game.

Market Information

DCF had conducted extensive market research into both the ice hockey and in-line hockey markets. This research included over 200 surveys as well as 10 focus group studies targeted at goaltenders from both markets. Further, various interviews were conducted with various players in the industry including manufacturers and retailers. It was from this research that the following conclusions were derived.

Ice Hockey

From data received from the Canadian Minor Hockey Association and the United States Minor Hockey Association, Flood estimated that there were approximately 80,500 goaltenders in North America in 1995 with a five per cent growth rate. Of this number, approximately 89 per cent were distributed in Canada and the Northern United States (Exhibit 3). With the expanding growth rates of sports such as Ringette and Women's Hockey, Flood felt these estimates were conservative.

Through data received from the International Ice Hockey Federation it was also determined that there were approximately 42,000 ice hockey goaltenders outside of North America. However, Flood felt that the North American market should be the initial launch area and a decision to launch in Europe would be made upon analysis of the performance of the product in North America.

The North American ice hockey goaltender market could be segmented into four categories: sponsored goaltenders, competitive minor hockey goaltenders, non-competitive minor hockey goaltenders, and men's league goaltenders.

Sponsored goaltenders were those who played in leagues for which goalie pads were provided by the company who had attained the rights to supply the league or particular team. Goaltenders from professional teams such as the National Hockey League (NHL), the International Hockey League (IHL), the American Hockey League (AHL), and from major amateur leagues such as Major Jr. "A," Canadian University (CIAU) and U.S. College (NCAA) made up the bulk of this category. This category represented approximately 5 per cent of the total North American market.

The largest category of goaltenders comprised those who played minor hockey. In Canada the age distribution of this category was between seven and 20 years of age. In the United States, the range was somewhat reduced because the final year of minor hockey coincided with the end of high school at the approximate age of 18. Market research indicated that most equipment purchased for this category was paid for by the goalie's parents. Thus the parent was determined to be the decision-maker and the goalie the influencer in the purchase of goalie equipment. This category could be further broken down into competitive and non-competitive goaltenders.

In North America, minor hockey teams were formed on the basis of age. Within each age category, teams and leagues were formed based

Total Number of Goalies: 83,000 Growth Rate per Annum: 5 Per Cent	
Region	*Percentage of Goalies*
Ontario	25
Prairie Provinces	14
Quebec	12
British Columbia	6
Maritimes	4
Mid Atlantic U.S. (Pa, R.I. , Del., Conn., N.Y., N.J., Maryland)	13
East North Central U.S. (Minn., Wis., Mich., Ind., Ill., Ohio)	11
New England U.S. (Mass., Vermont, N.H., Maine)	5
Pacific U.S. (Washington, Oregon, California)	3
West North Central U.S. (N.Dak., S.Dak., Idaho, Wyoming, Montana, Nebraska)	3
South Atlantic U.S. (Georgia, Florida, N.C., S.C., Va., W.Va)	2
Mountain U.S. (Colorado, Nevada, Utah)	1
West South Central U.S. (Ariz., N.Mex., Texas, Okla. Kansas)	.6
East South Central U.S. (Missouri, Ark., La., Miss., Ala., Tenn., Kentucky)	.4

Exhibit 3 Distribution of North American Ice Hockey Goalies (1995)

Source: Canadian and United States Hockey Associations.

on the abilities of the players. Competitive goaltenders included those who played in "AAA," "AA" and "A" hockey leagues in Canada and the U.S. These goalies who were considered to be the most talented for their age group and extremely serious about the game subsequently purchased higher end equipment. This segment made up approximately 35 per cent of the North American market.

Non-competitive minor hockey goaltenders were defined as those who played at the "B," "C" and "Houseleague" levels in Canada and the U.S. Since these leagues were more recreational in nature it was established that these goaltenders were less serious about the game and, therefore, were more prone to purchase used equipment or borrow equipment that was provided by their local hockey association. This segment made up approximately 45 per cent of the North American market.

Men's league goaltenders consisted of those who were too old to play minor hockey and thus ranged in age from 20 to about 60 years of age. While men's hockey leagues were not as strictly

Goalie Segment	*Purchase New*	*Purchase Used*	*Borrow From Association*
Competitive Minor	79%	14%	7%
Non-Competitive Minor	19%	29%	52%
Competitive Men's	72%	28%	0
Non-Competitive Men's	61%	39%	0

Exhibit 4 Aggregated Results of Market Research on Ice Hockey Goalie Pad Purchases

Source: DCF surveys and focus group studies.

Question: On a scale of 1-10 (1 low, 10 high) rank the following product features of goalie pads.

Product Feature	*Comp Minor Parents*	*Comp Minor Goalies*	*Non-Comp Minor Parents*	*Non-Comp Minor Goalies*	*Comp Men's*	*Non-Comp Men's*
Brand Name	7	8	5	7	8	7
Durability	8	5	6	5	8	8
Price	7	2	10	2	7	8
Weight	7	8	7	7	7	7
Aesthetics	3	8	1	7	7	5

Exhibit 5 Aggregated Results of Survey Regarding Significance of Product Features in Purchase Decision

Source: DCF surveys and focus group studies.

divided into age levels as minor hockey, leagues were set up to allow players to play at their desired level of competitiveness. In addition, this category could be further divided into competitive and non-competitive goaltenders. The competitive goaltenders, it was determined, were more prone to purchase higher quality equipment whereas the less competitive goalies were more conscious of price. This segment purchased their own equipment either new or used and were not offered the opportunity to borrow equipment from associations. This segment made up approximately 15 per cent of the North American goaltender market.

DCF's market research suggested that these various segments differed in terms of the types of goalie pads they purchased and used, as well as in the major criteria used in the purchasing decision (Exhibits 4 and 5). The main criteria listed by goaltenders during surveys and focus groups were price, weight, brand name, aesthetics, and durability.

Goalie pads ranged in price depending on size and model. The range was between $300 and $1,400. The price spectrum at a particular size range could vary by as much as $300. At particular size ranges prices varied according to the features and benefits provided by particular models.

Weight was one such feature and influenced both the price of the pad and its desirability. With flexibility and mobility crucial factors in the ability of a goaltender to play the position effectively, goaltenders sought goalie pads that were as light as possible. Less weight on their legs made them more mobile and flexible. They did not, however, want to sacrifice protection for weight and preferred that their goalie pads provide both features.

Manufacturers of hockey equipment spent millions of dollars annually on developing their brand names. The major brands for goalie pads were Vaughn, Koho, Cooper, Brians, Heaton, and Brown. The importance of brand name to goaltenders was evidenced by the premium price that top brand names could command.

Traditionally, goalie pads were made with brown leather exteriors devoid of any design features. Over the previous four years a trend had developed in which goalie pads were being offered in a variety of colors and designs. The aesthetic look of the pad was, therefore, becoming more and more important to goaltenders. The ability to purchase different colored pads allowed goaltenders to match their pads with their uniforms.

As a result of the cost of outfitting a goaltender with equipment and the wear and tear associated with continued use of goalie pads, durability was also a major consideration for goaltenders. Goalie pads varied in terms of their material construction and design that caused substantial differences in durability from model to model.

The competitive minor hockey segment was much less price-sensitive than any other. The majority of these goaltenders wore new goalie pads and considered brand name, weight and aesthetics to be of significant importance. Their parents too, felt that these criteria were of great importance although they were somewhat conscious of price considerations.

The non-competitive minor hockey segment was extremely price-sensitive. They wore primarily used pads or those borrowed from associations. Despite the price sensitivity, rooted from their parents, the goaltenders themselves were cognizant of brand name, weight and aesthetics.

Without the benefit of financial support or the ability to borrow pads from their respective associations, the goalies within the adult market were forced to purchase either new or used pads. All of the major purchasing criteria were of significant importance to this segment. The non-competitive goalies did, however, put less emphasis on aesthetics than their competitive counterparts.

In-Line Hockey

The in-line hockey market was much less organized than that of ice hockey. Leagues and associations were just forming and standardization was determined to be a couple of years away. Through the aid of the National In-Line Hockey Association (NIHA), Flood estimated the size of the North American goalie market to be approximately 183,000 with a growth rate of 27 per cent per annum. This market was almost entirely located in the United States with strong regional segmentation (Exhibit 6). The age distribution was more contained than the ice hockey market and ranged between the ages of seven and 30.

As a result of the fragmented and unorganized nature of the sport, customer segmentation was difficult. Flood divided the market into two different types of customers. The first were goaltenders that were converted from ice hockey and currently owned or had access to ice hockey pads. The first category was located primarily in the northern United States and in Canada. This segment represented approximately 25 per cent of the total market. It was felt that it would be easier to sell these goalies on the concept of goalie pad covers because they better understood the need for lateral movement, they had goalie pads they used for ice hockey and wanted to protect, and they would only have to make the purchase of the covers and not actual goalie pads as well.

The second category was made up of goaltenders that were new to the position or new to any form of hockey. This segment was primarily located in the southern and pacific regions of the United States and made up 75 per cent of the market. These goaltenders did not previously own goalie pads and were forced to purchase them in some form in order to play. They were just beginning to develop an understanding of the need for lateral mobility and had no other use for their goalie pads.

Total Number of Goalies: 183,000 Growth Rate per Annum: 27%	
Region	*Percentage of Goalies*
Canada	2
Mid Atlantic U.S. (Pa, R.I., Del., Conn., N.Y., N.J., Maryland)	25
East North Central U.S. (Minn., Wis., Mich., Ind., Ill., Ohio)	15
New England U.S. (Mass., Vermont, N.H., Maine)	4
Pacific U.S. (Washington, Oregon, California)	30
West North Central U.S. (N.Dak., S.Dak., Idaho, Wyoming, Montana, Nebraska)	7
South Atlantic U.S. (Georgia, Florida, N.C., S.C., Va., W.Va)	10
Mountain U.S. (Colorado, Nevada, Utah)	4
West South Central U.S. (Ariz., N.Mex.,Texas, Okla.Kansas)	2
East South Central U.S. (Missouri, Ark., La., Miss., Ala., Tenn., Kentucky)	1

Exhibit 6 Distribution of In-Line Hockey Goalies

Source: National In-Line Hockey Association (NIHA).

The market was growing from the grassroots and was compared directly with the skateboarding phenomenon. The popularity of in-line skating was a major factor in the development of this sport. Leagues were just beginning to form and most games were being played on an ad-hoc recreational basis. The sport and its players possessed a radical image and manufacturers attempted to focus their marketing efforts to adhere to these characteristics. Equipment was not yet standardized and varied both regionally and within different age groups. Flood felt that a major competitive advantage could be derived by those equipment manufacturers that helped in the organization and development of the sport.

Distribution Channels

Ice Hockey

National Chains

There were numerous ways for goaltenders to purchase goalie equipment in North America. National retail chains made up approximately 25 per cent of the sales of goalie equipment. National retail chains could be further divided into mass merchants and sporting good-specific stores.

In Canada, the two largest mass merchants, Canadian Tire and Wal-mart, were the two largest volume retailers of hockey equipment. Neither, however, carried a wide variety of goalie equipment.

These chains were focused on mass markets and the goaltender market did not represent a large enough opportunity to warrant carrying a large assortment. The bulk of goalie equipment sales for these retailers came from sticks and very limited low end lines of protective gear.

In the United States, the major volume retailers of hockey equipment included sporting good stores such as Sports Authority and Sport Mart. These retailers carried a much broader assortment of goalie equipment than did their Canadian mass merchant counterparts. Most brand names were available through these stores but inventory was not always carried on hand. Because goalie pads represented a large inventory investment, most stores limited the number of stock keeping units (SKUs) they carried in this category. However, they did offer their customers the opportunity to order product from their manufacturers' catalogues.

Play it Again Sports was also a major retail player in goalie equipment in Canada and the U.S. As a sporting goods-specific store, it offered both new and used equipment for sale to consumers. It offered a full range of both new and used goalie equipment, including goalie pads.

The national retail chain channel had very strong buying power and usually commanded margin levels of approximately 30 to 35 per cent on goalie equipment. Since space was at a premium in these stores, volume SKUs were preferred.

Independent Sporting Goods Stores

Independent sporting goods retailers made up 75 per cent of sales of goalie equipment in North America. These independents varied in size and commitment to ice hockey equipment. Most of the independents sold more than hockey equipment.

Their assortments would change dramatically throughout the year as different sports came into season. In Canada and the northern United States, most independents carried a broad assortment of hockey equipment during the ice hockey equipment selling season which peaked between August and February. Their goalie equipment inventory levels were higher than their national chain counterparts, but they too offered product through catalogue ordering. They had much less buying power but, due to lesser volumes, demanded a slightly higher margin of approximately 40 per cent on goalie equipment.

Minor ice hockey associations were approached directly by independent retailers to purchase larger quantities of product to be distributed within their organization. Goalie pads were a common purchase by associations. These pads were loaned to minor hockey goaltenders in the ice hockey association throughout the hockey season. The volume nature of these purchases would reduce the margin requirements of the retailer to approximately 25 per cent. Approximately 10 per cent of independent retailer sales were direct to associations.

In-Line Hockey

The channels were very similar for ice hockey and in-line hockey equipment. The major difference was the education of customers about what equipment was needed and where it could be purchased. Retailers, both independents and national chains, carried broad assortments of in-line skates but their assortments of in-line hockey protective gear, and especially goalie equipment, was limited. Ice hockey equipment was frequently recommended and used since specifically designed in-line equipment was just starting to be distributed.

Competition

Ice Hockey

Since the concept of goalie pad covers was completely novel, no direct competition existed. Indirect competition existed in the form of goalie pad painting, goalie pad reparation, and new and used goalie pad purchases. Each of these alternatives competed with one or more of the features offered by goalie pad covers. However, none provided them all.

Goalie pad painters were independent outfits and very difficult to find. The process which involved completely dismantling and reforming the pad compromised the pad's integrity. The price of re-painting ranged between $350 to $500 with an average price of $400. This alternative provided the aesthetics features available in goalie pad covers but did not provide the protection to the pads that the goalie pad covers offered.

Goalie pad reparation involved sewing or gluing patches of leather over worn areas of the pads. This method, while effective in rejuvenating the functionality of the pads, detracted from the aesthetic look of the pad. This alternative was provided by independent shoe repair shops and leather specialists and could range in price from $20 to $300 with an average price of $60.

New goalie pads were sold through independent and national retail chains. The retail price points ranged between $300 and $1,400 depending on size, make and brand. For junior sizes, servicing goaltenders between the ages of seven to 13, the average price was approximately $450. For senior sizes, servicing goaltenders above the age of 14, the average price was $800. New goalie pads would usually last for eight years. One particular goaltender would use a pair of goalie pads an average of three years, after which time the goalie pads would enter the used pad market. Although new goalie pads could be custom-made with both design and color, this customization would place the model at the high end of the new goalie pad price spectrum. Once purchased, new goalie pads would have to be broken in, in order to meet full functionality requirements. The established brands dominated the new goalie pad market. All of these brands possessed strong consumer recognition and were well represented in the retail channels.

Used goalie pads could be purchased at retail through independents dealing in used equipment or national chains such as Play it Again Sports. They were also purchased through word of mouth from other goaltenders. Further, minor hockey associations provided used pads for minor goaltenders to borrow. The purchase of used goalie pads was subject to what was currently available in the market. The goalie pads were already broken in but because of availability it was not always possible to purchase the desired color or design. The price of used goalie pads ranged from $200 to $800 depending on brand, model, size and degree of use. The average prices were $200 and $400 for junior and senior sizes, respectively.

In-Line Hockey

As a result of the fledgling nature of the sport, few goalie pads designed specifically for in-line hockey existed. Franklin, a major brand name in baseball equipment with some representation in hockey equipment, produced a goalie pad designed specifically for in-line hockey. It was lightweight and considered to be of lesser quality than most ice hockey goalie pads. It did not have a wide retail distribution but was available through the Franklin catalogue. It retailed for approximately $250.

New and used ice hockey pads were also available to in-line hockey goaltenders. They were available through the large retail chains as well as the independents. In the southern United States most sales of goalie pads were ordered through the catalogues because retailers did not carry inventory.

The only other alternative available to in-line hockey goalies were pads designed specifically for street hockey. These pads were plastic or vinyl-covered foam pads available in various designs. Though inexpensive, with an average price of $80, these pads did not provide much protection and were considered inferior to all other options.

None of the products that were currently available to in-line hockey goaltenders provided them with the sliding ability and durability provided by the goalie pad covers. From the conducted research, the main performance criteria for in-line goalie pads were: durability, weight, and sliding performance.

Decisions

To launch the two products, DCF had to make several key decisions in order to gain acceptance from both the end consumer and the retail channels.

Pricing

Pricing would have to be established based on DCF's unit cost estimates. The original prototypes were constructed from cordura nylon, which formed the bulk of the cover. This material was currently used as an alternative to leather for the outer surface of certain goalie pads on the market. Jenrino, a durable form of synthetic leather, was attached to the surface of the cordura nylon to detail the covers to resemble the outer surface of a goalie pad as well as to create any custom logo designs. Sportlight was a lightweight and flexible material that was used to make the "Gill System of Universal Fit." Once assembled, it too was attached to the cordura nylon on each side of the covers. A simple foam was chosen as filler to help contour the look of the Jenrino when it was sewn on to the cover. The in-line hockey model required the use of Duraflex plastic in the high wear areas of the surface and at the sides of the covers. The Duraflex was an additional cost but it reduced the amount of Jenrino required on the surface of the covers. As a result of the sewing involved in the construction of the units, the manufacture of the covers was quite labor-intensive. After receiving various cost quotations from suppliers and discovering a local area manufacturer with the capabilities to assemble the products, the following cost estimates were derived for the production of 5,000 units of each model:

Cost Component	*Ice Hockey Model*	*In-Line Hockey Model*
Cordura Nylon	9.00	9.00
Jenrino	10.47	7.72
Foam	.81	.81
Sport Light	1.37	1.37
Duraflex Plastic	0	2.25
Labor	25.00	25.00
Total	**46.65**	**46.15**

All of these costs were quoted in Canadian dollars and were sourced from solely Canadian suppliers. Flood felt that to reduce the unit costs DCF could pursue several alternatives. First, the materials that were used in the initial prototypes were extremely durable, and as a result, were more expensive than certain alternatives. He felt that a unit cost reduction of 15 per cent could be derived if durability was sacrificed and different materials were chosen. Further, the labor figure quoted was based on Canadian wage rates. Flood felt that if DCF could secure a manufacturing source outside of Canada that the unit cost for labor could be reduced by between 40 and 55 per cent depending on the country of origin and import duties.

Flood felt that DCF should command a margin of 50 per cent on the sale of each unit. He also wanted to establish pricing that he felt would allow the most market penetration. There appeared to be enough flexibility in the variable unit cost to allow a wide range of price points to be considered.

Branding

Branding was an issue that had to be addressed in order to penetrate this market. DCF did not have an established brand name and understood that the investment required to develop one was quite substantial. It was attempting to enter a market dominated by competitors with strong brand names. DCF had to develop a strategy to compete in this environment.

Merchandising

Understanding that one of the major benefits of goalie pad covers was the opportunity for custom design, Flood struggled to discover a way for them to be merchandised at the retail level. Both national retail chains and independents wanted to reduce the amount of SKUs they carried as much as possible. This made offering a wide variety of colors and designs on the shelf very difficult. It was not uncommon for goalie equipment to be ordered through a manufacturer's catalogue but this made visibility of the product limited at the store level. It was crucial that a merchandising strategy be developed to properly sell this product through the retail chain.

Advertising and Promotion

To support the retail channels, DCF had to come up with an advertising and promotion strategy that would create product awareness and customer acceptance. Various mediums were considered.

Print advertisements in magazines such as *The Hockey News* or *In-Line Skating Magazine* could range between $500 to $1,500 per ad depending on size and positioning. Sponsorship of ice and in-line hockey was also an option and could vary in cost from $10,000 to $100,000 depending on commitment. The National In-line Hockey association had Gold, Silver and Bronze sponsor categories with associated costs of $100,000, $50,000, and $25,000, respectively. Based on their category, sponsors would be given advertising space in all forms of communication including direct mail, print ads and television.

Endorsements from professional hockey players from the NHL were a medium often chosen by companies in this industry. Depending on the status of the athlete the costs associated with this could range between $10,000 and $250,000.

Direct marketing efforts could be implemented to target the end consumer through associations. Direct mail drops were expensive and depending on the quantities could range in cost between $25,000 to $100,000.

Further, sales support materials, samples and trade show participation were required to support the vast sales force needed to cover the North American market. Trade Show booths at events such as the World Sporting Goods Trade Show, held each July in Chicago, could cost between $10,000 and $100,000 depending on the size and location of the booth.

As he sat in his office, Flood looked over all of the information that DCF had collected. Based on the huge market potential and relatively low level of competition, Flood was sure that the goalie pad cover concept could work. What he had to do now was develop the marketing plan that would ensure DCF's success with its first products.

Note

1. Since the outer surface of goalie pads was made from various forms of leather, they were very stiff when first purchased. It took a period of time and continued use for the leather to stretch and the goalie pads to properly conform to the goaltender's legs.

Catfish Creek Canoe Company

Prepared by Robb McNaughton under the supervision of Dr. Russell Knight

Version: (A) 1999-09-29

In July 1998, Steve Davidson was preparing for the August opening of the Catfish Creek Canoe Company (CCC), a canoe manufacturing shop in St. Thomas, Ontario. Davidson planned to build 30 canoes per year and he wondered which pricing strategy would maximize his profits.

The initiative for CCC evolved from Davidson's canoeing and woodworking hobbies. Davidson had canoed recreationally for more than 20 years and had done woodworking for more than 15 years. In the past ten years, he had combined the two activities by building three canoes, which he sold for marginal profits after using them each for a season. When Davidson decided to purchase a canoe for the first time in the spring, he suffered what he described as "sticker shock." He could not believe the price and poor quality of retail canoes. Davidson saw an opportunity to build handcrafted cedar canoes, which would sell for a premium.

Entrepreneurial Manufacturing Generator

Davidson wanted assistance starting his company, so he enrolled in the 12-week business program at the Entrepreneurial Manufacturing Generator (EMG) in St. Thomas. The course was based on the case method and taught by faculty and graduates of the Richard Ivey School of Business and The University of Western Ontario Engineering Sciences. After completing the 12-week course, students had the opportunity (once they had drafted an acceptable business plan) to progress to a start-up and mentoring phase conducted on site. CCC would rent space at the EMG for $351 per month, starting in August 1998. The shared EMG facility gave Davidson access to a wide range of business resources, including the EMG instructors and another woodworking shop. Davidson hoped that the close proximity of these resources would give CCC a competitive advantage.

CCC was going to specialize in 16-foot Peterborough canoes, which were the classic Canadian design. Peterborough-type canoes were popular worldwide and had gained a reputation as agile, fast and stable. The canoes would be made from cedar strips and constructed with epoxy.[1] Davidson described building canoes as "relatively easy," although it took time and woodworking skill. Canoes produced at CCC would have executive features that included walnut decks, brass fasteners and cane seats. The finish would be hand-sanded, rubbed with epoxy and treated with Carnauba wax, which was a standard technique. In addition, customers would receive with each canoe a certificate of authenticity and canoes would be marked by serial numbers that identified the production number, similar to an art print. Canoes made by CCC would also be guaranteed for five years, which was long by industry standards.

Davidson planned to produce 30 canoes in the first year and average one canoe every ten days, which would leave 65 days to buffer any unforeseen production delays (an experienced craftsman could build 25 to 30 canoes per year). Davidson would have to work seven days a week to maintain the production pace; however, he felt that he could handle a seven-day schedule for two to three years. Although the first canoes were scheduled to take almost 12 days to build, throughput time (the time from start to finish) would decrease as production techniques improved. Davidson knew that he would have to invest in some equipment which would include an estimated $5,530 for power equipment and accessories; hand tools at $835; cutters, blades, and bits at $800; benches, stands, and cabinets for $1,600; forms and jigs for $160; and office equipment for $3,055. Although production costs were expected to decrease as the manufacturing process developed, Davidson projected that variable costs would total $1,161 per canoe and selected annual operating expenses including telephone and internet charges, supplies, insurance, and maintenance would total $8,644. Davidson projected almost $90,000 in sales in 1998, with gross profits of $52,000.

Market for Canoes

The market for canoes followed the business cycle. In recessions, canoe sales suffered as many prospective customers stopped recreational spending. Sales of premium-priced canoes were especially vulnerable. Davidson included statistics from Statistics Canada that showed the

Year	Firms in Business	Change Over Previous Year	Shipments (000,000)	Change Over Previous Year
1982	301	—	184.5	—
1983	342	14%	183.2	−1%
1984	369	8%	232.1	27%
1985	361	−2%	260.2	12%
1986	359	−1%	333.9	28%
1987	327	−9%	421.2	26%
1988	379	16%	463.4	10%
1989	326	−14%	440.9	−5%
1990	314	−4%	342.0	−22%
1991	252	−20%	250.6	27%
1992	233	−8%	221.3	−12%
1993	198	−15%	225.3	2%
1994	196	−1%	303.7	35%
1995	227	16%	428.1	41%
1996	249	10%	476.9	11%

Exhibit 1 Boat Building and Repair Industry (excluding watercraft)

Source: Statistics Canada.

number of companies categorized as manufacturing canoes of five tons or less displacement (which included companies that specialized in repairs as well as manufacturing) and the overall industry sales in his business plan (Exhibit 1).[2] The statistics showed that many companies were unable to survive the recession in the early 1990s; however, industry sales had been strong and improving over the last few years. Davidson was optimistic that growth would continue into the foreseeable future.

Marketing Strategy

Promotion would consist of a Web page, advertisements in canoeing magazines and press releases to industry and recreational associations. The World Wide Web would be the company's primary means of promotion and sale, and Davidson planned on establishing a Web page complete with photographs, diagrams and interactive order forms. Selling on the Web gave CCC access to thousands of prospective clients at virtually no cost. The company was also going to place advertisements in the "buyer's market" sections of the two most popular canoeing magazines, *Canoe & Kayak* and *Kanawa,* which were published in the U.S. and Canada, respectively. *Canoe & Kayak* had a monthly circulation of about 100,000. A one-inch advertisement cost US$140 per month. *Kanawa,* on the other hand, had a quarterly circulation of about 120,000. An equivalent one-inch advertisement cost Cdn$340

Company	# of Models	Size Range	Customize	High Price (CAD)	Low Price	Custom Price	Mean Price 16'–17' Boat
Northwoods (USA)	8	10'–17'	Limited to packages	$5,040	$1,820	$100–$600/ft.	$5,500
Laughing Loon (Cdn)	5	10'–17'	Yes	$4,258	$2,500	$252/ft.	$4,250
Franklin Cedar Canoes (USA)	4	12'–18–1/2'	Yes	$2,500	$1,700	Quote by the job	$2,200
Nashua River Craft (USA)	1	15'	Yes	$2,660	$2,660	Quote by the job	NA
Kevin Martin (USA)	6	15'–17'	Yes	$5,600	$2,800	$250–$1500/ft.	$4,700
Fletcher Canoes (Cdn)	2	15'–17'	Yes	$2,600	$2,400	$40–$485/ft.	$2,600
Bourquin Boats (USA)	3	16'6"–17'6"	Yes	$3,290	$3,430	$50–$725/ft.	$3,290
Bearwood Canoe Company (Cdn)	3	15'–16'	Limited to Dacron covering	$2,595	$2,425	$2,650	$2,595
Cheemaun Canoes (USA)	1	15'–20'	Limited to adding sail	$2,940	$2,940	$1,260	$2,940
Old Towne Classic Canoes (USA)	7	15'–20'	Yes	$4,473	$4,893	Quote by the job	$4,473
Nor West Canoes (Cdn)	22	12'–26'	Yes	$13,450	$2,165	Quote by the job	$3,100

Exhibit 2 Wood Strip Canoe Manufacturers

per year. Davidson calculated that he would only have to sell one canoe per 67,000 advertisement exposures if he produced 30 canoes per year. Finally, Davidson was going to issue press releases to Industry and Recreational Associations with the introduction of every new type of canoe at a cost of $300 per year.

Based on the promotion strategy, most sales would be direct from the shop to the customers. Professionals with above-average incomes, who canoed as a hobby, would be targeted. Canoeing for these professionals might be the hobby itself or part of another hobby such as fishing, hunting and camping. Although Davidson did not include an estimate of the size of this market segment, he cited statistics from Statistics Canada that Canadians owned over two million boats, including approximately 640,000 canoes. According to Davidson, "It would be difficult to find a Canadian who had not owned, ridden in or admired a cedar canoe." Indeed, the potential market was very large.

Pricing

Davidson included a price list of direct competitors who made wood strip canoes (Exhibit 2). In addition to the 11 companies listed in the business plan, there were many other small manufacturers listed on the World Wide Web. The price range of hand-crafted canoes sold on these Web sites ranged from under US$2,000 to over US$10,000. Most sites claimed to sell canoes made from cedar, comparable to the canoes made at CCC. The competition also included mass-produced canoes sold by well-known manufacturers such as Coleman and Alumicraft. Mass-produced canoes were lower quality and retailed between $750 and $3,000, depending on the make, model and size. Other types of watercraft, such as windsurfers, sailboats and motor boats, also competed with canoes for sales. Prices for small boats and watercraft started at under $1,000 for low-end windsurfers.

In all, the prices of products competing with canoes ranged widely. Davidson knew that canoes made by CCC would sell at a premium; however, he was unsure about the optimal price. Davidson did not want to price the canoes too high, since there would be no salesforce to promote the canoes and most sales would be direct to the customer; however, Davidson also wanted to maximize profits. Davidson analyzed the pros and cons of his pricing strategy and planned to calculate the sales projections and breakeven points for several different pricing scenarios.

Notes

1. Cedar strips are long narrow pieces of cedar. Epoxy is a resin that sets when heated.
2. Canoes made by CCC would be in the under five ton or less displacement. Displacement measured the weight of water moved by a stationary vessel.

WaveRider Communications, Inc.: Selling Wireless Internet Access Equipment

Prepared by Ken Mark under the supervision of Professor Don Barclay

Version: (A) 2001-01-31

Introduction

It was June 15, 2000, and WaveRider Communications, Inc., a Canadian wireless Internet access equipment provider, had just completed the first installation of its latest LMS3000 system. Charles Brown, vice-president (VP) marketing, although elated at this milestone, knew that he had to deal with two key sales issues that had recently surfaced. First, compared to initial expectations, it had been taking at least twice as long for WaveRider's salesforce to sell its new LMS portfolio of products. Second, Brown also noticed an upward spike in the number of customer complaints associated with selling the new system.

With its recent June 6 listing on the NASDAQ stock exchange, Brown knew that WaveRider, currently trading at US$8.00, would be under increasing scrutiny from the U.S. capital markets. WaveRider would have to provide quarter-by-quarter revenue and earnings per share guidance to analysts and institutional investors. The Last Mile Solution (LMS) portfolio of products would make up the bulk of revenues in the coming months, and Brown wanted to diagnose and solve these sales issues immediately.

↑ Customer complaints

With 17 years of experience in the telecommunications and cable communications industries, Brown, an MBA graduate from the Richard Ivey School of Business, had joined WaveRider in February 1998 as the firm's VP marketing. He was responsible for the development and execution of WaveRider's overall marketing and product strategy. Before joining WaveRider, Brown was VP and chief information officer (CIO) of Clearnet Communications.

WaveRider Communications

Founded in 1997, WaveRider's mission was to become the global leader in wireless information technology by developing, selling and supporting products that enabled Wireless Internet Service Providers (WISPs). WISPs were in the business of providing Internet access to businesses and consumers via wireless connections. More typically, both businesses and consumers accessed the Internet through hard-wired telephone lines or cable connections.

Brown commented,

> Only five per cent of the North American population has access to high-speed service. The other 95 per cent have to deal with 28.8 Kbps to 56 Kbps. Outside of North America, 80 per cent of the world has never heard a dial tone and fully 75 per cent of the world has never dialled a phone. We're targeting second and third tier markets that serve pockets of fewer than 50,000 users (500,000 users or less for the U.S. market). Our products can deliver high-speed access to these markets cost effectively.

During its first two years as a development stage company, WaveRider had raised US$27.5 million to finance ongoing product research and development, acquired U.S. Federal Communications Commission approval for its NCL[1] and LMS[2] products, and signed agreements and completed installations in over 30 countries. With over 100 employees by early 2000, including 14 salespeople, WaveRider was developing sales momentum. To gain even more momentum and to muster the necessary resources to develop business opportunities, WaveRider had embarked on a partnership drive with resellers and technology installers in early 2000. The financial outcomes of their efforts to date are reflected in Exhibit 1.

WaveRider focused on developing fixed Wireless Internet/Intranet Network access systems capable of providing high-speed access to businesses, organizations and consumers. WaveRider had recently launched its two main product families: NCL and LMS (see Exhibit 2).

NCL—In late October 1998, WaveRider received regulatory approval for its first product. The NCL 135 was a wireless high-speed router that provided secure, reliable connections to corporate computer networks, outlying offices and the Internet. It was designed to replace T1 or ISDN onsite communication lines. For example, if a customer had two offices, and one of the two had a local area network (LAN) with digital subscriber lines (DSL), then by using the NCL 135, both offices could share an Internet connection wirelessly. WaveRider had already launched a second version, the NCL 1135, enabling higher-speed broadband connections for LAN-to-Internet and LAN-to-LAN applications.

LMS—In March 2000, WaveRider introduced its LMS2000 product. The LMS system had been designed to provide "last mile" wireless Internet access to a user. The "last mile" referred to the difficulties that various technologies faced in delivering Internet access to consumers. To receive access by satellite, a dish was required; high-speed fibre optic access required trenching connecting lines at a high cost. Targeted at WISPs, the LMS system included network access points (NAPS) that accessed fibre optic lines, communication access points (CAPS) that accessed the network within a 10-mile radius, and modems for end-user computers. LMS2000 utilized license-free radio technology in the 2.4 GHz frequency band. Rémi Gaudet, business analyst, commented,

> The environment is changing every few months and, consequently, our products change. Our LMS product was a shift from our NCL product, which was developed to get our feet wet. Instead of being a pure developer of wireless technology, we're now a software development and system administration company.

(Text continues on page 282)

Quarterly Income Statement and Forecast
(US$ millions, except per share data)

	1999 (Actual)					2000	
	Q1	*Q2*	*Q3*	*Q4*	*Total Year*	*Q1A*	*Q2E*
Sales	$0.05	$0.19	$0.71	$0.77	$1.72	$0.81	$0.72
COGS	0.03	0.10	0.49	0.67	1.29	0.65	0.61
Gross Profit	0.02	0.09	0.22	0.09	0.42	0.16	0.11
SG&A	0.81	0.98	1.16	1.67	5.39	1.43	3.30
R&D	0.56	0.58	0.76	1.03	3.03	1.40	2.06
Total Expenses	1.37	1.56	1.91	2.70	8.42	2.83	5.36
Operating Income	(1.35)	(1.47)	(1.69)	(2.61)	(8.00)	(2.67)	(5.25)
Other Income	0.05	0.01	0.02	(0.03)	0.05	0.13	0.18
Pretax	(1.30)	(1.46)	(1.67)	(2.64)	(7.95)	(2.54)	(5.07)
Tax Expense	—	—	—	(0.50)	(0.50)	—	—
Net	(1.30)	(1.46)	(1.67)	(2.14)	(7.45)	(2.54)	(5.07)
EPS	(0.04)	(0.05)	(0.05)	(0.06)	(0.22)	(0.05)	(0.09)
Shares Outstanding	$31.59	$32.34	$35.04	$37.98	$34.26	$49.26	$53.43

SG&A-Q2E total of 3.30 includes extraordinary charge of US$1.3 million for an escrow release—there are approximately nine million more escrow shares to be released

ANNUAL STATEMENT OF CASH FLOWS (US$ MILLIONS)

	Dec-98	*Dec-99*
Operating		
Net Income	(4.48)	(7.45)
Deprec. & Amort.	0.30	0.74
Special Charges	0.64	0.94
Gain on Sales (Inv. & Assets)	—	—
Def. Taxes	—	(0.50)
Working Capital Changes	0.56	(0.85)
Net Cash From Operations	(2.98)	(7.12)
Investing Activities		
Purch. of Equipment	(0.61)	(0.38)
Investments	—	—
Acquisitions	—	(0.66)
Other	—	—
Net Cash From Investing	(0.61)	(1.03)
Financing Activities		
Borrowing/Payment	—	—
Issuance of Common	6.27	10.75
Other	(0.07)	(0.11)
Net Cash From Financing	6.20	10.65
Effects of Exchange Rate	—	—
Net Change in Cash	2.61	2.49
Cash in Beginning	0.44	3.05
Cash at End	3.05	5.54

Exhibit 1 WaveRider Communications, Inc. Financial Statements

WaveRider® NCL135 Bridge/Router

Take advantage of the wireless world – replace your fractional T1 or ISDN lines with WaveRider's wireless NCL135 bridge/router. The fully-featured NCL135 enables high-speed wireless connectivity for LAN-to-Internet and LAN-to-LAN applications and provides secure, reliable connections to corporate computer networks, outlying offices, and the Internet.

Using Frequency-Hopping Spread Spectrum modulation in the license-exempt 2.4GHz ISM band, the NCL135 can be deployed quickly and easily without applying for regulatory approvals, and without incurring licensing or monthly service charges. Compared to the cost of traditional leased lines, NCL135 wireless links typically deliver ROI payback in less than a year.

The NCL135 supports both point-to-point and point-to-multipoint communication, making it ideal for:

- Providing Internet access in areas without a suitable telecommunications infrastructure
- Linking remote offices to corporate offices without the recurring costs of leased lines
- Connecting academic or corporate campus buildings to each other and to the Internet
- Providing WAN or Internet services for temporary facilities, special events, etc.

NCL135 at a glance

- Operates in the 2.4GHz ISM band, license-exempt in the U.S., Canada, and many other countries
- Frequency-Hopping Spread Spectrum radio is highly resistant to interference and ensures secure communication
- Supports both point-to-point and point-to-multipoint applications
- Forwarding Modes: IP Routing and Bridging (default Learning Bridge Static Routing)
- Delivers over-the-air data rates of 1.6 Mbps and up to 800 Kbps of real world user data throughput
- Built-in SNMP functionality ensures trouble-free integration and management with existing networks
- Maintains optimal throughput up to 10 miles (16 kms)
- Routing features/protocols: RIP v2, Static IP

For more information on the NCL family of products, please visit our Website.

www.waverider.com

Exhibit 2 NCL and LMS Products *(Continued)*

NCL135 TECHNICAL SPECIFICATIONS

Models	NCL135	NCL135CU
Order Number (SKU)	100-0100	100-0101
Operating Frequency Range	2.400 to 2.4835 GHz	2.450 to 2.4835 GHz
Radio Type	Frequency-Hopping Spread Spectrum	
Radio Modulation	Quadrature and Binary Frequency Shift Keying	
Over-the-Air Data Rate	Up to 1.6 Mbps	
User Data Rate	Up to 800 Kbps	
Maximum Link Path Distance (typical)	Up to 10 Miles (16 km)	
Channels	15	
Bandwidth	1.0 MHz per channel	
RF Tx Output Power	+18 dBm at the antenna port	
RF Rx Threshold	-80 dBm	
Antenna Connector	Reverse Polarity TNC	
Network Interface	Ethernet 10BaseT RJ-45	
Configuration/Setup Port	RS232 DB9 (Console port-DCE)	
Flash Memory	4 MB	
LED Indicators	Fault, Power, RF link status, Ethernet tx/rx	
Power Supply Input	100-240 VAC, 50-60 Hz, auto-sensing	
Power Supply Output	+5 VDC/3.0 A	
OperatingTemperature	0° to 149° F (0° to 65° C)	
Humidity	5% to 95% relative humidity (non-condensing)	
Physical Size (LxWxH)	9.1" x 8.7" x 1.1" (230mm x 220mm x 27mm)	
Product Weight / Shipping Weight	5.01 lbs. (2.24 kg)	
Regulatory approvals		
NCL135	FCC Part 15, ETSI, CE	
NCL135CU	Industry Canada RSS-139, FCC Part 15, ETSI, CE	
Warranty	1 year limited parts and labor (see WaveRider Warranty Agreement)	

Note: WaveRider's Continuous Improvement Policy means that specifications are subject to change without notice.

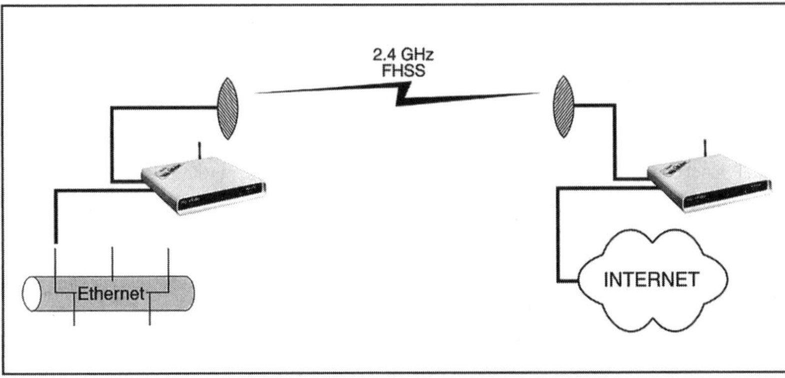

Exhibit 2 NCL and LMS Products *(Continued)*

Aimed at medium and large businesses and organizations requiring medium to high-speed throughput, combined with high availability, the LMS2000 provides the Wireless Internet Service Provider (WISP) with superior subscriber, equipment and network management, enhanced security, advanced billing support and a variety of maintenance features including real time alarms - all of which help to ensure that communication flows and profits soar - in a cost effective, easy to use, turnkey package.

LMS2000 at a glance

- *Is a complete system solution incorporating "best-in-class" components to maximize system capabilities and availability*
- *Provides sophisticated subscriber, network and equipment management for a cost effective solution which can be scaled to meet the long term needs of the WISP in a variety of environments*
- *Has superior maintenance features which allow operators to verify the configuration and operation of network modules on a scheduled or on-demand basis*
- *Generates real time alarms of failure of critical components*
- *Has automatic redundant fail over of key components to maximize system availability*
- *Provides environmentally hardened cabinets for key components to further enhance system availability and reduce maintenance costs*
- *Allows roll out of new system features from a central location in a controlled fashion*
- *Delivers IP communications links between a customer LAN and the Internet*
- *Operates in the 2.4 to 2.4835 GHz license exempt frequency band*
- *Has a raw data rate of 11 Mbps and provides access at speeds of up to 7.0 Mbps which is comparable to cable modems and xDSL*
- *Offers cost effective network infrastructure which can be easily scaled to meet the long term needs of the WISP*
- *Migrates easily to and from other LMS family products to ensure a long term solution and maximize return on investment*
- *Is a layer 3 end user modem to provide flexible, cost effective end user solutions*

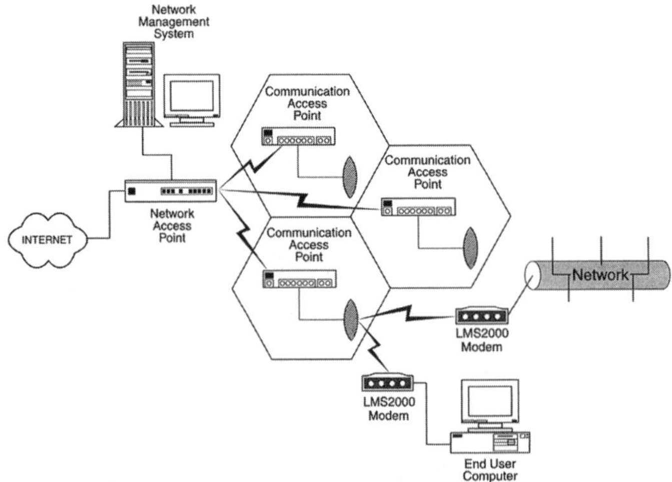

www.waverider.com

Exhibit 2 NCL and LMS Products *(Continued)*

LMS2000 TECHNICAL SPECIFICATIONS

NAP Specifications

The following tables list the technical specifications for the **LMS2000 NAP** including the NMS Workstation.

CAP-NAP Backhaul Interface Specifications	
Maximum Number of CAP-NAP Links	7
Physical Interface	10/100BaseTx auto-sense Ethernet
NAP-Internet Interface Specifications	
Maximum Number of NAP-Internet Links	1
Physical Interface	10/100BaseTx auto-sense Ethernet, full or half-duplex

The following tables list the technical specifications for the **LMS2000 CAP, CCU & EUM** configured for operation in the FCC/IC RF Regulatory Domain.

CAP Radio Specifications	
Maximum Number of Operational CCUs and Orthogonal Channels	3
Maximum Number of Standby CCUs	1
Ethernet Backhaul Interface Specifications	
Physical Interface	10/100BaseTx auto-sense, full or half-duplex

CCU and EUM Radio Specifications	
Minimum Channel Center Frequency	2.412 GHz
Maximum Channel Center Frequency	2.462 GHz
Channel Bandwidth	22 MHz
Center Frequency Spacing Increment	5 MHz
Minimum Separation Between Orthogonal Channels	25 MHz
Maximum Orthogonal Channels	3
Orthogonal Channel Set	1, 6, 11
Orthogonal Channel Set Center Frequencies	2.412 GHz, 2.437 GHz, 2.462 GHz
Maximum Output Power	+15dBm
Modulation Scheme	CCK (Complementary Code Keying) DSSS (Direct Sequence Spread Spectrum)
Receiver Sensitivity for BER < 10-5	-72 dBm
Maximum Over-the-Air, Raw Data Rate	11 Mbps
Ethernet Interface Specifications	
Physical Interface	10BaseTx half-duplex

Power Supply Specifications	**NAP**	**CAP & CCU**	**EUM**
AC Input	110/220 ±15% VAC single phase	110/220 ±15% VAC single phase	110/220 ±15% VAC single phase
AC Input Frequency	50/60 ±3 Hz	50/60 ±3 Hz	50/60 ±3 Hz
Maximum Input Power	1000 VA	1700 VA	1.5A
Maximum UPS Operating Time at full load	10 minutes	10 minutes	User defined
Environmental Specifications	**NAP**	**CAP & CCU**	**EUM**
Operating Temperature	10º to 40º C, indoor environment, 5% to 95%, RH non-condensing	10º to 40º C with integral fan cooling 10º to 55º C	10º to 55º C, indoor environment, 5% to 95%, RH non-condensing
Storage Temperature	-40º to 70º C	-40º to 70º C	-40º to 70º C

WaVeRider®
The World's Wireless Web Company

791-0001

Exhibit 2 NCL and LMS Products

Source: Company files.

Jim Chapman, VP Strategic Alliances, continued:

> Clients now buy from us because we've built software around optimizing technology itself. We've given them technology, opportunities and tools to optimize the level of service to their clients. Our competition says we have 2.4 GHz equipment and technology but it is more than that—we have created the tools to enable an installation as well. At the beginning, we were just building this radio for Internet access and as we got into product development and discussions with our customers, we saw that to distinguish ourselves we needed to add network management to our product suite. An interesting offshoot of this evolution was the impact on the sales task.

The Internet Wireless Access Industry

A number of factors were combining to generate demand for broadband access technologies capable of handling large amounts of data at high speeds. Use of the Internet was driving data traffic levels higher, with traffic on the Internet doubling every six months. The number of businesses and individual users on the net continued to climb at a staggering pace. In addition, the growing use of e-commerce and business productivity applications made high-speed local access networks more valuable than ever to companies and their employees.

There were thought to be four major factors driving demand for enhanced, high-speed, telecommunications services and equipment:

1. Internet growth and increased data traffic
2. An increase in demand for overall connectivity (especially in developing countries)
3. Upgrades to existing infrastructure as technology improved
4. Privatization and deregulation, which drove increased competition.[3]

As to the first factor, the U.S. fixed wireless market was expected to post a five-year compound annual growth rate of 65 per cent through 2003 to US$74 billion. The number of wireless data users in the United States alone was expected to increase from the current 2.9 million to 12.6 million by 2002, reported the Yankee Group in April 1999. As to the second factor, FreedomForum reported in early 1999 that Haiti had less than one phone line for every 100 people, and in Africa there were only 14 million telephone lines and 1.5 million users online for over 700 million people.

Although the penetration of broadband access among Internet users was still in the single digit percentages, the industry realized that consumers and businesses would soon demand access at speeds higher than a 128 Kbps rate due to the constant worldwide deployment of newer, richer online software applications. The demands on the part of businesses would be more stringent early on, since home users considered access at 56 Kbps or access via cable modems adequate to date.

WaveRider focused on the terrestrial-fixed wireless market, which was affected by the same drivers as the overall telecommunications market. Internet Service Providers (ISPs) had traditionally provided Internet access to small businesses and consumers via phone lines. Analysis by WaveRider indicated that there was a large gap between the "wired services" infrastructure currently available and what the worldwide marketplace desired. The gap was partially due to the reluctance of large telecommunications providers to rapidly upgrade their old networks. High-speed Internet access (one megabit per second or faster) was often unavailable outside dense metropolitan areas, and in fact, some underdeveloped regions of the world did not even have telecommunications infrastructure outside main cities. WaveRider intended to fill that gap with a viable, scalable alternative to wired access.

The Competitive Environment

Worldwide, telephone companies, cable operators, wireless operators and Internet service providers were deploying various high-speed access solutions to meet the needs of their end users. These included access through fibre optic lines, satellites, cable modems, DSL (Digital

Subscriber Lines), and wireless access technologies. Among these solutions, fixed wireless access[4] technology had emerged as a strong contender for solving the last mile access bottleneck.

WaveRider had to contend with wireless product competitors including Adaptive Broadband, Airspan, BreezeCOM, Cisco Systems, Lucent Technologies, Motorola, Nokia and Wi-Lan. Two typical competitors were:

BreezeCOM—Headquartered in Tel Aviv, Israel, BreezeCOM was a manufacturer of broadband wireless access equipment. With over 300 employees, 30 per cent of whom were in R&D, it had offices in North and South America, Uruguay, Hong Kong, China, Russia and Romania. It had a network of over 300 partners and distributors in more than 60 countries worldwide. Its BreezeACCESS solution delivered wireless connectivity in the licensed 3.5 GHz and MMDS 2.5–2.7 GHz frequency bands, as well as in the license-free 2.4 GHz ISM band. It also offered wireless network and modem solutions operating in the license-free 2.4 GHz ISM band.[5]

Wi-Lan—specialized in high-speed Internet access, LAN/WAN extensions and fixed wireless access. In June, Wi-Lan broke industry barriers with the launch of the "I.WiLL Access Point," a high-speed 30 Mbps wireless networking product. Targeting the demand for fixed wireless access products, the I.WiLL Access Point used Wi-Lan's patented technology to meet the stringent, industrial-strength demands of large telecommunications providers including telcos, fibrecos, cablecos, major ISPs and systems integrators. The I.WiLL 300–24 Access Point operated in the 2.4 GHz band to achieve a peak data rate of 30 Mbps in 20 MHz of bandwidth. This wireless product held many advantages over copper wire landlines, including low-cost, rapid installation and scalability.[6]

The Sales Environment

In the fast-paced, nascent world of wireless access providers, there were several general barriers to overcome, one of which was the long-term viability of WaveRider. In an industry with giant companies such as Nortel, Lucent and Cisco beginning to eye the wireless Internet access marketspace, WaveRider needed to demonstrate that it had staying power. At the present time, it could not show thousands of installations or a large market capitalization.

Second, WaveRider management noted that there was competitive "noise" in the marketplace, defined as unreachable promises made by the competition, which only served to confuse the market and lengthen the sales cycle. This "noise" frequently led customers to delay their decisions because they wanted to wait another two quarters for the "next version."

As a result of this noise, customers expected WaveRider salespeople to be on top of competitive developments and to provide information on the latest technologies. WaveRider salespeople had to work closely with product R&D staff to keep up to date on the latest news. WaveRider held quarterly sales seminars in Toronto to update its sales force on the latest developments. Brown stated, "When a customer casually mentions a competitive technology they're thinking of looking at, I want my salespeople to know about it."

Within this sales context, there were differences between selling the NCL and LMS product lines. Brown worried about this problem, as it seemed to be having significant implications for the length of the sell cycle, the sales support required, and perhaps even for the kind of salesperson best suited to selling the two lines.

Selling the NCL Product Line

Brown outlined WaveRider's approach to selling the NCL 135:

> While waiting for the LMS2000 product to be ready, we sold this product through our internal sales force along with our network of 75 Value-Added Resellers (VARs). The NCL 135 is simply a router that allows wireless access internally or between two office buildings. To install the product, one has to know how to hook two boxes up.

> I noticed that our salespeople never got comfortable selling the NCL 135 as they were more used to selling total solutions, not just hardware.
>
> In the last few months, we've noticed that this indoor wireless LAN marketspace is getting more competitive. Our potential customers are taking indoor LAN equipment made by our competitors and modifying it for outdoor usage. In addition, our large competitors like Lucent and Cisco are shipping hundreds of thousands of these wireless routers while we're shipping only in the thousands. Plus, at US$1,995, our solution is more expensive (but more robust) than our competition's products (costing roughly US$1,100).
>
> Therefore, one of the issues that we face in the NCL business is whether we should reposition our product as an outdoor wireless router. We could also take the NCL to an ISP at their Internet point of presence (POP), put an antenna up, and support 20 to 30 people. This would be a fourth or fifth tier market to us—for example, there are places in Iowa with 50 to 60 businesses in a closely knit cluster. We could never sell an LMS solution there, but we might be able to sell them the NCL if we packaged it up a little bit. Which brings us to the question—can I actually sell this product through distribution if packaged right?

With the increased competition, Brown wondered if it would be feasible to continue selling the NCL through VARs. He wanted to explore bundling the NCL with an installation package in the near future. Jim Chinnick, VP of engineering offered, "The NCL product really is not that complicated. There is a quick sell-in (30 days), it's relatively easy to manage, and once installed the only interface between engineering and sales is dealing with issues that arise as salespeople take products into new markets."

However, Brown was more concerned at this time with selling the LMS product line—the future growth engine of the company.

Selling the LMS Product Line

In the lead-up to the launch of the LMS product line, Brown observed that NCL salespeople were focused on margins and prices with the intent of quickly selling a set of 20 stocking units to the VAR, or an NCL unit to a customer (ISP). Brown knew that the selling strategy had to change for the LMS product.

He noted that selling the LMS solution was akin to selling a system to a large telephone company. There were more questions to answer, there was a formal decision-making process, and the sales process moved slower. The task required that the salesperson have professional selling skills, understand both the customer's application and, at the same time, the WaveRider business model. In addition, account management, product management and social-networking skills came into play. With these issues in mind, Brown originally estimated the LMS sales cycle to be 13 weeks—a far cry from the 30-day NCL cycle. Brown recounted:

> One of the realities about the sales process for our people on the LMS side was that our products are still really "leading edge stuff." It's not like cellular phones, which everybody by and large understands. We would meet with customers, show them a business plan, and then try to close the deal. If it was too expensive, we would negotiate price with them. Finally, we realized that the customer did not understand the fundamentals of the proposition. We were starting to close the sale when the customer was only starting to think, "Hey, this might be a good idea."
>
> What ended up happening was that our salespeople were talking about price way too soon and spent the next few months spinning their wheels because of this lack of understanding on the customer's part.

Even when an LMS sale was made, one of the more frequent complaints indicated that customers did not appreciate that they needed the whole LMS lineup of NAPs, CAPs and end-user modems. Customers were frustrated by their attempts to wirelessly connect computers to each other without deploying the full LMS lineup. Wondering why throughput rates for their Internet and LAN connections were so far below touted standards, they contacted WaveRider only to realize that they were not using the LMS product correctly. Chinnick stated:

> Right from the start, we knew that we had to deal with customer expectations carefully, especially from customers who had purchased something from us but expected more. Since our early missteps, we've learned that we can be much more honest with customers than we thought we could be. In most cases they are only looking for a bit more than what they have to start with. With the right specifications, an upgradable system, and a solution implemented in a timely, cost-effective manner, we can diffuse the pressure of negative customer satisfaction.

Over and above managing expectations, another customer concern focused on the installation of the new LMS2000 product line. This was one of the greatest hurdles that an ISP faced once it decided to deploy a fixed wireless system. This was no small task given the analysis required to minimize equipment costs, considering many variables such as uneven population densities over a given geographic area, topographical considerations, antenna locations, and roof right issues. WaveRider addressed this by establishing relationships with well-known RF engineering companies. WaveRider formed two separate strategic relationships to provide installation service and support to its customers. First, a three-way partnership with international wireless technology services companies SCIENTECH Inc. and Comsearch, a division of Allen Telecom Inc., was formed to provide engineering and installation services. Second, an alliance with General Dynamics Worldwide Telecommunications Systems was formed to integrate, install and support the LMS2000 product.[7]

Developing Additional Sales Support

Chinnick knew that for the LMS line, salespeople would not be the only ones involved in the sales process. To help customers understand product features and to develop suggestions for future products, a Product Line Management (PLM) section was created, with four people currently on staff. Ideally, PLM would set the direction for WaveRider product development by receiving information from the sales force and combining it with market research and discussions with some of the engineering staff—48 development engineers, six customer support engineers, and seven sales engineers.[8]

Acting as a bridge between the engineering and sales functions, PLM would manage information flows, develop product release plans and sales collateral materials. They would also make pricing and other critical decisions necessary to bring products to market. Other key parts of their role would be to work closely with salespeople to create a powerful demonstration of the product and create product manuals. PLM would also go on selected sales calls as a resource to answer technical questions (all of the PLM staff had engineering or technical backgrounds).

From the sales force perspective, Chinnick anticipated that the questions that would be most frequently posed to PLM would focus on: "When are the product and its associated features going to be available so that I can sell it?" and, "How do I sell this feature? How do I explain it to my customer in non-technical terms?"

Chinnick believed that the PLM group would help with the sales process and with customer credibility but was not entirely convinced that this was all that was needed to be successful with LMS2000 and beyond.

A Better Understanding of the LMS Sales Cycle

Reflecting on the past few months, Brown felt that by transferring product knowledge to the salespeople, they would be better prepared to pick up customer cues indicating that the customer understood the technology behind WaveRider products. This was a critical aspect of qualifying a prospect—understanding was fundamental to appreciating the value of the WaveRider LMS solution. Based on these cues, salespeople would have two options: invest more sales time or move on to the next prospect. With the rapidly growing awareness of the benefits of wireless Internet access technology, Brown knew that there was no shortage of prospects to pursue:

> One of the lessons that we learned from our early efforts selling the LMS2000 was that we have to invest time to figure out the sales process and experiment with different sales approaches. At the beginning, we closed LMS contracts in 13 weeks, but then we realized that the customer really did not know what to do with our product.

There was a need to avoid this problem in the future, to develop realistic sales forecasts, and to get a realistic picture of the LMS sales task and process. WaveRider senior management, in conjunction with the sales force, created "Standard Forecast Probability Indicators" (see Exhibit 3). This was an attempt to break down the typical sales process into stages, describe the positive customer behaviors associated with each stage, and estimate the probability of a sale closing if these behaviors were demonstrated. Brown continued:

> We now talk about the "sales funnel"—moving the "five per cent" customers to the next stage, qualifying them, investing time and training to get them to the next level . . . or dumping them if progress is not being made. We dump a lot of prospects at the "25 per cent" stage because we realize either that our solution does not fit their needs, or that they are not ready for a wireless solution.
>
> I estimate that to get customers to the "five per cent" stage requires three to four hours of a salesperson's time. To get to the "25 per cent" stage requires five days, progress to the "50 per cent" stage is another investment of 10 days, another 10 days to get to the "75 per cent" stage, and finally, it would take a day to get to the "100 per cent" stage. A typical LMS2000 sale is about US$200,000 (when fully deployed, it could be US$2,500,000),[9] and we pay our salespeople US$5,000 per month and three per cent of the sale. We now believe our sales cycle to be in the vicinity of six months.
>
> We were spending up to 10 days at the "25 per cent" stage trying to close when the probabilities were all wrong! Investing 21 days of a salesperson's time when there is a greater than 2:1 chance that the customer is going to say "no" is a bad investment. We expect our salespeople to eventually gross US$500,000 a quarter—we're not there yet since we have not been as productive as we'd like to be.
>
> There is also an overall company productivity issue. It doesn't take too many customer satisfaction issues to really slow down your whole sales and support process. If you skip steps in the sales process, you don't end up with the quality install you need. How do you move a prospect from a skeptic to somebody who is happy? It's a hundred times tougher with a new product category like LMS.

As another input to the concern about the lengthened sales cycle associated with LMS, Chinnick brought his past experience to the table. He had worked for a systems company that sold internationally, and he knew that sales cycles could be as long as 24 months. While working to understand the early frustration of salespeople and LMS customers alike, Chinnick concluded that WaveRider, as a whole, was "in denial" concerning the length of the sales process. He knew that with the development of the PLM function, the coordination of the sales engineers and sales account managers, and the use of the Standard Forecast Probability Indicators, more would be done to carefully document the sales process for future scrutiny.

Sales Cycle Longer Than Six Months?

The end of WaveRider's second quarter was approaching and Brown was forecasting sales estimates for the rest of the year. He had just conferred with a few salespeople as to their sales prospects and was concerned that there was a possibility that the LMS2000 sales cycle could be as long as 18 months.

WaveRider had plans to launch its next-generation LMS3000 and NCL1135 products in the next few weeks and Brown wanted to create sales forecasts for these new products. First, however, he had to resolve his sales cycle dilemma. How could he assuage Wall Street's and Bay

Probability of Sale	*Indicators*
5%	• We have met and discussed our solution with a senior decision maker • There appears to be a good fit for our solutions ***based upon client needs*** • The customer is interested in talking some more
25%	• The customer has been presented with details about our solution and we are on a shortlist of competitors • Corporate overview presentations reviewed with customer • The customer agrees we have a solution that meets their needs • The customer has identified that budget funds are available • The customer has a rough business plan for a solution like ours; estimated investment, estimated revenue, a rough roll-out schedule, a ***summary of needs*** and plans to go ahead with somebody's solution
50%	• We have identified an "internal coach" who is being helpful in promoting the WaveRider solution internally, and advising ***us*** on what we need to do to win the business. We have confirmed with the customer that our products meet their needs • The customer has a detailed implementation plan and business case that fits with the WaveRider solution • Preliminary Site analysis and a technical review of the customer's implementation plan have been completed • There are only one or two ***remaining*** competitors being seriously considered, if any • The planned date of implementation is set • Customer profile completed and forwarded to H/O • The customer has a clear plan on how they are financing the system, and the credit process has been initiated • Forecasted costing information to be included in the total summary of the forecast at 75% • The customer is working internally on approval
75%	• No ***remaining*** competition • The customer has verbally stated we have the best solution • The customer is negotiating price with us • Customer may have called other WaveRider reference sites • Most technical questions have been asked and answered • We have participated in building a detailed implementation plan
90%	• Customer has forwarded PO • Customer people are attending WaveRider training • Implementation steps (from our plan) are already being taken, i.e., site approvals, hiring, training, tower building, etc. • WISP Agreement has been signed • Project Manager assigned
100%	• Installed ***with formal*** customer acceptance received

Exhibit 3 Standard Forecast Probability Indicators (LMS2000 or a multi-unit NCL sale)

Street's concerns if he couldn't deliver sales until the end of an 18-month process? Could he in any way justify this long sales cycle?

Perhaps equally important, could he do anything to shorten the cycle and increase the odds of closing a sale? Did he have the right salespeople with the right credentials and training? Could WaveRider employ any technologies itself such as a Web site to enable the sales process? Was the sales support picture complete? What about changing the compensation plan? Life sure looked easier in the days of the NCL, but LMS was WaveRider's future.

Notes

1. NCL—Network Communication Link. Used primarily to create a Wide Area Network (WAN) by linking two or more Local Area Networks (LANs). This device is "plug and play" ready.
2. LMS—Last Mile Solution. Provides a complete solution for an ISP to provide high-speed wireless access for their customers.
3. First Security Van Kasper Research Report, 2000.
4. The term fixed wireless denoted wireless service that was delivered to the end-user via installed components.
5. Web site www.breezecom.com accessed June 1, 2000.
6. Web site www.wi-lan.com accessed June 1, 2000.
7. First Security Van Kasper, quoting company reports.
8. Sales engineers worked with sales account managers to handle ongoing technical issues with the product, most often concerning how to deploy and integrate the LMS product with the customer's network.
9. When customers first purchased the LMS suite, they tended to order a basic system—one NAP and three CAPs, for example. Fully-deployed, the LMS 3000 NAP could serve up to 15 CAPs.

Omega Paw Inc.

Prepared by Jannalee Blok under the supervision of Elizabeth M. A. Grasby

 Version: (B) 1999-10-06

Michael Ebert, president of Omega Paw (Omega) and inventor of the "Self-Cleaning Litter Box," reflected on the progress of his St. Mary's, Ontario-based company. In September 1996, after being in business for just over a year, Omega had reached a sales level of $1 million. Ebert knew that with Omega's current resources, the company could potentially target a much larger market. His goal was to "grow the business quickly," and in order to achieve these goals, Ebert knew Omega would have to expand its marketing initiatives and consider alternative channels of distribution.

The Cat Owners Market

In the mid-1990s, North America was home to approximately 66 million cats—60 million in the United States and six million in Canada. In 1996, approximately 33 per cent of the ten million households in Canada had, on average, two cats. The cat population had risen by seven per cent between 1994 and 1996, and was estimated to continue growing at an annual rate of four per cent for the next few years. A survey conducted by the American Pet Products Manufacturers Association, Inc. cited, as reasons for the growth, the increased trend in apartment and, more recently, condominium living. In addition, the survey pointed to the ever-increasing mobility of the workforce, the rising average age of the Canadian population (the typical cat owner was older than other pet owners), and the ease of care and maintenance for cats relative to other popular pets as reasons for the continued growth.

The typical cat owner spent approximately $520.00 annually on his or her feline pet.

Forty-four per cent was spent on food and 23 per cent on veterinarian visits. Cat supplies, such as litter, litter boxes, bowls, etc., accounted for 13 per cent of the yearly budget while 20 per cent was spent on flea and tick supplies, grooming, and toys. Just over 50 per cent of owners bought presents for their cats, of which the majority (88 per cent) were purchased and given during the Christmas season.[1]

Omega Paw's Consumer Groups

Based on experience and knowledge, Omega Paw had divided cat owners into three main consumer groups. The first group, five per cent of the total cat owner market, was the "new pet owner." These were consumers who had just acquired a cat or a kitten and who needed all the applicable pet care and maintenance products. They often did their own pet and product research, wanted good quality, long-lasting products and usually purchased items at the local pet stores or at the veterinarian's office.

The "existing cat owner," 80 per cent of the total cat owner market, was the second identifiable market. Having owned cats for some time, these consumers were experienced at caring for their cats and were well stocked with the traditional cat care and maintenance supplies. They purchased their cat products at a variety of locations such as pet stores, the veterinarian's office, household supply stores, and grocery stores.

The remaining 15 per cent of the cat owner market was labelled as the "gray zone." Most of this segment lived in the country and owned a variety of "outdoor" pets such as dogs and cats. Cats in this segment were not only one of many pets, but were also free to roam outside and, as a result, the owners usually did not concern themselves with purchasing specific cat products other than cat food.

The "Self-Cleaning Litter Box"

Two years ago, Ebert's brother and sister-in-law had gone on holidays, leaving Ebert to care for their cats. "There's got to be a better way," Ebert had thought as he held his nose while cleaning the cats' litter box. By September 1996, not only had Ebert "found a better way" by inventing a self-cleaning litter box, but he had set up a new company to distribute this product and other pet care products through pet store distribution channels all across North America.

The "Self-Cleaning Litter Box" was a moulded plastic box with rounded edges that allowed the cat to enter and leave through a large opening at the side. The box was available in two sizes, and the larger size was ideally suited for large or multiple cats. To clean the litter box, the cat owner would first roll the box onto its back, allowing all of the litter to pass through a filter screen and collecting any clumped litter separately in a long, narrow tray. The owner would then roll the box back to its normal position and allow the clean litter to flow back through the filter to the litter tray. At this point, the narrow tray could be removed by its handle, and the used cat litter could be dumped out. Exhibit 1 illustrates the simplicity of the process: roll back, roll forward, remove the tray and dump the waste.

The Competition

Direct Competition

The first of three main North American competitors, the "Everclean Self Scoop Litter Box," was an open litter box with rounded edges. In order to clean it, the rounded cover had to be attached and the box rolled. This allowed clean litter to fall through the filters and collected the clumped litter in the top half of the box. Following this, the entire top of the box was taken off, carefully maneuvered over a garbage can, and then angled so that the litter clumps would fall into the garbage. When finished, the top of the box was left detached and had to be stored until the next cleaning.

First Brands Corporation, the manufacturer of the "Everclean Self Scoop Litter Box," retailed its product for between \$53 and \$63.[2] It spent a lot of money advertising to pet stores via trade

Self-Cleaning Litter Box

"Consumers want a box that's easy to clean. They want a covered box that controls odors and is as low-maintenance as possible."
Source: Pet Product News July, 1997

Award Winning Design

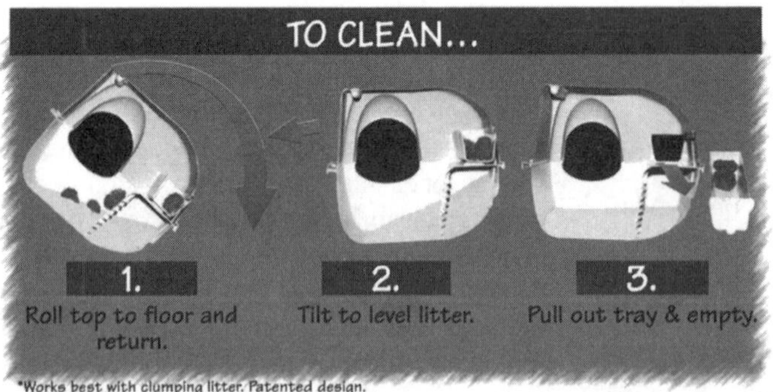

Omega Paw Inc.
P.O. Box 2979, 10 Thames Road North, St. Marys, Ontario N4X 1A6 CANADA
Phone 1-800-2 CAT BOX • 519-284-0513 • Fax 519-284-0509 • www.omegapaw.com

Exhibit 1 Omega Paw's "Self-Cleaning Litter Box"

magazines and had North American-wide distribution. First Brands also manufactured well-known home, automotive, and pet-care products, and recently reported annual sales revenues of just over $1 billion.

The second direct competitor, "Quick Sand," used a series of three trays—each with slanted slots on the bottom of the tray. These trays were layered in such a way that the slanted slots of the top and bottom were going in the same direction, and the slanted slots of the middle tray were facing the opposite direction. This layering technique formed a solid bottom to the litter box and prevented the clean litter from filtering through the trays prematurely. In order to clean the litter box, the first tray was lifted and sifted. Clean litter filtered down to the second tray, leaving the clumped litter in the top tray. The used litter was deposited into the garbage and the empty tray was replaced under the bottom until the process needed to be repeated.

The whole box required carrying and emptying which was awkward, and trays had to be replaced underneath each other with care so that litter did not leak out onto the floor. However, "Quick Sand" was competitively priced at $29 retail. In addition, it was shorter in length than other litter boxes and, as a result, was easier to place in a secluded spot. Introduced in March 1995, the product was endorsed by Dini Petty, a Canadian morning talk show host. It did not receive much attention, however, until Smart Inventions, an American company, bought the product in 1996 and launched an extensive media campaign. They spent between $200,000 to $300,000 per week for six months and gained exposure throughout Canada and the United States.

The last main competitor, "Lift & Sift," was very similar to the "Quick Sand" product. It was priced at $29 and also used the three-tray method. In addition, both products incorporated easy-to-follow directions as part of their packaging design. While "Lift & Sift" had been on the market for three years, it had limited advertising exposure. However, in 1996 it benefited from "Quick Sand's" extensive advertising and actually beat it into mass distribution outlets like Wal-Mart.

Indirect Competition

Despite the increasing number of "owner-friendly" cat litter boxes, many cat owners continued to favor the basic model. These products retailed for $10 to $15, were sold at numerous locations and represented the majority of the litter box market (approximately 90 per cent). Although cat litter boxes could be purchased in a variety of colors and sizes, compared to the more recent offerings they were awkward, messy, and smelly.

At the other end of the spectrum, a product named "Litter Maid" had also made its way into the market. With the aid of electric eyes and an automatic sifting comb, this computerized self-cleaning litter box combed through the litter, collected the waste and deposited it into a container at one end of the tray. The electric eyes reacted quickly and the litter box was cleaned within minutes of the cat leaving the box, thereby eliminating almost any odor. Its hassle-free process, benefits, and one-year manufacturer's warranty had all been heavily advertised on TV and in national magazines. "Litter Maid" could be purchased via mail order for $199.00 U.S.

From August 1995 to Present

Ebert realized that with such heavy competition, Omega would have to think carefully about its marketing campaign. Specifically, as it attempted to expand distribution, it would have to think carefully of the company's success and failures over the past year.

In August 1995, after four months of advertising the "Self-Cleaning Litter Box" via magazine advertisements (mail-order) and TV commercials, Omega pre-sold 2,500 units. These units were shipped to the customers as the orders came in; however, production problems with the initial moulds caused delays and, instead of the actual product, Omega had to send out letters stating that the product would be ready in a few weeks' time.

In late August 1995, the management group at Omega decided to end the "direct to customer" mail-order experiment and instead to target pet stores via distributors. Omega contacted Canadian Pet Distributors (CPD) in Cambridge, Ontario, who responded favorably and picked up the "Self-Cleaning Litter Box" line immediately. CPD distributed nationally and required a 40 per cent markup on the manufacturer's selling price; the pet stores, in turn, required a 100 per cent markup on the distributor's selling price.

CPD continued to sell Omega's prototype to pet stores in Canada from August through to December 1995. However, the initial run of products was not yet perfect and, as a result, slightly "dented" Omega's reputation. When asked why Omega continued to sell these prototype products, Ebert answered, "at that point we were happy to sell to anyone."

By December 1995, the "new and improved" "Self-Cleaning Litter Box" was ready. Omega sold it for $18. The variable costs for each box were $6.00 for production, $1.50 for shipping, and $1.38 for packaging. Since CPD only sold in Canada, Omega started looking for a distributor in the United States. After being introduced to the product at a trade show that Omega's management had attended, six of seven distributors contacted picked up the product right away. Interestingly, this favorable response made Omega the only "self-cleaning" litter box on the U.S. market in late 1995.

By January 1996, the management at Omega realized that they could not possibly continue their direct selling technique to the many potential pet store distributors across America. Instead, they chose to utilize the skills and industry contacts of manufacturer representatives. Manufacturer representatives required six per cent commission (on the MSP), and in return added Omega's product line to their existing product line portfolio for sale to pet store distributors across America.[3]

Throughout 1996, Omega continued to attend U.S. industry pet trade shows. The manufacturer representatives were working out very well for Omega and had secured 60 distributors across North America. By September 1996, Omega had sold approximately 50,000 "Self-Cleaning Litter Boxes" totalling $1 million in sales.

Alternatives for the Future

After being in business for just over a year, Omega had reached impressive sales levels. Ebert hoped to continue this favorable trend and aspired to reach sales of $1.7 million by the company's December 1996 fiscal year end, $3 million by December 1997, and $5.7 million by December 1998. He knew that such aggressive growth would not be easy and wondered, "Where do we go from here? Should we continue as we are, increase our penetration into pet stores, revisit mail order channels, pursue mass markets, or expand into grocery stores?"

Ebert wondered what changes to the existing strategy would be necessary to achieve market penetration and increased sales. Should Omega consider using different advertising mediums to attract attention, or should it simply increase the amount of existing advertising? Ebert knew of two or three good trade magazines that offered a one-shot deal (one month/one issue) at a cost of $3,000 to $4,000 including a one-time production fee. However, he wondered if there were any other creative marketing initiatives that could help increase sales among pet stores.

A mail order/TV campaign would cost $20,000 for an initial run. This cost included producing the commercial, a 1-800 phone number, the hiring of a company to answer the calls, and another company to collect the money. As a result of previous difficulties with mail order, a trial run would be conducted. Since Americans tended to be more receptive to mail order than Canadians, the trial would be launched on national television in the United States and would initially run for a two-week period. Then, if the trial went well, the TV campaign would continue. Ebert noted that under this alternative, Omega would produce and ship the product directly to the customer.

If Omega sold its "Self-Cleaning Litter Box" to mass distribution outlets such as Wal-Mart or Kmart,[4] it would cost an estimated $50,000 for additional tooling, different packaging and increased advertising. If this option was pursued, Ebert wondered what changes would have to be made to the product and how this might affect the product's selling price, image, and promotional plans.

If mass distribution outlets were pursued, there was also the decision of which trade route to use. With small to medium-sized accounts, Omega could continue using its existing manufacturer representatives to sell to the different stores. However, with large accounts, called "house" accounts, Omega would have to sell directly to the specific mass distribution buyers. The product would then be shipped by the buyers to store distribution centres, and only then would it be sent out to the individual stores. In addition to the added complexity of this trade route, Ebert was especially concerned about meeting the demands of buyers who required a 40-per cent markup (on the MSP), ample quantities, and on-time deliveries.

With 80,000 grocery stores in the United States alone, this relatively untapped market had considerable potential. However, if grocery store placement was pursued, Ebert knew the demands on Omega would be many.

In order to sell to grocery stores, Omega had to sell through a national broker, a regional broker, the distribution centres, and finally the grocery stores. The members of this trade channel respectively required the following:

- The greater of a four-per cent margin on the MSP, or a $2,000 monthly retaining fee (national broker);
- A four-per cent margin on the MSP (regional broker);
- A 20 to 25 per cent markup on the MSP (distribution centres); and
- A 40 per cent markup on the distributors' selling price (grocery stores).

In addition to the required margin, grocery stores wanted 10 per cent for co-operative advertising and for setting up point-of-purchase displays. Omega estimated a further cost of $3 to produce each of these displays.

Before he could seriously pursue this option, Ebert questioned whether the grocery industry was ready to accept "hard-good"[5] products. He knew some of the more aggressive stores, approximately 10 per cent, were expanding their pet sections, but would customers be willing to make an impulse buy of $30 as part of their weekly grocery shopping? It was evident that this distribution option had high potential, but Ebert questioned whether or not he wanted to be the one to develop it.

Decision Time

Omega had achieved considerable success to date, and the company's current financial resources and production capabilities positioned it well to service a larger market. A marketing budget of $100,000 was available and the manufacturing facilities had a capacity of 3,500 units per week. With all of this in mind, and the options to consider, Ebert wondered what decisions he should make to best position Omega Paw for the future.

Notes

1. "1996–1997 APPMA National Pet Owners Survey" Revised—American Pet Products Manufacturers Assoc., Inc.

2. All prices are in Canadian dollars unless noted otherwise.

3. American distributors and pet stores required the same markup as distributors and pet stores in Canada. (Distributors required 40 per cent markup on MSP. Pet stores required 100 per cent markup on DSP.)

4. Wal-Mart and Kmart each had 2,200 stores in the United States alone.

5. "Hard goods"—generally more durable products giving benefit to the consumer over an extended period of time.

6

Ongoing Venture Operations and Growth

The Process of Ongoing Operations and Growth

Ongoing operations leading to growth consists of a set of activities concerned with the continued and improved delivery of both the product(s) of the firm (Level 1) and the firm itself as a financial product (Level 2). According to noted economist Joseph Schumpeter (1934), who was one of the most respected commentators on entrepreneurship, "Everyone is an entrepreneur when he actually carries out new combinations, and loses that character as soon as he has built up his business, when he settles down to running it as other people run their businesses" (p. 78). From this we can gather that the entrepreneurial value added in this stage of the venture creation process is the continual addition of new combinations.

There are those who might assert that to qualify as entrepreneurial at this stage of the process, the venture must add new products or services. We are not convinced.

In our minds, we see that each time members of the venture team remove the frictions that prevent new transactions from occurring, this is entrepreneurial because new units *are* new combinations of transaction creator, work, and other persons. This is why, in our minds, the ongoing operations and growth stage of the venture creation process are very much an entrepreneurial phase in the venture life span.

Effectively bringing about continuing operation and growth includes the implementation of a visionary and flexibility-creating operations plan (Collins & Porras, 1995) and the use of this plan to achieve superior economic performance. This stage of venture development primarily involves at least the application of concepts related to continuous venture screening (e.g., the use of the New Venture Template™ [NVT] screening system to highlight the necessary venture viability attributes that may need attention), making market and industry assessments (e.g., brand management), ongoing financial assessment, and customer reputation and stakeholder relationship management. Through these activities, we believe that the processes of opportunity recognition that drive continuous improvement and growth can be stimulated.

Now out of print, but nevertheless an extremely useful handbook at this stage of venture creation, is a summary of what has been termed *organizational entrepreneurship* (Cornwall

& Perlman, 1990). According to these authors, the key to a vibrant organization is continual attention to the fundamentals of entrepreneurial organizations. These include

- managing total risk (sink-the-boat and miss-the-boat risk combined; e.g., Dickson & Giglierano, 1986);
- avoiding the traps of traditional organizations (e.g., defensive vs. proactive strategies, viewing change as a threat vs. as an opportunity, short- vs. long-term focus in control systems, protective vs. adaptive/innovative organizational culture, formal vs. informal communication structures, viewing people as expendable vs. as a key resource, mere toleration vs. fostering of creativity, etc.);
- fostering empowerment within the venture;
- minimizing bureaucracy;
- providing incentives versus constraints for innovation;
- enabling research and development (R&D) that is (a) balanced between basic, breakthrough-oriented research and applied research; (b) long term versus reactive to competitors; and (c) decentralized and integrated versus stand-alone and isolated;
- ethically and sustainability focused.

From our vantage point, we see the continuing operations and growth phase of the venture creation process to be somewhat "agricultural" in the sense that the first job of entrepreneurs remains the creation of new transactions, and, at this stage of venture creation, this can be best accomplished by providing the heat, light, water, and nourishment that the venture as a living organism requires. In our view, the sustainability and growth of the venture does not come from a restrictive, defensive, or mechanistic view of the business. Rather, it comes from developing the capabilities for reflective and reflexive awareness and responsiveness. We believe that opportunities for creating new value that is not restricted to economic value alone (Cohen & Winn, 2003) continue to surround the venture, and—as we explain in the next chapter—we believe that there are fundamental entrepreneurial thinking processes that exist and can be learned to make this happen.

A Student's View of the Operations and Growth Process

The operations and growth process, as viewed through the eyes of an entrepreneurship student, includes the following narrative that accompanies Figure 6.1. This narrative explains the figure and can be used to visualize many of the key elements we have just described to be essential to the setup process.

This student says the following:

Continuing operations have three key steps.

Step 1: NVT Analysis. This step involves periodically assessing the venture on the basis of the 15 questions that comprise the NVT. It is an excellent way to judge how well the venture fares on the 15 components and to engender thought about what could be done to improve the scores on the NVT analysis. In thinking about what could be done and in formulating plans to improve the venture, better ventures are being created.

Step 2: Market/Industry and Financial Assessment. This step involves two stages.

Stage 1: Market/industry assessment. This stage involves conducting a trend analysis, industry analysis, and market profile analysis (similar to what was conducted during the feasibility analysis

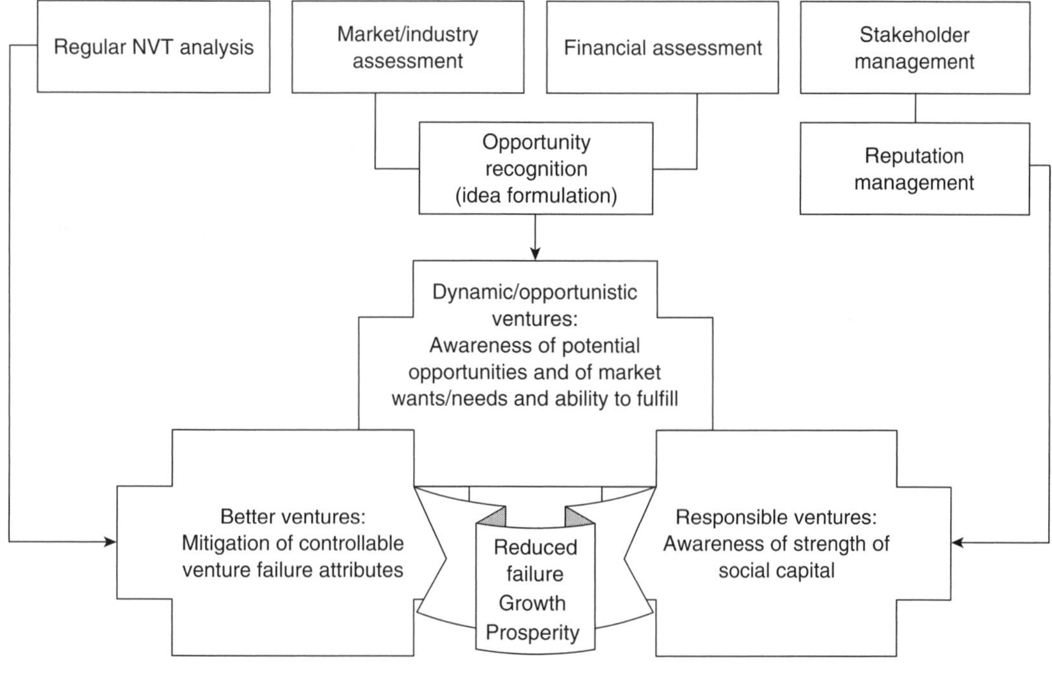

Figure 6.1 Ongoing/Continuing Operations

during the idea screening phase). Its purpose is to uncover potential opportunities/threats that may face the venture in the future. Planning should be conducted now to mitigate the threats and capitalize on the opportunities as they present themselves.

Stage 2: Financial assessment. This stage involves looking at the venture's profitability and internal operations.

- Is there a better way to produce the product/service (inputs)?
- Is there a better way to conduct workflow?
- Is there any way to reduce costs without inhibiting the performance of the venture?
- Is there any way in which the offering could be differentiated to increase net buyer benefit (NBB) and charge higher prices (or to leave prices constant and attain a larger market share)?

After conducting these two assessments, opportunities that present themselves should start at the idea screening stage, and the techniques that have not yet been conducted should be employed to stimulate more thought about how to capitalize on this opportunity. Conducting these analyses and recognizing opportunities creates a dynamic/opportunistic venture that is not stagnant and will not blossom into an overgrown bureaucracy. It creates an innovative, creative venture that will sustain itself through the recognition of emerging trends and opportunities.

Step 3: Stakeholder Management. The purpose of stakeholder management is to always be aware of the various groups that have vested interests in the company. Although not all groups can be satisfied all of the time, time must be devoted to acknowledging the interests of these groups. Doing so signals to these groups that you have a bearing on their lives and, at the absolute least, that you are aware that they exist. Ventures are not a closed box but exist within the framework of a larger society, and it is this society that gives the venture the license to operate. Effective stakeholder management is just one element that can sustain the venture. If the venture operates with complete disregard for the social setting in which it operates, its social license to operate may be in jeopardy.

Associated with this notion of the importance of stakeholders is the notion of reputation management. The reputation of the venture and its offering should be considered before every undertaking. Having a good reputation makes it easier to introduce new products and charge higher prices. Conversely, having a bad reputation will likely lead to the demise of the venture.

All in all, thinking about a firm's reputation and how the undertakings of the firm can affect that reputation, as well as acknowledging that the firm is a part of a larger society, leads to responsible ventures.

Operating a better, responsible, and dynamic venture reduces the chances for failure and induces growth prospects and chances for prosperity.

CASES

The following cases have been selected to help learners to develop and become more aware of their own thoughts on firm growth and ongoing operations.

EXTREME CCTV

Prepared by Ken Mark under the supervision of Professor Stewart Thornhill

 Version: (A) 2002-06-27

INTRODUCTION

On January 5th, 2001, Jack Gin, president and founder of Extreme CCTV, was considering acquiring Derwent Systems Ltd. of Newcastle, England. Derwent was Europe's leading manufacturer of infrared illuminators, and Extreme CCTV was its rapidly growing OEM distribution partner for sales in North America. At Extreme CCTV's head office in Burnaby, British Columbia, Gin knew that the acquisition of Derwent could provide Extreme CCTV with a solid foundation to tackle the European market of its own Extreme CCTV products. If a competitor purchased Derwent, Gin had the other option of working directly with U.K. distributors from his head office in Burnaby, but he would lose the advantage of having Derwent's unique UF500 infrared illuminator which had significant sales in Europe and had become important for Extreme CCTV sales in North America.

In the next few months, Gin had to manage rapidly growing sales and prepare Extreme CCTV for an initial public offering (IPO) in 2002. He needed to decide whether purchasing Derwent was the right decision.

THE CLOSED CIRCUIT TELEVISION INDUSTRY

With a global market estimated at Cdn$5 billion, the closed-circuit television (CCTV) industry served clients who were interested in using video surveillance devices for monitoring purposes. This industry was a subset of the larger security products industry which included the following categories: access control products, photo identification or badging, alarm systems and centralized monitoring systems, electronic locking devices and computer network/data security products. Separately, the North American and European CCTV markets were estimated to be worth Cdn$1.4 billion each.

The market for CCTV products had grown rapidly in the late 1990s. In 1999, revenues grew by approximately 12 per cent, and this trend was expected to continue into the future. The growing popularity of CCTV surveillance systems was attributed to their ability to provide a high level of security without the expense of security guards. A British study discovered that areas monitored by CCTV could deter crime by as much as 80 per cent. In fact, the United Kingdom was the most progressive country in its use of CCTV, with more than 150,000 cameras monitoring city streets and public places. Market growth had also been driven by the litigious culture in the United States which created a heightened demand for surveillance products that could be used as evidence in civil or criminal court cases.[1]

Products

CCTV products were offered in hundreds of varieties, with each manufacturer offering different special features on its equipment. General types of CCTV products included cameras, enclosures, domes, mounts, and pan/tilt units—everything necessary to implement, use and support video surveillance.

Distribution

Due to the complexity of the systems, most CCTV consumers made their purchases from a security products installer. These installers determined the client's needs and then prescribed adequate products. They were responsible for installing the system and servicing it when needed. Therefore, most manufacturers had little direct contact with their product's final users. Most installers were small to mid-sized, regionally based companies that would focus on installing traditional alarm systems, but offered CCTV systems as a component of their product offering. Many of the mid-sized installers also acted as the distributors for a number of different manufacturers' products, while the small installers would purchase the systems wholesale from a larger distributor. The large distributors were multinational corporations that carried a wide line of products from hundreds of different manufacturers.

Recent innovations in camera and digital technology had led to the development of CCTV systems that were easier to install and use than traditional products. This led to speculation that direct retailers would become a primary source of sales in the future. Such a development would have significant implications for the role of installers and distributors in the CCTV industry.[2]

Customers

From schools, government buildings and public spaces to retail, business offices and manufacturing, CCTV was being used to detect, deter and document operations, security incidents and crimes. There were more than two million security cameras in public places like U.S. airports and bus stations. Another five million CCTV devices were in private use, with both private and public markets for security devices growing for the foreseeable future.

Playing a large role in the growth of video security was the U.S. government. A 2001 study by the U.S. Department of Justice indicated that fixed-position CCTV cameras were in use by law enforcement in all 50 states. Bob Granger, manager of operation security with United Space Alliance, the private contractor that helps operate the Space Shuttle at Kennedy Space Center, uses CCTV extensively. He commented:

> At the Kennedy Space Center, we have "Ops TV" with hundreds of CCTV cameras throughout the complex. Today's digital CCTV goes far beyond anything before, both from a cost standpoint and with regard to overall system integration. Tied into access, motion detection and other physical security solutions, CCTV is an integral part of our overall security and documentation efforts.

Large corporations were also using the technology. An example was Procter & Gamble, which marketed a broad range of well-known consumer products worldwide. Ed Casey, director of corporate security-worldwide for Procter & Gamble, commented:

> We are continually evaluating our security posture and making modifications as appropriate. There's no doubt that CCTV is a vital part of our overall security program. Our primary benefits have been in reviewing history after an event has occurred and in using CCTV to permit access through visual observation.

Gin believed that the size of the future CCTV market was difficult to predict for many reasons. He had no doubt that the market was growing, but few understood how fast it was to grow and the reasons for it. It was Gin's belief that convergence of technologies and the world's acceptance of CCTV were the two key factors. Statistics were showing that crime was actually decreasing in America, due in part to CCTV technology. This decrease in crime would increase the desire for CCTV. Any amount of crime is not accepted or desired in a society that was becoming very technology-tolerant, thanks to convergence. Television news coverage of convictions made possible by CCTV would fuel more demand for the technology. If CCTV cameras could help deter crime at convenience stores, they would also deter vandalism at schools and be useful at hospitals, prisons and even in homes. A future world with PCs, LANs, high-bandwidth Internet, cell phones, satellite phones and PDAs would all make use of CCTV. In America, a litigious society would want CCTV cameras to protect owners from all kinds of concerns not even related to crime.

Competitors

Typically, CCTV equipment was sold to the customer through distributors or intermediaries. The market was highly fragmented, with no one supplier achieving majority share in any category. While customers paid distributors immediately or within 30 days, suppliers were generally paid 30 to 60 days after delivering product to distributors.

Pelco

An example of a significant competitor in Extreme CCTV's market space was Pelco, a large manufacturer from Southern California. It manufactured 2,500 CCTV products which were sold through a network of 3,500 dealers throughout the United States and in over 130 countries. These products included camera systems, cameras, lenses, enclosures, fixed domes, scanners, pan and tilts, mounts and adapters, and miscellaneous camera equipment. Pelco estimated that it had products in over 300,000 locations around the world. Privately held, with $600 million in annual sales, Pelco focused its efforts on providing excellent customer service, winning several top-supplier awards within the security industry, including Employer of the Year in 1998. In mid-2000, Pelco was expected to expand its workforce to 1,400 people by adding another manufacturing facility in California. In addition to its Californian base, Pelco had facilities in New York, training and sales offices in Las Vegas, Nevada, and in the Netherlands. It also operated a European distribution centre.

Silent Witness

Starting as a manufacturer of black-box data recorders for vehicles, Silent Witness Enterprises Ltd. (SW) was a Canadian public company trading on the Nasdaq. It sold products such as CCTV cameras, mobile surveillance equipment, video storage equipment, multiplexers and network transmission equipment. In 2000, SW had net profits of $5 million on sales of $40 million. It manufactured systems that could operate effectively in all types of weather and operating conditions. It had a worldwide network of 50 distributors and sold its systems to casinos, correctional institutions, government agencies, businesses and consumers. SW had increased its revenue at an average rate of 48 per cent per year since 1995, with earnings per share increasing 158 per cent over the same period.

The Creation of Extreme CCTV

While he was employed in the corporate world, Jack Gin never dreamed of owning his own business. If he had an entrepreneurial drive, it was satisfied through the "ownership" he took as a minority shareholder of the companies he worked in and in the challenges of his mandate, which had become his specialty: export business development. Trained as a structural engineer in British Columbia, Gin had become very successful in export sales of technology products and services. While at previous firms, Gin learned the security market inside and out and developed a thorough understanding of its technologies. But working for others proved to be increasingly stifling. Given an opportunity to start again, the engineer and marketer turned entrepreneur and founded Extreme CCTV in 1997. Larry Doan, director and sales manager, owned 10 per cent of Extreme CCTV and Jack Gin and his wife Sylvia Gin owned the other 90 per cent. All worked long hours and late nights designing prototypes, studying markets, identifying distributors and drafting business plans. Gin made sales calls, travelled to trade shows and wrote press releases, specification sheets and brochures. Gin recalled:

> We were driven to succeed, to build the company, but on our terms. I was a contrarian from the beginning—in a crowd of white sheep moving east, I was the black sheep walking west. Anyone else would have gone to Asia to pick up a CCTV product from Taiwan. I, however, flew to England, the most expensive place you could go to explore security products. I said to myself that since the British have the highest per capita usage of CCTV in the world it would stand to reason that they would be innovation leaders in the field. I cashed in some Air Canada Aeroplan Miles and flew over to England for free, stayed at cheap hotels and dropped off my business cards. Through the contacts with whom I reconnected, the idea for my Integrated Day/Night Camera came to fruition.

Extreme CCTV put a new twist on the surveillance camera. While other existing cameras captured video pictures by "seeing" the visible light, Gin's cameras emitted infrared light to allow them to "see" in the dark. His products would also correct for poor ambient lighting, much like a "fill-in flash" would make for a better photograph. Optimizing the latest LED-type, solid-state light sources, Gin and his tiny engineering team continued to hone what they called their "integrated day-night" technology. Compared with its competitors, Extreme CCTV cameras could penetrate further into the dark while consuming less power. There was no other product like it in the CCTV market. Within a month of starting in July 1997, Extreme CCTV released its first two products at the International Security Conference in New York. Soon after, the company had sold its first "Integrated Day/Night" CCTV cameras to a U.S. hospital to monitor patients who tended to wander.

From the first day of operations, Gin knew that the Canadian market would not be big enough to make his business profitable. Extreme CCTV began exporting to the United States, then to the United Kingdom, New Zealand and Taiwan.

A Tough Start Followed by Strong Growth

Gin found initial difficulty selling to the security industry. There were barriers to deal with that included credibility as a new company and impediments caused by competitors who were wary of Gin's track record of success in the industry. Not to be deterred, Gin focused on specialization and differentiation in order to gain industry notoriety while flanking the competitors. In the beginning, every sales order was special, but some offered great marketing "buzz." Applications that required the nighttime video monitoring of Apache military helicopters, wild lions in Africa and the backside of the HOLLYWOOD sign allowed the company to break through the credibility barrier.

With a tiny budget and a persistent sales and marketing effort, the international security community finally took notice of Gin's products. The infrared illuminators and Integrated Day Night™ cameras became known for their superb performance no other competitive product could come close to matching. Major distributors were compelled to take on Extreme CCTV's product line because of its unique edge and to satisfy a small-but-growing demand from significant end-users. Soon, Extreme CCTV technology was adopted by the Secret Service, the Drug Enforcement Agency, and several other government departments in the United States (see Exhibit 1).

In 1997, the first year of business, the company grossed Cdn$41,000. The following year, sales jumped to $416,000 and subsequently hit almost $3 million in 2000. By 2001, Gin was expecting to surpass $5 million in sales, employing 25 people in Burnaby. Extreme CCTV spent $150,000 annually in research and development expenses (see Exhibits 2, 3 and 4). In early 2001, Extreme CCTV continued to enjoy positive cash flow. When asked about Extreme CCTV's market share, Gin laughed:

> Market share suggests a finite concept, and most people think that your job as a marketing manager is to take other people's market and increase your share. I never go there. We prefer to create market. As engineers, we create products for new market categories. This takes creative ingenuity and a lot of marketing work, but then we get to own the category. On this basis, there would be no sharing; we would get it all until someone copies us!

Derwent Systems Ltd.

During his 1997 trip to the United Kingdom, Gin met Trevor Duffy, owner of Derwent Systems Ltd. (Derwent). Derwent had introduced an innovative product providing "even-illumination" to the security world. Even illumination from infrared light sources was key in producing effective coverage of monitored areas. Focused solely on the U.K. market, Derwent had thus far ignored the North American market.

Derwent was created in 1991 and was primarily owned by Anthony Whiting and Trevor Duffy. Based in Newcastle, United Kingdom, Derwent focused on building infrared illuminators. With a staff of two engineers working with them, Whiting and Duffy had been able to develop and commercialize world-class technology. Derwent had grown steadily, with sales of approximately $2.0 million in 1998 to $4.5 million in 2000. Both owners attended major product shows worldwide and kept abreast of competitive product development. With 20 employees in Newcastle, Derwent spent $150,000 annually in research and development expenses.

Since Gin was interested in expanding Extreme CCTV's reach beyond what could be achieved with North American-based distributors, both principals were interested in distributing each other's products in their respective markets, signing a distribution agreement. Derwent had recently introduced its new, even illumination UF500 infrared lamp, generating significant interest in the European security market. This lamp was considered by security industry experts to be the highest quality, highest performance infrared illuminator in the world (see Exhibit 5). The UF500 would be a great complement to Extreme CCTV's integrated day/night camera equipment, thought Gin. Gin sketched out how Derwent products would fit in Extreme CCTV's offering to North American dealers:

Extreme CCTV's Proposed Product Offering			
	Extreme CCTV	*Derwent*	*Competitor—Pelco*
Stand-Alone Cameras	X		X
Integrated Day/Night Cameras	X		
Infrared Low-Powered Illuminators	X	X	
Infrared High-Powered Illuminators		X	X

(Text continues on page 307)

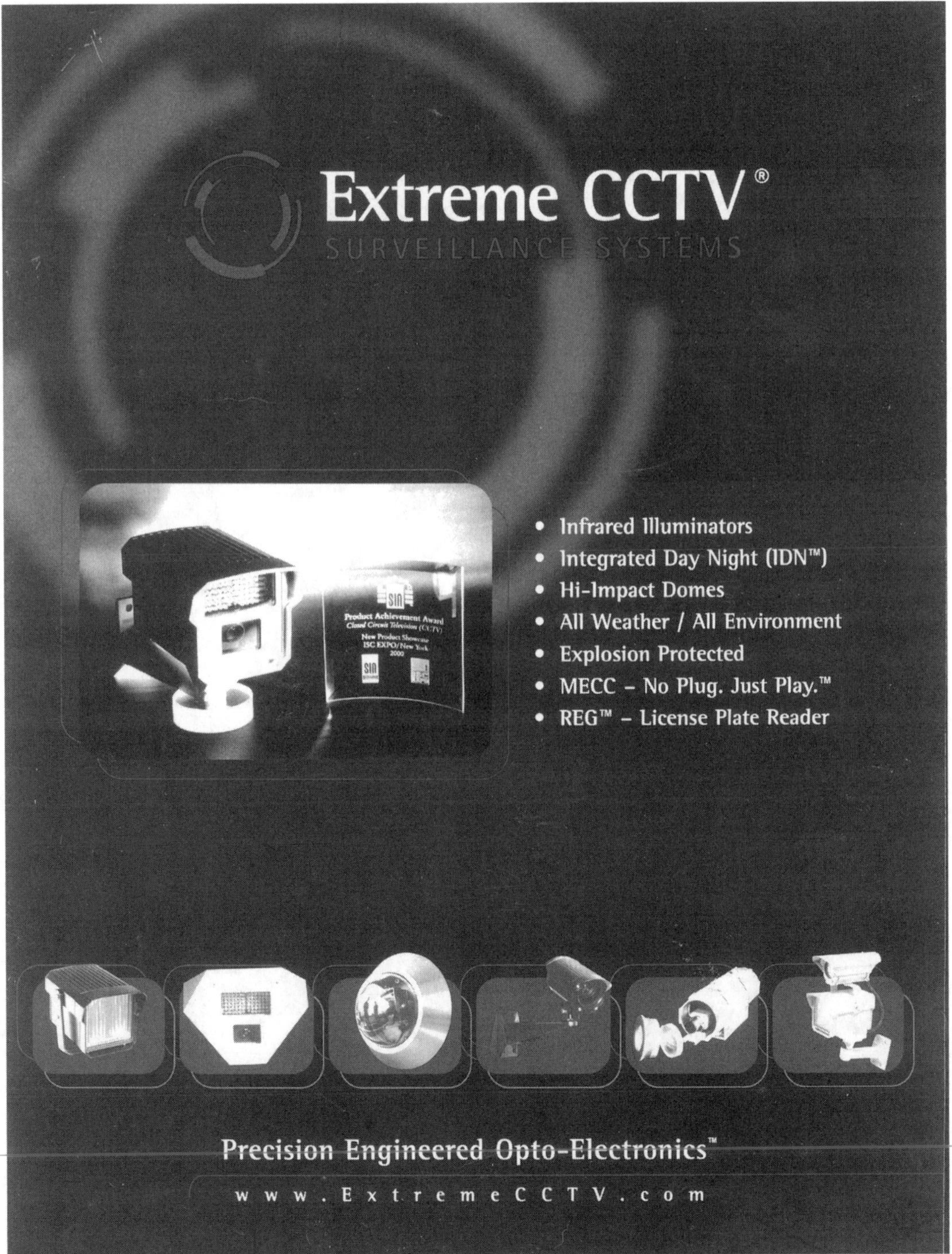

Exhibit 1 Extreme CCTV Products *(Continued)*

INTEGRATED

IDN™ by Extreme CCTV

Integrated Day Night Cameras

Designed specifically for a relentless 24/7 digital world, a new category of camera is introduced by the engineers of Extreme CCTV. When most security cameras sold today are "plug and play" for the optimum conditions of a daytime scene, customers are usually left with a poor or useless picture at night. A demanding 24/7 world would regard that as half a solution. In the world of Extreme CCTV, the IDN camera will get you a total solution.

Integrated into a single housing, the IDN camera by Extreme CCTV will create light, capture light and control the light to ensure a high-signal / low-noise picture under all day and all night conditions.

Today's security provider is expected to be a professional videographer. It is not enough to plug and play to take video-photos of whatever the ambient light allows.

"You don't take a photograph, you make it." ... Ansel Adams

And if there is no light, there can be no picture.

The IDN by Extreme CCTV raises the professional standard of video surveillance to a 24/7 day/night - all condition level.

IDN: Integrated for Day and Night Performance

We integrate a camera, lens, infrared illuminator, photocell, power regulator, control relay and a vandal resistant environmental housing. You make the simple BNC video connection and low voltage power leads.

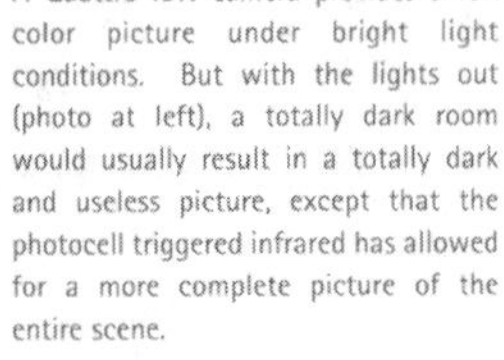

A Quattro IDN camera provides a full color picture under bright light conditions. But with the lights out (photo at left), a totally dark room would usually result in a totally dark and useless picture, except that the photocell triggered infrared has allowed for a more complete picture of the entire scene.

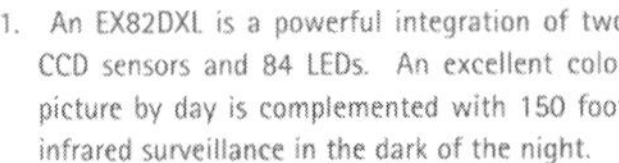

1. An EX82DXL is a powerful integration of two CCD sensors and 84 LEDs. An excellent color picture by day is complemented with 150 foot infrared surveillance in the dark of the night.

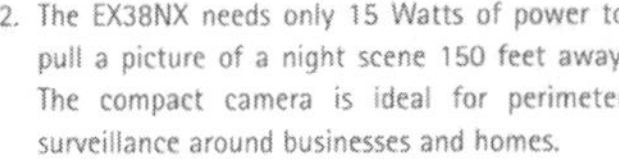

2. The EX38NX needs only 15 Watts of power to pull a picture of a night scene 150 feet away. The compact camera is ideal for perimeter surveillance around businesses and homes.

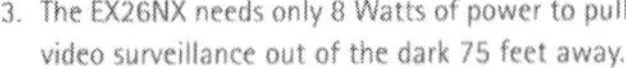

3. The EX26NX needs only 8 Watts of power to pull video surveillance out of the dark 75 feet away.

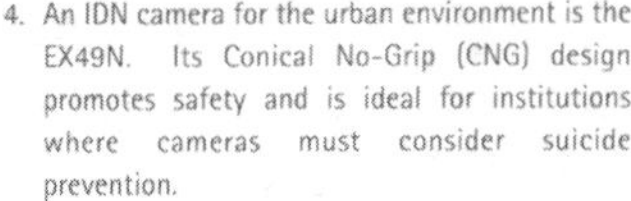

4. An IDN camera for the urban environment is the EX49N. Its Conical No-Grip (CNG) design promotes safety and is ideal for institutions where cameras must consider suicide prevention.

* denotes Patent Pending designs.

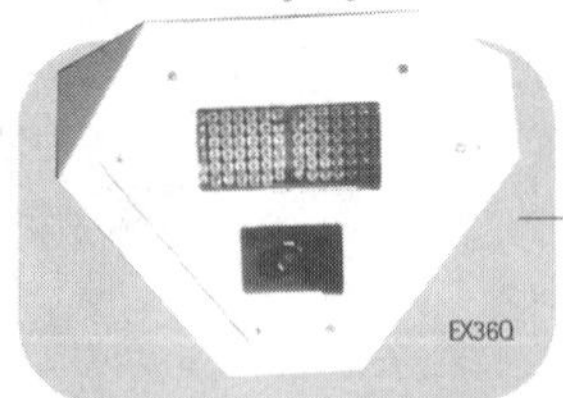

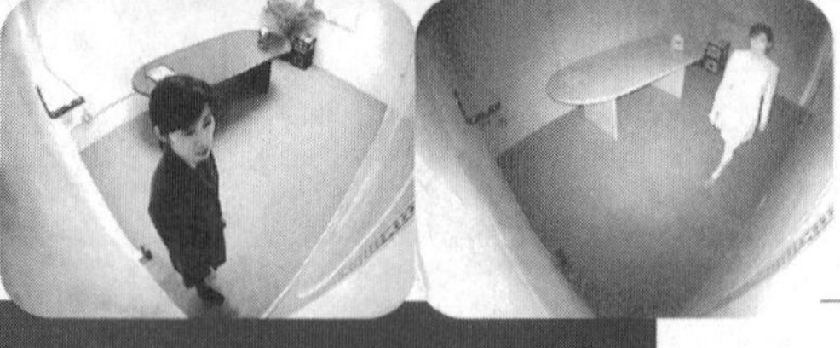

The EX36Q is a corner No-GRIP camera designed to get the full view of an entire room, its 4 walls and all of its floor on a 24 hour - day / night basis.

The unique design (patents pending) is specified for use in psychiatric rooms of hospitals and prisons. A color daytime scene (at far left) shows the entire room. The same room at night in total darkness is also within full view through even illumination in the infrared at 940 nanometers.

Exhibit 1 Extreme CCTV Products *(Continued)*

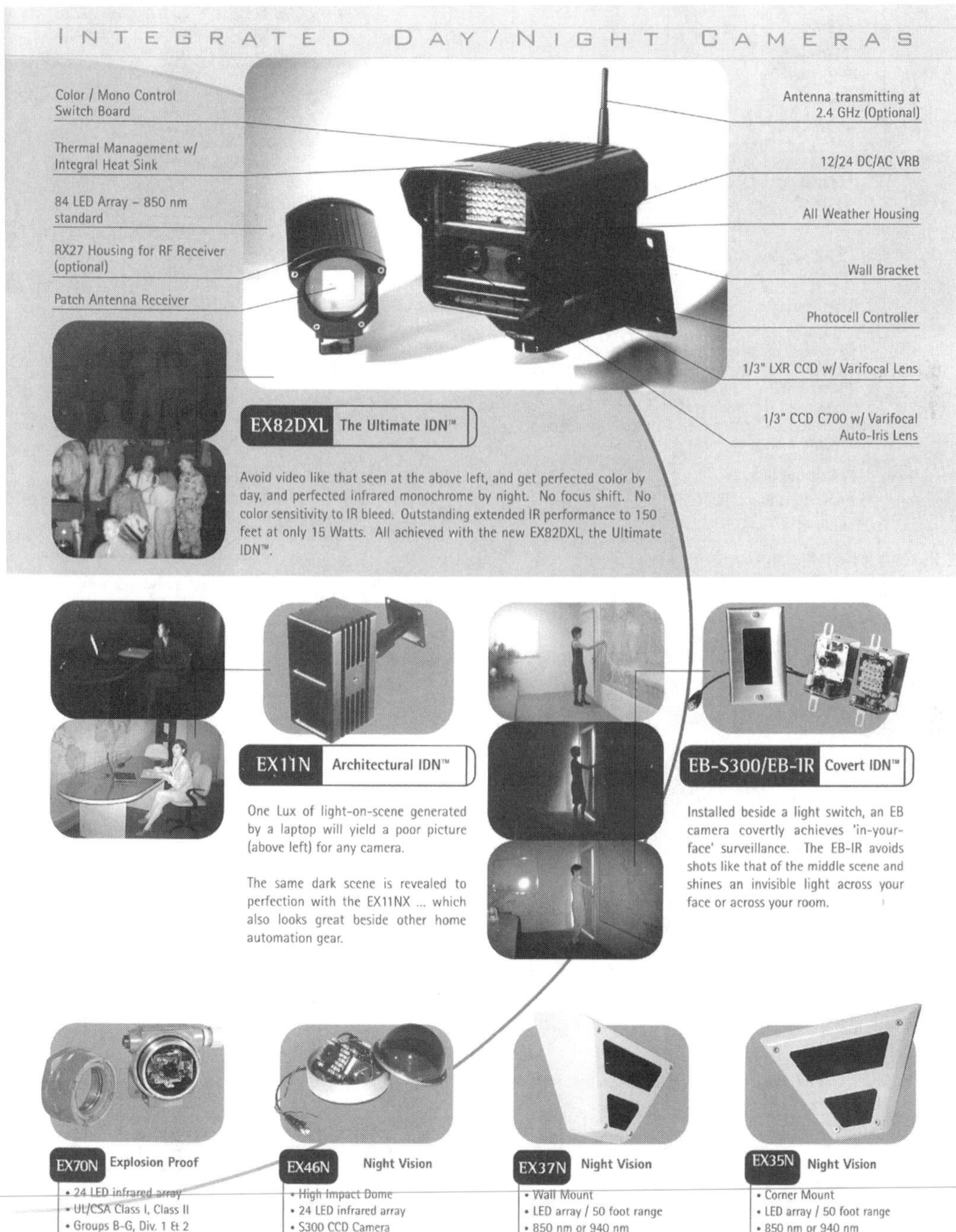

Exhibit 1 Extreme CCTV Products

Source: Company files.

Revenue	
Cost of Sales	$5,107,907
Gross Margin	2,836,843
Expenses	
Sales and Marketing	638,940
General and Administrative	465,143
Research and Development	37,401
Amortization of Capital Assets	47,806
Financing	16,783
	1,206,073
INCOME (Loss) Before Other Items, Provision for (Recovery of) Income, Taxes and Non-Controlling Interest	1,064,991
Other Items	
Bonuses	(500,000)
Gain (Loss) on Disposal of Assets	(17,436)
INCOME (Loss) Before Provision for (Recovery of) Income Taxes and Non-Controlling Interest	547,555
Provision for (Recovery of) Income Taxes	221,553
Income (Loss) Before Non-Controlling Interest	326,002
Non-Controlling Interest	9,093
Net Income (Loss)	335,095
Retained Earnings (Deficit)	
Beginning of Period	294,549
Retained Earnings (Deficit)	
End of Period	629,644

Exhibit 2 Extreme CCTV Inc. Consolidated Statement of Operations and Retained Earnings for the Period Ended February 28, 2001

Source: Company files.

Assets	
Current Assets	
Cash	$ 234,334
Accounts Receivable	1,418,377
Inventories	940,805
Future Income Taxes	—
Prepaid Expenses	19,363
	2,612,879
Capital Assets	78,545
Future Income Taxes	13,000
Total Assets	2,704,424
Liabilities	
Current Liabilities	
Accounts Payable and Accrued Liabilities	1,347,528
Income Taxes Payable	252,362
	1,599,890
Due to Program for Export Market Development	76,500
Due to Shareholders	394,432
Non-Controlling Interest	3,938
Total Liabilities	2,074,760
Shareholders' Equity	
Total Shareholders' Equity	629,664

Exhibit 3 Extreme CCTV Inc. Consolidated Balance Sheet as at February 28, 2001

Source: Company files.

Operating Activities	
Net Income (Loss)	335,095
Items Not Affecting Cash	
Amortization of Capital Assets	47,806
Loss (Gain) on Sale of Capital Assets	17,436
Non-Controlling Interest	(9,093)
Future Income Taxes	(13,000)
	378,244
Changes in Non-Cash Operating Accounts	(464,372)
	(86,128)
Investing Activities	
Purchase of Capital Assets	(105,994)
Financing Activities	
Due to Shareholders	61,158
Due to Program for Export Market Development	55,336
	116,494
Increase (Decrease) in Cash	(75,628)
CASH, Beginning of Period	309,962
Cash (Bank Indebtedness)	
End of Period	234,334
Cash Flows Include the Following Elements	
Interest Paid	16,783
Income Taxes Paid	3,000

Exhibit 4 Extreme CCTV Inc. Consolidated Statements of Cash Flows for the Period Ended February 28, 2001

Source: Company files.

Thus, the UF500 would give Gin an entry into another product segment: it would allow customers with existing video surveillance equipment to capture long-distance, outdoor, night-time images using infrared light. A customer could potentially purchase UF500 for use with current camera equipment (to monitor large spaces) and Extreme CCTV's Integrated Day/Night camera (to monitor confined spaces).

Gin recalled his initial dealings with Derwent:

> Through references in the security industry, Trevor and Tony (from Derwent) located me. It was June 1997, and they showed me their initial marketing plan to launch their products into North America. I said, "Trevor, you've got it wrong. I wouldn't do it that way. This is how you're going to have to do it." The byproduct of my being candid and showing them how to strategically position their product in North America was a gaining of their respect. At the time, I wasn't really interested in their product since I was developing my own, but they subsequently chased me down to represent their products in North America.
>
> The challenge for the Derwent brand was that our market lacked an appreciation for the benefits of infrared illumination. "The quality is evident but there's no market for your products in North America," said one prominent security distributor. I was reminded that distributors are averse to new technologies and sell what already sells—I would have to create a market for the UF500, which we thought was an opportunity instead of a problem! In September 1997, I picked a trade show in St. Louis, sold the UF500 to our first customer and never looked back (until now).

Over the past year, Derwent sold $220,000 worth of Extreme CCTV equipment in the United Kingdom, and Extreme CCTV sold nearly a million dollars worth of Derwent equipment in North America (see Exhibit 6).

INFRARED

Infrared Illuminators

Precision Engineered for Night Surveillance

If there is no light,
... there can be no picture.

Still photography is the art of capturing light. Surveillance photography is the art of capturing moving light.

In the convergence of a digital world, the technologies have become the same. In both cases, if there is no light, there can be no picture.

No portrait photographer in the world works without lighting equipment, the essential tools to "making" photos by creating and controlling light effects.

Yet most surveillance photographers today, simply "plug and play" to "take" video photos and accept whatever the ambient light allows.

At Extreme CCTV, we are raising the performance standard of video surveillance to a 24 hour – day/night, all-condition level.

We have mastered the art of creating infrared light for today's CCD camera. We filter the near-infrared. And we reflect it, shape it and control it to give you the power to get your picture under bright light, low light or no-light. With mastery of this "invisible light", we create the conditions that are necessary for optimal CCD camera performance.

Model UF500 is unlike any other illuminator. Recently awarded a U.S. Patent, its testimony to its high performance is its user list that includes the highest levels of government in the U.S., U.K. and Canada.

In the video-stills below, the human eye sees nothing in the dark scene at left, while the infrared supported camera (at right) sees it all. Uncovered at 700 feet (225 m) away, a government helicopter is monitored in the dark using twin UF500 infrared illuminators and an FSX800 camera.

See the Light. Get the Picture.™

1. Detected at 150 meters (500 feet) in total darkness, a runner is tracked with video motion detection (VMD). Even illumination in the infrared spectrum allows for pixel change detection which is vital for VMD. (videoprint copy, actual resolution is better)

2. Twin UF500 infrared illuminators are specified for proactive police surveillance throughout Europe. In the Americas, the UF500 has become the benchmark for high performance infrared and is used by defense, police and industry. It is the world's only patented infrared illuminator, unique in its ability to evenly illuminate a dark scene with infrared energy.

3. The UF-LED uses solid-state LEDs to achieve durable long life illumination to 200 feet. (60+ m).

4. The UF100 is a compact version of the UF500. It operates at 12 VDC and utilizes 70 Watts for its 250 foot (80 m) performance.

5. The EX25LED matches well with conventional CCTV cameras to achieve 24-7 day/night video at new or existing camera locations.

6. The EX60LED is an explosion-proof infrared illuminator commonly used in hazardous factory applications where additional lighting is required to support CCTV or machine vision.

The REEL DEAL™

All of the video-photos in this document are video-stills taken from real video surveillance to demonstrate Extreme CCTV equipment. (The performance you will see on your monitor will actually be BETTER.) We use no simulations. There are no fake portrayals. Even the animal shots are of the real wild. REEL DEAL video-stills are available to Extreme CCTV dealers to support your sales.

Exhibit 5 Derwent's UF500 (as seen in Extreme CCTV'S North American brochure) *(Continued)*

INFRARED NIGHT SURVEILLANCE

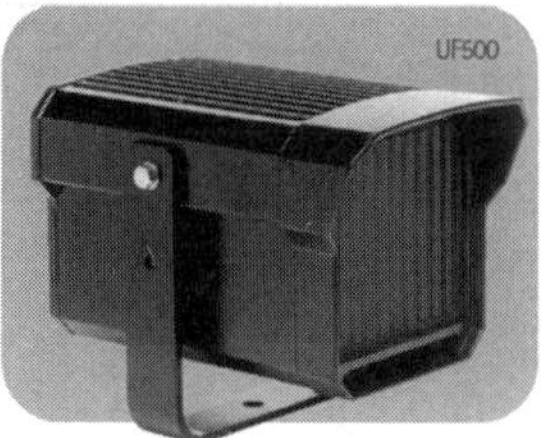

UF500 FEATURES:
- High output even-illumination
- No foreground overexposure
- Gold optics for greater I.R. efficiency
- 730 nm, 830 nm and 950 nm Filter models
- Spot, 10 deg, 30 deg and Flood Beam models
- Integrates with Pan/Tilt motors
- Low operating voltage / Long bulb life
- Uses 220 watts to outperform other 500 watt brands

UF500 Even-Distribution Infrared Illuminator

Patented design allows an even distribution of I.R. light for unsurpassed night viewing over 200 meters with dual illuminators (with twin lamps). This very special feature allows good infrared sensitive cameras to operate with a greater dynamic range to receive clear, low-noise pictures from foreground to a distant background in complete darkness.

Full Scene Even Illumination in the Infrared

Above: In the monitor photo of a dark night-time scene, the vehicle at 150 feet (50 m), the person at 300 feet (100 m) and the fence at 500 feet (160 m) are all clearly visible because of the even-illumination provided by dual 830 nm UF500 infrared lamps.

The MATRIX Chart
Night-Time Video Performance
for usable 20 db Signal/Noise video

Illuminator	Filter	Beam Shape	Camera Type	Distance Meters	Distance Feet
UF500 Twin	730 nm	10 deg Cosec	EX27SX800	245	760
UF500 Twin	730 nm	10 deg Cosec	Ikegami ICD47	245	760
UF500 Twin	730 nm	10 deg Cosec	Sanyo VCB-3574IR	220	680
UF500 Twin	830 nm	10 deg Cosec	EX27SX800	210	650
UF500 Twin	950 nm	10 deg Cosec	EX27SX800	165	510
UF500 Single	730 nm	10 deg Cosec	EX27SX800	170	525
UF500 Single	830 nm	10 deg Cosec	EX27SX800	150	465
UF500 Single	950 nm	10 deg Cosec	EX27SX800	115	355
UF500 Single	830 nm	30 deg Cosec	EX27SX800	100	310
UF500 Single	730 nm	10 deg Cosec	Mid-Performance	105	465
UF500 Single	730 nm	30 deg Cosec	Mid-Performance	75	230
UF500 Single	730 nm	60 deg Flood	Mid-Performance	55	170
UF100 Twin	730 nm	10 deg	EX27SX800	125	400
UF100 Twin	730 nm	10 deg	EX27S300	70	220
UF100 Single	830 nm	30 deg	EX27SX800	60	200
UFLED Single	850 nm	30 deg	EX27SX800	60	200
EX25LED Single	850 nm	30 deg	EX27SX800	30	100
EX12LED Single	850 nm	30 deg	EX12S300	15	45

- Infrared performance is affected by choice of cameras and lenses, and by atmospheric weather conditions.
- Specifications for cameras and lenses subject to change without notice.
- The entire MATRIX Chart is a valuable resource for infrared video performance data on many CCTV cameras. The MATRIX Chart is available only to Extreme CCTV dealers and their customers, and is updated regularly by Extreme engineers in Canada and the UK.

Why is Infrared Important?

1. Infrared allows for proactive policing by capturing night-crime events in locations of high crime-probability.
2. Infrared night-time surveillance is demanded in a 24/7 digital world.
3. Infrared allows for video evidence not possible to attain with visible light.
4. Night surveillance is often more important than daytime surveillance.
5. Infrared allows Video Motion Detection (VMD) functions in DVRs to work better at night by decreasing picture noise.
6. The alternative of using bright lighting of large areas is much more expensive than strategically placed infrared lighting.

Recent Applications:

US DEA	Traffic monitoring on river
US DOD	Undisclosed sites
US Secret Service	Undisclosed sites
US National Guard	Military equipment security
UK Royal Navy	Perimeter surveillance at base
UK Government	Embassies worldwide
Canadian Prisons	Perimeter surveillance
Windsor Castle	Queen's residence security
City of Hollywood	HOLLYWOOD sign security

EX45LED
- High Impact Dome
- ~~42 LED infrared array~~
- Pan/Tilt adjustable
- local area illuminator

EX12LED
- Anodized Aluminum
- ~~42 LED infrared array~~
- Weatherproof CNC Case
- local area illuminator

LED BULLET™
- Discreet IR
- ~~30 LED infrared array~~
- Universal Bracket
- local area illuminator

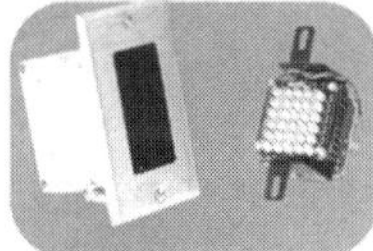

EB-IR
- Discreet Gang Box IR
- ~~32 LED infrared array~~
- Pan/Tilt adjustable
- local area illuminator

Exhibit 5 Derwent's UF500 (as seen in Extreme CCTV'S North American brochure)

Source: Company files.

	*Extreme CCTV Products Sold in United Kingdom via Derwent**	*Derwent Products Sold in North America via Extreme CCTV*
1999	$215,154	$656,546
2000	$220,344	$993,161

Exhibit 6 Extreme CCTV/Derwent Distribution Agreement Sales

*£1 = Cdn$2.265

	2000 (Actual)	*1999 (Actual)*	*1998 (Actual)*
Turnover	$4,514,372	$3,126,413	$2,677,361
Cost of Sales	2,692,675	1,987,562	1,538,506
Gross Profit	1,821,696	1,138,851	1,138,856
Administrative Expenses	1,495,546	915,821	770,419
Operating Profit	326,151	223,030	368,436
Profit on Sale of Fixed Assets	5,352	3,398	—
Interest Receivable	10,673	9,062	21,769
Interest Payable	(6,331)	(4,202)	(4,990)
Profit on Ordinary Activities Before Taxation	335,845	231,288	385,215
Tax on Ordinary Activities	71,973	58,682	73,599
Profit on Ordinary Acitivites After Taxation	263,873	172,607	311,616
Dividends	(104,761)	(11,325)	(19,046)
Retained Profit	159,111	161,282	292,570

Exhibit 7 Derwent Systems Ltd. Profit and Loss Accounts* for the Years Ending December 31

*Generally accepted auditing standards as applied to the audit of Derwent Systems Ltd. financial statements were substantially equivalent to generally accepted auditing standards in Canada as established by the Canadian Institute of Chartered Accountants.

Note: All amounts have been converted to Canadian dollars at Cdn$2.265 per British pound.

The Derwent Purchase Opportunity

Duffy had contacted Gin in early 2001, saying that he wanted to retire from the security business. That meant that Derwent would have to be sold. He proposed that Gin acquire Derwent for one million British pounds (about Cdn$2.26 million) in cash (see Exhibit 7 and 8). Facing explosive growth in his own company, Gin was hesitant at first. What was he buying in Derwent? Since he would be expected to pay for the acquisition in cash, how would he ensure that there was adequate cash for both companies to grow?

Gin planned to go ahead with an Extreme CCTV IPO in early 2002—could he afford to let this consume his attention? Lastly, Gin wondered how he would manage both companies in the coming months.

Notes

1. Taken from the Ivey #9B00M004—"Silent Witness Enterprises" by Professor Charlene Nicholls-Nixon and Adam Fremeth.
2. Ibid.

	2000 (Actual)	*1999 (Actual)*	*1998 (Actual)*
Fixed Assets			
Tangible Assets	$257,431	$224,933	$239,882
Current Assets			
Stock and Work in Progress	540,354	270,874	181,359
Debtors	1,323,168	894,548	573,444
Cash at Bank and in Hand	489,591	228,287	480,495
	2,353,113	1,393,709	1,235,297
Creditors: Amounts Falling Due Within One Year	(1,498,402)	(652,950)	(659,582)
Net Current Assets	854,711	740,759	575,715
Total Assets Less Current Liabilities	1,112,142	965,692	815,597
Creditors: Amounts Falling Due After More Than One Year	(36,267)	(42,910)	(2,682)
Net Assets	1,075,875	922,781	788,680
Capital and Reserves			
Share Capital	33,975	54,360	81,540
Other Reserves	61,155	40,770	13,590
Profit and Loss Account	980,745	827,651	693,550
Total Shareholders' Funds	$1,075,875	$922,781	$788,680

Exhibit 8 Derwent Systems Ltd. Balance Sheets for the Years Ending December 31

Source: Company files.

Note: All amounts have been converted to Canadian dollars at Cdn$2.265 per British pound.

VanCity Savings Credit Union: Corporate Venturing Into Uncharted Waters

Prepared by Devkamal Dutta and Diane Friedman under the supervision of Professor Stewart Thornhill

Version: (A) 2002-10-18

On the morning of September 15, 1998, Bob Williams, board member at VanCity Savings Credit Union (VanCity) and chair of the three-member corporate venturing committee (CVC), was giving finishing touches to the presentation he and his two colleagues had lined up for the board meeting in about an hour. Williams believed that this was going to be one of the most important strategic decisions the VanCity board would be making in the years to come. Much would depend on how effectively he was able to articulate the findings of the CVC. Today's board meeting would bring to culmination months of intensive strategic deliberations by Williams and his team about whether VanCity needed to venture into the previously uncharted waters of mezzanine financing.

VanCity: A Successful Story in Community Banking

With $7.5 billion in assets, 275,000 members and 39 branches throughout Greater Vancouver, the Fraser Valley and Victoria, VanCity was Canada's largest credit union. It was founded in 1946 to provide financial services to people from all walks of life and served as a major financial institution in British Columbia.

Values

VanCity prided itself on being a member-oriented organization, serving the communities where it is based. Its corporate philosophy was to be "a democratic, ethical and innovative provider of financial services to its members." Being member-controlled, it was committed to delivering solutions that would help its members and communities achieve their financial goals, with the members participating in the decisions that affected their credit unions operations. VanCity's statement of values and commitments is depicted in Exhibit 1.

Current Performance

In 1998, VanCity's consolidated assets stood at $5.9 billion, representing a growth of $328 million during the year. Deposits grew by $672 million and earnings from operations were $38.6 million. Net earnings for the year stood at $23.5 million. VanCity was able to distribute $6.8 million in earnings to its members and to the communities with which it did business. In keeping with its philosophy of corporate social responsibility, VanCity also contributed $1.6 million to fund various community projects during the year.

In 1998, VanCity released its first comprehensive social audit report. The year also marked the VISA Centre's first year of operations, which helped VanCity to increase its credit card base by 44 per cent. During the year, VanCity co-hosted "Standards for the New Millennium," the first North American conference on social and ethical auditing, accounting and reporting. This was done in partnership with the Ethics Practitioners Association of Canada and the U.K.-based Institute of Social and Ethical Accountability. VanCity exceeded its sales objectives for the Family of Ethical Funds by 29 per cent and launched a new advertising and promotion campaign that positioned it as the right and smart choice for financial services. The Credit Union coined the statement "It's right here" to depict its commitment of corporate social responsibility and its desired role as a quality financial services provider. To improve its operational efficiency, VanCity installed a centralized automated teller machine administration that enabled branch staff to spend more time on developing member relationships.

The financial highlights of the year 1998, as well as those of the two preceding years, are provided in Exhibit 2.

Emerging Strategic Priorities

1997–98 had been an eventful period for VanCity. The pace of globalization in financial services, increased competition and changing expectations of members had forced that the Credit Union to rethink its methods of conducting business for the coming years. Comparatively higher levels of unemployment and social stress in the region demanded that the organization look for innovative ways to assist its members and communities achieve their financial goals. To be able to meet these environmental pressures, it was time for VanCity to initiate a transformation process that would prepare for and lead into the future.

VanCity management identified relationship building as the key strategy of the future. This initiative would aim at strengthening the Credit Union's member relationships and would be achieved by proactively anticipating member needs, providing knowledgeable and responsive service, and assisting members to achieve their financial goals. By 1998, VanCity had outlined its change program and had implemented that program in 24 of its branches.

The benefits of the Internet and communication technologies allowed routine transactions to shift to electronic support systems, thus

As VanCity grows and changes, there are some things that will never change—our purpose and values. VanCity's Statement of Values and Commitments was created in consultation with our members, staff and communities and provides a framework for how we do business. It will guide our business decisions and strategies, ensuring that we stay true to the values that have made us strong.

Our Mission

To be a democratic, ethical, and innovative provider of financial services to our members.
Through strong financial performance, we serve as a catalyst for the self-reliance and economic well-being of our membership and community.

Our Purpose

Working with people and communities to help them thrive and prosper.

Our Values

Integrity: We act with courage, consistency and respect to do what is honest, fair and trustworthy.
Innovation: We anticipate and respond to challenges and changing needs with creativity, enthusiasm and determination.
Responsibility: We are accountable to our members, employees, colleagues and communities for the results of our decisions and actions.

Our Commitments

We make the following commitments in order to live our purpose and values in how we do business. Our aim is to strengthen VanCity's long-term business while contributing to the well-being of our members, staff, communities and the environment.

We will be responsible and effective financial managers so VanCity remains strong and prospers.

This means we will:

- Make sound business decisions to achieve solid financial results;
- Manage risks responsibly to safeguard vancity's assets;
- Prudently exercise fiduciary responsibility with members' deposits.

We will provide you with outstanding service and help you achieve your financial goals.

This means we will:

- Treat you with respect and dignity;
- Give you trustworthy advice about your financial options;
- Offer products and services that meet your unique needs and provide good value;
- Protect your right to privacy;
- Ensure that low income and marginalized members have access to necessary financial services.

We will provide meaningful opportunities for you to have input in setting the direction of the credit union.

This means we will:

- Make it easy and straightforward to vote and provide you with information to make informed decisions;
- Offer multiple channels for you to provide us with input and feedback;
- Address your concerns in a timely manner.

We will ensure that VanCity is a great place to work.

This means we will:

- Create a workplace that is healthy, diverse, stimulating and rewarding;
- Provide the leadership, tools, resources and opportunities for employees to do their best work;
- And achieve their full potential;
- Respect and honour employees' responsibilities to their families, friends and communities.

We will lead by example and use our resources and expertise to effect positive change in our communities.

This means we will:

- Leverage our unique skills and expertise as a financial institution to create solutions to social, environmental and economic issues;
- Model and advocate socially and environmentally responsible business practices;
- Seek business partners who practise progressive employee relations, contribute to the well-being of their communities and respect the environment;
- Invest our dollars responsibly in the communities where we live and work.

We will be accountable for living up to our commitments.

This means we will:

- Make continuous and measurable progress in meeting our commitments;
- Involve our members, staff and communities in measuring our performance and report the findings in a public, externally verified report.

Exhibit 1 VanCity's Statement of Values and Commitments

	1998	*1997*	*1996*
Assets			
Cash and Securities	550,722	503,940	385,030
Loans	5,212,914	4,946,842	4,299,867
Other Assets	154,514	139,758	117,732
Total Assets	5,918,150	5,590,540	4,802,629
Liabilities and Members' Equity			
Deposits and Equity Shares	5,359,291	4,687,703	4,081,405
Debentures and Loans Payable	187,710	559,951	414,780
Other Liabilities	144,322	139,591	120,357
Retained Earnings	226,827	203,295	186,087
Total Liabilities and Members' Equity	5,918,150	5,590,540	4,802,629
Statements of Earnings			
Net Interest Income	149,751	140,668	118,025
Charge for Impairment of Loans	(5,516)	(5,101)	(3,553)
Other Income	41,619	32,837	27,632
Net Interest and Other Income	185,854	168,404	142,104
Salaries and Employee Benefits	78,415	68,263	55,986
Other Operating Expenses	68,864	69,523	51,038
Total Operating Expenses	147,279	137,786	107,024
Earnings From Operations	38,575	30,618	35,080
Donations to Foundation	600	775	600
Distribution to Members	6,420	8,641	7,835
Income Taxes	8,023	3,944	6,037
Net Earnings for the Year	23,532	17,258	20,608
Statistics			
Average Assets	5,738,457	5,112,619	4,631,941
Growth of Total Assets (%)	5.86	16.41	9.94
Return on Assets (%)	0.41	0.34	0.45
Dividends per Equity Share	5.0	5.0	5.0
Dividends per Investment Share	5.6	6.0	7.3
Membership	261,613	252,638	231,558
Number of Employees (full-time eqvt.)	1,513	1,417	1,265
Number of Branches	42	42	38

Exhibit 2 VanCity Credit Union—Consolidated Financial Performance

challenging staff to adopt the role of planners, advisors and consultants. The branches were fast becoming financial hubs where members would plan their financial futures with VanCity's staff as advisors. An important part of the corporate change program was to provide staff with training, not only to upgrade their technical and operational skills but also to make them better facilitators of relationship management.

An important offshoot of the new strategy was to re-establish VanCity's high commitment to the small business sector. To better serve those members who had difficulty accessing traditional business loans, VanCity took the significant step of integrating its micro-lending programs into its business services group. The result was that even members who lacked a credit history or collateral could obtain financing to set up their own businesses.

In tandem with its strategic renewal program, VanCity also committed substantial resources to make all its internal systems and installations Y2K ready. Specialized internal teams were formed to extend this preparedness through to VanCity's suppliers as well.

Mezzanine Financing and SMEs

Small and medium enterprises (SMEs), especially in fast growth industries, play an important role in terms of innovation and introduction of new products and services. In 1998, SMEs in Canada were facing challenges brought about by increasing competitive pressures due to globalization, liberalization of trade and infusion of new technology. It was believed that the next few years would lead to a general shake-out in the economy, and only those companies that would reach out to customers with higher quality products and services at competitive prices would survive. This meant there would be an increasing requirement by SMEs to upgrade themselves technologically as well as organizationally, which would call for financial resources that could aid in their growth.

Financing needs of SMEs vary according to the stage in their business life cycle. Depending on the life cycle of the enterprise, merchant banking services to SMEs comprise several kinds of financial assistance. Exhibit 3 provides more details. Mezzanine financing is a kind of hybrid finance that fits between senior debt and common equity. It is a useful route to raising additional funds when available assets have already been pledged as collateral, but free cash flows can be leveraged. Mezzanine financing typically resembles debt in its structure but can have some equity features. The debt instrument is subordinated to senior creditors and, to compensate an investor for higher risk (relative to secured debt), the return on mezzanine financing is correspondingly higher. An investor will realize their return with a combination of coupon interest and equity participation, where the latter can take the form of warrants or shares that entitle the investor (lender) to buy shares of the firm's stock at a stated price.

Mezzanine financing becomes especially important when enterprises are looking for financing to support their objectives of rapid growth. Mature businesses obtain bank financing because of their track record, asset base and equity. But given that conventional lenders require collateral in the form of tangible assets rather than innovative ideas and potential before they lend money, fast growing SMEs may require capital above and beyond the capacity of conventional financing. This is where mezzanine financing can help a company with immediate working capital requirements to fund increases in inventory, accounts receivables, marketing expenses, ongoing research and development, etc. Mezzanine financing assists such enterprises because lenders accord more importance to characteristics such as a strong management team, industry growth opportunities and profitability, rather than to balance sheet figures. Accordingly, with sufficient due diligence, funds are loaned without collateral support.

Major Players in Mezzanine Financing

In 1998, the following players provided mezzanine financing in British Columbia:

Primary Source	*Development*	*Startup*	*Early*	*Rapid Growth*	*Exit Growth*
Entrepreneur	■				
Friends and Family	■				
Angel Investors	■	■			
Strategic Partner	■	■			
Venture Capital		■	■	■	
Asset-Based Lender		■	■	■	
Equipment Lessor		■	■	■	
Small Business Investment Companies			■	■	
Trade Credit			■	■	
Factor			■	■	
Mezzanine Lender				■	■
Public Debt					■
IPO					■
Acquisition, LBO, MBO					■

Exhibit 3 Life Cycle Model of New-Venture Financing

Source: Smith, J. K. and Smith, R. L. (2000): *Entrepreneurial Finance.* New York: John Wiley & Sons, Inc.

Business Development Bank of Canada

The Business Development Bank of Canada (or BDC), a financial institution wholly owned by the Government of Canada, delivered financial and consulting services to SMEs, primarily in high-tech, export-oriented and rapid-growth businesses. The BDC's mission was to "make a unique and significant contribution to the success of dynamic and innovative entrepreneurship for the benefit of all Canadians."[1] With over 80 branches and a virtual branch (BDC Connex) spread across Canada, BDC had prided itself as Canada's bank for small business for over 50 years.

In 1995, when the BDC initiated a program of strategic change, its legislation was updated and the bank was given a revised mandate. No longer the "lender of last resort," the bank's role was redefined so that it could fulfil a role complementary to other commercial functions.

The BDC provided a range of term loan and consulting products and services to the small business sector: secured loans (available on easier terms than conventional bank loans), subordinated debt financing (focused on fast-growing manufacturers, exporters, new economy enterprises and management buyouts), venture capital (equity investments in high-tech and biotech sectors), and consulting (services to potential borrowers so that they implement effective strategies to compete and grow).

RoyNat Capital

Formed in 1962, RoyNat Capital (or RoyNat) was the merchant-banking arm of Scotiabank. It was a provider of term debt, subordinated debt, mezzanine financing and equity to SMEs. RoyNat promised "more than money" and helped in the growth efforts of successful businesses through creative financial solutions, strong customer relationships and active referral networks.

RoyNat's target customers were enterprises with revenues in the $5 million to $200 million range. It provided them with a full range of financing services: funds for acquiring fixed assets, refinancing existing borrowings, working capital, mergers and acquisitions and succession planning. Where necessary, RoyNat could also provide customers with consulting support. RoyNat's service groups included:

- RoyNat Business Capital (the U.S. merchant bank headquartered in Cleveland, Ohio, and focused on assisting Canadian companies that required financing for their U.S. operations, expansion and acquisition, and U.S. companies that required similar services in Canada).
- RoyNat Capital Corporate Finance (worked with clients to execute mergers, acquisitions and divestitures, arranged strategic partnerships, helped raise capital for both private and public companies).
- RoyNat Capital Partners (provided a forum by which owners of mid-market companies could evaluate the underlying value of their business and the issues and opportunities that challenged them).

Bank of Montreal Capital Corporation

In 1966, the Bank of Montreal set up the Bank of Montreal Capital Corporation (BMO Capital). The objective was to provide specialized financing and venture capital to small- and medium-sized Canadian businesses to reach their full potential.

BMO Capital provided quasi-equity and equity financing of up to $5 million to businesses that had a strong growth potential. It provided these funds at all stages of the business life cycle of an enterprise.

HSBC Capital

HSBC Capital offered both private equity financing and shorter term capital (or bridge financing) to companies with strong cash flow or high prospects for more permanent financing.

With respect to equity investments, HSBC's objective was to substantially increase the value of the investee company by introducing new capital, as well as by offering strategic and financial advice. They were medium-term, minority investors, generally looking to employ capital for three to seven years, with ownership limited to not more than 49 per cent and a clear exit strategy developed at the outset. Investments were chosen on the basis of potential return, and capital could be provided for a variety of purposes, including: internal growth financing, leveraged and management buyout transactions, shareholder reorganizations and financing for acquisitions. Selected turnarounds would be considered but they did not invest in startup or early-stage situations.

Mercantile Bancorp Limited

Mercantile Bancorp Limited (Mercantile) was a private merchant investment company with offices in Vancouver and Calgary. Mercantile specialized in providing capital and advisory services to emerging and mid-sized businesses and had been investing in Western Canada since 1989. Mercantile invested capital on behalf of some of Canada's largest institutional investors in conjunction with the personal capital of its management team, with a principal focus in Western Canada and selective involvement in other geographic areas.

Mercantile was capitalized with $48.5 million, which was targeted at investing in businesses in the industrial, service and consumer products sectors. Target companies included both private and "micro-cap" public companies, with sales typically ranging from $3 million to $50 million. Mercantile was registered as a portfolio manager with the British Columbia Securities Commission.

Mercantile invested between $1 million and $7 million per transaction in emerging, middle-market, private and public companies for management and leveraged buyouts, acquisitions and divestitures, growth and project-related expansions, and restructurings and turnarounds. Mercantile provided capital in the form of debt, mezzanine debt, equity and/or bridge debt financing and may initiate or participate in larger syndicated transactions.

The Mezzanine Venture Proposal

In early 1998, VanCity was wrestling with the question of how to expand its service to SMEs and achieve growth within the Credit Union. It was decided that senior board member Bob Williams would assemble a team to work on the question of emerging regional opportunities and the creation of a new subsidiary of VanCity. The new subsidiary, initially named the Regional Development Corporation (RDC), would deal with mezzanine financing and subordinated debt, while keeping to VanCity's overall objective of generating additional employment and regional and economic development in British Columbia.

The next few months went by with Williams and his team meeting every month. The basic objective was to identify the market niche, if any, where VanCity could play a bigger role. Williams believed that the best opportunities would be found within the business sector. In addition, other issues required consideration as well: the new RDC would need to absorb the culture of VanCity and at the same time be distinct from it. Would that mean it would continue to support not-for-profit organizations? If so, would it become an extended arm of the parent or should it instead be distinct and look at only for-profit businesses? These were the issues upon which the RDC's business plan would hinge. Williams felt that by supporting non-profit organizations, albeit in a professional manner as if they were business organizations, the RDC would retain its roots with VanCity. This would also help the business create value in the marketplace and differentiate itself from its competitors.

> It does seem to me that a fair number of the principles around venturesome lending could apply to the non-profit sector. We need to think about it in the context of asset development that's going on with individuals in the United States and pilot projects we have here. I think we have to find a few different routes than those we have applied so far, in terms of making this idea work. I think our goal should be something like 10 per cent of our business from the new entity would be from non-profits. Many business leaders to whom we have spoken informally have said that they're not really sure that there's enough demand here, that there's a real need, or that we have that amount of entrepreneurial talent here that would benefit from this new entity. I think it's a neat question in terms of how big the market is, but I don't think there's much doubt in terms of who we are that there's a real need, and it's going to continue to grow. I think it has to be about seeing the opportunity out there in the marketplace.

In the course of his work within and outside VanCity, Williams met a few officials from Shore Bank Chicago at a conference on SMEs and financing. He decided to consult with them as they had recently gone through the same kind of questions before they ventured into business lending. Shore Bank had pioneered banking in the south side of Chicago, essentially an African-American neighborhood. In the exercise of doing their work, they discovered that if they were to be more relevant in the neighborhood, they had to understand the neighborhoods of industry around them as well, at least in terms of generating employment for the people in those communities who generally weren't part of the industrial neighborhood game. So, in turn, Shore Bank became superb industrial commercial lenders and developed a capacity with subordinated debt and similar instruments.

By July, Williams and his team were giving shape to the basic contours of a business plan for the new RDC.

Excerpts From the Business Plan

The business plan drafted by Williams and his team recommended that the new entity would begin its operations in January 1999, with an initial capitalization of $11.5 million. At the end of three years of operations, additional capital of $10 million to $15 million would be required to make the RDC self sufficient. However, as the lump sum payment of $11.5 million would not optimize capital adequacy and taxation issues for VanCity, the capital would be arranged through staged payments over the first three years of the RDC's operations. Additionally, the credit union management would have to provide an operating subsidy to the RDC for the first three years, after which it was expected to become profitable.

The overall vision for RDC was coined as: "To create a profitable source of risk capital and management support to successful business people who can ultimately strengthen the communities they operate in."[2] In order to operationalize this vision, the RDC would attempt to leverage and spread the value and recognition of the VanCity brand into the business community. Similarly, in the non-profit and co-operative sectors, the RDC would endeavor to develop an innovative package of services to bring to its borrowers.

It was anticipated that in its first year of operations, the RDC would make 20 loans approximating $4.1 million, generating an operating loss of $900,000. With additional capital, this would progressively increase to 45 loans for $9 million in year five, generating an operating profit of $400,000. The RDC would breakeven in its fourth year of operation.

Based on a critical analysis of the mezzanine financing industry in Canada and the players operating within it, Williams and his team identified the target market for the new RDC as "well-managed companies with some track record of success, who are at a threshold in the development of their business." This was meant to include the following categories of fast-growth ventures in the SME sector:

- Expansion to new markets,
- Entry into export markets,
- Development of new products,
- Acquisition of a complementary business,
- Purchase of assets to expand or improve operations,
- Working capital to accommodate growth, and
- Venture-backed companies whose planned IPO is delayed.

After initial deliberations, Williams and his team decided that while the RDC would consider funding startup situations, these would usually be avoided unless there was a strong business reason for doing so. In line with the scope of and the demand for mezzanine financing, the RDC would fuel the growth of fast-growing, existing businesses. Also, the nature of the products and services being offered (high-yield debt) was not well suited to startup situations. Exhibit 4 provides details of the package of products and services that the RDC would offer to its target customers. The business plan suggested that buy-out financing would be considered for management groups to facilitate succession planning issues or where a new management team could revitalize and grow an existing business.

In terms of its market entry strategy, the RDC would establish industry specializations based on market intelligence. The plan suggested that the strategy's core would be built around being opportunistic in finding the best companies and management teams to finance. As the portfolio grew, sectors of significant opportunity would emerge, and the RDC would capitalize on these. With the RDC being complementary to other lenders, referrals could be sought from chartered banks and credit unions, while partnering on some deals with competitors such as the BDC.

Williams and his team determined that in the first year of operations, the RDC would seek to underwrite 16 loans, eight loans per lender. This was slightly higher productivity than that of similar lenders, but given that the RDC would operate as a flexible structure with the requisite level of independence, it was still an achievable goal. In fact, Williams expected it would be possible to achieve a more ambitious productivity target of 12 loans per year per lender in the future.

Initial calculations suggested that the expected average loan size of $200,000 to $250,000 would produce a volume $3.5 million to $4 million. An additional four loans in the civil and co-operative sector would be sanctioned in the first year.

Amount:	$50,000 to $500,000 (average size is expected to be in the $250,000 range). Opportunities over $500,000 will be syndicated for portfolio diversification.
Pricing:	Prime plus 6%–10% (combination of interest, premiums, royalties, options, bonuses, etc.)
	Application fee of 1%, annual administration fee .5%
Amortization:	24 to 60 months, usually no principal payments for six to 12 months
Security:	GSA ranking behind senior creditors, specific charge on fixed assets we finance, intellectual property if available. No security value will usually be assigned.
Location:	Lower mainland targeted. The venture can operate anywhere in British Columbia if an opportunity arises.
Exclusions:	Real estate development, natural resource extraction

Exhibit 4 Suggested Products and Services Package for the Venture

Source: Company files.

Borrowers in this category would be eligible for lower interest premiums than those for regular commercial clients. The actual number and dollar volume of loans generated would be affected by the economic conditions in the market as well as by pricing, specifically whether customers would accept the cost versus opportunity rationale and whether other players would undercut prices. Recently, it had been brought to Williams' attention that some institutions, backed by government guarantees, were attempting significantly riskier deals at artificially low pricing.

However, Williams felt the risk of a price war was mitigated by the fact that the RDC would do relatively low volume, only 16 deals per year. The RDC's objective would be to set its sights on unique opportunities with companies that would be willing to pay for a creative structuring process and a nimble approach. Rather than succumb to downward price pressure, the RDC would seek to understand markets and companies and find a niche where other players lacked expertise.

Promotional activities for the RDC would, for the most part, be geared towards creating awareness of its existence and its products within key constituencies, with focus on the following:

- VanCity business services,
- VanCity branch network,
- Business professionals (accountants, lawyers, etc.),
- Business associations,
- Other non-competing financial institutions, and
- Competing institutions (syndication opportunities).

A series of personal visits and presentations to potential sources of referral business would mark the beginning of an intensive effort to launch the new RDC. To communicate the RDC's offering, the business plan recommended that the services of a public relations and communications consultant be sought, especially to suggest ways and means of leveraging the VanCity name among the target business community in co-ordination with the entire VanCity group of companies.

Exhibit 5 details the RDC's projected scale of operations as identified in the business plan. While financial reports would be maintained as if the full $11.5 million of capital was paid in on January 1, 1999, Williams assumed that idle capital (funds not loaned out) would earn a deposit rate of interest (i.e., bankers' acceptances) and that initial years' losses would be charged against retained earnings.

During the first three to four years of its operations, the RDC would operate in a startup phase. Initial startup losses were anticipated to be

Balance Sheet ($ 000's)	*1999*	*2000*	*2001*	*2002*	*2003*	*2004*	*2005*	*2006*	*2007*	*2008*
Cash	$6,338	$1,976	($1,632)	$8,320	$4,468	$2,271	$1,349	$1,458	$1,319	$1,466
Portfolio Outstanding	$4,080	$8,110	$11,633	$16,440	$21,140	$24,265	$26,198	$27,065	$28,040	$28,731
Provision	$303	$718	$1,131	$1,629	$2,120	$2,498	$2,764	$2,902	$2,992	$3,065
Assets	$10,115	$9,369	$8,869	$23,131	$23,487	$24,038	$24,783	$25,621	$26,367	$27,132
Capital	$11,000	$11,000	$11,000	$25,200	$25,200	$25,200	$25,200	$25,200	$25,200	$25,200
R/E	($885)	($1,631)	($2,131)	($2,069)	($1,713)	($1,162)	($417)	$421	$1,167	$1,932
Total Liabilities	$10,115	$9,369	$8,869	$23,131	$23,487	$24,038	$24,783	$25,621	$26,367	$27,132
Income Statement ($ 000's)	*1999*	*2000*	*2001*	*2002*	*2003*	*2004*	*2005*	*2006*	*2007*	*2008*
Operating Revenue	$343	$979	$1,564	$2,227	$2,971	$3,573	$3,962	$4,178	$4,327	$4,453
Interest Earned (Theoretical)	$340	$163	$7	$410	$251	$132	$71	$55	$54	$55
Net Revenue	$683	$1,142	$1,570	$2,636	$3,222	$3,705	$4,033	$4,233	$4,381	$4,508
Operating Expenses	$1,264	$1,395	$1,410	$1,644	$1,697	$1,855	$1,918	$1,988	$2,168	$2,247
Community Partnership Development	$170	$171	$172	$174	$175	$176	$177	$179	$180	$181
Loss Provision	$303	$494	$659	$930	$1,169	$1,299	$1,370	$1,407	$1,466	$1,495
Net Profit (Loss) Before Taxes	($885)	($747)	($499)	$62	$356	$551	$745	$838	$746	$765
Cumulative Loans Issued - $	$4,080	$8,620	$13,720	$21,320	$30,400	$39,480	$48,560	$57,640	$67,510	$77,380
- #	20	42	67	104	148	192	236	280	328	376

Exhibit 5 Projected Scale of Operations for the RDC

$885,000 for 1999, $747,000 for 2000, and $499,000 for 2001. Williams expected that break-even would be realized by 2002. Total cumulative startup losses were estimated to be $2.1 million. These would be recouped by 2006, by when the RDC would begin adding to its capital base through operational gains. In the fourth year of its operation, the RDC would receive a further capitalization of approximately $14.2 million, as it progressed towards achieving long-term sustainability in its lending and development operations.

While loan losses would be a major determinant of profitability, Williams and his team felt that an ultimate loss rate of 15 per cent of total authorizations (spread over the expected five-year life of the loans) was a fair assumption to make. Other assumptions made in the business plan are laid out in a series of excerpts from the business plan in Exhibits 6, 7 and 8. Pro-forma financials are presented in Exhibits 9 to 11.

Organizational Issues

While Williams and his team were reasonably sure that the financials developed for the RDC gave them a winning business case, organizational factors would play a critical role in deciding the new venture's degree of success. An important factor would be to retain the overall VanCity commitment to customers and the community, and yet create a venture that would be intensely business focused and collegial in its operational culture.

The RDC team would be small: a chief executive officer (CEO), three investment managers and an administrative assistant. The investment managers would be expected to be intensively involved in sourcing, negotiating, writing and administrating deals. Since the RDC was a new venture in a new market niche, it was determined that an outsider with market experience would need to be sourced to fill the CEO role and develop a new organizational culture.

The one CEO candidate who rose above the others was Dave Mowat of the BDC. Mowat was well recognized in the field and was then a member of the BDC's senior management team. Williams had a discussion with Mowat to get some of his viewpoints on lending in both the for-profit and non-profit sectors. Mowat explained that he was both interested and challenged by the notion that the new venture would earmark 10 per cent of its capital to advance to non-profits. Mowat believed that if the non-profit sector were to get better at its business, then it would have to learn to build capacity in exactly the same way as a business would learn how to raise capital or debt. Furthermore, as had happened in the business sector, this growth and learning would be facilitated by a financial institution leading the way.

Williams was pleased with Mowat's observation and turned the conversation to the issue of culture, and how the RDC could develop its own personality while still fitting within the culture of the credit union. Mowat explained that it would be necessary to build a new culture and incubate it for a while so that it would stand on its own legs. At the same time, he foresaw that a separate corporate structure would become redundant after a period of time. Ultimately, that point was one of mechanics, and Mowat explained that the RDC could become a division today and still keep a unique character, have its own confidence and its own way of doing things. Mowat felt that it would be best to start from scratch and get the new business formed, rather than trying to make it an offshoot of an existing business. The latter would be less likely to realize a pure response to (and from) the market.

Williams was confident that he and his team had performed the appropriate due diligence on the RDC's corporate venturing idea and had a well-developed business plan to present to VanCity's board. As a new company, the RDC would need to be aggressive and returns-focused and yet retain the core values of VanCity. Similarily, the lenders managing the new business would need to be highly focused and motivated; they would need to be competitive and should recognize the need to set ambitious targets and work towards achieving them so they could go home

(Text continues on page 330)

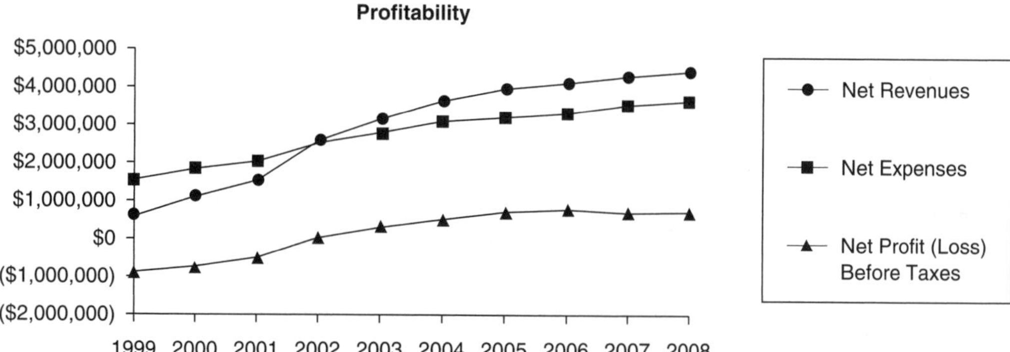

Break-Even occurs when Net Revenues and Net Expen the $2,500,000 level.

Both Net Revenues and Net Expenses remain at a near of about $800,000 per year by year 7 of operations.

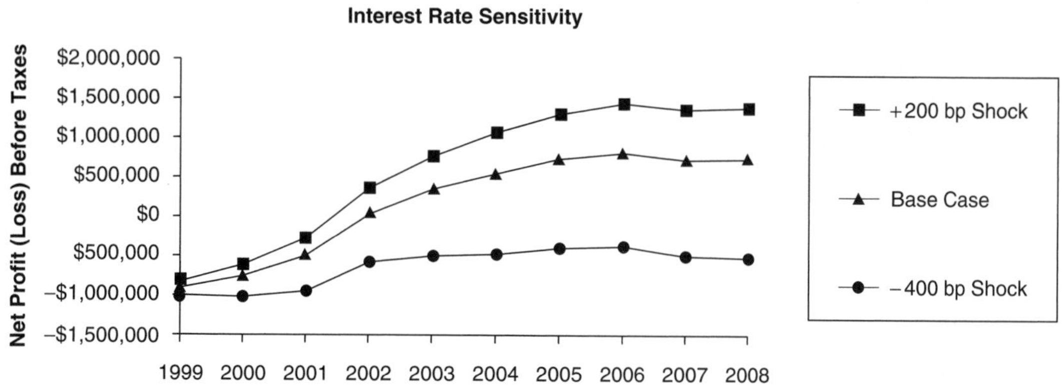

Under current business plan expectations (Base Case), is expected to be positive by year 3 or 4 of operations, a sustainable level near the $800,000 level.

+ 200 bp Shock

If interest rates were to rise by 2%, the RDC nearly 6 months earlier than expected, and d

– 400 bp Shock

If interest rates were to decrease by 4%, the solvency under the current business model.

In this scenario, the RDC would have to adju and apply cost-cutting strategies to break even

Exhibit 6 RDC Profitability and Interest Rate Sensitivity

Note: This exhibit has been directly extracted from the RDC business plan that was forwarded to the Board of Directors.

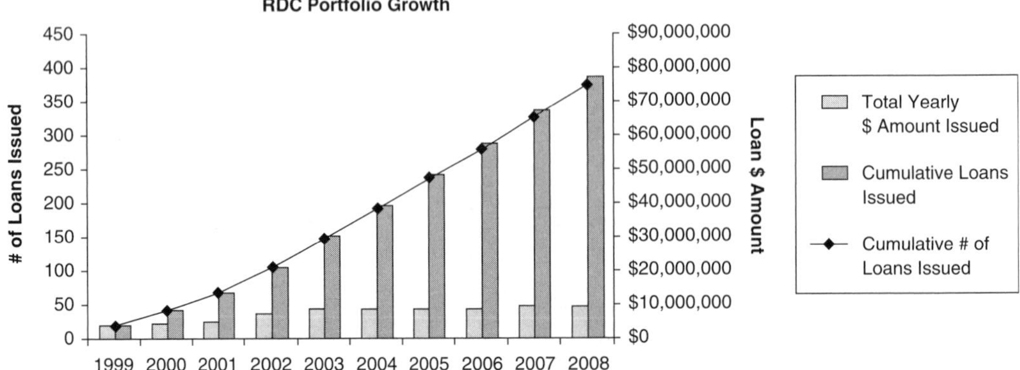

During the first 3 years of operations, the RDC will issue $13 over 67 loan placements

1999 Loan Issues

$4,080,000 20 Placements

2000 Loan Issues

$4,540,000 22 Placements

2001 Loan Issues

$5,100,000 25 Placements

The RDCís Portfolio is expected to mature at levels sustaini $10,000,000 in new loan issues per year

The 10 year forecast estimates $78,000,000 in toal Loans I placements

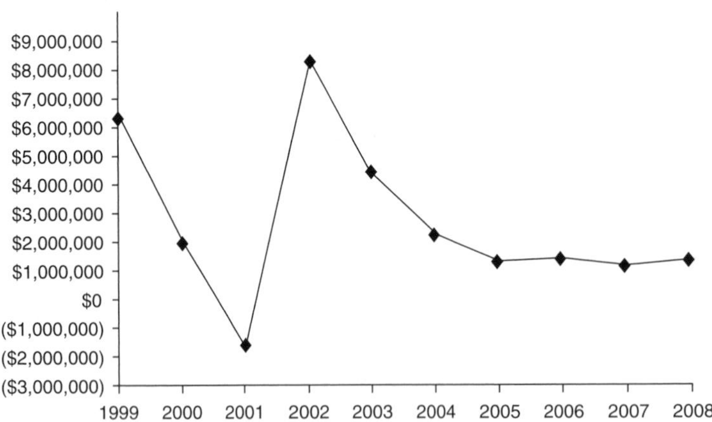

The RDCís initial $11,000,000 in capital is expected to be for by the end of year 3 of operations.

A requirement of further capitalization will need to be injected beginning of the RDCís 4th year of operations.

This second capital infusion of approximately $14.2 Million/sufficient funding to bring the RDC to long-term sustainability

Portfolio maturity will occur by year 7 of operations, whereup maintain an outflow of capital equal to its inflow, thus sustainability

Exhibit 7 RDC Portfolio Growth and Capital Utilization

Note: This exhibit has been directly extracted from the RDC business plan that was forwarded to the Board of Directors.

Lending & Investment Portfolio Schedule		*1999*	*2000*	*2001*	*2002*	*2003*	*2004*	*2005*	*2006*	*2007*	*2008*
Beginning Balance		$0	$3,680,000	$7,360,000	$10,522,500	$14,892,500	$19,205,000	$22,080,000	$23,862,500	$24,667,500	$25,530,000
New Loans		$3,680,000	$4,140,000	$4,600,000	$6,900,000	$8,280,000	$8,280,000	$8,280,000	$8,280,000	$8,970,000	$8,970,000
Sub Total		$3,680,000	$7,820,000	$11,960,000	$17,422,500	$23,172,500	$27,485,000	$30,360,000	$32,142,500	$33,637,500	$34,500,000
Principal Repayment		$0	$460,000	$1,437,500	$2,530,000	$3,967,500	$5,405,000	$6,497,500	$7,475,000	$8,107,500	$8,366,250
Principal Repayment Reduction Due to Write-Off		$0	($69,000)	($215,625)	($379,500)	($595,125)	($810,750)	($974,625)	($1,121,250)	($1,216,125)	($1,254,938)
Net Principal Repayment		$0	$391,000	$1,221,875	$2,150,500	$3,372,375	$4,594,250	$5,522,875	$6,353,750	$6,891,375	$7,111,313
Write-Off		$0	$69,000	$215,625	$379,500	$595,125	$810,750	$974,625	$1,121,250	$1,216,125	$1,254,938
Closing Balance		$3,680,000	$7,360,000	$10,522,500	$14,892,500	$19,205,000	$22,080,000	$23,862,500	$24,667,500	$25,530,000	$26,133,750
Loan Loss Provision	15.00% net										
Allowance as a Percentage of Portfolio for Period		7.19%	5.92%	5.49%	5.49%	5.37%	5.20%	5.08%	5.02%	5.06%	5.04%
Opening Provision		$0	$264,500	$631,063	$993,313	$1,431,750	$1,868,750	$2,206,563	$2,445,188	$2,561,625	$2,637,094
Provision for the Year		$264,500	$435,563	$577,875	$817,938	$1,032,125	$1,148,563	$1,213,250	$1,237,688	$1,291,594	$1,317,469
Less: Write-Off	1 year lag	$0	($69,000)	($215,625)	($379,500)	($595,125)	($810,750)	($974,625)	($1,121,250)	($1,216,125)	($1,254,938)
Net Provision		$264,500	$631,063	$993,313	$1,431,750	$1,868,750	$2,206,563	$2,445,188	$2,561,625	$2,637,094	$2,699,625
Interest Revenue		$280,021	$840,064	$1,360,728	$1,933,897	$2,594,572	$3,141,489	$3,495,890	$3,692,780	$3,819,665	$3,931,236
Fees											
Processing Fee		$36,800	$41,400	$46,000	$69,000	$82,800	$82,800	$82,800	$82,800	$89,700	$89,700
Annual Fee		$0	$27,600	$44,706	$63,538	$85,244	$103,213	$114,856	$121,325	$125,494	$129,159

Exhibit 8 RDC Loan Portfolio Schedule

(Continued)

Civil Portfolio Schedule		*1999*	*2000*	*2001*	*2002*	*2003*	*2004*	*2005*	*2006*	*2007*	*2008*
Beginning Balance		$0	$400,000	$760,000	$1,110,000	$1,547,500	$1,935,000	$2,185,000	$2,335,000	$2,397,500	$2,510,000
New Loans		$400,000	$400,000	$500,000	$700,000	$800,000	$800,000	$800,000	$800,000	$900,000	$900,000
Sub Total		$400,000	$800,000	$1,260,000	$1,810,000	$2,347,500	$2,735,000	$2,985,000	$3,135,000	$3,297,500	$3,410,000
Principal Repayment		$0	$50,000	$150,000	$262,500	$412,500	$550,000	$650,000	$737,500	$787,500	$812,500
Principal Repayment Reduction Due to Write-Off		$0	($10,000)	($30,000)	($52,500)	($82,500)	($110,000)	($130,000)	($147,500)	($160,000)	($167,500)
Net Principal Repayment		$0	$40,000	$120,000	$210,000	$330,000	$440,000	$520,000	$590,000	$627,500	$645,000
Write-Off		$0	$10,000	$30,000	$52,500	$82,500	$110,000	$130,000	$147,500	$160,000	$167,500
Closing Balance		$400,000	$750,000	$1,110,000	$1,547,500	$1,935,000	$2,185,000	$2,335,000	$2,397,500	$2,510,000	$2,597,500
Loan Loss Provision	20.00% net										
Allowance as a Percentage of Portfolio for Period		9.58%	7.78%	7.32%	7.24%	7.06%	6.86%	6.73%	7.06%	6.96%	6.85%
Opening Provision		$0	$38,333	$86,667	$137,917	$197,500	$251,667	$291,667	$318,750	$340,417	$355,000
Provision for the Year		$38,333	$58,333	$81,250	$112,083	$136,667	$150,000	$157,083	$169,167	$174,583	$177,917
Less: Write-Off	1 year lag	$0	($10,000)	($30,000)	($52,500)	($82,500)	($110,000)	($130,000)	($147,500)	($160,000)	($167,500)
Net Provision		$38,333	$86,667	$137,917	$197,500	$251,667	$291,667	$318,750	$340,417	$355,000	$365,417
Interest Revenue		$22,041	$63,367	$102,489	$146,433	$191,892	$227,019	$249,060	$260,769	$270,412	$281,432
Fees											
Processing Fee		$4,000	$4,000	$5,000	$7,000	$8,000	$8,000	$8,000	$8,000	$9,000	$9,000
Annual Fee		$0	$2,875	$4,650	$6,644	$8,706	$10,300	$11,300	$11,831	$12,269	$12,769
Total RDC Portfolio Schedule		*Year 1*	*Year 2*	*Year 3*	*Year 4*	*Year 5*	*Year 6*	*Year 7*	*Year 8*	*Year 9*	*Year 10*
Beginning Balance		$0	$4,080,000	$8,120,000	$11,632,500	$16,440,000	$21,140,000	$24,265,000	$26,197,500	$27,065,000	$28,040,000
New Loans		$4,080,000	$4,540,000	$5,100,000	$7,600,000	$9,080,000	$9,080,000	$9,080,000	$9,080,000	$9,870,000	$9,870,000
Sub Total		$4,080,000	$8,620,000	$13,220,000	$19,232,500	$25,520,000	$30,220,000	$33,345,000	$35,277,500	$36,935,000	$37,910,000

Exhibit 8 RDC Loan Portfolio Schedule

Assets	*1999*	*2000*	*2001*	*2002*	*2003*	*2004*	*2005*	*2006*
Cash Available for Operations	$6,338,278	$1,976,343	($1,632,063)	$8,320,480	$4,467,510	$2,271,410	$1,349,484	$1,457,958
Total S.T. Liquid Assets	**$6,338,278**	**$1,976,343**	**($1,632,063)**	**$8,320,480**	**$4,467,510**	**$2,271,410**	**$1,349,484**	**$1,457,958**
L & I Loan Portfolio								
Performing L & I Loans	$3,680,000	$7,360,000	$10,522,500	$14,892,500	$19,205,000	$22,080,000	$23,862,500	$24,667,500
Non Performing	$3,680,000	$7,360,000	$10,522,500	$14,892,500	$19,205,000	$22,080,000	$23,862,500	$24,667,500
Book Value of L & I Loans								
Less: Net Provisions	$264,500	$631,063	$993,313	$1,431,750	$1,868,750	$2,206,563	$2,445,188	$2,561,625
Net Book Value of L & I Portfolio	**$3,415,500**	**$6,728,938**	**$9,529,188**	**$13,460,750**	**$17,336,250**	**$19,873,438**	**$21,417,313**	**$22,105,875**
Civil Loan Portfolio								
Performing Civil Loans	$400,000	$750,000	$1,110,000	$1,547,500	$1,935,000	$2,185,000	$2,335,000	$2,397,500
Non Performing	$400,000	$750,000	$1,110,000	$1,547,500	$1,935,000	$2,185,000	$2,335,000	$2,397,500
Book Value of Civil Loans								
Less: Net Provisions	$38,333	$86,667	$137,917	$197,500	$251,667	$291,667	$318,750	$340,417
Net Book Value of Civil Portfolio	**$361,667**	**$663,333**	**$972,083**	**$1,350,000**	**$1,683,333**	**$1,893,333**	**$2,016,250**	**$2,057,083**
Net Book Value of RDC Portfolio	**$3,777,167**	**$7,392,271**	**$10,501,271**	**$14,810,750**	**$19,019,583**	**$21,766,771**	**$23,433,563**	**$24,162,958**
Total Assets	**$10,115,445**	**$9,368,614**	**$8,869,208**	**$23,131,230**	**$23,487,093**	**$24,038,181**	**$24,783,047**	**$25,620,917**
LIABILITIES & EQUITY								
Liabilities	**$0**	**$0**	**$0**	**$0**	**$0**	**$0**	**$0**	**$0**
EQUITY								
Net Capital for Community Development	$0	$0	$0	$0	$0	$0	$0	$0
Paid in Capital From VanCity	$11,000,000	$11,000,000	$11,000,000	$25,200,000	$25,200,000	$25,200,000	$25,200,000	$25,200,000
Retained Earnings	($884,555)	($1,631,386)	($2,130,792)	($2,068,770)	($1,712,907)	($1,161,819)	($416,953)	$420,917
Total Equity	**$10,115,445**	**$9,368,614**	**$8,869,208**	**$23,131,230**	**$23,487,093**	**$24,038,181**	**$24,783,047**	**$25,620,917**
Total Liabilities & Equity	**$10,115,445**	**$9,368,614**	**$8,869,208**	**$23,131,230**	**$23,487,093**	**$24,038,181**	**$24,783,047**	**$25,620,917**

Exhibit 9 RDC Forecast Balance Sheet

	1999	2000	2001	2002	2003	2004	2005	2006	2007	2008
Revenue										
L & I and Civil Loan Revenue										
Interest Income	$302,062	$903,431	$1,463,218	$2,080,330	$2,786,464	$3,368,508	$3,744,950	$3,953,549	$4,090,077	$4,212,668
Processing Fee Income	$40,800	$45,400	$51,000	$76,000	$90,800	$90,800	$90,800	$90,800	$98,700	$98,700
Annual Fee Income	$0	$30,475	$49,356	$70,181	$93,950	$113,513	$126,156	$133,156	$137,763	$141,928
Total Operating Revenue	$342,862	$979,306	$1,563,574	$2,226,511	$2,971,214	$3,572,820	$3,961,906	$4,177,506	$4,326,539	$4,453,296
Interest Earned (Charged) on Capital	$339,966	$163,032	$6,751	$409,577	$250,745	132,136	$70,998	$55,048	$54,455	$54,616
Net Revenues	**$682,828**	**$1,142,338**	**$1,570,325**	**$2,636,088**	**$3,221,959**	**$3,704,956**	**$4,032,904**	**$4,232,554**	**$4,380,994**	**$4,507,912**
Expenses										
L & I	$858,750	$870,441	$881,631	$1,090,960	$1,122,636	$1,257,611	$1,295,362	$1,339,008	$1,491,195	$1,539,042
Civil	$169,800	$287,179	$289,659	$306,591	$320,778	$336,188	$352,992	$371,389	$391,617	$413,954
Other	$236,000	$237,652	$239,316	$246,495	$253,890	$261,507	$269,352	$277,432	$285,755	$294,328
Total Operating Expenses	**$1,264,550**	**$1,395,272**	**$1,410,606**	**$1,644,045**	**$1,697,304**	**$1,855,306**	**$1,917,706**	**$1,987,829**	**$2,168,567**	**$2,247,323**
Operating Profit (Loss)	**($581,722)**	**($252,935)**	**$159,719**	**$992,043**	**$1,524,655**	**$1,849,651**	**$2,115,199**	**$2,244,724**	**$2,212,427**	**$2,260,589**
Loan Loss Provision Charges										
L & I	$264,500	$435,563	$577,875	$817,938	$1,032,125	$1,148,563	$1,213,250	$1,237,688	$1,291,594	$1,317,469
Civil	$38,333	$58,333	$81,250	$112,083	$136,667	$150,000	$157,083	$169,167	$174,583	$177,917
Total Loan Loss Provision	**$302,833**	**$493,896**	**$659,125**	**$930,021**	**$1,168,792**	**$1,298,563**	**$1,370,333**	**$1,406,854**	**$1,466,177**	**$1,495,385**
Net Expenses	**$1,567,383**	**$1,889,168**	**$2,069,731**	**$2,574,066**	**$2,866,095**	**$3,153,868**	**$3,288,039**	**$3,394,683**	**$3,634,744**	**$3,742,709**
Net Profit (Loss) Before Taxes	**($884,555)**	**($746,831)**	**($499,406)**	**$62,022**	**$355,863**	**$551,088**	**$744,865**	**$837,870**	**$746,250**	**$765,203**

Exhibit 10 RDC Forecast Statement of Profit and Loss

	Year 1	*Year 2*	*Year 3*	*Year 4*	*Year 5*	*Year 6*	*Year 7*	*Year 8*	*Year 9*	*Year 10*
Cash Provided by (used in):										
Operations:										
Net Profit (Loss) for the Period	($884,555)	($746,831)	($499,406)	$62,022	$355,863	$551,088	$744,865	$837,870	$746,250	$765,203
Adjust: Non Cash Items Loan Loss Provision	$302,833	$493,896	$659,125	$930,021	$1,168,792	$1,298,563	$1,370,333	$1,406,854	$1,466,177	$1,495,385
	($581,722)	($252,935)	$159,719	$992,043	$1,524,655	$1,849,651	$2,115,199	$2,244,724	$2,212,427	$2,260,589
Investments:										
Portfolio Outstanding	$4,080,000	$4,030,000	$3,522,500	$4,807,500	$4,700,000	$3,125,000	$1,932,500	$867,500	$975,000	$691,250
Write-Off for the Period	$0	$79,000	$245,625	$432,000	$677,625	$920,750	$1,104,625	$1,268,750	$1,376,125	$1,422,438
	$4,080,000	$4,109,000	$3,768,125	$5,239,500	$5,377,625	$4,045,750	$3,037,125	$2,136,250	$2,351,125	$2,113,688
Financing:										
Equity Financing	$11,000,000	$0	$0	14,200,000	—	—	—	—	—	—
	$11,000,000	$0	$0	$14,200,000	$0	$0	$0	$0	$0	$0
Change in Cash	$6,338,278	($4,361,935)	($3,608,406)	$9,952,543	($3,852,970)	($2,196,099)	($921,926)	$108,474	($138,698)	$146,901
Opening Cash Balance	$0	$6,338,278	$1,976,343	($1,632,063)	$8,320,480	$4,467,510	$2,271,410	$1,349,484	$1,457,958	$1,319,261
Cash at the End of the Period	$6,338,278	$1,976,343	($1,632,063)	$8,320,480	$4,467,510	$2,271,410	$1,349,484	$1,457,958	$1,319,261	$1,466,162

Exhibit 11 RDC Statement of Changes in Financial Position

having earned substantial bonuses. Williams was optimistic that the business plan was sound.

The Decision

The morning of September 15, 1998, found Williams going through the presentation material that he and his team members had spent so much time preparing. In about an hour, the Board was going to meet—to take a decision on whether VanCity should take a corporate venturing decision in the area of mezzanine financing. Williams shut his laptop and prepared to leave for the boardroom. This would be a crucial step that could create history for VanCity.

Notes

1. Source: BDC Web site.
2. Source: RDC 1999 Business Plan.

Krave's Candy Co.—Clodhoppers (A)

Prepared by Chris Sturby under the supervision of Professor Stewart Thornhill

 Version: (A) 2004-09-02

Introduction

> *Everyone in the world knows what a Kit Kat is; everyone will know what a Clodhopper is.*
>
> —Chris Emery, 1997

In April 1999, Chris Emery and Larry Finnson were gearing up for another busy season. Over the previous three years, their company, Krave's Candy (Krave's), had enjoyed tremendous success and was now Manitoba's fastest growing company. Krave's product, Clodhoppers, had been successfully distributed across Canadian Wal-Mart stores in 1998, and Chris and Larry were hoping to build on their success for the upcoming Christmas season. Knowing that their product was a hit with consumers, the partners had dreams of becoming known as Canada's candy company. In order to finance their ambitious growth targets, they knew they would require additional capital in the upcoming months.

Clodhoppers

Best friends Chris Emery and Larry Finnson grew up in Winnipeg dreaming about going into business together and becoming millionaires. After high school, Chris and Larry followed different paths. Chris went to The University of Manitoba where he studied economics for three years before dropping out and taking an office job. Larry entered community college where he graduated in electronics before taking a job in construction.

While at The University of Manitoba, Chris often received care packages from his grandmother, Edith Baker. One of his favorite treats was a cluster of white chocolate, cashews and graham wafers. Not only did Chris enjoy the clusters, his roommates and friends would frequently bother him for samples. After seeing how popular the candy was with his friends, Chris figured that the product would be popular commercially. Chris approached his good friend and associate, Larry Finnson, and together they founded the Krave's Candy Company (Krave's) in 1996.

The pair had difficulty coming up with a name for their flagship product. Once at a party, a friend of Chris's put his boots on the furniture. After somebody asked the friend to remove his "clodhoppers" from the table, Chris felt that he had come across a quirky and fun name that would represent his candy well. Knowing they had a great product, the partners rushed into production despite a lack of business experience, no business plan and no marketing strategy. They received $20,000 from friends and family in exchange for shares in the company, and they started operations.

THE CHOCOLATE MARKET IN CANADA

Chocolate was a subsector within the large confectionery industry in Canada (for statistics, see Exhibits 1 and 2). Within the chocolate subsector, there were two major types of products: boxed chocolates and chocolate bars. The majority of boxed chocolate sales came from holiday sales or from gifts for special occasions. In 2000, the size of the boxed chocolate market was approximately $160 million to $200 million. Among the top brands of boxed chocolate in Canada were Pot of Gold (Hershey), Turtles (Nestle), Black Magic (Nestle), Russell Stover, Lindt, Godiva and Ferrero-Rocher.

The chocolate bar market was not as seasonal but was highly fragmented. The most successful chocolate bars in Canada had market shares no greater than 5.2 per cent, and most of the top 10 brands in the bar market had been among the top 10 for close to 60 years (Exhibit 3).

The chocolate market was dominated by foreign-controlled enterprises, including Cadbury,

	1997	*1998*	*1999*
Chocolate	$971.50	$917.30	$1,118.40
Sugar Confectionery	$317.80	$292.10	$299.30
Gum	$206.00	$198.10	$212.50

Exhibit 1 Confectionery Sales in Canada (millions of dollars)
Source: Candy Industry, January 2001, p. 33.

	$	*Share (%)*
Hershey Foods Corp.	679.5	44.9
Mars Inc.	401.1	26.5
Nestle S.A.	102.8	6.8
Brachs Confections	61.4	4.1
Philip Morris Co. Inc.	28.5	1.9
Ferrero USA Inc.	26.2	1.7
American Specialty Foods	20.5	1.4
Stock USA	19.6	1.3
Favorite Brands Intl.	19.6	1.3
Private label	29.2	1.9

Exhibit 2 Top Chocolate Bag/Box Leaders (United States) (millions of dollars)
Source: The Manufacturing Confectioner, September 2000, p. 3, from Information Resources Inc.
Note: Data are for the greater than 3.5 oz segment.

Caramilk	5.2%
Kit Kat	5.0%
Oh Henry	5.0%
M&Ms	4.9%
Mars	4.2%
Coffee Crisp	4.2%
Hershey Milk Chocolate	4.1%
Reese Peanut Butter Cups	4.1%
Smarties	4.1%
Cadbury Milk Chocolate	3.9%
Other	55.3%

Exhibit 3 Top Chocolate Candy Bars in Canada, 2000 Market Share (%)

Source: Marketing Magazine, June 4, 2001.

Note: Market shares are shown in per cent based on estimated sales of $744.9 million.

Hershey, Nestle, and Effem Foods (parent of Mars Inc.). According to Agriculture and Agri-Food Canada, these firms competed on the basis of brand name, product advertising and promotion, specialty products, quality and cost of production.[1] Because confectionery products were usually discretionary and high-impulse purchases, promotion played a substantial role in establishing brand-name presence in Canadian markets.

Beginning Operations

Initially, Chris and Larry manufactured small batches of Clodhoppers in their garage and marketed the product door-to-door to local convenience, drug and grocery stores and to individual consumers. Soon after, the duo rented a facility that provided them with 350 square feet of factory space along with 300 feet of office space. Chris and Larry purchased an old candy mixer for $3,500 and re-engineered it for their needs. The piece of machinery was 34 years old and had been converted by Larry from a Frito Lay packaging machine. Manufacturing capacity was 50 pounds per hour. The partners decided to package the product in 300-gram peanut butter jars to compete in the boxed chocolate market, and they realized $59,000 in sales in their first year.

While they were fairly pleased with their first year of operations, Chris and Larry quickly learned from some of their early mistakes. They received feedback that their packaging looked sloppy and didn't do justice to their high-quality product. Also, stores had placed Clodhoppers alongside popcorn-type snacks instead of boxed chocolates. Larry's wife suggested that Clodhoppers should be packaged in a box, and the duo radically revamped the packaging to a 300-gram shiny black box with foil embossment. On the side of the box there was a story about a fictional Krave's company that lived in a castle in the Alps and developed a secret chocolate recipe. The story was inspired by characters such as the Keebler elves.

The new packaging was popular and sales began to take off. With the help of a local snack food distributor, Chris and Larry managed to bypass the normal purchasing procedure and sneak their product into Wal-Mart stores in Winnipeg. Although the Wal-Mart Canada head office was not thrilled with the "back-door" approach, sales in Winnipeg were so strong that Wal-Mart agreed to have Clodhoppers appear on the shelves at Wal-Mart stores across Canada for the 1998 holiday season. The 60,000-box deal was Krave's first big break. Soon thereafter, deals with Safeway and Shoppers Drug Mart materialized. Initially, Clodhoppers retailed at $5.87 per box.

Due to the fact that Clodhoppers were new to the marketplace and relatively unknown, Chris and Larry knew they had to build brand awareness and loyalty by sampling their product to consumers. As a result, they initiated a coast-to-coast sampling program through Wal-Mart. Although the program was extremely expensive, it proved to be a worthwhile investment. The first year of sales at Wal-Mart proved to be a success, as the chain sold approximately two-thirds of its initial order.

By the end of 1998, annual sales at Krave's had grown to $650,000, representing an increase of 958 per cent over three years. Approximately

85 per cent of annual sales had been earned during the Christmas season. Krave's was now the fastest-growing company in Manitoba. By April 1999, Wal-Mart had reordered for the upcoming Christmas season. After declining the previous year, Zellers had also committed to a substantial order for the holiday season. Together, the two orders totalled over $500,000.

Looking Forward

After three years of building Krave's into a successful and well-respected local company, Chris and Larry had long-term plans to grow annual sales to over $20 million and eventually become known as Canada's candy company. In order to do so, they knew that they would eventually require additional financing. With that in mind, Chris and Larry were extremely curious to see how well their company would be received by prospective investors.

Note

1. http://atn-riae.agr.ca/supply/3298_e.pdf. September 2003.

Trojan Technologies Inc.: Organizational Structuring for Growth and Customer Service

Prepared by Greg Upton under the supervision of Professor John Eggers

Version: (A) 1999-08-19

In March 1998, a group of Trojan Technologies Inc. (Trojan) employees grappled with the issue of how to structure the business to effectively interact with their customers and to manage the company's dramatic growth. The London, Ontario manufacturer of ultraviolet (UV) water disinfection systems believed that strong customer service was key to its recent and projected growth and had come to the realization that changes would have to be made to continue to achieve both simultaneously. The group hoped to develop a structure to address these issues. Marvin DeVries, executive vice-president, was to lead the development and implementation of the new structure. The transition to the new structure was to begin as of September 1998 to coincide with the new fiscal year.

The Business

Technology

Since 1977, the company had specialized in UV light applications for disinfecting water and wastewater. In essence, Trojan's products killed micro-organisms using high-intensity UV lamps. Water was channeled past the lamps at various speeds, based on the clarity of the water and the strength of the lamps, to achieve the required "kill" rate.

Trojan's UV technology had proven to be an environmentally safe and cost-effective alternative to chlorination, and was gaining wider recognition and acceptance. Even so, a significant market remained to be tapped, as the company estimated "... that only five per cent to 10 per cent of municipal wastewater sites in North America use UV-based technology ... [and] of the approximate 62,000 wastewater treatment facilities operating worldwide, only 2,500 currently utilize UV disinfection systems."[1]

Trojan Technologies Inc.[2]

Trojan was established in 1977 with a staff of three with the goal of developing a viable UV wastewater disinfection technology. Following several years of work, the first UV disinfection system (System UV2000™) was installed in Tillsonburg, Ontario, in 1981. It took another two years, however, before the regulatory approvals were in place to market the technology for municipal wastewater treatment in Canada and the United States. During this time, the company generated revenues through the sale of small residential and industrial cleanwater UV systems.

By 1991, the company had sales in excess of $10 million and had introduced its second-generation technology in the System UV3000™ wastewater disinfection system. As the company's growth continued, a staff of 50 was in place by 1992. The following year, due to capital requirements created by the company's strong growth, an initial public offering on the Toronto Stock Exchange was completed. Also in 1993, a branch office was established in The Hague, Netherlands, expanding Trojan's reach across the Atlantic.

1994 saw the launch of the System UV4000™, the construction of a new head office and sales exceeding $20 million. In 1995, a branch office was opened in California to service the enormous market for wastewater treatment in that state. Two years later, an expansion doubled head office capacity to house 190 staff and to meet the demand for sales of more than $50 million.

Well into 1998, the expectation was that sales would reach $70 million by year-end and continue to grow by more than 30 per cent per year over the next five years, reaching $300 million by 2003. The company was in the process of planning additional capacity expansion in the form of building and property purchases adjacent to head office, and expected to quadruple its headcount by 2003 to more than 1,000 employees.

Products

In 1997, 93 per cent of Trojan's sales were of wastewater products (System UV4000™ and System UV3000™). These systems were designed for use at small to very large wastewater treatment plants and more complex wastewater treatment applications with varying degrees of effluent treatment. The remaining seven per cent of sales were cleanwater products (primarily the System UV8000™ and Aqua UV™) for municipal and residential drinking water and industrial process applications. Growth in the coming year would be driven by increased sales of the wastewater disinfection products in both current and new geographic markets. In the longer term, new products such as the A•I•R• 2000™, which was to use UV light with an advanced photocatalytic technology to destroy volatile organic compounds in the air, were expected to further Trojan's sales growth.

Products were typically assembled from component parts at Trojan head office. The complexity of the product design, manufacture and service arose from the integration of skills in electronics, biology, controls programming and mechanical engineering. The company owned patents on its products and was prepared to defend them to preserve its intellectual capital.

Customers

Trojan sold its wastewater treatment products to contractors working on projects for municipalities or directly to municipalities. Typically, the process involved bidding on a project based on the Trojan products required to meet the municipality's specifications, and, therefore, engineering expertise was required as part of the selling process. Project sales typically fell in a $100,000 to $500,000 range, and given the large value of each sale, the sales and marketing function was critical to the company's success. However, for marketing to be effective, this new technology had to be well supported. Municipalities purchasing the wastewater disinfection systems required rapid response to any problems and expected superior service, given the consequences of breakdowns for the quality of water being discharged from their facility. Municipalities also had the ability to discuss Trojan and their UV products with other municipalities before deciding to make their purchase, further underlining the importance of warranty and aftermarket service to customers to ensure positive word-of-mouth advertising.

Trojan's smaller product line, the cleanwater segment, focused on a different customer base from wastewater, and it was difficult to generalize about the nature of this segment's customers. These customers ranged from municipalities to industrial companies to individuals.

Interaction With Customers

The Process

The main points of customer interaction in the wastewater product line included:

1. Quote/bid process
2. Configuration of project structure
3. Project shipment and system installation
4. Technical support and warranty claims
5. Parts order processing

Each of these is described briefly below:

The quote/bid process was a major function of the marketing department, with support from the project engineering department. Although the marketing department took the lead role in assembling the appropriate bid and pricing, the customer would on occasion wish to speak directly to the project engineering department on specific technical questions related to the function of the UV unit within the particular wastewater setting.

After winning a bid, the configuration of project structure involved working with the customer on the detailed specifications for the project and applying the appropriate Trojan systems in a configuration that would meet the customer's needs. The project engineering department took the lead role in this work, and either worked through the marketing representative in transmitting technical information to and from the customer or communicated directly with the customer's technical personnel.

Once the project had been configured, it was scheduled for manufacture by the operations department. On completion, and when the customer was ready to integrate the UV system into their wastewater facility, the service department completed the installation and start-up of the unit. The service department would also be involved in demonstrating the proper use of the system to the customer.

After the system was in use by the customer, further interaction came in the form of technical support. The service department would deal with phone calls, site visits and warranty claims and was the primary contact point for the customer. By its nature, most service work at this stage of the process was completed on an "as-needed" basis by the first available service representative. As a result, it was difficult or impossible to have the same service representative available to respond to a particular customer on every occasion. The service department, therefore, kept a detailed file on each UV installation and all customer contact to ensure the most informed response on each service call.

The final stage of customer interaction was the ordering of replacement parts by the customer after the warranty period was complete. This was handled by a call centre at Trojan head office in London that was separate from the other departments that had dealt with the customer. The call centre was staffed to receive orders for Trojan replacement parts, but not to provide technical support as with the service department, and would generally not access customer service files in taking the order.

In summary, customers would deal with as many as four different departments during their interaction with Trojan. During the early days of Trojan's growth, the "close-knit" nature of Trojan's workforce allowed a seamless transition between "departments." However, as described below, the company's continued growth began to complicate the transition between departments.

Customer Support in the Early Days

In the 1980s and early 1990s, when Trojan had less than 50 employees and worked on a limited number of wastewater bids and projects during the course of the year, customer support was a collective effort across the entire company. In fact, it was not unusual that virtually everyone in Trojan knew the details of all the major projects in process at any given time. There was a common knowledge base of customer names and issues, which resulted, in DeVries' words, in an "immediate connectivity" to the job at hand. At times, during those early days, there were as few as two employees in a "department." Under these conditions every project received immediate and constant attention from start to finish, ensuring the customer was satisfied and potential issues were addressed in a proactive manner.

Challenges Created by Growth

As the company grew, departments grew. Very quickly the number of projects multiplied and it became impossible for everyone to know all the customers and active projects, or even all the people in the organization. As departments grew from two to five to 10 people, communications became focused internally within the departments. This made it progressively more difficult to ensure timely and effective communication on project status between departments, and the "immediate connectivity" described by DeVries began to break down. The situation was described by many as one where "things began to slip between the cracks" in terms of customer service excellence, because it was no longer possible for employees to shepherd a project through the company from start to finish as had been done in the early days. Once a particular department had finished their component of a project, they immediately had to turn their attention to the other projects they had ongoing, creating the potential for a lag before the next department picked up the customer file.

Project Engineering

Project engineering was one example of a department that had begun to experience problems maintaining service levels to the end-customer as a result of growth. By 1997, there were seven engineers in the department handling the regular support to the marketing department and acting as "specialists" for the various technical components of the products. When engineers were hired into this group, there was no formal training or apprenticeship program in place. The new hire would simply follow along as best he or she could and attempt to learn the complex product line through observation and assistance from others in the department. This type of training was strained by the demand for project engineering services brought on by Trojan's growth.

A "specialist" role, in addition to their support of the marketing department's project bids, had evolved within the project engineering group. To handle specific technical requests, this informal addition to the project engineer's role had occurred somewhat spontaneously within the department. For example, if one of the project engineers had developed a detailed understanding of the electronics included in the System UV4000™ products, that employee acted as the reference point for most detailed queries on this subject and was considered the "electronics specialist." There was no specific training or support to develop these specialists for their roles in place in 1997, nor was hiring particularly targeted at filling the specialist roles described above, as it was a secondary role for the department. As a result of the dual roles and the company's rapid growth, project engineers could not take responsibility to guide a project from bid through customer queries to production and commissioning of the project. The demand for assistance on many bids, coupled with the need to respond to queries in their "specialist" area on active projects prevented project engineers from acting as a steward on specific projects as they passed through the company. Instead, the department operated more as a pooled resource that was accessed as needed by the marketing department to support bids and by the service group to assist with product support.

Service

The growth of the company and the establishment of new product lines had caused an amplified growth in the service group, because for each new project installed there was a long-term source of potential queries and service needs. The service group covered a broad spectrum of needs, from the initial setup of UV systems to emergency responses to equipment problems or queries (which frequently required site visits). A formal training program had been instituted during early 1998 when the new service manager recognized the need to quickly develop new employees to ensure they could contribute a strong technical background and familiarity with the product. An existing service group member typically instructed new employees for approximately one week, and new employees learned the balance "on the job" through observation and discussion of issues with other service employees. Again, company growth had caused some difficulty in ensuring that new employees received adequate training before they were needed to actively service customer inquiries.

There was a fundamental structuring conflict within the service area on how to best serve the customer. On one hand, customers appreciated the ability to contact one person whenever they had a concern or question. Also, customers frequently needed quick response times to their site for in-person assessments and action by the service employee. This appeared to suggest a need to place service employees physically as close to the end-customer as possible, especially given the company's expanded geographic marketing area. However, the timing of service work was very uncertain. Whereas the project engineering department had some ability to prioritize and schedule their workload, the service department typically had to respond to customer calls immediately, and the geographic distribution of calls was not predictable. Therefore, if Trojan received significant service requests in California, the company could be forced to respond by sending all available service employees there. The uncertainty of the timing and geographic distribution of service calls lent itself more to the centralized pooling of resources that Trojan currently used.

As Trojan had a significant geographic distribution of sales, service work involved substantial travel. In fact, the constant travel presented an additional risk of "burnout" that was unique to the department. To address this, and to ensure a reliable response to calls for assistance from customers, a head office call centre was created in 1998. The call centre was staffed by service technicians who could respond to many customer situations over the phone and by using sophisticated remote monitoring of the UV installments in some cases. The call centre also provided a place where experienced service personnel who were at risk of "burn out" from constant travel could use their expertise. Also, the call centre provided another opportunity to train new employees before dispatching them directly to customer locations on service calls.

Related Issues

Career Ladders

In a small company, career progression and satisfaction typically comes with successes achieved that significantly affect the organization. There was generally not the expectation or the possibility of significant promotion or role development, but this was offset by the potential for involvement of everyone in several major components of company activity. This was certainly the case at Trojan in the early days. As the company grew, however, a need to distinguish between and recognize the various levels of experience developed. The current department structure did not provide for much differentiation of job requirements within the departments and, therefore, did not recognize the significant difference in experience levels between new and veteran employees.

Training Issues

As Trojan's sales continued to grow, the need to increase staffing was accelerating. In the early days, the addition of a person to the company was informal and supportive. The new employee would be introduced to everyone and would easily be able to approach the appropriate person to ask questions and to learn their role within the company. Given the rapid expansion of the company, this informal introduction to the company and its processes was rapidly becoming insufficient to allow new employees to become effective in their new position. Training, therefore, needed to be addressed in many areas.

Decisions

Given the issues developing as Trojan grew, the structuring issue was becoming steadily more important. The structuring team under DeVries envisioned a regional, team-based approach to customer interaction that would replicate the structure used by the company in the early days. One of the difficulties in implementing such a structure, however, would be ensuring that the groups still operated as though they were one company, sharing knowledge and resources as appropriate. Another would be determining what level of centralized support would be appropriate, bearing in mind the need to avoid duplicating activities at head office that should be handled by the regional teams. Employees were now aware that there would be a change in the company structure, and there was a need to come to some conclusions on the new structure quickly to reduce anxiety about the change within the organization.

Notes

1. From Trojan 1998 annual report.
2. The information in this section was primarily gathered from Trojan 1997 annual report.

Mainstreet Equity Corp. (A)

Prepared by Professor Terry H. Deutscher

 Version: (A) 2004-04-21

It was March 23, 2001, and the board of directors of Mainstreet Equity Corp. was nearing the end of a two-hour meeting.

Bob Dhillon, president and chief executive officer (CEO) of the firm summarized:

> The issue boils down to this: Is now the time that Mainstreet should rapidly expand its holdings in the market in order to become the leading brand and largest, most profitable owner of multifamily apartment properties in Canada? If so, where and how fast should we grow? If not, what do we need to do first, before we can go into a phase of very rapid growth?

The Corporation

The Founding of Mainstreet

Mainstreet Equity Corp. was incorporated as a numbered company in Alberta on May 21, 1997. It began trading on the Alberta Stock Exchange a year later and on the Toronto Stock

Exchange (under the stock symbol MEQ) on May 31, 2000. The firm commenced active operation as a real estate company involved in the acquisition, management and divestiture of multifamily residential rental properties with its first major real estate transaction on December 7, 1998. At that time, Mainstreet acquired 10 buildings consisting of 271 units in Calgary, Alberta.

Bob Dhillon

The key person responsible for developing and executing Mainstreet's strategy was Bob Dhillon, president and CEO of the corporation. With more than 20 years of experience in the real estate industry, Dhillon had bought and sold more than $150 million in real estate (80 per cent of it in Calgary) before he founded Mainstreet. Besides his extensive dealings in the Calgary real estate market, Dhillon had wide-ranging interests and experience. He had owned a travel consolidation business, was currently the exclusive distributor of Tabasco™ products in South Asia, and served as the Honorary Consul of Belize for Alberta.

These features have characterized Dhillon's ventures:

- They were very profitable, enabling Dhillon to maintain a comfortable lifestyle without the need for any compensation from Mainstreet. (His earnings from the corporation came from appreciation of the shares—he owned 38.7 per cent of the approximately nine million outstanding shares of Mainstreet, as well as share options of the company.)
- They required expert skills in developing and maintaining a business network, an aspect that Dhillon greatly enjoyed.
- Success in the ventures required considerable expertise in negotiation.

Currently, Dhillon divided his time among Mainstreet (his main interest, consuming 80 per cent of his normal 65-hour workweek), his work for McIlhenny Company as their distributor of Tabasco products in South Asia (which consumed 10 per cent of his time, mostly in three or four trips annually to Asia or to the firm's headquarters in Louisiana), and his activities in Belize, where he was spearheading a 2,300-acre island resort development (five per cent of his time), and numerous other ventures (five per cent).

In 1998, Dhillon graduated with an MBA degree from the Richard Ivey School of Business at The University of Western Ontario. As one of his classmates in the program described it:

> Before the Executive MBA Program, Bob was a "flipper," very successful at buying and selling apartment buildings in the Calgary market. Starting from a very small base, he did larger and larger deals, eventually earning the respect of the major players in the market. It was in the EMBA program that Bob conceived the initial Mainstreet concept. Instead of simply buying and selling properties, Mainstreet would upgrade and manage them, thereby enhancing their value.

Dhillon was aggressive, ambitious and entrepreneurial. He was known among his classmates for his stated goal of becoming the world's first Sikh billionaire.

Managing Mainstreet

Dhillon gratefully acknowledged the role of the EMBA program in the launch of Mainstreet and the strategic contribution of David Mitchell, who preceded him by one year in the Calgary section of the program.

> I used every single course at Ivey to build the strategy for Mainstreet. Whether it was building a brand, running an efficient operation, financing growth or making a speech, I thought about the lessons from the courses in terms of what they meant for Mainstreet. Every major decision about our strategy was discussed, debated, and tested with Dave (Mitchell).

Mitchell became a major shareholder in Mainstreet. Although he did not have a formal role in the corporation, his discussions with Dhillon continued throughout the initial years of operation of the company—in the same penetrating, no-holds-barred, politically incorrect tone as always. He continued to be Dhillon's principal sounding board outside the organization.

"Mainstreet has always been a very lean organization," Mitchell commented. "In the early days, it operated out of the trunk of Dhillon's car, then subsequently out of the studio apartment in Mainstreet's first building that was also used by contractors for storing building materials." Dhillon definitely intended to keep Mainstreet lean and agile as the firm grew. "For every dollar we spend we ask ourselves: is that the best way to spend money on the business, or could that dollar be more efficiently used elsewhere?"

In 1999, Mainstreet built itself an office on the ground floor of one if its apartment buildings, just outside the Calgary downtown area. Late in 2000, the office was remodelled and expanded. From it, eight people ran Mainstreet's corporate office and its Calgary operations; two others ran a satellite operation in Edmonton. Brief descriptions of their areas of responsibility are presented with the organization chart in Exhibit 1.

Besides Dhillon, there were two senior internal managers in the corporation, Johnny Lam (chief financial officer) and Don Murray (operations manager). Lam held a certified accounting designation and more than 20 years of financial management experience in Europe, Asia and North America. He worked for Coopers & Lybrand and HBM Holdings in Singapore before joining Mainstreet in 1999. As CFO, his major responsibilities were financial strategy and reporting. He supported Dhillon in evaluating property purchases and sales and in negotiations with lenders.

Before joining Mainstreet in April 2000, Murray had consulted with the company for the previous year. Through most of the 1990s, he held positions of increasing responsibility in the operations area of Boardwalk Equities. Boardwalk was a Calgary-based firm that grew rapidly in the 1990s and, by 2001, owned more than 25,000 multifamily units, the largest portfolio of residential property in Canada. Like Lam, Murray was attracted to Mainstreet by Dhillon's vision of rapidly growing a major Canadian real estate business while preserving the values of a small entrepreneurial firm. Operating clean, efficient and profitable buildings was a major part of that vision, and that was Murray's focus.

Dhillon also relied heavily on Mainstreet's board of directors for advice on major strategic decisions like the one he faced in March 2001. Brief biographical sketches of the five board members are presented in Exhibit 2.

Dhillon, his advisors and the Mainstreet management team shared the view that it was imperative for the success of the company that it stay non-bureaucratic and quick to react as it grew. Murray explained the difference between Mainstreet's culture and the industry's:

> The multifamily rental sector in Canada is comprised mainly of property management companies that manage the apartments for owners who do not want the headaches of the daily operations. These fee management companies become somewhat bureaucratic and are not quick decision-makers. To make a decision to do any major work or improvements requires the approval of the owner of the individual apartment building.
>
> Fee managers typically work for several different properties whose owners have differing levels of capital available to them. Therefore, the consistency of product, the co-ordination of the staff, and the affordability of supplies change building by building, making the property manager's job a difficult one.
>
> In contrast, Mainstreet owns all its properties; therefore, decisions are made on a global basis. Quality control, consistent service levels, bulk buying, and staffing efficiencies are all possible. Mainstreet can change direction to fix a problem very quickly without having to consult a large number of individual owners.

THE MULTIFAMILY REAL ESTATE SECTOR IN CANADA

There were five main sectors in the Canadian Real Estate industry: commercial, retail, industrial, residential housing, and multifamily. Each had its own distinctive financing, operating and valuation methods. The multifamily sector

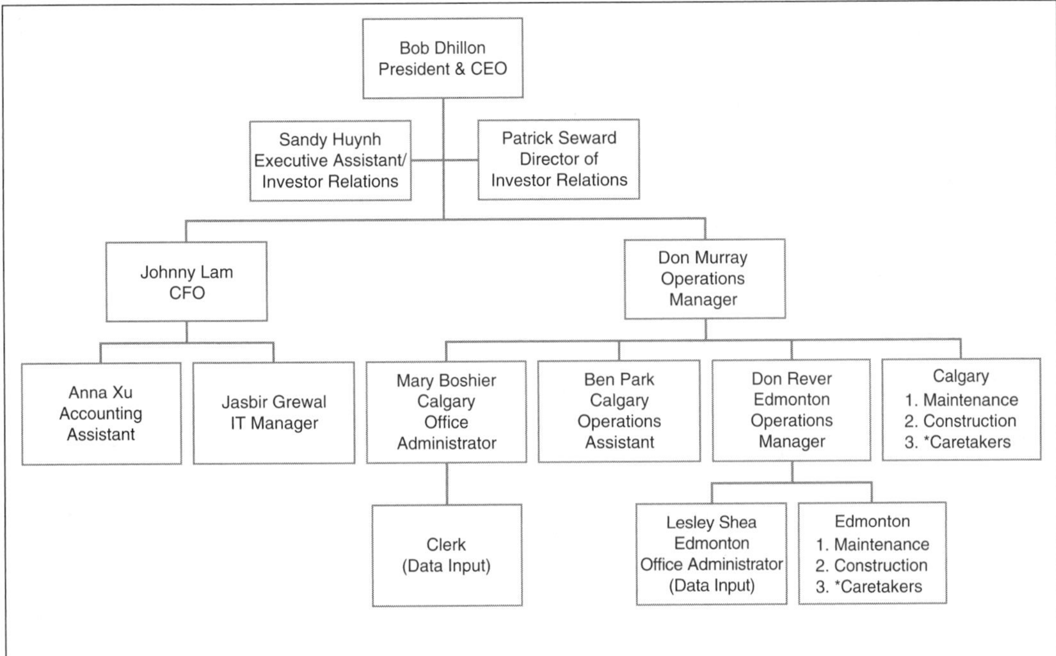

Mary Boshier, office administrator: Computer input, handling tenant and resident manager problems and inquiries, monthly autodebit for rent collection.

Sandy Huynh, executive assistant to Bob Dhillon: Duties included management of Tabasco distribution, pro forma analysis, investor relations at an administrative level (quarterly reports, annual filings, annual general meeting, press releases, compiling mail-outs).

Ben Park, operations assistant: Renovation scheduling, inspection of units, communicating with contractors, co-ordinated with Don Murray and Mary Boshier.

Patrick Seward, director of Investor Relations, based in Toronto: Background in investment banking (CIBC Wood Gundy, Deloitte & Touche), specializing in real estate. Relationships with financial analysts and media. Sourcing large real estate and financing deals.

Anna Xu, accounting assistant to Johnny Lam: Payroll, payables, receivables, maintaining and organizing accounting records with accounting and property management software.

Don Rever, Edmonton operations manager: Co-ordinates Edmonton operations.

Lesley Shea, Edmonton office administrator.

Exhibit 1 Organization Chart

*Please note that the operations managers in each city are supervisors for all caretakers in their city. For example, Don Murray is responsible for 40 caretakers, a large construction crew and a three-man maintenance engineering team. (To be a member of the maintenance team, members must maintain boiler/mechanical certificates.)

Joe Amantea is senior partner at the law firm Warren Tettensor in Calgary. He acts as corporate counsel on behalf of Mainstreet.

Frank Boyd is chairman of The Apex Corporation, a real estate development company based in Calgary and operating in Canada and the United States. Apex, which is the largest land development company in Western Canada, has recorded 39 consecutive quarters of earnings increases. Its major businesses are in single-family residential homes and land development.

Darrell Cook is president of Gibraltar Mortgage Ltd. A Fellow of the Certified General Accountants' Association of Canada with an MBA from University of Calgary, he has more than 25 years of experience in real estate acquisition and development. He is a substantial investor in Mainstreet, owning 25.6 per cent of the outstanding common shares.

Bob Dhillon is president and CEO of Mainstreet Equity Corp.

Rowland Fleming is the former president and CEO of the Toronto Stock Exchange (1994 to 1999). He has more than 30 years of experience in the financial services industry in Canada, including terms as vice-president of the Bank of Nova Scotia, president and CEO of National Trust Company, and president and CEO of the Dominion of Canada General Insurance Company.

Larry Tapp is dean of the Richard Ivey School of Business at The University of Western Ontario. In 1985, he initiated what was then the largest leveraged buy-out outside of the United States, a $552 million deal that created Lawson Mardon Group, one of the world's largest packaging conglomerates. As CEO of the group, he took it public in one of the largest international share offerings ever by a Canadian company.

Exhibit 2 Board of Directors

Table 1 Multifamily Units by Building Size, Canada 2000

Building Size	*Number of Units*	*Proportion of All Units*
6–19	437,316	30.4%
20–49	346,125	24.0%
50–199	471,996	32.8%
200+	184,329	12.8%

consisted of apartment buildings and row housing (also called townhouses). In Canadian urban centres with populations over 50,000, it was estimated that there were 1.44 million multifamily residential units available for rent in 2000. Table 1 shows how these units were distributed according to size of the property.

The Canadian multifamily sector in early 2001 had some distinctive characteristics:

Vacancy Rates

As of October 2000, the overall apartment vacancy rate in Canada was at 1.6 per cent, down from 2.6 per cent the previous year, and at its lowest level since 1987. Furthermore, these low vacancy rates characterized the whole country, with 22 of Canada's 26 major urban centres recording lower vacancy rates in Fall 2000 than in 1999. Exhibit 3 shows vacancy rates for 1998–2000 in 15 major metropolitan areas across Canada (part A) and a 10-year history and projection of vacancy rates in Calgary and Edmonton (part B). In the 10-year period from 1991 to 2001, which was a period of high gains in employment in Alberta's two major cities, the number of rental units per capita in Calgary and Edmonton had actually declined by more than 20 per cent.

Future Supply of Residential Rental Units

It would not appear that new construction in the short run was likely to address the need for apartments in Canada. Why not? Costs of development (including land and construction costs, development charges, building permit fees and taxes) were so high that developers would have to charge rents far beyond what the market would support.[1] As Dhillon described it, "I can buy a building in Calgary today for $60,000 a door (i.e., a unit) that would cost $100,000 a door to build. Therefore, there will be no new supply on the market until rents go up significantly." The reasons for this disparity, which Dhillon estimated to be from 40 per cent to 100 per cent of current property values in Canadian cities, can be traced back to the late 1970s. Dhillon explained:

> At that time, there was a building boom in the multifamily sector because the federal government provided significant tax incentives for construction of new units. The resulting oversupply, and then the recession of the early 1980s, resulted in high vacancy rates and low rents. Consequently, there has been very little new construction in the multifamily sector in the last 15 years, and the rent structure in the Canadian marketplace is still significantly below what would be required to make new building economically feasible.

Another factor affecting the supply of multifamily rental units was the trend to convert rental properties into condominiums, effectively removing them from the rental market. For example, in Edmonton, throughout most of the 1990s, the supply of rental units declined by about one per cent per year, largely due to condominium conversion. By the turn of the century, however, the pace of conversion had slowed somewhat because most of the properties that were deemed to be "ownership quality" had already been changed over to condominiums.[2]

In summary, according to Dhillon:

> What would it take for us to see substantial increases in the supply of multifamily rental units in Canada? A lot! Rents would have to increase by 50 per cent or more in most cities. Interest rates would have to stay low—because interest is the biggest single cost factor in these properties. And, finally, construction costs and localized economics (land availability and prices, and development fees) would have to be reasonable.

Canadian Demographic Trends

Between 1981 and 2001, a period during which the increase in stock of multifamily residential rental units was virtually zero, the Canadian population grew by almost 25 per cent. Exhibit 4 shows projected population growth by age group in Canada for 2001 to 2016. It is noteworthy that the young adult population (aged 20 to 29), who are primarily renters, was expected to grow by 9.5 per cent during this period, although this is slightly under the overall growth in the country of 11 per cent. The other demographic factor affecting the rental market was immigration, which was expected to stay at high levels for the foreseeable future. Immigration was a key driver of the rental market, because immigrants were much more likely than Canadians of similar demographic profiles to rent apartments.

Property Ownership and Management

Ownership of multifamily properties in Canada was highly fragmented. The largest portfolios of these properties were held by the aforementioned Boardwalk Equities (approximately 25,000 units, primarily in Alberta) and Minto Management (approximately 10,000 units in Ottawa and 8,000 more in Southern Ontario). With its 1,600 units, Mainstreet was one of 10

A) By Census Metropolitan Area 1998–2000			
Census Metro Area	*1998*	*1999*	*2000*
Calgary Alberta	0.6	2.8	1.3
Edmonton Alberta	1.9	2.4	1.4
Halifax Nova Scotia	5.5	3.6	3.6
Hamilton Ontario	3.2	1.9	1.7
Kitchener Ontario	1.5	1.0	0.7
London Ontario	4.5	3.5	2.2
Montreal Quebec	4.7	3.0	1.5
Ottawa Ontario	2.1	0.7	0.2
Quebec Quebec	5.2	3.3	1.6
Regina Saskatchewan	1.7	1.4	1.4
St. John's Newfoundland	15.4	9.2	3.8
Toronto Ontario	0.8	0.9	0.6
Vancouver British Columbia	2.7	2.7	1.4
Victoria British Columbia	3.8	3.6	1.8
Winnipeg Manitoba	4.0	3.0	1.5
Canada	3.5	2.6	1.6

B) Ten-Year History for Edmonton and Calgary

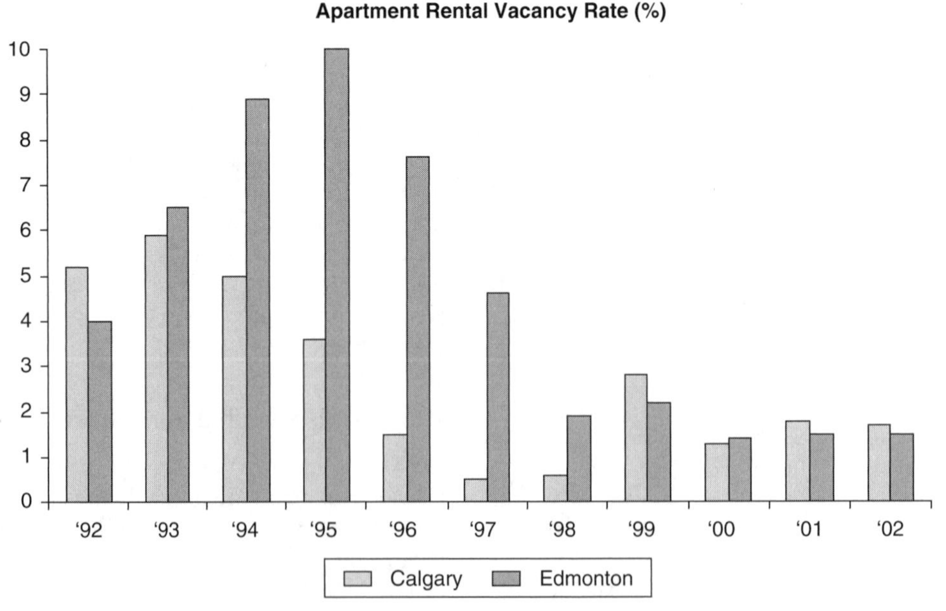

Exhibit 3 Apartment Vacancy Rates

Source: Canada Mortgage and Housing Corporation Rental Market Report for Edmonton, 2001.

Age	*2001*	*2006*	*2011*	*2016*
0–4	1,715.9	1,640.2	1,666.4	1,708.7
5–9	2,026.6	1,790.4	1,715.8	1,741.8
10–14	2,076.6	2,096.4	1,863.6	1,790.1
15–19	2,081.0	2,155.3	2,175.0	1,945.5
20–24	2,097.0	2,167.6	2,241.4	2,261.2
25–29	2,100.3	2,194.1	2,263.5	2,336.4
30–34	2,252.5	2,201.6	2,293.0	2,360.0
35–39	2,641.7	2,326.8	2,278.1	2,367.1
40–44	2,659.1	2,675.7	2,370.3	2,324.0
45–49	2,384.9	2,663.7	2,681.7	2,385.2
50–54	2,114.7	2,362.9	2,637.4	2,657.5
55–59	1,625.9	2,073.7	2,318.3	2,588.5
60–64	1,291.1	1,578.1	2,011.3	2,251.4
65–69	1,137.8	1,222.4	1,495.8	1,907.4
70–74	1,012.0	1,030.5	1,112.7	1,365.7
75–79	815.2	858.7	879.7	957.2
80–84	525.7	627.5	666.2	688.1
85–89	295.2	351.3	422.5	452.9
90 and over	149.2	211.8	269.0	331.0
Total	**31,002.40**	**32,228.70**	**33,361.7**	**34,419.8**

Exhibit 4 Canadian Population (thousands)
Source: Statistics Canada.

largest owners of multifamily units in the country. Private investors, whose principal careers were not in real estate, held the great majority of apartments and row housing properties.

The major multifamily rental firms managed their properties themselves. However, most private investors had careers and busy lives aside from their real estate holdings. "The last thing these people want," according to Dhillon, "is a phone call at midnight about a toilet that isn't working. Therefore, most private investors outsource the actual management of their properties to Property Management companies." For a fee that was typically three to five per cent of the rent, plus a modest percentage of outside maintenance and capital improvement charges, these firms managed a building. They hired a resident manager, contracted for maintenance and repairs, advertised for new tenants, etc. In Dhillon's opinion, the preponderance of private ownership of smaller properties and reliance on so-called "fee managers" created a real opportunity for consolidation and professional management.

> In theory, a "mom and pop" owner of a small property with 20 to 50 units thinks the fee manager will take over all the headaches, and they will just be able to cash a nice cheque every month. But reality can be very different. First, the fee manager isn't paid particularly well and can be fortunate to clear 0.5 per cent from the management fees. Second, the owners aren't eager to spend money on the building for regular maintenance, let alone improvements such as energy-efficient devices. They'd rather go to Hawaii, or buy a new Cadillac than replace the carpets or upgrade the appliances. What *has* to get done is done; what isn't critical is deferred. Over time, what results is a building with a lot of deferred maintenance (carpets, paint, appliances, common areas) that starts to be uncompetitive at the rental rates for its market segment. It gets more difficult to rent vacant units because the building looks "tired." In order to keep the building full, the fee manager doesn't want rents to be increased with the market, and so the building slips into a lower market segment with a lower class of tenant. The net effect of these inefficiencies and the downward economic cycle that appears to be under way in March 2001 is an opportunity for Mainstreet to acquire property and make the necessary investments to unlock its true potential.

Don Murray, Mainstreet's operational manager, listed several reasons for Mainstreet to have a competitive advantage over property management companies:

1. Economies of scale, for example, through bulk purchases.
2. Proprietary software, including accounting programs for financial control and property management programs for control of everyday operations.
3. A computer network system that was online in all Mainstreet properties, eliminating paperwork and providing an immediate information updates at any location.
4. Branding to give consistent quality, level of service and recognition across the board:
   a. Common color scheme at entrances of buildings
   b. Intercom system and security
   c. Uniforms for Mainstreet managers and maintenance staff
   d. Common signage
5. Web site: in the past six months, the percentage of inquiries and subsequent rentals through www.mainstreetequities.com had grown from zero to 15 per cent.
6. Operational synergies among properties located in the same vicinity.
7. Potential for internal tenant transfers between properties.
8. Ability to provide "24-7" service to tenants.

The Mainstreet Strategy

As Dhillon described:

> Mainstreet is focused solely on the multifamily segment of the Canadian real estate sector, and we aim to be the best in the industry. "Apartments are us." We are reinventing a dinosaur business by investing in capital improvements, re-engineering operations and branding the properties. It's a great opportunity for a well-managed company to create shareholder value. Where else are government-guaranteed loans at interest rates of six per cent[3] available for investments with significant potential for capital appreciation?

Mainstreet's financial objective was to deliver consistent returns that were well above the average for a real estate company. There were six linked components of the company's strategy.

Step One: Acquisitions

A key element of Mainstreet's strategy was to buy properties that were under-performing but had a high potential for appreciation under the Mainstreet brand. Unlike residential properties, where the vast majority of homes were sold through the local MLS (Multiple Listing Services) real estate board, the market for multifamily units was not efficient. Trades were done exclusively, and it was difficult to get information on transactions. Consequently, it was very difficult to put a price on an apartment building. Value depended on a host of variables, such as location, construction type, condition, presence of assumable financing, suite sizes, curb appeal and taxation.

Typically, the buildings Mainstreet targeted were apartment or townhouse developments in the middle to lower sector of the multifamily segment, in good locations. Dhillon knew the Calgary market so well that when he received a call from a broker (or a bank receiver) about a given property, he knew instinctively whether or not it was worth further investigation. If so, operations manager Murray would do a workup on what investments would have to be made to bring the property under the Mainstreet brand, and CFO Lam would run the financial analysis. The final call on whether to proceed with an offer was made by Dhillon.

Of course, as Dhillon moved further afield from Calgary, he was not able to rely on local knowledge and instinct about the available deals. However, he believed the multifamily residential segment in Canada was controlled by a tight network of about 100 people (10 big landlords and 90 key real estate players, of which he was one). He was well acquainted with many of these major players, and they would be the primary sources of deals if Mainstreet were to decide to expand outside Alberta.

Step 2: Capital Improvements

Once Mainstreet had purchased a new property, a "swat team" of Mainstreet employees and contractors moved immediately to bring the building under the Mainstreet brand. Murray co-ordinated the effort, which rapidly upgraded the property by renovating the common areas of the development in the characteristic Mainstreet manner. A distinctive Mainstreet sign was placed in front of the building, initially labelled "Under New Management." A uniquely designed canopy was immediately placed over the front entrance to the building, and the common areas (front lobby and hallways) were renovated using a combination of Mainstreet's signature colors, a vibrant forest green and a deep shade of purple. Typically, the floor in the front lobby was replaced with ceramic tile, and lighting in the lobby and hallways was upgraded. Vacant units were also completely renovated before they were rented again. This typically included a new energy-efficient refrigerator and dishwasher, new kitchen cupboards, countertops, paint and carpets. Generally, Mainstreet spent about $4,000 inside each unit in upgrading a newly purchased property. As a high-volume purchaser, Mainstreet obtained both significant price concessions from suppliers and reliable supply on a just-in-time basis so that Mainstreet did not require a high inventory investment.

Step 3: Operational Efficiency

Next, in a program that was organized and managed by Murray, Mainstreet installed energy-efficient devices in the building, such as:

- Replacing incandescent light fixtures with fluorescent (for example, installing a $20 fluorescent fixture cut electricity consumption from $30 per year for a 60-watt light bulb to $8);
- Installing aerators on shower heads and water faucets that cut water flow rates by more than half;
- Replacing toilets with modern, low-volume fixtures that reduced water consumption from six gallons per flush to 1.6.

Murray had data on costs and savings for each of the upgrades, and paybacks were usually less than one year.

As well as the physical changes in the buildings, Mainstreet changed the manner in which the property operated. A new resident manager was installed, consistent with the targeted group of tenants, and the property was moved to an efficient management system with a dedicated maintenance team, an automatic debit rent collection system, and integrated accounting and property management software. The net effect of these changes was to cut annual operating costs, which were typically about $2,400 per unit in a purchased property, by 20 to 25 per cent.

Exhibit 5 portrays Mainstreet's operational procedures diagrammatically. Each apartment building was set up as a separate business unit. A computer, Internet connection and proprietary software were installed at the property. These devices allowed just-in-time information to reach the head office. All deposits, work orders for problems, and tenant information were input directly at the site level. Double entry was eliminated, and information about the project was available at the head office at the touch of a button.

Rent collection at Mainstreet was simplified with automatic debit from tenant bank accounts on the first of the month, unlike mom-and-pop operations where it might well be the 10th or 15th before the entire rent was deposited. This system required no manpower except for inputting of data into the system.

Step 4: Value Enhancement

Along with the significant improvements in the property came an increase in rents, typically in the order of 25 per cent to 50 per cent, but sometimes even more. Alberta was not subject to legislated rent controls, an issue which could become a factor should Mainstreet decide to expand beyond the province. However, Dhillon believed, even if a protesting tenant brought Mainstreet to court, the corporation could easily justify the rent increase by the improvements in the property.

Rental increases were not always perceived negatively. Typically, 70 per cent of tenants moved out and 30 per cent accepted the increase, feeling that it was worthwhile because of the value-enhancing improvements. Mainstreet would transfer a current tenant into a renovated suite as well as do some renovations in an occupied suite. In one recent instance, Mainstreet had implemented a 40 per cent rent increase in one of its Edmonton properties but had no net increase in the vacancy rate because the higher rents were justified by renovations and enhancements. As well as the immediate cash flow effects, the rent increases had one other significant benefit for Mainstreet: the least desirable renters moved out, and they were easily replaced a better class of tenant.

Step 5: Financing

Based on the increased value of the property, Mainstreet could obtain long-term, government-insured mortgages at favorable interest rates. This freed up capital for acquisition of new high-potential properties. Mainstreet's account manager at People's Trust described how this worked:

> Bob is an astute buyer. Mainstreet typically buys properties that have high deferred maintenance, but good upside potential. It can obtain a first mortgage for 75 per cent of the purchase price from us at a favorable rate of interest, say prime plus 1.25 per cent. Furthermore, Mainstreet could obtain a second mortgage for 15 per cent of the purchase price, at a higher interest rate—say 13 per cent—and sometimes a third mortgage at an even higher rate. Sometimes, a highly motivated vendor provides some financing for the transaction with a vendor take-back mortgage.
>
> Next, Bob invests a significant amount, say 30 per cent of the cost of the building, in a complete renovation of the property, which justifies a substantial rent increase, of 30 per cent to 50 per cent. But because the investment has also produced energy savings and Mainstreet has scale economies in operations, operating income for the building has actually increased by more than the dollar amount of the rent increase. This improved cash flow makes the property now worth substantially more; it could easily be appraised at 75 per cent to 100 per cent over the purchase price, based on the improved operating income alone. Now Bob can refinance the

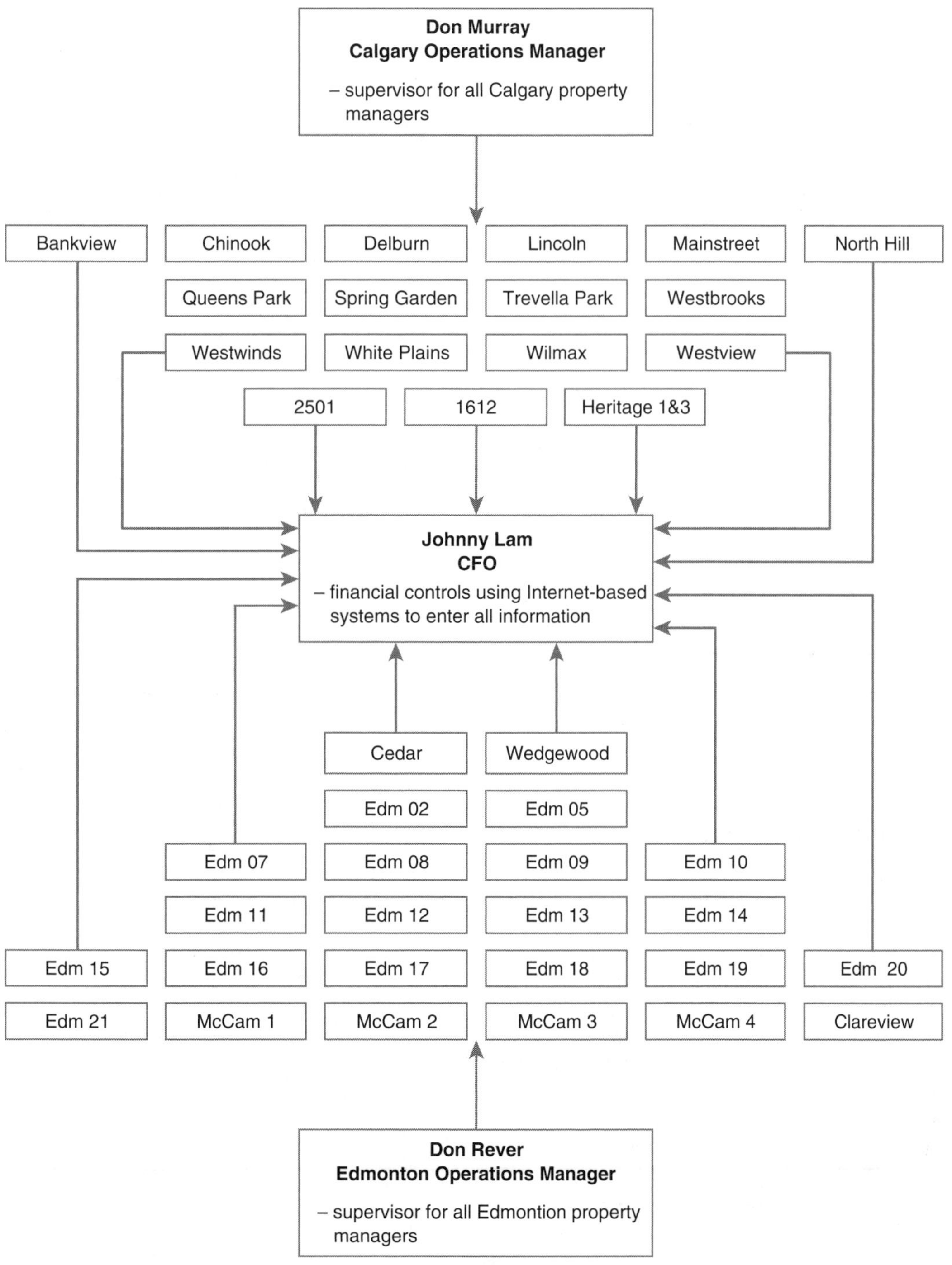

Exhibit 5 Operational Procedure

> property with a CMHC (Central Mortgage and Housing Corporation) guaranteed loan, at 6.1 per cent interest,[4] for 75 per cent of the new market value. Mainstreet pays off the original mortgages, recovers its investment for improvements, and owns an asset with substantial cash flow. The surplus cash goes into the next round of building purchases and capital improvements.

See Exhibit 6 for an actual example of what Mainstreet calls the value creation process.

Step 6: Divestitures

Most mature assets are held for cash flow purposes, but Mainstreet does selectively sell some properties that do not offer sufficient potential value.

Results

Exhibit 7 portrays the financial results of Mainstreet's first years of operation, while Table 2 below shows Mainstreet's growth in units. The results were generated through internal growth alone, with no new equity issues.

The Growth Opportunity in March 2001

At the March 23, 2001, board meeting, Dhillon wanted to get feedback from his directors on what he felt was the critical choice that Mainstreet faced: how rapidly to expand. Should Mainstreet be satisfied with steady growth in Alberta, and plan to add 300 to 400 units in the next year? Or, he thought, was this the time to "bet the farm," extend the Mainstreet brand outside Alberta, and double the size of the company in the next year?

Dhillon was aggressively pro-expansion, and he opened the discussion by making the case for it. He summarized arguments on both the supply (low vacancy rates, low property values compared with replacement costs, and low and falling interest rates) and demand (population growth in the renter segment, and increasing immigration) sides. Furthermore, he believed,

> The end result of a slowdown in the economy or even a full-fledged recession, is that liquidity dries up and the volume of buy-and-sell transactions for rental properties slows down as well. However, that is also a time of opportunity for Mainstreet. As the old saying goes, "Cash is king in a recession."

However, Dhillon also listened carefully to the comments of his board members who, for the most part, were more cautious:

- The U.S. economy seems to be going into a deep freeze. My instincts tell me that this might be the time to go slowly rather than expand rapidly.
- We need more data. Let's take the time to digest the numbers from the economy before we move precipitately, and plan carefully before shooting from the hip in an immediate aggressive expansion.
- There's still room to expand right here in Alberta, in your own back yard. Going into other markets is a lot riskier. And these markets are much more regulated than Alberta. I know that in the Vancouver area, development costs are 20 per cent higher than Calgary, just because of the additional bureaucracy—permits, local regulations, etc.

On the other hand, there were also arguments in favor of aggressive expansion. As one board member expressed:

> Go for it! The fundamentals in this market—vacancy rates, new construction costs, interest rates—have never been better. We're cyclical players in the market. When the economy turns down, it's a great time for us to buy. Furthermore, we benefit from lower interest rates, since our major expense is interest on our debt. In fact, if interest rates go where we expect, in the next year we will refinance two-thirds of our mortgage portfolio, at interest rates averaging two per cent less than we are currently paying. Now is the time to move.

As CEO of Mainstreet and by far its largest shareholder, Dhillon had to make the call on

West Wind, a 31-unit apartment in Calgary

Stage 1—Acquisition

	Amount	**Per unit**
Purchase price	$1,080,000	$34,839
1st Mortgage loan 75% @ 7%/yr.	810,000	
2nd & 3rd Mortgage 25% @ 12.5%/yr.	270,000	
Equity	—	
Rent	163,000	5,258
Vacancy and bad debt allowance (3%)	4,890	158
Operating expenses	77,500	2,500
Operating income	80,610	2,600
Mortgage interest	90,450	
Depreciation	7,709	
Income before income taxes	$(17,549)	

Stage 2—Value enhancement through capital improvement. Actual annualized income after capital expenditure of $315,000, increased rents and operational efficiency improvements.

	Amount	**Per unit**
Capital expenditure	$315,000	$10,161
Rent	255,708	8,249
Vacancy & bad debt allowance (3%)	7,671	247
Operating expenses	71,484	2,306
Operating income	176,553	
Mortgage interest	90,450	
Depreciation	10,324	
Income before income taxes	$75,779	

Stage 3—Consolidate mortgage loans

		Per unit
Appraised market value of the property with operating income of $176,553	$2,046,000	$66,000
CMHC insured mortgage @ 6.1%/yr. on 75% of appraised value	$1,534,500	

These funds will pay off the original mortgages of $1.08 million and leave $454,500 for further purchases and capital improvements. With an investment of $315,000, Mainstreet has acquired an asset that provides positive cash flow and is worth $2 million; furthermore, by refinancing with a low-interest CMHC guaranteed loan, it has generated $454.5 thousand in cash for further investments.

Exhibit 6 Example of Value Creation

Source: Adapted from Mainstreet Equity Corp. internal documents.

CONSOLIDATED BALANCE SHEETS (Thousands of dollars)			
As at	*December 31, 1998*	*September 30, 1999*	*September 30, 2000*
Assets			
Real estate properties	$10,789	$37,152	$66,034
Cash	1,506	1,415	898
Other current assets	34	526	569
Deferred charges	152	359	1,178
	$12,482	$39,452	$68,679
Liabilities			
Mortgages payable	$10,219	$34,127	$63,122
Bank indebtedness	80	—	396
Accounts payable	161	286	532
Refundable security deposits	145	366	—
Income taxes payable	—	426	931
Deferred income taxes	7	264	
	10,613	36,469	64,981
Shareholders' Equiity			
Share capital	1,859	1,869	1,869
Retained earnings	9	1,114	1,829
	1,869	2,983	3,698
	12,482	39,452	68,679

CONSOLIDATED STATEMENTS OF INCOME AND RETAINED EARNINGS (Thousands of dollars, except per share amounts)			
As at	*December 31, 1998 (9 months)*	*September 30, 1999 (12 months)*	*September 30, 2000 (12 months)*
Revenue			
Rental income	$1,778	$2,971	$7,740
Sale of real estate properties	—	3,223	2,609
Interest income	71	84	41
	1,849	6,277	10,390
Expenses			
Property operating expenses	643	904	2,077
Cost of sales, real estate properties	—	1,778	2,002
General and administrative expenses	230	327	858
Financing cost	773	1,210	3,382
Depreciation and amortization	186	273	711
	1,832	4,492	9,030
Income before income taxes	16	1,786	1,360
Income taxes			
– Current	—	426	(23)
– Deferred	7	256	667
Net income	9	1,104	716
Retained earnings, beginning of year	—	9	1,113
Retained earnings, end of year	$9	$1,113	$1,829
Earnings per share			
– Basic	*	$0.12	$0.08
– Fully diluted	*	$0.12	$0.08

Exhibit 7 Financial Statements

*Less than 1 cent per share

Source: Mainstreet Equity Corp. annual reports.

Table 2 Growth in Mainstreet Holdings 1998–2001

	Dec. 31, 1998	*Sept. 30, 1999*	*Sept. 30, 2000*	*Jan. 1, 2001*
# of Units				
• Calgary	271	548	816	874
• Edmonton	0	356	554	670
Total	271	904	1,370	1,544
Market Value	$17 million	$50 million	$90 million	$100 million

the biggest decision in Mainstreet's short but successful history.

Notes

1. "New Ottawa high rise ends drought," *Toronto Globe and Mail,* March 27, 2001, p. B17.

2. Canada Mortgage and Housing Corporation Rental Market Report for Edmonton, 2001.

3. In March 2001, the Bank of Canada overnight rate (for funds loaned to Canadian chartered banks) was five per cent and the banks' prime rate was 5.75 per cent.

4. Interest rate on CMHC guaranteed loans were typically 0.75 per cent above Canadian long-term bond rates.

7

Venture Analytics

Beyond Venture Creation

Background

In this chapter, we intend to demonstrate how you can apply your new knowledge of the venture creation process as an analytical tool to the identification of new opportunity or to solving virtually any venturing problem that relates to creating new units of value. As we have previously asserted, the first job of the entrepreneur is to create new units of value. Anyone who has prepared a financial projection and has begun with the "top line" (revenues) has observed that the gross revenue for a product or service can be computed by multiplying *units* times price. Although price setting is the job of the marketer, unit creation is the job of the entrepreneur.

What are new units?

As illustrated in Figure 7.1, the most basic unit in business is the transaction, which consists of a creative person or team creating a work that is sold to other persons or entities in the marketplace. Thus, entrepreneurs add value because they can bring units into existence, which—prior to their intervention—did not exist.

As explained in more detail below, transaction cognition entrepreneurship theory (Mitchell, 1999, 2001, 2003) proposes that three sets of cognitions working together are sufficient for an individual to create a successful transaction:

- Competition cognitions
- Promise cognitions
- Planning cognitions

The combined experience (Vesper, 1996) of expert entrepreneurs suggests a master venture creation process, or "script," that contains at least the six skill subscripts that have been discussed in Chapters 1 through 6:

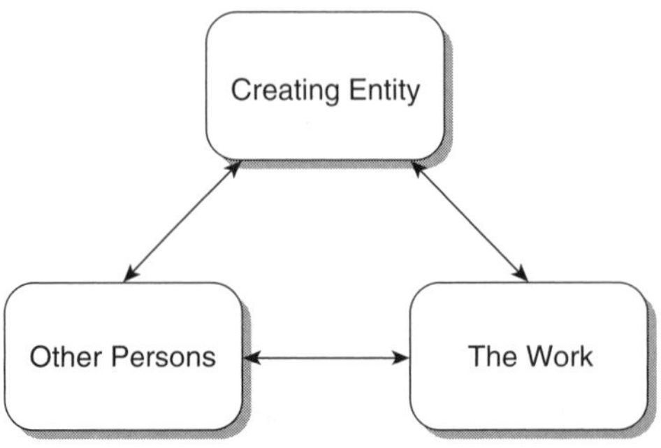

Figure 7.1 The Elements of a Basic Transaction

Source: Based on Gardner (1993).

- Searching
- Screening
- Planning/financing
- Setup
- Start-up
- Ongoing orchestration and growth

This seventh chapter of the casebook is written to explain how the six skill subscripts link to planning, promise, and competition cognitions, as suggested by transaction cognition entrepreneurship theory, and furthermore how these linkages make it possible for entrepreneurs to recognize unit-driven opportunity or to diagnose unit-based problems. And in doing so, it explains how the venture creation process is the sequential application of transaction cognitions that, with the same power these cognitions have to bring transactions into existence, brings a venture (as a new economic unit at the firm level of analysis) into existence.

Transaction Cognition Entrepreneurship Theory

Transaction cognitions consist of specialized mental models or scripts (Arthur, 1994; Neisser, 1967; Read, 1987) that guide individuals' economic responses to three principal sources of market imperfection: specificity (S), opportunism (O), and bounded rationality (BR) (Williamson, 1985). In the real world, markets are not perfect because transactions do not occur instantaneously, and information is incomplete. Because each product or service in the real world is specific, it takes time (e.g., shopping) versus being instantaneous to match a buyer with a product/service. Because at least once in their real-world experience someone has been cheated, each party must also take time in a new transaction to try to minimize the possibility of opportunism. And because in the real world there are limits to how much information we possess and how effectively we use it, our intention to be "rational" in a transaction is, in effect, bounded or limited. The extent to which transaction time is extended and rationality is bounded creates a kind of transaction-preventing

Table 7.1 Some Attributes of the Contracting Process

Behavioral Assumption			
Asset Specificity	*Opportunism*	*Implied Bounded Rationality*	*Contracting Process*
0	+	+	Competition
+	0	+	Promise
+	+	0	Planning
+	+	+	Governance

Source: Adapted from Williamson (1985, p. 31).
Note: 0 = absence, + = presence.

friction in socioeconomic relationships known as *transaction costs,* which have actually been compared by Kenneth Arrow, winner of the Nobel Prize in Economics, to "friction in physical systems" (Arrow, 1969, p. 48; Williamson, 1985, p. 19). Therefore, for transactions to occur, the parties must think of ways to reduce the transaction costs caused by S, O, and BR, so that a transaction is not prevented from happening by socioeconomic friction. The thinking that is used by people to help them to make helpful transacting responses is what we call *transaction cognitions,* or transaction thinking. The three general transaction-thinking sets/transaction cognitions can be logically derived from work in transaction cost economics conducted by noted scholar Oliver Williamson.

Williamson (1985, p. 31) argues that transacting responses, such as the ones discussed in the preceding paragraph, take the form of contracting processes in the transacting world and include (a) competition, (b) promise, (c) planning, and (d) governance/hierarchy-creating processes, depending (respectively in each instance) on the presence/absence combination of the foregoing market attributes (S, O, and BR) (Williamson, 1985), as shown in Table 7.1.

The framework presented in Table 7.1 suggests three sets of attribute-process relationships: (a) between specificity and competition, (b) between opportunism and promise, and (c) between bounded rationality and planning. Interestingly, although each relationship is shown to be by nature bidirectional, Williamson (1985) uses only one direction in his analysis of hierarchies versus markets. That is, he suggests (for example) that the "absence" of asset specificity in the "presence" of opportunism and bounded rationality implies competition but leaves underused the reverse idea that competition should also reduce transaction costs from specificity in situations characterized by those same two conditions. The same conclusion follows for market imperfections created by opportunism and bounded rationality. The logic represented in Table 7.1 suggests that the level of transaction costs from opportunism should be affected by promise processes (e.g., trust creation; Barney & Hansen, 1994) among stakeholders (Agle, Mitchell, & Sonnenfeld, 1999; Mitchell et al., 1997) and the level of transaction costs from bounded rationality by planning processes (Simon, 1979).

Thus, the cognitions, or thinking models, that individuals possess about (a) competition (defined as mental models that reduce transaction costs from specificity-friction to create sustainable competitive advantage), (b) promise (defined as mental models that reduce transaction costs from opportunism-friction to help in promoting trustworthiness in relationships with stakeholders; Agle et al., 1999; Mitchell et al., 1997), and (c) planning (defined as the mental models that reduce transaction costs from bounded rationality-friction to assist in developing analytical structure to solve previously unstructured problems) are expected to affect the success of transacting.

Entrepreneurial opportunity (Kirzner, 1982) occurs when entrepreneurs use entrepreneurial thinking (planning, promise, and competition cognitions) to reduce transaction costs/socioeconomic frictions such that transactions that would otherwise fail due to transaction costs now are able to occur. Entrepreneurship may in this respect be conceptualized as an essentially cognitive process (Mitchell, Smith, Seawright, & Morse, 2000).

According to the above definitions, then, a transaction occurs when a creating entity (e.g., an individual) produces a "work" (some product or service) and then enters into an exchange relationship with other persons (the marketplace) for the sale or acceptance of that work (Gardner, 1993), as illustrated in Figure 7.1. And transaction cognitions are the mental models or scripts (Arthur, 1994; Read, 1987) that are used in this process. Thus, when the objective of entrepreneurship is to discover (Kirzner, 1982) and enact successful transactions/units, the job of the entrepreneur is to use transaction cognitions to create new units of value—new transactions.

This reasoning produces a definition of entrepreneurship that is highly useful in recognizing opportunity and in solving real-world unit-creation problems:

> Transaction cognition theory defines entrepreneurship to be: the use of transaction cognitions (competition, promise, and planning mental models/scripts) to organize exchange relationships (among the work, other persons, and creating entities) that utilize the sources of market imperfections (specificity, opportunism, and bounded rationality) to create new units of value. (Mitchell, 2003, pp. 190–191)

This definition is illustrated in Figure 7.2.

The Six Skill Subscripts

After more than 25 years of studying entrepreneurs, Vesper (1996) suggests six skill subscripts that experienced venturers use in venture creation. These have been presented previously in Chapters 1 through 6 and include searching, screening, planning/financing, setup, start-up, and ongoing orchestration/growth. As previously explained, each of these skill sets contains unique knowledge and, when combined, forms an entrepreneur's master script.

In the following paragraphs, we analyze each of the skill subscripts according to the transaction cognition model, producing a definition of the skill subscript that can be stated in terms of transaction cognition theory. And to help you to better visualize these relationships, we also provide a diagram explaining the link between transaction cognition theory and each skill subscript. We encourage you to try to imprint these visualizations in your mind so that you will be prepared to take the knowledge you have gained in Chapters 1 through 6 and use it for more than simply understanding the venture creation process itself. In this chapter, we hope that you will also learn how to apply your new knowledge of the venture creation process as an analytical tool to the identification of new opportunity or to solving virtually any venturing problem that relates to creating new units of value.

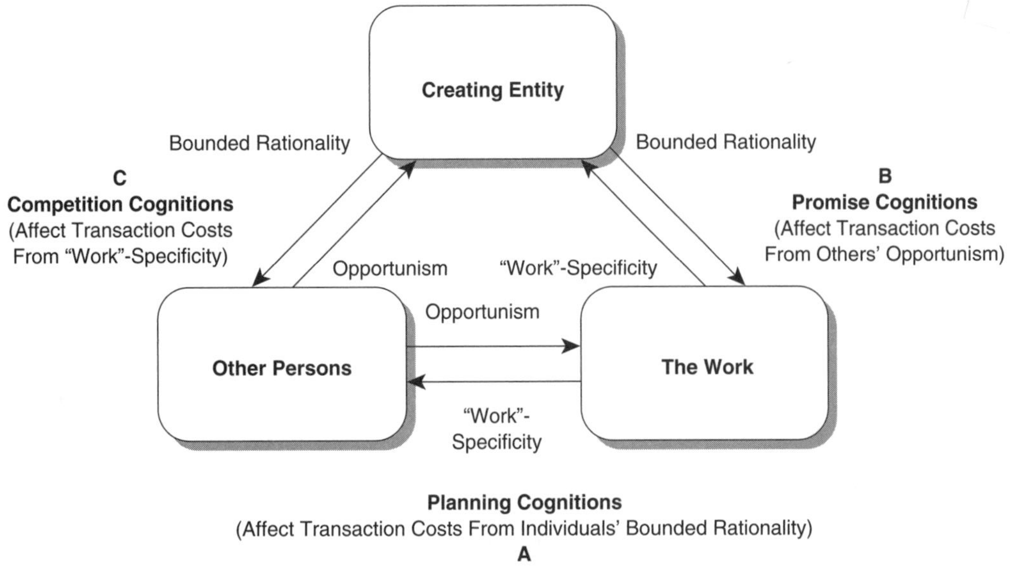

Figure 7.2 The Three Transaction Cognitions Needed to Create Value Based on New Units (Transactions)

Source: Mitchell (2002).

Searching

In the search process, an individual (the transaction creator) connects with other persons (the marketplace) and identifies works (products or services that these persons want) that this individual can produce competitively. As illustrated in the diagram below, searching skill primarily concerns finding "the work" that the market wants and, as shown in Figure 7.3, is a type of competition cognition.

Screening

In the screening process, an individual (the transaction creator) assesses the proposed work (products or services that other persons might want) to estimate their promise to profitably satisfy the wants of other persons (the marketplace). As illustrated in the diagram below, screening skill primarily involves understanding the wants of "other persons" and, as shown in Figure 7.4, is a type of promise cognition.

Planning/Financing

In the planning/financing process, an individual (the transaction creator) must gather, process, understand, and use the information necessary to organize the delivery of the work (Level 1: products or services that other persons want; Level 2: the venture as a finance product) to other persons (the marketplace). This includes the writing of the business plan and the use of this plan to finance the venture. As illustrated in the diagram below, planning/financing skill primarily involves overcoming the limitations of "the individual"

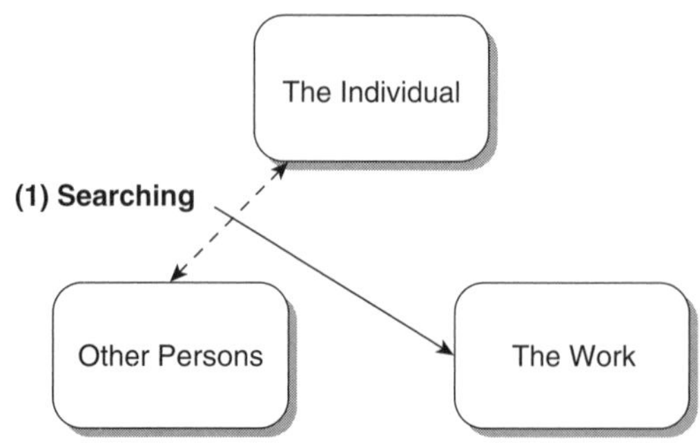

Figure 7.3 Searching Skill Is a Competition Cognition

Source: Based on Gardner (1993).

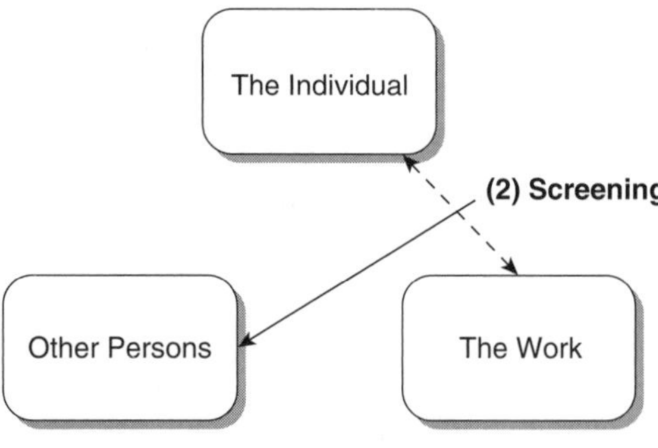

Figure 7.4 Screening Skill Is a Promise Cognition

(transaction creator) through planning the connection of the work (Level 1: products or services that other persons want; Level 2: the venture as a finance product) to the "other persons" (marketplace) and, as shown in Figure 7.5, is a type of planning cognition.

Setup

In the setup process, an individual (the transaction creator) connects with other persons (the marketplace) and creates the venture that will produce competitively the works (products or services that these persons want). As illustrated in the diagram below, setup skill primarily concerns the production of "the work" that the market wants and, as shown in Figure 7.6, is a type of competition cognition.

Start-Up

In the start-up process, an individual (the transaction creator) focuses on the wants of other persons (in the marketplace) and begins the process of production and sale of the

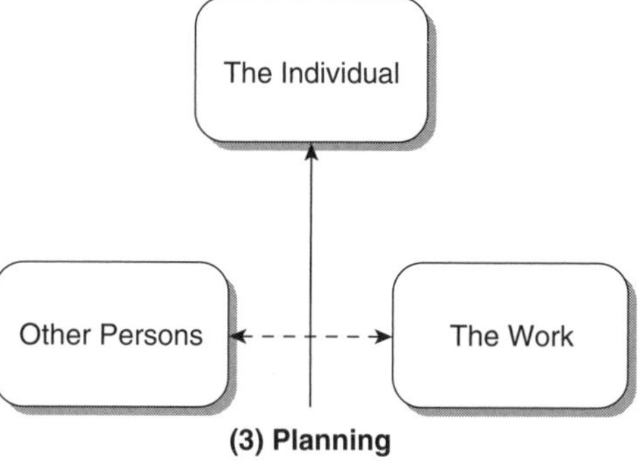

Figure 7.5 Planning/ Financing Skill Is a Planning Cognition

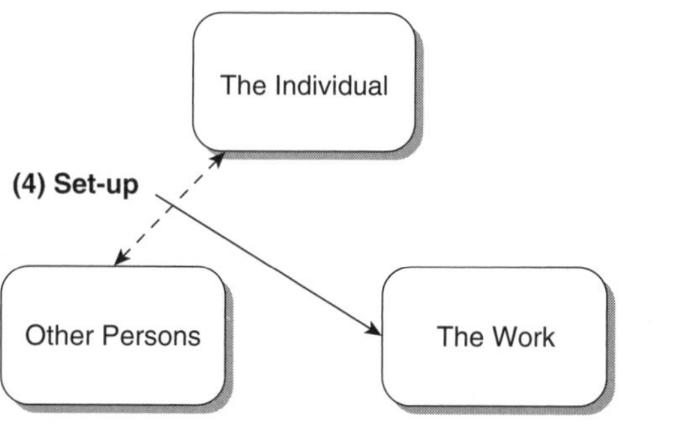

Figure 7.6 Setup Skill Is Competition Cognition

work (products or services that the venture produces) to satisfy the wants of other persons (the marketplace). As illustrated in the diagram below, start-up skill primarily involves understanding "other persons" (the marketplace) and, as shown in Figure 7.7, is a type of promise cognition.

Ongoing Operations and Growth

In the ongoing/growth orchestration process, an individual (the transaction creator) must gather, process, understand, and use the information necessary to continue the delivery of the work (Level 1: products or services that other persons want; Level 2: the venture as a finance product) to other persons (the marketplace). This includes the implementation of the operations plan and the use of this plan to produce the results that the venture was created to accomplish. As illustrated in the diagram below, ongoing/growth orchestration skill primarily involves a continuous process of overcoming the limitations of "the individual" (transaction creator) through planning for, assessing, and maintaining the connection of the work (Level 1: products or services that other persons want; Level 2: the venture as a

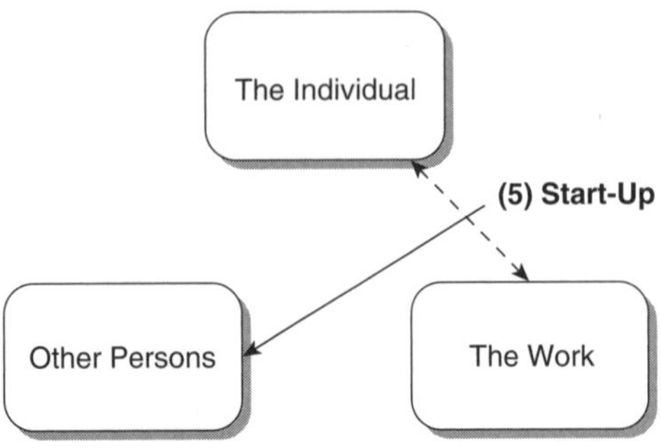

Figure 7.7 Start-Up Skill Is a Promise Cognition

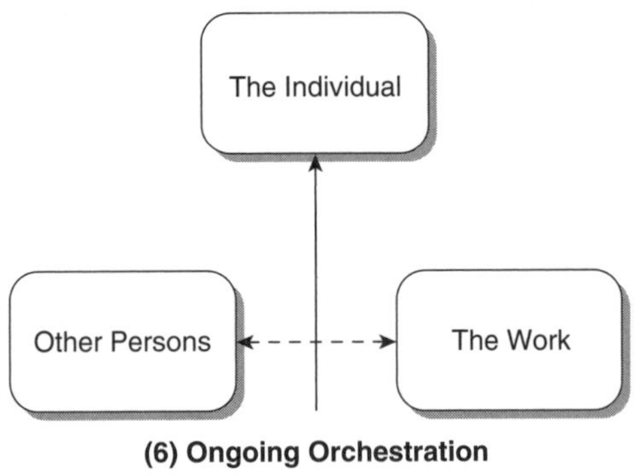

Figure 7.8 Ongoing Operations/Growth Skill Is a Planning Cognition

finance product) to the "other persons" (marketplace) and, as shown in Figure 7.8, is a type of planning cognition.

Venture Analytics: Putting It All Together

In this section of the chapter, we explain how to apply the knowledge that you have gained in learning the six skill subscripts of searching, screening, planning/financing, setup, start-up, and operations/growth to the challenge of identifying new opportunity or of solving unit-based venture value creation problems. The key to this analysis method is to use the transaction cognition definition of entrepreneurship to create an analysis framework that relates your knowledge to the key elements of entrepreneurship contained in the definition, as illustrated in Figure 7.9.

The analysis proceeds in two phases: In Phase 1, the first three columns are filled in; in Phase 2, connections are made across rows to complete column 4. As illustrated in Figure 7.9, the column phase of this analytical method starts first with column 2, then moves on to columns 3, 1, and 4. The logic behind this approach is to use the matrix format to

(3) Use Transaction Cognitions	*(1) To Organize Exchange Relationships*	*(2) That ↓ Transaction Cognitions Due To the Following*	*(4) To Create New Units of Value*
Competition cognitions:	The work:	Specificity:	
Promise cognitions:	Others:	Opportunism:	
Planning cognitions:	Transaction creators:	Bounded rationality:	

Figure 7.9 The Venture Analytics Transaction Analysis Worksheet

organize the information available in a given situation. Most easily identified is information about the exchange itself: the work, the others, the transaction creators. A little more difficult is to extract from the details of the situation the nature of the socioeconomic frictions—the transaction costs—that may be hindering the occurrence of, or an increase in, the flow of transaction units.

Once these two sets of information have been specified, it is then possible to begin exploring the three categories of cognitions—competition, promise, and planning—for possible thought → action combinations that will alter the nature of the exchange such that transaction costs will be removed and transaction occurrence will be expedited. Finally, column 4 is completed as columns 1 to 3 are connected, where transaction cognitions modify exchange relationships to decrease transaction costs and yield increased units of value.

Here are the steps behind this method. You'll notice that your first step begins in column 2. We do this because the information to fill in column 2 is the most concrete. Once column 2 is known, then the next easiest column to fill out is column 3 because we can see what problems are arising from the entities involved. After that, we can go to column 1. To complete this column, use the information learned in Chapters 1 through 6. Last, proceed to column 4, but this time, use row analysis to go across the columns in order (1, 2, 3) following the definition of entrepreneurship in the column headings. If you do this, it sets you up to have the insights necessary to use your new knowledge (Chapters 1–6), to organize exchange relationships (column 2), and to solve the transaction problems (column 3) with your new value-adding insights (column 4).

Column 2: Organize Exchange Relationships. The first step in a transaction cognition analysis is to fill in column 1 by identifying the work (product or service), the others (customers and other stakeholders), and the transaction creators (those individuals who have control of the transacting process).

Column 3: The Transaction Costs. Second, fill in column 3 by listing next to the work, others, and creators, the sources of transaction costs that these three elements of the transaction contribute to the opportunity or problem situation.

Column 1: Transaction Cognitions. Third, fill in column 1 with the competition, promise, and planning cognitions that come from your venture knowledge/script as follows:

- Competition cognitions: from searching and setup
- Promise cognitions: from screening and start-up
- Planning cognitions: from planning/financing and ongoing operations/growth

As noted above, these cognitions consist of possible thought → action combinations that will alter the nature of the exchange (column 2) such that transaction costs will be removed or reduced (column 3), and transaction occurrence will be expedited (i.e., units will increase).

Column 4: Increased Units of Value. Fourth, explicitly explain how the entrepreneurial thinking from column 1 changes the exchange parameters, such that socioeconomic frictions decrease and new units are made possible.

Student Applications Example

In an assignment designed to facilitate practice of the transaction cognition approach to venture analytics, students are asked to find a case in the business/entrepreneurship press (please see Table 7.2 for an example [Anderson, 2004], as marked up by the student, that describes the unit-based entrepreneurial problems of Celestia, Inc.) where a venturing problem was solved (a lot of new value was created) and to apply the matrix analysis method to this success to explain how and why it occurred.

Along with their completed worksheet (see Figure 7.10), students are asked to hand in a three-paragraph analysis that explains what they learned, the possible underlying pattern in that specific situation, and ways they can see to generalize this pattern to future situations that they might encounter.

The following analysis comes from a student in the University of Victoria 2004 Entrepreneurship Program:

(Text continues on page 368)

Table 7.2 Sample Student Case

casestudy

subject: Celestica Inc.

company: The world's fourth largest electronics manufacturing services firm
problem: Proving a sudden turnaround after a two-year slump is for real
question: How can Celestica build on its momentum, and avoid repeating history?
By Mark Anderson

AS THE TECH ECONOMY RECOVERS FROM ITS PROTRACTED slump, an unlikely company has been flirting with market-darling status: Celestica Inc. As recently as three months ago, analysts wondered aloud whether the Toronto-based electronics manufacturing services firm — the fourth largest in the world — would ever return to health. It had grown robust during the tech boom, assembling high-end servers, monitors and optical networking gear for clients such as IBM Corp., Sun Microsystems Inc., Nortel Networks Corp. and Cisco Systems Inc. But when it crashed, it crashed hard. And no amount of cost-cutting could stop the erosion of earnings as demand for its services dried up. Revenues went into a two-year slide, and Celestica closed the books on 2003 with a US$266-million loss, followed by the abrupt departure of its long-time CEO, Eugene Polistuk.

Even though Celestica was winded, it wasn't entirely knocked out. On April 22, it posted its results for the first quarter of 2004 — and the numbers vastly exceeded expectations. Revenues stood at US$2 billion, up 27% from 2003's first quarter. They also rose 5% over the third quarter, in which a loss had been predicted. Adjusted earnings, meanwhile, came in at 2 cents U.S. per share, compared to an expected loss of 3 cents U.S. The next day, investors boosted Celestica stock to $26.97 from $22.52 on the TSX.

Where did the turnaround come from? Celestica attributed the performance to a pair of factors: the ongoing effects of cost cutting, and a rising demand for electronic manufacturing services — or EMS — as telecom companies and major corporations started spending on network technology again. Although things are looking up, Celestica still faces challenges. The most important? Building on the momentum it has finally started to show.

IBM Canada created Celestica in 1994, and sold it two years later to Onex Corp., the Toronto-based leveraged buyout firm led by Gerald Schwartz. At the time, large computer and telecom equipment makers — the so-called OEMs, or original equipment manufacturers — were starting to outsource their manufacturing and assembly work, selling in-house capabilities to firms that would then carry out the work under contract. The rationale behind the trend was simple: If the OEMs got out of manufacturing and assembly, a low-margin business, they could concentrate on high-value activities like design, engineering, sales and marketing. Manufacturing could be consolidated in the hands of a few mega-sized EMS firms, which could then use their economies of scale to squeeze out costs.

Onex floated Celestica on the public markets in 1998 — the largest tech IPO in Canadian history. The company spent the remainder of the decade buying up manufacturing capacity from OEMs in Asia, Europe and North America. (Overall, Celestica has made more than 30 acquistions.) The business model worked, at least in the early years. In the boom of the late 1990s, investors were only too happy to reward EMS companies that showed strong revenue growth and global scale, especially since the industry was rapidly consolidating in the hands of a few major players.

And all major EMS companies were enjoying impressive revenue growth, although they continued to operate on razor-thin margins. Several attempted to reduce costs and improve profitability by purchasing the manufacturers of the components that went into EMS products. But the strategy proved ill-advised, as tech crashed and demand for manufacturing evaporated. Companies such as Flextronics Corp., Selectron Corp., Sanmina-SCI Corp. and C-MAC Industries Inc., which had been buying up suppliers, were hit hard as they found themselves carrying the costs of maintaining increasingly idle factories, and with few opportunities to reduce costs by shopping around for deals on components.

Celestica, by contrast, had not gone on a supplier-buying spree, and weathered the first months of the downturn. But by 2002, it could no longer avoid the impact of what had become a long-term slump in its industry, and a worldwide glut in EMS capacity. CEO Polistuk responded by shuttering facilities and slashing thousands of jobs — roughly one-third of Celestica's force. But the cuts came too late and didn't go deep enough to reverse the slide. Celestica's overall earnings, revenues, and margins declined in

(Continued)

Table 7.2 (Continued)

Illustration by Zach Trenholm

2003, leading Standard & Poor's Ratings Services, earlier this year, to downgrade the company's credit rating to BB — junk status, two levels below investment grade. The downgrade might have been expected by some, but the sudden resignation of Polistuk wasn't. He stepped down on January 29, 2004, the same day Celestica released its dismal year-end results for 2003. Officially, Polistuk's departure was called a retirement, but it was widely believed Celestica's board of directors forced the issue, due to his inability to reverse the firm's fortunes. Without a successor waiting in the wings, the board turned to Stephen Delaney, the company's president of American operations, and made him interim CEO until a permanent replacement for Polistuk could be found.

If there were concerns over Delaney's leadership, they proved short-lived as he embarked on an aggressive cost-cutting program, promising to close more redundant plants in Europe and North America, and to trim a further 5,000 jobs from the payroll. Then he delivered 2004's surprising first quarter results.

Looking forward, Delaney promised more good news in the second-quarter: Revenue would grow by 12% over the preceeding three months, while earnings per share would come in between 7 cents U.S. and 13 cents U.S. — more than double most analysts' predictions. The long-awaited comeback, it appeared, had finally arrived. Celestica's board called off their CEO search and offered Delaney a permanent home in the top executive suite.

And yet ... there are concerns for the industry in general, and Celestica in particular. First, there are fears that the firm's ongoing restructuring efforts will cost more than anticipated. Layoffs and plant closures are expected to yield annual savings of US$125 million. But the company faces between US$175 million and US$200 million this year in restructuring charges, and there's speculation that estimate is low.

Celestica has also vowed to eliminate 20% of its senior management team. The move is generally viewed as a positive, though largely symbolic, gesture. Still, it could cause disruptions in the months ahead. Likewise, Celestica is making a move to tie executive compensation to the company's financial peformance. In theory, this should lead to more rigourous efforts to control costs. But this can have unforeseen consequences, as the accounting scandal at Nortel Networks Corp. has shown.

More serious issues centre on Celestica's product mix. During the tech downturn, the firm focussed on its core products: sophisticated electronics, especially Unix servers and optical telecommunications gear, products that were hit especially hard when large corporations stopped investing in large networks. As a result, Celestica suffered losses disproportionate to those of many of its competitors, especially those involved in manufacturing consumer electronics. Looking ahead, Celestica must broaden its customer base, as well as its product base, if it is to grow sales and soften the risk of a future downturn.

And what exactly are the future growth engines to be, not only for Celestica, but also for the electronics manufacturing industry in general? Only one thing is certain: The growth-through-acquisition model that reigned in the 1990s will no longer play. Most of the large OEMs have already gotten rid of their manufacturing operations. There isn't a lot left to buy.

More importantly, investors stung by the tech collapse no longer accept revenue growth as the key indicator of EMS health. Today, they look at earnings, and, more rigorous yet, return on invested capital. The focus on investment return is particularly challenging, given that contract electronics manufacturing has become increasingly competitive. It remains to be seen whether Celestica can get back to the point where the business is sustainable, let alone profitable, over the long term.

Q: What should Celestica do to grow its sales, improve its margins and protect itself from future tech downturns?

Jeff Rath

Analyst • Canaccord Capital Corp.

Electronics manufacturers face a set of fundamental problems in addition to high costs and low margins, says Toronto-based analyst Jeff Rath. In supplying services to OEMs, they must do more than carry the costs of the bricks, mortar and labour of their own factories: They also carry high inventories. "The dirty secret of the EMS business is that it doesn't create shareholder value," Rath says. "Your weighted average cost of capital [the average cost of equity and debt] is 10% to 12%. The industry as a whole, Celestica included, hasn't generated sufficient returns to cover that."

Complicating matters is the fact that companies like Celestica have a limited ability to improve their margins by raising prices. The reason? In many cases, they are competing against their own customers. "IBM knows how to manufacture things better, and has been doing it longer, than Celestica," Rath says. "Until Celestica's customers become virtually fab-less — meaning they have no internal [fabrication] capabilities any more — Celestica will be constrained in its ability to set prices."

But there is an out, Rath says. And to take advantage of it, Celestica will have to soften its focus on manufacturing and move increasingly into the high-margin realm of electronics design. In doing so, it would be borrowing a strategy from the automotive parts industry, where companies such as Magna International Inc. sell specialized design services in addition to manufacturing capability. "But while it's healthy, it's very difficult to do organically," Rath says. "It's expensive, and it's a drag on earnings because you end up having to invest future earnings."

Accordingly, Celestica should consider buying companies with design capabilities in addition to building its own in-house capabilities. Then it can leverage their expertise to win new customers and drive traffic through assembly plants. "They can look at some design shops that are specific to telecommunications and networking, but I'd also like to see them do something outside their traditional markets where they don't currently have a footprint," Rath says. "They probably need bigger exposure in the consumer market, someone building handsets or perhaps innovative automotive electronics for next-generation vehicles."

Celestica will also have to become more efficient in its core assembly work to reduce costs, Rath adds. To do that, it should implement the kind of "lean manufacturing" processes pioneered by Toyota, and widely used by all automotive manufacturers. "The whole idea behind lean manufacturing is that everything is triggered by demand. Instead of building to budgets, which leads to oversupply and inventory gluts, every time someone buys something it triggers a supply chain response, which is tremendously efficient. Lean manufacturing is something Celestica and the entire EMS industry has to do, because each year they have to deliver cost improvements to their customers."

Thomas Astle

Analyst • National Bank Financial

Celestica's most pressing issue heading into the second half of 2004 will be proving to the markets that it can repeat and build on its first-quarter results, says Toronto-based analyst Thomas Astle. "They have to show they have all the metrics going in the right direction, that gross margins are improving, they have costs under control, and that they're maintaining their top-line growth, which has been doing reasonably well. The external conditions are in place. It's really just a matter of internal execution in line with their peer group."

Despite the knock that Standard & Poor's delivered to Celestica's credit rating, Astle says he doesn't think cash is going to be a major issue for the company in the coming months. "The credit downgrade by S&P is a concern, but not something they need to panic over. Their balance sheet is still pretty strong, and they shouldn't have to raise capital in the near term."

Astle, however, believes that Celestica can do more to diversify its product base. "Product mix was part of the problem over the last couple years. They had a high exposure to Unix servers through Sun and IBM, and that isn't a growth business. So we'd like to see less of that, and more emphasis on things like automotive and consumer products."

Selective acquisitions might also be in order, he says, particularly in Japan and Europe, where there are still OEM companies with manufacturing capabilities to buy. "In North America the major OEMs in the IT world are pretty outsourced at this point. But the Japanese haven't outsourced yet, and the Europeans haven't to the extent we've seen in North America."

Finally, Celestica can get more aggressive about winning business from its core customers, especially Nortel Networks, which recently awarded a major assembly contract to rival Flextronics.

"I'm sure Celestica would have been interested in that business, and disappointed they didn't get it," Astle says. "But it's not terribly surprising. Celestica has a really strong relationship with [Nortel competitor] Lucent Technologies, and Nortel might have said, 'I'm not sure we want to put our stuff in the same plant as Lucent.'"

Keith Dunne

Analyst • RBC Capital Markets

Keeping costs down must be Job One at Celestica, says California-based analyst Keith Dunne. "They've been one of the best-performing stocks in their sector this year," he says. "And that's because it looks like they're finally getting costs under control." That being the case, Dunne expects Celestica to close more plants in Western Europe and North America, and consolidate the production in lower-cost regions — China being one of several options.

"They're under-represented in China relative to many of their competitors, but that's not necessarily a bad thing," Dunne says, while noting that Celestica will need to keep an eye on shipping issues as it selects manufacturing locations. "It makes sense for a company like Flextronics to be in China in a big way because 30% of their business is cell phones, commodities with very small form factors [physical size and shape] that can be cost effectively put on container ships. If they spend a week or two in transit, it doesn't really matter."

Delivering larger and more complex products raises other issues, Dunne continues: "A product line like Celestica's ... is a lot more complex, has a much bigger form factor, and goes through more engineering changes through the developmental life cycle. You often want your manufacturing facilities closer to the OEM." For that reason, Dunne says, it may make sense for Celestica to beef up operations in Eastern Europe and Mexico, "even though I think they'll ultimately put more capacity in China, as well."

In order to grow sales, meanwhile, Celestica should expand both its customer base and product line, particularly in the areas of defence, aerospace, medical and industrial electronics. "That'll boost your margins, add some percentage points to your top-line growth. It will also mitigate the risk that any one sector will be particularly hard hit going forward."

But there's a caveat: Celestica has to manage its diversification in a way that does not detract from the core businesses of serving communications and computing companies. "If you won 100% of the aerospace, defence and medical electronics outsourcing contracts ... [over] the next 10 years, it still wouldn't be as important as communications and computing." **B**

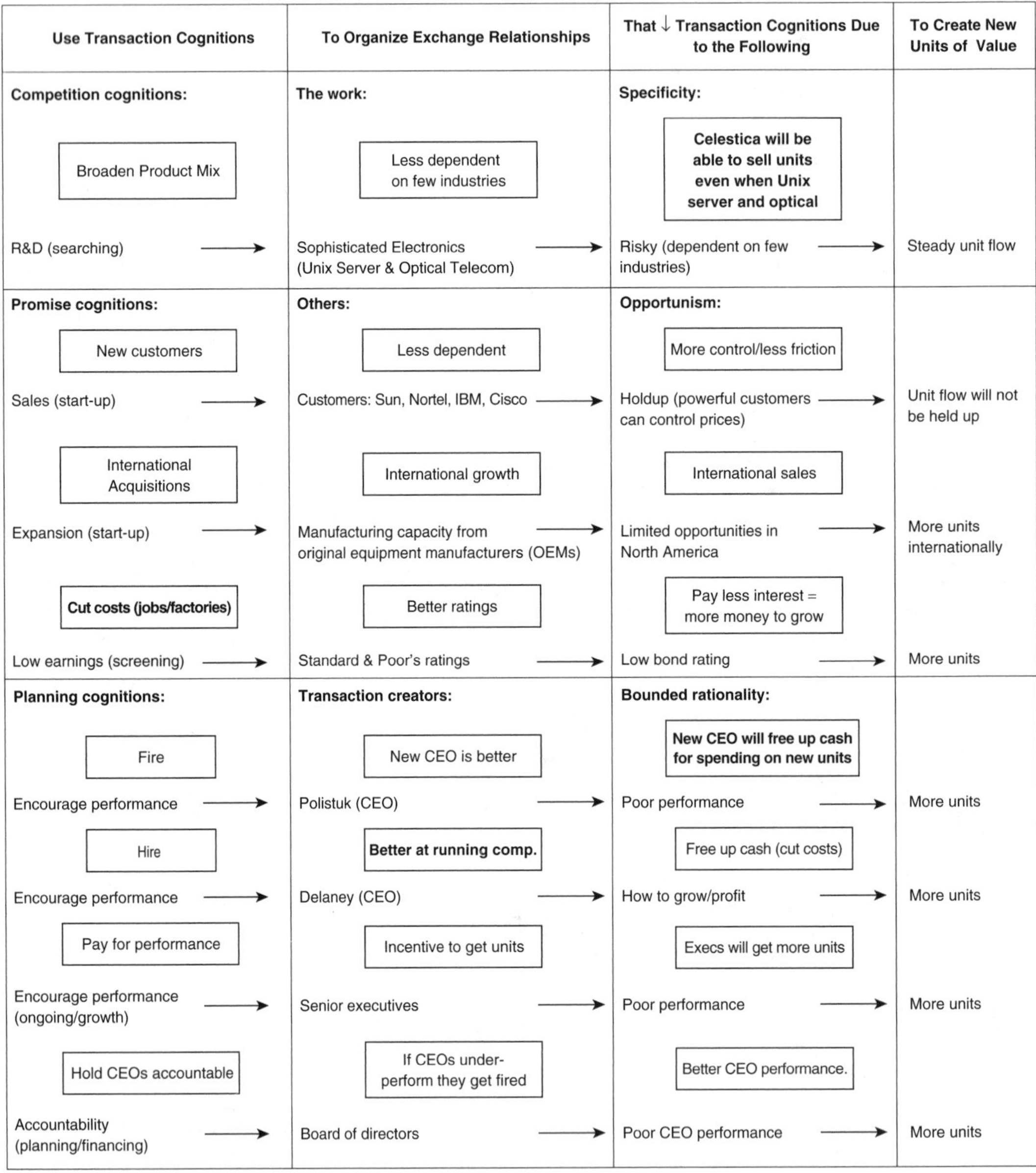

Figure 7.10 Example: Transaction Analysis Worksheet

Learning

While I was doing this assignment, there were two fields of learning going on. First, I was learning about how Celestica overcame the tech crash and what it has to do to build momentum in the future. Second, and more important, I learned a great deal about how transaction cognitions can organize relationships to reduce transaction costs and ultimately lead to more units. I learned how to identify the cognitions, the work, the others, the transaction creators, the specificity, the opportunism, and the bounded rationality in the case. Once these items had been identified, I could read the case and understand what was done to fix the problems that were holding back transactions and ultimately holding back units. For example, first I identified the work, others, and transaction creators; then I identified what was causing these items not to produce the maximum number of units (specificity, opportunism, bounded rationality); then I identified the transaction cognitions that were related to these elements; and then I explained how the company (Celestica) made changes that would ultimately lead to increased units.

Patterns

The pattern that is specific to Celestica is that when its financial statements get in trouble, it responds by firing executives, cutting costs, and thinking of ways that will help the company avoid this problem in the future. I think it's important to note that this pattern can be observed in many companies across many industries. For example, Bombardier has followed a similar pattern. Bombardier's financial statements got in trouble (a loss), the company fired their CEO, the new CEO cut costs (fired employees, closed plants), and then Bombardier came up with new ways to avoid the problem in the future.

The other pattern I noticed was that everything depends on units. Whether Celestica knew it or not, when it got in trouble, it made changes that increased their units.

Generalization of Patterns to Other Situations

This first pattern that I have observed in Celestica, Bombardier, and other corporations can be generalized and used in other situations. Basically, these companies wait for something to go wrong and make appropriate changes that will fix the problem. This generalization could be used in any situation. For example, someone driving on an icy road slips on some black ice and crashes into the snow bank. If the person driving survives the crash, that person buys a different car with different tires and continues with his or her life. However, I have a recommendation for the companies and person following this pattern. On a macro level, this pattern seems very reactive. My recommendation is that rather than wait for your financial statements to go down the drain, a company should be implementing solutions to avoid future problems and ultimately avoid having their statements go down the drain (units stop). For example, Celestica almost went bankrupt because it was 100% dependent on a few customers and a few products. I think it's obvious that these customers and products were going to run into trouble (nothing stays perfect forever). So instead of waiting for its customers and products to run into trouble, Celestica should have thought of ways to expand its customers and products (protect their units). Also, the person driving the car on the slippery road should have purchased good snow tires or waited for better road conditions before driving. The only problem with this recommendation is that it can very costly to be highly proactive. This pattern almost seems analogous to second-order operations (what you must do to protect your units).

This second pattern is analogous to first-order operations (what you must do to get your units). This second pattern can also be carried forward to other situations. Basically, this pattern shows that getting more units is always the end goal. Whatever you do, somehow it has to lead to more units.

As a conclusion, I will link both these patterns. Once a company gets units (first order), it has to protect its units (second order).

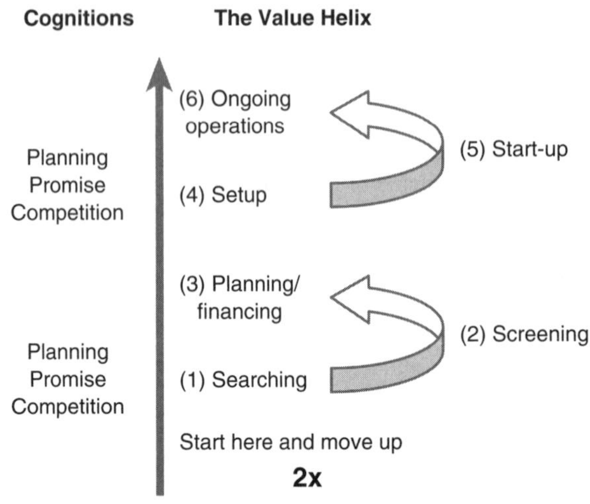

Figure 7.11 The Venture Creation Process Value Helix

Summary

In this chapter, we have explained that the venture creation process is, in actuality, the sequential application of transaction cognitions that, with the same power these cognitions have to bring transactions into existence, brings a venture (as a new economic unit at the firm level of analysis) into existence. Thus, the venture creation process of searching, screening, planning/financing, setup, start-up, and ongoing operations and growth can be shown to consist of a type of "value helix," where venture creators repeat the competition, promise, and planning sequence two full times (see Figure 7.11).

These key thinking skills (or transaction cognitions)—competition, promise, and planning cognitions—are necessary to support the venture creation process. These skills are unique and may be distinguished from the more general areas of strategic thinking (competitive analysis); marketing, law, human resource management, and so on (building venture relationships); and accounting, organization design, operations and production management, and so forth (business planning) because they focus *only* on the unit-creating aspect of these core business disciplines. We think of these as "first-order" cognitions (Williamson, 1991) because they deal with the first order of business: creating new units. The following cases may be used to practice and refine the transaction analytic skills that are at the core of the entrepreneur's job: creating new units of value.

Cases

The following cases have been selected to help learners to develop and become more aware of their own capabilities for synthesizing the steps in the venture formation process through transaction analytics to produce new units of value—the first job of the entrepreneur.

Creemore Springs Brewery: Branding Without Advertising

Prepared by Ken Mark under the supervision of Professor Niraj Dawar

Version: (A) 2000-01-11

Introduction

"We're at a crossroads," remarked Howard Thompson, vice-president of marketing at Creemore Springs Brewery in April, 1999. "We can either stay at our current capacity of 27,000 hectolitres (hl) (100 litres = 1 hl) or expand to the next feasible level of 50,000 hl, at a cost of three million dollars or more." At his office in sleepy Creemore, Canada, Howard pondered how the specialty image of the Creemore Springs brand was going to be managed through this expansion.

Creemore Springs Brewery

In 1987, Creemore Springs Brewery (Creemore) was started by John Wiggins, a retired advertising consultant in the town of Creemore which was located between Toronto, Canada's largest city with over three million inhabitants, and the town of Collingwood, a destination for summer cottage dwellers. Under the care of brewmaster Doug Babcook, Creemore developed the "Creemore Springs Premium Lager," a continental-style lager sold in oversize glass bottles and kegs. The brewery also brewed "urBock," a seasonal brew available only during the winter months. Creemore Springs beer quickly attracted a loyal Toronto base of customers seeking a specialty image beer. The brewery turned a profit in its first year.

In this advertising-intensive business, the Creemore Springs brand was built entirely without traditional advertising. "We have no sales force either," said Thompson. "The beer is delivered fresh to the bars by a small, dedicated fleet of trucks." Despite this, Creemore had managed to increase its brew sales annually, in a beer market that was otherwise stagnant. "In fact, we actually ran out of beer in '91 and '93 and had to convince bar owners not to take our beer. We're successful because most of the bar staff like our beer and recommend it. Those who try it like the flavour and tell their friends about it." By 1999, Creemore had increased its beer production and sales to 27,000 hl from 7,000 hl in 1987 (see Exhibit 1 and Exhibit 2). With total revenue at Cdn$13.5 million, staffing had increased to 40 in 1999: 13 in trucking, 13 in brewing, four in management, 10 in selling and administration.

The Ontario Beer Market

Beer sales in Ontario had leveled off at seven million hectolitres over the past five years. In 1998, Creemore sales had grown eight per cent in a stagnant market. The two large national brewers, Molson and Labatt, each held roughly 40 per cent of the Ontario market (see Exhibit 3). Microbreweries (also known as "craft brews") were growing but still accounted for less than five per cent of the market. Within this segment, main competitors included Sleeman (which also owned the Upper Canada brand) and Big Rock. Creemore did not use market share as a measure for success. In fact, it was rather difficult to define the competition for market share purposes: "I never think market share in craft beer," Thompson offered. "Some of the craft brews are not premium, and their product profiles do not reflect a premium positioning. Some are owned by the majors, which conflicts with a "pure craft" operating mandate."

	Year to Date	*$/hl*
Revenue		
Beer	$13,309,987	530.0
Gifts Revenue	135,891	5.4
Dispensing Equipment—Revenue	9,923	0.4
Under/Over	27	0.0
Full Goods Returned	(19,179)	–0.8
Bottle Refunds	66,183	1.6
Other Revenue	25,984	1.0
Total Revenue	$13,528,816	537.6
Cost of Sales		
Salaries—Manufacturing	$622,202	24.8
Employee Benefits—Mftg	60,071	2.4
Sales Taxes	3,548,478	141.3
Factory Overhead	1,443,371	57.5
Hospitality Beer Gifts	(81,397)	–3.2
Materials Consumed	1,609,045	64.1
Inventory Changes (Beer)	(17,752)	–0.7
Total Cost of Sales	$7,184,018	286.2
Gross Profit	$6,344,798	251.4
Expense		
Distribution Expenses	$2,482,473	98.9
Selling & Administrative Costs	2,098,424	83.6
Operation Expense	$4,580,897	182.5
Net Profit Before Tax	$1,763,901	68.9
Income Tax	$86,911	3.3
Net Profit After Tax	$1,676,990	65.6

Exhibit 1 Creemore Springs Brewery Income Statement—September 30, 1998

"We operate mainly in the Ontario market—that is our world," Thompson continued. "We believe in operating as a local phenomenon, with our local identity. If we double capacity to 50,000 hl, we would still have to sell all of it in the local market."

THE CREEMORE BRAND

Creemore's lager had won consecutive national and international awards in the 1990s. Creemore prided itself on having a "100 years behind the times" small town, unhurried image, which Creemore emphasized by doing things differently from its provincial competitors. Whereas other brewers distributed their beer mainly through the two government-controlled outlets, the Liquor Control Board of Ontario (LCBO) and Brewer's Retail, Creemore delivered its beer to bars, restaurants and taverns within a day's trucking distance. While competitors relied on "traditional" television, radio and print advertising, Creemore encouraged word-of-mouth promotion,

Assets		Liabilities	
Current Assets		**Current Liabilities**	
Pallet/Skid Deposits	10,151	Accounts Payable	1,444,584
Receivables	571,151	Accrued Liabilities	106,264
Prepaid Expenses	55,821	Taxes Payable	(18)
Cash on Deposit	969,818	Current Portion—Other/Vehicles	409,265
Inventories	634,078	Customer Deposits	264,435
Total Current Assets	2,241,019	**Total Current Liabilities**	2,224,530
		Long-Term Liabilities	
		Current Portion—Long-Term	679,288
		Current Portion—Vehicles	274,876
Fixed Assets			
Properties	3,119,531		
Waste Disposal System	32,139	**Total Long-Term Liabilities**	954,164
Equipment	3,498,948		
Leasehold Improvement	—	**Equity**	
Other Equipment	1,223,386	Retained Earnings	(1,573,835)
Less: Accumulated Depreciation	(2,670,020)	Class A Non-Voting Shares	1,194,070
		Common Shares	2,969,084
Total Fixed Assets	5,203,984	Net Profit/(Loss)	1,676,990
		Total Equity	4,266,310
Total Assets	$7,445,003	**Total Liabilities and Equity**	$7,445,003

Exhibit 2 Creemore Springs Brewery—Balance Sheet—as at September 30, 1998

preferring that new customers "discover" Creemore for themselves. Part of the brand's allure was that it was known only to a select few. For its loyal fans, Creemore produced a newsletter, "Froth Talk," and used it to promote the Creemore Springs and its seasonal urBock product (Exhibit 4). The newsletter and a Web site (www.creemoresprings.com) dedicated to the discussion of Creemore news created a sense of community among loyal Creemore drinkers.

> Creemore is the most expensive domestically produced beer. Access to it is limited and growth only by word-of-mouth necessitates gradual expansion. If we move towards the majority of the market in terms of our taste, positioning, and advertising, we stand to alienate our loyal consumers and customers and attract the attention of Labatt or Molson. Now on the other hand, Sleeman (another popular beer in Ontario) has pulled it off by focusing on its distinct, clear bottle, which is great from a packaged goods standpoint. Even then, Molson is still 200 times the size of Sleeman.
>
> Our brand image has painted us into this corner, into this "aww shucks country bumkin" image. And we've got to nurture that image. We get people to come and visit the Creemore town, and our website, and live this image. However, in order to absorb the added capacity, we will probably need a smartly executed marketing event that catapults us up a few thousand hectolitres. We haven't yet hit upon what this will be.

Creemore Consumer Behaviour

Thompson continued,

> I don't think we can get significantly more from our current purchasers. I don't think the market

Labatt Breweries of Canada

- Capacity—9,800,000 hl
- Brands—Blue, Blue Dry, Blue Light, Bud Light, Budweiser, Carlsberg Light, Classic, Classic Wheat, Crystal, Extra Stock, Genuine Draft, Labatt .5, Labatt Ice, Labatt Lite, Labatt Maximum Ice, PC Draft, PC Draft Light, PC Draft Strong, PC Ultimate Dry, Select, Twist Shandy, Lucky Lager, Labatt 50, Extra Dry, Guiness, Carlsberg Dark (draft only), Labatt Copper, Schooner, Wildcat, Wildcat Dry, Wildcat Light, Wildcat Mountain Ale, Wildcat Strong, Oland Export, Oland Schooner, Keith's India Pale Ale, Keith's Light, Keith's Special Dry, Jockey Club, Blue Star, Blue Star Glacier Cold, Black Label, Club, Labatt Lite, Kokanee, Kokanee Gold, Kokanee Light, Kootenay Ale

Molson Breweries

- Capacity—13,000,000 hl
- Brands—Black Ice, Black Label, Carling, Carling Ice, Carling Light, Carling Pilsner, Carling Strong, Coors, Coors Light, Excel, Extra Old Stock, Miller High Life, Miller Lite, Miller Genuine Draft, Miller Genuine Draft Light, Molson Canadian, Molson Canadian Light, Molson Canadian Ice Draft, Molson Special Dry, Molson XXX, Old Vienna, OV Light, Pilsner, Rickard's Red, Rickard's Pale Ale, Red Dog, Foster's, Black Horse, Dominion Ale, India Beer, Brador, Molson Export, Molson Golden, Toby, Ultra, Molson Stock Ale, Champlain Porter, Dow Ale, Grand Nord, Laurentide, Bohemian, Calgary

Algonquin Brewing Company

- Capacity—100,000 hl
- Brands—Algonquin Light, Black and Tan, Bruce County Lager, Country Lager, Formosa Draft, Formosa Draft Light, Honey Brown Lager, Royal Amber Lager, Special Reserve Dark Ale, Bank's Lager, Formosa Bavarian Bock

Big Rock Brewery

- Capacity—450,000 hl
- Brands—Black Amber Ale, Buzzard Breath Pale Ale, Grasshopper Wheat Ale, Magpie Rye Ale, McNally's Extra Ale, Pale Ale, Traditional Ale, Warthog Ale, Cold Cock Winter Porter, Expo Ale

Moosehead

- Capacity—1,000,000 hl
- Brands—Alpine, Alpine Genuine Cold Filtered, Alpine Light, Clancy's Amber Ale, Moosehead Beer, Moosehead Canadian Ice, Moosehead Canadian lager, Moosehead Canadian Light, Moosehead Dry Ice, Moosehead Light, Moosehead Mariner Ale, Moosehead PaleAle, Moosehead Premium Dry, Ten Penny Old Stock Ale

Sleeman Brewing and Malting Company

- Capacity—225,000 hl
- Brands—Arctic Wolf, Nordik Wolf Light, Schlitz, Silver Creek Lager, Sleeman Cream Ale, Sleeman Light, Sleeman Original Dark, Stroh's Lager, Stroh's Light Lager, Sleeman's Honey Brown Ale

Upper Canada Brewing Company (owned by Sleeman)

- Capacity—150,000 hl
- Brands—Dark Ale, Lager, Light Lager, Natural Point 9, Pale Ale, Publican's Special Bitter, Rebellion Ale, Rebellion Lager, Woody's Wild Ale, Colonial Stout, Summer Brew, Pilsner, True Bock, Wheat Beer, Winter Brew, Strong Lager

Exhibit 3 A List of Selected Beer Producers in the Ontario Beer Market

Issue # 15

Loyal Order of Frothquaffers official newsletter

www.creemoresprings.com

The new site is launched! Creemore Springs official web site has undergone a serious redesign. Hats off to Dale Douglas for his great work. The new and improved 'homepage' is iteractive, dynamic and intense (well about as intense as a sunny porch and a cool beer can get).

New features:

- *Take a brewery tour*
- *Read updated copies of the Frothtalk...online!*
- *Purchase your official Creemore Springs gear from our online store (see back page)*
- *Register as a Loyal Order of Fothquaffers member*
- *Direct questions and comments to the crew at Creemore*
- *Check out upcoming Creemore Spings events*
- *Search for bars and restaurants in your area featuring Creemore Springs on tap*
- *Book group tours and tastings*
- *Link to other interesting beer sitess*

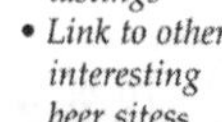

Exhibit 4 Froth Talk

will grow. We need to get the word out to more people, but we have to be careful about how we do this. To date, we've effectively led people to the conclusion that they discovered us. I often hear that they fondly remember the first time they discovered Creemore. They were interested in the unique cultural and geographic image that this premium brand brings. People like the brand because it is like a well-guarded secret. We at Creemore have to be incredibly sensitive to that. If we were to do overt advertising, it would be as if we opened our trench coats to the marketplace. That's the way, I think, people would feel about Creemore advertising—they would feel that they'd just been flashed.

Pondering Capacity Expansion

Thompson explained,

> Our bottleneck used to be the fermentation process. But we've since expanded it to 30,000 hl, so that is not the issue anymore. The reality is that we cannot just make the kettle bigger. Everything will have to change with it. To make the brew house bigger, we have to make all our vessels bigger.
>
> We've pegged a 50 hl kettle as the next logical move. The expansion of the brew house will cost us $3 million alone. But our land area can support this—we've bought the property south of us. We can get more warehouse space in the fall and move things around (see Exhibit 5).

Creemore's Distribution Format

Thompson continued,

> People know us as the "milkmen of the beer industry." We phone every one of our customers at least once a week and deliver beer to them. Our trucks get our people in front of them—they're part of our branding. Although we want to sell our draft beer within a day's trucking distance, an alternative is to expand our bottle sales through Brewer's Retail. We can choose to deliver to our draft customer through Brewer's Retail, costing us $45.3 per hl for handling and delivery charges. Now, we distribute our draft for $98.9 per hl ourselves, so delivery through Brewer's Retail would only cost slightly less once incremental trucking and holding costs are taken into account (we'd have to get our draft to Brewer's warehouses ourselves). Actually, we do deliver through Brewer's Retail for 10 of our bar customers in Ottawa, but rely on our own trucks for the rest of the 560 bars and 240 Brewer's Retail outlets we service.

Bottled or Draft?

> Currently, 80 per cent of our bottle sales are sold through Brewer's Retail and the LCBO, with the rest at bars, restaurants, and taverns. We sell more draft beer than bottled, but we make better margins on the bottles. If we could grow our bottle sales, that would be great. Brewer's Retail and the LCBO are not as fickle as the bars. To get into a bar, and remain one of the beers on offer, brewers often give special deals, such as a number of kegs free.

In contrast, Thompson offered,

> We still don't do "special" deals in our draft market. The price is set, take it or leave it. We know that our competitors give incentives, but we don't do that.
>
> Still, our popularity attracted LCBO stores. We used to stay away from them because of their large handling charges. But then we weren't at capacity one year, so we provided those stores with bottles. Something happened last year in Collingwood that led me to believe that we can expand our bottle business. We had Creemore in Brewer's Retail, and then began stocking Creemore in the Liquor store (LCBO). Instead of cannibalisation, our sales went up in both stores! Our bottle sales alone grew 26 per cent in March 1999!
>
> Keg sales are flat year over year; I think it is the same people buying our beer. But last summer, it was so hot that I think that as cottage country folk left Toronto they grabbed a case of Creemore instead of Ex (Molson Export). I think that's why our sales went up last year.
>
> But we're in a different bottle size than other beers—500 ml versus the standard 341 ml. If we had to do it over again, we'd probably be in the regular bottle. What I mean to say is that if we could

Item	*Mth 1*	*Mth 2*	*Mth 3*	*Mth 4*	*Mth 5*	*Mth 6*	*Mth 7*	*Mth 8*	*Mth 9*	*Mth 10*	*Mth 11*	*Mth 12*	*Other*	*Total*
Brewhouse			98		67	124	125	100						$514
Fermentation Cellar			204		50	255	200	250					210	$1,169
Packaging					54	80	145	50					248	$577
Utilities			16	10	45	62	78	80						$291
Land & Buildings				89	137	66	18							$310
Organizational Costs	65	65	5											$135
Total Capital Expenditures														$2,996

Exhibit 5 Expansion Expenditures

> start all over again, we'd seriously think about the regular 341 ml bottle size. On balance, we've probably restricted our market. The 500 ml bottle gave us an initial competitive advantage, but is so far from standard that it hinders our sales. At bars, I know we sell less because of its different size. This does not affect our home consumer much, however, as we believe they are less particular about the larger size. Now we wouldn't think of switching because the cost of switching is very high—including the purchase of new equipment, a bottle float . . . the return on investment is not good.

The Creemore Management Team

The head of Creemore, John Wiggins, focused on the strategic, non-operating side of the business. Curtis Zeng, Gord Fuller, and Howard Thompson were the operating officers, sharing operating decisions of significance such as investments above Cdn$25,000, staffing, and administration concerns. Otherwise, Zeng specialised in running the facility, Fuller ran the product and brewing, and Thompson took care of the distribution, marketing, sales, and service issues.

Thompson remarked,

> My existence here was greeted with initial skepticism. But, we carved out a management style that worked really well because it relied on the three of us to agree on everything. In the first year, I was just another body. With my business background, however, I sorted that out immediately.

Recent Events at Creemore Springs Brewery

John Wiggins had decided, in early 1999, to sell his shares and retire in September 2000. Most of his shares went towards two minority (and soon to be majority) shareholders. These shareholders were well aware that Creemore was reaching maximum capacity with its current equipment. They knew that an investment had to be made if a decision to grow sales was reached.

On April 19, a big consideration for Thompson was trying to understand the strategic approach of the new shareholders with regards to the Creemore franchise. If they were aligned to the current strategy, then Thompson was willing to spend Cdn$3 million and plan for 20 years of expansion, taking steps to protect the integrity of the brand. He thought the shareholders were not unsympathetic to that. He would not blame them, however, if they sought more aggressive growth targets. Thompson hoped that a consensus agreement could be reached.

Options Available

"How should we grow profits?" Thompson asked.

> We're thinking about that daily. Raising our prices doesn't feel right. Rewarding our fans for getting us to 30,000 hl by raising our price is NOT the Creemore way. We can seek to expand our bottle sales. We could do that rather quickly. But how would we do that without destroying the Creemore brand for the long term?
>
> We could brew another brand—like a pale ale. This would appeal to lots of people in our segment. It would still be a premium beer, we wouldn't suffer our margins, and the beer would be ready in 14 days instead of 21. I think we could market other brands if they're premium and they did not distract us from what we do. urBock did nothing but improve our image. But we only sold 400 hl this year, so you see we're not going to get thousands of hectolitres from this brand!
>
> We're still getting growth of five to six per cent a year, and we're going to run into a new brewhouse because we don't want to run our operations "round the clock." If we change our brewhouse, it would get us a lot more capacity. Why don't we just cap production? Then what about stock-outs? Or customers who open another bar? If we were to cap it, it would be extremely difficult later on to "uncap" it. If we did, we'd be seen as too arrogant. The bigger question is once we spend the money, do we suffer a return on capital investment and keep a good thing (i.e., slow but profitable growth—the Creemore way),

or do we pursue quick growth? Once we spend the money, we'll have capacity for 38,000 hl, with an option for 50,000 hl once more tanks are added.

Personally, I think we can grow to 50,000 hl without sacrificing our shareholder return. Fundamentally, we shouldn't aim to grow while selling our beer less profitably. That dictates a growth path that is less steep but a heck of a lot more meaningful in the long-term.

Thompson concluded:

What is the logical and reasonable size for Creemore five years from now? Who knows? Radical change has been the downfall of two major breweries. They hurt themselves in quality because they were driven by "shareholder return." Sales continued to be flat, and they weren't making consistently good beer after a while and meeting share targets.

No question in my mind that if we were to spend $3 million, that would influence expectations of growth. Any other alternative is inconceivable. We don't know the expectations of our soon-to-be majority shareholders. In preparation for that meeting, I'm going to create, in the next six months, a full outline of what's going to happen and a growth plan that does not depart from our operating philosophy too significantly.

Fernando Rego and the Fitter

Prepared by Professor Murray J. Bryant

 Version: (A) 2004-11-11

Fernando Rego was a very successful owner of a retail menswear store located in the central business district of Toronto. In 2000, when Rego contemplated the possibility of retirement after 40 years in retail and 16 years of running his own clothing business, he thought about the future of the business and the possibility of passing it on to his sons. He realized that the menswear retail industry was in difficulty, specifically that there was a lack of tailors in the retail trade to adjust off-the-rack suits for customers. Rego saw the potential to replace the on-site tailors with a device, later termed the Fitter, so that all customers could obtain made-to-measure, well-fitting suits at reasonable prices.

By January 2004, the Fitter had completed successful beta testing at the store and had been adopted by other major retailers. A major retail chain with over 150 stores in the United States was contemplating purchase. Rego wondered how he could convince all middle- and upper-end men's retailers to change the way they do business to better serve their customers by providing suits that fitted and by allowing customers to select from a wide range of fabrics as well.

The Clothing Industry

During the dot-com boom, business people shed the traditional suit in favor of a more casual approach to business, i.e., business casual. However, with the demise of the dot-com in 1999, the suit had now once again become *de rigueur* of attire of the male business executive.

Traditionally, business executives would purchase a suit from available suits stocked by a retailer. A business executive would purchase four to five suits a year. The suit would be selected off the rack with advice from the retailer. Thus, the customer would select a size based generally upon chest size and select the color and type of fit (slim, comfortable or easy) and the fabric. The retailer would have the customer try on the suit, and an on-site tailor would make adjustments, let out seams, lift the shoulder, etc., and the customer would purchase the suit based upon the tailoring required. The customer would collect the suit a few days later.

What the customer did not see was the process by which the suit was designed, manufactured and distributed. The process generally started with the production and sale of wool. In general, the wool was produced by Australian merino sheep that gave a long, fine, staple fibre. The wool was auctioned on a worldwide basis, and, in general, prices for wool had fallen over the past 20 years.[1] In an effort to arrest this decline, the Wool Marketing Authority had promoted the qualities of wool—comfort, drape, ease of care, etc.—to customers to encourage them to buy natural fabrics.

At the auction house, buyers for the woolen mills sampled the wool from bales and then bid for the completed product. A typical price per kilogram in 2003 for high quality wool that could go into a Super 100 or Super 110 cloth for a man's suit was A$9.50.[2] One kilogram of raw wool would produce three metres[3] of 300 grams of material. Thus, the cloth had a weight, and 300 grams was a typical weight for a high-end, all-season men's suit. In addition, the feel of the wool and, to some extent, the weight was determined by the number of cross weaves (warp and web) in a square inch of fabric. The most common suiting fabric was Super 100 or Super 110s, but extremely fine, soft suiting material could be made from Super 180s.

The buyers for the high-end mills, (the major mills were still located in the United Kingdom and Italy) and include such names as Holland and Sherry,[4] Scabal, and Loro Piana take the wool, process it, dye it and produce bolts of cloth—a typical bolt was 60 inches wide by 80 yards in length. The buyer would buy wool at auction by determining the length of staple, the fineness of the staple and the condition of the wool. The mill processed the wool bought by the buyers. A metre is 1.094 yards. The industry was characterized by high skill barriers to entry, notwithstanding the utilization of technology, due to skill levels required to transform the fibre and dye it into a finished bolt of cloth. There were only a few milling firms producing for a world market.

The mills worked on a two- to three-year cycle as the major suiting manufacturers in Europe, United States, Canada and China visited the mills and gave the mills an indication of what fabrics would be required in two to three years—thus color, style (pin-stripe, herringbone, solids, etc.), were required. The mills then produced test runs, and once these were approved by the buyers, the clothing manufacturers were in essence, committed to both quantity and price.

The value-added process from unprocessed wool to finished clothing bolt took one kilogram of wool to make three metres of the bolt. The processing and milling operations added value as the bolt sold for prices from $4,000[5] to $40,000. A typical bolt had a selling price of around $10,000. This price included shipping costs of $60 a bolt and duty of 16 per cent on the fee on board price. The higher prices were reserved for fine woolen cloth termed Super 180s. In addition, the high-end fabrics were often woven with a mix of other natural fabrics (e.g. silk, cashmere, angora and vicuna) all with the objective of making the fabric soft so that it would drape the body in the finished suit so the suit moved and accommodated the wearer. The lower end bolts of fabric were generally lower quality, coarser weaves.

A suit manufacturer bought the bolts of cloth from the mill and manufactured the suit, employing standard sizing and patterns. It took three to four yards[6] of fabric to make a suit; thus, a bolt yielded an average of 18 to 20 North American males' suits.

The clothing manufacturer employed a great deal of technology—laser or water cutting (i.e., cutting up to 12 suits at a time), fairly automated sewing, etc., to keep costs low. North American manufacturers were increasingly finding that labor costs in China were causing them to really work hard to keep costs low. The responsiveness of North American companies to retailers who employed the Fitter may provide advantages to them.

A typical mid-priced suit delivered to a Canadian retailer sold for $600 to $750, i.e., a wholesale price.

As Canada and the United States had taken steps to dismantle trade barriers, suit manufacturers had, in some instances, closed and, in other instances, moved jobs offshore. The tariff protection for Canadian manufacturers was, until 2002, 18 per cent. The reduction of this tariff, coupled with increases in minimum wages, particularly in Quebec, had meant that the suit manufacturing industry was restructuring. Peerless, the largest suit manufacturer in Quebec, had recently outsourced 1,000 jobs from its factory workforce of 2,500 in Montreal to Asia, Eastern Europe and South Africa. (Peerless manufactured 8,000 men's suits per day.) The clothing industry in Canada represented a $7-billion industry in 2003, roughly equal to the pharmaceutical/medicine industry, and provided jobs for 55,000 Canadians or three per cent of the Canadian manufacturing workforce.

The retailer bought suits from the manufacturer based upon local knowledge of the client—a retailer such as Rego Clothier would provide a different assortment, given his location, than a retailer located in a shopping mall, for example. The retailer promoted the store and, through on-site tailoring, provided the service component such that the suit, including alterations, sold for $1,000 to $1,500. A retailer such as Rego would have a store of roughly 450 square metres in length and would carry an inventory (at wholesale) of approximately $800,000.

The Fitter

In 2000, Rego realized that traditional tailors were a dying breed. In the 1950s and 1960s in North America, most tailors had been trained in Italy and the United Kingdom and could make a suit from scratch—the term bespoke tailoring goes back to the custom in the 18th and 19th century of gentlemen aristocrats going to Savile Row in London and "bespeaking" or committing to a new cloth and then returning several months later for fitting and up to five or six fittings of the suit. Thus, in those times, buying an annual suit was as much a social occasion as a purchase[7]—i.e., the customer spoke/committed for four to five yards or so for his suit—hence the term bespoke.[8]

Tailors were employed by retailers such as Rego, and they essentially altered an off-the-rack suit to make it customized. The tailor was highly skilled and would look at items such as posture—eyeing the customer's body to see how well the suit fit. The tailor then had to decide what adjustments were necessary (typically, a jacket in the chest or trousers in the waist can be adjusted up to two inches) and then mark the adjustments. The tailoring process of an off-the-rack suit would necessitate unpicking, cutting, sewing and pressing—all requiring a high level of skill.

A typical retailer would employ two to three tailors and also two to three people who assisted the tailors. All were in short supply. Rego recognized the shortage of supply and determined that he could replace the tailoring.

The Fitter as a Product

Exhibits 1 and 2 describe the Fitter. Essentially the customer would stand in front of the product while a salesperson took 46 different measurements. The process for the customer took about five to 10 minutes and was highly accurate. The salesperson did have to ensure that the customer leaning against the back of the machine was relaxed or that his chin was not extended military style.

The measurements were made using a bar reader that went into the customer profile on the computer. The computer software had smart features such that if a salesperson unintentionally misread a measurement, the program would suggest retaking that measurement.

The client would stand in front of the machine; the arms of the machine would go up and down such that critical measurements, for example height, waist, sleeve length, underarm sleeve length, trouser rise and trouser length, were taken with speed and accuracy. A salesperson could be trained very quickly to use the machine.

(Text continues on page 385)

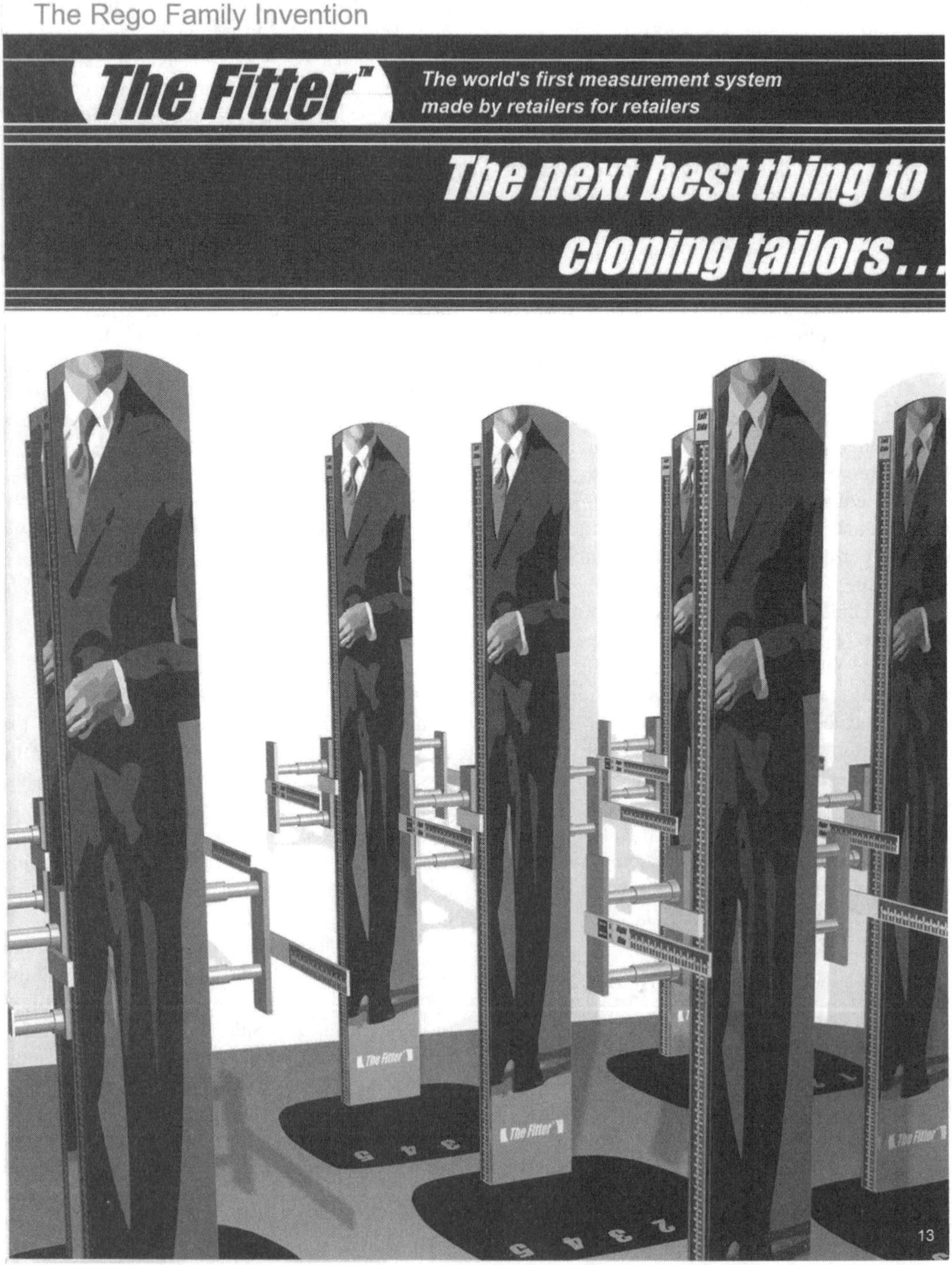
The Rego Family Invention
The Fitter™
The world's first measurement system
made by retailers for retailers
The next best thing to
cloning tailors...
13

Exhibit 1 The Fitter: The Next Best Thing to Using Tailors *(Continued)*

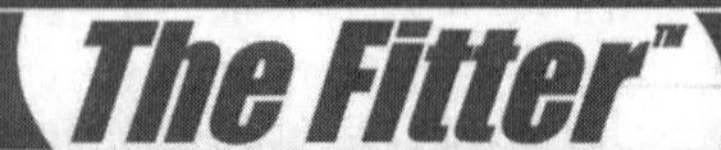

Sartorial Instruments & Technology Inc.

FEEL the Tailor's Fit

The Fitter Measurement System has been quickly catching the attention of both retailers and manufacturers. One of the most frequently asked questions of course is "How do you know that the system's recommended measurements will produce a suit that fits well"? The answer . . . experience. When you've measured approximately 20,000 customers over a 42 year period, you learn a thing or two about measuring. The Fitter Measurement System is based on the experience gained by SIT's C.E.O. Fernando Rego Sr. over the past 4 decades. The Tailor's Fit refers to our exclusive set of formulas that are applied to your customer's body measurements to generate recommended measurements for an excellent custom fit. We have been using the system in our own store and are delighted with the results.

What do we mean by recommended measurements? It would be impossible for us to say that the measurements generated by our system will ALWAYS be perfect, because people do have preferences that can vary. You could have 10 different customers who are 5'10" and wear a 42 Regular off the rack, but prefer their garment to fit differently. The system recommends a terrific set of measurements based on your customer's body measurements. Through asking your customer how he likes his garment to fit, you can enter his preferences in the system and fine tune the measurements to your customer's exact liking. If your customer has no clue how he likes his clothes to fit (and we all know there's lots of these guys), or requires a try-on size that you don't have in stock, you can rely on the system's recommended measurements to yield a great result. If the garment does require any minor adjustments when it arrives, you enter these adjustments in the system and the next time the fit will be perfect.

Many consumers have tried a made-to-measure suit before with disappointing results because they ended up with a suit made to a set of measurements that did not include their own preferences. After all, the idea behind getting an individually tailored suit is that you get exactly what you want.

The Fitter makes it easy for anyone to obtain accurate body measurements, which are used as the foundation for building the perfect set of measurements for your customer in what we call "The Fitting Room" section of the software. The Fitting Room is an extremely powerful tool that will take you just minutes to learn to use because it works like a real fitting.

- After measuring your customer, the first step is to select a garment Brand and Model from the list of supported manufacturers, for example, the "Andrew" model from Samuelsohn. If the brand that you want to sell your customer isn't supported in the system yet, you can use our generic garment specs based on the averages of different North American and Italian made garments that we have studied. Let's call this the virtual try-on garment.
- Next our unique "fit to chest" or "fit to shoulders" approach coaches your staff by recommending the correct try-on size to use for showing the customer how his new suit will fit his chest AND his shoulders. This is particularly important, as many customers require a different size to fit their shoulders than their chest.
- Once the customer is wearing the try-on garment in the recommended size, the salesperson can ask the customer if he wants any changes to the sleeve length, shoulder width, coat length or coat waist from the measurements already recommended by the system.
- If the customer requires a size that is not in stock, the salesperson can load up their own measurements into the system, and try-on a garment themselves, to show the customer how the garment fits compared to his own recommended measurements.
- Now the customer can accurately quantify what he likes or dislikes about the fit of the stock garment. If his preferences differ from the recommendations of the system, those differences are saved as plus/minus values in the system.
- These preferences can be recalled or changed at any time, and you can save as many different sets of preferences as you wish to reflect his varying tastes for a casual suit vs. a business suit, for example.

(continued – see reverse)

Sartorial Instruments & Technology Inc. Exchange Tower, 130 King St. W. Suite 1800 Toronto, ON Canada M5X 1E3 Tel: (416) 366-5669 Fax: (416) 366-2531

Exhibit 1 The Fitter: The Next Best Thing to Using Tailors *(Continued)*

■ *Sartorial Instruments & Technology Inc.*

If your customer has gained or lost weight since his last visit, The Fitter prompts you to re-measure the weight-related measurements only, and will merge all other measurements with the newly-taken ones as one file again. Since any preferences previously saved are stored as plus/minus values above or below the recommended measurements of the system, your customers preferences will still apply even if his new measurements have turned him into "a new man" or one that just looks "happily married."

Customers with wide shoulders often have to size up when buying a suit off the rack in order to get a comfortable fit, and those with small shoulders either size down or end up with a suit that matches their chest measurement but has shoulders that are far too wide. And really, when it comes to a perfectly fitted suit, isn't it all about the shoulders? In addition, sizing up for the shoulders often means putting the customer in a pair of pants that are at least 2–4 sizes too large, and your tailor has to take them in. Not only does this cost you extra money, but the customer is never completely satisfied.

The Fitter measures the customer's shoulders perfectly, indicating the following:

- the exact amount of slope or high shoulder correction required
- which one is low and by how much
- recommends the best point-to-point measurement to fit the customer's shoulder width.

For manufacturers with today's modern cutting equipment, The Fitter will be able to provide participating manufacturers with the exact angle that the customer's shoulder declines, in addition to indicating that the customer has a right low by half an inch, for example. The factory will cut the suit to the exact angle that matches your customer's physique, providing an unparalleled upper body fit, that "suits your customer perfectly."

As you can tell, we're very enthusiastic about our system and we want to explain why. We look forward to answering any questions you may have in person. Feel free to give us a call on our toll free number, 1-866-4FITTER (1-866-434-8837), or you can email us at *info@thefitter.com*

We look forward to hearing from you.

Fernando Rego Sr.
CEO
Sartorial Instruments & Technology

Exhibit 1 The Fitter: The Next Best Thing to Using Tailors

Source: Company files.

Custom fitting has never been so easy, or so quick, **DICK SNYDER** reports

High-tech tailoring

For businessmen who don't blink at dropping $2,000 on a custom-made suit, Fernando Rego has come up with a way to give them something that money can't buy.

Time.

Rego has invented a device that measures a man's body with astonishing accuracy. The timesaving comes when the client returns in three weeks and finds that his customized Brioni or Samuelsohn suit is ready to wear out of the store.

"Up until now," Rego said, "people just expected that they'd have to come in for a second fitting, so that's the way everyone measured. But as has been said, 'The best alteration is no alteration.' Now we can do it right the first time."

David Forbes, vice-president at BMO Nesbitt Burns, has been a client since Rego opened his shop 18 years ago in Toronto's financial district. "For customers at this level," he said, "what's a couple thousand bucks? It's popcorn money. The most precious commodity is time. Do I really want to spend it having three fittings for a suit?"

Rego's device, called the Fitter, looks like an upended surfboard with two metal arms. As a customer stands against the board, a salesperson uses the arms and a bar-coded tape to take 46 measurements, about 30 more than during a conventional fitting. Each measure is scanned and stored digitally.

In the fusty world of tailoring, where methods have remained unchanged for 200 years, this is revolutionary stuff. It's also a lifeline.

"There are just no more tailors," says Rego, who was in New York this week for the men's wear collections, pitching his device to an industry that is facing a stark reality. Through his 40 years in the business — first in his native Portugal, then at Tip Top Tailors and Harry Rosen in Toronto — Rego has seen the end of the Old World apprenticeship system. Manufacturers saw the tailor drought coming, and over the past 20 years have introduced computerized cutting machinery.

But a market still exists for the more refined fit of a bespoke suit. A few years ago, 62-year-old Rego realized that he and his tailor would both retire at the same time. He worried there would be nothing to pass on to his sons, Fernando Jr. and Paul, who both work in the shop. When he began to develop the Fitter, Paul wrote the software.

What the Fitter does best is quantify a subjective art. In the past, for example, only the most experienced eye could detect the intricacies of posture. With its rigid board, the Fitter provides a point of reference so that curvatures of the neck, back and seat can be noted numerically.

"I felt like I was taking my car for its emission test," says software designer Doug Sutherland of his fitting. But three weeks later, he was handed a pressed pair of cuffed pants and a finished sports jacket. "They truly fit. I don't just mean the size, but they fit my shape. No bumps. No bulges." He ordered another suit on the spot.

Special to The Globe and Mail

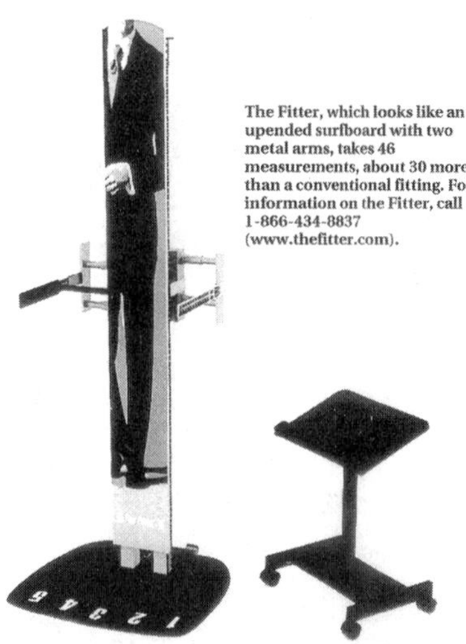

The Fitter, which looks like an upended surfboard with two metal arms, takes 46 measurements, about 30 more than a conventional fitting. For information on the Fitter, call 1-866-434-8837 (www.thefitter.com).

Exhibit 2 High-Tech Tailoring

Source: Dick Snyder, *The Globe and Mail,* January 31, 2004.

Rego tested this product against his measurements (by hand) on 300 customers at a menswear show in July 2003. At that stage, the product had gone through beta testing, but a critical adjustment that was made as a consequence of the show and the 300 "mannequins" was the importance of posture and the location of the chin. Rego wondered whether he should patent his invention in terms of both hardware and software.

In addition, after the show, Rego and his contract manufacturers made suits for customers to prove the accuracy of the Fitter. All customers were delighted with the results and made positive commendations that Rego employed in his material; see Doug Sutherland's comments in Exhibit 2.

Rego was active in two further international shows in getting a buzz going around the benefits of the Fitter. Articles in major newspapers also helped increase the awareness of the product (see Exhibit 3).

Rego targeted key chains such as Saks and Nordstrom in the United States as potential customers for the product. Saks saw many benefits for the Fitter. A key element of Saks's retail strategy was consistency across all its stores; the Fitter made that feasible, as Saks too had been affected by the lack of tailors. At present, many Saks tailors were aged over 70 and were hired on a part-time basis.

The other advantage that Saks saw with the Fitter was cash flow. Traditionally a small percentage of the company's sales were in made-to-measure, about 10 per cent, but the charge was generally $200 to $300 more for a made-to-measure suit. These costs covered individual fitting, cutting, pressing and the proportion of rejects, termed "kills" in the trade. Such costs would not exist with the Fitter as the made-to-measure costs were the same or less than the off-the-rack costs.

The key retail prospects, for Rego, saw the Fitter as a way to increase cash flow and profits. Traditionally, a retailer such as an individual Nordstrom store would stock up to 800 to 1,000 suits at an average cost of $700. The target gross margin on a suit is 55 per cent, or a markup of 2.3 times. An average retailer would obtain two and a half

April 16, 2004

Fashion Enters a New Era: Toronto Company Invents the Virtual Tailor

By Mike Drach

TORONTO, Digital Journal—If there was ever an "endangered species" in the ecosystem of commerce, that title would have to go to today's master tailor.

Tailors, especially the North American variety, are an aging population with tendencies towards fatigue and impatience. Many began learning their craft at a very young age and have practiced it for decades, often at the entreaties of a desperate boss. They've watched fashions come and go but always understood the value of a good, made-to-measure suit.

Though their numbers are dwindling rapidly, Toronto firm Sartorial Instruments and Technology thinks it has the solution. No, they're not cloning tailors, but they've come up with the next-best thing: the Fitter Measurement System.

Essentially, the Fitter consists of a tall backboard standing on a 36-inch-wide base, a pair of arms that measure posture and levelness and some high-tech measuring tape with barcodes at quarter inch intervals.

In about 10 minutes, a trained employee can use it to take 46 measurements that are automatically inputted into a sophisticated software program. It makes some recommendations, spits out an order form and it's off to the manufacturers who will eventually deliver the perfect suit.

The Fitter was developed over the last four years by father-and-son retailers Fernando Rego Sr., Fernando Rego Jr. and Paul Rego, owners of the successful Rego Bespoke Clothiers in Toronto's Exchange Tower. Fernando Sr. has been in the business for 42 years and first came up with the Fitter as a brilliant exit strategy.

Exhibit 3 Typical Promotional Article

(Continued)

Made in Canada (with some parts imported from Germany), the physical unit is a fairly simple tool. More impressive, however, is the included software and Web-based ordering system co-developed by Paul Rego, the company's young president.

Incorporating the standard set of measurements used by an old-world tailor, it also takes into account various styles, customer preferences, even posture and variations in shoulder incline. These tweaks can be entered into the system and it adjusts accordingly. If the customer returns six months later having gained a few pounds, his data can be altered in an instant.

At $10,000 per unit (including a customizable backboard), Paul Rego says it pays for itself in efficiency, lower tailor shop expenses, customer satisfaction and return rates. The Fitter will immediately tell the salesperson what, out of your current inventory, will fit the customer. It also turns each employee into a master tailor—a breed Paul Rego predicts will be extinct within 10 years.

Another bonus is the "helping hand" effect of its arms: A female tailor no longer has to physically hug customers to measure their chests. She can also hand the tape over to the shopper when it comes time to complete the always-awkward inseam measurement.

Currently, Samuelsohn Ltd of Montreal, Quebec is the first manufacturer to officially support the Fitter. However, Paul Rego estimates that there are about 2,000 finer clothing stores in North America that would be well-matched to incorporate this system.

"Tailored suits used to be associated with those more mature in age or bank account," chuckles Rego, whose store targets the more upscale of the Bay Street crowd. "But we find awareness, especially among younger people, is increasing." Manufacturers these days can easily adjust a stock pattern, Rego says, making a custom suit only $100 or $200 more than ready-to-wear.

Rego says sales have increased by more than a third since integrating his Fitter system. That kind of figure would suit any aspiring businessman just fine.

Exhibit 3 Typical Promotional Article

Source: http://www.digitaljournal.com/print.htm?id=4000

inventory turns a year; a good retailer would obtain three inventory turns; a superior retailer, greater than three. The assumption was that these were real inventory turns at normal prices not obtaining another turn due to significant discounting. Nordstrom achieved an inventory turn of three times. On other items, Nordstrom achieved a turn of greater than four. With the Fitter, Nordstrom would need to stock only 50 to 100 suits—a real saving in working capital.

The retailer bought the inventory generally twice a year, paying 30 days after receipt in the store. Thus, the retailer had to commit to color, size, fabric and style six months ahead of potential sales.

In contrast, with the Fitter, the customer paid one-third of the suit on order. The choice of fabrics, styles, color was made based on free sample books, and a retailer such as Saks or Nordstrom could have available 50 or so fabric books (at no cost to the store) covering some 2,500 fabrics. One challenge was that retailers now had to sell to customers on the basis of a sample book. The order was taken from the customer and was e-mailed to Canadian or U.S. manufacturers such as Coppley or Samuelsohn. They then took four to five weeks to manufacture the suit, and then it was delivered to the store. When the suit arrived at the retailer, the retailer called his customer in for a final "celebratory" fitting (no adjustment required), and the customer paid the remainder of the invoice. The retailer then had 30 days to pay the manufacturer—a real cash flow boon.

A further benefit of having the customer select the fabric from a fabric book was that the retailer could up-sell on the cloth or up-sell on the manufacturer. A leading made-to-measure Italian manufacturer was Brioni, located in Milan, in which case if Rego or Nordstrom sold a Brioni made-to-measure suit, the price was more than the Samuelsohn manufacturer and, just as importantly, Brioni allowed 60 days after receipt of the suit before Rego had to pay. A Samuelsohn suit retailed for $1,500; Brioni retailed for $3,600 to $4,500.

Thus, the value proposition of Rego's Fitter was to solve the tailoring problem, up-sell, perfect fit and provide cash flow and profit advantages. Rego thought that, with the Fitter, it was possible to adopt a Dell Computers business model in the men's retail clothing industry, i.e., receive the cash from the customer before the store had to pay the supplier.

Summary

Rego felt proud of his achievement. He knew that, with the Fitter, each customer of a store could obtain a suit that was made for them, rather than for someone like them. He needed a business plan including an economic analysis of the Fitter so as to market the concept to Nordstrom. Nordstrom was a very successful Seattle-based retailer. Annual sales were US$6.46 billion, net income in 2003 was US$243 million. Total investment in inventory was US$901 million over 156 stores. The theme of Nordstrom was "I want to make Nordstrom a great experience for every customer." The business plan needed to outline the business case for Nordstrom to adopt the Fitter in all their stores. The adoption by Nordstrom would be a major coup for a small entrepreneurial Canadian retailer to really crack a major account in the United States. Rego put several thousand dollars of his own money into the Fitter's development plus sweat equity and sweat equity by his son in terms of the software. He wanted to know how much he should charge a national retail chain such as Nordstrom, knowing that if the store adopted the Fitter, it could lead to a rapid adoption cycle. The manufacturing cost of each Fitter was $3,000. Thus Rego really needed to show Nordstrom the benefits of the Fitter to its customers and to the store itself.

Notes

1. Australian wool industry market outlook: With wool supply falling because of drought in Australia, world wool prices rose by around 27 per cent in 2002–03. Wool prices were expected to remain strong in 2003–04. However, the market was likely to remain highly volatile as market participants responded in particular to new supply information such as revisions to Australian flock numbers and wool production forecasts. The Australian eastern market indicator was forecast to average 910 cents a kilogram (clean) in 2003–04.
2. January 2004, A$1 = Cdn$0.915.
3. One metre = 1.094 metres.
4. The mills are largely privately held. Holland and Sherry is partly owned by a U.S. consortium, the Individualized Apparel Group (IAG), who purchased their share in Holland and Sherry in February 2003. IAG was a major client of Holland and Sherry before the deal. IAG also owns a ready-made suit manufacturer, H. Freeman and H. Oritsky. Holland and Sherry provide suiting fabric as well as fabric for interiors, annual sales of over £13 million and pretax profits of £1.4 million. Holland and Sherry employs roughly 200 people, largely in the United Kingdom. January 2004, £1 = Cdn$2.28.
5. All monies in Cdn$ unless otherwise specified.
6. A yard (Imperial measure) = 0.9144 metres. In tailoring, the use of imperial measure was still the industry norm, perhaps, due to the large influence of the U.K. woolen mills.
7. "Bespoke, a garment cut by an individual, for an individual, is one definition of the word that is synonomous with Savile Row," from *Savile Row,* Walker R., Rizzoli, 1989.
8. "The coat of the mid-1700s had been a simple, loose attire; more sophisticated garments called for more sophisticated methods of cutting. In the nick of time, somebody—nobody knows exactly who—invented the tape measure. This little item, to the tailor what the stethoscope is the doctor, drew tailoring into the third dimension. A wholly new approach to cutting based on a geometric appreciation of anatomy sprang from the realization that the various body measurements were in a constant ratio to each other," from *Savile Row,* Walker R., Rizzoli, 1989.

Drawn and Quarterly

Prepared by Professor Fernando Olivera

 Version: (A) 2000-10-19

It was June of 2000 and Chris Oliveros, founder and only employee of Montreal-based Drawn and Quarterly (D&Q), wondered what actions he should take to keep his publishing company afloat. Volume 3 of the D&Q anthology had arrived from the press and was now on its way to distributors and comic book specialty stores in Canada, the United States and Europe. A US$50,000 investment, Oliveros knew that publishing this volume was putting his company at risk. He was convinced that Volume 3 was the best international anthology of comics, but it would have to sell well in the next few months for him to continue publishing.

The Comic Book Industry

By the year 2000, many considered the comic book industry to be in a state of crisis. Sales in Canada and the United States had dropped from $1 billion in 1993 to almost half that amount. The number of comic book specialty stores in North America had experienced a similar drop, from about 8,000 in 1993 to 4,000. Several publishers had gone out of business in the last few years and even Marvel, one of the largest comic book publishers, had declared bankruptcy.

The state of the industry in 2000 was a sharp contrast to what it had been just a few years prior. In 1993, comic book sales had reached their peak with the emergence of a strong speculator market. Collectors were buying unprecedented amounts of comic books, expecting the value of their investment to increase as the books became rare items. But this speculator market was short-lived. Reacting to the high demand, publishers increased the number of print runs and began publishing "collector's edition" versions of popular titles. Collectors soon realized that most of the comic books they were accumulating were not becoming more valuable and, in some cases, they were even decreasing in value. Taking the industry by surprise, collectors suddenly stopped buying comics. Thousands of retailers were left with large quantities of unsold, non-returnable comic books and went out of business. Publishers were also left with a large production of unsold titles.

One of the key challenges the North American comics industry faced by the year 2000 was attracting new readers. There were several reasons why attracting new readers was challenging. First, comic books did not have much visibility and did not get much attention from the popular media. Although movie franchises had made some titles popular (e.g., *Batman, The Mask*), they had generally failed at converting movie fans into regular comic book readers. One of the difficulties that new readers faced was becoming familiarized with characters and story lines that had developed in serialized titles over the years. Since back issues were often out of print, expensive or hard to find, new readers often lost interest in becoming acquainted with the comics medium. A second problem was accessibility—comic books were sold mainly in specialty stores, typically located in downtown areas. Finally, comics faced strong competition from other media, such as television, the Internet, movies and books, for the attention of new readers, particularly children. Many industry experts believed that getting children to read comics was the most critical factor in the long-term survival of comic books.

In the year 2000, the industry was made up of four large and several small, independent publishers. The four large companies (Dark Horse, DC, Marvel, and Image Comics) published primarily superhero comics (e.g., *Batman, Superman* and *The X-Men*) and accounted for approximately 80 per cent of industry sales. There was wide variation among the smaller companies in the types of comics they published, including superhero comics, mysteries, science fiction, horror, adventures, fantasy and Japanese (or Manga).

A small group of the independent publishers, which included Drawn and Quarterly, Fantagraphics, Highwater Books, Oni Press, and Top Shelf, specialized in "alternative" comics (i.e., non-mainstream) for adult readers. The content of these comics was varied and ranged from journalistic accounts of war to autobiographies and humor. These publishers accounted for approximately one per cent of industry sales, with Fantagraphics being the largest player in terms of sales and number of titles.

Company Background

Drawn and Quarterly was founded in 1990 by Chris Oliveros, a Montreal-based art school graduate and former bicycle courier. Oliveros conceived D&Q as an anthology of high-quality alternative comics. His goal had been, as he put it simply, "to publish the best cartoonists around." He explained:

> When I was starting, the goal was to have a magazine that came out quarterly and focused on short stories. I was influenced by magazines like *The New Yorker* and *Harpers,* but I wanted to do it in comics.

Oliveros found cartoonists by placing ads in magazines and using his personal network of friends. Borrowing money from his father, he published the first issue of Drawn and Quarterly in the spring of 1990. Although he had not yet recovered his investment, he managed to publish a second issue in October of the same year. Oliveros soon realized that it would be very difficult to make a living out of publishing the magazine. He explained:

> I didn't realize that doing this was financially impossible. The magazine business is tough. It's hard to get started. If you go to a magazine store you may think there are lots of magazines, but there are actually very few good ones and they tend to have been around for many years. It's virtually impossible to start a magazine as an individual without having thousands and thousands of dollars to finance it.

Oliveros had by then met several cartoonists and decided to begin publishing the work of some of them in the form of serialized titles. Among these cartoonists were Chester Brown, who already had a strong following among readers of alternative comics, and two new, promising cartoonists: Julie Doucet and Seth.

Although Oliveros had to borrow money from his father a few more times, by the end of 1992, he had published 10 issues of the anthology (which formed the first volume) and a total of 15 issues from four serialized titles.

D&Q quickly developed a strong reputation for the high quality of the work it published, both in its anthology and the serialized titles. Peter Bagge, a renowned cartoonist, wrote in the introduction to 1993's "Best of Drawn and Quarterly" collection:

> Not only has Drawn and Quarterly been a consistently satisfying read during its entire run, but the [serialized] titles . . . make up the most consistent, high-quality imprint I have ever known. . . . The "secret" to Olivero's success is that he chooses the artists he uses very carefully.

A second volume of the anthology, which comprised six issues, was published between 1994 and 1998. Over the years, new cartoonists came on board, adding to the catalogue of D&Q titles. In addition, Oliveros began publishing books (also known as graphic novels) that followed complete story lines from the serialized titles. For example, Issues 4 through 9 of Seth's series *Palooka-Ville* were collected in the graphic novel "It's a good life if you don't weaken." (Exhibit 1 is a sample of this work.)

By the year 2000, the D&Q catalogue included the first two volumes of the anthology, 13 serialized titles (see Exhibit 2) and 25 graphic novels.

Having won several industry awards, D&Q was widely recognized as one of the most prestigious graphic art publishing companies and Oliveros as one of the most influential publishers in the industry (see Exhibit 3).

D&Q titles were considered among the high-minded, literary version of comics. Their content ranged from autobiographical accounts of contemporary urban life to historical events and fiction. For example, Seth's *It's a good life if you don't weaken* story was an introspective account of the author's search for meaning in the life of a 1940s cartoonist. Chester Brown's *Louis Riel* was a biography of the 19th century Canadian historical figure. Adrian Tomine's *Optic Nerve* narrated short stories of modern, urban life. Oliveros' own *The Envelope Manufacturer* was the story of a man struggling to keep his company afloat. Common to all the titles published by D&Q was the high quality of its cartoonists' craftsmanship. Oliveros considered the quality of his cartoonists of critical importance:

> The reputation I want for the company is of publishing the best cartoonists around. People trust Drawn and Quarterly. They know if they pick a Drawn and Quarterly book, it will be good. This is not true with other companies.

In addition to the high quality of the cartoonists, D&Q held high production standards. Oliveros explained:

> Production and design quality are a priority, as it is for art books. It is possible to do it cheaply, by using cheap paper and only black and white. But I want Drawn and Quarterly to be known for high design and quality standards.

Despite its successes and wide recognition, D&Q remained a small company. Although sales from the D&Q back catalogue were a steady source of income, the company was not breaking into profits. Oliveros explained the situation succinctly:

> The main problem is that not many people buy comics.

Publishing Comics

Publishing comic books involved three distinct sets of tasks: managing the relationship with cartoonists, production work and sales.

Managing Relationships With Cartoonists

D&Q published the work of some of the best cartoonists in the world. Oliveros attributed to luck the fact that he had met Brown, Doucet and Seth in the early days of the company. The work of these artists had received several industry awards and was listed in the *Comics Journal,* an industry publication, among the 100 most important comics of the 20th century.

Luck aside, Oliveros had been able to consistently bring top talent to D&Q. He described how he began publishing the work of two of his cartoonists:

> There is a fellow that publishes in French, Michel Rabagliatti. He is from Montreal. I picked up his book, liked it and decided I wanted to publish him. I called him up and said, "Can I publish you?" He said "Sure!" He knew me because he reads our comics.
>
> Another example is Adrian Tomine. He had been sending me his stuff for over a year. I didn't publish him right away. I was waiting and monitoring his development. I didn't know this, but at the time, he was 18 or 19. He was 20 when I finally called him. I knew that if I did not call him then, someone else, probably Fantagraphics, would have signed him up. When you start a relationship with an artist it tends to go on and on, so I would have lost him. Adrian's *Optic Nerve* is our best-selling title.

Tomine, who was based in California and had worked with Oliveros since 1993, explained his interest in being published by D&Q.

> Part of my inspiration for doing comics was the comics that Drawn and Quarterly publishes; the work of Chester Brown and Julie Doucet. I was a big fan of Drawn and Quarterly and had as an

(Text continues on page 396)

Exhibit 1 Sample From "It's a good life if you don't weaken" by Seth *(Continued)*

Exhibit 1 Sample From "It's a good life if you don't weaken" by Seth

Source: Reproduced with permission from the publisher.

Author & Title	Issue #													
	1	2	3	4	5	6	7	8	9	10	11	12	13	14
Chester Brown														
Louis Riel	Jun-99	Sep-99	Dec-99	May-00										
Underwater	Aug-94	Dec-94	May-95	Sep-95	Feb-96	May-96	Aug-96	Dec-96	Apr-97	Jun-97	Oct-97			
Yummy Fur	Jul-91	Oct-91	Jan-92	May-92	Aug-92	Apr-93	Sep-93	Jan-94						
Julie Doucet														
Dirty Plotte	Jan-91	Mar-91	Jul-91	Oct-91	May-92	Jan-93	Sep-93	Feb-94	Apr-95	Dec-96	Sep-97	Aug-98		
Debbie Drechsler														
Nowhere	Oct-96	Apr-97	Oct-97	Jun-98	Apr-99									
Max														
The Extended Dream of Mr. D	Sep-98	Jan-99	May-99											
Joe Matt														
Peepshow	Feb-92	May-92	Nov-92	Apr-93	Oct-93	Apr-94	Feb-95	Jul-95	Apr-96	Jul-97	Jun-98	Apr-00		
Jason Lutes														
Berlin	Apr-96	Jul-96	Feb-97	Feb-98	Dec-98	Aug-99	Apr-00							
Seth														
Palooka-Ville	Apr-91	Sep-91	Jun-93	Dec-93	May-94	Nov-94	Apr-95	Dec-95	Jun-96	Apr-97	Oct-97	May-98	Jul-99	May-00
Adrian Tomine														
Optic Nerve	Apr-95	Nov-95	Aug-96	Apr-97	Feb-98	Feb-99								
Archer Prewitt														
SofBoy	Sep-97	Aug-98												
Joe Sacco														
Stories from Bosnia	Feb-98													
Chris Oliveros														
The Envelope Manufacturer	Oct-99													
Drawn and Quarterly														
Volume 1	Spr-90	Oct-90	Jan-91	Mar-91	Jun-91	Oct-91	Mar-92	Apr-92	Jul-92	Dec-92				
Volume 2	Aug-94	Dec-94	May-95	Dec-95	Apr-96	Jun-97								

Exhibit 2 Drawn and Quarterly Titles and Publication Dates

Source: Drawn and Quarterly catalogue, June, 2000.

Drawn and Quarterly

"... [displays] a fine editorial taste as well as an outstanding design sense."

—*The San Francisco Chronicle Book Review*

"Let's face the fact: Drawn and Quarterly is, without a doubt, the single best English-language anthology comic of the past decade . . . Drawn and Quarterly simply never missed."

—*The Comics Journal*

"... collects stories by some of today's best comic artists . . . beautifully produced."

—*Publishers Weekly*

"Drawn and Quarterly presents material that busts out of the term 'comics' and leaves it in the dust. Each issue has knockout stories, rich but never slick art work, and generous design, paper, and printing . . . the classiest comics anthology on the market."

—*Geist Magazine*

Chester Brown

"Like all of Brown's work, *Louis Riel* has a serious, adult sensibility and, as in the best comics, the book encourages readers to fill in the gaps between panels, to think and arrive at their own understanding of the characters' motives."

—*The Globe And Mail*

"... as delightful as comics get."

—*Rolling Stone*

"This beautiful book ensnares the agony of youth, the awkwardness of the body, and the burden of knowing that you are alone in your skin . . . *I Never Liked You* brilliantly illuminates the tenuous connection between words and actions."

—*The San Francisco Bay Examiner*

"... a minimalist, but haunting, memoir of the artist's troubled adolescence and his mother's progressive schizophrenia."

—*The New York Times Book Review*

"... an engrossing memoir by one of the most talented artists working in alternative comics today."

—*Publishers Weekly*

Seth

"While reading *Palooka-Ville,* a magically beautiful line will come out of nowhere or a gorgeous image will captivate."

—*Eye Magazine*

"... the stories unfold as a tranquil anecdote to the furious tempo at which we live our lives."

—*The Boston Phoenix*

"Seth inks and letters *Palooka-Ville* with a fluid brushwork whose grace invites the reader to linger cozily in his ruminative, patient stories, each of which grows from Seth's obsession with the past. He hand cuts and overlays black and blue tones over his brushwork onto paper the color of yellow candlelight. *Palooka-Ville* tells the story of what the past was, and of its ripe possibilities that were never borne out."

—*The Village Voice*

"... rich and evocative . . . characterized by small moments revealing the author's sharp eye for detail."

—*The Globe & Mail*

Adrian Tomine

"... easily the most prodigious talent to burst on the alternative scene in several years . . ."

—*The Comics Journal*

"... deftly rendered character sketches. In these narratives, we see a keen, expanding intelligence at work."

—*Wired*

"... great art and a soft, smooth page that's slick to the touch . . . reading *Optic Nerve* is like peeking into someone's diary or flipping through your favorite photo album."

—*The New York Daily News*

Exhibit 3 Critical Praise for Drawn and Quarterly and Its Artists

> aspiration to be published by them so I sent them my work. Initially, I got no response, but I continued to send it. In '91, I got a letter from Chris thanking me for sending my work and offering some feedback on what I could do to improve. I persisted, and in '93 he gave me a call telling me that I was ready.

In addition to being able to attract cartoonists, Oliveros had maintained long-term working relationships with his artists. He explained:

> A good chunk of them have been working with me since the beginning. The contracts are for a specific number of issues and then they can leave, but they have stayed. At least eight or nine have continued with me.
>
> There is not much reason for the artists to go elsewhere. We have the mutual interest of showing the best work. Our interests are in harmony. They may take a book elsewhere if they got an offer from a larger publisher. I would actually encourage them to do that because it gives them exposure and that would also benefit me. I wouldn't hold them back.

Tomine's reasons for staying with D&Q were consistent with Oliveros':

> I've had such a positive experience working with Chris that I've never felt even the slightest temptation to work with another publisher. The market has withered so that there's really one other competitor for Chris, Fantagraphics. I'm friends with them but I prefer Drawn and Quarterly. It's a small operation, there's no bureaucracy—when I call up, I get Chris. Drawn and Quarterly has a significantly better royalty scale. On a personal level, I feel I've become good friends with Chris.

D&Q cartoonists worked on a royalty system. They received a percentage of the retail price of every copy sold on a sliding scale by volume. For example, an artist would get an eight per cent royalty for the first 3,000 copies of an issue, 12 per cent for the next 3,000, and so on. These royalties were slightly higher than in other publishing companies. The contracts were the same for all artists.

Artists had full control over the content of their comics. Oliveros explained:

> Content is typically not a problem. One interesting case was Chester Brown's "Underwater" series. His sales plummeted after the first few issues. He was doing something very different, the characters spoke in a language that doesn't exist and I guess the readers got frustrated. He was selling 9,000 of "Yummy Fur" and then went to 4,000 for "Underwater." But that is rare. You need to have confidence in your artists.

Artists also had full control over the appearance of their comics. Seth explained:

> Chris plays a role in the choice of production aesthetics, but it is a collaboration where we talk about, for example, paper types, colors and design. He doesn't try to impose anything. He'll just give me options.

Given Oliveros' high production standards, cost was generally not an obstacle when making decisions about the comics' appearance. Tomine observed:

> The most impressive thing to me is that whether it's good or bad for his finances, Chris is more concerned with aesthetics than money. He is more of an artist. He always wants to make the comics look as good as possible.

One of the challenges of working with artists was the unpredictability of their output. Most cartoonists took several months to produce each new issue (see Exhibit 2). Oliveros explained:

> Frequency is a problem because cartoonists are slow. But my philosophy is, they are creating something based on artistic expression. You can't crank them out. Do the best you can. If it takes six, 12 or 15 months, so be it.

When asked why he continued to publish his work with D&Q, Seth offered three reasons:

> First, Chris doesn't interfere with the creative process. His philosophy is he picks the artists he likes and assumes he will like the work they do. This is really important for me. I don't want an editor.
>
> Second, I have respect for the company itself. It's a company that has a great deal of integrity in all

> that it publishes. It has the most coherent line of publications; it's all work that Chris likes. He doesn't publish a not so good title that sells well so he can keep the ones he likes. I actually like everything he publishes. The high quality of the work gives the company integrity.
>
> Third, Chris has a long-term belief in what I'm doing. He's willing to put the time, believing that the rewards may come in the long run. I know he's not going to call me one day to tell me that he'll cancel my title. He actually likes what I do and has faith in me. There isn't much money to be made publishing comics, so there is a real commitment from him to produce this material without expecting much in terms of rewards.

Production

Production of comic books involved generating electronic versions of the work done on paper by cartoonists. Some artists did the production work themselves, sending only electronic files to the publisher. Other artists sent paper originals that Oliveros scanned and put together in his computer. Producing the D&Q anthology and catalogues also required design and editorial work for captions and descriptions. Once the electronic files were generated, they were sent to press.

Oliveros determined the print run for each issue based on the volume of preorders and his estimation of sales over the next few years. Given that the start-up costs for printing were high, he tried to print enough copies to cover the initial demand from preorders while not having too many copies left in stock. Most print runs were of 5,000 or 6,000. For *Optic Nerve,* his best-selling title, he would print 15,000 copies (his preorders for this title were about 9,000). Most issues were sold out within four years of printing.

Book volumes (i.e., graphic novels) had a print run of 5,000. Initial orders were usually low, but reorders tended to be frequent and stable. Thus, although publishing books meant losing money in the short run, Oliveros considered them a steady source of revenue for the company. In addition, he believed book volumes were a good way to attract new readers. Books were sold at several large bookstore chains and thus were visible to people who did not frequent comic book stores. Also, because graphic novels contained full, stand-along stories, new readers did not need to be familiar with the characters and story lines from the comic books.

Sales

D&Q products were sold primarily through four channels: distributors, direct orders from comic book stores, mail catalogue, and Internet Web site.

Distributors accounted for approximately 80 per cent of sales. Of these, about 80 per cent were done through Diamond, a major distributor of comic books for the United States and Canada. The remaining 20 per cent were done through smaller distributors, mainly for the European market, and a book distributor that sold to large bookstore chains. Distributors typically got a 55 per cent discount over retail price.

Direct orders from comic book stores accounted for approximately 15 per cent of sales. These orders usually received a 50 per cent discount.

The remaining five per cent of sales were direct orders through the mail catalogue or Web site. Depending on volume, these orders would receive a discount of up to 10 per cent. Oliveros expected electronic sales to go up in the coming months as the site had been relaunched just six months prior.

About 80 per cent of sales were in the United States, 10 per cent in Canada, and the remainder in Europe, mostly in England, France, Finland and Holland.

The retail price of serialized comic books was between $2.99 and $3.50 per issue. Issues were typically 24 pages long. The price of graphic novels ranged from $9.99 to $19.99. (All prices in U.S. dollars.)

D&Q sales had remained relatively stable during the 1990s. Unlike the case of mainstream superhero comics, there was no speculative market for D&Q titles. Oliveros observed, however, that comic book stores had become cautious and tended to order conservatively.

The readership for alternative comic books was hard to define. Oliveros believed that readers were mostly in their 20s, probably in college, and about two-thirds male. Some comic book retailers observed that D&Q readers tended to be in their 30s and well educated. They also observed that perhaps up to 50 per cent of readers were female, an atypical proportion given that most comic book readers were male. Cartoonists also had difficulty describing their readership. Tomine believed his readers were evenly divided between male and female and were probably teenagers or in their 20s. Seth also made an attempt at describing his readership:

> I have an idea based on people who may come up to me or send letters. They are probably young, in their mid-20s; urban; interested in cartooning rather than casual readers; maybe into alternative music. It's hard to tell. I do hear from older readers, but it's hard for me to know if they are representative of my readers in general.

D&Q Volume 3

After publishing the six issues that comprised the second volume of the D&Q anthology, Oliveros decided to relaunch the series in a new format. Rather than publishing multiple issues, Volume 3 would be one book of almost 200 pages and a large 9″ × 12″ format. (Issues of D&Q Volume 2 had been 40 to 60 pages long and 7″ × 10.″ The retail price was US$6.95 per issue for Issues 1 through 5 and $9.95 for the 60-page Issue number 6.) Oliveros explained the concept for Volume 3:

> The idea was to make it like a coffee-table art book. I wanted to publish more international cartoonists and include a section on the history of comics. The risk is that it's expensive, it requires a $50,000 budget. If it goes badly, I risk the entire company.

Oliveros explained his approach to promoting the book:

> I tried to get media coverage. About 100 people will get complementary copies. They go to a few industry publications and to newspapers and magazines, like *Time, Entertainment Weekly,* the *New York Times* and the *New Yorker,* and to radio stations. I placed ads in trade publications, like the *Comics Journal* and in Diamond's catalogue. The main problem with advertising in the general media is that the costs are very high. Also, I would need to convince non-comics readers that comics are worthwhile, that the medium is interesting.

The print run for Volume 3 was 6,000. The retail price was US$24.95. Initial orders from comic book stores were 2,400 (through distributors and direct orders). In addition, 1,000 copies were shipped to the bookstore distributor, but it was difficult to predict how many of those would actually be sold. Oliveros' hope was that, in six months, he would have sold 4,500 copies, which was the break-even point. The remainder would be a profit but would likely take another year and a half to sell.

Considerations for Growth

Oliveros explained his views about growth for D&Q:

> This is a small industry. There just aren't many great cartoonists out there, maybe 15 or 20 in the world and I publish most of them. The industry grows very slowly. I wouldn't even measure it in years. I would say that every five years, you may get a couple of promising cartoonists. So you can't really say "I'm going to quadruple in size in the next year." I could in theory, but because the talent isn't there, the work would be of lesser quality.

In terms of sales, Oliveros had recently joined an initiative with the book distributor and five other small publishers, including Highwater Books and Oni Press, to produce a promotional tabloid that would be distributed in bookstores. The idea was to increase the visibility of graphic novels in the growing book market.

His personal lifestyle was an important factor in his views on growth. Oliveros ran D&Q from his apartment, which he shared with his partner, Marina, who worked as a school teacher, and his three-year-old son, Miguel. Oliveros described his daily life:

I drop off my son in day care every day and check my e-mail in the morning when I get back. But after that, there are so many different things to do. Every day is different. I'm not sure there is a typical day. If I have a big job, I'll just work on that all day. Yesterday I worked for eight hours on the new catalogue and sent it out to the press. I was at the computer, scanning, designing, writing the captions. I usually have letters to write. I fill out the mail orders. I fill out orders for the warehouse. A big chunk of it is production work. I spend a lot of time on the computer.

Oliveros reflected on the things he liked and disliked about his job and on his goals for the future:

I like the work I do. Some of the people I publish are my favorite cartoonists, and that is very rewarding. I've liked comics since I was a kid. If someone had told me I would end up doing what I do I wouldn't have believed it. This is the best job I could have hoped for.

The other things I like are probably common to people who work independently: working for yourself, not having to go into some office from nine to five, being your own boss. When I go downtown during traffic hour I think, "How do people do this?"

In terms of what I don't like, it's hard to say. It tends to be the little details you need to stay on top of. It can be overwhelming. There are j
things, like the finances, keeping tra
and orders. I have an accountant, but
lot of paper and numbers. I also som
go after people who have not paid their bills. We are not breaking into profits. It's very, very tight. I have these bills to pay and only so much money, so I really need to keep on top of things.

My goals now are similar to when I started. I still want to publish the best cartoonists working today. I guess what's changed is that my taste is more refined and I have a better idea of what works and what doesn't.

I don't think in terms of sales. I like the idea of what I want to do, publish these great books that I can take and show to other people. I want to have the freedom to keep doing this.

Oliveros knew that his ability to invest in new projects depended in part on getting enough revenue from sales. As copies of the D&Q Volume 3 were on their way to retailers, he wondered if changing the format of the anthology from multiple issues to a coffee-table style volume had been the right decision. He also wondered if there were things that he could do differently to guarantee the success of future publications.

InnoMedia Logic Inc.

Prepared by Warren Roll under the supervision of Professor James E. Hatch

Version: (A) 2002-05-16

In just two years, InnoMedia Logic Inc. ("IML" or "the Company") had grown from a small eight-person operation, developing Voice over Internet Protocol (VoIP) hardware for products that transferred voice through the Internet, to a fully operational producer and worldwide distributor on the cusp of becoming a multimillion-dollar high-tech company. This exponential growth had placed great strain on the Company and uncertainty over the direction it should take in the coming months.

It was September 1999, and Michel Laurence, president and chief executive officer (CEO) of IML, was staring at his company's production and testing facility as he sat back in his office chair, pondering a number of issues his company was facing. His two-year-old high-tech start-up venture had blossomed into a fast growing VoIP card producer, with technology that was becoming very attractive in the industry. Earlier that day, Laurence had received an unsolicited offer of US$38 million cash, to purchase 100 per cent of his company's shares from CT Networks, one of the three leading suppliers of telephony and components (see Exhibit 1). With this offer in hand, Laurence began to evaluate his options.

The Technology

Organizations around the world were increasingly concerned with their rising communications costs. Consolidation of separate voice and data networks offered an opportunity for significant savings and was becoming a priority for many network managers. Organizations were pursuing solutions that would enable them to take advantage of excess capacity on broadband networks for voice and data transmission, as well as utilize the Internet as an alternative to costlier media.

To address these demands, IML focused on converging high-speed Internet with voice communication. IML believed the next generation of long-distance calling would be carried out through the use of the Internet as the vehicle to transfer voice data and not through the traditional public switched telephone networks. This could be accomplished by using VoIP through Computer Telephony (CT).[1]

Voice information could now be sent and received in digital form. These digital "packets" of information could be delivered through different speeds, depending on bandwidth capability. IML focused on Voice over Digital Subscriber Line (VoDSL),[2] as Digital Subscriber Line (DSL)[3] was the broadband Internet connection most medium-sized businesses were using.

IML was a provider of a group of different technologies that were required for the implementation of a VoIP network for small and medium-sized businesses. They offered packet voice networking solutions for current and next generation communications networks. The Company had a family of adapters that were integrated into multimedia gateways. These adapters supported voice switching and voice traffic conversion for applications over DSL networks. (The Company also provided adapters for voice processing services normally required in packet voice networks, such as compression and echo cancellation.) All of the equipment that IML produced for the CT market was sold to companies that developed the full network solution for VoIP, which was then sold to distributors and deployed to the consumer.

Customers could realize significant savings on a variety of fronts when they deployed a VoIP network, including: reduced access lines costs, better customer support, high-speed Internet access and one network for local/long-distance calling and Internet.

Background

Laurence and his partner, Michel Brule, were professors from École Technologie Supérieure in Montreal. Both entrepreneurs had strong academic and professional backgrounds in electronic engineering, obtained while working for numerous top tier telecommunication providers and equipment manufacturers in the 1980s. Between 1989 and 1996, Laurence gained his credibility in the CT industry by developing communications systems for a law enforcement agency. He eventually recognized that this market was too small to make any substantial returns and decided to turn to consulting, taking on various contracts in Canada and in Silicon Valley. Laurence was dedicated to developing more effective and more efficient ways of voice communication using computers. His keen sense of the industry told him that the next generation of telecommunications technology would incorporate the Internet and PC technology.

Laurence realized that there was an untapped market of small businesses currently using telephone lines for local and long-distance calling and broadband for Internet connections, such as DSL. He was confident that once these firms understood the substantial cost savings and the increased voice data capacity they could obtain, they would switch from using old telephone lines to VoIP.

Purchase Price:	US$9.00/share for outstanding common stock and vested options • $4.50/share—at closing • $4.50/share—on first anniversary of closing (no performance conditions)
Transaction Structure:	Structured to achieve tax-deductible goodwill for CT Networks, while maximizing tax benefits to sellers.
Operating Structure:	Existing organization, except Sales, operates as a unit of CT Networks. Technology, Data Technology Division, reporting to Michel Laurence. Michel Laurence sets local policies, consistent with CT Network's company practices. All personnel remain in present location. *Sales:* Company sales staff (including sales engineers and equivalent technical staff) report to CT Sales organization; reporting structure to be determined. Company products are sold by any CT Sales person designated by CT Sales management. CT Networks intends for IML to honor all existing development, distribution and other contractual agreements. Where appropriate, these relationships will be managed by Michel Laurence directly. *Marketing:* Company marketing programs coordinated with CT marketing programs and implemented through CT Corporate Communications. CT may initiate additional marketing programs. *Finance & Administration:* Adopt CT Networks processes and procedures and eliminate redundancies where possible, subject to mutual agreement. *Manufacturing:* May be consolidated with CT Networks Technology's operations
Employees:	All employees become employees of CT Networks. All employees receive current compensation program (assuming all are at market value). In addition, they will receive newly issued CT Networks Incentive Stock Options consistent with the current practices at CT Networks (see below: Incentives for Employees Remaining with Business).
Key People Employment Agreements:	Key individuals (assumed to be Michel Laurence, vice-president of engineering and sales and the directors of Hardware and Software Engineering) agree to two-year employment with CT Networks. Employment can be terminated early, by mutual agreement between the individuals and the president of CT Networks.
Incentives for Employees Remaining With Business:	Two programs: **CT Networks Stock Options:** Options will be allocated to the employees of IML who remain with CT Networks. This includes converting unvested IML options to options in CT Networks and making additional grants in order to make everyone's position consistent with CT Networks practices. The allocation of the shares will be agreed upon by Michel Laurence and the president of CT Networks, but shall include options on 40,000 shares for Michel Laurence. Vesting of Michel Laurence's shares will accelerate upon achievement of the revenue & profit objectives below (50 per cent in year 1, 50 per cent in year 2). **Performance Bonus:** A bonus pool will be created for the shareholders of IML business who remain with CT Networks until the first and second anniversary of the closing. The available bonus will be 25 per cent of the total revenue in excess of: • $16.1 million in 2000 • $22.5 million in 2001.

Exhibit 1 Terms of the Unsolicited Offer *(Continued)*

	The available bonus pool will be reduced if expenses exceed the approved business plan. This bonus pool will be distributed pro rata, according to the number of IML shares held by each employee at closing.
IML Systems:	IML Systems shall be incorporated by existing IML shareholders as described in IML's November 23, 1999, letter to CT Networks. IML's convertible loan to Systems shall be included in the assets of the business purchased by CT Networks (including all conversion privileges). CT Networks will honor product supply agreements and will make other CT Networks products available: to Systems on substantially similar terms. Up to four of the current IML employees may be transferred to Systems.
Assumptions:	**Balance Sheet at Closing:** Working Capital (minimum): Cdn$4.5 million Book Value Net Worth (minimum): Cdn$6 million Revenue: CT Networks will support IML in maximizing revenues from existing development and distribution agreements.

Exhibit 1 Terms of the Unsolicited Offer

The Birth of IML

IML was a spinoff of IML Research (IMLR), a company created in 1994 to develop a PC card that allowed voice to be carried over data networks. In 1996, IMLR closed a deal to design a computer card that allowed voice signals to be carried over a data-transmission system for a major North American call center located in Atlanta, Georgia. The new card represented breakthrough technology that Laurence's client and many other companies worldwide had been demanding.

Laurence knew he was onto something revolutionary with this new PC card. He was confident that VoIP hardware and software sales would continue to grow exponentially, as he had recently read that international VoIP call volumes were expected to reach 1.7 billion minutes in 1999.

Laurence wanted to spin off a company from IMLR with the exclusive license to distribute VoIP cards worldwide. However, his client from Atlanta, who had funded IMLR's development thus far, believed they had control over the intellectual property (IP). Ownership of the IP had not been made clear within the precedent contracts and his client wanted royalties on any future sales of these cards. Laurence was not clear regarding the strength of his IP claim and decided that he would pay a negotiated royalty fee based on future sales. This agreement would eliminate any potential liability for intellectual property infringement.

The final validation of the technology occurred while producing cards for the Atlanta Company. Laurence took IMLR's modified technology to an industry-wide CT trade show in Los Angeles and received the "Best of Show" award. The products were also receiving rave reviews from the call center industry, just from the one card that they had recently developed on contract. This positive feedback from the industry was exactly the support that was needed to justify mass marketing of the voice cards.

Starting Up and Growing IML

The dream finally became a reality in early 1996, when Laurence and his partner each put up Cdn$100,000 of their own savings and started

IML. IML secured from IMLR, an exclusive, irrevocable and perpetual license on the originally developed products and technology and spun off the new company from IMLR, taking eight of the 15 employees with them.

IML, now a privately owned corporation, located in Montreal, Quebec, focused on developing, manufacturing and selling these specialized network products. The first commercial products were released in December 1996, and at the end of March 1998, IML had shipped over Cdn$1.8 million of its products to 56 customers around the world.

The Competition

In 1999, the competitive market for VoIP technology was heating up quickly. There were dozens of companies in the sector that had gone public on American and Canadian stock exchanges over the last two years. The capital markets had recognized VoIP as a revolutionary technology and there was a mass influx of institutional and venture capital injected into this industry. The race for market share was beginning and more and more companies were emerging with similar technology, although there were very few players that had reached the production stage. IML faced mostly indirect competition from several large companies. Each was already selling similar technology and some had distinct advantages, including wider product lines, diverse client portfolios and larger pools of capital. There were some signs of consolidation beginning within the VoIP industry and Laurence felt that if he played his cards right, his competitors could turn into possible acquirers. Among the stronger competitors were:

Jetstream Communications, San Jose, CA

IML's biggest customer was the leading provider of VoIP. Jetstream's solutions had driven the standard for bundled voice and data service delivery over DSL and wireless broadband access networks. Although Jetstream did not build IML's technology internally, there was a risk that they could eventually produce IML's VoIP cards by themselves.

First Virtual Corporation (FVC), Santa Clara, CA

FVC provided rich media communications solutions, enabling interactive voice, video and data collaboration over IP-based networks. First Virtual provided cost-effective, integrated end-to-end solutions for large-scale deployments to enterprise desktops. FVC had recently gone public on Nasdaq and raised over US$40 million. Although they were not yet a major threat, their strategy was not perfectly clear. One possibility was to increase their strength in IML's direct market. As a public company, they could easily use their shares to make acquisitions in order to gain market share and were also more visible to customers.

Sphere Communications (Sphere), Lake Bluff, IL

Sphere, a private company, was founded in 1994 and provided voice and data communications solutions on broadband networks. Sphere was primarily a software development company. Their products were not compatible with any computer telephony hardware interface standards. Sphere was not currently a competitor with IML, and in order for Sphere to compete, it would have needed to drastically change the direction of their business and develop brand new technologies. Sphere was looking to go public in the near future with a Nasdaq listing.

Xinex, Vancouver, BC

Xinex was a small Vancouver-based company that had recently entered the VoIP market. It was marketing a product that was very similar to Sphere's offering. To achieve their target price, they had decided to use a proprietary technology variant. There was no public offering for Xinex in the foreseeable future and Xinex was not considered a competitive threat.

Financing History

Round One

In 1996, finding adequate financing to get IML on its feet proved to be an arduous and time-consuming task. Laurence visited a number of Canadian banks and institutional investors, but no one showed interest, due to the inherent risk in the early stage company.

Novacap

Novacap was a Quebec venture capital group that was created in 1981 and managed over Cdn$100 million in capital. They focused on early stage high-tech companies that were developing "next generation" technology, concentrating mostly on the telecommunications hardware sector. They typically structured their financing using common and preferred shares, as well as debentures, and usually invested $1 million to $5 million per company.

Novacap began negotiations with IML for a small equity investment. They had one condition though. Dialogic Corp. of Parsippany, N.J., also had expressed an interest in investing in IML and Novacap would invest in IML if Dialogic would partner with them in the financing.

Dialogic Inc.

Dialogic was one of the three leading suppliers of telephony cards and components to large telecommunications networking companies. With over US$300 million in sales, Dialogic could be an eventual suitor for IML; Dialogic was not currently in the VoDSL market but wanted eventually to be a leader in this sector. An early investment in IML would be strategic and could give them a lock on this revolutionary new card for the future.

In April 1997, while Novacap was still completing their due diligence, Dialogic took a minority equity position of approximately 15 per cent for US$600,000 or $1.37 per share. A better understanding of the market had allowed them to move much quicker than Novacap.

Then in June, Novacap came to the table, but not at the same valuation. Laurence saw that the valuations for public companies in this industry were beginning to rise substantially on little or no earnings; he concluded that his company was also worth more with Dialogic as a shareholder, even within just two months. IML closed its second round of financing, with Novacap providing US$300,000 at a price of $1.37 and US$300,000 at $1.87 for 12 per cent of the total equity. Laurence remembers:

> We had to be tough with investors. We knew we had a winning technology and we were confident that we could get financing elsewhere at our valuation if Novacap didn't want to participate. I remember how cheated Novacap felt when they came back to participate in an equity financing and we told them that the price had just gone up. The tension between us didn't last long though; it turned out that they wanted to invest in us even more because of our keen business sense and sharp negotiation skills.

Round Two

When Dialogic invested in IML, part of the deal was a commitment from Dialogic to sell a specified number of IML's cards. If Dialogic could reach Cdn$9 million in sales within three years, they would have been granted the right to purchase 30 per cent more of IML at a price of $1.37. Laurence felt that this option was a good strategy to increase sales and future funding sources for the Company. Unfortunately, Dialogic was unable to meet the agreed sales targets and the partnership began to deteriorate:

> Dialogic wanted to prevent its biggest competitor, NMS Communications, from gaining the technology in the future. But the Dialogic partnership just wasn't working out as planned and our relationship with them grew increasingly frustrating. In fact, we

ended up selling $1 million of their $1.3 million sales commitment in the first year of the agreement.

By early 1998, it was clear that IML would need more money if it was going to achieve its potential in the marketplace; Laurence decided to take advantage of the market's appetite to invest in IML's technology. In the spring of 1998, Laurence set out with a brand new business plan and presentation, including up-to-date financials, intending to raise additional funds to finance growth. The target was US$3.5 million, and Laurence felt that the minimum pre-money value of equity was US$15 million. Laurence made presentations across Canada and California to numerous banks and venture capital companies. Offers received ranged from US$1 million to US$3 million with pre-money valuations of US$15 million. However, due to the established strong relationship and familiarity with IML, it was Novacap that was chosen to participate in this second strategic round of financing. They matched IML's best offer of US$3.5 million at a price of $5.00 per share because of their familiarity with the Company. Dialogic decided to exercise their matching right and split the financing with Novacap. The standard due diligence requirement was waived. The financing history of IML is summarized in Exhibit 2.

Employee Stock Option Plan

Laurence knew that in order to build a loyal team and attract strong talent from the telecommunications industry he would have to create large incentives. Stock options were also allotted to employees, amounting to approximately 10 per cent of the outstanding common stock. Options were priced at the time of each financing, and typically each employee was allotted 3,000 shares for three years.

Taking IML to the Next Level

Armed with cash in the bank, a proven product and a loyal customer base, Laurence wanted to take IML to the next level. Sales needed to be ramped up and the Company needed to turn a profit by the first quarter of 1998.

> Our timing couldn't have been more perfect. We had already secured the financing we needed to attain our sales goals for the year. Meanwhile business spending was up for the year and international demand for VoIP products was heating up. Internet companies were the largest percentage of IPOs on Nasdaq and there was a tremendous amount of capital being invested in all technology sectors. It was a very exciting time for us as we were right in

	Financing ($000)	*Price/Share (US$)*	*Pre-Money Valuation (US$)*	*Shares*	*Ownership*
Michel Laurence (Founder)	100,000			1,000,000	24%
Michel Brule (Founder)	100,000			1,000,000	24%
Dialogic	600,000	1.37	2,740,000	437,956	10%
Novacap	300,000	1.37	3,340,000	218,978	5%
Novacap	300,000	1.87	4,968,467	160,428	4%
Angel Investors	390,000	1.87	5,268,467	208,556	5%
Novacap	1,750,000	5.00	15,129,591	350,000	8%
Dialogic	1,750,000	5.00	15,129,591	350,000	8%
Convertibles, Warrants & Options				500,000	12%
Total				**4,225,918**	**100%**

Exhibit 2 IML Financing History

Source: Company files.

the middle of this technological revolution with a very healthy company. The industry was expecting the number of IP telephony minutes to reach 135 billion by 2004, and revenue for this service would rise from an expected US$480 million in 1999 to US$19 billion by 2004.

By April 1998, IML began turning a profit each quarter (see Exhibits 3 and 4). IML was enjoying 80 per cent margins as they were still one of the few companies competing in this space. IML was able to keep overhead quite low compared to the industry, given that their head office was situated in Montreal (where costs were relatively low) and there were substantial government tax incentives.

Laurence believed his sales initiative could expand even further to take advantage of the strong demand for VoIP products that was being fuelled by hundreds of distributors capitalizing on the growing opportunities in this brand new market. He hired more salespeople and engineers, bringing the total head count to 30 employees.

	1997	*1998*	*1999*	*Forecast 2000*
Assets				
Current				
Cash	4	119	—	918
Short-term investments	—	131	2,210	3,134
Accounts receivable	207	411	801	6,854
Income taxes receivable	—	546	865	123
Inventory	—	330	697	1,706
Prepaid expenses and deposits	13	55	54	187
	224	1,592	4,627	12,922
Capital assets	6	337	567	1,933
	230	1,929	5,194	14,855
Liabilities				
Current				
Demand loan	—	262	—	—
Accounts payable and accrued charges	212	177	506	2,265
Advances from affiliated companies	3	—	—	—
Current portion of long-term debt	—	26	32	210
Income taxes payable	—	—	—	244
Deferred revenues	—	—	—	1,170
	215	465	538	3,889
Deferred income taxes	—	—	—	127
Long-term debt	—	281	560	517
	215	746	1,098	4,533
Shareholders' Equity				
Capital stock	0	1,567	3,960	5,808
Share options	35	35	35	1
Retained earnings	(21)	(418)	101	4,513
	14	1,184	4,096	10,322
	229	**1,930**	**5,194**	**14,855**

Exhibit 3 Balance Sheet as at March 31 ($000s)

Source: Company files.

	1997 *$*	*1998* *$*	*1999* *$*	*Forecast 2000* *$*
Revenue:				
Sales	214,025	1,606,582	3,641,391	13,825,000
Other revenue	—	5,536	42,899	1,443,000
	214,025	1,612,118	3,684,290	15,268,000
Cost of sales	185,871	667,139	959,217	3,553,000
Gross margin	28,154	944,979	2,725,073	11,715,000
Research and development	—	366,930	612,323	2,068,000
Marketing and sales expenses	30,378	489,415	799,064	1,893,000
Administrative expenses	18,719	462,185	755,662	1,365,000
Financial expenses	165	23,581	12,643	—
	49,262	1,342,111	2,179,692	5,326,000
Net income (loss) for the year	(21,108)	(397,132)	545,381	6,389,000
Income taxes	—	—	(25,864)	(1,977,000)
Retained earnings (deficit) At beginning of year	—	(21,108)	(418,240)	101,277
Retained earnings (deficit) at end of year	(21,108)	(418,240)	101,277	4,513,277

Exhibit 4 Statement of Income and Deficit Year Ended March 31

Challenges of Growth

IML's strongest year, since its inception, was 1999. IML and many other high-tech companies were able to benefit from the strong public and private capital markets, the rapid growth in the demand for technology products and the overall booming economy. In spite of this prosperity, IML was facing a number of internal challenges resulting from the Company's quick development and intensified competition in the industry.

Internal Issues

Overt conflict between sales and engineering was becoming more of an issue, especially when sales began to pick up in 1999. Engineering, which would have to design and deliver the technology specifications on a fixed time and price basis, wanted to limit customers' expectations about the products' capacity and design. Sales, on the other hand, was often tempted to sell capabilities and possibilities that were not achievable. Management attempted to deal with this conflict by clearly demarcating the roles of sales and engineering within the design and delivery cycle.

Further to this issue was the concern around compensation. There were feelings of inequality, particularly among the engineering employees. Engineers were feeling underpaid and overworked, compared to sales, who were being paid high commissions. As well, many of them knew of engineers, working elsewhere, who were better compensated. Although the issues between engineering and sales were being managed, the disparity between these two groups continued to grow as sales continued to increase.

External Issues

IML was still too small to be considered an important client by any of the big contract manufacturers, and therefore had to settle for the second- and third-tier contractors to manufacture and package the VoDSL chips. Problems with suppliers began to develop in 1999 with the increase in demand. The Company began to experience quality control issues, as more and more defective cards were being shipped to customers. As the quality of the cards continued to diminish, Laurence began spending more and more time with these local contractors trying to reduce the level of defects. Laurence began to worry about maintaining the high customer service satisfaction that he had established over the years and knew he could not access the top contract manufacturers in the near future.

IML's biggest customers were companies building VoDSL and VoIP gateways for small and medium-sized businesses. The value proposition was to allow local exchange carriers (LEC) to offer voice services in competition with Bell, using new broadband access services and high-speed Internet access. In 1999, there was a significant number of LECs emerging; however, because of IML's lack of resources, the Company was not expanding its sales initiative and new customer acquisition was slow. Instead, increased sales were coming from their current customer base. In fact over 50 per cent of IML's sales were from one particular customer. Moreover, as demand continued to grow, major suppliers of these VoIP gateways, including some of Laurence's best customers, were considering making their own VoIP cards rather than outsourcing. This could pose a major threat to IML's sales projections and would likely cause a reduction in the high margins they had enjoyed.

Market Conditions

North America was witnessing an equity bull market. With the Nasdaq Composite Index reaching 3,000 points, and the DOW escalating to 11,000, each index was posting record highs (see Exhibit 5). Nasdaq volumes were at their all-time highs in 1999, with significant amounts of capital being transferred from the fixed income markets.

After posting a rise of 29 per cent through the first three quarters of the year, the high-tech sector now represented almost 25 per cent of the value of the S&P 500, up from 13 per cent at year-end 1997. Equity prices had increased enormously over the past four years to levels that challenged previous valuation standards.[4] The world had never seen such high stock prices in the equity markets and analysts weren't sure what to expect in the near future. One thing was certain however, investors had a strong appetite for technology plays and they continued to finance all types of companies through private placements and public offerings. All of these healthy growth signals, coupled with lower interest rates, a low rate of inflation and heavy consumer spending, confirmed an exceptionally strong economy. The only worry was how long this boom would last.

Within this industry, Voice over Internet Protocol (VoIP) was driving the convergence of voice and data networks and promised to deliver significant cost-savings to both end-users and service providers. According to Cahners In-Stat Group, a high-tech market research firm, equipment vendors and service providers would benefit most from VoIP. Fuelled by improvements in quality, interoperability and applications, VoDSL would become a US$1 billion market by the end of 2000, VoIP gateway sales would increase 280 per cent during the next five years, reaching $3.8 billion in 2003. Many analysts, however, felt that the high-tech bubble was about to burst and optimistic projections would never be realized, as consumer demand would soon begin to decline.

The Surprise Offer

After experiencing four consecutive quarters of rapid growth, and achieving positive earnings,

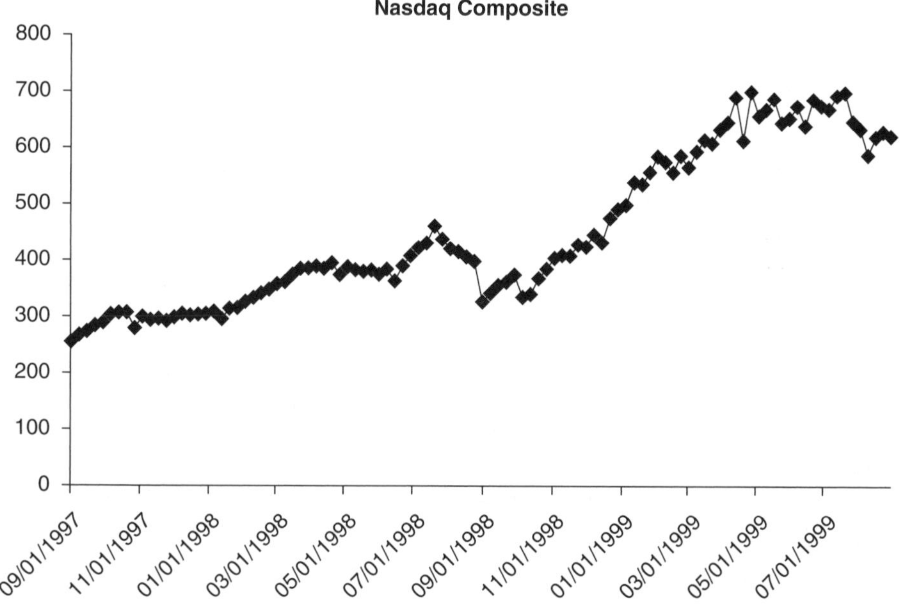
Nasdaq Composite
800
700
600
500
400
300
200
100
0
09/01/1997
11/01/1997
01/01/1998
03/01/1998
05/01/1998
07/01/1998
09/01/1998
11/01/1998
01/01/1999
03/01/1999
05/01/1999
07/01/1999

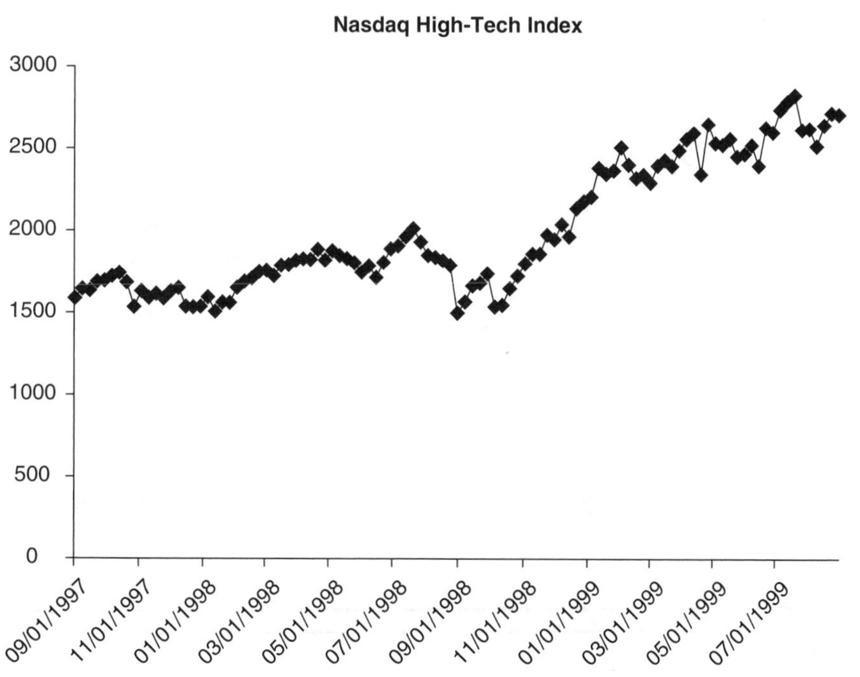
Nasdaq High-Tech Index
3000
2500
2000
1500
1000
500
0
09/01/1997
11/01/1997
01/01/1998
03/01/1998
05/01/1998
07/01/1998
09/01/1998
11/01/1998
01/01/1999
03/01/1999
05/01/1999
07/01/1999

Exhibit 5

Laurence received a fax one afternoon in early September. It was an unsolicited offer to buy 100 per cent of IML shares in return for US$38 million (see Exhibit 1) from one of the three biggest telecommunications subsystems suppliers in North America. The suitor was a networking and communication equipment supplier that designed and developed network quality hardware and software components. The suitor wanted, like Dialogic, to expand into the VoDSL market and needed IML's proven technology in order to penetrate the market successfully.

The US$38 million offer was equal to approximately $9 per share. Laurence was unsure what the best decision was for his company and his shareholders. His ultimate responsibility was to maximize the shareholders' value, and this offer, although not a substantial valuation increase from the last round, would still give his shareholders an exceptional return on investment and an effortless passage to exit his company.

Michel Brule, IML's second biggest shareholder and Laurence's long-time partner, indicated that he would abide by whatever decision Laurence took.

Novacap, the Company's biggest shareholder, would be willing to exit; however, they were used to staying with their investments for longer periods of time. The venture capitalist (VC) had also mentioned on numerous occasions the expectation that this company would go public on Nasdaq giving Laurence the impression that his biggest investor did not want to sell out yet. Still, if Laurence would begin to prepare for an initial public offering (IPO) or an even bigger private acquisition, he wondered if Novacap would provide his company with the necessary bridge financing.

The relationship between Dialogic and IML was still weak and it was unlikely that Dialogic would match the proposed offer. Dialogic had hinted over the year at a lack of interest in investing further in IML. Dialogic only had one seat on the board of directors and Laurence expected that they would accept the proposed offer. It was essential for Laurence to examine the original shareholders agreement to see whether Dialogic had a right of co-sale and/or any other restrictions that might be a factor in accepting the proposed offer.

Laurence wanted to ensure that if the deal was accepted, all of his employees' positions would be safe in the merged company and they would have an equivalent incentive plan. It was also essential for both Laurence and his partner to receive a portion of the selling price in stock (for tax purposes) and to receive additional purchase options based on performance.

Still, Laurence was concerned that IML was worth much more, given that public share prices relative to book value were extremely high and that the investment community had been very enthusiastic and receptive with early stage VoIP-related technology ventures. The Company needed to consider any other alternative exit strategies that could optimize the value of the Company shares.

Financial Projections

IML exhibited fundamentals that nearly all of the new public high-tech companies lacked. Current sales had reached over Cdn$3.5 million and earnings were positive. Laurence felt that, at the very least, his sales could reach Cdn$2.3 million for the next quarter, ending December 31. If market trends continued, Laurence was confident the Company could surpass their revenue projection of Cdn$13.8 million for 2000, double that by 2002 and maintain over 20 per cent net margins after tax. With what he believed to be conservative financial projections, Laurence continued to question whether the Company was worth only US$38 million.

Laurence needed to put his own value on the Company and the most widely used valuation tool was the discounted cash flow (DCF) model. However, the DCF did not appear to be applicable in this instance, due to the Company's early stage and unpredictable cash flow. Therefore, Laurence used the multiples approach. Multiples based on the stock price of comparable companies were calculated and applied to the financial

	Symbol	Share Price ($)	Shares O/S	Market Cap ($)	P/E (TTM)	Price/ Sales (last yr)	EPS (TTM)	SPS (last yr)
Virata Corpt.	VRTA (NASD)	14.93	46.57	695.29	64.84	4.99		9.26
First Virtual Corp.	FVCX (NASD)	15.75	16.83	265.07	118.85	7.67	(0.87)	2.78
Sphere Communications	Private							
Texas Instruments	TXN (NYSE)	45.43	17.00	772.31	53.53	8.17	0.86	5.81
NMS Communications	NMSS (NASD)	64.00	25.52	1,633.28	16.44	6.79	(0.81)	3.46
Dialogic		31.12	15.89	494.50	28.48	2.41		
Brooktrout (BRKT)			10.76		33.57	1.44	1.76	11.77
Jetstream	Private							
Average					52.62	5.25	0.24	6.62

Exhibit 6 Valuation of Selected Companies Based on the Multiples Approach

*Sales per share–SPS

results of the issuer. The most applicable multiples were the price-to-EBITDA and price-to-sales, as most of the emerging technology companies were not and did not anticipate to be profitable in the near future (see Exhibit 6).

As Laurence prepared for his board meeting, he pondered whether US$38 million cash was a fair value for a company. Although this sum would enable Laurence to retire or allow him to start a new company (he had only invested $100,000 just three and a half years ago), he wondered if he could continue to manage IML and take the current operation from a $4 million dollar company to the expected $35 million dollar company he was projecting by 2001.

He questioned the Company's ability to expand its sales initiative, and the reliability of his current suppliers to produce cards at an increasingly rapid rate, to meet this high market demand. He also questioned the timing and if there were better deals in the marketplace and how long the "window" would stay open. As the markets continued to heat up, was it the right time to take advantage of Nasdaq and complete an initial public offering or was it too risky and should the Company continue to seek private funding?

Notes

1. CT refers to the use of computers to manage telephone calls and VoIP (Voice over IP) refers to voice that is delivered using the Internet Protocol.
2. VoDSL refers to transferring voice data packets using a type of high-speed Internet access for home and office use.
3. DSL is a technology for bringing high-bandwidth information to homes and small businesses over ordinary copper telephone lines.
4. Robert A. Dennis, "The Perac Financial Bulletin," *C.F.A. Financial Market Review,* 3rd Quarter, 1999.

Quadra Logic Technologies Inc. (A)

Prepared by Warren Roll under the supervision of Professor James E. Hatch

 Version: (A) 2002-05-30

In late June 1987, Ron MacKenzie, Executive Vice-President of Quadra Logic Technologies Inc. (QLT), located in Vancouver, was thinking over the firm's latest opportunity to commercialize a product. The small company's research group had come up with a drug which, when combined with laser technology, could be used in the treatment of cancer. He muttered to himself:

> Killing malignant tumours with beams of light . . . it's right out of science fiction. We've got to market this product. But how? Can we do it ourselves or should we sell it to someone else? Maybe we should wait until we're in a better position to support it.

Ron knew that QLT's product presented a major opportunity for his firm because it was potentially superior to alternative treatments for several forms of cancer. Their decision on which direction to take with this product could not be delayed. Ron wanted to have a well-developed marketing strategy worked through before entering into serious negotiations on any of the alternatives. He decided to have the strategy worked out in time to present it at the next board meeting, slated for July 10th.

The Company

Quadra Logic Technologies Inc. (QLT) was considered a rising star in the biotechnology industry in Canada. In five years, it had gone from existing only on paper to being the only publicly traded biotechnology firm in Canada and the 12th largest publicly-traded biotechnology firm in North America.

The company was formed in February 1981 by five individuals who believed that considerable improvements could be made in the existing links between academic research and commercialization of discoveries. Four were university professors with specialties in biology and medicine. The fifth, Ron MacKenzie, was a business executive who held chemical engineering and MBA degrees and who had experience as a health care management consultant.

The firm's primary goal was to be a leader in the field of medical diagnostics and therapeutics. This would be achieved through developing products that featured unique biological materials and product formats. QLT specialized in the development, production, and marketing of human and veterinary health products, mainly through the application of monoclonal antibody and genetic engineering technology. Essentially, these technologies consisted of the manipulation of cells and/or the DNA purified from the cells. From the beginning, the partners' objective had been to identify and exploit those areas of their research that represented the greatest commercial potential. They aggressively pursued opportunities by acquiring technologies or the right to further develop products which had demonstrated feasibility in the lab and apparent market potential for the end product.

"The fact that we're totally market-driven is not so unusual. Scratch almost any academic and you'll find a latent entrepreneur," Julia Levy, VP and Director of Research, was heard to comment. A colleague in the financial area of QLT had described the concept slightly differently in an interview with *B.C. Business* magazine: "Rather than pure researchers, our people could more accurately be called developmental scientists."

During the first five years, QLT had focused on research, funded predominantly by government

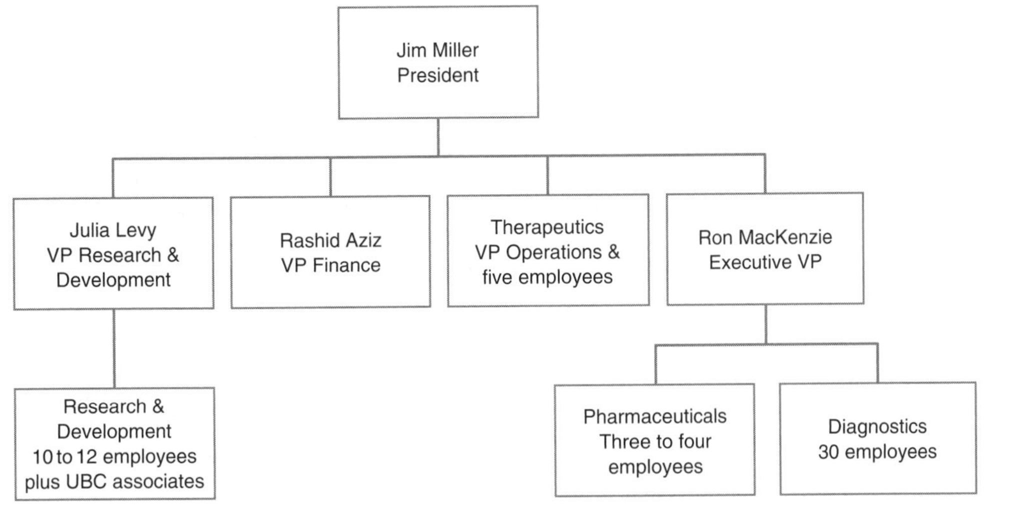

Exhibit 1

grants with some income resulting from royalties generated from licensing of early products. The major change occurred late in 1986 when the firm went public. It raised $4.7 million and three of the five principals became employees of the company in anticipation of the commercialization of their own products. In addition to three of the founding members, the company had 60 employees, 15 of whom were Ph.D.s or medical doctors (see Exhibit 1).

QLT Product Lines

The company handled three main product areas: diagnostics, pharmaceuticals, and therapeutics. The products were directed at three market segments:

- the over-the-counter (OTC) segment, consisting of end users treating themselves;
- the professional segment, in which sales were made to the medical practitioner treating patients in his or her office; and
- the clinical segment, in which sales were made to hospitals or clinics for treatment, testing and diagnostic services.

QLT's diagnostic products included pregnancy and ovulation test kits, infectious disease testing (e.g., AIDS), and microbiological testing (to determine the antibiotic profile of bacteria). They were particularly popular in less developed countries because of their fast application, accuracy, and inexpensive prices.

Through its pharmaceutical area, QLT also functioned as a bulk commodity distributor of pharmaceutical products, predominantly for the North American market. QLT was in a 50 per cent partnership with Guangdong Enterprises in China where the drugs were manufactured, and it aimed to become a key supplier of pharmaceuticals to the generic drug industry in North America. At first, easily imported commodity products such as Aspirin, Vitamin C, and Acetaminophen had been produced, but QLT planned rapid expansion to higher-risk/higher-return products such as Tetracycline and Lincomycin.

By 1986, diagnostics and pharmaceuticals had begun to provide a source of income which QLT regarded as financing to be used to develop its therapeutic product line. While most companies concentrated on either diagnostics or therapeutics, QLT worked on both to provide a more diverse product portfolio and to give greater insulation from competitive advances that could threaten the future of individual QLT products. However, developing therapeutic products was a high priority for QLT, as they were perceived as the long-term moneymakers. They were considered key to long-term growth because a higher sales volume was likely and profit margins were more favourable. (See Exhibit 2 for financial statements and forecasts.) Within therapeutics, QLT concentrated on three major areas:

- photodynamic therapy for the treatment of cancer tumours;
- growth promoters to stimulate animal growth rates; and
- immune modulation to regulate the body's immune system in humans and in animals and to provide greater protection against infections and diseases.

QLT was considered to have several potential "blockbuster" products in developmental stages. In the world of pharmaceuticals, a blockbuster product is one whose annual sales volume is expected to exceed US$100 million. Margins for these products are very comfortable, generally in the neighbourhood of 95 per cent. Production is economic at relatively low volumes. Research and development, as well as marketing costs, are the major expenses related to these products. It is not uncommon for the total costs of $80 million to be expended in developing a new drug and bringing it through the clinical trial process.

The Industry

Through the 1980s, the biotechnology industry experienced unprecedented growth and it played a major role in many other industries, from agriculture to mining. The health care industry especially felt the impact of biotechnology. In North America alone, there were over 200 small firms which operated on the basis of research only. They licensed or sold the results of their work to a handful of firms who had the resources to produce and market the product; and, they subsequently retained approximately 90 per cent of the profits. Very few small firms combined research and commercialization like QLT.

Drug Development and Testing

Therapeutic products, developed for treating diseases, were administered to induce certain biological changes in a patient. Developing any therapeutic drug was a five to 10 year process requiring substantial investment of both human and financial resources, with no assurance that the end result would be approved for marketing by government agencies. Competitive risk was also high. The product development efforts of one company might reach the final stages only to find that an equivalent or superior competitive product had beaten it to the market.

After developing a product, a firm had to subject it to three phases of clinical trials which were monitored by a government agency: the FDA (Food and Drug Administration) in the United States, and the HPB (Health Protection Branch) in Canada. The trials alone generally spanned a five year period: six to 12 months in phase 1, in which the safety of the drug was established; eight to 12 months in phase 2, in which a pilot study determined the drug's effectiveness; and 24 to 36 months in phase 3, in which it was determined whether the proposed treatment was superior to existing ones. The drug had to complete all three phases successfully before the agency would allow its release on the market.

Conventional wisdom was that of 100 products which began the process of FDA approval, only 25 would reach phase 3. Of those 25, 92 per cent would receive final approval.

Photodynamic Therapy (PDT)

PDT involved the use of light-sensitive drugs, in combination with light, to treat a range of conditions including cancer in both humans and animals. It differed from other light therapies in that cancerous tissue destruction resulted from changes induced by the photosensitizing drug, not from thermal effects of the light source or

CONSOLIDATED STATEMENTS OF LOSS & DEFICIT

	1987	*1986*	*1985*
Research and development	$1,190,062	422,872	209,830
Costs less:			
Government grants and contracts	350,463	249,872	253,467
Interest income	95,758	3,242	5,846
Gross margin on sales	4,411	9,677	11,745
	450,632	262,791	271,058
(Loss) Income before taxes and extraordinary items	(739,430)	(160,081)	61,228
Income tax recovery and extraordinary items	30,330	49,939	(80,269)
Net loss for the year	$(709,100)	(110,142)	(19,041)

CONSOLIDATED BALANCE SHEETS
Year Ended January 31

	1987	*1986*
Assets		
Current assets		
Cash and term deposits	$3,603,688	18,101
Receivables and prepaid expenses	134,543	120,716
Investment tax credits recoverable + loans receivable	261,562	170,300
	3,999,792	309,117
Fixed assets	201,030	94,126
	$4,200,823	403,243
Liabilities		
Current liabilities	140,265	174,605
Debenture payable, government grants & deferred income taxes	31,128	235,120
	171,393	409,725
Shareholders' equity		
Share capital	5,042,488[1]	322,476
Contributed surplus	47,743	12,743
Deficit	(1,060,801)	(351,701)
	4,029,430	(6,482)
	$4,200,823	403,243

Exhibit 2

1. Share issue—in November 1986, $4.7 million in shares was issued in a public offering.

laser. Consequently, treatment left the surrounding normal tissues intact.

QLT's version of PDT, Benzoporphyrin Derivative or BPD, was the second one developed in the world. The original PDT product was being developed by Photomedica, a division of Ortho Pharmaceuticals (a subsidiary of Johnson and Johnson), and had been in phase 3 of clinical trials for almost two years. Photomedica's product, Photofrin II, had been demonstrated effective in the treatment of cancers of the lung, skin, esophagus, bladder, breast, colon, and rectum, and was expected to receive FDA approval by early 1989. QLT's BPD product was known to be superior to Photofrin II, as it could access tumours up to five centimetres deep, rather than the one to two centimetres achieved by Photofrin II. BPD had a greatly reduced affinity for skin tissue, causing minimal discomfort and damage due to light sensitivity. In addition, it was a singular synthesized molecule, so distinct that its actual form was promising from a patenting perspective. This was an advantage relative to Photofrin II, which was more of a "soup" of many different molecules.

Said Ron MacKenzie:

> Imagine the body as a doughnut. The sterile envelope is contained on the outside by the skin and the inside by the walls of the digestive and respiratory systems. The respiratory and digestive systems are themselves "exterior" to the body as they allow foreign substances such as food and air in. We can access many forms of cancer by entering the "hole" from either end.

The implication was that BPD could treat any cancer within five centimetres of the internal or external surface, anywhere but in the brain.

PDT involved development of a porphyrin compound, a light-sensitive chemical derived from red blood cells. The solution, containing modified porphyrins and sterile water, was injected into the cancer patient. Then it circulated in the patient's blood stream and, over the course of two to three days, accumulated in greater concentration in the cancerous tissue. A specific wavelength of light was introduced to the area through the use of fibre optics and laser technology. The light caused the porphyrins to be activated, which resulted in cell necrosis or death, effectively "killing" the tumour.

It was expected that Quadra Logic's BPD drug would successfully complete the phase 2 clinical trials within six months, and phase 3 trials would begin immediately thereafter, early in 1988.

In addition to synthesizing and developing the light-activated chemical BPD, Dr. Levy and Dr. David Dolphin, her colleague from UBC, inserted radioisotopes in the porphyrins so that tumours could be detected through radio-imagery (scanning). A procedure was also developed to link the compound to monoclonal antibodies, which could ultimately be designed to improve the efficiency of delivery by seeking out specific types of cancer cells, for example, squamous lung cancer. As a result, the compound could be used simultaneously for the localization and treatment of cancers. Thus, significantly improved delivery efficiency by this manner signalled the birth of a third generation of this PDT drug. The third generation was only in the early stages of research and not yet ready to begin clinical trials.

The "product" itself consisted of three parts: the laser and fibre optic linking equipment (capital investment), fibre optics which delivered the laser beams to the cancer site, and the drug which was injected into the patient's bloodstream.

An example of the use of BPD or second generation compound was in the case of lung cancer. After the drug had circulated for two to three days and accumulated in the area of the tumour, the patient was prepared for the procedure through the use of a local anaesthetic. A bronchoscope was then inserted down the throat to the lungs so as to accurately locate the tumour(s) visually. A six foot, flexible pipe/channel (fibre optic) was then inserted. It has a specially designed head which diffused light through radial distribution. That head was pushed into the tumour so the doctor could be sure it would impact the tumour to the maximum extent before turning the laser on. Light was applied for eight to 12 minutes to kill the tumour. The procedure was repeated with any other tumours that still existed. Visual confirmation of efficacy and removal of dead tumour tissue was made one to two days later and, if necessary, the procedure was repeated for any remaining tumour tissue.

The Market

Cancer therapy piqued the public's interest more than any of QLT's other therapeutic product areas, not just because it promised to replace chemotherapy and other procedures, but because it brought the prospect of actual cure within the realm of possibility. In that context, potential market demand was conceivably as great as the number of new cancer cases in a given year. Estimates based on cancer data indicated that there were one million new cases of cancer per year in the United States alone. The rest of the world had twice that number. These figures did not include skin cancer, which was readily treatable through existing means. This initial data suggested a market large enough to support any activity QLT could generate.

The direct customer for the product, however, was not the patient, but large hospitals or specialized cancer facilities. QLT estimated that there were three potential customer sites in British Columbia, approximately 30 in the rest of Canada, and a few hundred in the United States. A purchase decision involved a number of individuals in the facility. There needed to be at least one doctor who indicated a strong interest in performing the new procedure, either as a result of treating many cancer patients or because of a strong interest in lasers. Unless both the administrative and the medical staff supported the purchase, the sale was unlikely to be successful. Although the company would be selling to the hospital, it would influence the doctors through pharmaceutical retailers. These were company representatives who would describe the product and its features without actually selling it.

A sale would be complicated by the fact that a purchase decision would not only entail purchasing the drug, but would also require a capital investment in the laser and related equipment. Exhibit 3 contains QLT's estimates of those costs.

Because of the high cost and lengthy decision making process, it was estimated that sales efforts would involve six to 12 visits to each potential customer per year to initiate the relationship and then half as many to maintain it.

QLT estimates were:

Capital Costs

$100,000	laser
10,000	instrumentation to link laser & fibre optics
$110,000	

Annual Costs

$40,000–50,000	technician
15,000–20,000	service contract/year
5,000	training (repeated annually as refresher)
$60,000–75,000	

Drug Costs per Treatment

$150	fibre optics
to be priced	PDT compound (drug itself)

Exhibit 3 Cost of Cancer Treatment With PDT

A salesperson could only be expected to make one to two calls per day because in most regions of North America, medical centres are not located close enough to permit three visits during business hours. QLT felt that there were so many variables involved in making the initial sale that the buyer/seller relationship would be complex, rather than superficial; thus the first firm marketing a PDT drug had a competitive advantage. Most customers were expected to continue purchasing the drug from the same company that coordinated the total package and trained their staff rather than switch to a "new, improved version"—unless it had major advantages. It was expected that a specialist operating with a trained staff at a medical facility would draw large numbers of referrals from the general practitioners in the local system.

Segmentation

QLT management segmented the global health care market along geographical lines. The segments, in order of priority, were:

1. Canada/United States
2. Western Europe
3. Japan
4. Developing countries, with China singled out because of its unique relationship with QLT through the pharmaceutical division

QLT management knew very little about most of these segments and, in some cases, did not know who to approach to find out more. As they already had contacts in North America and some knowledge of the market there, they hired a New York market research firm to assemble market data. As of late June 1987, many of the tentative results were already available. A complete report was expected by the end of the summer.

After deciding to focus on the North American market, QLT estimated that it would cost $3 million to $12 million to put PDT through the clinical trial process. Further, it was thought that it would take up to five years before they could reasonably expect to put PDT on the market.

Competition

The health care industry was dominated by firms with financial, technical, and marketing resources greater than QLT's. Its competitors were thus better equipped than QLT to develop diagnostic and therapeutic products. For example, within the field of cancer treatment alone, researchers in 25 countries were developing products and processes which could eventually compete with those QLT was developing. This competition would extend well beyond Johnson & Johnson's expected rivalry in the photodynamic therapy market. Although QLT management had not invested time or resources in evaluating competition other than that expected from Photomedica in PDT therapy, they expected strong competition from other forms of cancer treatment such as surgery, radiation and chemotherapy.

QLT felt that its major advantage in such a highly competitive race was the product itself. In addition, however, QLT was developing leading edge products in a number of major areas so as not to be "caught out" if another firm experienced early success in PDT therapy.

Alternative Strategies

By June 1987, Ron MacKenzie felt QLT knew enough to make a decision on what they should do with their new PDT compound. The management group perceived several alternatives:

1. **Go-it-alone**—Escalate development of the PDT compound with the objective of getting it to the market as soon as possible, relying exclusively on the company's resources to do so. This would involve spending $3 million to $12 million over three to five years in clinical trails, hiring someone well-versed in running trials and in dealing with the FDA ($100,000 to $150,000 per year), developing a sales force to handle the Canadian and U.S. markets, and pursuing arrangements with laser and fibre optic companies to ensure that the other parts of the product would also be ready once the compound was approved for market. This alternative would likely include further government research grants in bringing the product to a marketable stage. Grants had been consistently available and were not expected to dry up at this stage.

QLT had strong production capability in place. They considered the sales/marketing function to be their weakest area; they had a number of strong individuals, but no sales force of any consequence. Products had only recently begun to reach the commercialization stage. In pursuing this go-it-alone alternative, QLT would need a sales force on board in approximately four years, when they would expect to have received FDA approval. At that stage, they would expect to raise money on the public market in addition to using revenues from diagnostic kits and pharmaceuticals to fund the marketing of PDT.

Ron felt that this alternative could best meet some important company objectives, as it would preserve QLT's autonomy and realize the original goal of linking discovery and commercialization. By pursuing this alternative, QLT would develop a marketing capability and receive full public recognition for the result of their work. However, Ron was concerned about the following:

a. developing and supporting an international sales force on a single compound; and

b. the requirement for additional capital funding:
   - QLT did not want to raise large amounts of money on public markets at the current price (just under $5 a share) as it could significantly dilute the current shareholders' equity
   - QLT was reluctant to rely on future capital markets because of the uncertainty of these markets to deliver capital when required, due to the U.S. trade deficit, interest rate uncertainty, etc.
   - the consequence of program success but financing failure would be a great opportunity for another company, not QLT.

2. **License**—Cease research and development and license the PDT product out as it was. QLT had proceeded this way with a number of previous discoveries and inventions. Every deal was slightly different but, under this arrangement, over the life of the product QLT expected to receive about five to 10 per cent of revenues stemming from its sale. Some audit costs to monitor the purchaser would be involved.

There were a number of firms interested in taking on a license from QLT. Pursuing this alternative would simplify things considerably for QLT as they would effectively drop any further market development of the product. There would be no need to develop marketing capability. They would remain focused on research and development. Furthermore, licensing out PDT would provide financing for further R&D in other areas of research.

3. **Do nothing**—continue to develop the drug, wait and see how things unfolded in this market. Then, cash in on a new improved version once Photofrin II, the first PDT drug, was on the market (expected approval date of early 1989).

4. **Joint venture**—continue to develop the product, but in a joint venture with another firm with stronger marketing and distribution resources. QLT would retain ownership, continue R&D and do the manufacturing. The partner would market and distribute the product. Criteria which would be used in considering a joint venture include:

- a firm truly interested in the technology;
- a reputable company that QLT could work with; and
- the prospects for QLT to retain control of the program and the manufacturing.

QLT management were reluctant to return to the equity market as they had just raised $4.7 million in November, 1986. Returning so soon with so much unresolved would not be a strong signal.

To be certain that these were all viable alternatives, QLT management had done some legwork. They felt that getting PDT to the market, regardless of the alternative chosen, required the following:

- development of all three product components: the drug, the laser, and the fibre optics. Only the drug had been developed. Without the right kind of equipment in place, the drug could not be put to use.
- access to expertise and financial resources to get through the FDA process.
- development of a sales force and distribution system that could handle sales. (Whereas Johnson & Johnson could take advantage of its existing sales force, QLT would have to develop its own from scratch, unless it were to benefit from another company's infrastructure.)

Preliminary discussions had taken place with various laser and fibre optic companies to determine whether they could work together on a product package. It appeared that the time frame necessary to complete clinical trials for the drug allowed plenty of scope to modify laser equipment and to develop fibre optics to meet the needs of QLT. QLT was entirely satisfied with the way arrangements were shaping up with regards to the equipment. It could, therefore, concentrate on the further development and marketing of the drug itself.

The market research was almost completed. Preliminary results gave QLT a much better sense of what they could expect from the North American market. The study identified their

Market	*Estimated Treatments/Year*	
	Most Likely Case	*Best Case*
Lung Cancer	42,800	100,000
Bladder Cancer	20,400	47,600
Esophageal Cancer	18,000	18,000
Head/Neck	7,400	7,400
Basal Cell Carcinoma	25,000	25,000
Melanoma	—	—
Breast Cancer	2,600	2,600
Cervical Cancer	33,800	33,800
Total	**150,000**	**234,400**

Exhibit 4 Market Research Results Summary—Realistic Market Potential for Photodynamic Therapy

initial market as being 15 per cent or 150,000 cases per year in the United States. This was calculated on the basis of selecting eight forms of cancer, comparing alternative treatments available, cost of treatments, and success rates. They assumed that there was no particular reason for using their new treatment for cancers which were already being effectively treated with another method (see Exhibit 4).

In arriving at these market estimates, the research firm had assumed a per patient treatment price of $600 to $1,000 for the QLT product. By way of comparison, drug costs for chemotherapy treatments were in the range of $2,500 to $5,000 per person. However, QLT needed to consider the pricing issue much more closely. To what should they relate this product when there were no equivalent products on the market? There was no standard margin in the industry. Production costs were expected to run at $25 to $75 per treatment. The most recent drug to be marketed in the biotechnology field was one reducing tissue damage after heart attacks. It was being sold for US$2,200 per treatment and it was causing some controversy about unethical pricing practices. Other firms were pricing new therapeutic biotech products in the range of $1,000 to $2,000.

Although cost was not a primary decision-making criteria when compared with effectiveness, Ron MacKenzie noted that the "retail" cost of PDT treatment was less than $10,000, which compared well with the cost of surgery ($20,000 to $25,000). The breakdown is as follows (assuming Canadian rates that hospitals use to bill the health insurance plans):

– five inpatient days @ $500 to $600 per day	2,500–3,000
– five to six hours doctor's time @ $300 to $400 per hour	1,500–2,400
– tests, etc., @ $50 to $75 per day × five days	250–375
– laser amortization (machine obsolete in three years)	250–300
– technician salary + overhead ($80,000 per year, with 800 treatments per year at capacity)	100
– service contract	100
– PDT compound	600–2,200
– fibre optics	150
Total	**$5,450–$8,625**

From February through June, 1987, QLT had approached three pharmaceutical firms in turn to explore their interest in the possibility of a joint venture to market the product. All three were initially interested. However, two were obliged to terminate the discussions, one because it had been acquired by another company and the second because of poor communications between the American parent and Canadian subsidiary. The third, American Cyanamid (AC), was of particular interest to Ron as AC had already established a working relationship with QLT in assessing other product offerings. AC had particularly strong industry expertise and was generally recognized in the industry as a major distributor of oncology products. In addition, QLT had gained an understanding of Cyanamid's R&D interests and capabilities during technical discussions held several months earlier. There were several other similar potential venture partners which QLT could pursue if AC turned out not to be a favourable choice.

An agreement with American Cyanamid would likely give them all marketing rights for QLT's PDT products for cancer only, current and future, in exchange for a percentage of revenues. Unlike licensing out fully, this option would allow QLT to retain product ownership. Under a joint venture, QLT would receive 30 to 40 per cent of sales revenue from the PDT compound, with responsibilities to include: research for clinical trials and regulatory approvals, manufacturing scale-up, and manufacturing. In comparison, under a licensing agreement, QLT revenues would equal five to 10 per cent of PDT sales revenue with no accompanying responsibilities other than sharing ongoing R&D support and financial administration. Ron believed that American Cyanamid would prefer to have control of the clinical trials and research that they would receive under the licensing alternative, but that they were still interested in the joint venture possibility as well.

With the knowledge that any of the alternatives could be pursued, Ron felt it was time to make a decision and to develop a comprehensive strategic plan for the product in line with the decision. His intention was to present it at the next board meeting, slated for July 10, 1987.

REFERENCES

Agle, B. R., Mitchell, R. K., & Sonnenfeld, J. A. (1999). Who matters to CEOs? An investigation of stakeholder attributes and salience, corporate performance, and CEO values. *Academy of Management Journal Special Research Forum on Stakeholder Theory, 42*(5), 507–525.

Anderson, M. (2004, July). Casestudy subject: Celestica Inc. *National Post,* pp. 26–30.

Arrow, K. J. (Ed.). (1969). *The organization of economic activity: Issues pertinent to the choice of market versus nonmarket allocation* (Vol. 1). Washington, DC: Government Printing Office.

Arthur, W. B. (1994). Complexity in economic theory: Inductive reasoning and bounded rationality. *AEA Papers and Proceedings, 84*(2), 406–411.

Barney, J. B., & Hansen, M. H. (1994). Trustworthiness as a source of competitive advantage. *Strategic Management Journal, 15,* 175–190.

Block, Z., & MacMillian, I. C. (1985, September/October). Milestones for successful venture planning. *Harvard Business Review,* pp. 184–196.

Charness, N., Krampe, R., & Mayer, U. (1996). The role of practice and coaching in entrepreneurial skill domains: An international comparison of life-span chess skill acquisition. In K. A. Ericsson (Ed.), *The road to excellence: The acquisition of expert performance in the arts and sciences, sports, and games* (pp. 51–80). Mahwah, NJ: Lawrence Erlbaum.

Cohen, B. D., Smith, J. B., & Mitchell, R. K. (2004, June). *New venture value creation strategies: Outcome comparisons.* Paper presented at the Babson Kauffman Entrepreneuship Research Conference, Glasgow, Scotland.

Cohen, B. D., & Winn, M. (2003, October). *Market imperfections, opportunity, and sustainable entrepreneurship.* Paper presented at the Greening of Industry Network Conference, San Francisco.

Collins, J. C., & Porras, J. I. (1995). Building a visionary company. *California Management Review, 37*(2), 80–100.

Cornwall, J. R., & Perlman, B. (1990). *Organizational entrepreneurship.* Homewood, IL: Irwin.

Csikszentmihalyi, M. (1988). Society, culture, and person: A systems view of creativity. In R. J. Sternberg (Ed.), *The nature of creativity* (pp. 325–339). New York: Cambridge University Press.

Dean, T. J., & McMullen, J. S. (2002). Market failure and entrepreneurial opportunity. In *Best Paper Proceedings of the Academy of Management.*

Deming, W. E. (1986). *Out of crisis.* Cambridge: MIT Center for Advanced Engineering Study.

Dickson, P. R., & Giglierano, J. J. (1986). Missing the boat and sinking the boat: A conceptual model of entrepreneurial risk. *Journal of Marketing, 50,* 58–70.

Drucker, P. F. (1985). Entrepreneurial strategies. *California Management Review, 27*(2), 9–25.

Freeman, R. E. (1984). *Strategic management: A stakeholder approach.* Boston: Pitman.

Gardner, H. (1993). *Creating minds.* New York: Basic Books.

Ghemawat, P. (1991). *Commitment: The dynamics of strategy.* New York: The Free Press.

Hindle, K. (1997). *An enhanced paradigm of entrepreneurial business planning: Development, case applications and general implications.* Melbourne, Australia: Swinburne University of Technology.

Hunt, S. D., & Morgan, R. M. (1995, April). The comparative advantage theory of competition. *Journal of Marketing, 59,* 1–15.

Kirzner, I. M. (1982). The theory of entrepreneurship in economic growth. In C. A. Kent, D. L. Sexton, & K. H. Vesper (Eds.), *Encyclopedia of entrepreneurship* (pp. 272–276). Englewood Cliffs, NJ: Prentice Hall.

Lenn, J. (1993, March). *Discussion of stakeholder theory and entrepreneurship.* Paper presented at the IABS Conference, San Diego.

Magnier, M. (1999, October 25). Rebuilding Japan with the help of 2 Americans. *Los Angeles Times,* p. U-8.

Mainprize, B., & Hindle, K. (2003). *A systematic approach to writing and rating entrepreneurial business plans.* Paper presented at Academy of Social Sciences Canada (ASAC), St. Mary's University, Halifax, Nova Scotia.

Mainprize, B., Hindle, K., Smith, B., & Mitchell, R. (2002). Toward the standardization of venture capital investment evaluation: Decision criteria for rating investee business plans. In W. D. Bygrave, C. G. Brush, P. Davidsson, J. Fiet, P. G. Greene, R. T. Harrison, et al. (Eds.), *Frontiers of entrepreneurship research 2002* (Vol. 22). Babson Park, MA: Babson College. Accessed from http://www.babson.edu/entrep/fer/Babson2002/XIII/XIII_P4/XIII_P4.htm

Mainprize, B., Hindle, K., Smith, B., & Mitchell, R. (2003). Caprice versus standardization in venture capital decision making. *Journal of Private Equity, 7*(1), 15–25.

McGrath, R. G. (1999). Falling forward: Real options reasoning and entrepreneurial failure. *Academy of Management Review, 24*(1), 13–30.

Michener, J. A. (1982). *Space.* New York: Ballantine.

Mintzberg, H. (1987). The strategy concept II: Another look at why organizations need strategies. *California Management Review, 30*(2), 25–32.

Mintzberg, H. (1994). *The rise and fall of strategic planning.* New York: The Free Press.

Mitchell, R. K. (1999). *A transaction cognition theory of entrepreneurship.* Working paper, University of Victoria.

Mitchell, R. K. (2001). *Transaction cognition theory and high performance economic results.* Victoria, British Columbia: International Centre for Venture Expertise. Accessed from www.ronaldmitchell.org/publications.htm

Mitchell, R. K. (2002). Entrepreneurship and stakeholder theory. *Business Ethics Quarterly (The Ruffin Series), 3,* 175–196.

Mitchell, R. K. (2003). A transaction cognition theory of global entrepreneurship. In J. A. Katz & D. A. Shepherd (Eds.), *Advances in entrepreneurship, firm emergence and growth: Cognitive approaches to entrepreneurship research* (Vol. 6, pp. 181–229). Greenwich, CT: JAI Press.

Mitchell, R. K., Agle, B. R., & Wood, D. J. (1997). Toward a theory of stakeholder identification and salience: Defining the principle of who and what really counts. *Academy of Management Review, 22*(4), 853–886.

Mitchell, R. K., Morse, E. A., & Sharma, P. (2003). The transacting cognitions of non-family employees in the family business setting. *Journal of Business Venturing, 18*(2), 3–22.

Mitchell, R. K., Smith, J. B., Morse, E. A., Seawright, K. W., Peredo, A. M., & McKenzie, B. (2002). Are entrepreneurial cognitions universal? Assessing entrepreneurial cognitions across cultures. *Entrepreneurship Theory & Practice, 26*(4), 9–32.

Mitchell, R. K., Smith, B., Seawright, K. W., & Morse, E. A. (2000). Cross-cultural cognitions and the venture creation decision. *Academy of Management Journal, 43*(5), 974–993.

Neisser, U. (1967). *Cognitive psychology.* New York: Appleton-Century-Crafts.

Penrose, E. (1959). *The theory of the growth of the firm.* New York: John Wiley.

Porter, M. E. (1980). *Competitive strategy: Techniques for analyzing industries and competitors.* New York: The Free Press.

Read, S. J. (1987). Constructing causal scenarios: A knowledge structure approach to causal reasoning. *Journal of Personality and Social Psychology, 52,* 288–302.

Sahlman, W. A. (1997, July/August). How to write a great business plan. *Harvard Business Review,* pp. 99–108.

Sarasvathy, S. D. (2001). Causation and effectuation: Toward a theoretical shift from economic inevitability to entrepreneurial contingency. *Academy of Management Review, 26*(2), 243–264.

Schumpeter, J. (1934). *The theory of economic development.* Cambridge, MA: Harvard University Press.

Simon, H. A. (1979). Rational decision making in business organizations. *The American Economic Review, 69,* 493–513.

Stevenson, H. H., Roberts, M. J., & Grousbeck, H. I. (1994). *New business ventures and the entrepreneur.* Homewood, IL: Irwin.

Stinchcombe, A. L. (1965). Organizations and social structure. In J. G. March (Ed.), *Handbook of organizations* (pp. 142–193). Chicago: Rand-McNally.

Tortorella, M. J. (1995, July 16). The three careers of W. Edwards Deming. *SIAM (Society for Industrial and Applied Mathematics) News.*

Vesper, K. H. (1996). *New venture experience.* Seattle, WA: Vector Books.

Williamson, O. E. (1985). *The economic institutions of capitalism.* New York: The Free Press.

Williamson, O. E. (1991). Strategizing, economizing, and economic organization. *Strategic Management Journal, 12*, 75–94.

World Commission on Environment and Development (WCED). (1987). *Our common future.* Oxford, UK: Oxford University Press.

Ziglar, Z. (1982). *Zig Ziglar's secrets of closing the sale.* Grand Rapids, MI: Baker Book House Company.

About the Editors

Eric A. Morse, Ph.D., is the JR Shaw Professor of Entrepreneurship and Family Owned Business and the Director of the Institute for Entrepreneurship at the Richard Ivey School of Business. He is the Academic Director for Ivey's *Quantum Shift* Executive Program for High Potential Entrepreneurs, and he teaches in several other custom executive programs. His research focuses on entrepreneurial cognition, entrepreneurial strategy, and family business and has been published in the *Academy of Management Journal, Entrepreneurship Theory & Practice,* the *Journal of Business Venturing,* the *Journal of Management,* and the *MIT Sloan Management Review.*

He has served on the board, been an adviser to, founded, or been an investor in a variety of entrepreneurial start-ups and actively consults with both private and government enterprises.

Ronald K. Mitchell, CPA, Ph.D., is Professor of Entrepreneurship in the Rawls College of Business at Texas Tech University and holds the J. A. Bagley Regents' Chair in Management. His research has been published in the *Academy of Management Journal, Academy of Management Review, Business Ethics Quarterly, Entrepreneurship Theory & Practice,* the *Journal of Business Venturing*, and other respected outlets. He is a specialist in entrepreneurial cognition, entrepreneurial finance, entrepreneurial teaching program design, global entrepreneurship, stakeholder theory, and venture management, and he researches, consults, and lectures worldwide.

Active in entrepreneurship throughout his career (venture advising, founding, investment, turnaround, and value creation), Professor Mitchell's interests currently focus on creating strategies for increasing economic well-being in society through the study of entrepreneurs, the development of transaction cognition theory, and the further development of stakeholder theory.

w/This particular product

Boxed Chocolate → opportunities for increased seasonal sales
- Christmas
- V-Day
- Easter

-VS-

Choc. Bars → Fragmented Sales

- Need - Collaborative Effort - w/CCAH Neighborhood network
- Legal issues
- Dedication - work on through & and not 4 ppl.

- Evening Soup Kitchen
- Partner w/Caux St John's
- Secure additional Grant

children

CPR Program

- No-Load
- T-Rowe Price
- Vanguard
* Mutual Funds

- Entrepreneurship
- Social Enterprise
- Microcredit
- Leadership
- Behavioral Science

Business Basics Nonprofits

Socialinvest.org

- Business
- Am. History
- Pol Science
- Af Am. History/MLK
- Sex
- Religion
- Geography
- Mythology
- Math
- Haiti
- France
- Astronomy
- Bible
- Vocabulary

Dudleys Hair Growth

Wemix.com

At the end of the day we're all just shades of Brown